IN SHARK YEARS
I'M DEAD

Other Books by Jim Toomey

Sherman's Lagoon: Ate That, What's Next?

Poodle: The Other White Meat

An Illustrated Guide to Shark Etiquette

Another Day in Paradise

Greetings from Sherman's Lagoon

Surf's Up!

The Shark Diaries

Catch of the Day

A Day at the Beach

Surfer Safari

Treasury

*Sherman's Lagoon 1991 to 2001:
Greatest Hits and Near Misses*

In Shark Years I'm Dead

Sherman's Lagoon Turns Fifteen

by Jim Toomey

**Andrews McMeel
Publishing, LLC**

Kansas City

Sherman's Lagoon is distributed internationally by King Features Syndicate, Inc. For information, write King Features Syndicate, Inc., 888 Seventh Avenue, New York, New York 10019.

08 09 10 SDB 10 9 8 7 6 5 4 3 2

ISBN-13: 978-0-7407-5702-0
ISBN-10: 0-7407-5702-4

Library of Congress Control Number: 2005936148

www.andrewsmcmeel.com

Sherman's Lagoon may be viewed on the Internet at
www.shermanslagoon.com.

ATTENTION: SCHOOLS AND BUSINESSES

Andrews McMeel books are available at quantity discounts with bulk purchase for educational, business, or sales promotional use. For information, please write to: Special Sales Department, Andrews McMeel Publishing, LLC, 4520 Main Street, Kansas City, Missouri 64111.

Don't want to end up a cartoon,
In a cartoon graveyard . . .

—Paul Simon

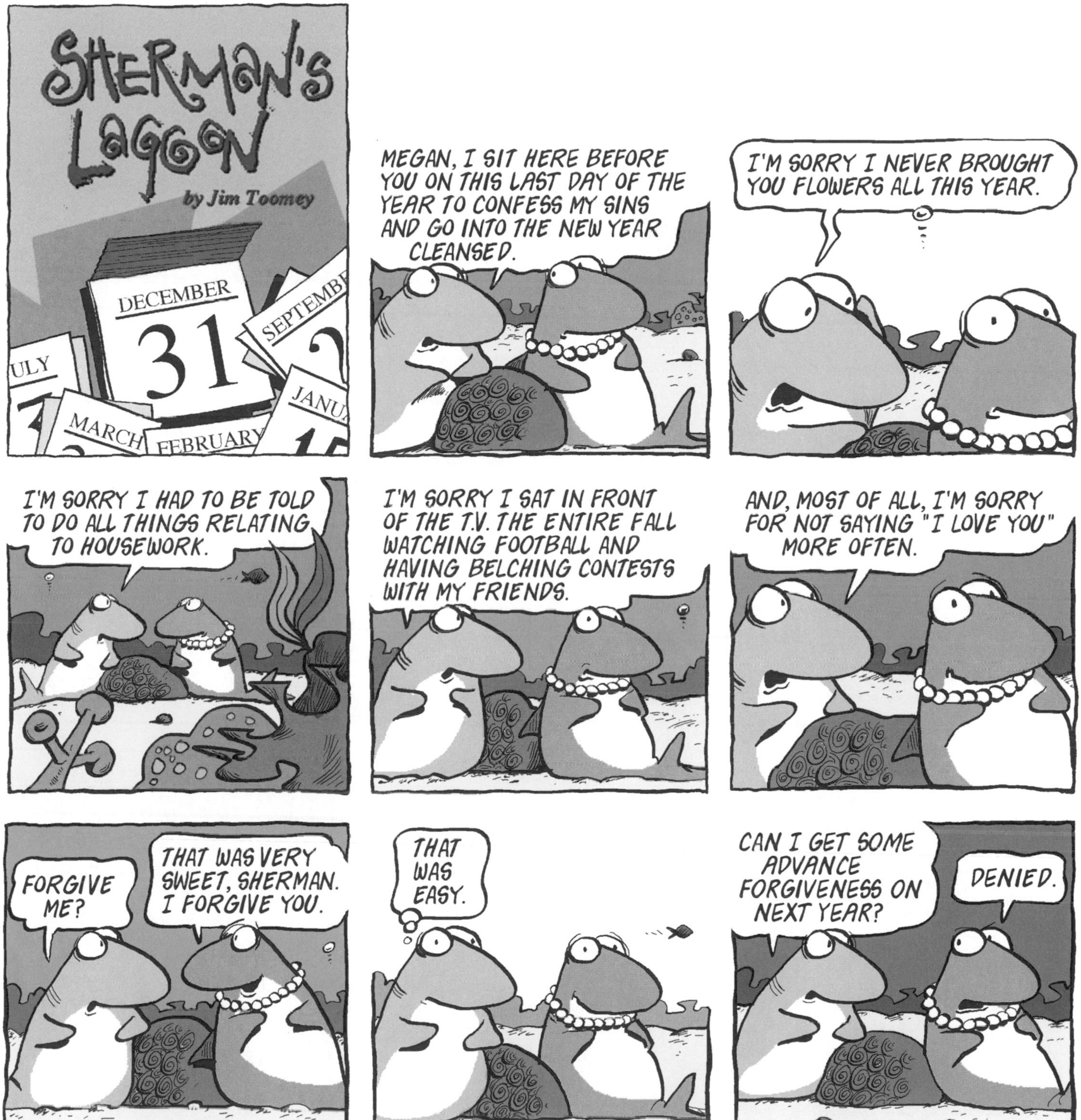
SHERMAN'S LAGOON
by Jim Toomey
DECEMBER
31
SEPTEMBER
JULY
JANU
MARCH
FEBRUARY
MEGAN, I SIT HERE BEFORE YOU ON THIS LAST DAY OF THE YEAR TO CONFESS MY SINS AND GO INTO THE NEW YEAR CLEANSED.
I'M SORRY I NEVER BROUGHT YOU FLOWERS ALL THIS YEAR.
I'M SORRY I HAD TO BE TOLD TO DO ALL THINGS RELATING TO HOUSEWORK.
I'M SORRY I SAT IN FRONT OF THE T.V. THE ENTIRE FALL WATCHING FOOTBALL AND HAVING BELCHING CONTESTS WITH MY FRIENDS.
AND, MOST OF ALL, I'M SORRY FOR NOT SAYING "I LOVE YOU" MORE OFTEN.
FORGIVE ME?
THAT WAS VERY SWEET, SHERMAN. I FORGIVE YOU.
THAT WAS EASY.
CAN I GET SOME ADVANCE FORGIVENESS ON NEXT YEAR?
DENIED.

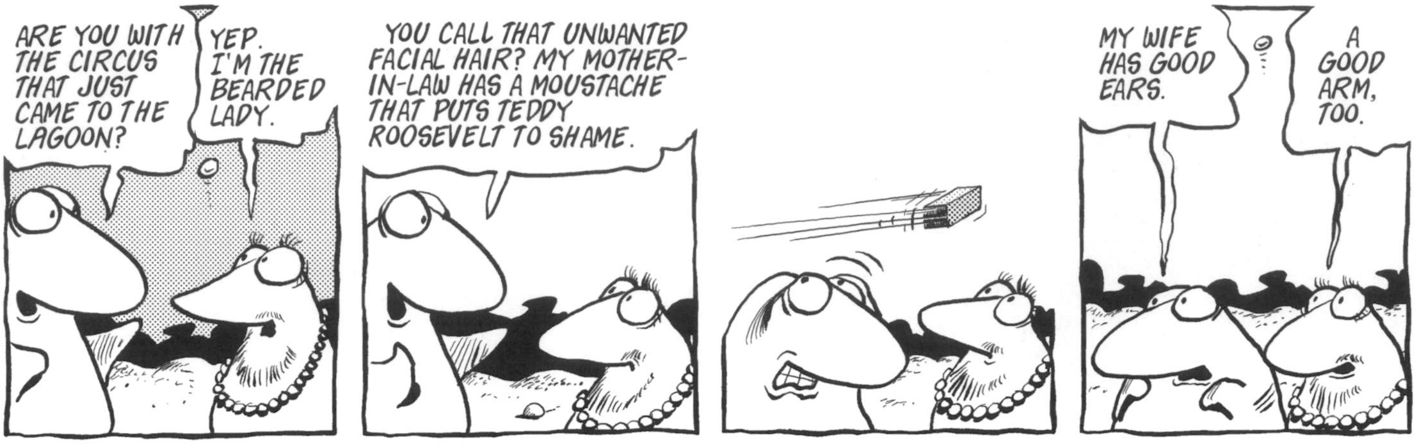
ARE YOU WITH THE CIRCUS THAT JUST CAME TO THE LAGOON?
YEP. I'M THE BEARDED LADY.
YOU CALL THAT UNWANTED FACIAL HAIR? MY MOTHER-IN-LAW HAS A MOUSTACHE THAT PUTS TEDDY ROOSEVELT TO SHAME.
MY WIFE HAS GOOD EARS.
A GOOD ARM, TOO.

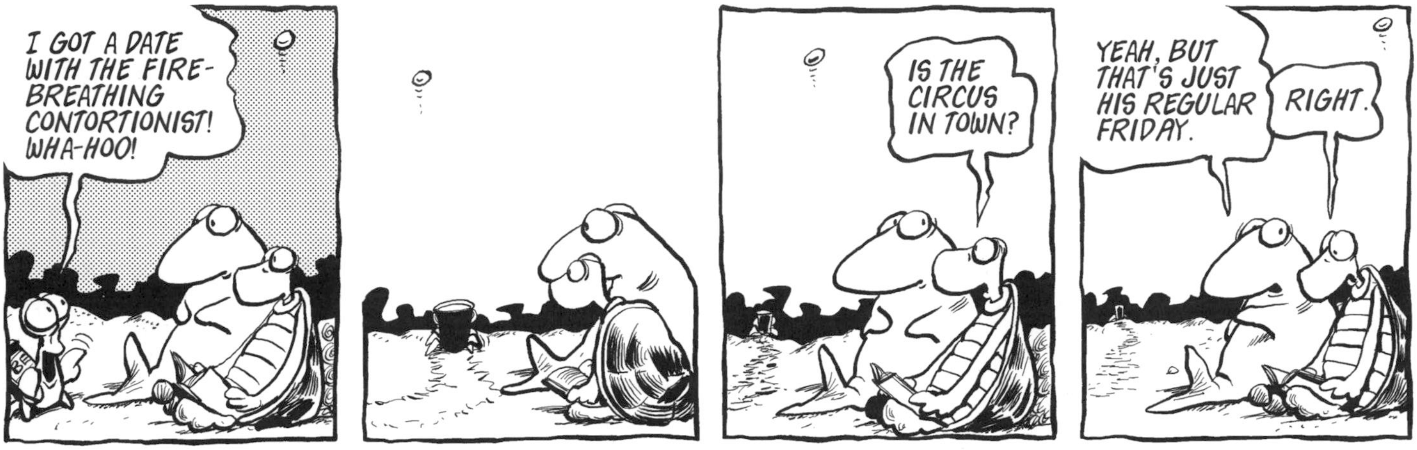
I GOT A DATE WITH THE FIRE-BREATHING CONTORTIONIST! WHA-HOO!
IS THE CIRCUS IN TOWN?
YEAH, BUT THAT'S JUST HIS REGULAR FRIDAY.
RIGHT.

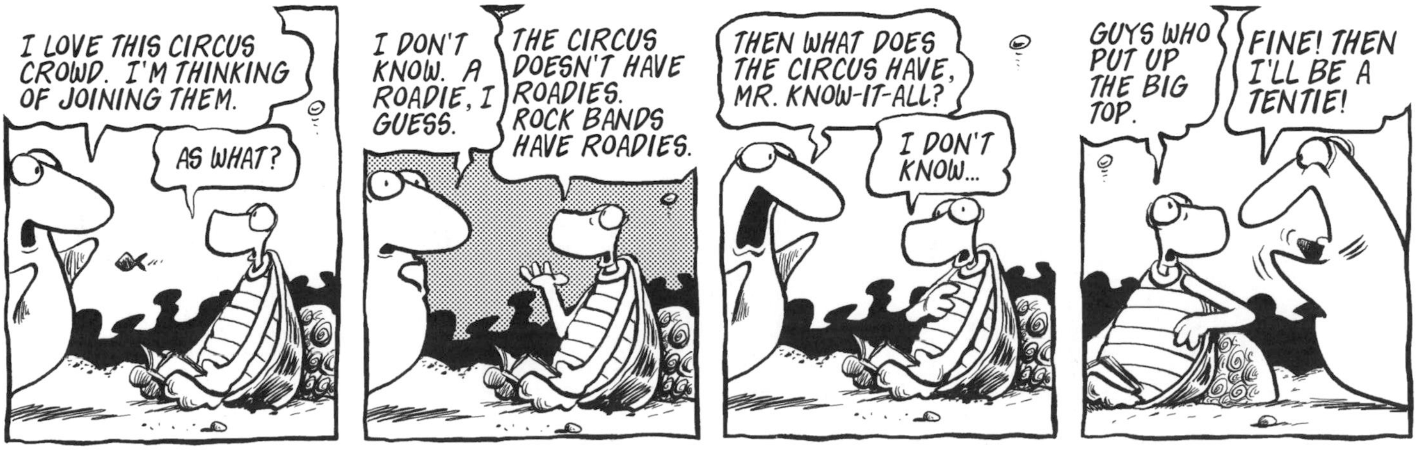
I LOVE THIS CIRCUS CROWD. I'M THINKING OF JOINING THEM.
AS WHAT?
I DON'T KNOW. A ROADIE, I GUESS.
THE CIRCUS DOESN'T HAVE ROADIES. ROCK BANDS HAVE ROADIES.
THEN WHAT DOES THE CIRCUS HAVE, MR. KNOW-IT-ALL?
I DON'T KNOW...
GUYS WHO PUT UP THE BIG TOP.
FINE! THEN I'LL BE A TENTIE!

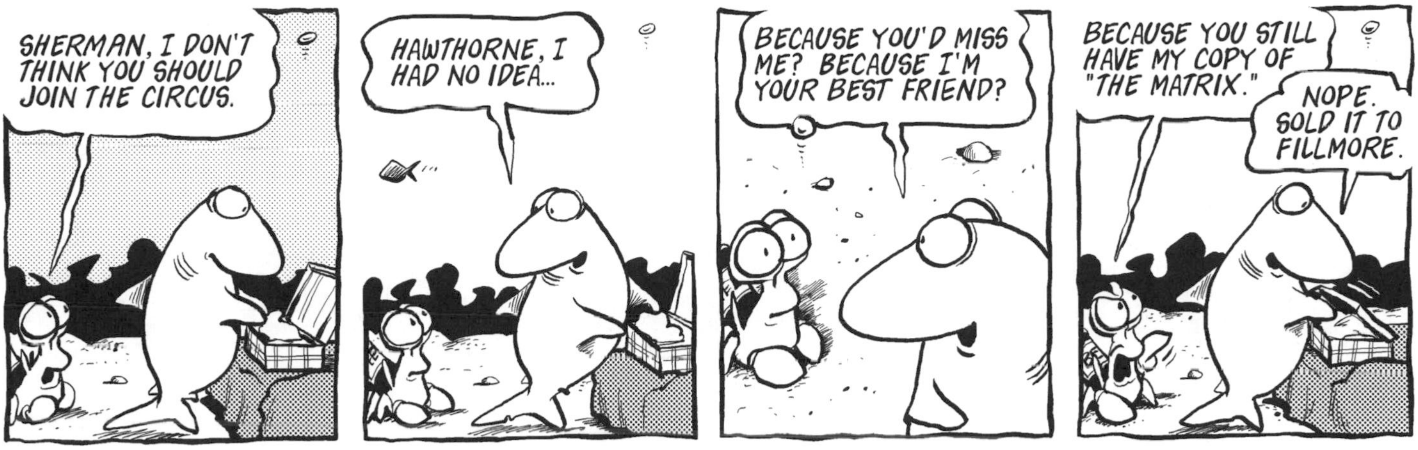
SHERMAN, I DON'T THINK YOU SHOULD JOIN THE CIRCUS.
HAWTHORNE, I HAD NO IDEA...
BECAUSE YOU'D MISS ME? BECAUSE I'M YOUR BEST FRIEND?
BECAUSE YOU STILL HAVE MY COPY OF "THE MATRIX."
NOPE. SOLD IT TO FILLMORE.

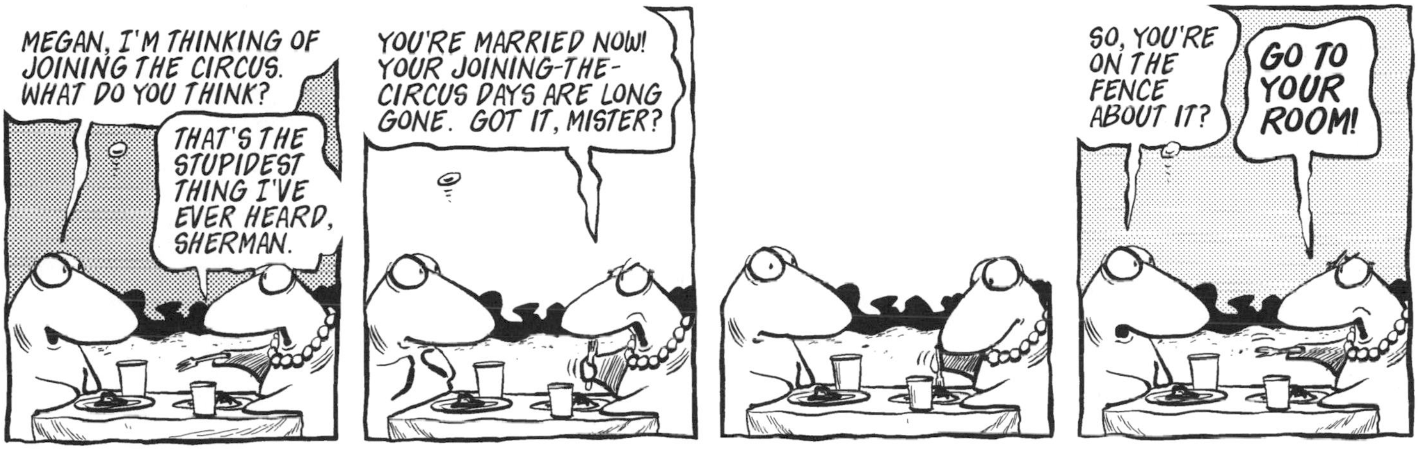
MEGAN, I'M THINKING OF JOINING THE CIRCUS. WHAT DO YOU THINK?
THAT'S THE STUPIDEST THING I'VE EVER HEARD, SHERMAN.
YOU'RE MARRIED NOW! YOUR JOINING-THE-CIRCUS DAYS ARE LONG GONE. GOT IT, MISTER?
SO, YOU'RE ON THE FENCE ABOUT IT?
GO TO YOUR ROOM!

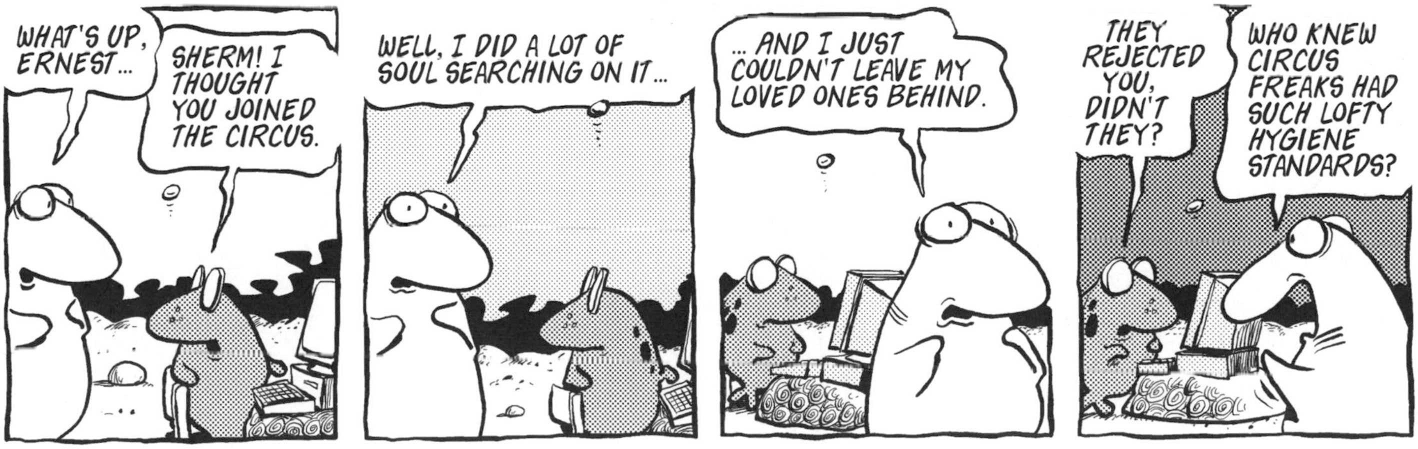
WHAT'S UP, ERNEST...
SHERM! I THOUGHT YOU JOINED THE CIRCUS.
WELL, I DID A LOT OF SOUL SEARCHING ON IT...
... AND I JUST COULDN'T LEAVE MY LOVED ONES BEHIND.
THEY REJECTED YOU, DIDN'T THEY?
WHO KNEW CIRCUS FREAKS HAD SUCH LOFTY HYGIENE STANDARDS?

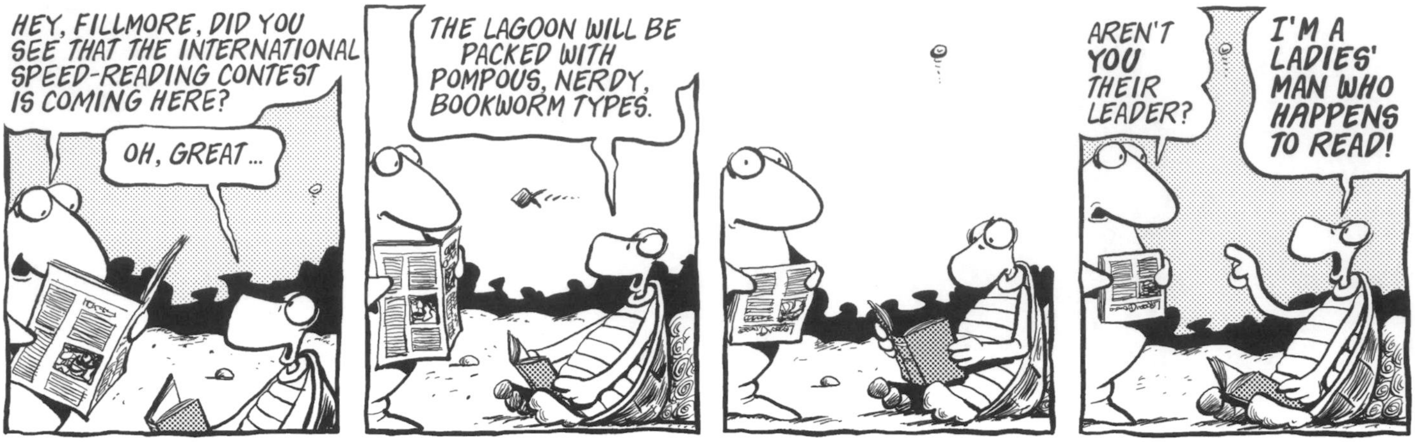
HEY, FILLMORE, DID YOU SEE THAT THE INTERNATIONAL SPEED-READING CONTEST IS COMING HERE?
OH, GREAT...
THE LAGOON WILL BE PACKED WITH POMPOUS, NERDY, BOOKWORM TYPES.
AREN'T YOU THEIR LEADER?
I'M A LADIES' MAN WHO HAPPENS TO READ!

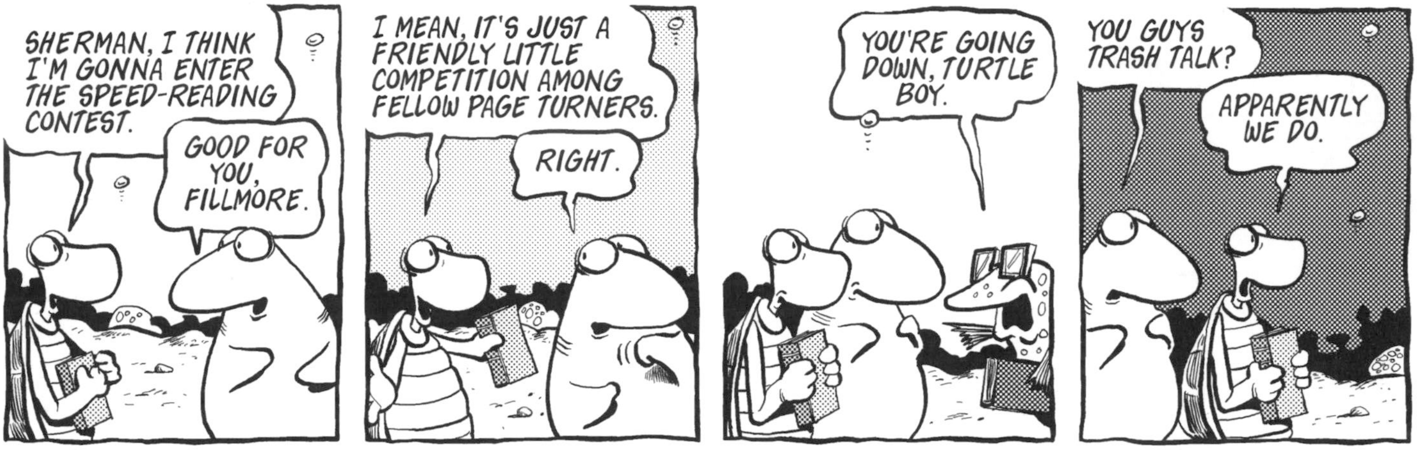
SHERMAN, I THINK I'M GONNA ENTER THE SPEED-READING CONTEST.
GOOD FOR YOU, FILLMORE.
I MEAN, IT'S JUST A FRIENDLY LITTLE COMPETITION AMONG FELLOW PAGE TURNERS.
RIGHT.
YOU'RE GOING DOWN, TURTLE BOY.
YOU GUYS TRASH TALK?
APPARENTLY WE DO.

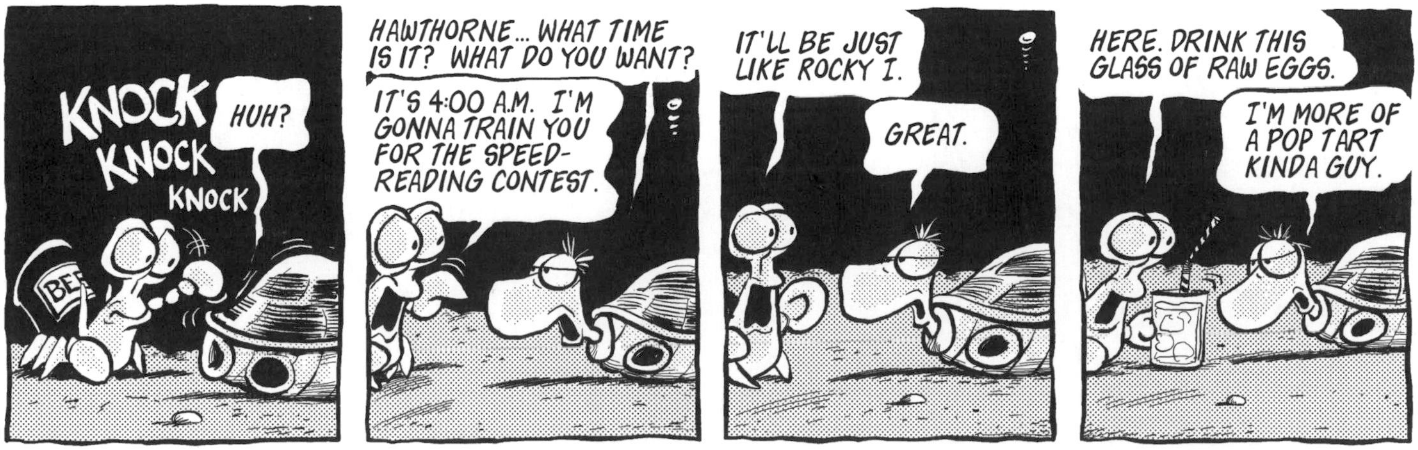
KNOCK KNOCK KNOCK
HUH?
HAWTHORNE... WHAT TIME IS IT? WHAT DO YOU WANT?
IT'S 4:00 A.M. I'M GONNA TRAIN YOU FOR THE SPEED-READING CONTEST.
IT'LL BE JUST LIKE ROCKY I.
GREAT.
HERE. DRINK THIS GLASS OF RAW EGGS.
I'M MORE OF A POP TART KINDA GUY.

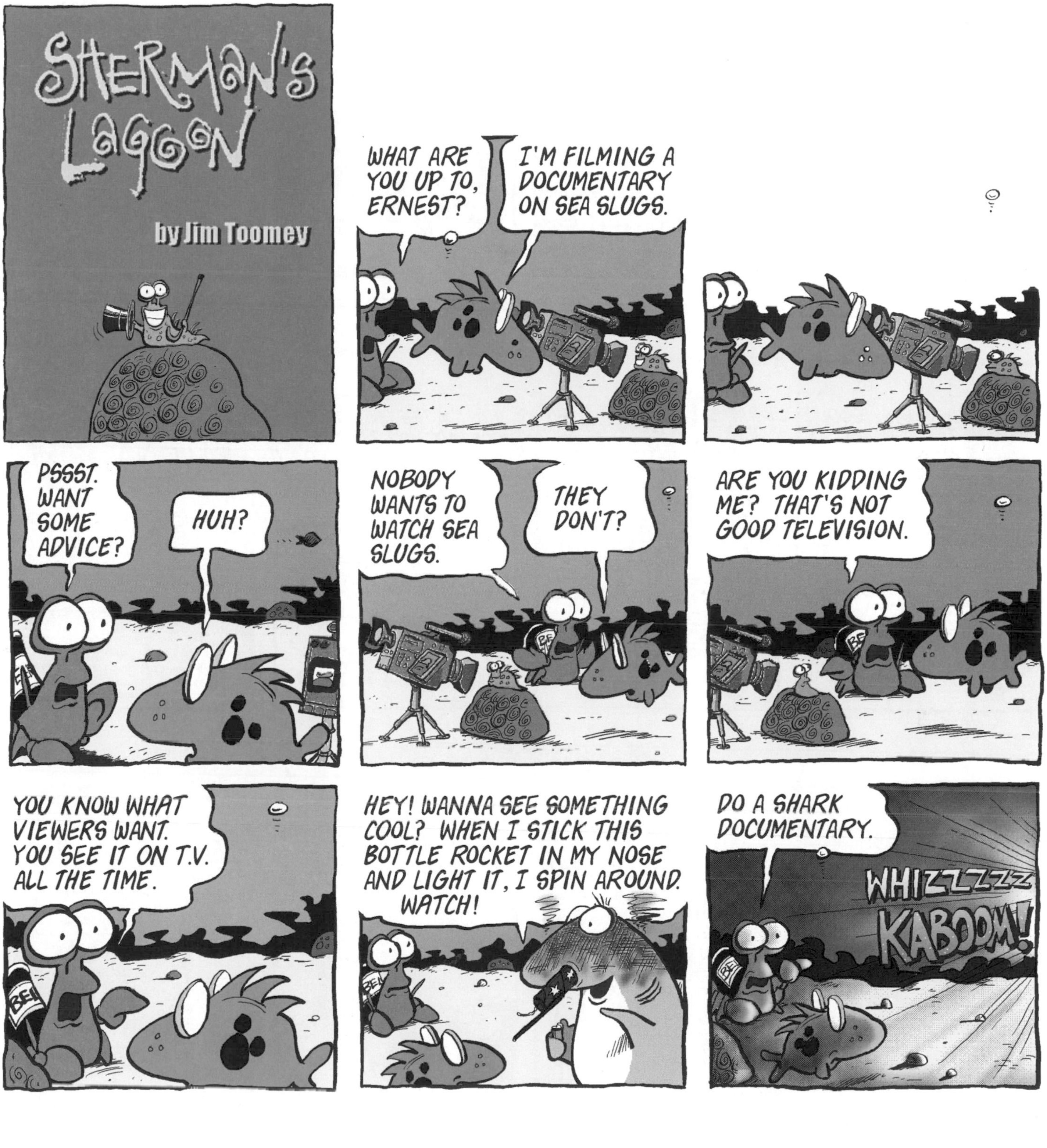
SHERMAN'S LAGOON
by Jim Toomey
WHAT ARE YOU UP TO, ERNEST?
I'M FILMING A DOCUMENTARY ON SEA SLUGS.
PSSST. WANT SOME ADVICE?
HUH?
NOBODY WANTS TO WATCH SEA SLUGS.
THEY DON'T?
ARE YOU KIDDING ME? THAT'S NOT GOOD TELEVISION.
YOU KNOW WHAT VIEWERS WANT. YOU SEE IT ON T.V. ALL THE TIME.
HEY! WANNA SEE SOMETHING COOL? WHEN I STICK THIS BOTTLE ROCKET IN MY NOSE AND LIGHT IT, I SPIN AROUND. WATCH!
DO A SHARK DOCUMENTARY.
WHIZZZZZ
KABOOM!

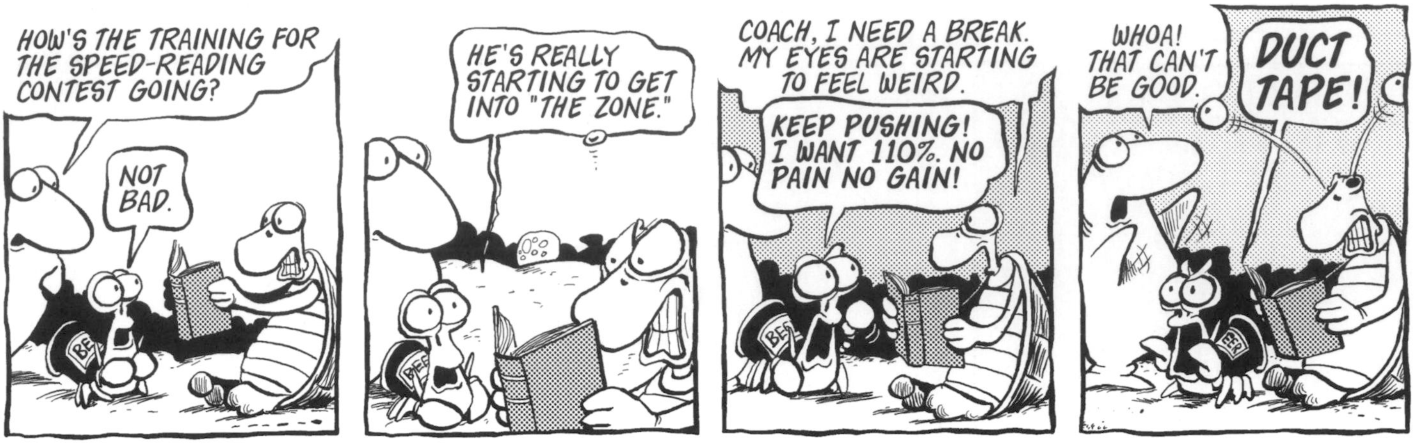
HOW'S THE TRAINING FOR THE SPEED-READING CONTEST GOING?
NOT BAD.
HE'S REALLY STARTING TO GET INTO "THE ZONE."
COACH, I NEED A BREAK. MY EYES ARE STARTING TO FEEL WEIRD.
KEEP PUSHING! I WANT 110%. NO PAIN NO GAIN!
WHOA! THAT CAN'T BE GOOD.
DUCT TAPE!

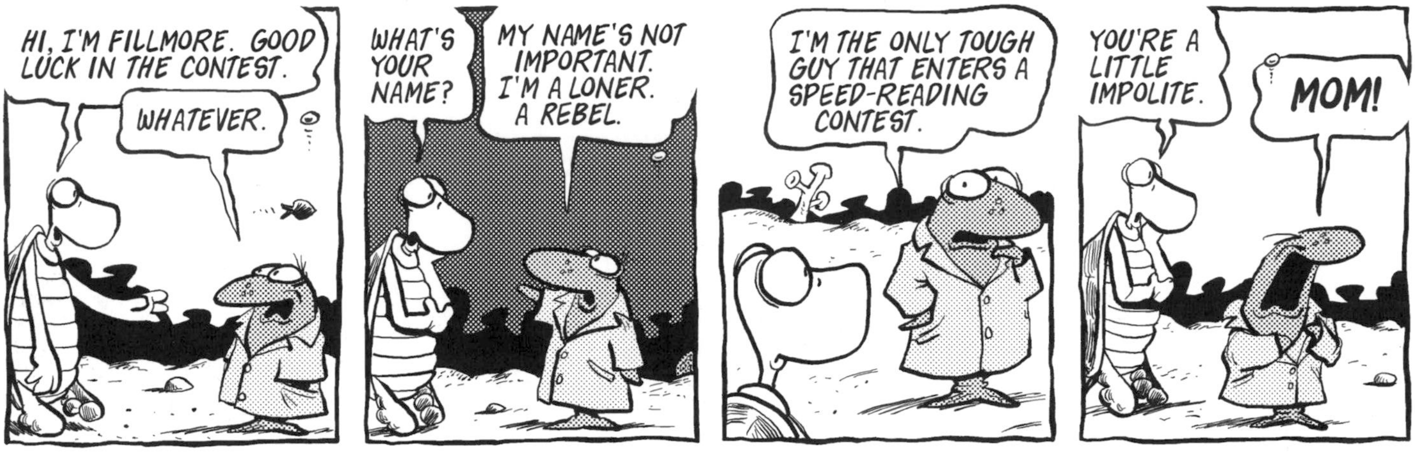
HI, I'M FILLMORE. GOOD LUCK IN THE CONTEST.
WHATEVER.
WHAT'S YOUR NAME?
MY NAME'S NOT IMPORTANT. I'M A LONER. A REBEL.
I'M THE ONLY TOUGH GUY THAT ENTERS A SPEED-READING CONTEST.
YOU'RE A LITTLE IMPOLITE.
MOM!

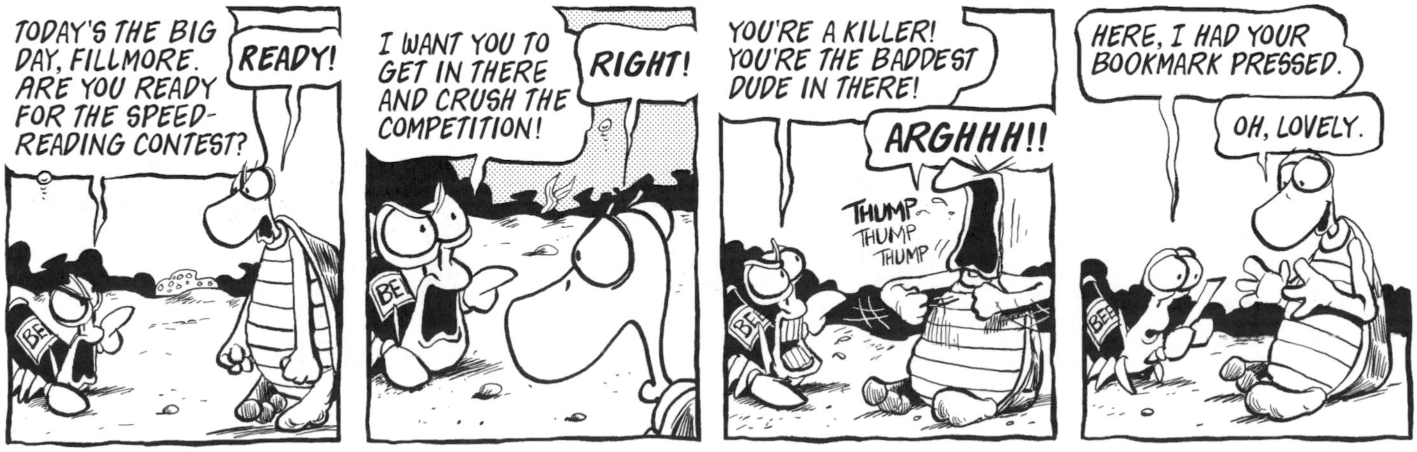
TODAY'S THE BIG DAY, FILLMORE. ARE YOU READY FOR THE SPEED-READING CONTEST?
READY!
I WANT YOU TO GET IN THERE AND CRUSH THE COMPETITION!
RIGHT!
YOU'RE A KILLER! YOU'RE THE BADDEST DUDE IN THERE!
ARGHHH!!
THUMP THUMP THUMP
HERE, I HAD YOUR BOOKMARK PRESSED.
OH, LOVELY.

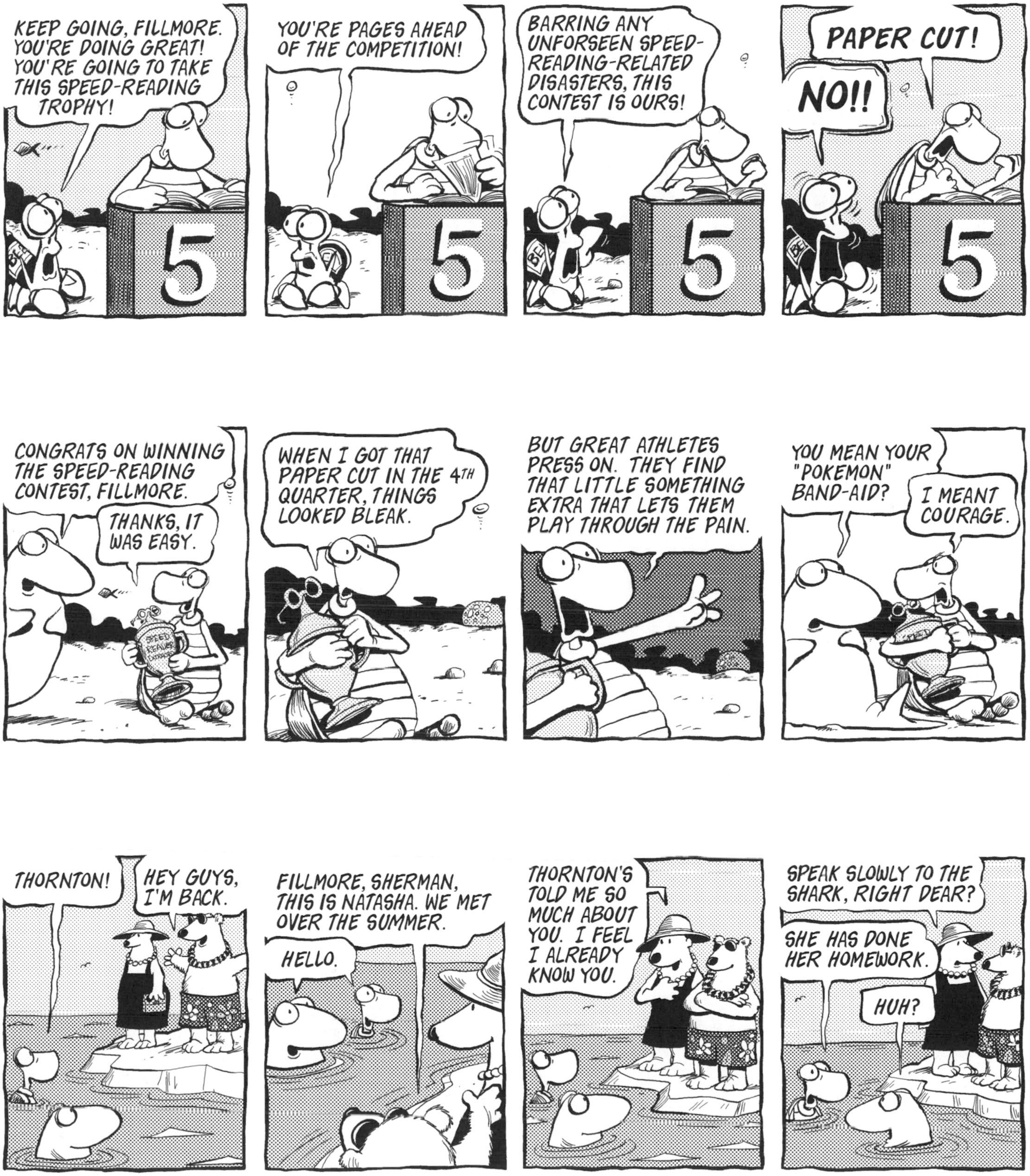
KEEP GOING, FILLMORE. YOU'RE DOING GREAT! YOU'RE GOING TO TAKE THIS SPEED-READING TROPHY!
YOU'RE PAGES AHEAD OF THE COMPETITION!
BARRING ANY UNFORSEEN SPEED-READING-RELATED DISASTERS, THIS CONTEST IS OURS!
PAPER CUT!
NO!!
CONGRATS ON WINNING THE SPEED-READING CONTEST, FILLMORE.
THANKS, IT WAS EASY.
WHEN I GOT THAT PAPER CUT IN THE 4TH QUARTER, THINGS LOOKED BLEAK.
BUT GREAT ATHLETES PRESS ON. THEY FIND THAT LITTLE SOMETHING EXTRA THAT LETS THEM PLAY THROUGH THE PAIN.
YOU MEAN YOUR "POKEMON" BAND-AID?
I MEANT COURAGE.
THORNTON!
HEY GUYS, I'M BACK.
FILLMORE, SHERMAN, THIS IS NATASHA. WE MET OVER THE SUMMER.
HELLO.
THORNTON'S TOLD ME SO MUCH ABOUT YOU. I FEEL I ALREADY KNOW YOU.
SPEAK SLOWLY TO THE SHARK, RIGHT DEAR?
SHE HAS DONE HER HOMEWORK.
HUH?

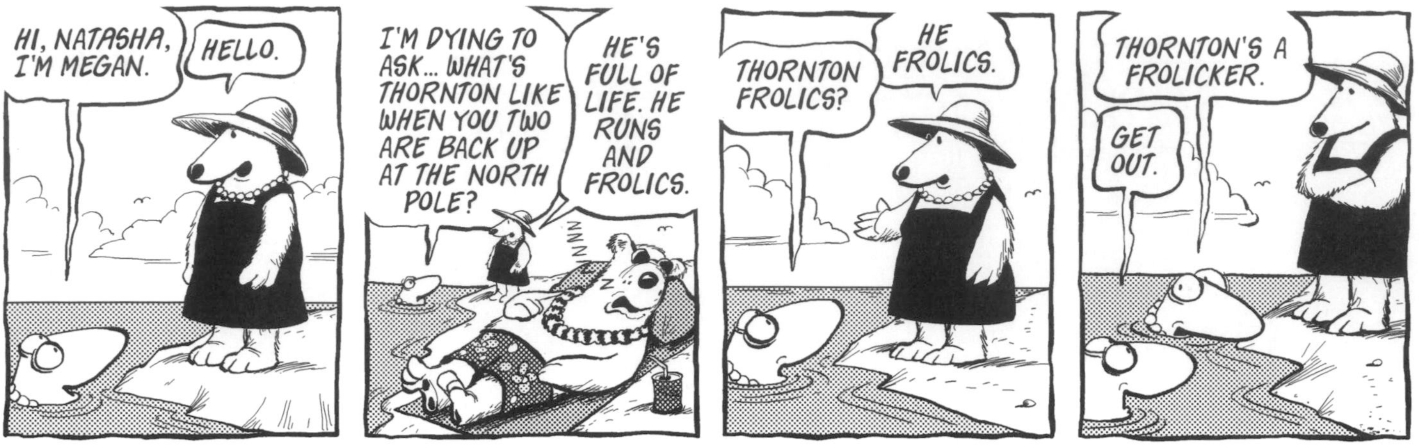
HI, NATASHA, I'M MEGAN.
HELLO.
I'M DYING TO ASK... WHAT'S THORNTON LIKE WHEN YOU TWO ARE BACK UP AT THE NORTH POLE?
HE'S FULL OF LIFE. HE RUNS AND FROLICS.
THORNTON FROLICS?
HE FROLICS.
THORNTON'S A FROLICKER.
GET OUT.

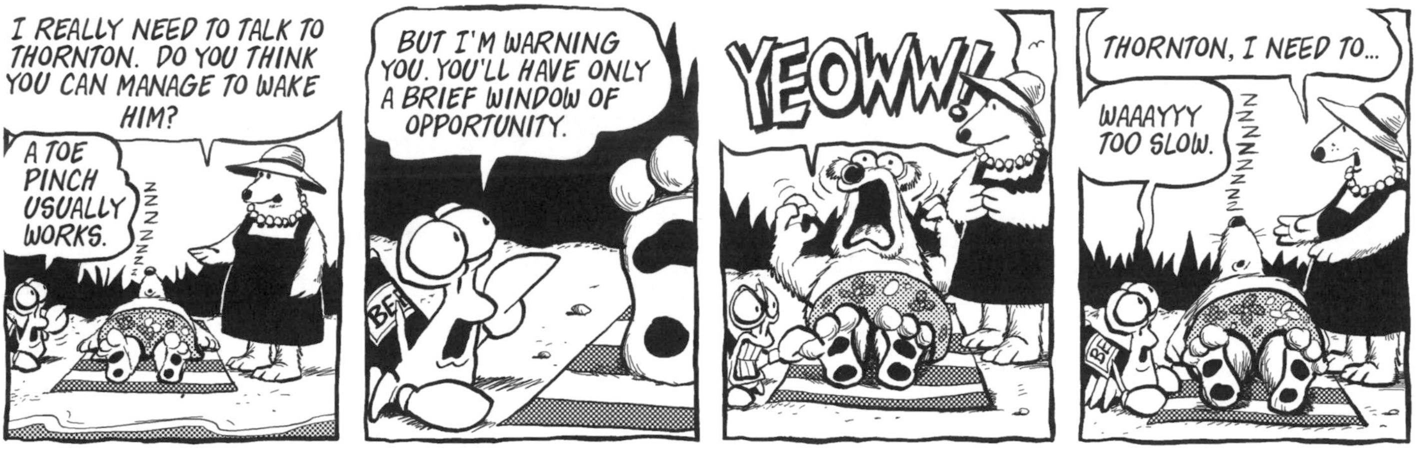
I REALLY NEED TO TALK TO THORNTON. DO YOU THINK YOU CAN MANAGE TO WAKE HIM?
A TOE PINCH USUALLY WORKS.
BUT I'M WARNING YOU. YOU'LL HAVE ONLY A BRIEF WINDOW OF OPPORTUNITY.
YEOWW!
THORNTON, I NEED TO...
WAAAYYY TOO SLOW.

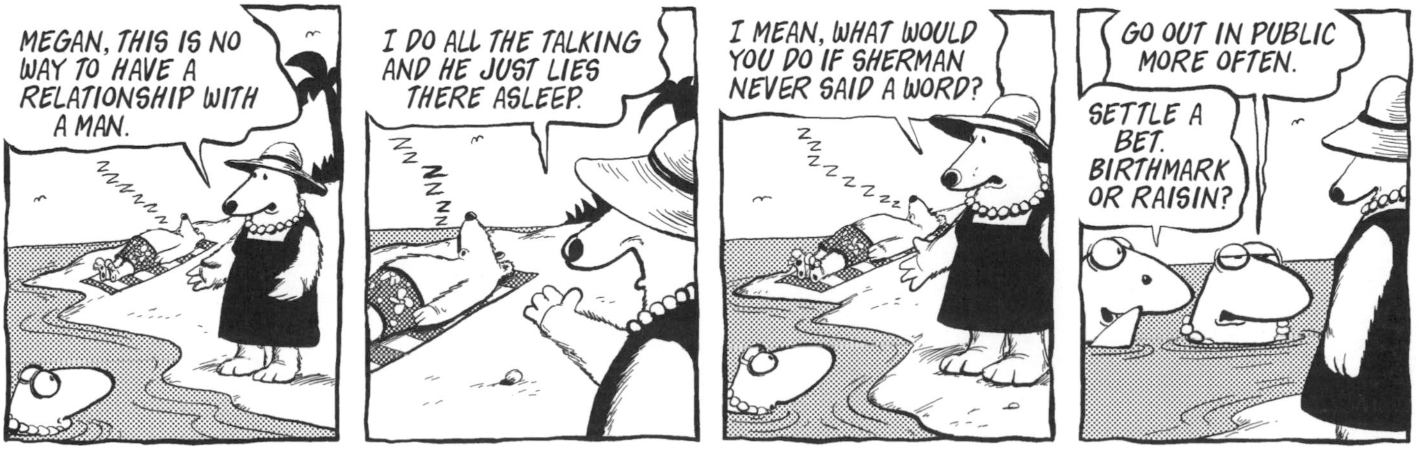
MEGAN, THIS IS NO WAY TO HAVE A RELATIONSHIP WITH A MAN.
I DO ALL THE TALKING AND HE JUST LIES THERE ASLEEP.
I MEAN, WHAT WOULD YOU DO IF SHERMAN NEVER SAID A WORD?
GO OUT IN PUBLIC MORE OFTEN.
SETTLE A BET. BIRTHMARK OR RAISIN?

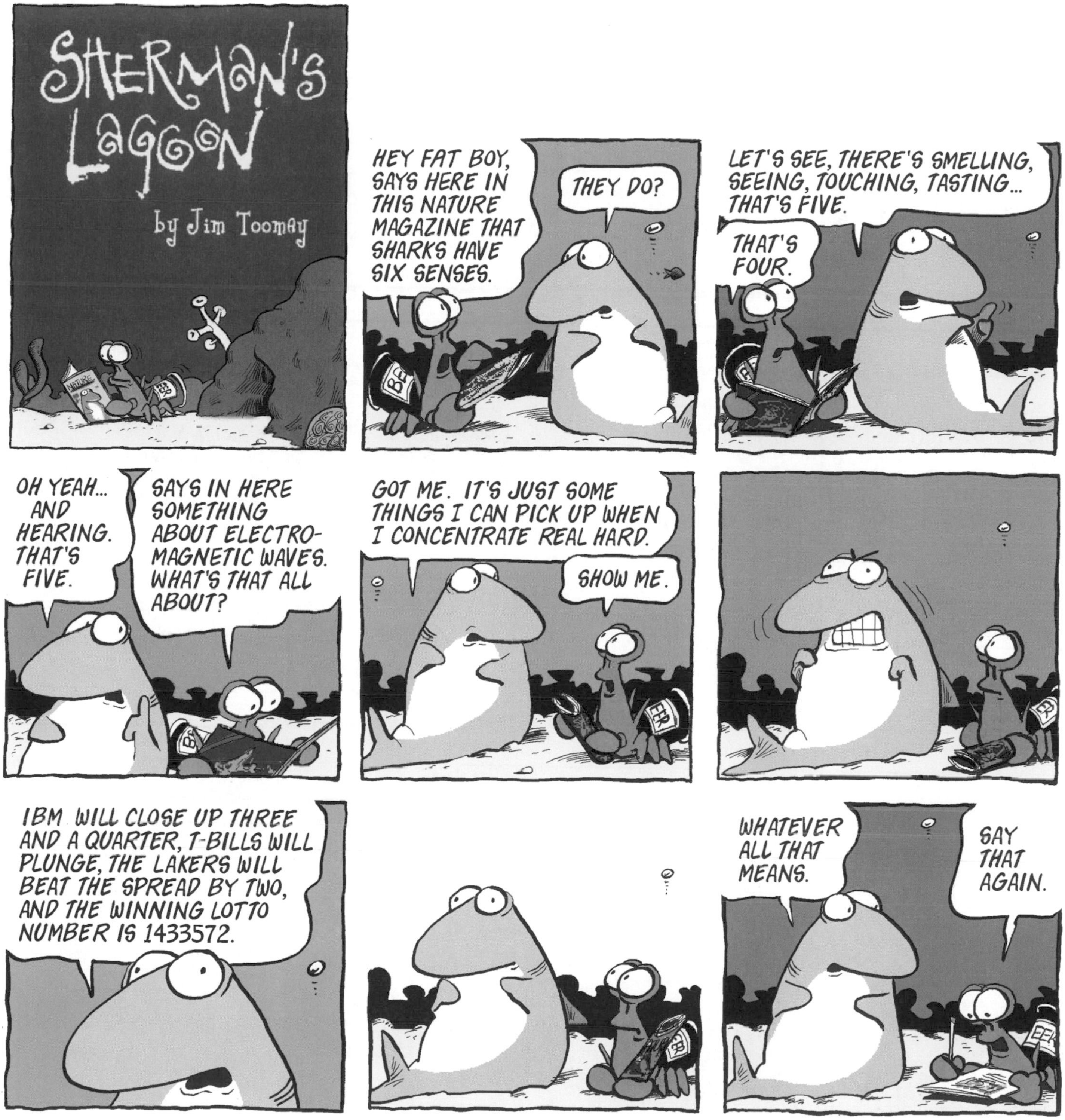
SHERMAN'S LAGOON
by Jim Toomey
NATURE
BEER
HEY FAT BOY, SAYS HERE IN THIS NATURE MAGAZINE THAT SHARKS HAVE SIX SENSES.
THEY DO?
LET'S SEE, THERE'S SMELLING, SEEING, TOUCHING, TASTING... THAT'S FIVE.
THAT'S FOUR.
OH YEAH... AND HEARING. THAT'S FIVE.
SAYS IN HERE SOMETHING ABOUT ELECTRO-MAGNETIC WAVES. WHAT'S THAT ALL ABOUT?
GOT ME. IT'S JUST SOME THINGS I CAN PICK UP WHEN I CONCENTRATE REAL HARD.
SHOW ME.
IBM WILL CLOSE UP THREE AND A QUARTER, T-BILLS WILL PLUNGE, THE LAKERS WILL BEAT THE SPREAD BY TWO, AND THE WINNING LOTTO NUMBER IS 1433572.
WHATEVER ALL THAT MEANS.
SAY THAT AGAIN.

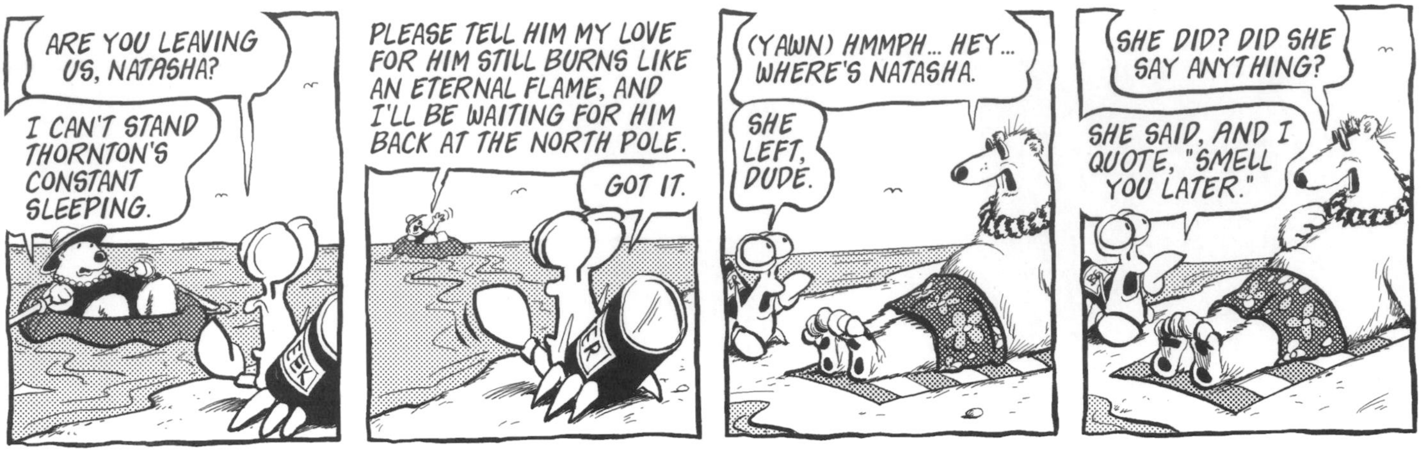
ARE YOU LEAVING US, NATASHA?
I CAN'T STAND THORNTON'S CONSTANT SLEEPING.
EEK
PLEASE TELL HIM MY LOVE FOR HIM STILL BURNS LIKE AN ETERNAL FLAME, AND I'LL BE WAITING FOR HIM BACK AT THE NORTH POLE.
GOT IT.
(YAWN) HMMPH... HEY... WHERE'S NATASHA.
SHE LEFT, DUDE.
SHE DID? DID SHE SAY ANYTHING?
SHE SAID, AND I QUOTE, "SMELL YOU LATER."

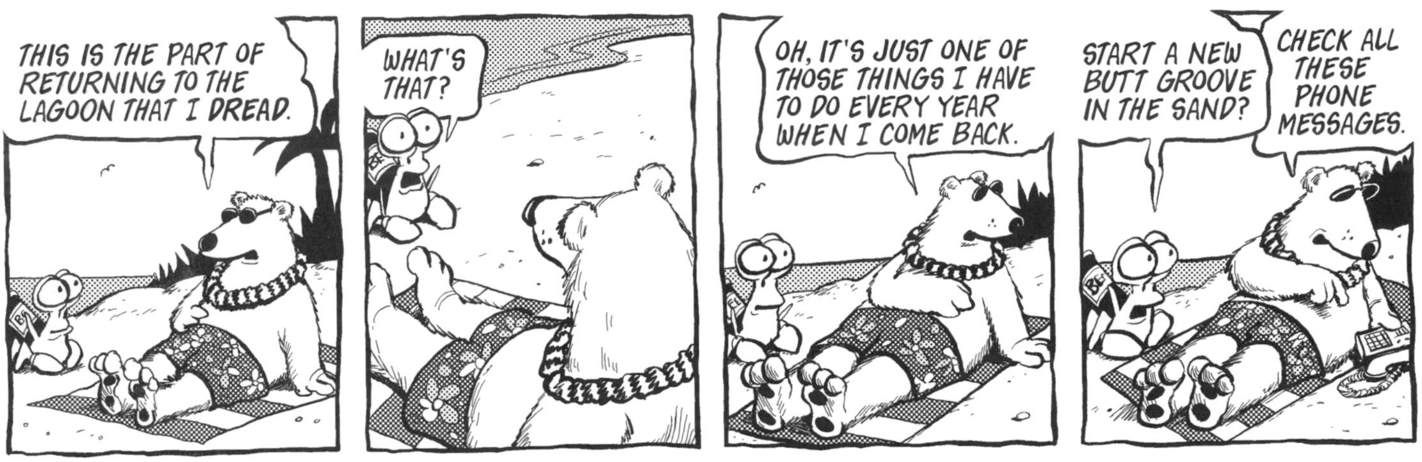
THIS IS THE PART OF RETURNING TO THE LAGOON THAT I DREAD.
WHAT'S THAT?
OH, IT'S JUST ONE OF THOSE THINGS I HAVE TO DO EVERY YEAR WHEN I COME BACK.
START A NEW BUTT GROOVE IN THE SAND?
CHECK ALL THESE PHONE MESSAGES.

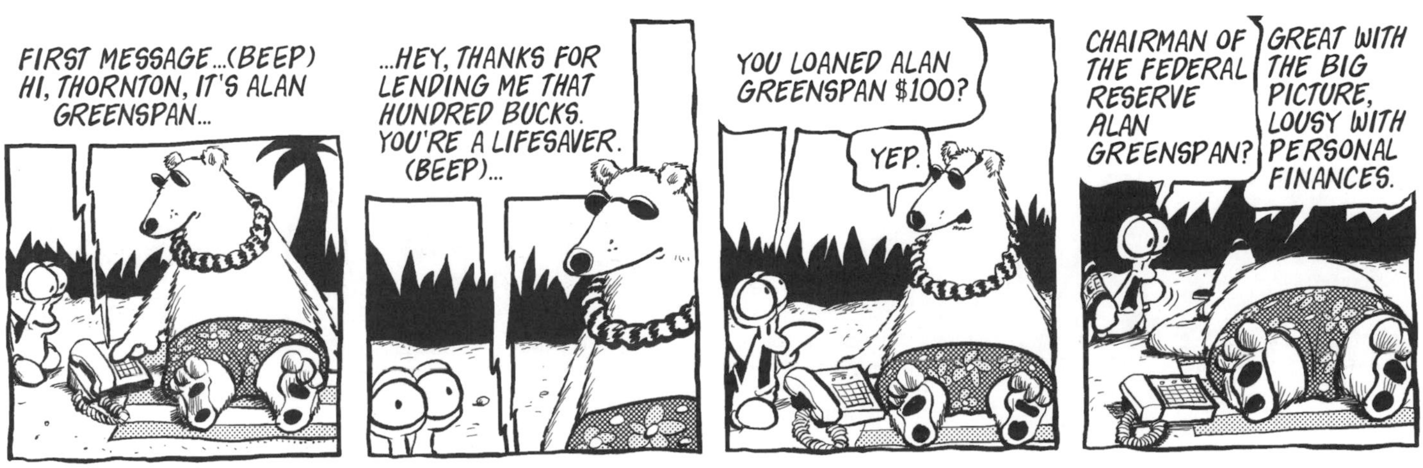
FIRST MESSAGE...(BEEP) HI, THORNTON, IT'S ALAN GREENSPAN...
...HEY, THANKS FOR LENDING ME THAT HUNDRED BUCKS. YOU'RE A LIFESAVER. (BEEP)...
YOU LOANED ALAN GREENSPAN $100?
YEP.
CHAIRMAN OF THE FEDERAL RESERVE ALAN GREENSPAN?
GREAT WITH THE BIG PICTURE, LOUSY WITH PERSONAL FINANCES.

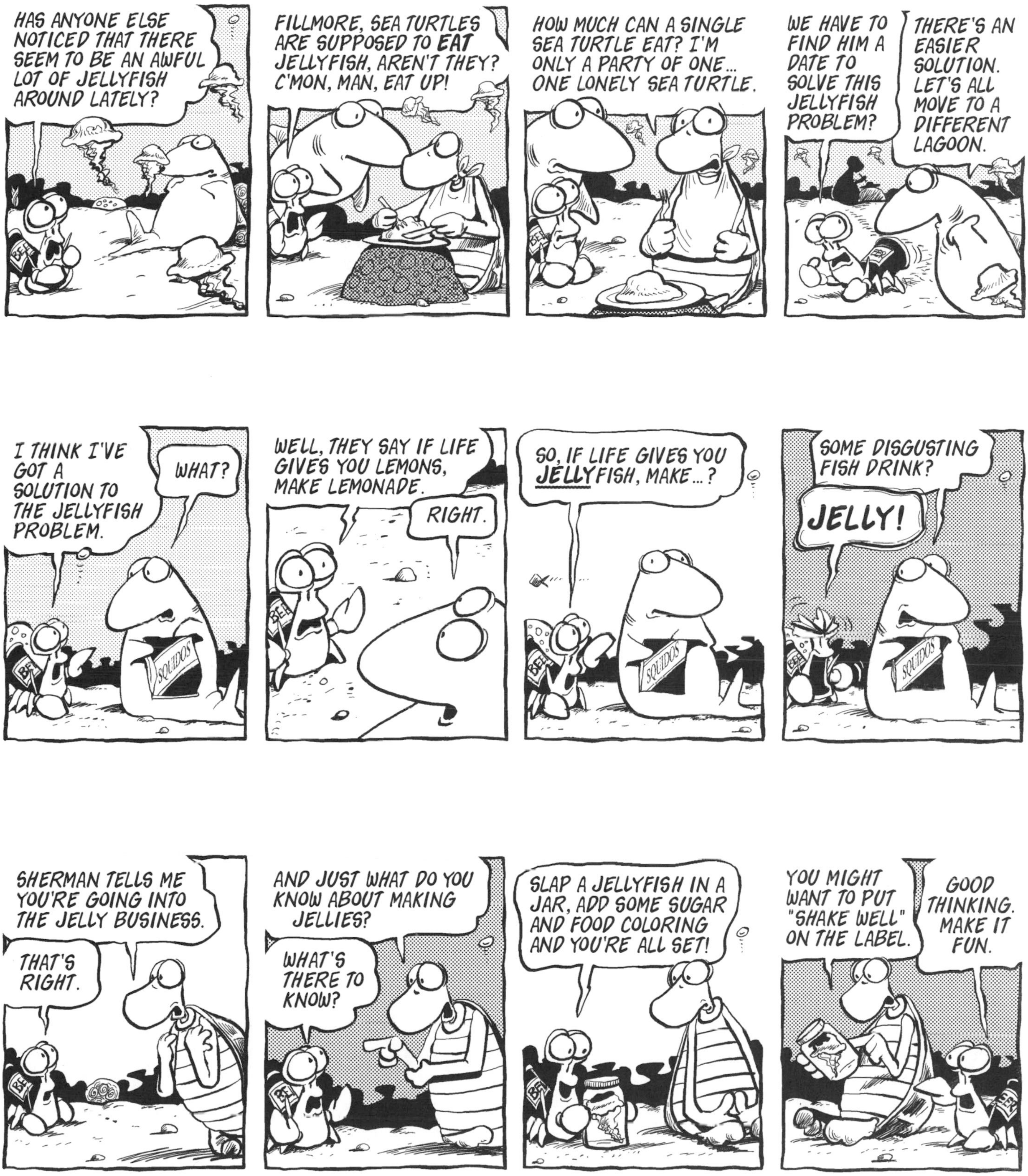
HAS ANYONE ELSE NOTICED THAT THERE SEEM TO BE AN AWFUL LOT OF JELLYFISH AROUND LATELY?
FILLMORE, SEA TURTLES ARE SUPPOSED TO EAT JELLYFISH, AREN'T THEY? C'MON, MAN, EAT UP!
HOW MUCH CAN A SINGLE SEA TURTLE EAT? I'M ONLY A PARTY OF ONE... ONE LONELY SEA TURTLE.
WE HAVE TO FIND HIM A DATE TO SOLVE THIS JELLYFISH PROBLEM?
THERE'S AN EASIER SOLUTION. LET'S ALL MOVE TO A DIFFERENT LAGOON.
I THINK I'VE GOT A SOLUTION TO THE JELLYFISH PROBLEM.
WHAT?
SQUIDOS
WELL, THEY SAY IF LIFE GIVES YOU LEMONS, MAKE LEMONADE.
RIGHT.
SO, IF LIFE GIVES YOU JELLYFISH, MAKE...?
SOME DISGUSTING FISH DRINK?
JELLY!
SHERMAN TELLS ME YOU'RE GOING INTO THE JELLY BUSINESS.
THAT'S RIGHT.
AND JUST WHAT DO YOU KNOW ABOUT MAKING JELLIES?
WHAT'S THERE TO KNOW?
SLAP A JELLYFISH IN A JAR, ADD SOME SUGAR AND FOOD COLORING AND YOU'RE ALL SET!
YOU MIGHT WANT TO PUT "SHAKE WELL" ON THE LABEL.
GOOD THINKING. MAKE IT FUN.

YOUR NEW JELLY BUSINESS HAS CERTAINLY CLEARED UP THE JELLYFISH PROBLEM.

AND IT'S GOING TO BE HUGE.

I'VE COME UP WITH OVER A DOZEN DIFFERENT FLAVORS.

I THOUGHT I'D NAME MY JELLIES AFTER CELEBRITIES, LIKE THOSE ICE CREAM GUYS.

"RUDOLPH JELLYANI"?

TRY "CHUNKY CHENEY."

I'VE GOT A GREAT HOOK FOR MARKETING MY NEW JELLIES.

I'LL SAY THEY'RE MEDICINAL JELLIES.

BUT THEY'RE JUST MADE FROM BLENDED JELLYFISH.

YEAH, BUT EVERYONE LIKES TO THINK THEY'RE DOING SOMETHING GOOD FOR THEMSELVES.

IT STINGS YOUR MOUTH.

THAT TELLS YOU IT'S WORKING.

GOOD MORNING, FILLMORE. HOW CAN I HELP YOU TODAY?

GOURMET JAMS & JELLIES
$6.95 per jar

I'D LIKE ANOTHER JAR OF "RUDOLPH JELLYANI" PLEASE.

GOURMET JAMS & JELLIES
$6.95 per jar

WAIT! TRY THIS NEW CELEBRITY FLAVOR I'VE JUST INVENTED. IT'S PART OF MY 60'S SERIES.

GOURMET JAMS & JELLIES
$6.95 per jar

IT'LL DISAPPEAR, AND YOU WON'T KNOW WHERE IT WENT.

JAMMY HOFFA?

GOURMET JAMS & JELLIES
$6.95 per jar

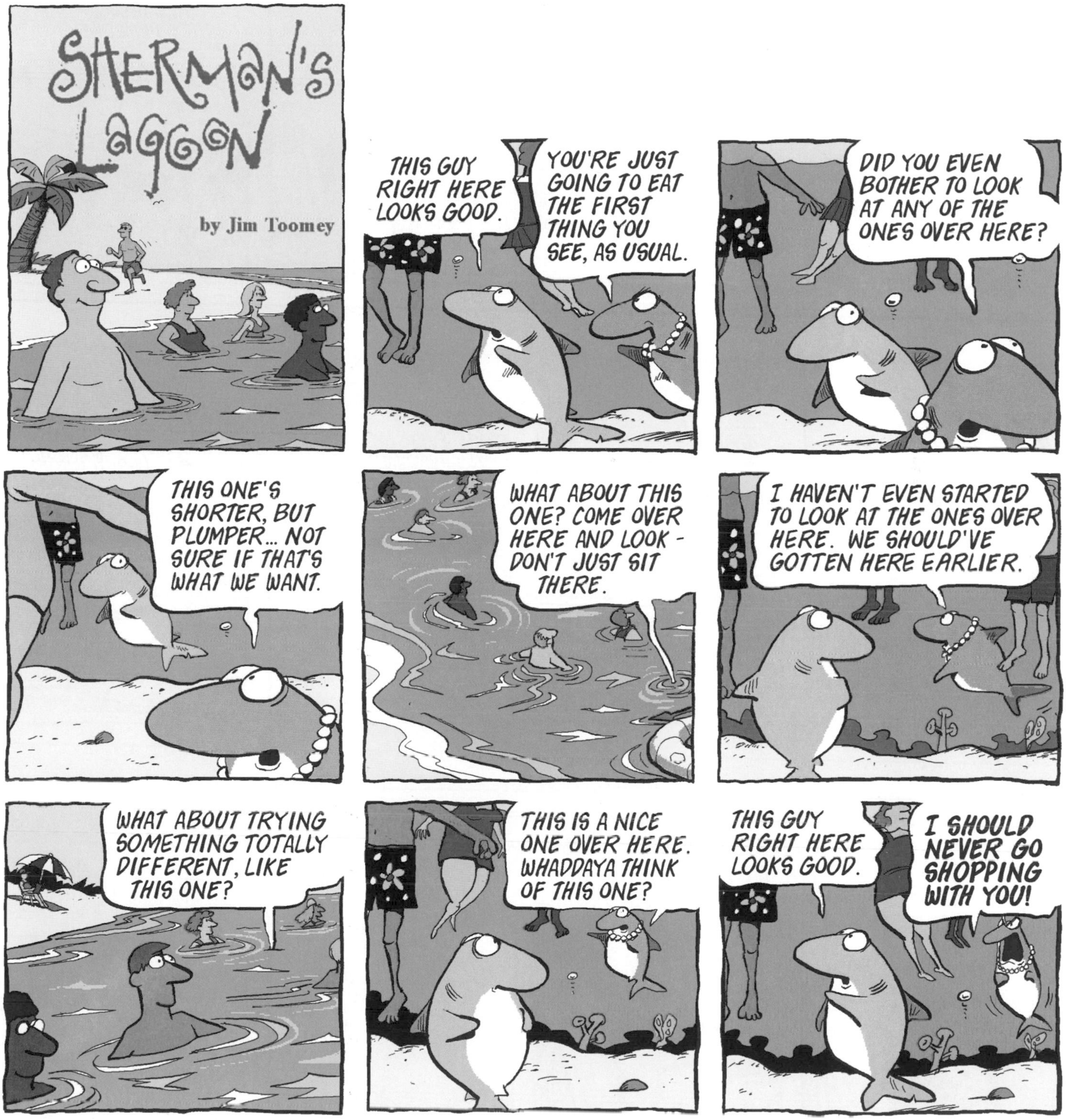
SHERMAN'S LAGOON
by Jim Toomey
THIS GUY RIGHT HERE LOOKS GOOD.
YOU'RE JUST GOING TO EAT THE FIRST THING YOU SEE, AS USUAL.
DID YOU EVEN BOTHER TO LOOK AT ANY OF THE ONES OVER HERE?
THIS ONE'S SHORTER, BUT PLUMPER... NOT SURE IF THAT'S WHAT WE WANT.
WHAT ABOUT THIS ONE? COME OVER HERE AND LOOK - DON'T JUST SIT THERE.
I HAVEN'T EVEN STARTED TO LOOK AT THE ONES OVER HERE. WE SHOULD'VE GOTTEN HERE EARLIER.
WHAT ABOUT TRYING SOMETHING TOTALLY DIFFERENT, LIKE THIS ONE?
THIS IS A NICE ONE OVER HERE. WHADDAYA THINK OF THIS ONE?
THIS GUY RIGHT HERE LOOKS GOOD.
I SHOULD NEVER GO SHOPPING WITH YOU!

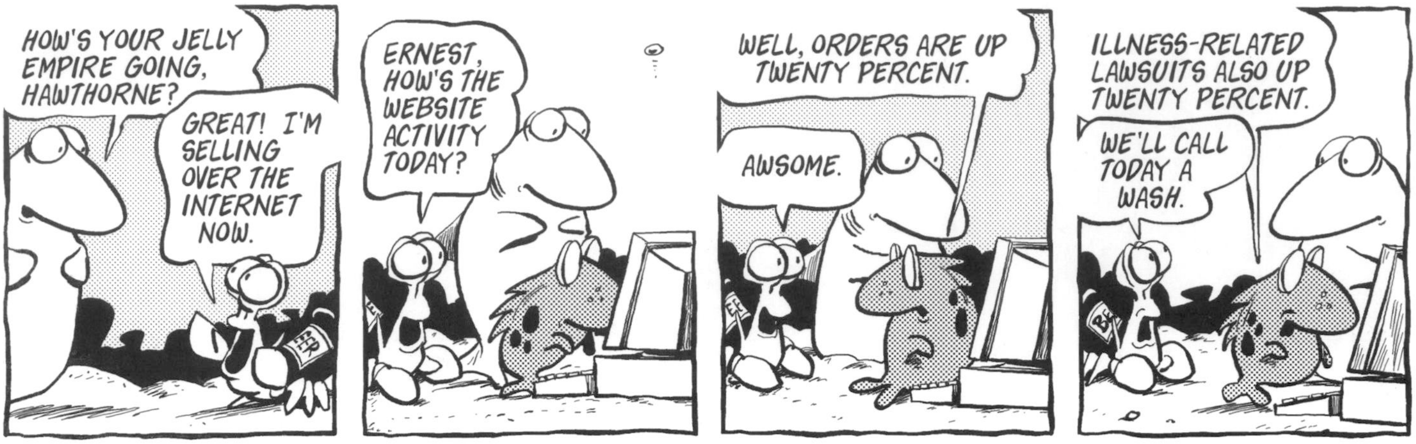
HOW'S YOUR JELLY EMPIRE GOING, HAWTHORNE?
GREAT! I'M SELLING OVER THE INTERNET NOW.
ERNEST, HOW'S THE WEBSITE ACTIVITY TODAY?
WELL, ORDERS ARE UP TWENTY PERCENT.
AWSOME.
ILLNESS-RELATED LAWSUITS ALSO UP TWENTY PERCENT.
WE'LL CALL TODAY A WASH.

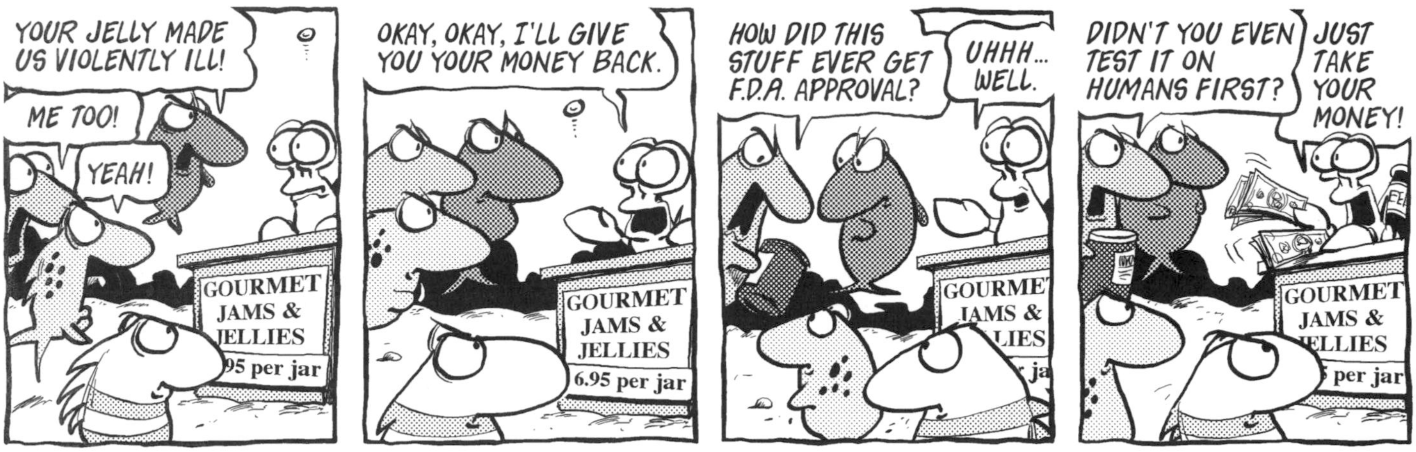
YOUR JELLY MADE US VIOLENTLY ILL!
ME TOO!
YEAH!
GOURMET JAMS & JELLIES
OKAY, OKAY, I'LL GIVE YOU YOUR MONEY BACK.
GOURMET JAMS & JELLIES 6.95 per jar
HOW DID THIS STUFF EVER GET F.D.A. APPROVAL?
UHHH... WELL.
DIDN'T YOU EVEN TEST IT ON HUMANS FIRST?
JUST TAKE YOUR MONEY!

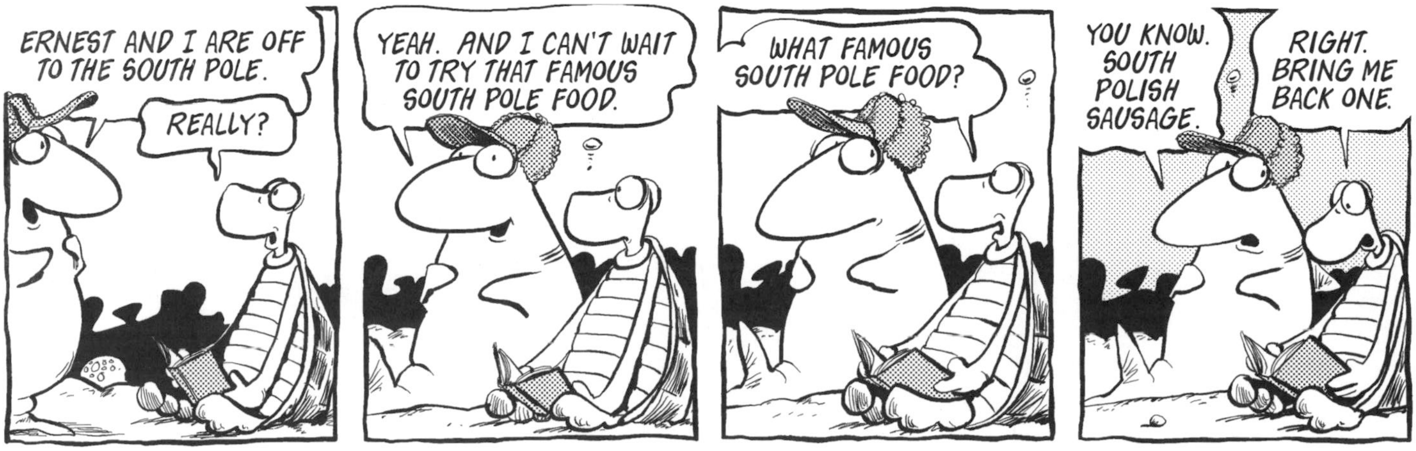
ERNEST AND I ARE OFF TO THE SOUTH POLE.
REALLY?
YEAH. AND I CAN'T WAIT TO TRY THAT FAMOUS SOUTH POLE FOOD.
WHAT FAMOUS SOUTH POLE FOOD?
YOU KNOW. SOUTH POLISH SAUSAGE.
RIGHT. BRING ME BACK ONE.

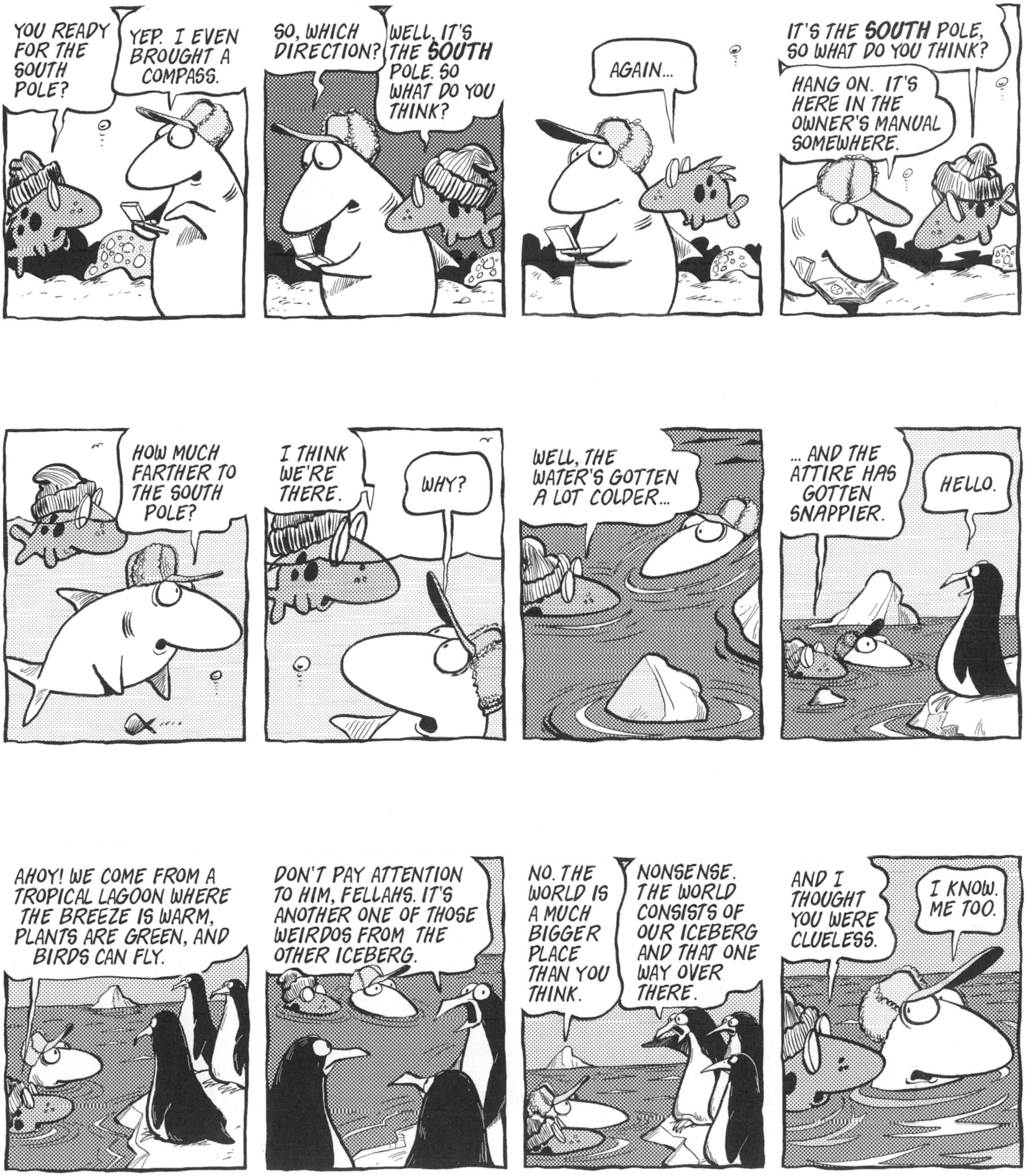
YOU READY FOR THE SOUTH POLE?
YEP. I EVEN BROUGHT A COMPASS.
SO, WHICH DIRECTION?
WELL, IT'S THE SOUTH POLE. SO WHAT DO YOU THINK?
AGAIN...
IT'S THE SOUTH POLE, SO WHAT DO YOU THINK?
HANG ON. IT'S HERE IN THE OWNER'S MANUAL SOMEWHERE.
HOW MUCH FARTHER TO THE SOUTH POLE?
I THINK WE'RE THERE.
WHY?
WELL, THE WATER'S GOTTEN A LOT COLDER...
... AND THE ATTIRE HAS GOTTEN SNAPPIER.
HELLO.
AHOY! WE COME FROM A TROPICAL LAGOON WHERE THE BREEZE IS WARM, PLANTS ARE GREEN, AND BIRDS CAN FLY.
DON'T PAY ATTENTION TO HIM, FELLAHS. IT'S ANOTHER ONE OF THOSE WEIRDOS FROM THE OTHER ICEBERG.
NO. THE WORLD IS A MUCH BIGGER PLACE THAN YOU THINK.
NONSENSE. THE WORLD CONSISTS OF OUR ICEBERG AND THAT ONE WAY OVER THERE.
AND I THOUGHT YOU WERE CLUELESS.
I KNOW. ME TOO.

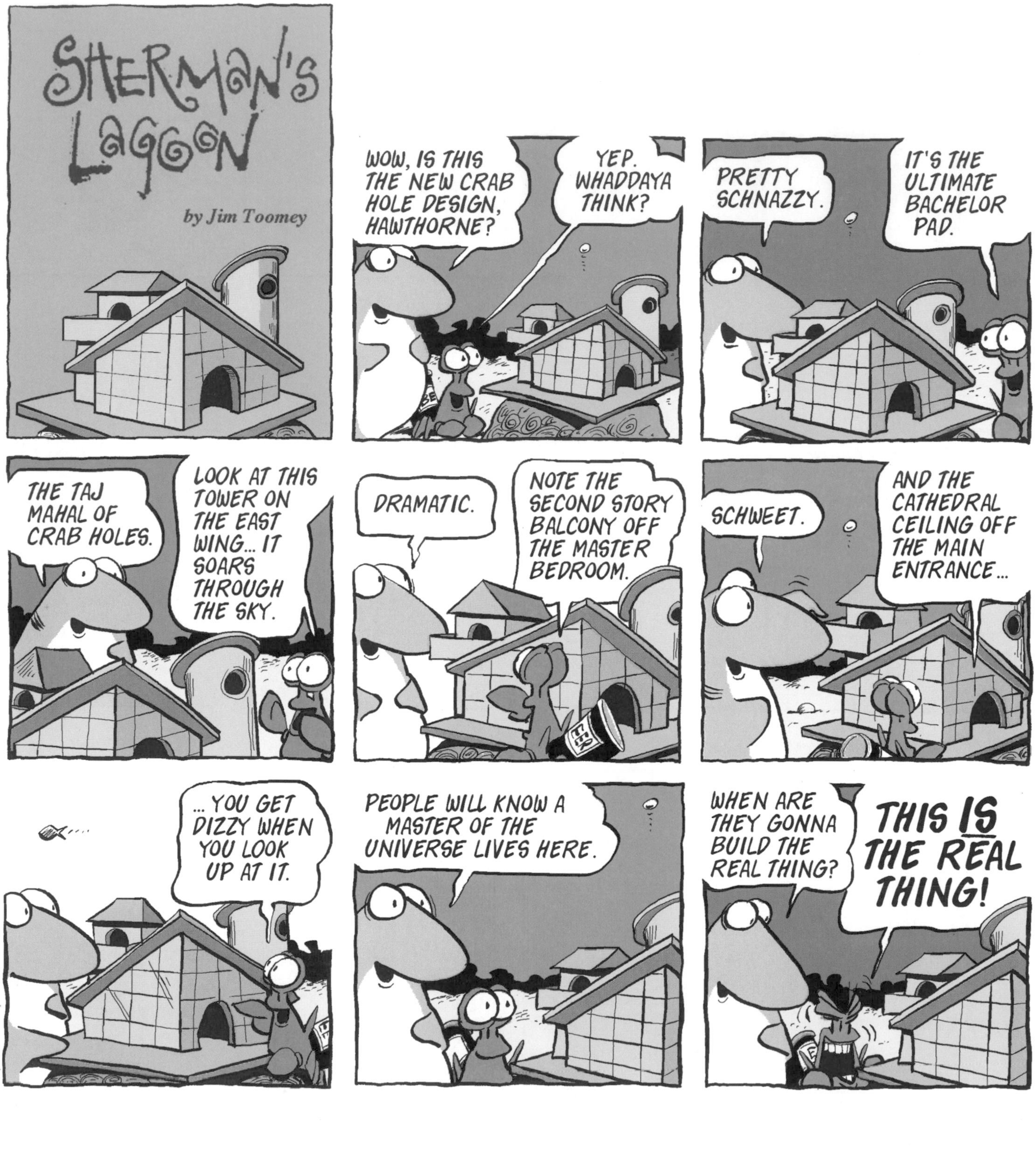
SHERMAN'S LAGOON
by Jim Toomey
WOW, IS THIS THE NEW CRAB HOLE DESIGN, HAWTHORNE?
YEP. WHADDAYA THINK?
PRETTY SCHNAZZY.
IT'S THE ULTIMATE BACHELOR PAD.
THE TAJ MAHAL OF CRAB HOLES.
LOOK AT THIS TOWER ON THE EAST WING... IT SOARS THROUGH THE SKY.
DRAMATIC.
NOTE THE SECOND STORY BALCONY OFF THE MASTER BEDROOM.
SCHWEET.
AND THE CATHEDRAL CEILING OFF THE MAIN ENTRANCE...
... YOU GET DIZZY WHEN YOU LOOK UP AT IT.
PEOPLE WILL KNOW A MASTER OF THE UNIVERSE LIVES HERE.
WHEN ARE THEY GONNA BUILD THE REAL THING?
THIS IS THE REAL THING!

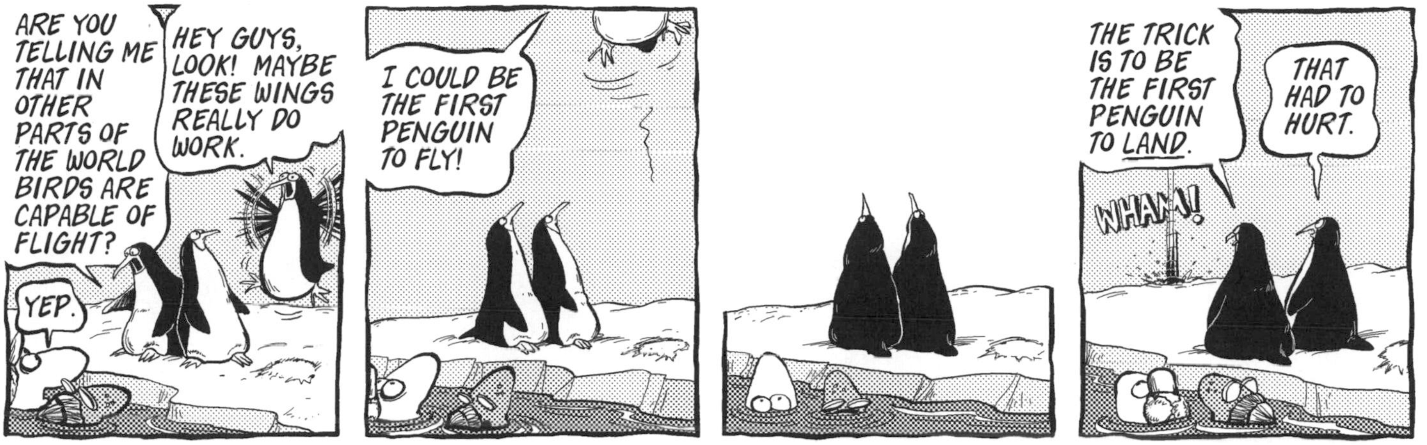
ARE YOU TELLING ME THAT IN OTHER PARTS OF THE WORLD BIRDS ARE CAPABLE OF FLIGHT?
YEP.
HEY GUYS, LOOK! MAYBE THESE WINGS REALLY DO WORK.
I COULD BE THE FIRST PENGUIN TO FLY!
WHAM!
THE TRICK IS TO BE THE FIRST PENGUIN TO LAND.
THAT HAD TO HURT.

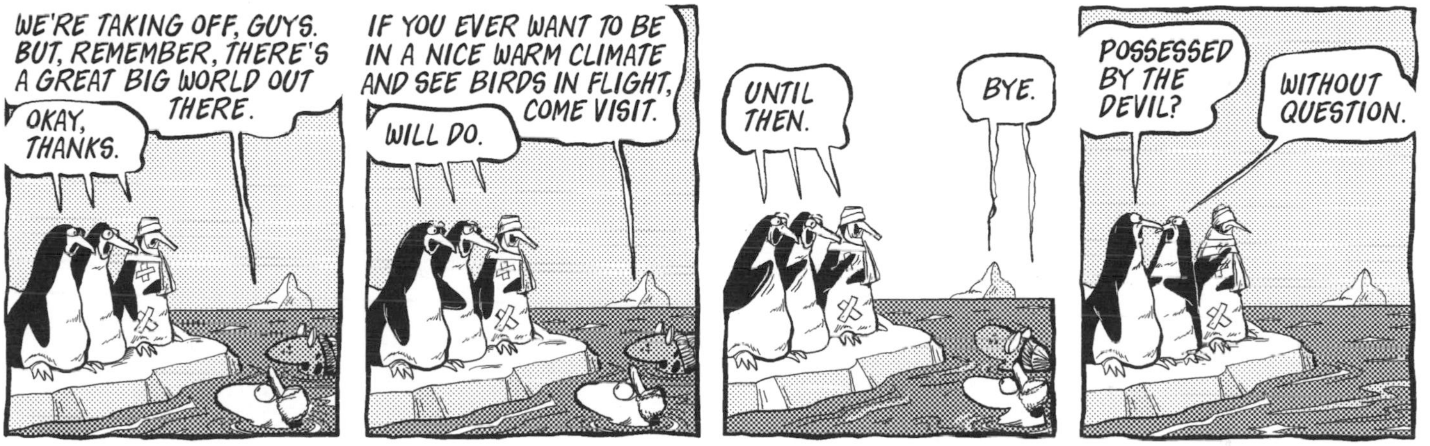
WE'RE TAKING OFF, GUYS. BUT, REMEMBER, THERE'S A GREAT BIG WORLD OUT THERE.
OKAY, THANKS.
IF YOU EVER WANT TO BE IN A NICE WARM CLIMATE AND SEE BIRDS IN FLIGHT, COME VISIT.
WILL DO.
UNTIL THEN.
BYE.
POSSESSED BY THE DEVIL?
WITHOUT QUESTION.

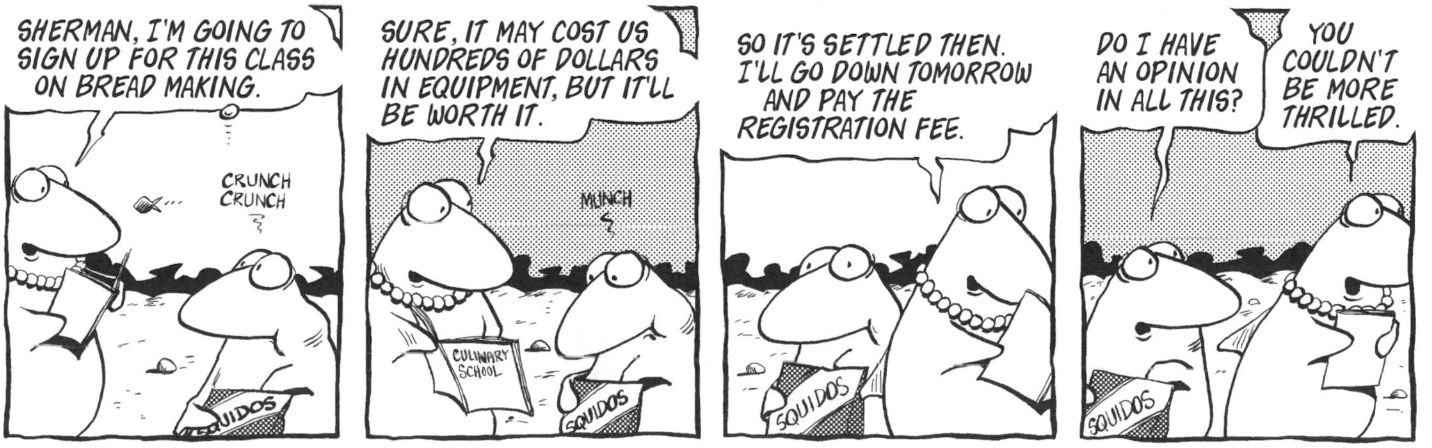
SHERMAN, I'M GOING TO SIGN UP FOR THIS CLASS ON BREAD MAKING.
CRUNCH CRUNCH
SQUIDOS
SURE, IT MAY COST US HUNDREDS OF DOLLARS IN EQUIPMENT, BUT IT'LL BE WORTH IT.
MUNCH
CULINARY SCHOOL
SQUIDOS
SO IT'S SETTLED THEN. I'LL GO DOWN TOMORROW AND PAY THE REGISTRATION FEE.
SQUIDOS
DO I HAVE AN OPINION IN ALL THIS?
YOU COULDN'T BE MORE THRILLED.
SQUIDOS

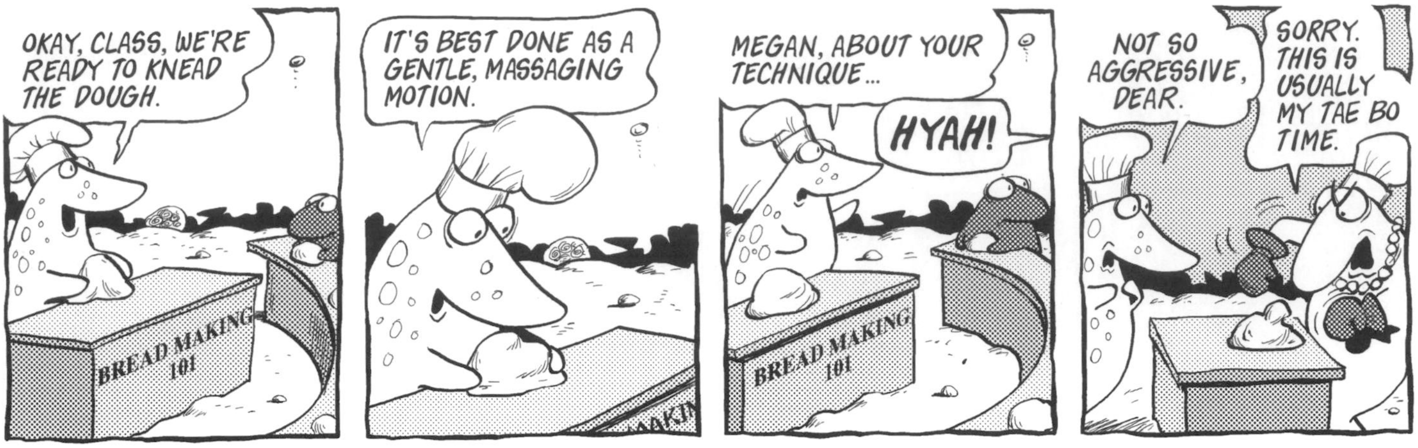
OKAY, CLASS, WE'RE READY TO KNEAD THE DOUGH.
BREAD MAKING 101
IT'S BEST DONE AS A GENTLE, MASSAGING MOTION.
MEGAN, ABOUT YOUR TECHNIQUE...
HYAH!
BREAD MAKING 101
NOT SO AGGRESSIVE, DEAR.
SORRY. THIS IS USUALLY MY TAE BO TIME.

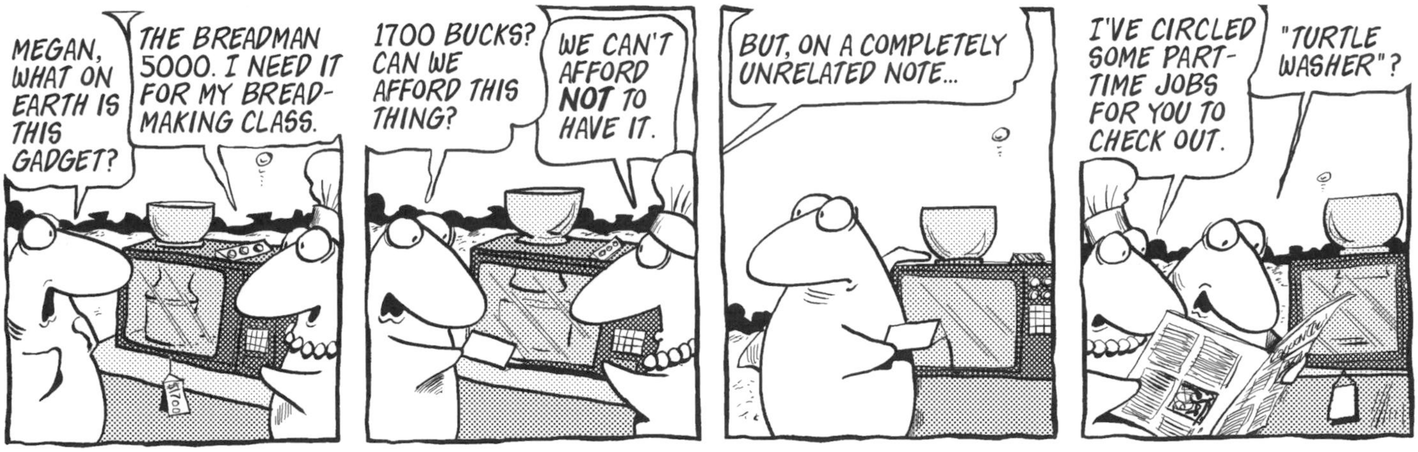
MEGAN, WHAT ON EARTH IS THIS GADGET?
THE BREADMAN 5000. I NEED IT FOR MY BREAD-MAKING CLASS.
1700 BUCKS? CAN WE AFFORD THIS THING?
WE CAN'T AFFORD **NOT** TO HAVE IT.
BUT, ON A COMPLETELY UNRELATED NOTE...
I'VE CIRCLED SOME PART-TIME JOBS FOR YOU TO CHECK OUT.
"TURTLE WASHER"?

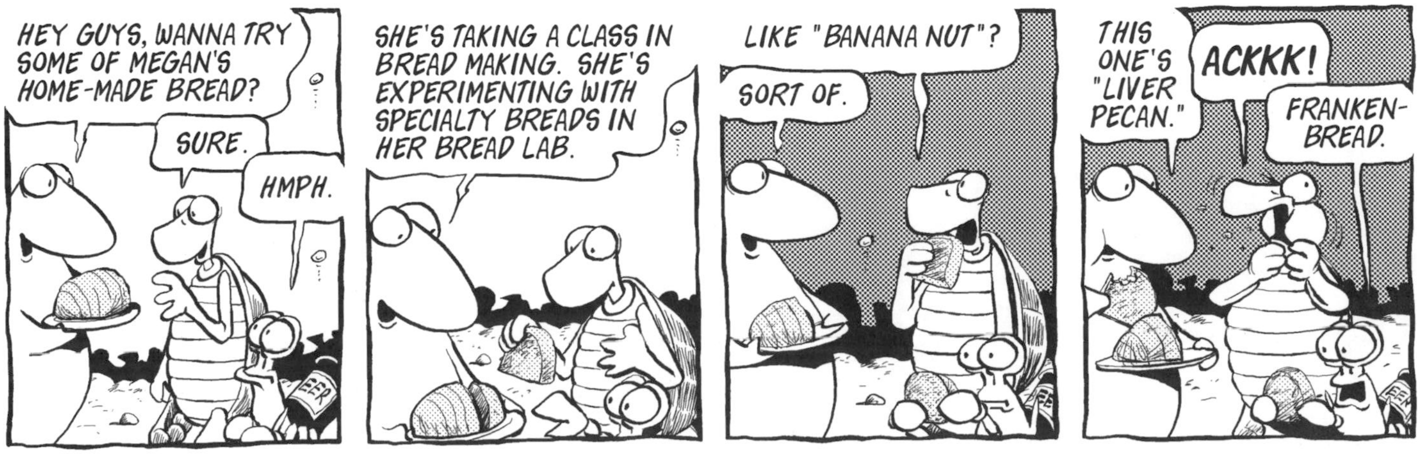
HEY GUYS, WANNA TRY SOME OF MEGAN'S HOME-MADE BREAD?
SURE.
HMPH.
SHE'S TAKING A CLASS IN BREAD MAKING. SHE'S EXPERIMENTING WITH SPECIALTY BREADS IN HER BREAD LAB.
LIKE "BANANA NUT"?
SORT OF.
THIS ONE'S "LIVER PECAN."
ACKKK!
FRANKEN-BREAD.

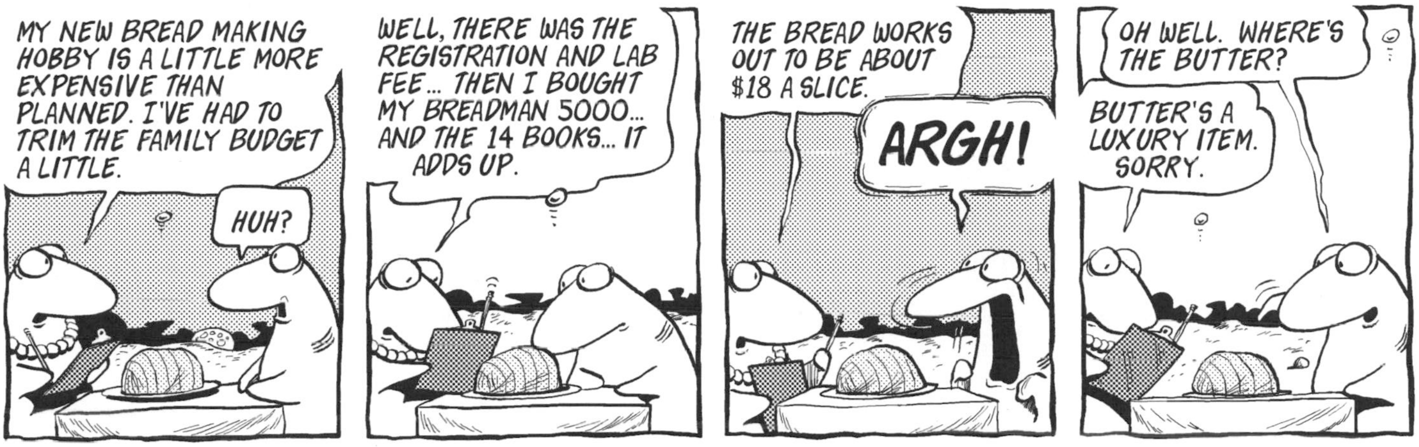
MY NEW BREAD MAKING HOBBY IS A LITTLE MORE EXPENSIVE THAN PLANNED. I'VE HAD TO TRIM THE FAMILY BUDGET A LITTLE.
HUH?
WELL, THERE WAS THE REGISTRATION AND LAB FEE... THEN I BOUGHT MY BREADMAN 5000... AND THE 14 BOOKS... IT ADDS UP.
THE BREAD WORKS OUT TO BE ABOUT $18 A SLICE.
ARGH!
OH WELL. WHERE'S THE BUTTER?
BUTTER'S A LUXURY ITEM. SORRY.

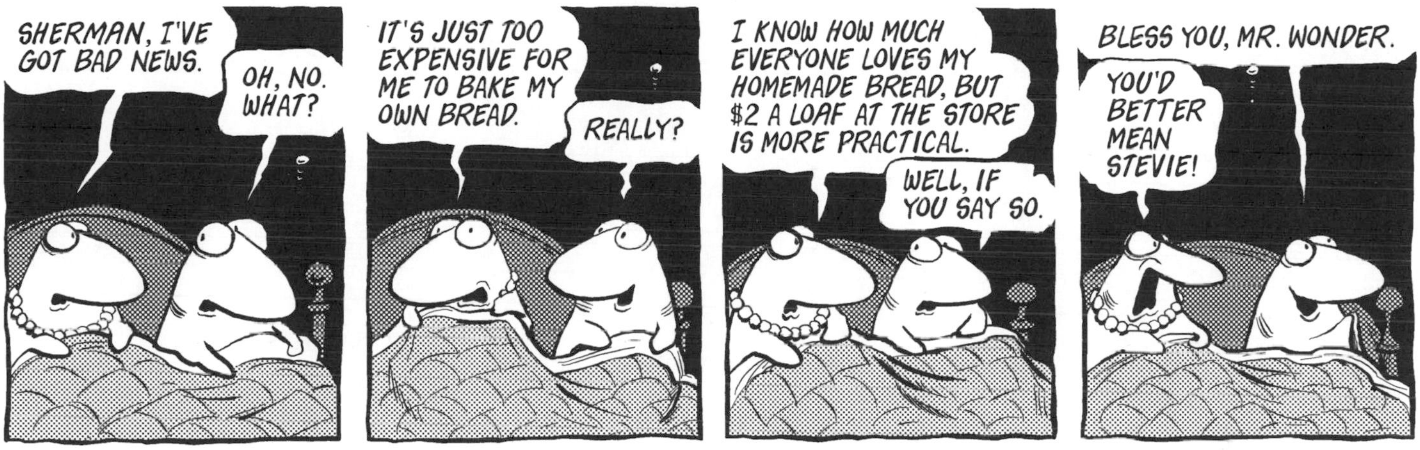
SHERMAN, I'VE GOT BAD NEWS.
OH, NO. WHAT?
IT'S JUST TOO EXPENSIVE FOR ME TO BAKE MY OWN BREAD.
REALLY?
I KNOW HOW MUCH EVERYONE LOVES MY HOMEMADE BREAD, BUT $2 A LOAF AT THE STORE IS MORE PRACTICAL.
WELL, IF YOU SAY SO.
BLESS YOU, MR. WONDER.
YOU'D BETTER MEAN STEVIE!

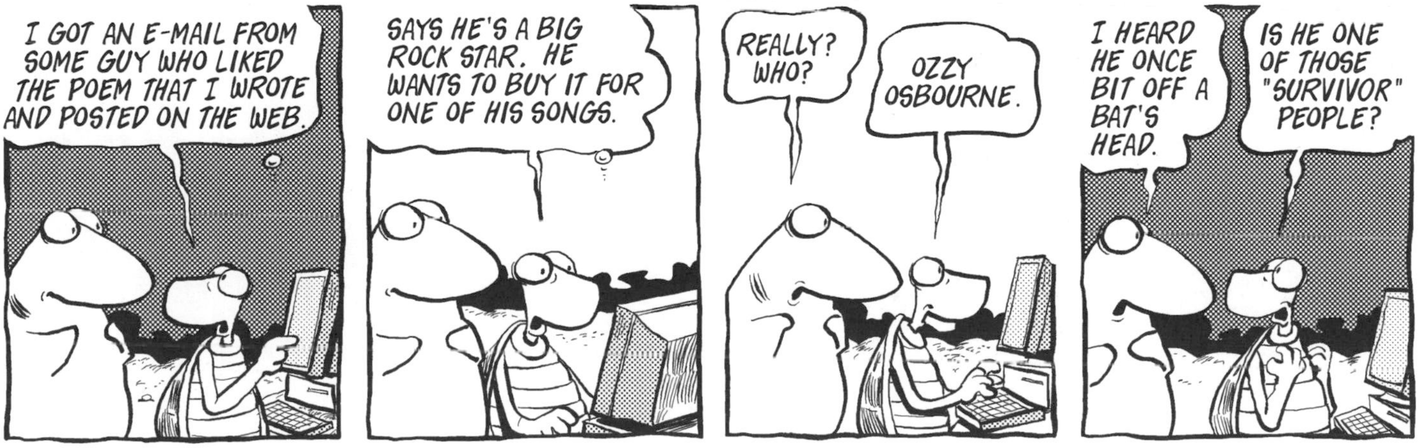
I GOT AN E-MAIL FROM SOME GUY WHO LIKED THE POEM THAT I WROTE AND POSTED ON THE WEB.
SAYS HE'S A BIG ROCK STAR. HE WANTS TO BUY IT FOR ONE OF HIS SONGS.
REALLY? WHO?
OZZY OSBOURNE.
I HEARD HE ONCE BIT OFF A BAT'S HEAD.
IS HE ONE OF THOSE "SURVIVOR" PEOPLE?

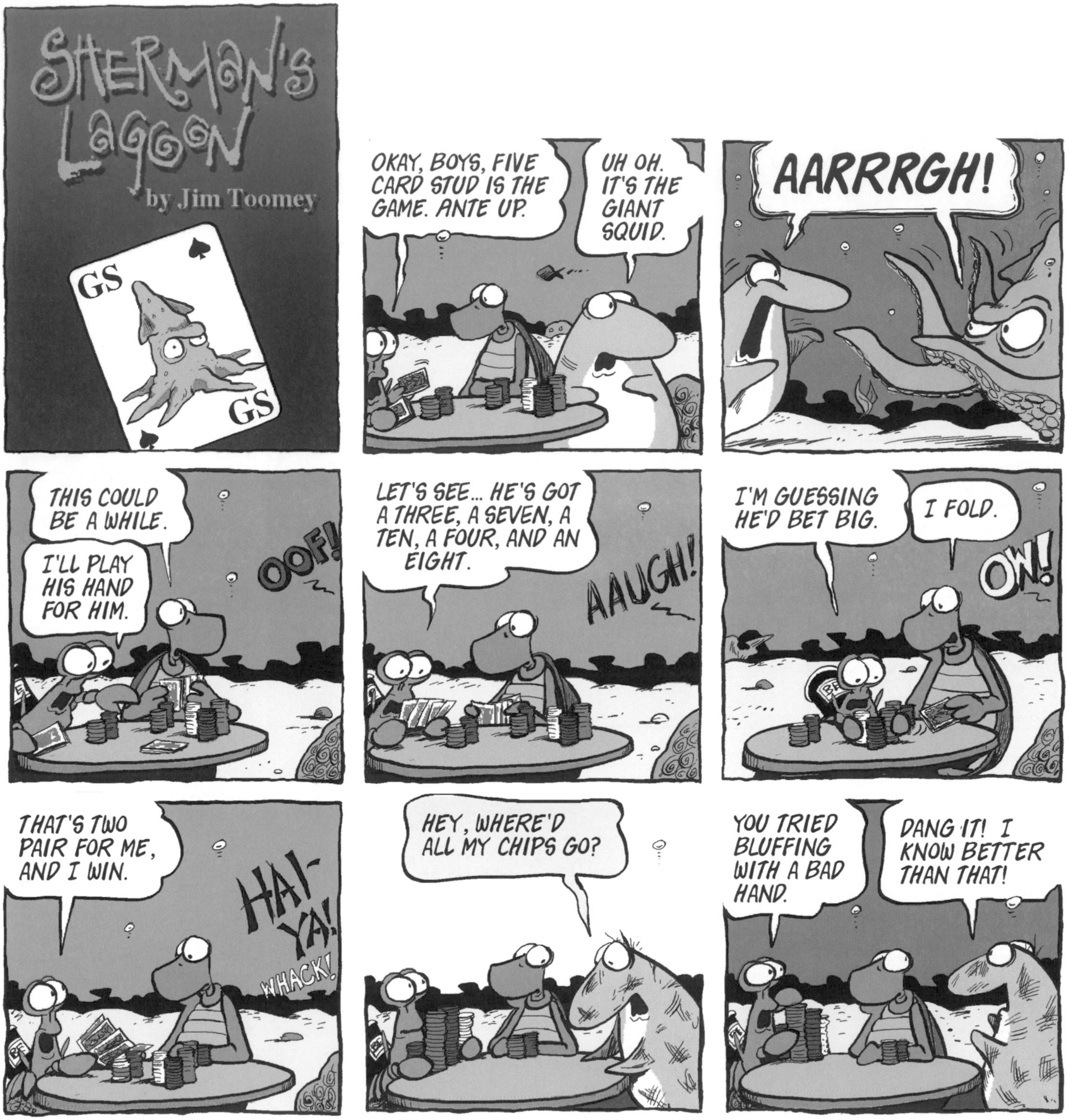
SHERMAN'S LAGOON
by Jim Toomey
GS
GS
OKAY, BOYS, FIVE CARD STUD IS THE GAME. ANTE UP.
UH OH. IT'S THE GIANT SQUID.
AARRRGH!
THIS COULD BE A WHILE.
I'LL PLAY HIS HAND FOR HIM.
OOF!
LET'S SEE... HE'S GOT A THREE, A SEVEN, A TEN, A FOUR, AND AN EIGHT.
AAUGH!
I'M GUESSING HE'D BET BIG.
I FOLD.
OW!
THAT'S TWO PAIR FOR ME, AND I WIN.
HAI-YA!
WHACK!
HEY, WHERE'D ALL MY CHIPS GO?
YOU TRIED BLUFFING WITH A BAD HAND.
DANG IT! I KNOW BETTER THAN THAT!

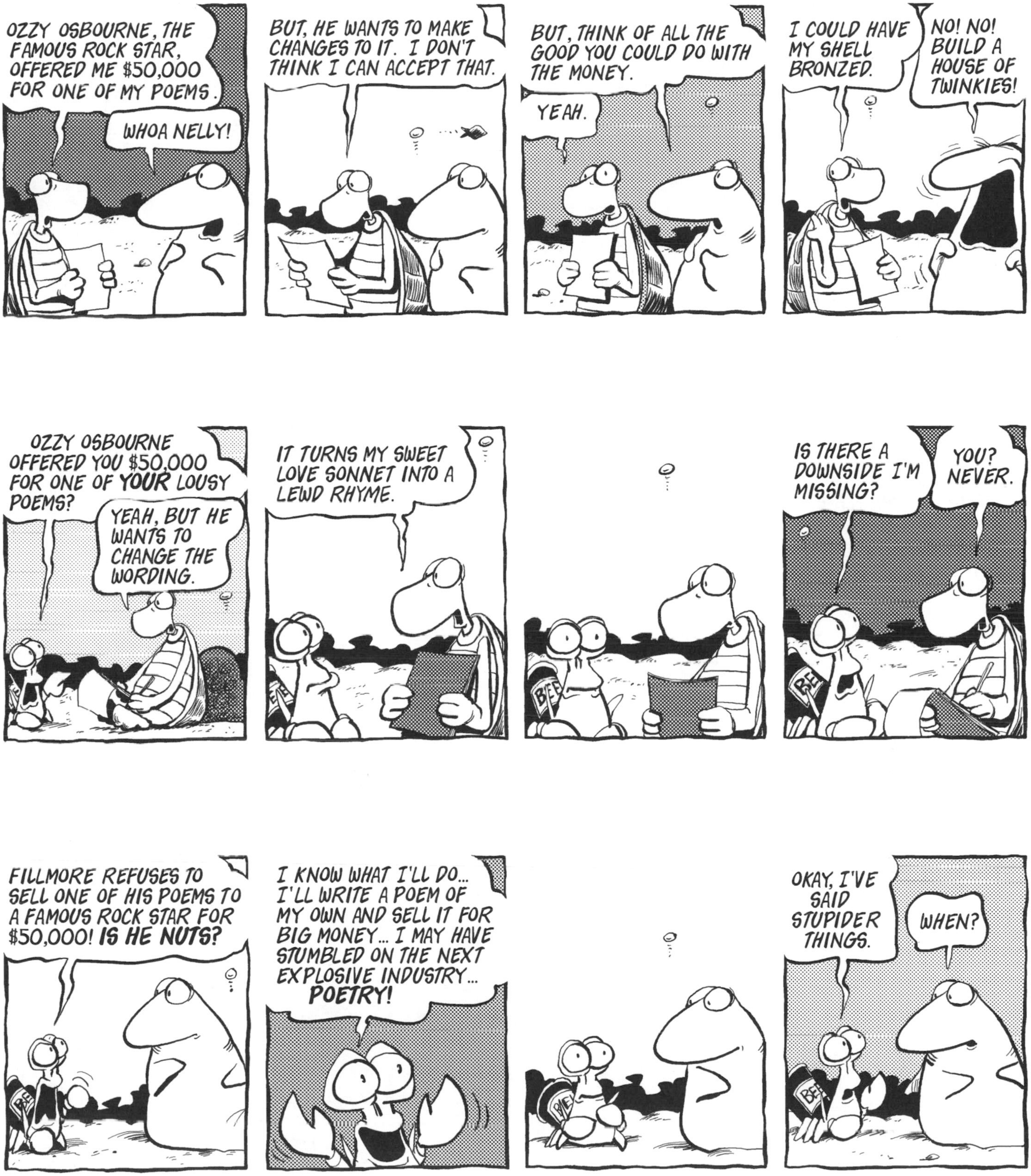
OZZY OSBOURNE, THE FAMOUS ROCK STAR, OFFERED ME $50,000 FOR ONE OF MY POEMS.
WHOA NELLY!
BUT, HE WANTS TO MAKE CHANGES TO IT. I DON'T THINK I CAN ACCEPT THAT.
BUT, THINK OF ALL THE GOOD YOU COULD DO WITH THE MONEY.
YEAH.
I COULD HAVE MY SHELL BRONZED.
NO! NO! BUILD A HOUSE OF TWINKIES!
OZZY OSBOURNE OFFERED YOU $50,000 FOR ONE OF YOUR LOUSY POEMS?
YEAH, BUT HE WANTS TO CHANGE THE WORDING.
IT TURNS MY SWEET LOVE SONNET INTO A LEWD RHYME.
IS THERE A DOWNSIDE I'M MISSING?
YOU? NEVER.
FILLMORE REFUSES TO SELL ONE OF HIS POEMS TO A FAMOUS ROCK STAR FOR $50,000! IS HE NUTS?
I KNOW WHAT I'LL DO... I'LL WRITE A POEM OF MY OWN AND SELL IT FOR BIG MONEY... I MAY HAVE STUMBLED ON THE NEXT EXPLOSIVE INDUSTRY... POETRY!
OKAY, I'VE SAID STUPIDER THINGS.
WHEN?

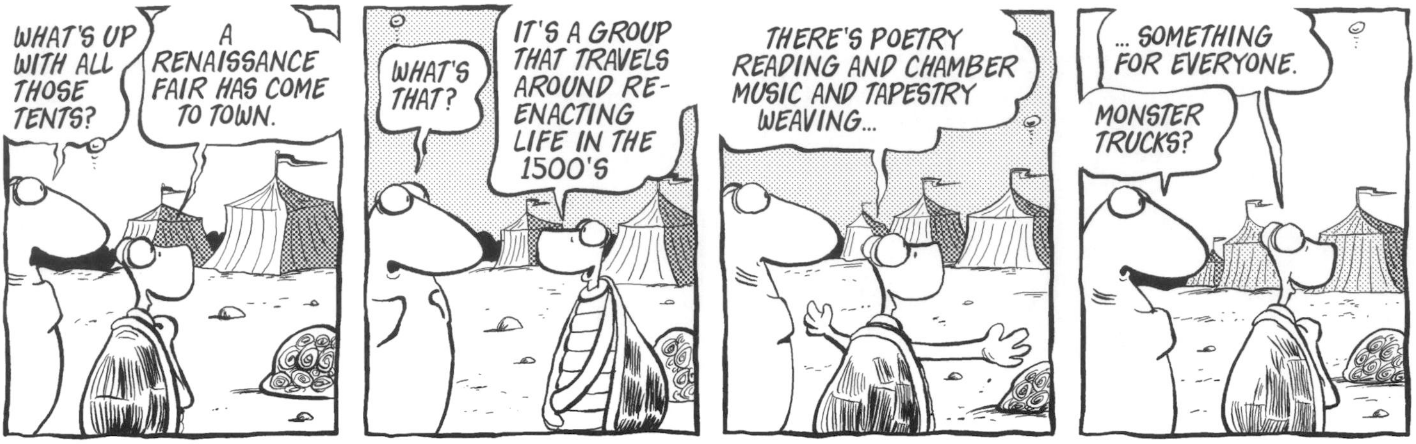
WHAT'S UP WITH ALL THOSE TENTS?
A RENAISSANCE FAIR HAS COME TO TOWN.
WHAT'S THAT?
IT'S A GROUP THAT TRAVELS AROUND RE-ENACTING LIFE IN THE 1500'S
THERE'S POETRY READING AND CHAMBER MUSIC AND TAPESTRY WEAVING...
... SOMETHING FOR EVERYONE.
MONSTER TRUCKS?

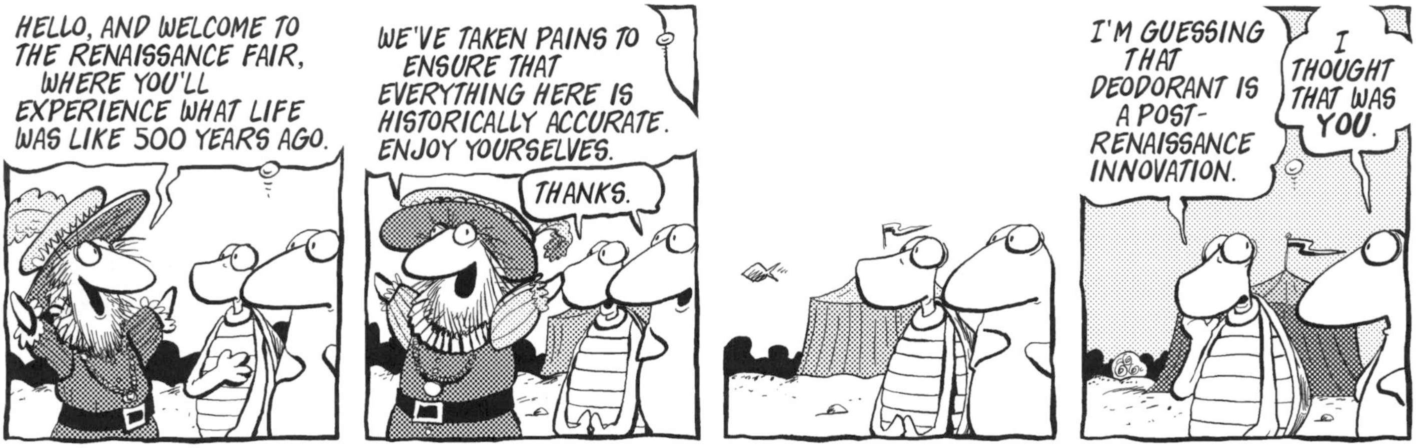
HELLO, AND WELCOME TO THE RENAISSANCE FAIR, WHERE YOU'LL EXPERIENCE WHAT LIFE WAS LIKE 500 YEARS AGO.
WE'VE TAKEN PAINS TO ENSURE THAT EVERYTHING HERE IS HISTORICALLY ACCURATE. ENJOY YOURSELVES.
THANKS.
I'M GUESSING THAT DEODORANT IS A POST-RENAISSANCE INNOVATION.
I THOUGHT THAT WAS YOU.

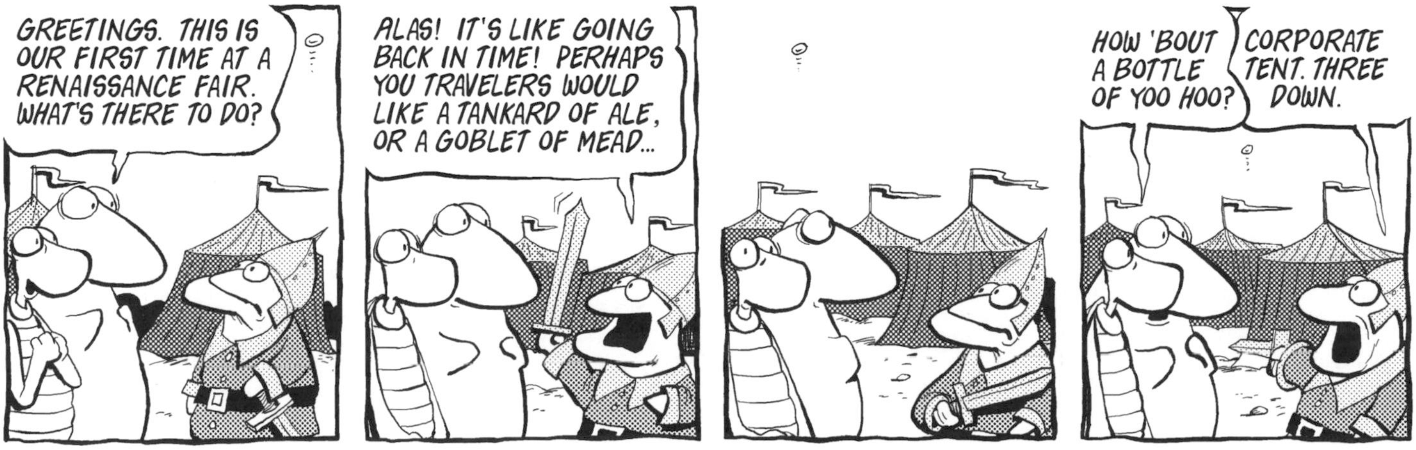
GREETINGS. THIS IS OUR FIRST TIME AT A RENAISSANCE FAIR. WHAT'S THERE TO DO?
ALAS! IT'S LIKE GOING BACK IN TIME! PERHAPS YOU TRAVELERS WOULD LIKE A TANKARD OF ALE, OR A GOBLET OF MEAD...
HOW 'BOUT A BOTTLE OF YOO HOO?
CORPORATE TENT. THREE DOWN.

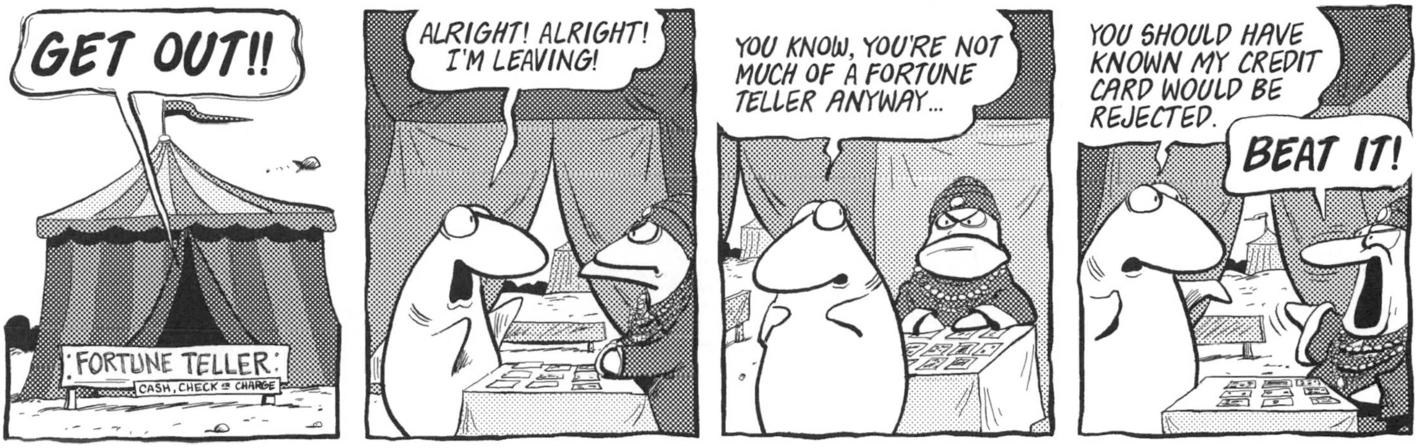
GET OUT!!
FORTUNE TELLER
CASH, CHECK OR CHARGE
ALRIGHT! ALRIGHT! I'M LEAVING!
YOU KNOW, YOU'RE NOT MUCH OF A FORTUNE TELLER ANYWAY...
YOU SHOULD HAVE KNOWN MY CREDIT CARD WOULD BE REJECTED.
BEAT IT!

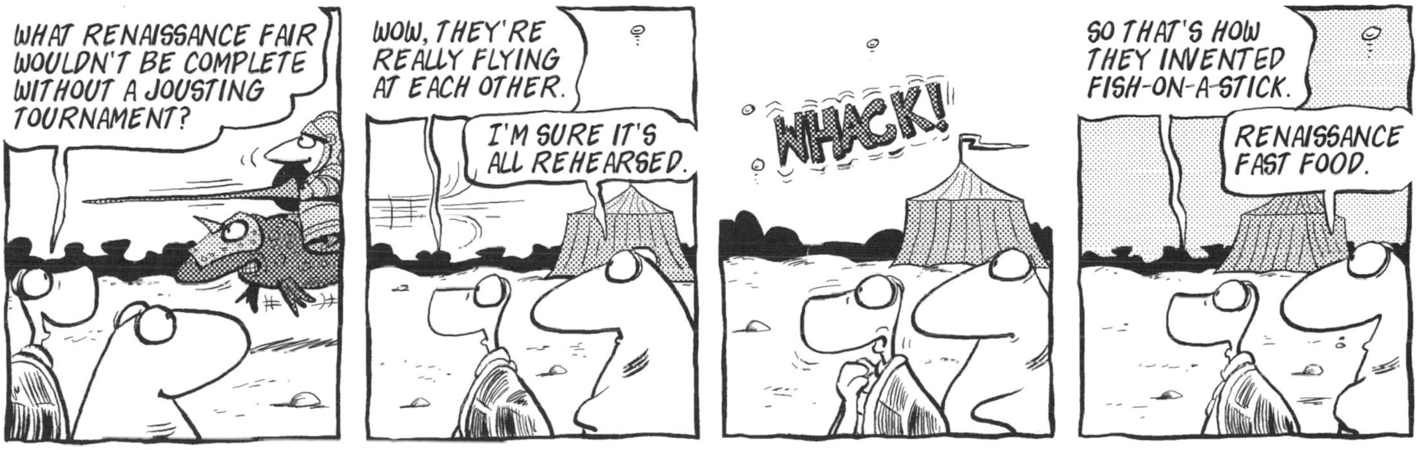
WHAT RENAISSANCE FAIR WOULDN'T BE COMPLETE WITHOUT A JOUSTING TOURNAMENT?
WOW, THEY'RE REALLY FLYING AT EACH OTHER.
I'M SURE IT'S ALL REHEARSED.
WHACK!
SO THAT'S HOW THEY INVENTED FISH-ON-A-STICK.
RENAISSANCE FAST FOOD.

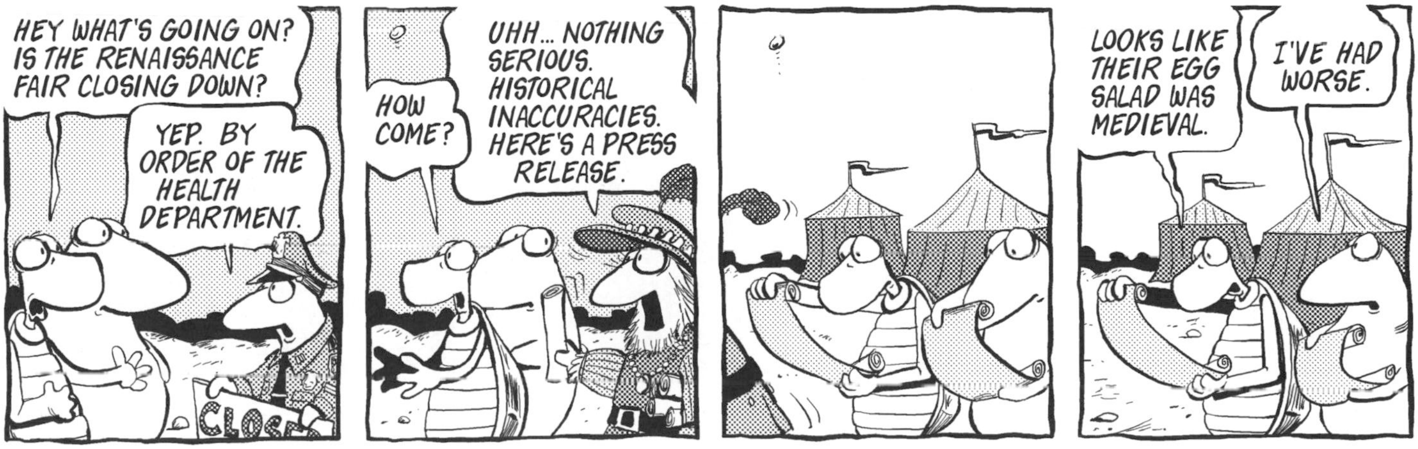
HEY WHAT'S GOING ON? IS THE RENAISSANCE FAIR CLOSING DOWN?
YEP. BY ORDER OF THE HEALTH DEPARTMENT.
HOW COME?
UHH... NOTHING SERIOUS. HISTORICAL INACCURACIES. HERE'S A PRESS RELEASE.
LOOKS LIKE THEIR EGG SALAD WAS MEDIEVAL.
I'VE HAD WORSE.

SHERMAN'S LAGOON
by Jim Toomey
HEY! I WAS ABOUT TO EAT THAT GUY AND HE DISAPPEARED ON ME!
HE'S UP ON THE BEACH. HIS WIFE NEEDED HELP WITH THE BEACH UMBRELLA.
DO YOU KNOW THE MORAL TO THIS STORY, SHERMAN?
WHAT'S THAT?
WHEN YOUR WIFE NEEDS HELP WITH SOMETHING, YOU SHOULD HELP HER RIGHT AWAY.
OH REALLY?
YOU NEVER KNOW. IT MAY SAVE YOUR LIFE.
WHY DON'T YOU EAT THAT GUY OVER THERE?
I'M GOING TO WAIT FOR THIS GUY TO COME BACK.
HIGH FIVE.

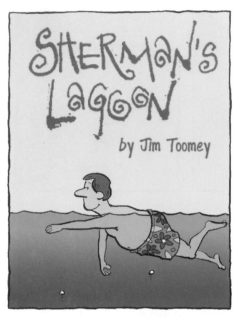

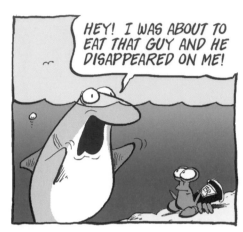

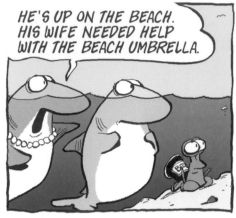

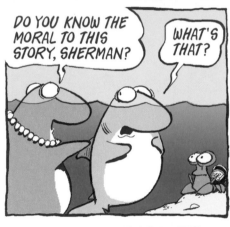

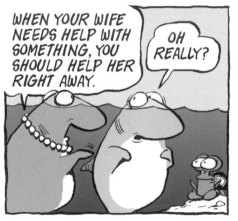

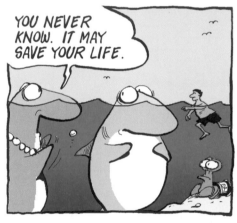

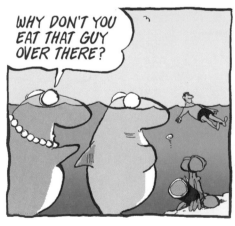

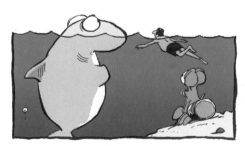

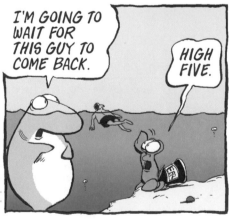

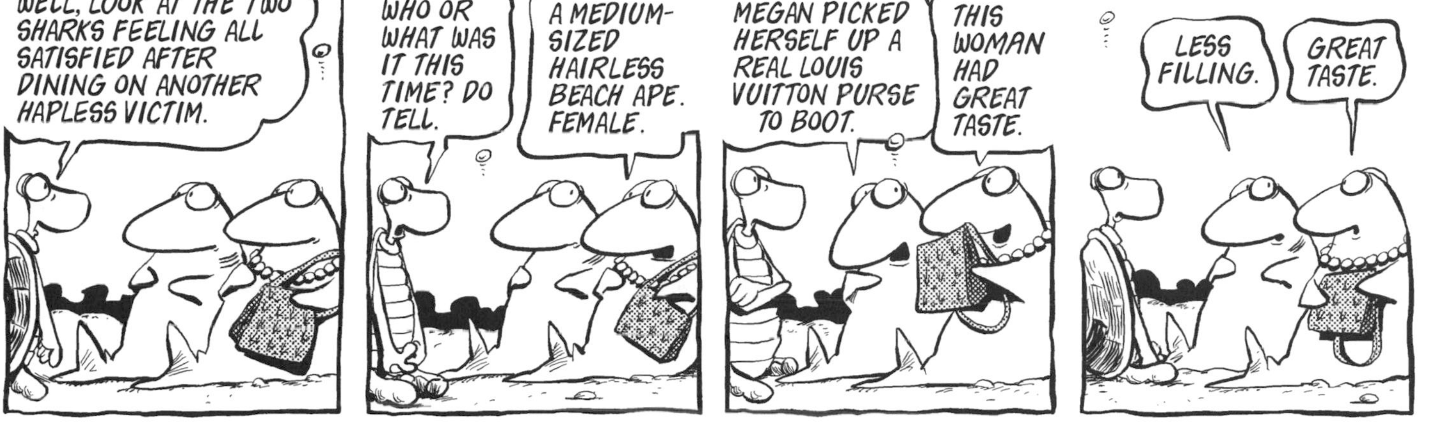
WELL, LOOK AT THE TWO SHARKS FEELING ALL SATISFIED AFTER DINING ON ANOTHER HAPLESS VICTIM.
WHO OR WHAT WAS IT THIS TIME? DO TELL.
A MEDIUM-SIZED HAIRLESS BEACH APE. FEMALE.
MEGAN PICKED HERSELF UP A REAL LOUIS VUITTON PURSE TO BOOT.
THIS WOMAN HAD GREAT TASTE.
LESS FILLING.
GREAT TASTE.

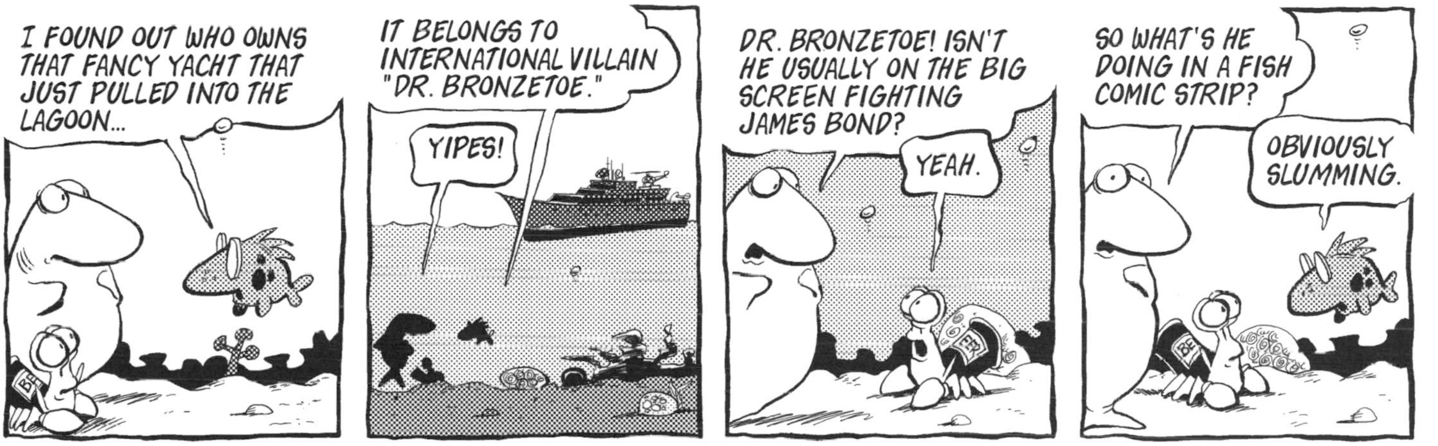
I FOUND OUT WHO OWNS THAT FANCY YACHT THAT JUST PULLED INTO THE LAGOON...
IT BELONGS TO INTERNATIONAL VILLAIN "DR. BRONZETOE."
YIPES!
DR. BRONZETOE! ISN'T HE USUALLY ON THE BIG SCREEN FIGHTING JAMES BOND?
YEAH.
SO WHAT'S HE DOING IN A FISH COMIC STRIP?
OBVIOUSLY SLUMMING.

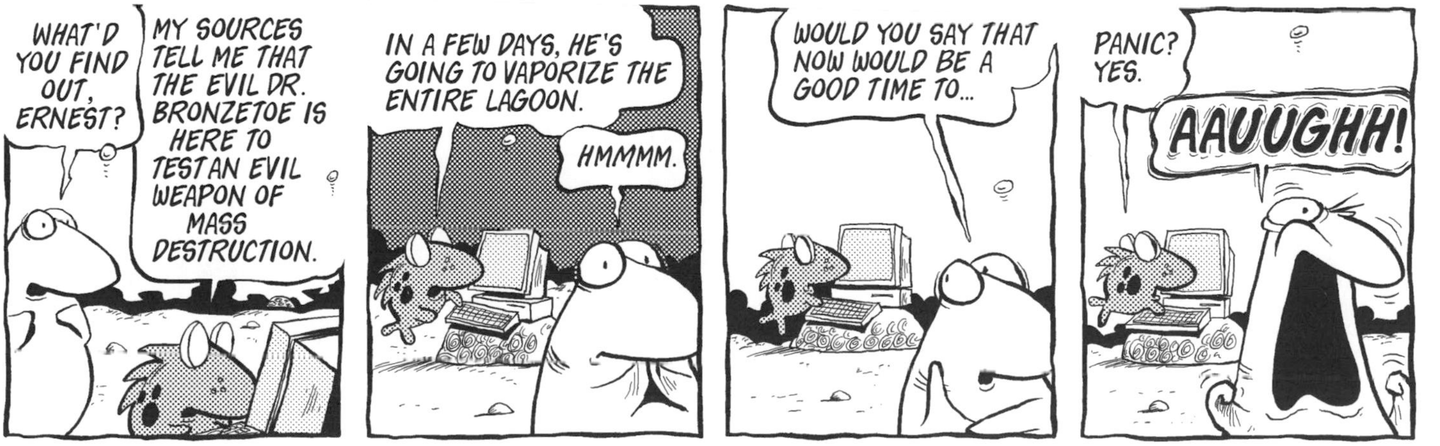
WHAT'D YOU FIND OUT, ERNEST?
MY SOURCES TELL ME THAT THE EVIL DR. BRONZETOE IS HERE TO TEST AN EVIL WEAPON OF MASS DESTRUCTION.
IN A FEW DAYS, HE'S GOING TO VAPORIZE THE ENTIRE LAGOON.
HMMMM.
WOULD YOU SAY THAT NOW WOULD BE A GOOD TIME TO...
PANIC? YES.
AAUUGHH!

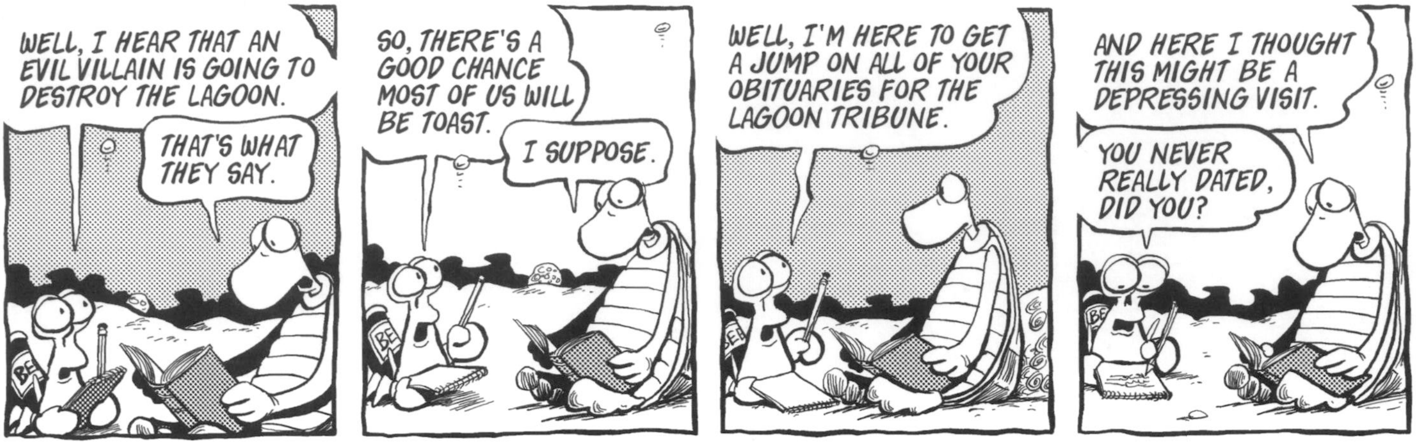
WELL, I HEAR THAT AN EVIL VILLAIN IS GOING TO DESTROY THE LAGOON.
THAT'S WHAT THEY SAY.
SO, THERE'S A GOOD CHANCE MOST OF US WILL BE TOAST.
I SUPPOSE.
WELL, I'M HERE TO GET A JUMP ON ALL OF YOUR OBITUARIES FOR THE LAGOON TRIBUNE.
AND HERE I THOUGHT THIS MIGHT BE A DEPRESSING VISIT.
YOU NEVER REALLY DATED, DID YOU?

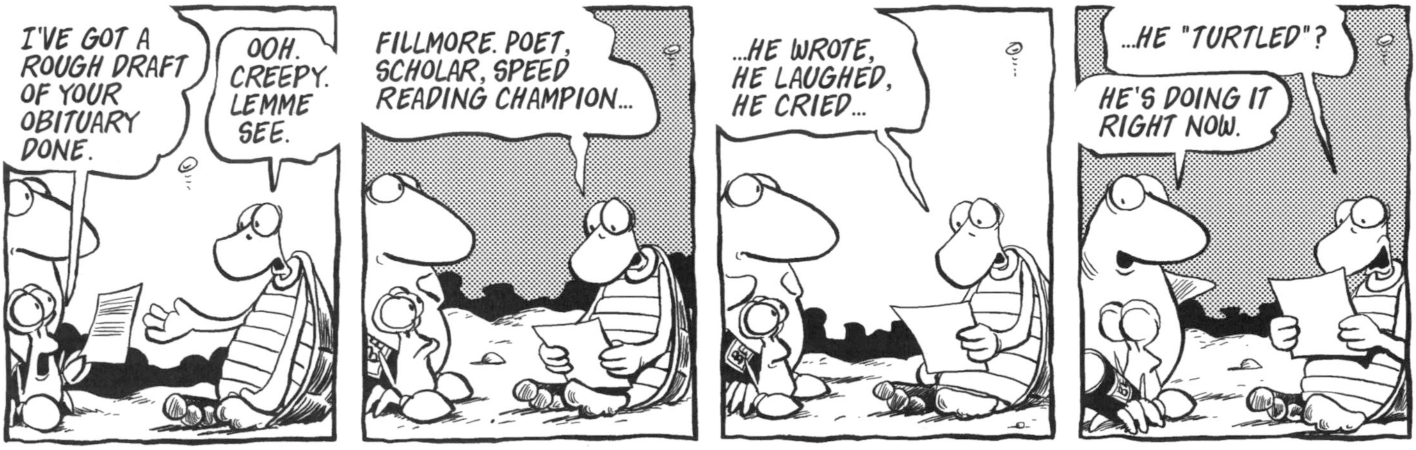
I'VE GOT A ROUGH DRAFT OF YOUR OBITUARY DONE.
OOH. CREEPY. LEMME SEE.
FILLMORE. POET, SCHOLAR, SPEED READING CHAMPION...
...HE WROTE, HE LAUGHED, HE CRIED...
...HE "TURTLED"?
HE'S DOING IT RIGHT NOW.

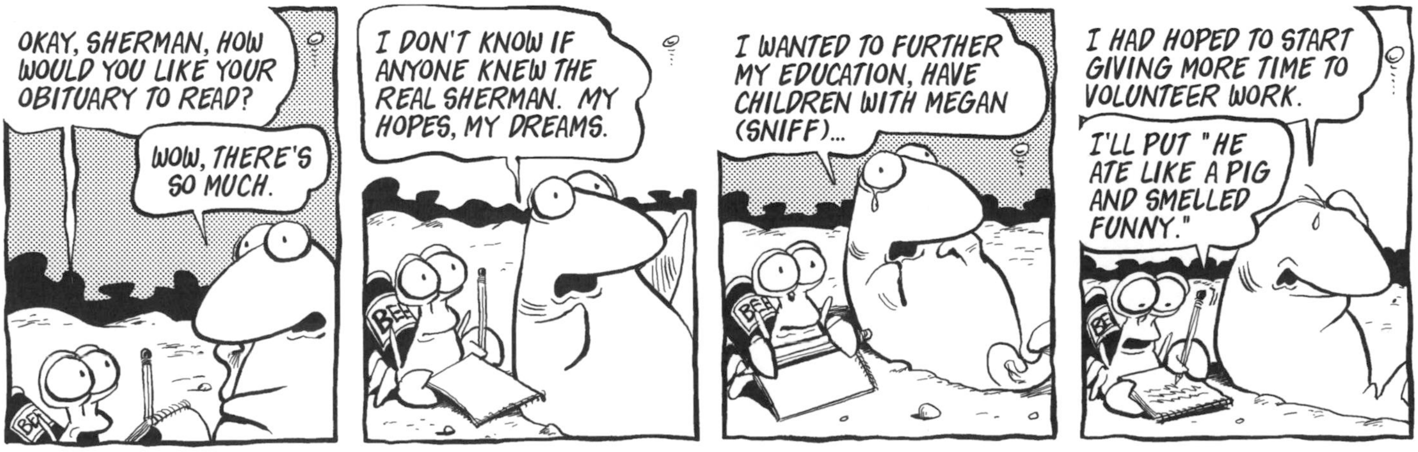
OKAY, SHERMAN, HOW WOULD YOU LIKE YOUR OBITUARY TO READ?
WOW, THERE'S SO MUCH.
I DON'T KNOW IF ANYONE KNEW THE REAL SHERMAN. MY HOPES, MY DREAMS.
I WANTED TO FURTHER MY EDUCATION, HAVE CHILDREN WITH MEGAN (SNIFF)...
I HAD HOPED TO START GIVING MORE TIME TO VOLUNTEER WORK.
I'LL PUT "HE ATE LIKE A PIG AND SMELLED FUNNY."

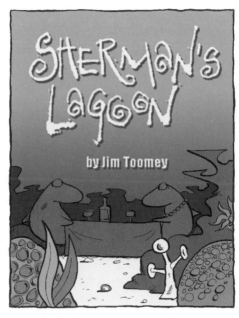

SHERMAN'S LAGOON

by Jim Toomey

OH MY, EVERYTHING LOOKS SO GOOD.

I THINK I BETTER STICK WITH A SALAD. I'M ON A DIET.

ARE YOU READY TO ORDER?

YES, I THINK I'M JUST GOING TO HAVE A SALAD.

ALRIGHT.

BUT, WITH EXTRA CROUTONS...

OKAY.

...AND DON'T SKIMP ON THE BLUE CHEESE DRESSING.

YES, MA'AM.

OOH. AND PUT SOME MUSHROOMS ON IT.

AND, SINCE WE'RE ADDING MUSHROOMS, PUT A CHEESEBURGER ON IT AS WELL.

GOT IT.

AND, FOR YOU, SIR?

SALAD SOUNDS GOOD.

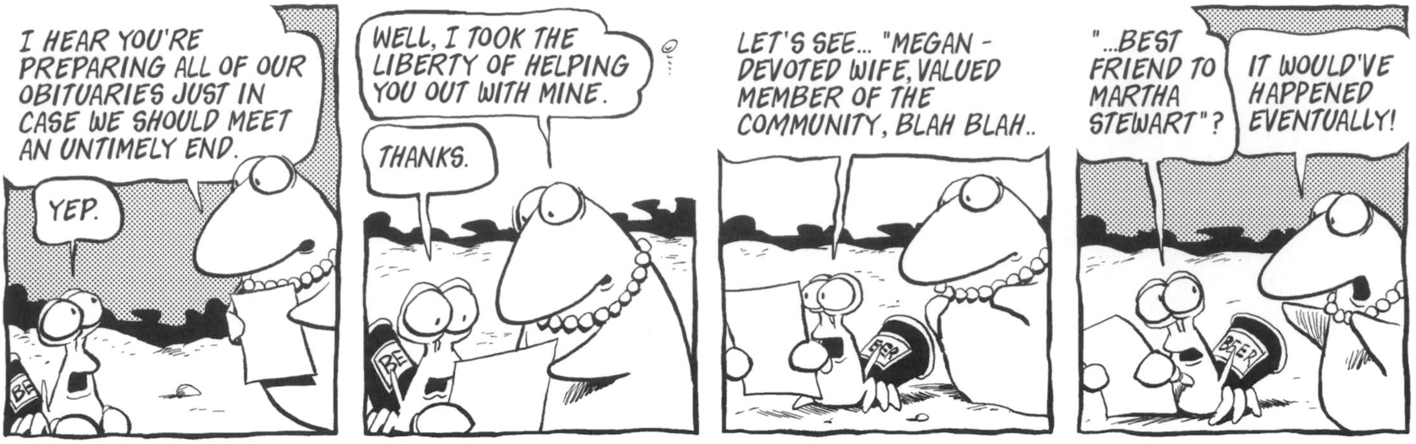
I HEAR YOU'RE PREPARING ALL OF OUR OBITUARIES JUST IN CASE WE SHOULD MEET AN UNTIMELY END.
YEP.
WELL, I TOOK THE LIBERTY OF HELPING YOU OUT WITH MINE.
THANKS.
LET'S SEE... "MEGAN - DEVOTED WIFE, VALUED MEMBER OF THE COMMUNITY, BLAH BLAH..
"...BEST FRIEND TO MARTHA STEWART"?
IT WOULD'VE HAPPENED EVENTUALLY!

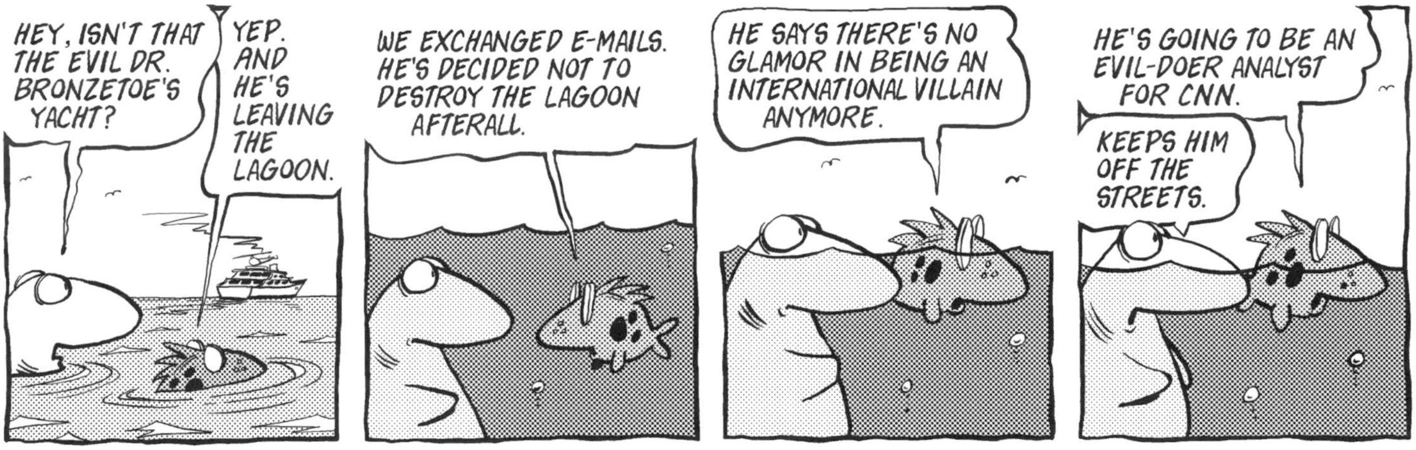
HEY, ISN'T THAT THE EVIL DR. BRONZETOE'S YACHT?
YEP. AND HE'S LEAVING THE LAGOON.
WE EXCHANGED E-MAILS. HE'S DECIDED NOT TO DESTROY THE LAGOON AFTERALL.
HE SAYS THERE'S NO GLAMOR IN BEING AN INTERNATIONAL VILLAIN ANYMORE.
HE'S GOING TO BE AN EVIL-DOER ANALYST FOR CNN.
KEEPS HIM OFF THE STREETS.

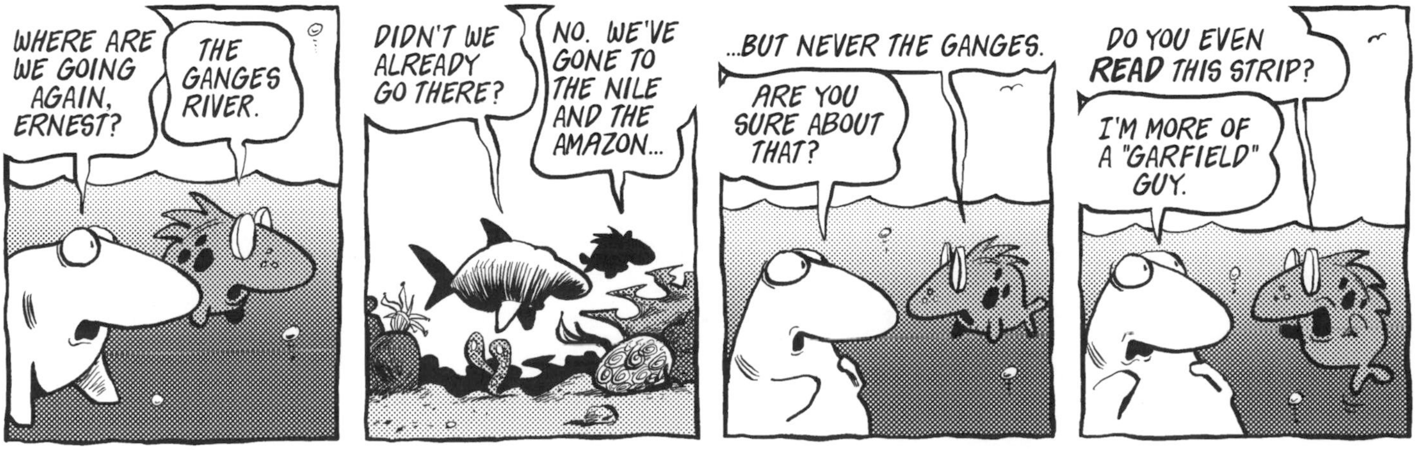
WHERE ARE WE GOING AGAIN, ERNEST?
THE GANGES RIVER.
DIDN'T WE ALREADY GO THERE?
NO. WE'VE GONE TO THE NILE AND THE AMAZON...
...BUT NEVER THE GANGES.
ARE YOU SURE ABOUT THAT?
DO YOU EVEN READ THIS STRIP?
I'M MORE OF A "GARFIELD" GUY.

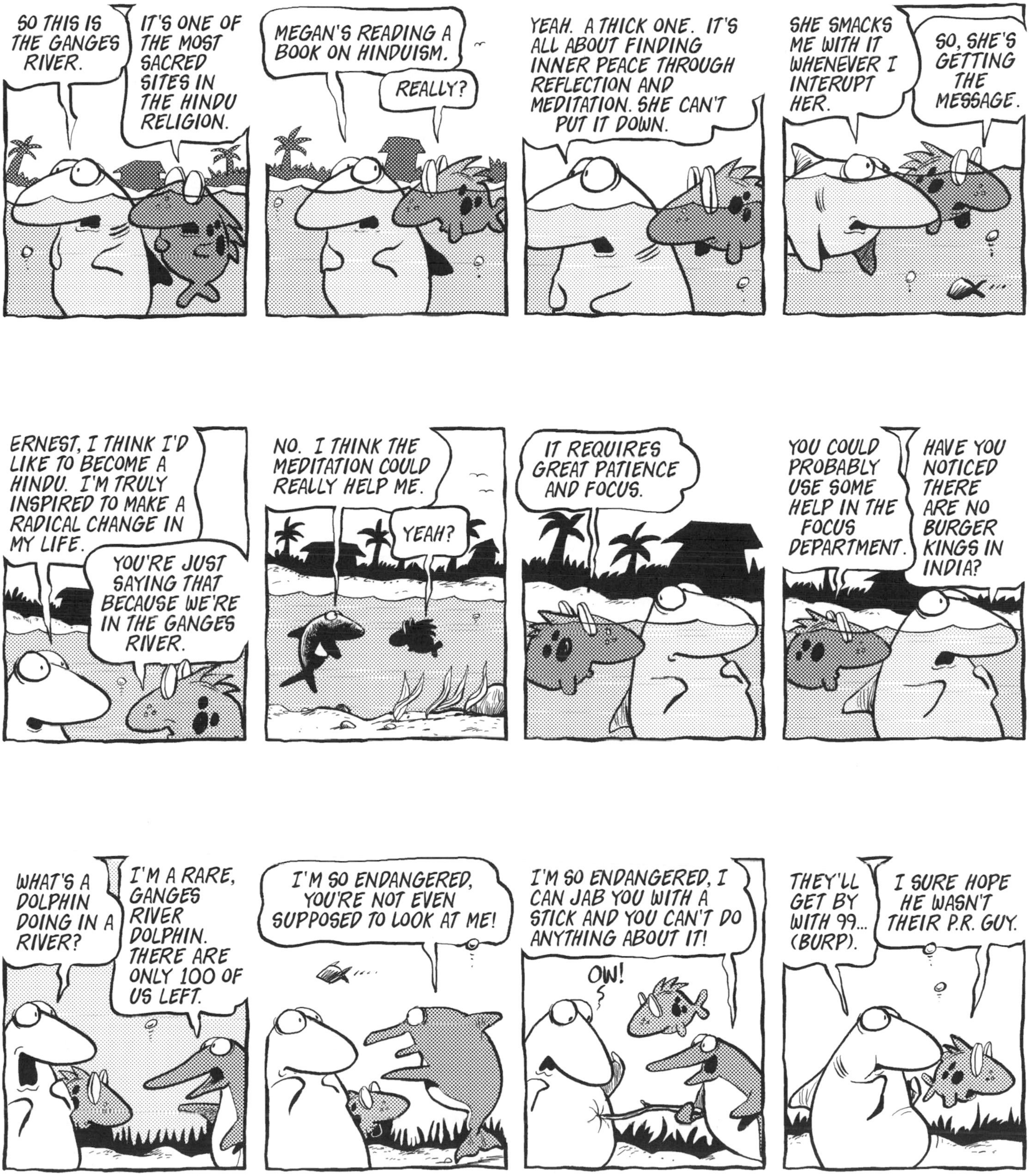

SO THIS IS THE GANGES RIVER.
IT'S ONE OF THE MOST SACRED SITES IN THE HINDU RELIGION.
MEGAN'S READING A BOOK ON HINDUISM.
REALLY?
YEAH. A THICK ONE. IT'S ALL ABOUT FINDING INNER PEACE THROUGH REFLECTION AND MEDITATION. SHE CAN'T PUT IT DOWN.
SHE SMACKS ME WITH IT WHENEVER I INTERUPT HER.
SO, SHE'S GETTING THE MESSAGE.
ERNEST, I THINK I'D LIKE TO BECOME A HINDU. I'M TRULY INSPIRED TO MAKE A RADICAL CHANGE IN MY LIFE.
YOU'RE JUST SAYING THAT BECAUSE WE'RE IN THE GANGES RIVER.
NO. I THINK THE MEDITATION COULD REALLY HELP ME.
YEAH?
IT REQUIRES GREAT PATIENCE AND FOCUS.
YOU COULD PROBABLY USE SOME HELP IN THE FOCUS DEPARTMENT.
HAVE YOU NOTICED THERE ARE NO BURGER KINGS IN INDIA?
WHAT'S A DOLPHIN DOING IN A RIVER?
I'M A RARE, GANGES RIVER DOLPHIN. THERE ARE ONLY 100 OF US LEFT.
I'M SO ENDANGERED, YOU'RE NOT EVEN SUPPOSED TO LOOK AT ME!
I'M SO ENDANGERED, I CAN JAB YOU WITH A STICK AND YOU CAN'T DO ANYTHING ABOUT IT!
OW!
THEY'LL GET BY WITH 99... (BURP).
I SURE HOPE HE WASN'T THEIR P.R. GUY.

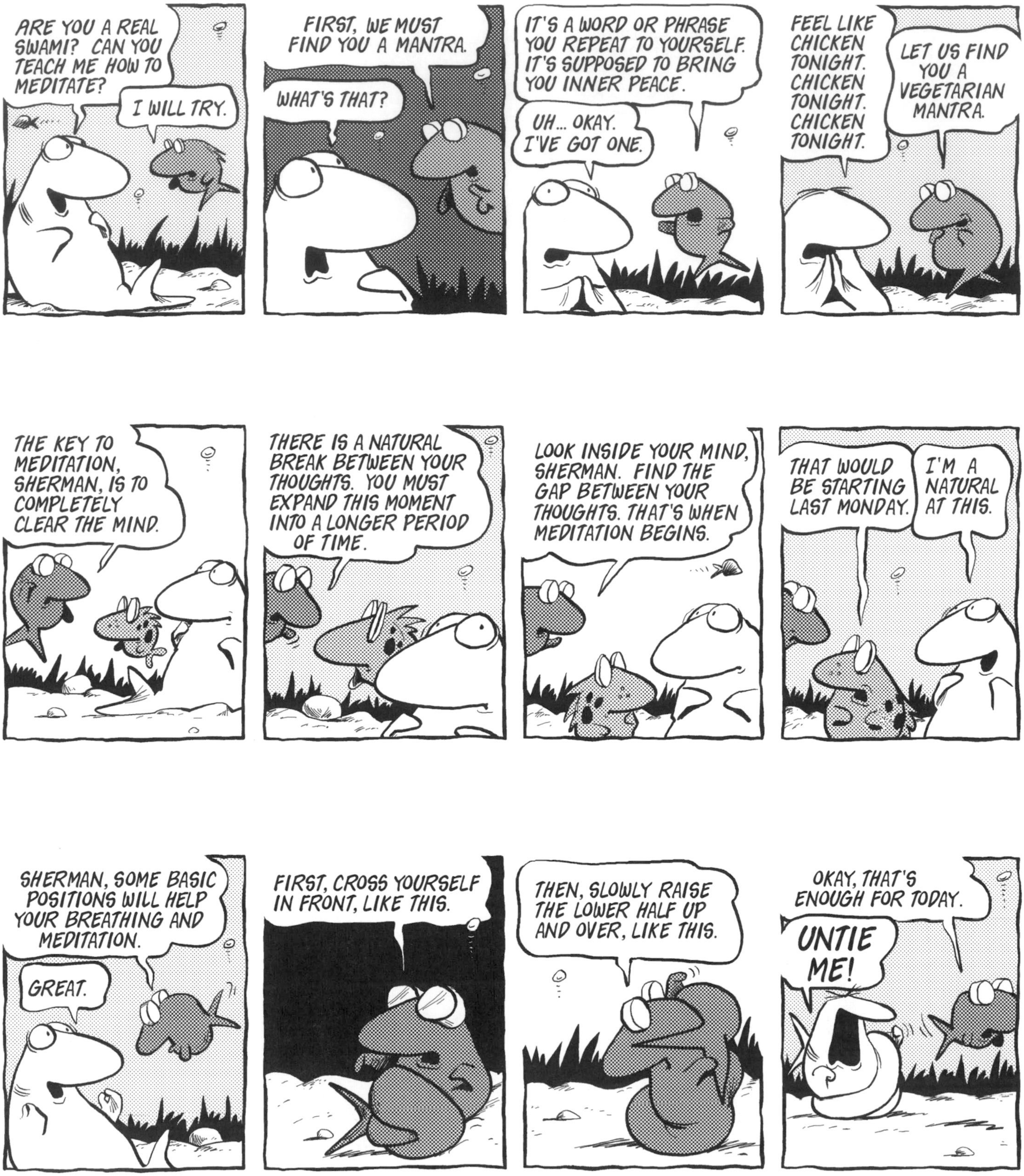
ARE YOU A REAL SWAMI? CAN YOU TEACH ME HOW TO MEDITATE?
I WILL TRY.
FIRST, WE MUST FIND YOU A MANTRA.
WHAT'S THAT?
IT'S A WORD OR PHRASE YOU REPEAT TO YOURSELF. IT'S SUPPOSED TO BRING YOU INNER PEACE.
UH... OKAY. I'VE GOT ONE.
FEEL LIKE CHICKEN TONIGHT. CHICKEN TONIGHT. CHICKEN TONIGHT.
LET US FIND YOU A VEGETARIAN MANTRA.
THE KEY TO MEDITATION, SHERMAN, IS TO COMPLETELY CLEAR THE MIND.
THERE IS A NATURAL BREAK BETWEEN YOUR THOUGHTS. YOU MUST EXPAND THIS MOMENT INTO A LONGER PERIOD OF TIME.
LOOK INSIDE YOUR MIND, SHERMAN. FIND THE GAP BETWEEN YOUR THOUGHTS. THAT'S WHEN MEDITATION BEGINS.
THAT WOULD BE STARTING LAST MONDAY.
I'M A NATURAL AT THIS.
SHERMAN, SOME BASIC POSITIONS WILL HELP YOUR BREATHING AND MEDITATION.
GREAT.
FIRST, CROSS YOURSELF IN FRONT, LIKE THIS.
THEN, SLOWLY RAISE THE LOWER HALF UP AND OVER, LIKE THIS.
OKAY, THAT'S ENOUGH FOR TODAY.
UNTIE ME!

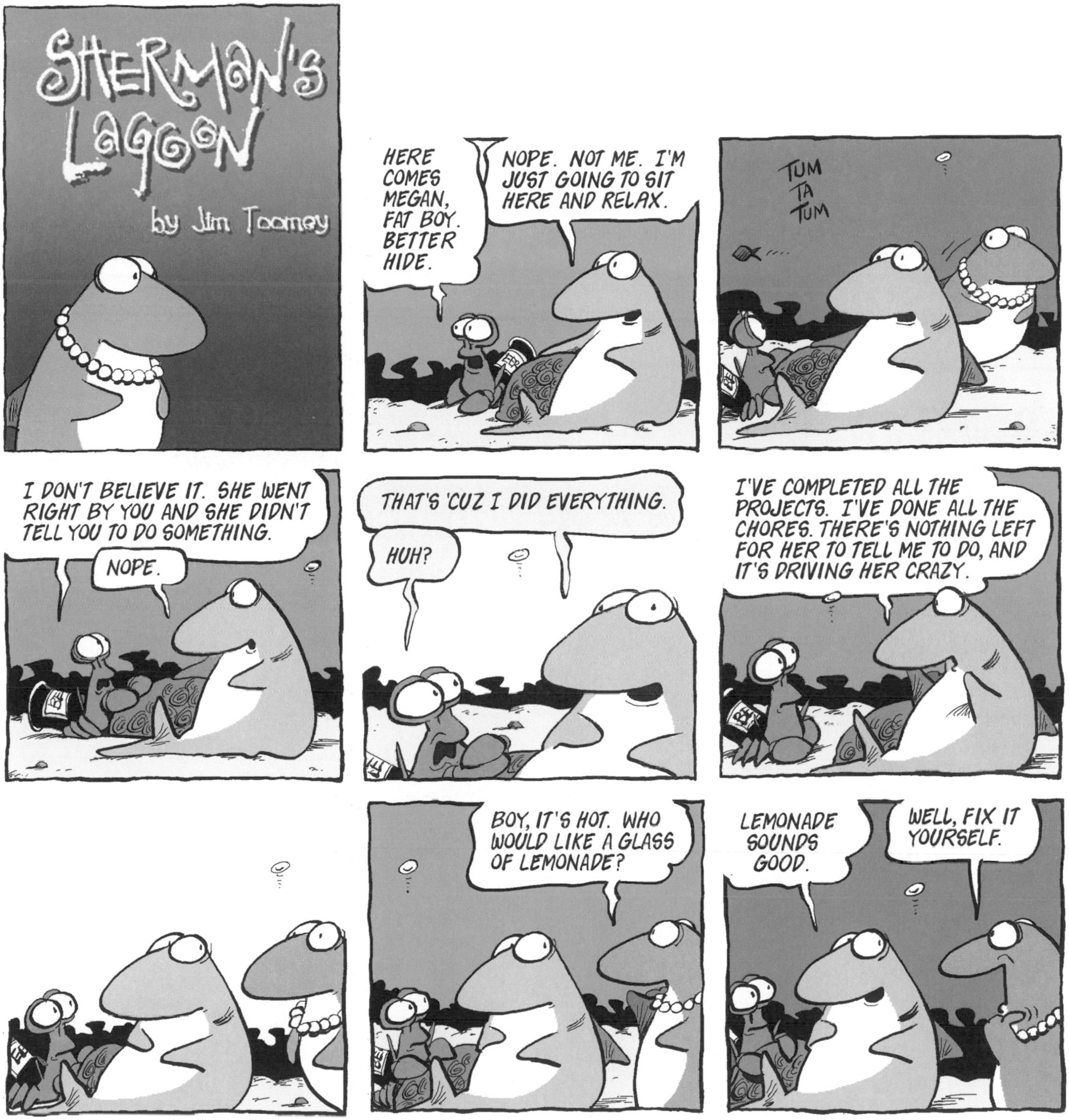
SHERMAN'S LAGOON
by Jim Toomey
HERE COMES MEGAN, FAT BOY. BETTER HIDE.
NOPE. NOT ME. I'M JUST GOING TO SIT HERE AND RELAX.
TUM TA TUM
I DON'T BELIEVE IT. SHE WENT RIGHT BY YOU AND SHE DIDN'T TELL YOU TO DO SOMETHING.
NOPE.
THAT'S 'CUZ I DID EVERYTHING.
HUH?
I'VE COMPLETED ALL THE PROJECTS. I'VE DONE ALL THE CHORES. THERE'S NOTHING LEFT FOR HER TO TELL ME TO DO, AND IT'S DRIVING HER CRAZY.
BOY, IT'S HOT. WHO WOULD LIKE A GLASS OF LEMONADE?
LEMONADE SOUNDS GOOD.
WELL, FIX IT YOURSELF.

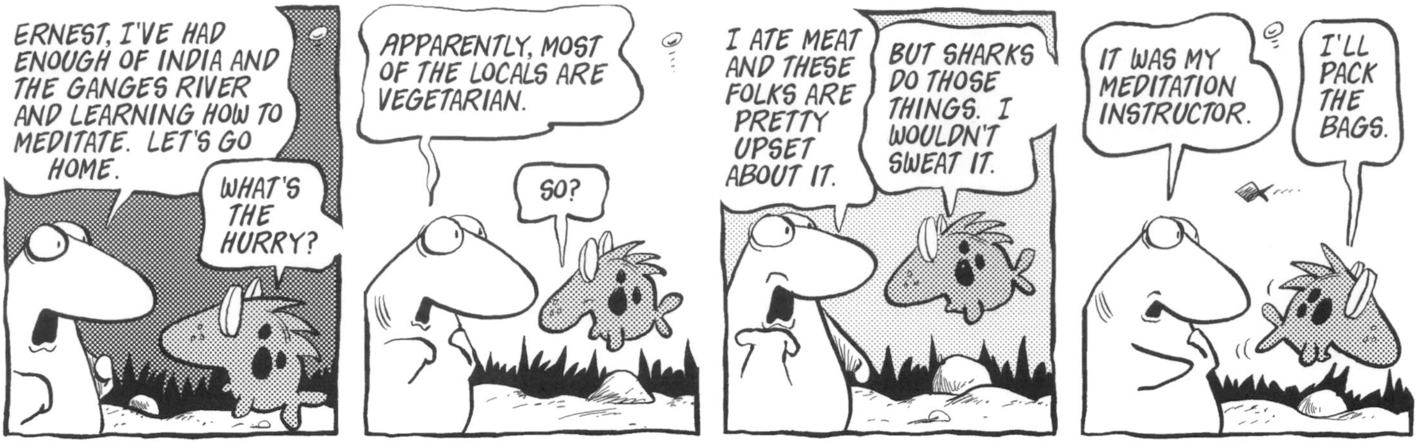
ERNEST, I'VE HAD ENOUGH OF INDIA AND THE GANGES RIVER AND LEARNING HOW TO MEDITATE. LET'S GO HOME.
WHAT'S THE HURRY?
APPARENTLY, MOST OF THE LOCALS ARE VEGETARIAN.
SO?
I ATE MEAT AND THESE FOLKS ARE PRETTY UPSET ABOUT IT.
BUT SHARKS DO THOSE THINGS. I WOULDN'T SWEAT IT.
IT WAS MY MEDITATION INSTRUCTOR.
I'LL PACK THE BAGS.

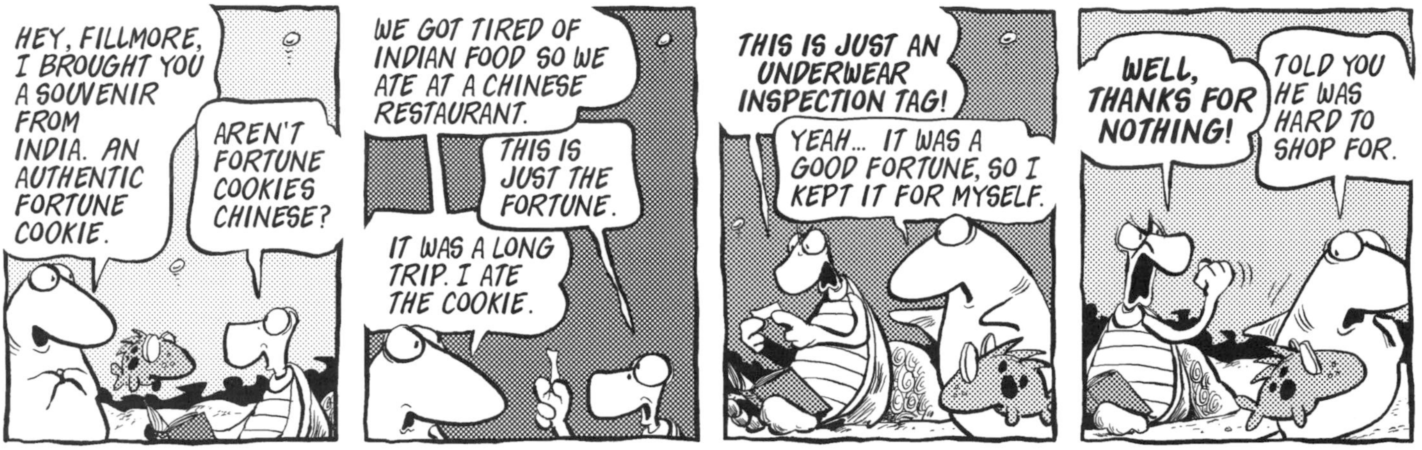
HEY, FILLMORE, I BROUGHT YOU A SOUVENIR FROM INDIA. AN AUTHENTIC FORTUNE COOKIE.
AREN'T FORTUNE COOKIES CHINESE?
WE GOT TIRED OF INDIAN FOOD SO WE ATE AT A CHINESE RESTAURANT.
THIS IS JUST THE FORTUNE.
IT WAS A LONG TRIP. I ATE THE COOKIE.
THIS IS JUST AN UNDERWEAR INSPECTION TAG!
YEAH... IT WAS A GOOD FORTUNE, SO I KEPT IT FOR MYSELF.
WELL, THANKS FOR NOTHING!
TOLD YOU HE WAS HARD TO SHOP FOR.

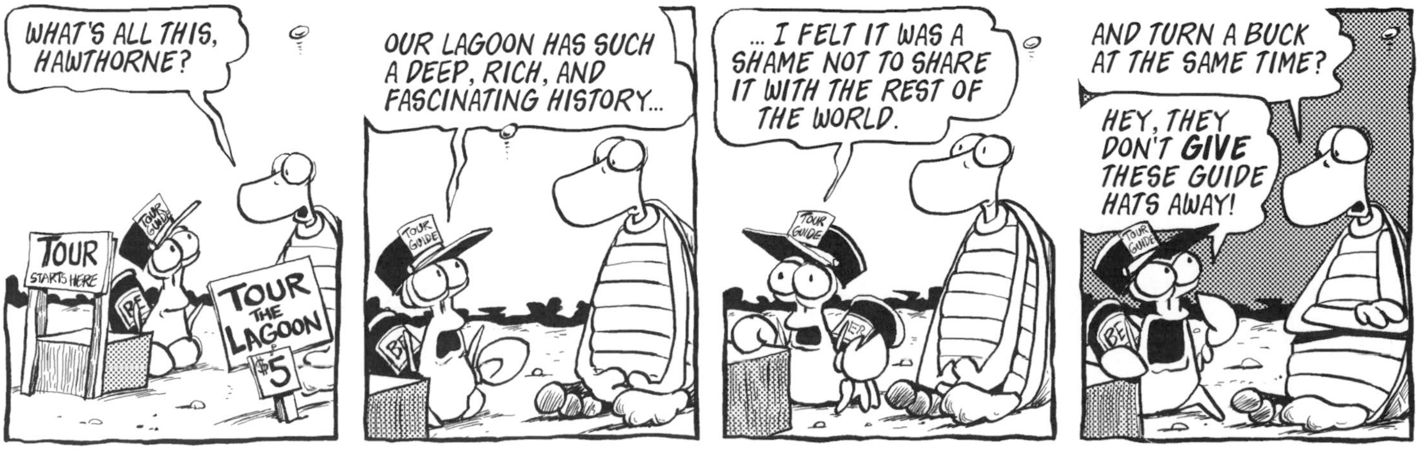
WHAT'S ALL THIS, HAWTHORNE?
TOUR STARTS HERE
TOUR GUIDE
TOUR THE LAGOON $5
OUR LAGOON HAS SUCH A DEEP, RICH, AND FASCINATING HISTORY...
... I FELT IT WAS A SHAME NOT TO SHARE IT WITH THE REST OF THE WORLD.
AND TURN A BUCK AT THE SAME TIME?
HEY, THEY DON'T GIVE THESE GUIDE HATS AWAY!

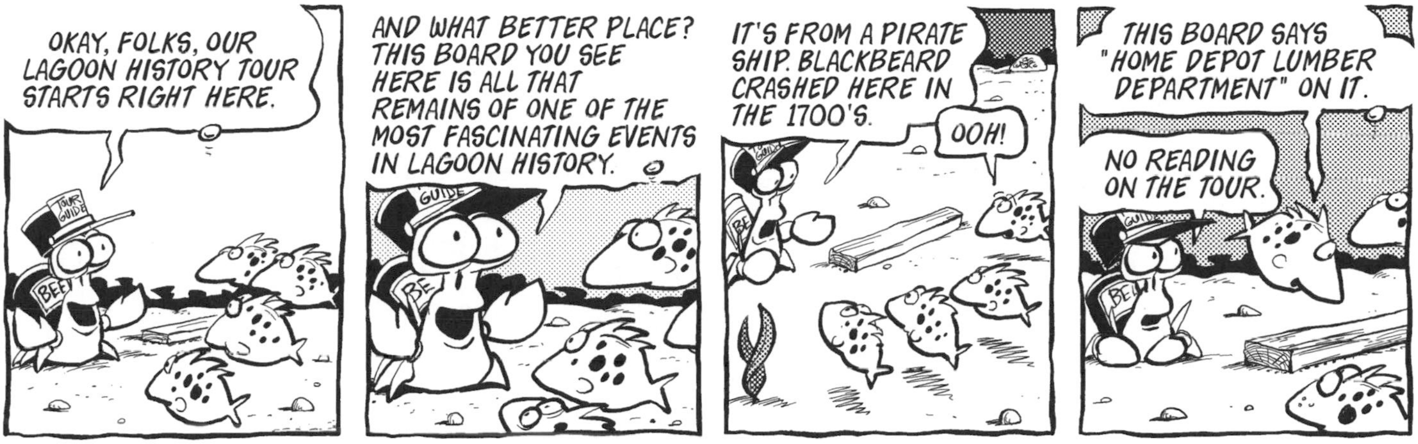
OKAY, FOLKS, OUR LAGOON HISTORY TOUR STARTS RIGHT HERE.
TOUR GUIDE
AND WHAT BETTER PLACE? THIS BOARD YOU SEE HERE IS ALL THAT REMAINS OF ONE OF THE MOST FASCINATING EVENTS IN LAGOON HISTORY.
IT'S FROM A PIRATE SHIP. BLACKBEARD CRASHED HERE IN THE 1700'S.
OOH!
THIS BOARD SAYS "HOME DEPOT LUMBER DEPARTMENT" ON IT.
NO READING ON THE TOUR.

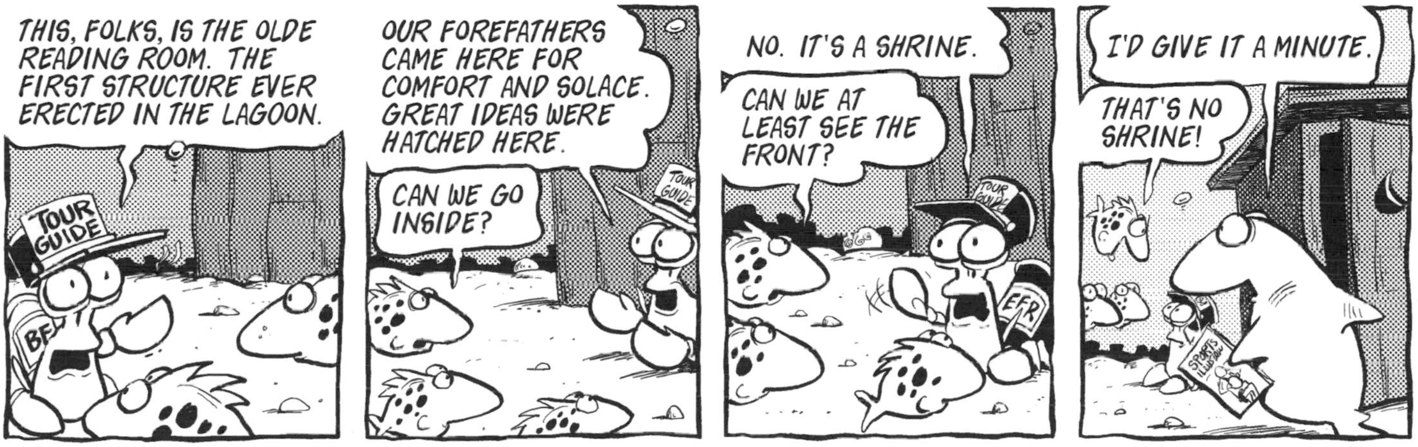
THIS, FOLKS, IS THE OLDE READING ROOM. THE FIRST STRUCTURE EVER ERECTED IN THE LAGOON.
TOUR GUIDE
OUR FOREFATHERS CAME HERE FOR COMFORT AND SOLACE. GREAT IDEAS WERE HATCHED HERE.
CAN WE GO INSIDE?
NO. IT'S A SHRINE.
CAN WE AT LEAST SEE THE FRONT?
I'D GIVE IT A MINUTE.
THAT'S NO SHRINE!

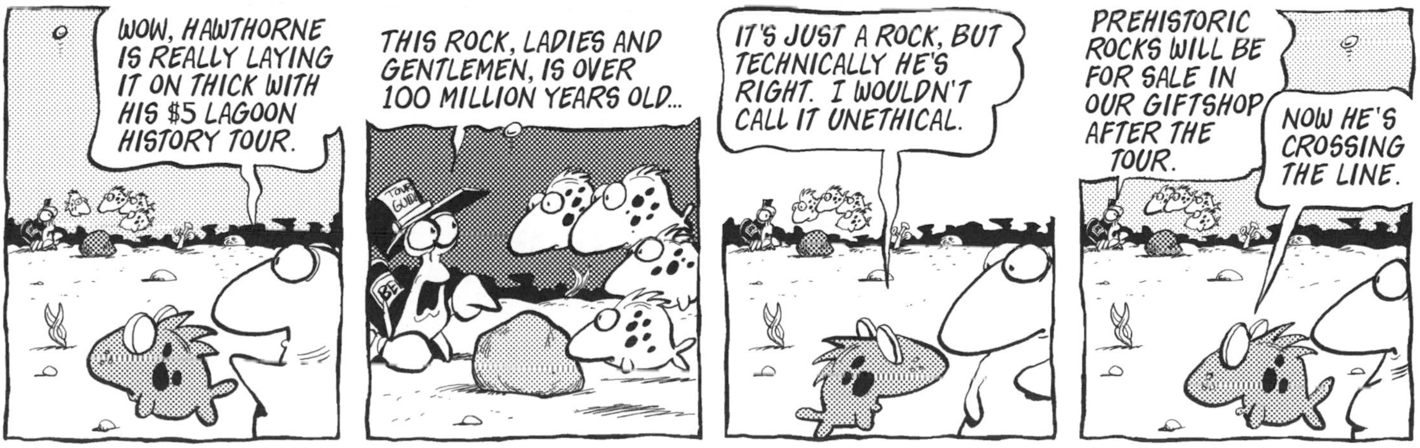
WOW, HAWTHORNE IS REALLY LAYING IT ON THICK WITH HIS $5 LAGOON HISTORY TOUR.
THIS ROCK, LADIES AND GENTLEMEN, IS OVER 100 MILLION YEARS OLD...
IT'S JUST A ROCK, BUT TECHNICALLY HE'S RIGHT. I WOULDN'T CALL IT UNETHICAL.
PREHISTORIC ROCKS WILL BE FOR SALE IN OUR GIFTSHOP AFTER THE TOUR.
NOW HE'S CROSSING THE LINE.

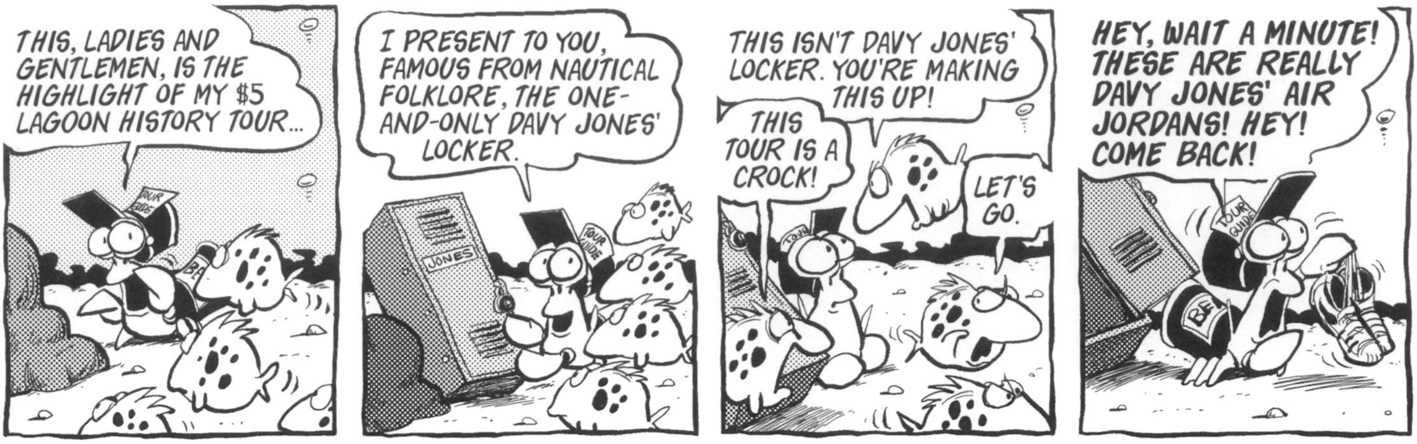
THIS, LADIES AND GENTLEMEN, IS THE HIGHLIGHT OF MY $5 LAGOON HISTORY TOUR...
I PRESENT TO YOU, FAMOUS FROM NAUTICAL FOLKLORE, THE ONE-AND-ONLY DAVY JONES' LOCKER.
JONES
THIS ISN'T DAVY JONES' LOCKER. YOU'RE MAKING THIS UP!
THIS TOUR IS A CROCK!
LET'S GO.
HEY, WAIT A MINUTE! THESE ARE REALLY DAVY JONES' AIR JORDANS! HEY! COME BACK!

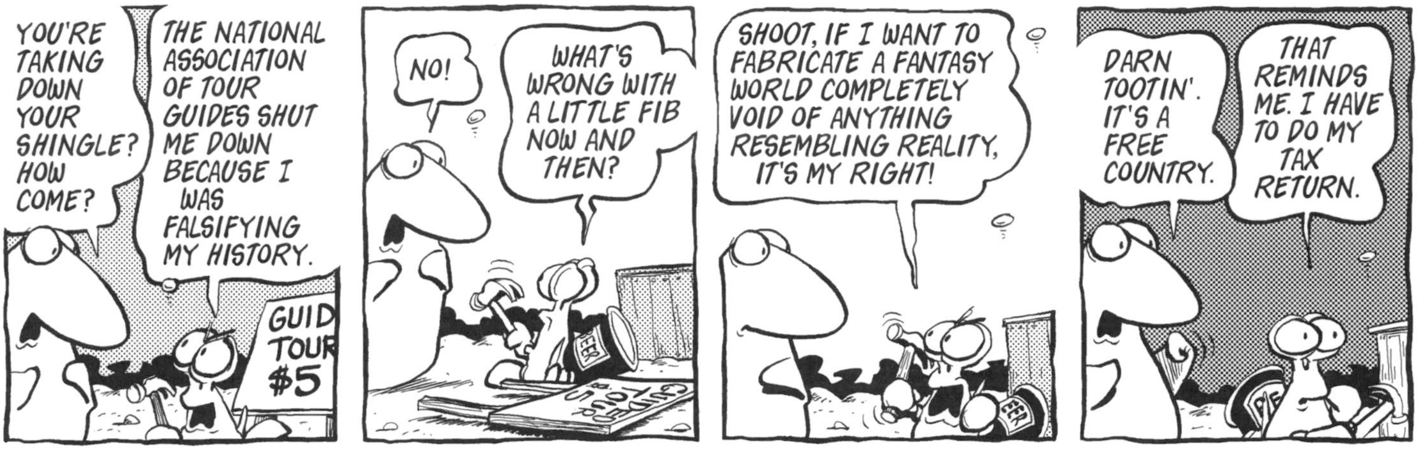
YOU'RE TAKING DOWN YOUR SHINGLE? HOW COME?
THE NATIONAL ASSOCIATION OF TOUR GUIDES SHUT ME DOWN BECAUSE I WAS FALSIFYING MY HISTORY.
GUID TOUR $5
NO!
WHAT'S WRONG WITH A LITTLE FIB NOW AND THEN?
SHOOT, IF I WANT TO FABRICATE A FANTASY WORLD COMPLETELY VOID OF ANYTHING RESEMBLING REALITY, IT'S MY RIGHT!
DARN TOOTIN'. IT'S A FREE COUNTRY.
THAT REMINDS ME. I HAVE TO DO MY TAX RETURN.

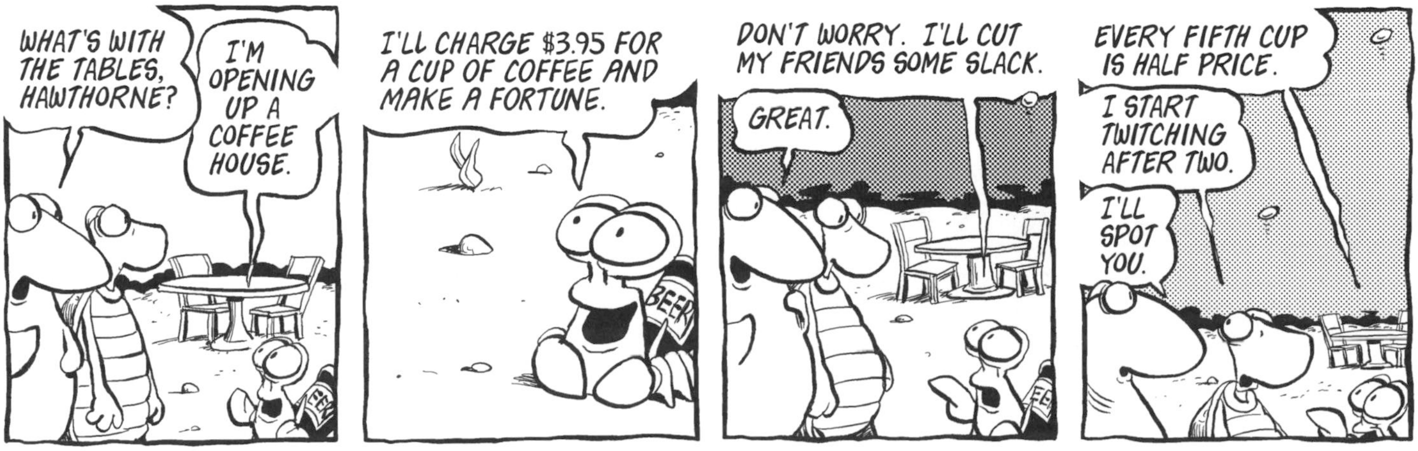
WHAT'S WITH THE TABLES, HAWTHORNE?
I'M OPENING UP A COFFEE HOUSE.
I'LL CHARGE $3.95 FOR A CUP OF COFFEE AND MAKE A FORTUNE.
BEER
DON'T WORRY. I'LL CUT MY FRIENDS SOME SLACK.
GREAT.
EVERY FIFTH CUP IS HALF PRICE.
I START TWITCHING AFTER TWO.
I'LL SPOT YOU.

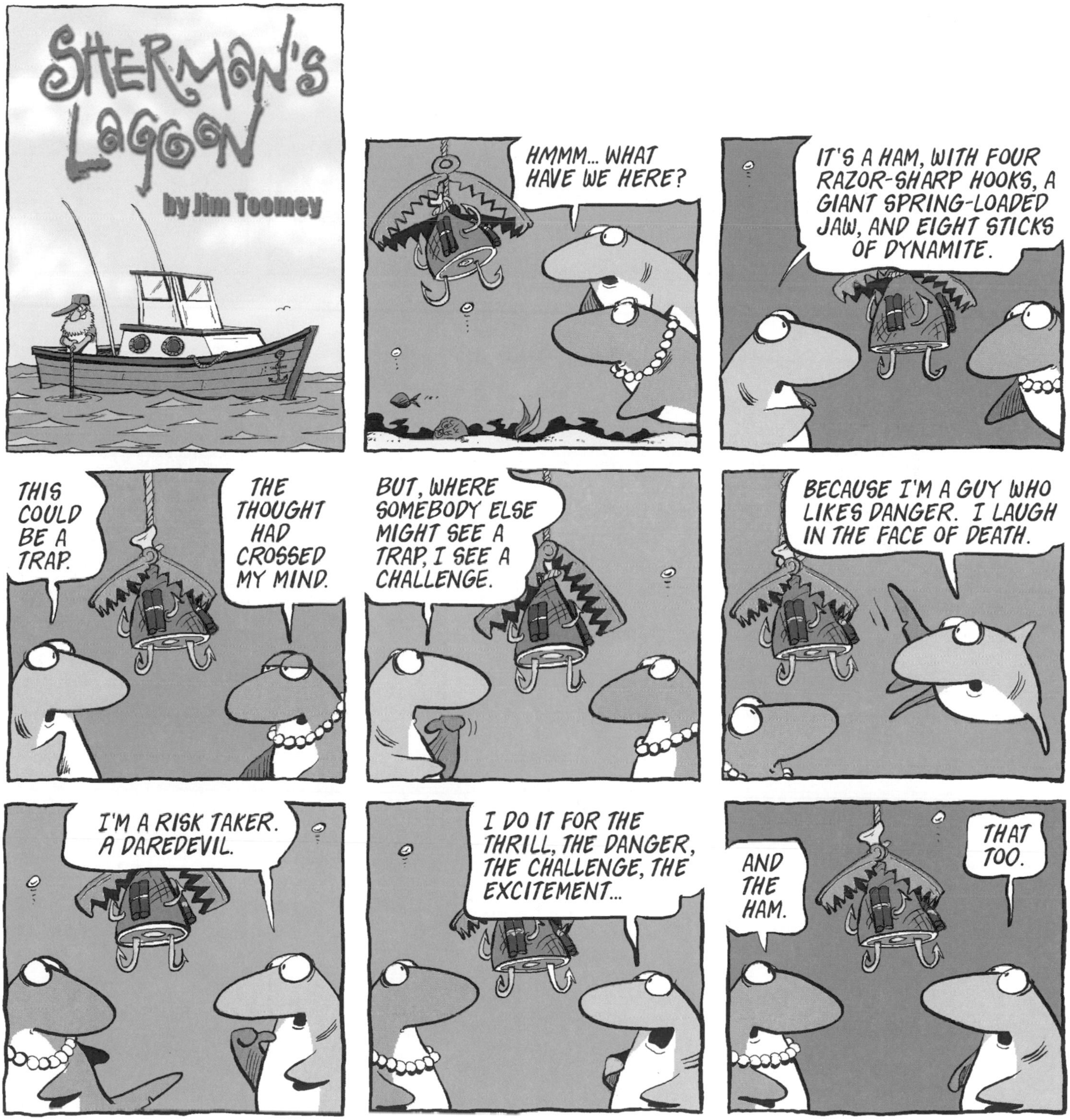
SHERMAN'S LAGOON
by Jim Toomey
HMMM... WHAT HAVE WE HERE?
IT'S A HAM, WITH FOUR RAZOR-SHARP HOOKS, A GIANT SPRING-LOADED JAW, AND EIGHT STICKS OF DYNAMITE.
THIS COULD BE A TRAP.
THE THOUGHT HAD CROSSED MY MIND.
BUT, WHERE SOMEBODY ELSE MIGHT SEE A TRAP, I SEE A CHALLENGE.
BECAUSE I'M A GUY WHO LIKES DANGER. I LAUGH IN THE FACE OF DEATH.
I'M A RISK TAKER. A DAREDEVIL.
I DO IT FOR THE THRILL, THE DANGER, THE CHALLENGE, THE EXCITEMENT...
AND THE HAM.
THAT TOO.

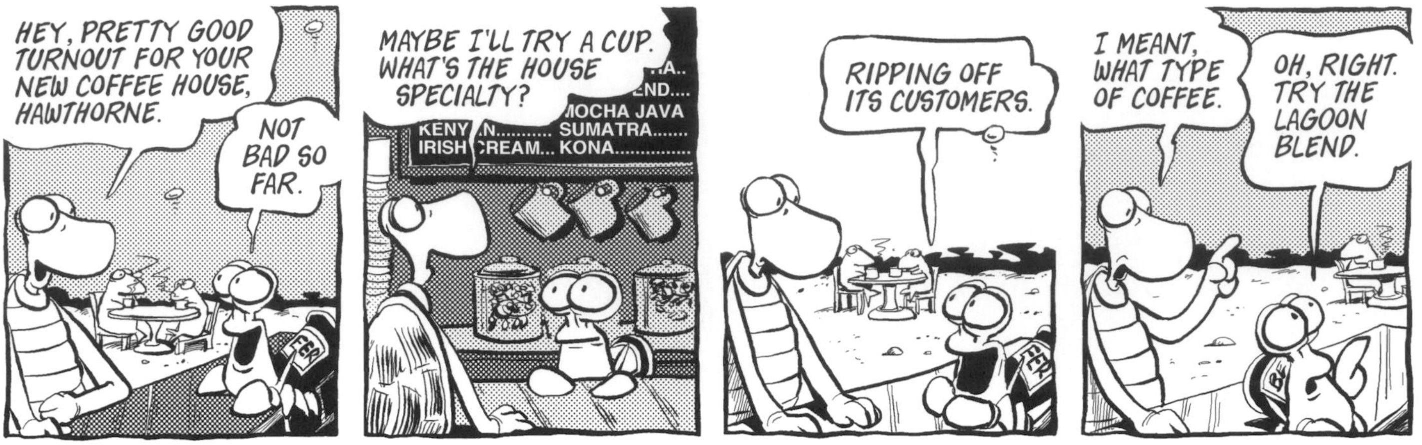
HEY, PRETTY GOOD TURNOUT FOR YOUR NEW COFFEE HOUSE, HAWTHORNE.
NOT BAD SO FAR.
MAYBE I'LL TRY A CUP. WHAT'S THE HOUSE SPECIALTY?
MOCHA JAVA
SUMATRA
KONA
RIPPING OFF ITS CUSTOMERS.
I MEANT, WHAT TYPE OF COFFEE.
OH, RIGHT. TRY THE LAGOON BLEND.

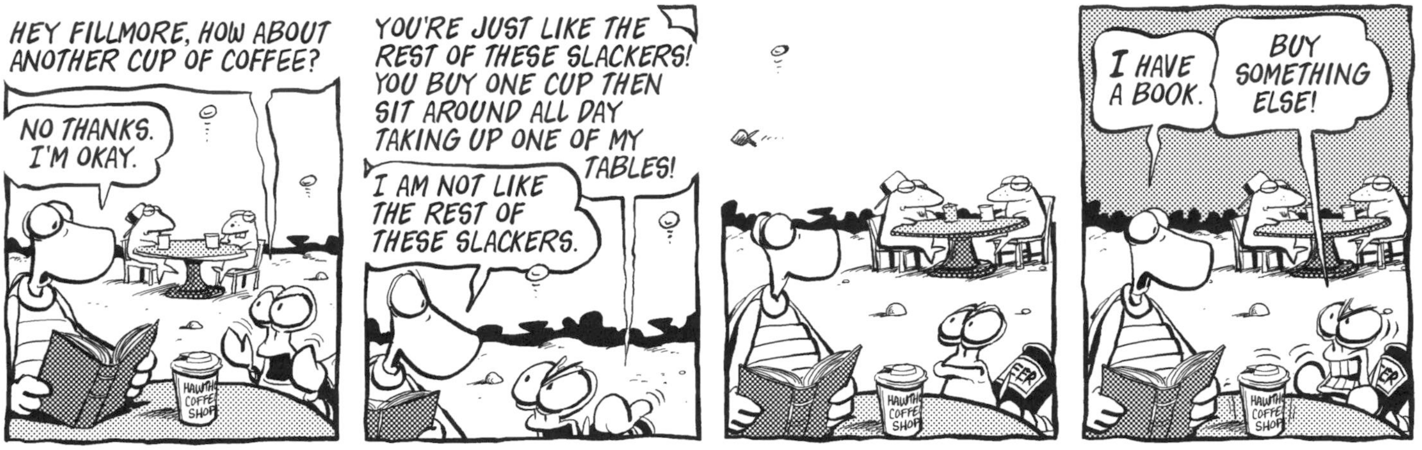
HEY FILLMORE, HOW ABOUT ANOTHER CUP OF COFFEE?
NO THANKS. I'M OKAY.
YOU'RE JUST LIKE THE REST OF THESE SLACKERS! YOU BUY ONE CUP THEN SIT AROUND ALL DAY TAKING UP ONE OF MY TABLES!
I AM NOT LIKE THE REST OF THESE SLACKERS.
I HAVE A BOOK.
BUY SOMETHING ELSE!

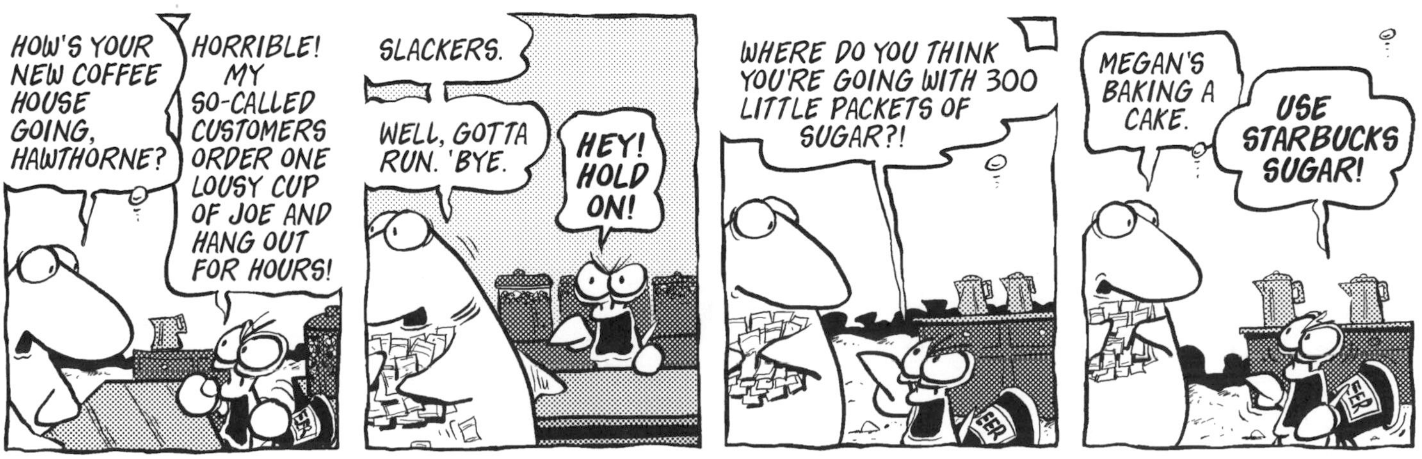
HOW'S YOUR NEW COFFEE HOUSE GOING, HAWTHORNE?
HORRIBLE! MY SO-CALLED CUSTOMERS ORDER ONE LOUSY CUP OF JOE AND HANG OUT FOR HOURS!
SLACKERS.
WELL, GOTTA RUN. 'BYE.
HEY! HOLD ON!
WHERE DO YOU THINK YOU'RE GOING WITH 300 LITTLE PACKETS OF SUGAR?!
MEGAN'S BAKING A CAKE.
USE STARBUCKS SUGAR!

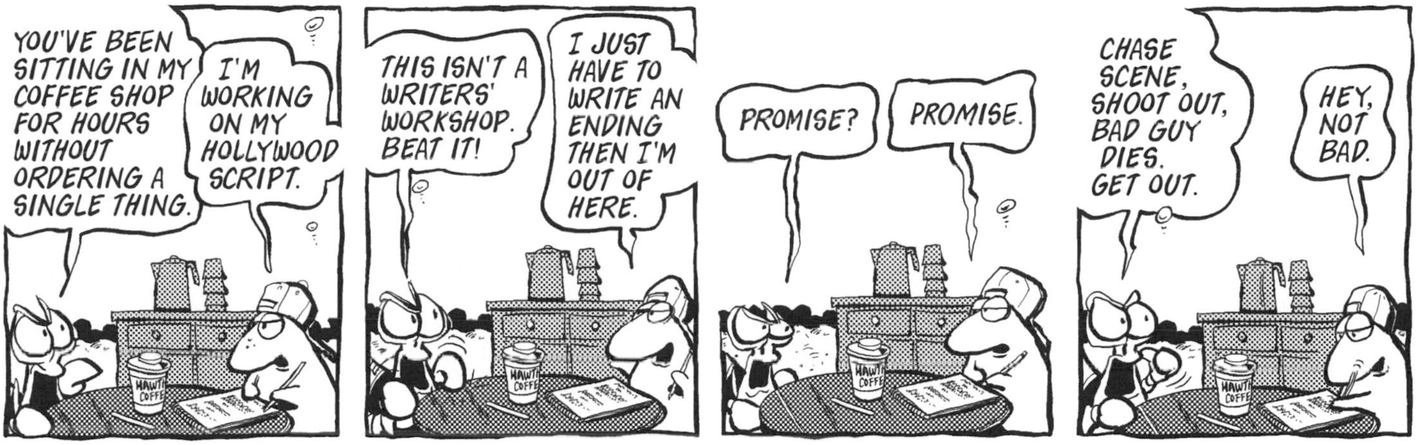
YOU'VE BEEN SITTING IN MY COFFEE SHOP FOR HOURS WITHOUT ORDERING A SINGLE THING.
I'M WORKING ON MY HOLLYWOOD SCRIPT.
THIS ISN'T A WRITERS' WORKSHOP. BEAT IT!
I JUST HAVE TO WRITE AN ENDING THEN I'M OUT OF HERE.
PROMISE?
PROMISE.
CHASE SCENE, SHOOT OUT, BAD GUY DIES. GET OUT.
HEY, NOT BAD.

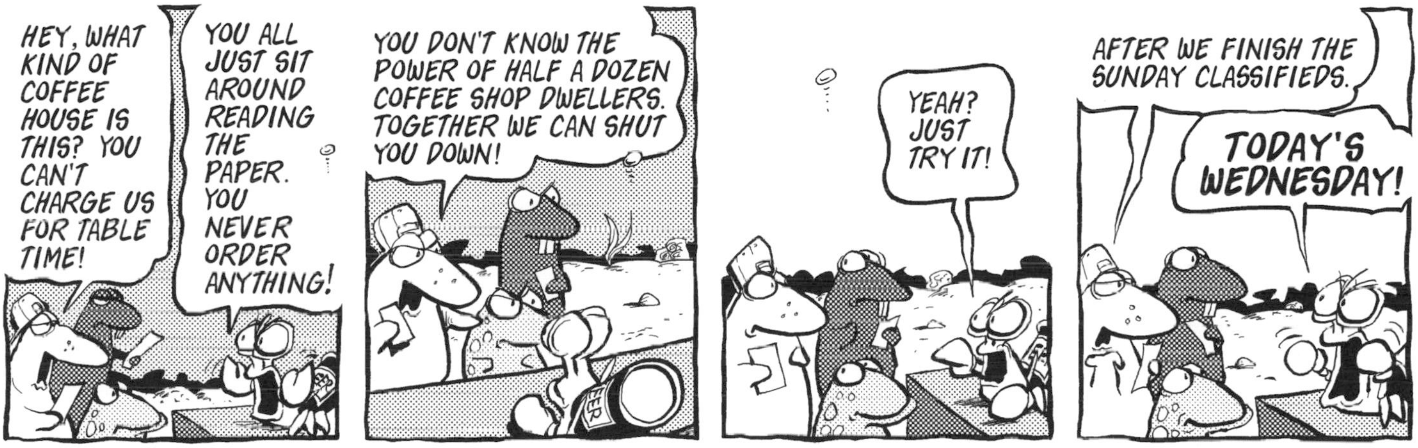
HEY, WHAT KIND OF COFFEE HOUSE IS THIS? YOU CAN'T CHARGE US FOR TABLE TIME!
YOU ALL JUST SIT AROUND READING THE PAPER. YOU NEVER ORDER ANYTHING!
YOU DON'T KNOW THE POWER OF HALF A DOZEN COFFEE SHOP DWELLERS. TOGETHER WE CAN SHUT YOU DOWN!
YEAH? JUST TRY IT!
AFTER WE FINISH THE SUNDAY CLASSIFIEDS.
TODAY'S WEDNESDAY!

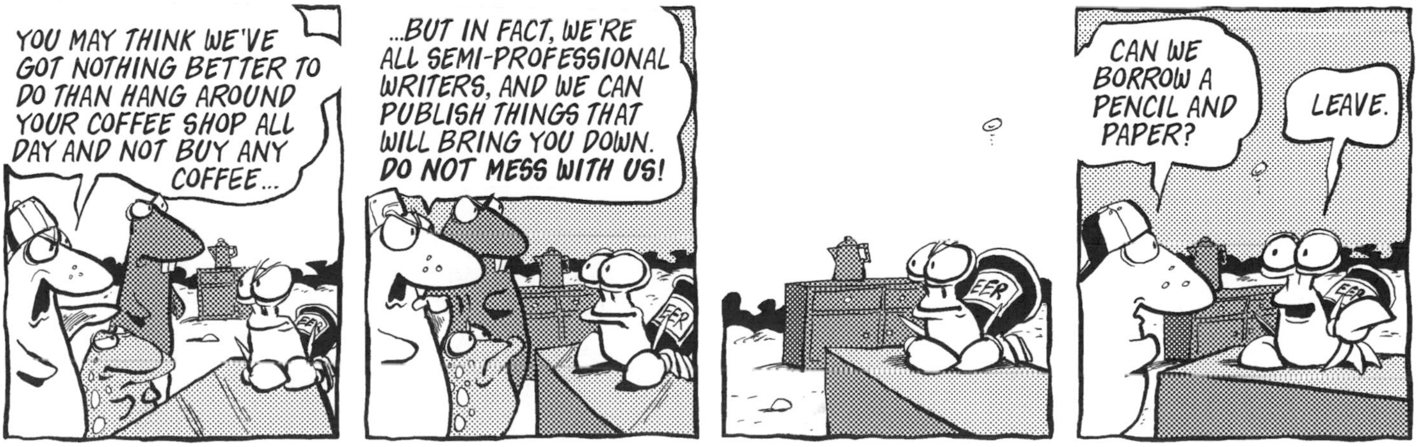
YOU MAY THINK WE'VE GOT NOTHING BETTER TO DO THAN HANG AROUND YOUR COFFEE SHOP ALL DAY AND NOT BUY ANY COFFEE...
...BUT IN FACT, WE'RE ALL SEMI-PROFESSIONAL WRITERS, AND WE CAN PUBLISH THINGS THAT WILL BRING YOU DOWN. DO NOT MESS WITH US!
CAN WE BORROW A PENCIL AND PAPER?
LEAVE.

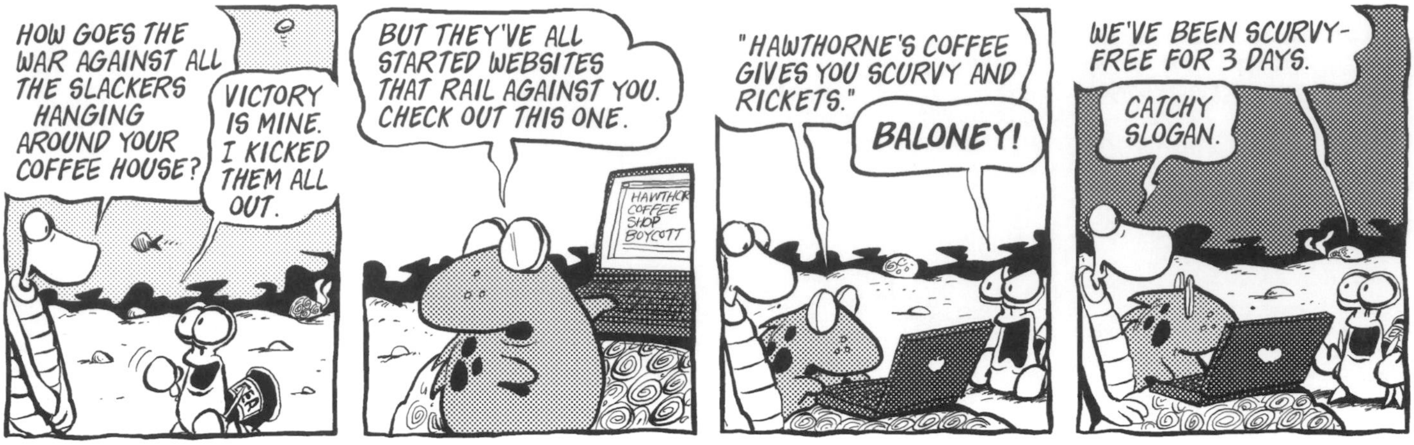
HOW GOES THE WAR AGAINST ALL THE SLACKERS HANGING AROUND YOUR COFFEE HOUSE?
VICTORY IS MINE. I KICKED THEM ALL OUT.
BUT THEY'VE ALL STARTED WEBSITES THAT RAIL AGAINST YOU. CHECK OUT THIS ONE.
HAWTHORNE COFFEE SHOP BOYCOTT
"HAWTHORNE'S COFFEE GIVES YOU SCURVY AND RICKETS."
BALONEY!
WE'VE BEEN SCURVY-FREE FOR 3 DAYS.
CATCHY SLOGAN.

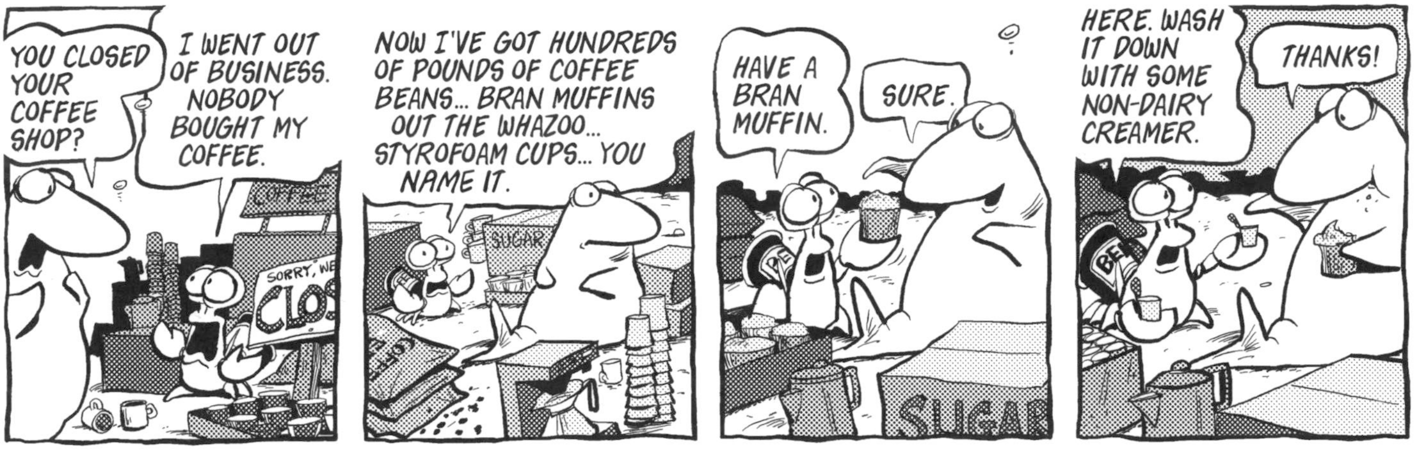
YOU CLOSED YOUR COFFEE SHOP?
I WENT OUT OF BUSINESS. NOBODY BOUGHT MY COFFEE.
SORRY, WE CLOS
NOW I'VE GOT HUNDREDS OF POUNDS OF COFFEE BEANS... BRAN MUFFINS OUT THE WHAZOO... STYROFOAM CUPS... YOU NAME IT.
SUGAR
HAVE A BRAN MUFFIN.
SURE.
SUGAR
HERE. WASH IT DOWN WITH SOME NON-DAIRY CREAMER.
THANKS!

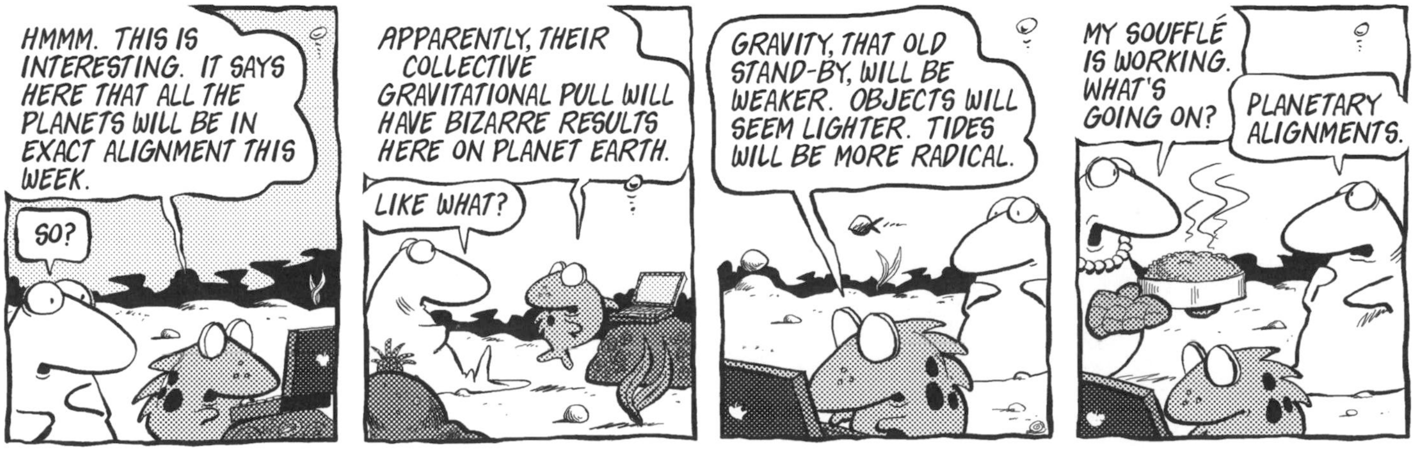
HMMM. THIS IS INTERESTING. IT SAYS HERE THAT ALL THE PLANETS WILL BE IN EXACT ALIGNMENT THIS WEEK.
SO?
APPARENTLY, THEIR COLLECTIVE GRAVITATIONAL PULL WILL HAVE BIZARRE RESULTS HERE ON PLANET EARTH.
LIKE WHAT?
GRAVITY, THAT OLD STAND-BY, WILL BE WEAKER. OBJECTS WILL SEEM LIGHTER. TIDES WILL BE MORE RADICAL.
MY SOUFFLÉ IS WORKING. WHAT'S GOING ON?
PLANETARY ALIGNMENTS.

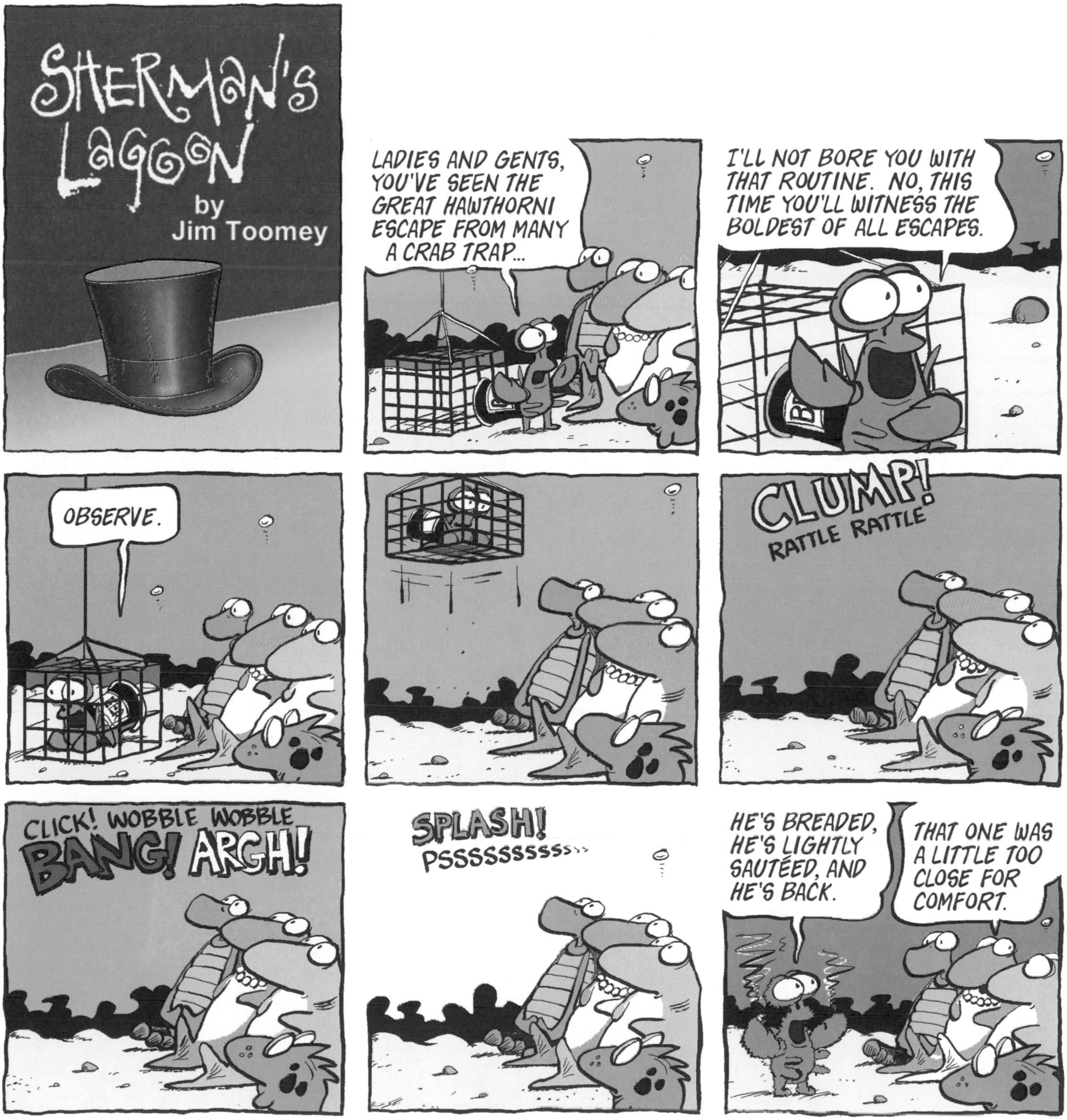
SHERMAN'S LAGOON
by
Jim Toomey
LADIES AND GENTS, YOU'VE SEEN THE GREAT HAWTHORNI ESCAPE FROM MANY A CRAB TRAP...
I'LL NOT BORE YOU WITH THAT ROUTINE. NO, THIS TIME YOU'LL WITNESS THE BOLDEST OF ALL ESCAPES.
OBSERVE.
CLUMP! RATTLE RATTLE
CLICK! WOBBLE WOBBLE BANG! ARGH!
SPLASH! PSSSSSSSSSSsss
HE'S BREADED, HE'S LIGHTLY SAUTÉED, AND HE'S BACK.
THAT ONE WAS A LITTLE TOO CLOSE FOR COMFORT.

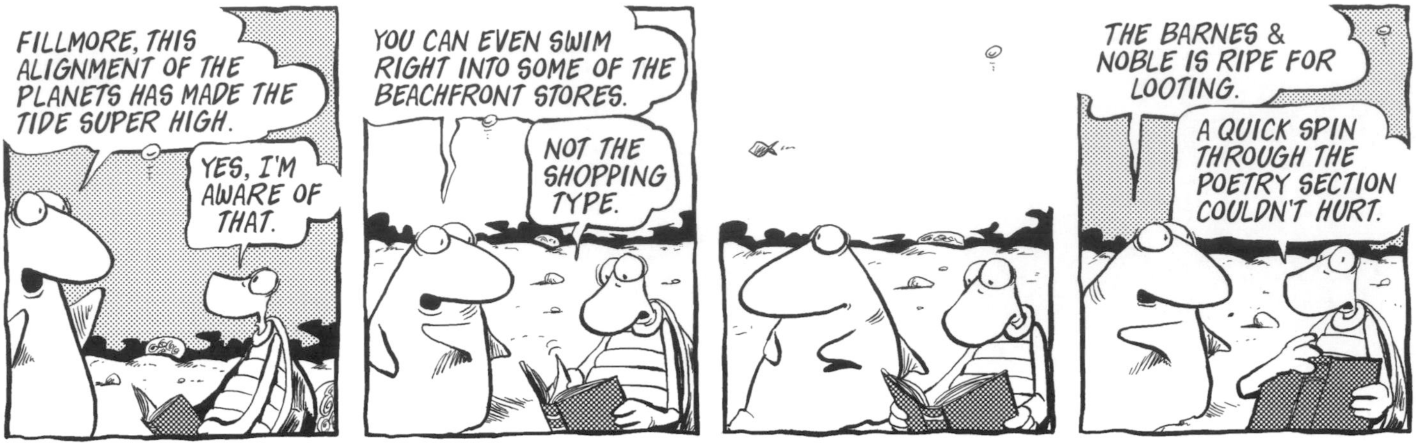
FILLMORE, THIS ALIGNMENT OF THE PLANETS HAS MADE THE TIDE SUPER HIGH.
YES, I'M AWARE OF THAT.
YOU CAN EVEN SWIM RIGHT INTO SOME OF THE BEACHFRONT STORES.
NOT THE SHOPPING TYPE.
THE BARNES & NOBLE IS RIPE FOR LOOTING.
A QUICK SPIN THROUGH THE POETRY SECTION COULDN'T HURT.

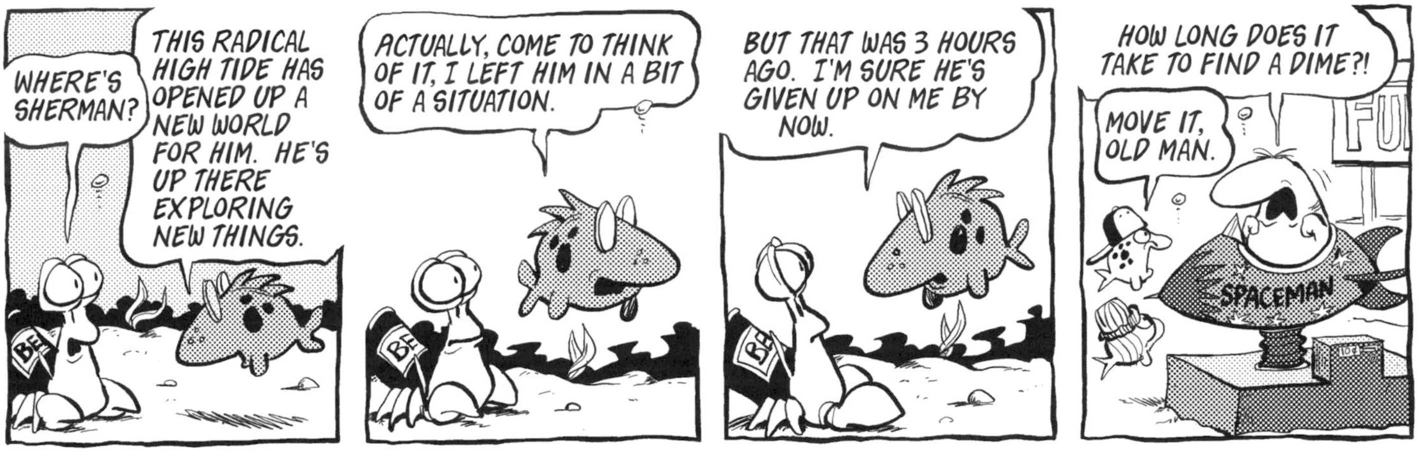
WHERE'S SHERMAN?
THIS RADICAL HIGH TIDE HAS OPENED UP A NEW WORLD FOR HIM. HE'S UP THERE EXPLORING NEW THINGS.
ACTUALLY, COME TO THINK OF IT, I LEFT HIM IN A BIT OF A SITUATION.
BUT THAT WAS 3 HOURS AGO. I'M SURE HE'S GIVEN UP ON ME BY NOW.
HOW LONG DOES IT TAKE TO FIND A DIME?!
MOVE IT, OLD MAN.
SPACEMAN

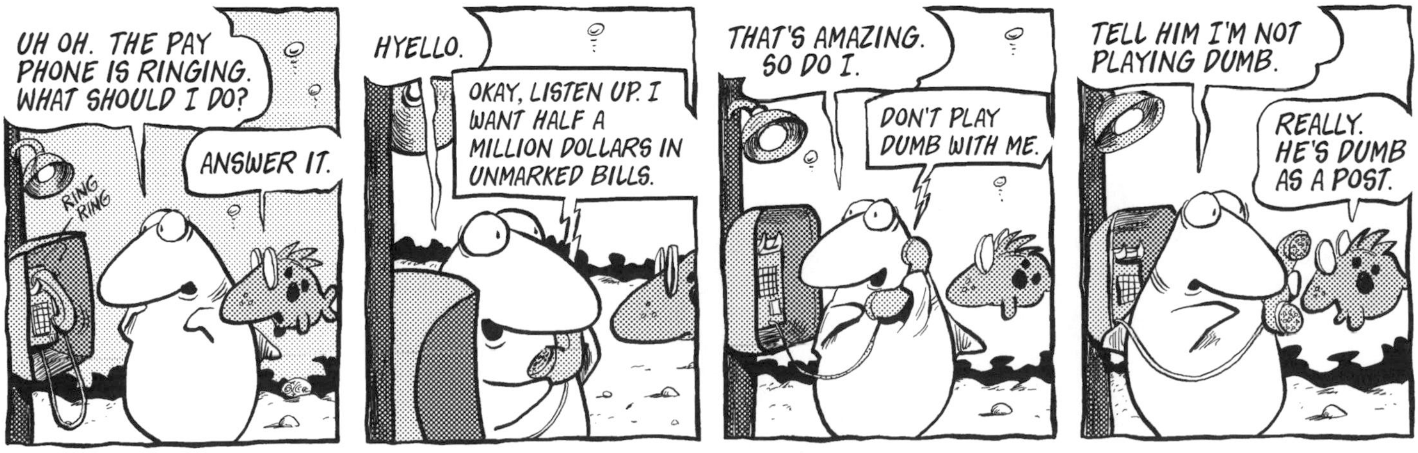
UH OH. THE PAY PHONE IS RINGING. WHAT SHOULD I DO?
ANSWER IT.
RING RING
HYELLO.
OKAY, LISTEN UP. I WANT HALF A MILLION DOLLARS IN UNMARKED BILLS.
THAT'S AMAZING. SO DO I.
DON'T PLAY DUMB WITH ME.
TELL HIM I'M NOT PLAYING DUMB.
REALLY. HE'S DUMB AS A POST.

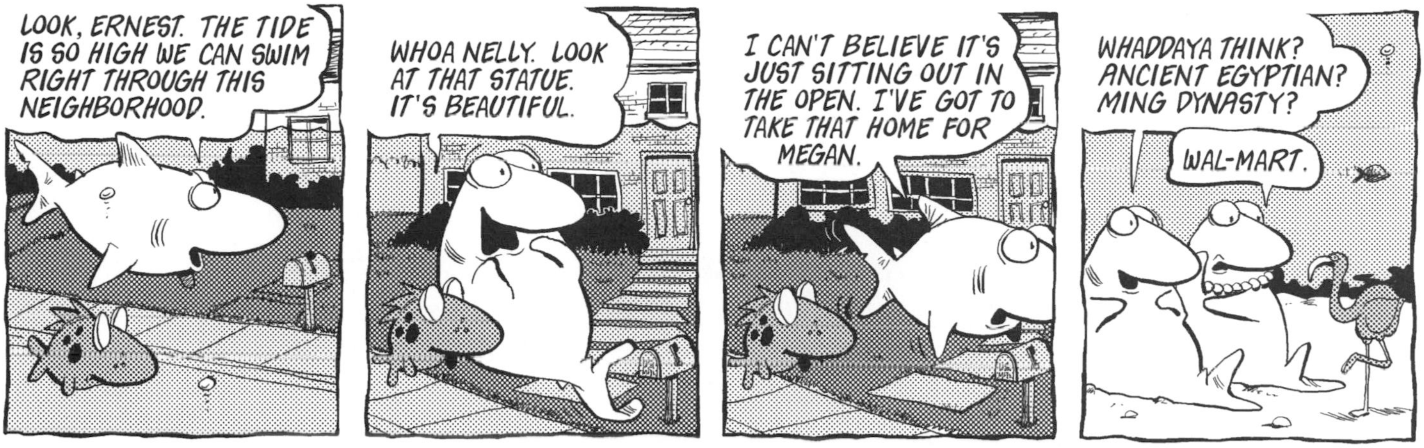
LOOK, ERNEST. THE TIDE IS SO HIGH WE CAN SWIM RIGHT THROUGH THIS NEIGHBORHOOD.
WHOA NELLY. LOOK AT THAT STATUE. IT'S BEAUTIFUL.
I CAN'T BELIEVE IT'S JUST SITTING OUT IN THE OPEN. I'VE GOT TO TAKE THAT HOME FOR MEGAN.
WHADDAYA THINK? ANCIENT EGYPTIAN? MING DYNASTY?
WAL-MART.

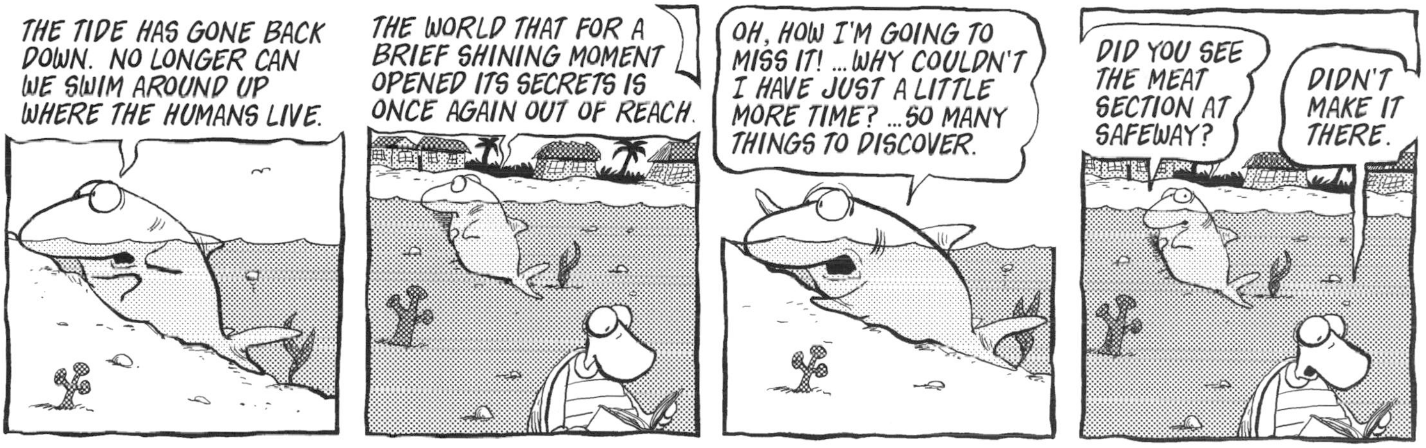
THE TIDE HAS GONE BACK DOWN. NO LONGER CAN WE SWIM AROUND UP WHERE THE HUMANS LIVE.
THE WORLD THAT FOR A BRIEF SHINING MOMENT OPENED ITS SECRETS IS ONCE AGAIN OUT OF REACH.
OH, HOW I'M GOING TO MISS IT! ...WHY COULDN'T I HAVE JUST A LITTLE MORE TIME? ...SO MANY THINGS TO DISCOVER.
DID YOU SEE THE MEAT SECTION AT SAFEWAY?
DIDN'T MAKE IT THERE.

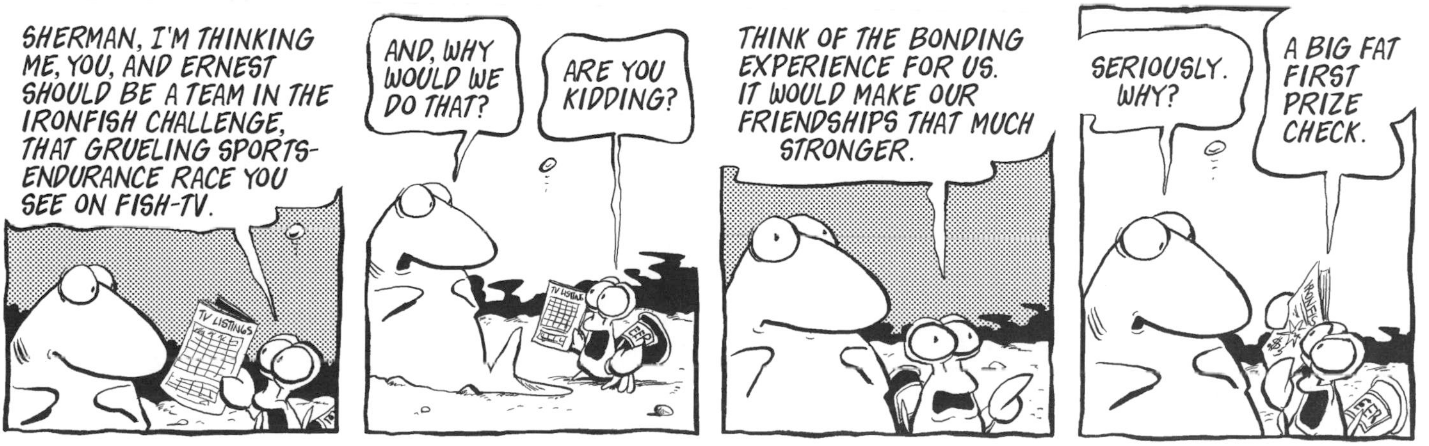
SHERMAN, I'M THINKING ME, YOU, AND ERNEST SHOULD BE A TEAM IN THE IRONFISH CHALLENGE, THAT GRUELING SPORTS-ENDURANCE RACE YOU SEE ON FISH-TV.
AND, WHY WOULD WE DO THAT?
ARE YOU KIDDING?
THINK OF THE BONDING EXPERIENCE FOR US. IT WOULD MAKE OUR FRIENDSHIPS THAT MUCH STRONGER.
SERIOUSLY. WHY?
A BIG FAT FIRST PRIZE CHECK.

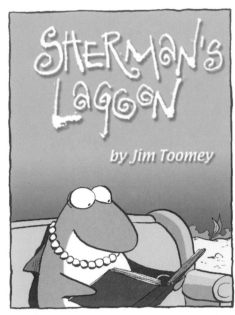

SHERMAN'S LAGOON

by Jim Toomey

WHATCHA DOIN', MEGAN?

JUST LOOKING AT SOME OLD VACATION PHOTOS.

OOH, THERE'S THE MEDITERRANEAN. THAT WAS FUN.

AND THERE'S HAWAII.

AND THE BAHAMAS. THAT WAS ROMANTIC.

LOOK HOW HAPPY WE WERE THERE.

THAT'S NOT ME.

"WE" DOESN'T NECESSARILY MEAN "US".

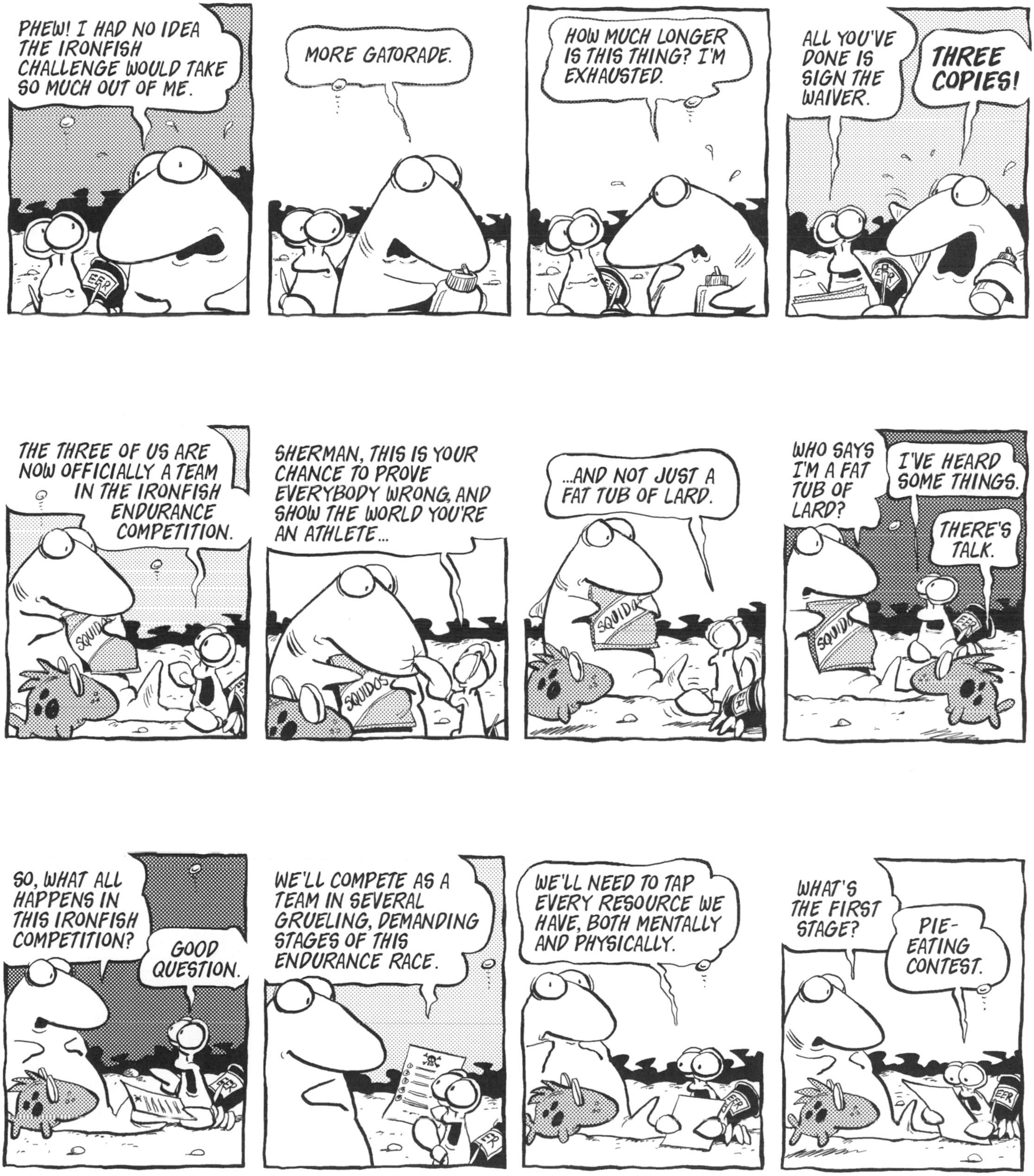
PHEW! I HAD NO IDEA THE IRONFISH CHALLENGE WOULD TAKE SO MUCH OUT OF ME.
MORE GATORADE.
HOW MUCH LONGER IS THIS THING? I'M EXHAUSTED.
ALL YOU'VE DONE IS SIGN THE WAIVER.
THREE COPIES!
THE THREE OF US ARE NOW OFFICIALLY A TEAM IN THE IRONFISH ENDURANCE COMPETITION.
SHERMAN, THIS IS YOUR CHANCE TO PROVE EVERYBODY WRONG, AND SHOW THE WORLD YOU'RE AN ATHLETE...
...AND NOT JUST A FAT TUB OF LARD.
WHO SAYS I'M A FAT TUB OF LARD?
I'VE HEARD SOME THINGS.
THERE'S TALK.
SO, WHAT ALL HAPPENS IN THIS IRONFISH COMPETITION?
GOOD QUESTION.
WE'LL COMPETE AS A TEAM IN SEVERAL GRUELING, DEMANDING STAGES OF THIS ENDURANCE RACE.
WE'LL NEED TO TAP EVERY RESOURCE WE HAVE, BOTH MENTALLY AND PHYSICALLY.
WHAT'S THE FIRST STAGE?
PIE-EATING CONTEST.

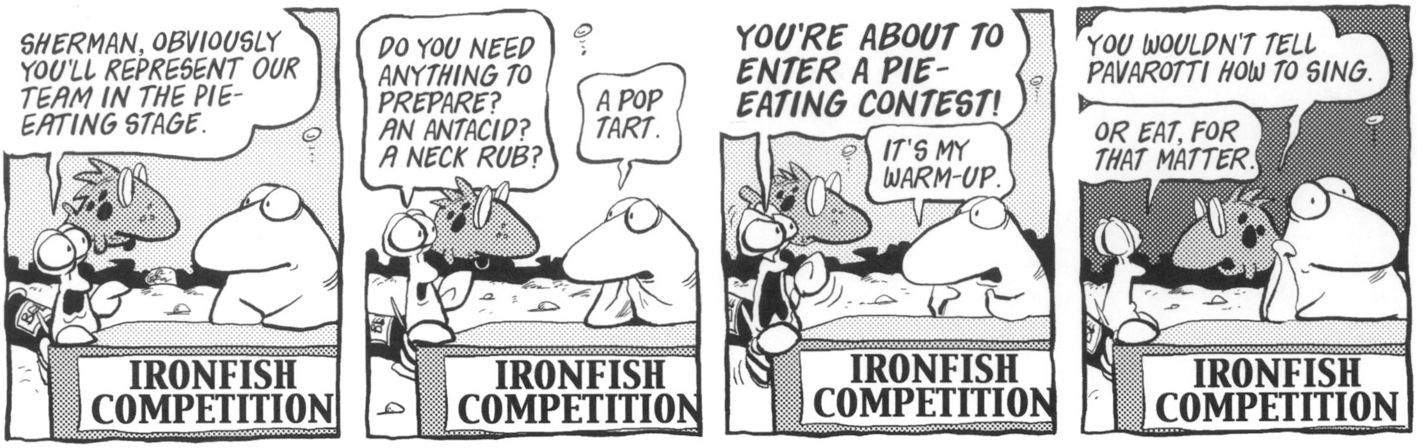
SHERMAN, OBVIOUSLY YOU'LL REPRESENT OUR TEAM IN THE PIE-EATING STAGE.
IRONFISH COMPETITION
DO YOU NEED ANYTHING TO PREPARE? AN ANTACID? A NECK RUB?
A POP TART.
IRONFISH COMPETITION
YOU'RE ABOUT TO ENTER A PIE-EATING CONTEST!
IT'S MY WARM-UP.
IRONFISH COMPETITION
YOU WOULDN'T TELL PAVAROTTI HOW TO SING.
OR EAT, FOR THAT MATTER.
IRONFISH COMPETITION

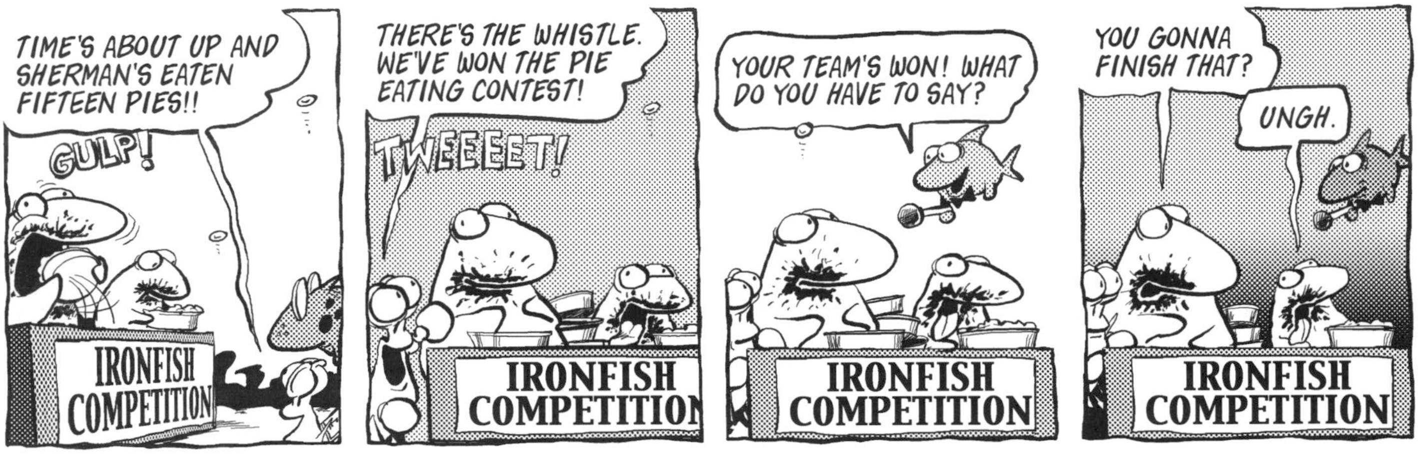
TIME'S ABOUT UP AND SHERMAN'S EATEN FIFTEEN PIES!!
GULP!
IRONFISH COMPETITION
THERE'S THE WHISTLE. WE'VE WON THE PIE EATING CONTEST!
TWEEEEET!
IRONFISH COMPETITION
YOUR TEAM'S WON! WHAT DO YOU HAVE TO SAY?
IRONFISH COMPETITION
YOU GONNA FINISH THAT?
UNGH.
IRONFISH COMPETITION

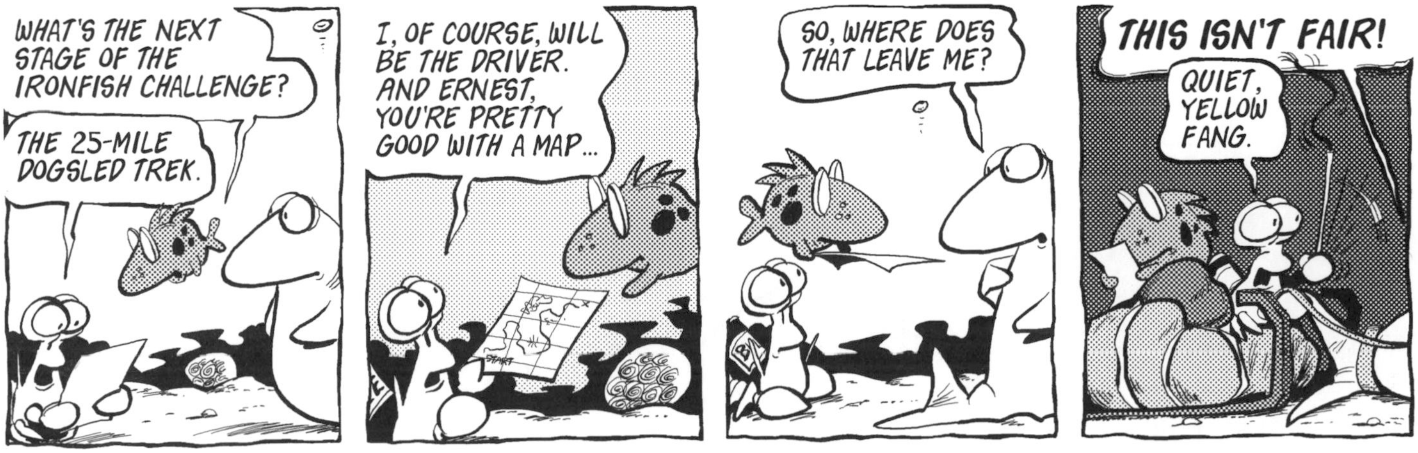
WHAT'S THE NEXT STAGE OF THE IRONFISH CHALLENGE?
THE 25-MILE DOGSLED TREK.
I, OF COURSE, WILL BE THE DRIVER. AND ERNEST, YOU'RE PRETTY GOOD WITH A MAP...
SO, WHERE DOES THAT LEAVE ME?
THIS ISN'T FAIR!
QUIET, YELLOW FANG.

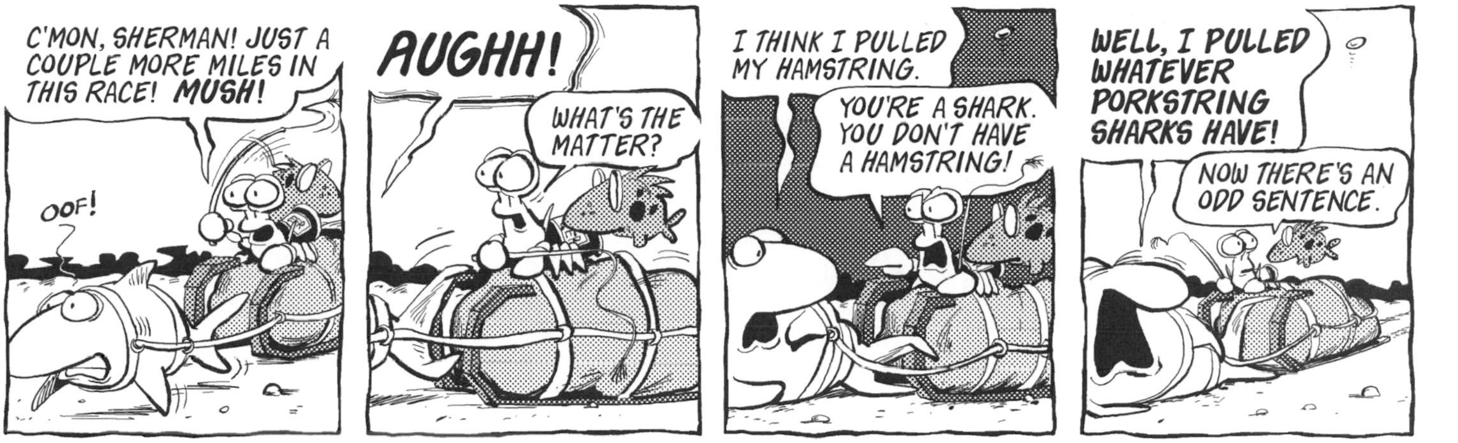
C'MON, SHERMAN! JUST A COUPLE MORE MILES IN THIS RACE! **MUSH**!
OOF!
AUGHH!
WHAT'S THE MATTER?
I THINK I PULLED MY HAMSTRING.
YOU'RE A SHARK. YOU DON'T HAVE A HAMSTRING!
WELL, I PULLED WHATEVER PORKSTRING SHARKS HAVE!
NOW THERE'S AN ODD SENTENCE.

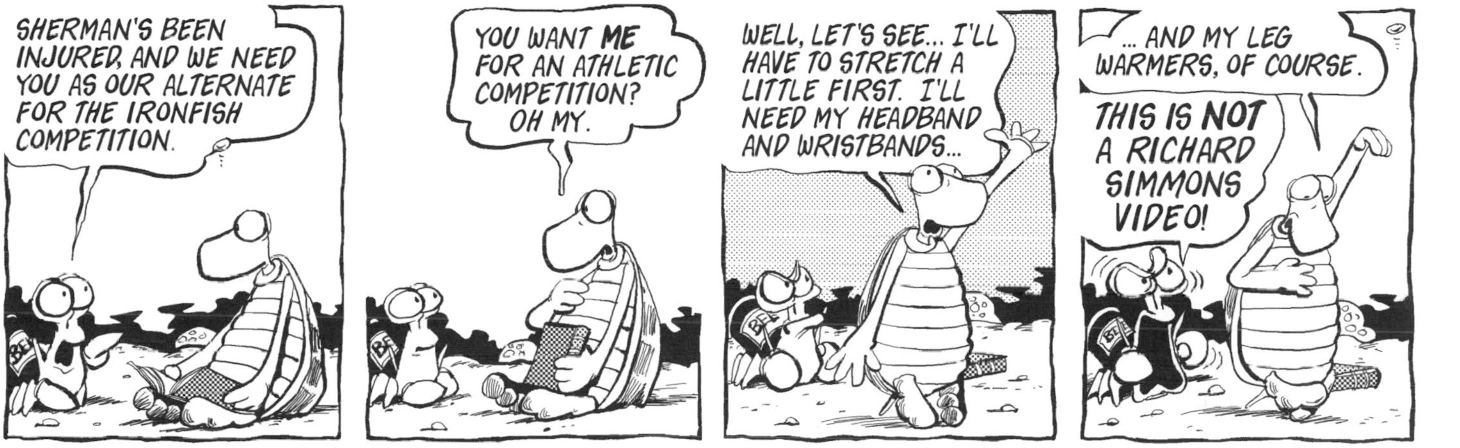
SHERMAN'S BEEN INJURED, AND WE NEED YOU AS OUR ALTERNATE FOR THE IRONFISH COMPETITION.
YOU WANT **ME** FOR AN ATHLETIC COMPETITION? OH MY.
WELL, LET'S SEE... I'LL HAVE TO STRETCH A LITTLE FIRST. I'LL NEED MY HEADBAND AND WRISTBANDS...
... AND MY LEG WARMERS, OF COURSE.
THIS IS **NOT** A RICHARD SIMMONS VIDEO!

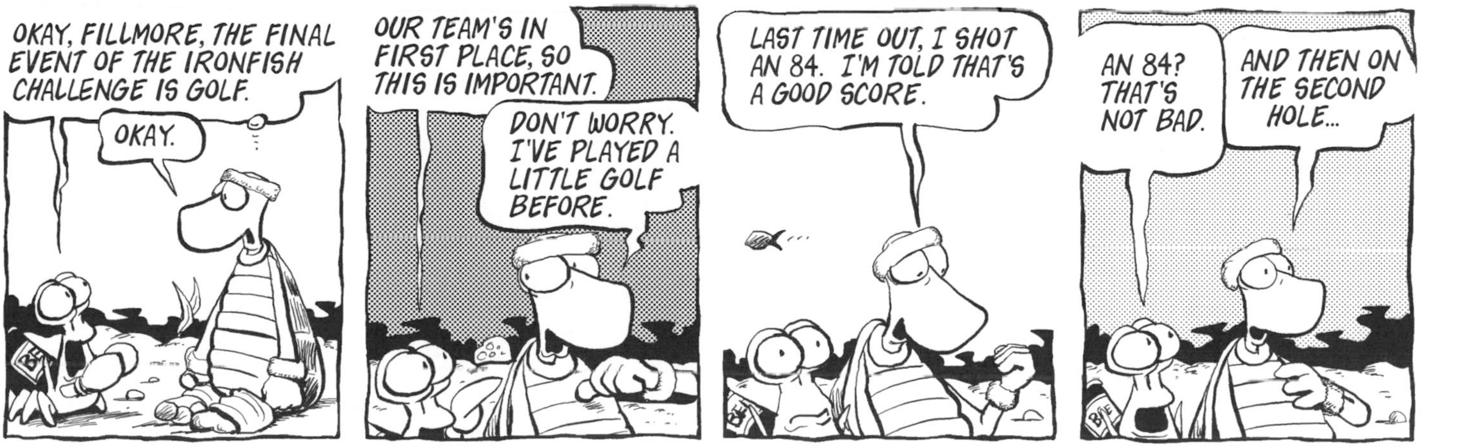
OKAY, FILLMORE, THE FINAL EVENT OF THE IRONFISH CHALLENGE IS GOLF.
OKAY.
OUR TEAM'S IN FIRST PLACE, SO THIS IS IMPORTANT.
DON'T WORRY. I'VE PLAYED A LITTLE GOLF BEFORE.
LAST TIME OUT, I SHOT AN 84. I'M TOLD THAT'S A GOOD SCORE.
AN 84? THAT'S NOT BAD.
AND THEN ON THE SECOND HOLE...

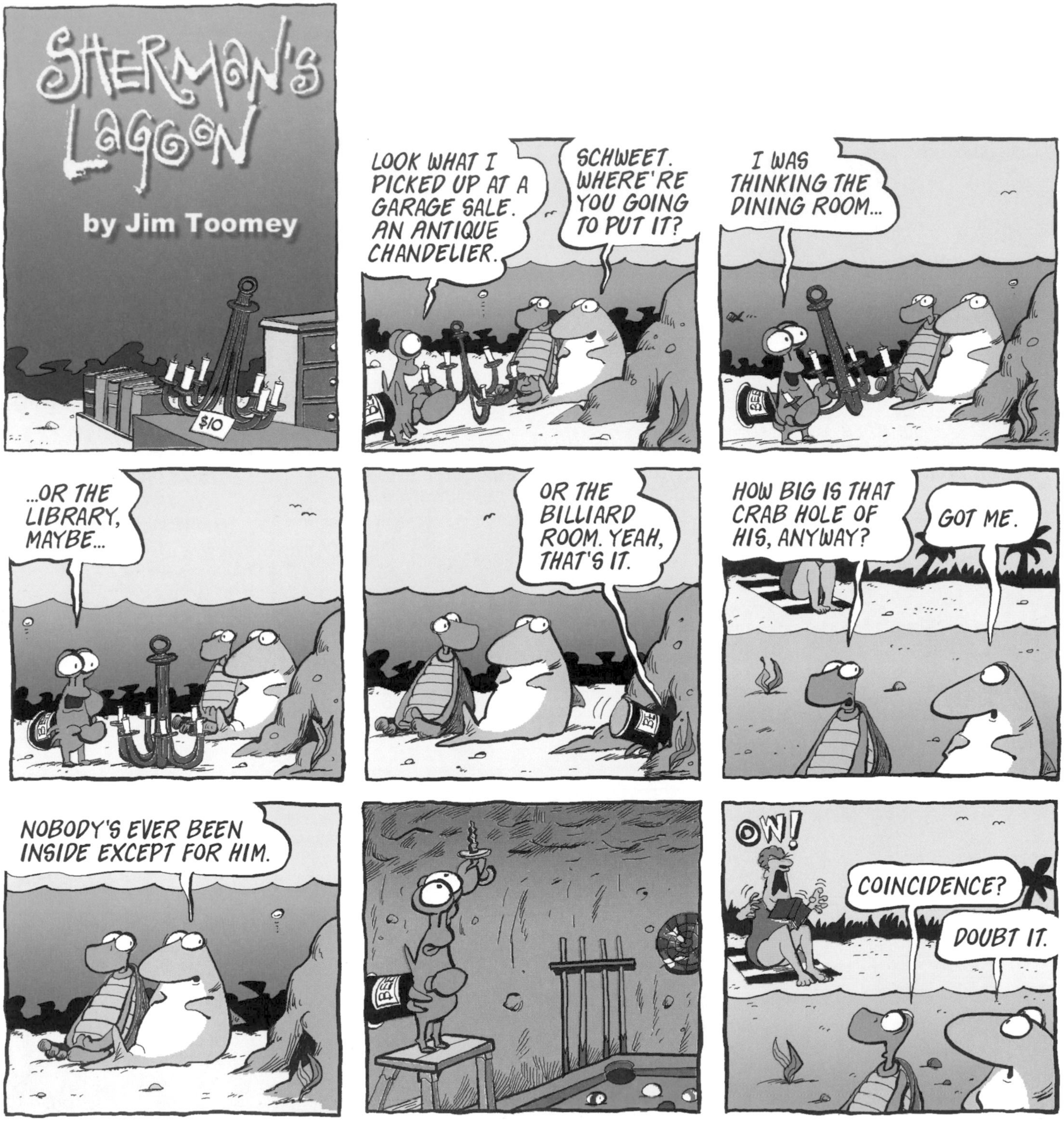
SHERMAN'S LAGOON
by Jim Toomey
$10
LOOK WHAT I PICKED UP AT A GARAGE SALE. AN ANTIQUE CHANDELIER.
SCHWEET. WHERE'RE YOU GOING TO PUT IT?
I WAS THINKING THE DINING ROOM...
...OR THE LIBRARY, MAYBE...
OR THE BILLIARD ROOM. YEAH, THAT'S IT.
HOW BIG IS THAT CRAB HOLE OF HIS, ANYWAY?
GOT ME.
NOBODY'S EVER BEEN INSIDE EXCEPT FOR HIM.
OW!
COINCIDENCE?
DOUBT IT.

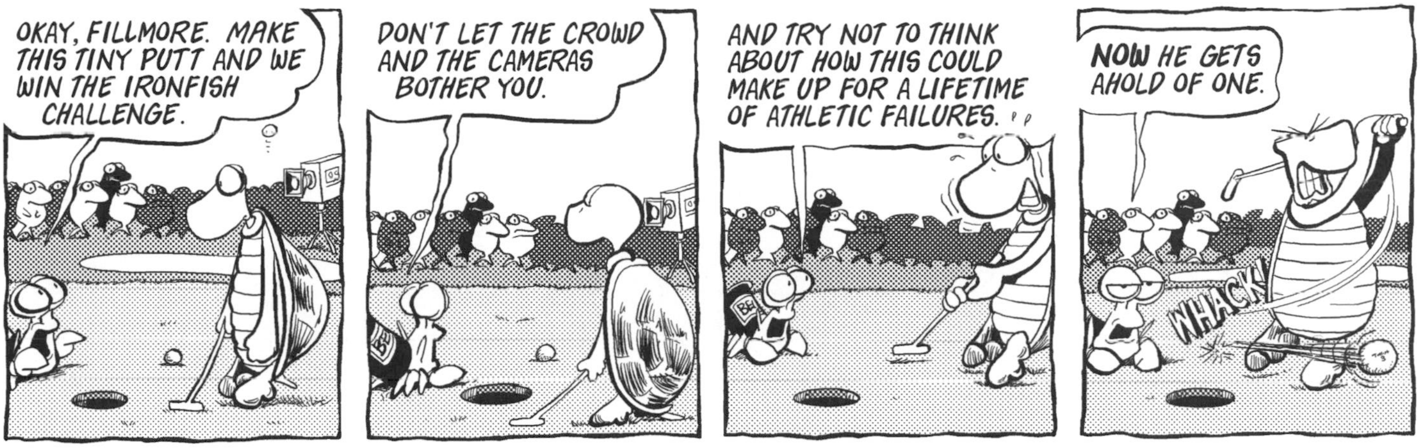
OKAY, FILLMORE. MAKE THIS TINY PUTT AND WE WIN THE IRONFISH CHALLENGE.
DON'T LET THE CROWD AND THE CAMERAS BOTHER YOU.
AND TRY NOT TO THINK ABOUT HOW THIS COULD MAKE UP FOR A LIFETIME OF ATHLETIC FAILURES.
NOW HE GETS AHOLD OF ONE.
WHACK!

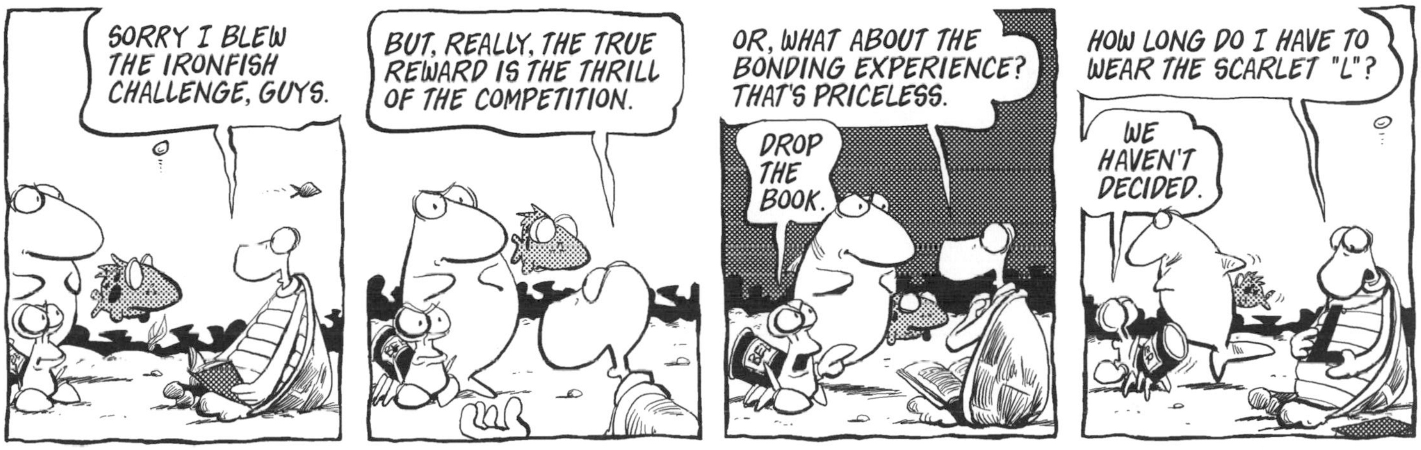
SORRY I BLEW THE IRONFISH CHALLENGE, GUYS.
BUT, REALLY, THE TRUE REWARD IS THE THRILL OF THE COMPETITION.
OR, WHAT ABOUT THE BONDING EXPERIENCE? THAT'S PRICELESS.
DROP THE BOOK.
HOW LONG DO I HAVE TO WEAR THE SCARLET "L"?
WE HAVEN'T DECIDED.

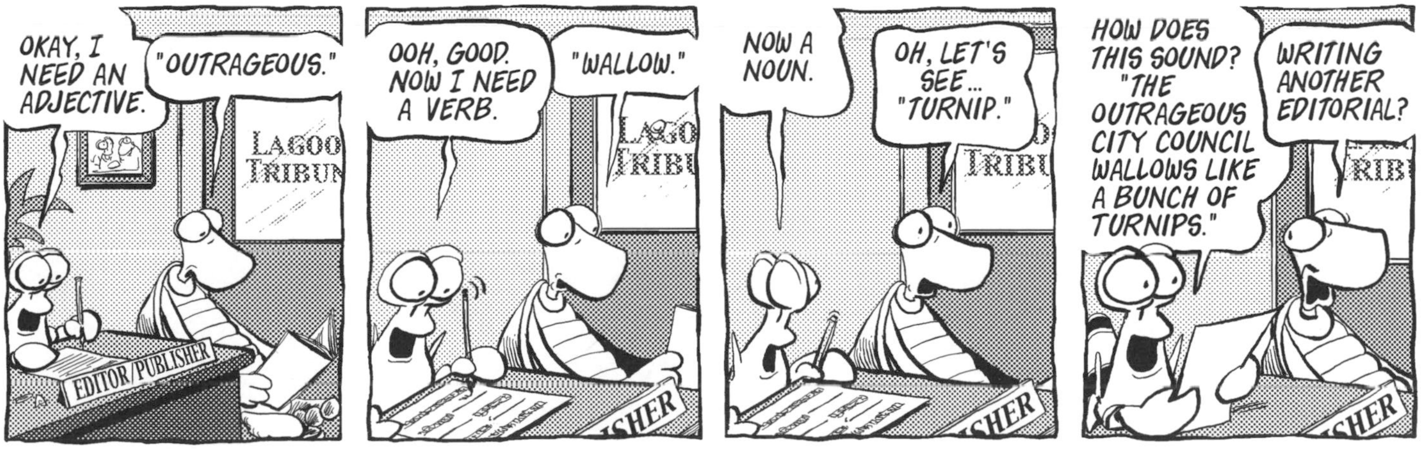
OKAY, I NEED AN ADJECTIVE.
"OUTRAGEOUS."
LAGOON TRIBUNE
EDITOR/PUBLISHER
OOH, GOOD. NOW I NEED A VERB.
"WALLOW."
NOW A NOUN.
OH, LET'S SEE... "TURNIP."
HOW DOES THIS SOUND? "THE OUTRAGEOUS CITY COUNCIL WALLOWS LIKE A BUNCH OF TURNIPS."
WRITING ANOTHER EDITORIAL?

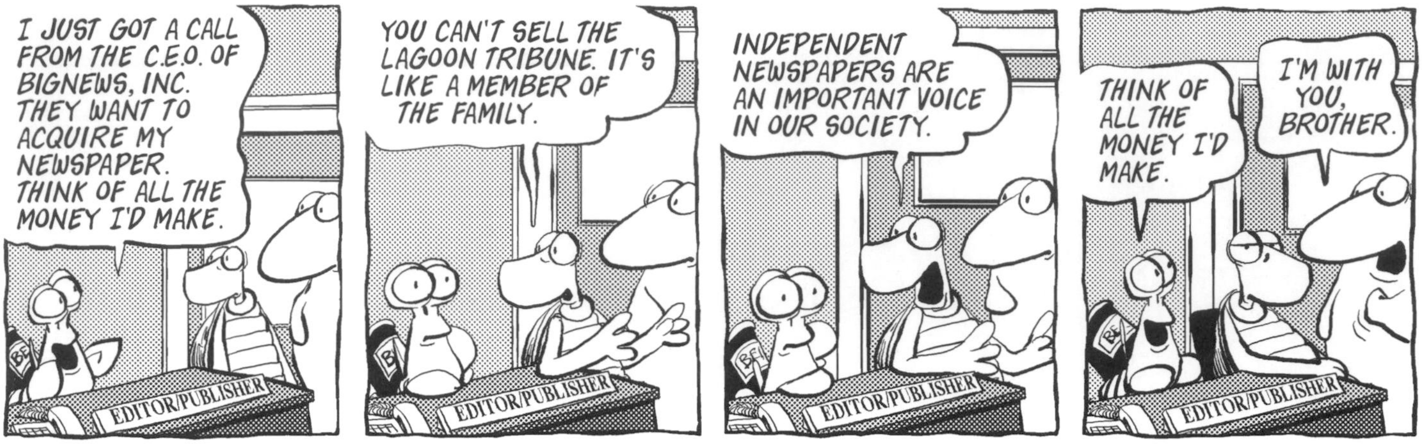
I JUST GOT A CALL FROM THE C.E.O. OF BIGNEWS, INC. THEY WANT TO ACQUIRE MY NEWSPAPER. THINK OF ALL THE MONEY I'D MAKE.
EDITOR/PUBLISHER
YOU CAN'T SELL THE LAGOON TRIBUNE. IT'S LIKE A MEMBER OF THE FAMILY.
INDEPENDENT NEWSPAPERS ARE AN IMPORTANT VOICE IN OUR SOCIETY.
THINK OF ALL THE MONEY I'D MAKE.
I'M WITH YOU, BROTHER.

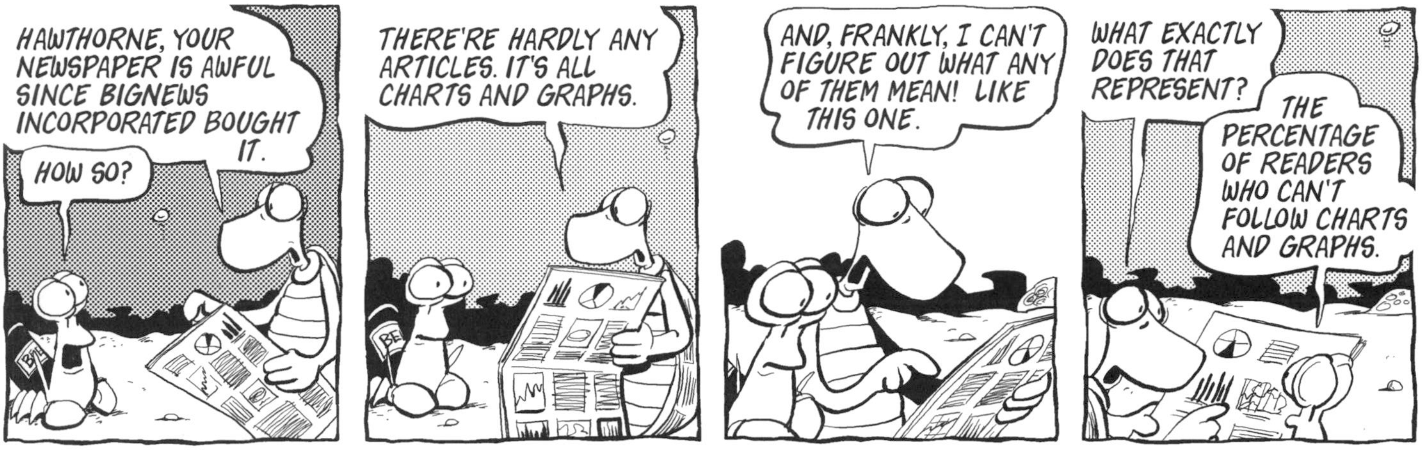
HAWTHORNE, YOUR NEWSPAPER IS AWFUL SINCE BIGNEWS INCORPORATED BOUGHT IT.
HOW SO?
THERE'RE HARDLY ANY ARTICLES. IT'S ALL CHARTS AND GRAPHS.
AND, FRANKLY, I CAN'T FIGURE OUT WHAT ANY OF THEM MEAN! LIKE THIS ONE.
WHAT EXACTLY DOES THAT REPRESENT?
THE PERCENTAGE OF READERS WHO CAN'T FOLLOW CHARTS AND GRAPHS.

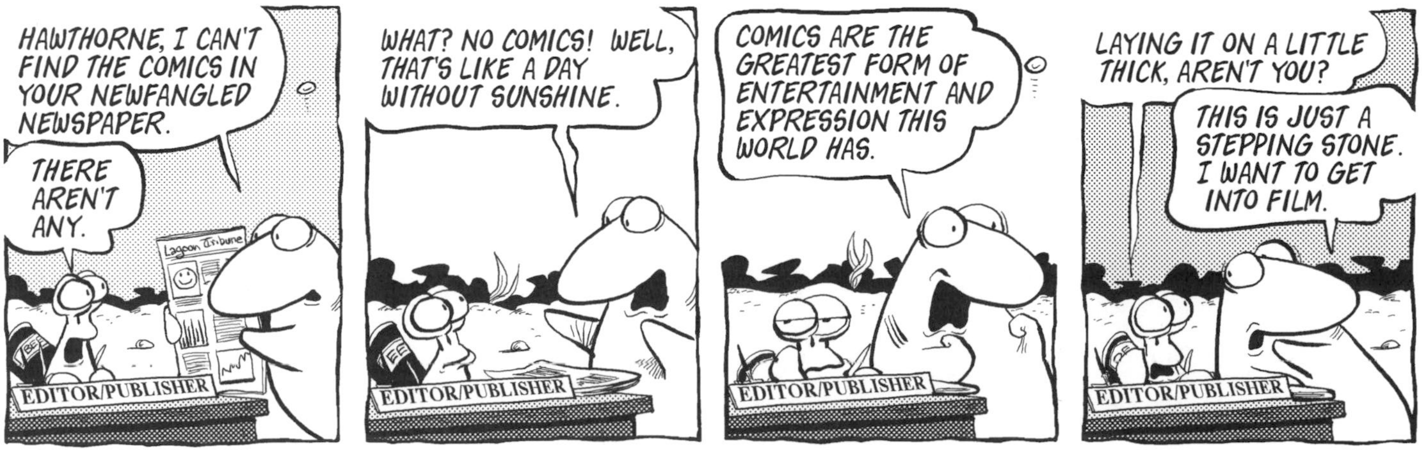
HAWTHORNE, I CAN'T FIND THE COMICS IN YOUR NEWFANGLED NEWSPAPER.
THERE AREN'T ANY.
Lagoon Tribune
EDITOR/PUBLISHER
WHAT? NO COMICS! WELL, THAT'S LIKE A DAY WITHOUT SUNSHINE.
COMICS ARE THE GREATEST FORM OF ENTERTAINMENT AND EXPRESSION THIS WORLD HAS.
LAYING IT ON A LITTLE THICK, AREN'T YOU?
THIS IS JUST A STEPPING STONE. I WANT TO GET INTO FILM.

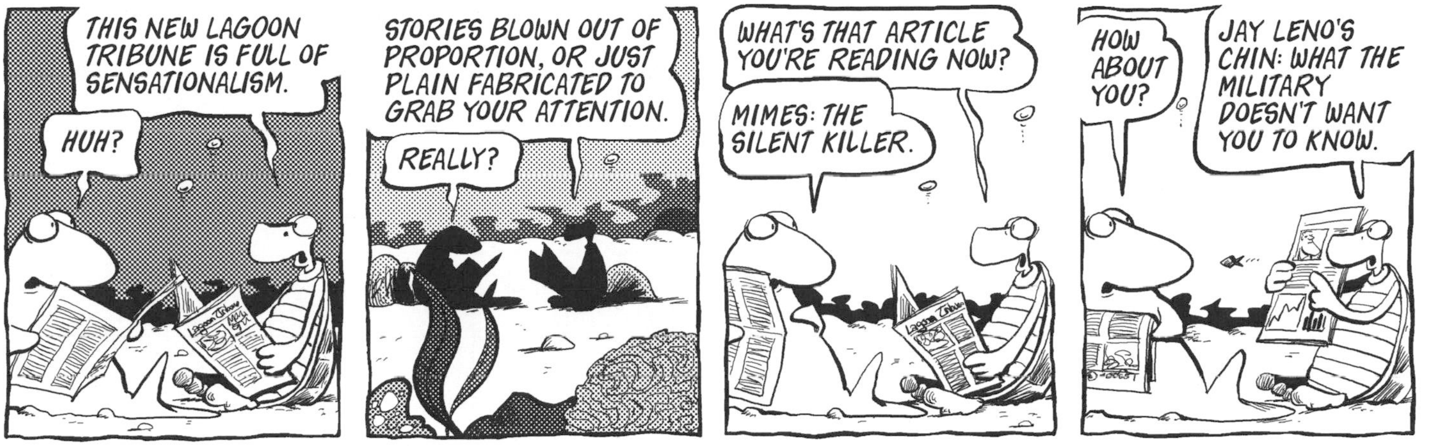
THIS NEW LAGOON TRIBUNE IS FULL OF SENSATIONALISM.
HUH?
STORIES BLOWN OUT OF PROPORTION, OR JUST PLAIN FABRICATED TO GRAB YOUR ATTENTION.
REALLY?
WHAT'S THAT ARTICLE YOU'RE READING NOW?
MIMES: THE SILENT KILLER.
HOW ABOUT YOU?
JAY LENO'S CHIN: WHAT THE MILITARY DOESN'T WANT YOU TO KNOW.

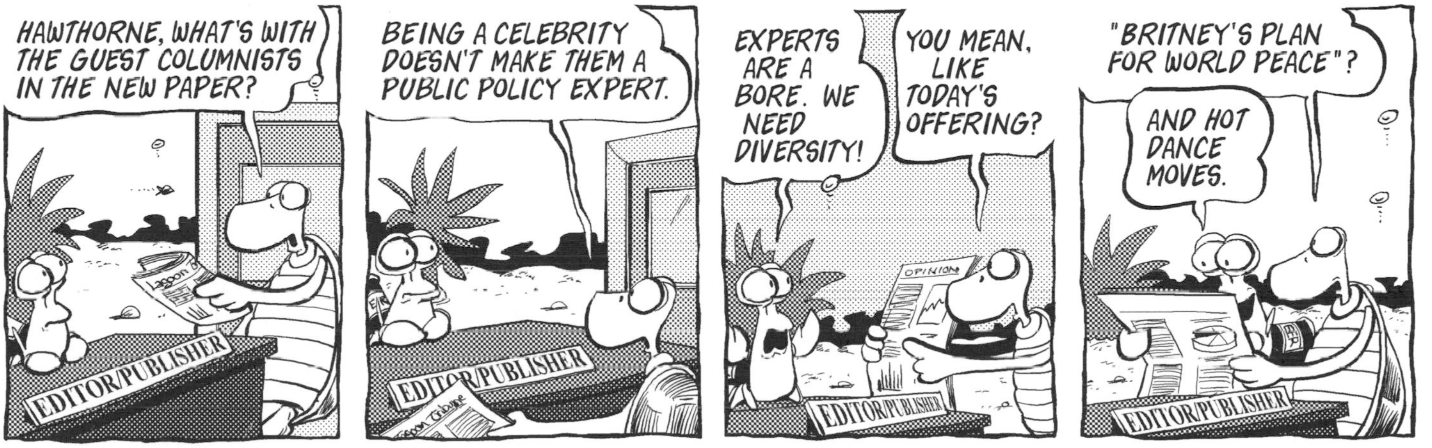
HAWTHORNE, WHAT'S WITH THE GUEST COLUMNISTS IN THE NEW PAPER?
EDITOR/PUBLISHER
BEING A CELEBRITY DOESN'T MAKE THEM A PUBLIC POLICY EXPERT.
EDITOR/PUBLISHER
EXPERTS ARE A BORE. WE NEED DIVERSITY!
YOU MEAN, LIKE TODAY'S OFFERING?
OPINION
EDITOR/PUBLISHER
"BRITNEY'S PLAN FOR WORLD PEACE"?
AND HOT DANCE MOVES.
EDITOR/PUBLISHER

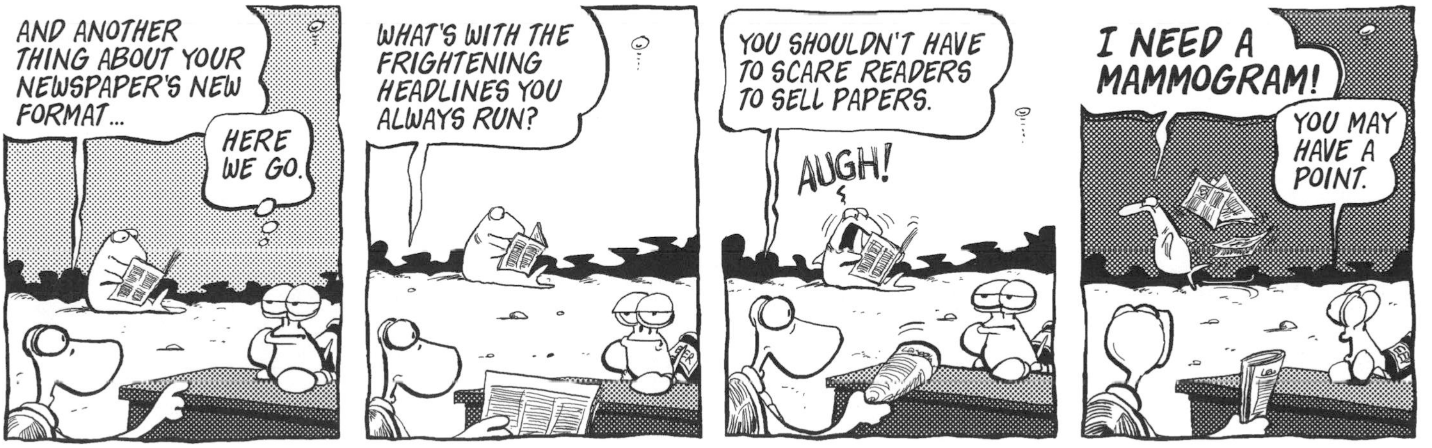
AND ANOTHER THING ABOUT YOUR NEWSPAPER'S NEW FORMAT...
HERE WE GO.
WHAT'S WITH THE FRIGHTENING HEADLINES YOU ALWAYS RUN?
YOU SHOULDN'T HAVE TO SCARE READERS TO SELL PAPERS.
AUGH!
I NEED A MAMMOGRAM!
YOU MAY HAVE A POINT.

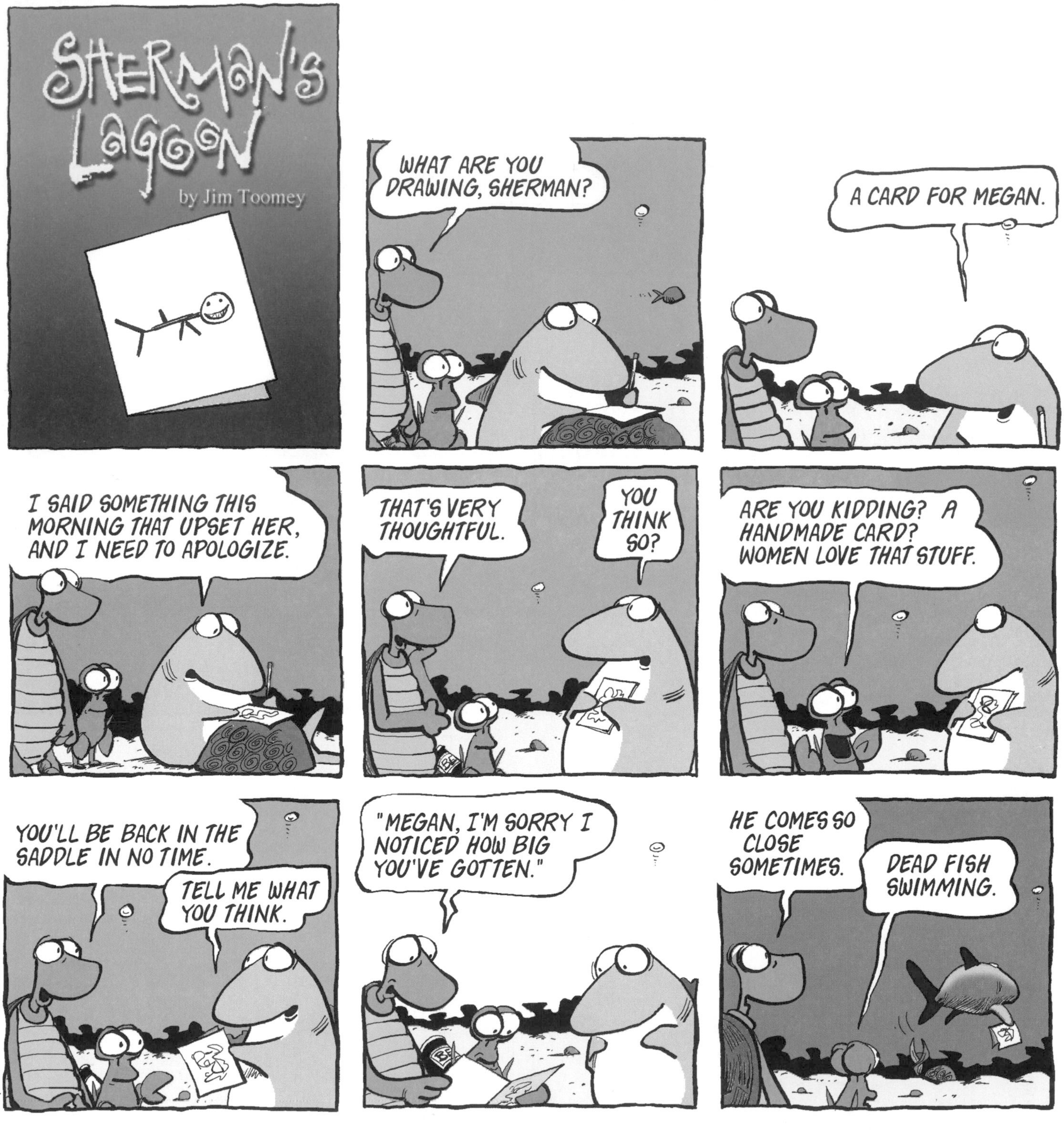
SHERMAN'S LAGOON
by Jim Toomey
WHAT ARE YOU DRAWING, SHERMAN?
A CARD FOR MEGAN.
I SAID SOMETHING THIS MORNING THAT UPSET HER, AND I NEED TO APOLOGIZE.
THAT'S VERY THOUGHTFUL.
YOU THINK SO?
ARE YOU KIDDING? A HANDMADE CARD? WOMEN LOVE THAT STUFF.
YOU'LL BE BACK IN THE SADDLE IN NO TIME.
TELL ME WHAT YOU THINK.
"MEGAN, I'M SORRY I NOTICED HOW BIG YOU'VE GOTTEN."
HE COMES SO CLOSE SOMETIMES.
DEAD FISH SWIMMING.

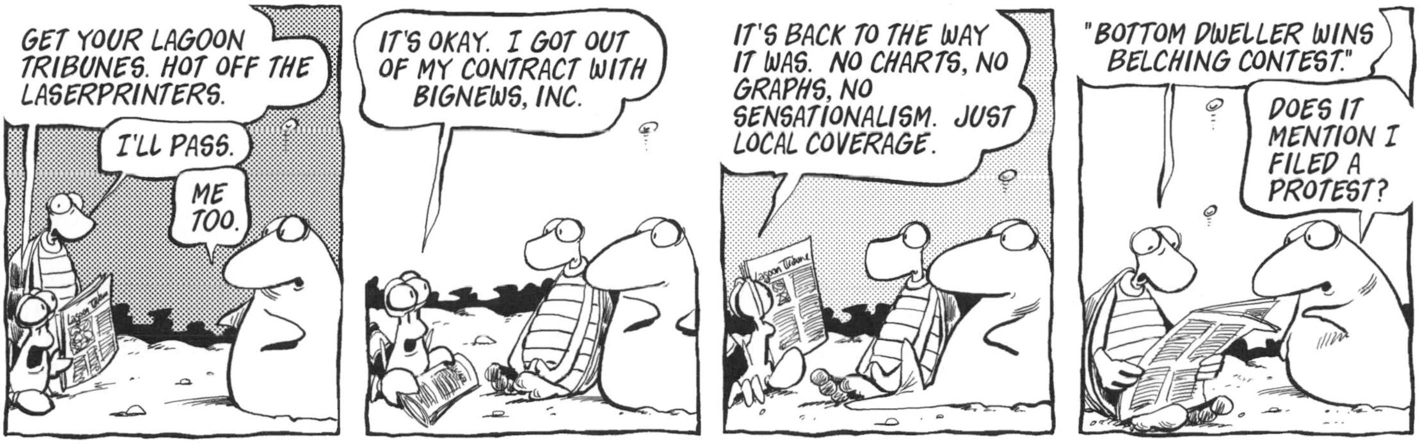
GET YOUR LAGOON TRIBUNES. HOT OFF THE LASERPRINTERS.
I'LL PASS.
ME TOO.
IT'S OKAY. I GOT OUT OF MY CONTRACT WITH BIGNEWS, INC.
IT'S BACK TO THE WAY IT WAS. NO CHARTS, NO GRAPHS, NO SENSATIONALISM. JUST LOCAL COVERAGE.
"BOTTOM DWELLER WINS BELCHING CONTEST."
DOES IT MENTION I FILED A PROTEST?

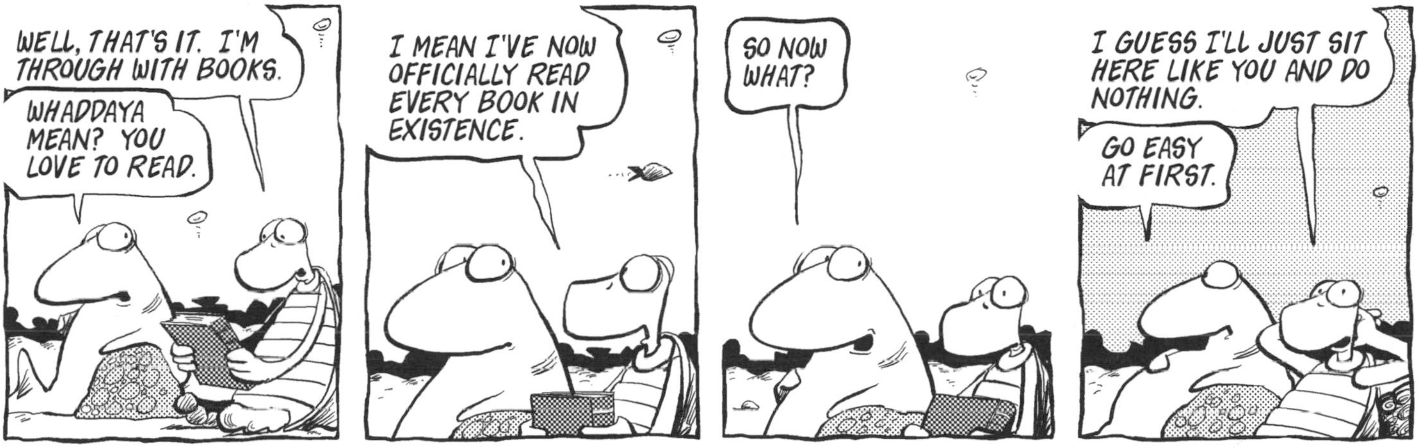
WELL, THAT'S IT. I'M THROUGH WITH BOOKS.
WHADDAYA MEAN? YOU LOVE TO READ.
I MEAN I'VE NOW OFFICIALLY READ EVERY BOOK IN EXISTENCE.
SO NOW WHAT?
I GUESS I'LL JUST SIT HERE LIKE YOU AND DO NOTHING.
GO EASY AT FIRST.

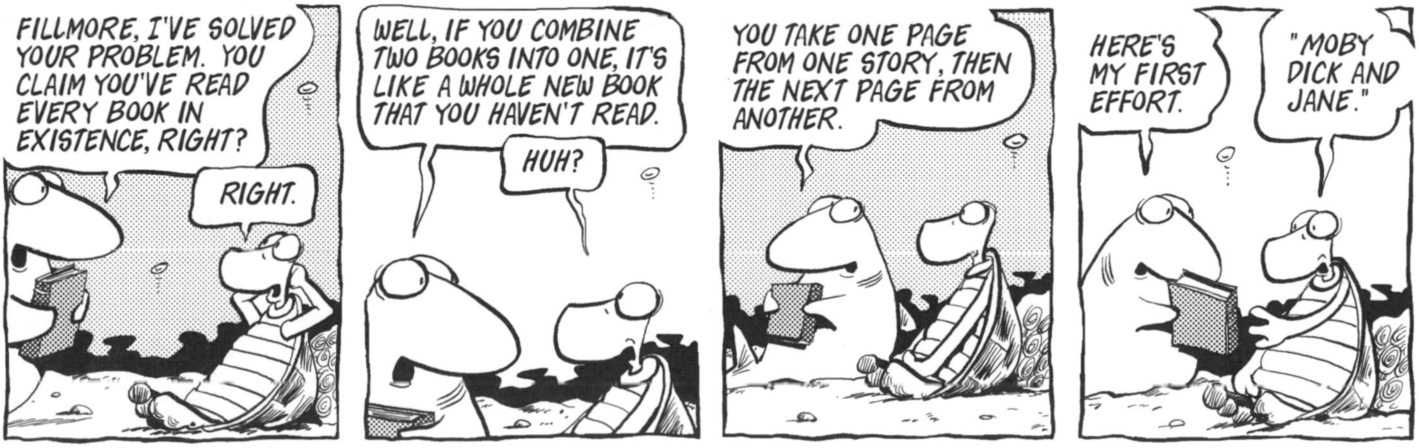
FILLMORE, I'VE SOLVED YOUR PROBLEM. YOU CLAIM YOU'VE READ EVERY BOOK IN EXISTENCE, RIGHT?
RIGHT.
WELL, IF YOU COMBINE TWO BOOKS INTO ONE, IT'S LIKE A WHOLE NEW BOOK THAT YOU HAVEN'T READ.
HUH?
YOU TAKE ONE PAGE FROM ONE STORY, THEN THE NEXT PAGE FROM ANOTHER.
HERE'S MY FIRST EFFORT.
"MOBY DICK AND JANE."

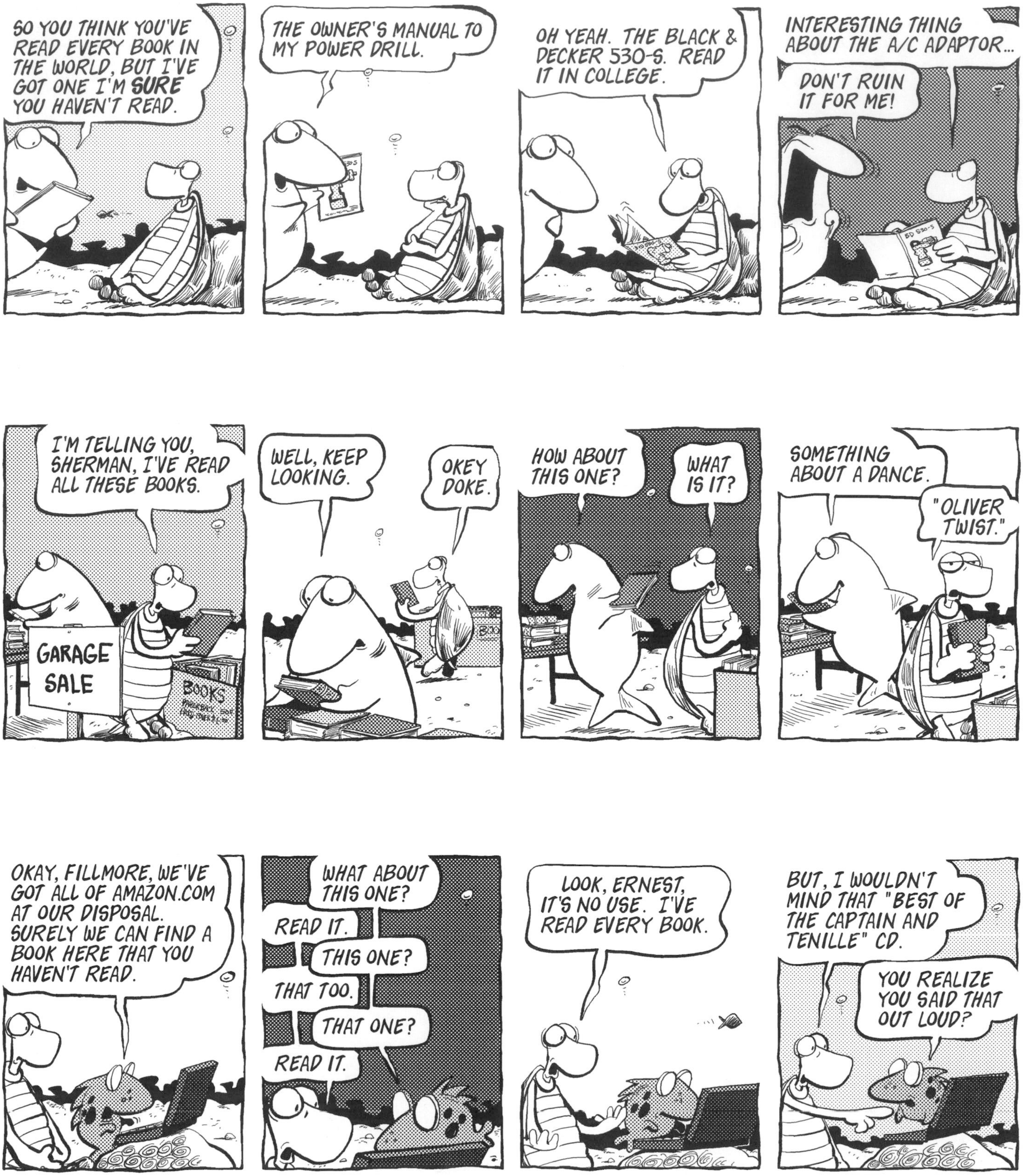
SO YOU THINK YOU'VE READ EVERY BOOK IN THE WORLD, BUT I'VE GOT ONE I'M SURE YOU HAVEN'T READ.
THE OWNER'S MANUAL TO MY POWER DRILL.
OH YEAH. THE BLACK & DECKER 530-S. READ IT IN COLLEGE.
INTERESTING THING ABOUT THE A/C ADAPTOR...
DON'T RUIN IT FOR ME!
I'M TELLING YOU, SHERMAN, I'VE READ ALL THESE BOOKS.
GARAGE SALE
BOOKS
WELL, KEEP LOOKING.
OKEY DOKE.
HOW ABOUT THIS ONE?
WHAT IS IT?
SOMETHING ABOUT A DANCE.
"OLIVER TWIST."
OKAY, FILLMORE, WE'VE GOT ALL OF AMAZON.COM AT OUR DISPOSAL. SURELY WE CAN FIND A BOOK HERE THAT YOU HAVEN'T READ.
WHAT ABOUT THIS ONE?
READ IT.
THIS ONE?
THAT TOO.
THAT ONE?
READ IT.
LOOK, ERNEST, IT'S NO USE. I'VE READ EVERY BOOK.
BUT, I WOULDN'T MIND THAT "BEST OF THE CAPTAIN AND TENILLE" CD.
YOU REALIZE YOU SAID THAT OUT LOUD?

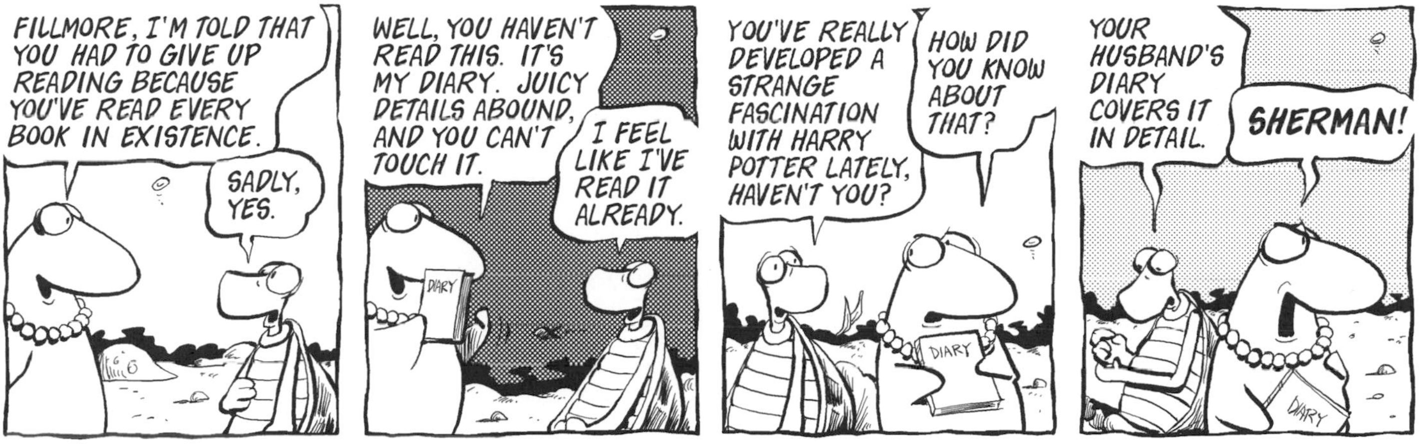
FILLMORE, I'M TOLD THAT YOU HAD TO GIVE UP READING BECAUSE YOU'VE READ EVERY BOOK IN EXISTENCE.
SADLY, YES.
WELL, YOU HAVEN'T READ THIS. IT'S MY DIARY. JUICY DETAILS ABOUND, AND YOU CAN'T TOUCH IT.
DIARY
I FEEL LIKE I'VE READ IT ALREADY.
YOU'VE REALLY DEVELOPED A STRANGE FASCINATION WITH HARRY POTTER LATELY, HAVEN'T YOU?
HOW DID YOU KNOW ABOUT THAT?
DIARY
YOUR HUSBAND'S DIARY COVERS IT IN DETAIL.
SHERMAN!
DIARY

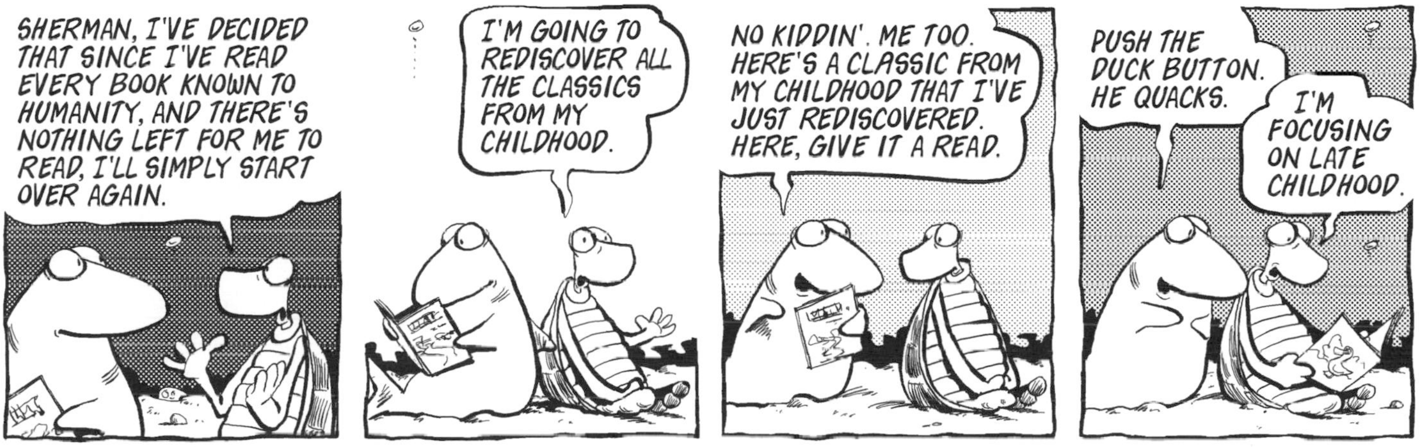
SHERMAN, I'VE DECIDED THAT SINCE I'VE READ EVERY BOOK KNOWN TO HUMANITY, AND THERE'S NOTHING LEFT FOR ME TO READ, I'LL SIMPLY START OVER AGAIN.
I'M GOING TO REDISCOVER ALL THE CLASSICS FROM MY CHILDHOOD.
NO KIDDIN'. ME TOO. HERE'S A CLASSIC FROM MY CHILDHOOD THAT I'VE JUST REDISCOVERED. HERE, GIVE IT A READ.
PUSH THE DUCK BUTTON. HE QUACKS.
I'M FOCUSING ON LATE CHILDHOOD.

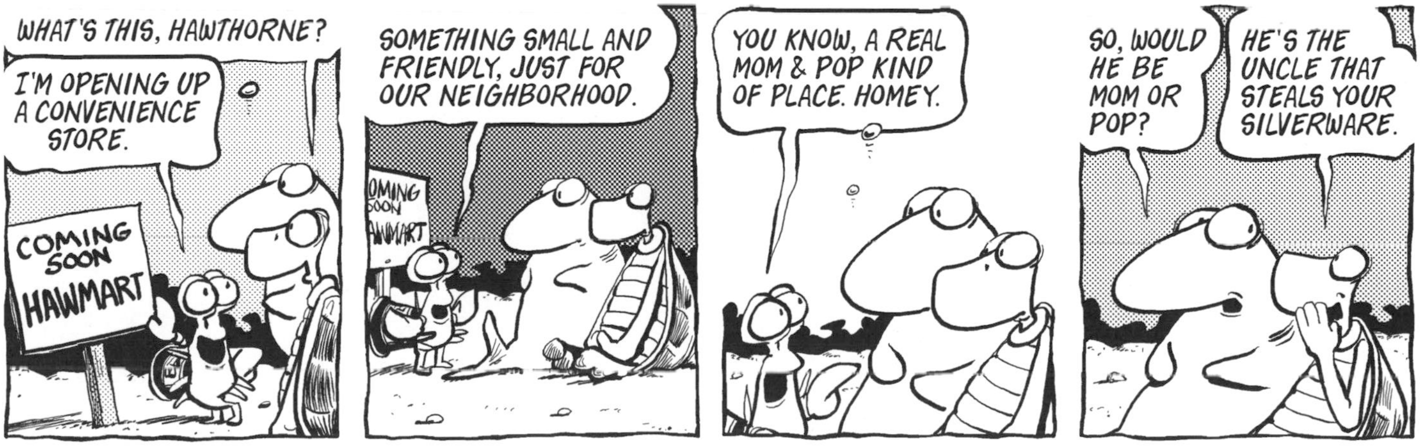
WHAT'S THIS, HAWTHORNE?
I'M OPENING UP A CONVENIENCE STORE.
COMING SOON HAWMART
SOMETHING SMALL AND FRIENDLY, JUST FOR OUR NEIGHBORHOOD.
YOU KNOW, A REAL MOM & POP KIND OF PLACE. HOMEY.
SO, WOULD HE BE MOM OR POP?
HE'S THE UNCLE THAT STEALS YOUR SILVERWARE.

SHERMAN'S LAGOON
by Jim Toomey
WHAT'S UP WITH THE FANCY SCHMANCY DINNER SETTING?
TONIGHT'S SPECIAL, HAWTHORNE.
IT'S THE ANNUAL HERRING MIGRATION.
HERE THEY COME NOW.
EXTEND HERRING FORKS.
HERRING IS A ONCE-A-YEAR DELICACY.
FIRST, YOU CAREFULLY FILET IT. THEN, YOU ADD A DASH OF HERRING SAUCE.
MMMMM... DELICIOUS.
FROM NOW ON, EVERYTHING YOU EAT HAS TO TOUCH A PLATE.
MPHT.

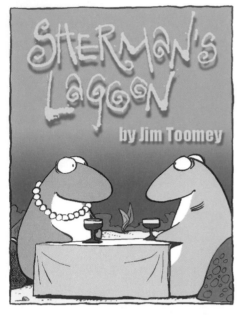

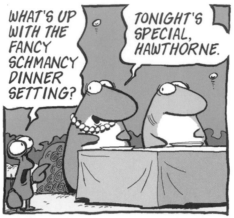

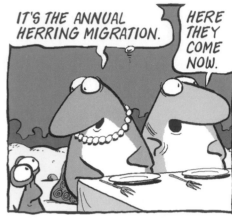

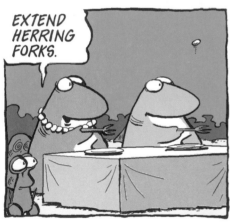

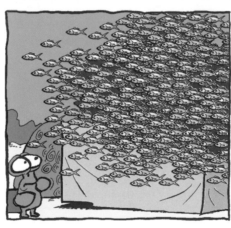

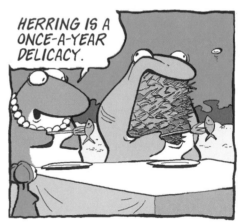

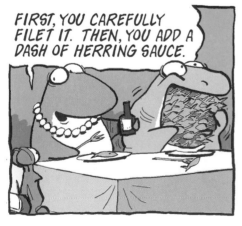

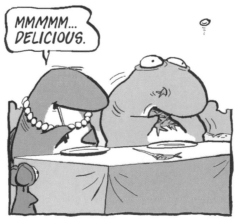

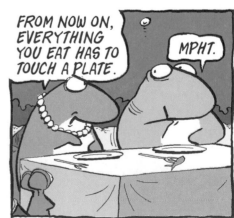

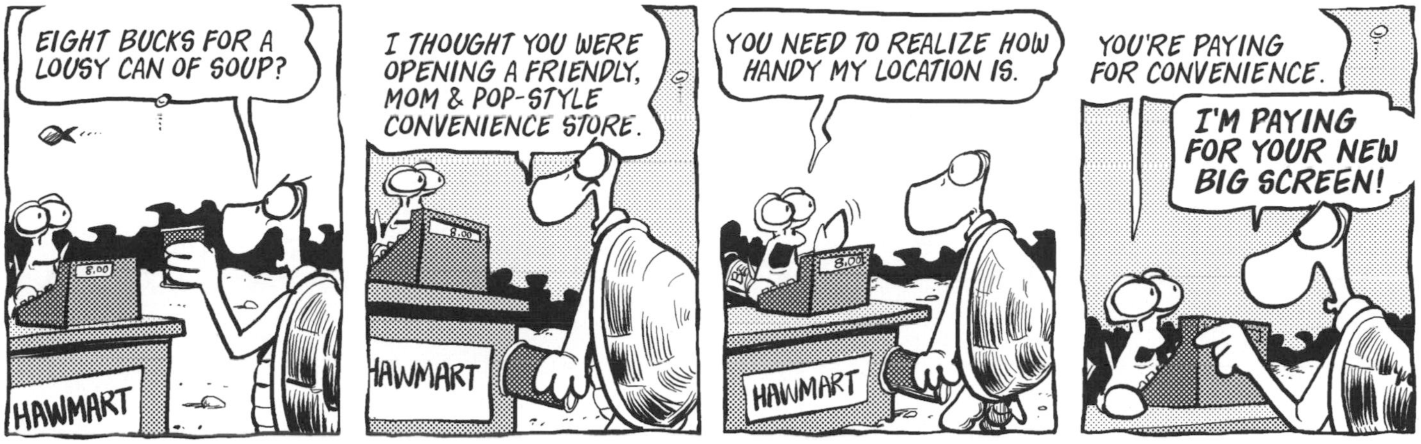
EIGHT BUCKS FOR A LOUSY CAN OF SOUP?
HAWMART
I THOUGHT YOU WERE OPENING A FRIENDLY, MOM & POP-STYLE CONVENIENCE STORE.
HAWMART
YOU NEED TO REALIZE HOW HANDY MY LOCATION IS.
HAWMART
YOU'RE PAYING FOR CONVENIENCE.
I'M PAYING FOR YOUR NEW BIG SCREEN!

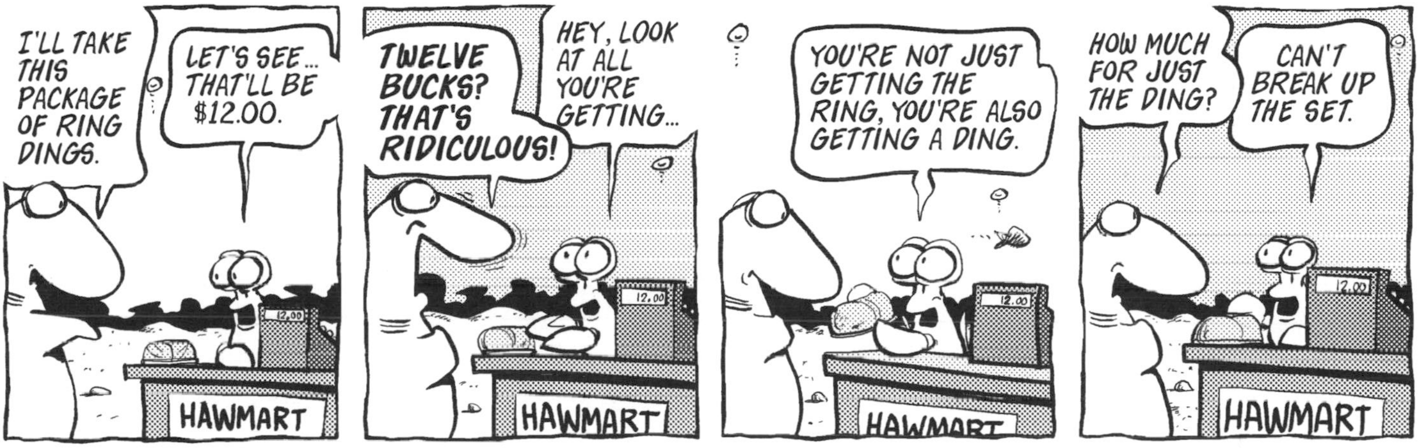
I'LL TAKE THIS PACKAGE OF RING DINGS.
LET'S SEE... THAT'LL BE $12.00.
HAWMART
TWELVE BUCKS? THAT'S RIDICULOUS!
HEY, LOOK AT ALL YOU'RE GETTING...
HAWMART
YOU'RE NOT JUST GETTING THE RING, YOU'RE ALSO GETTING A DING.
HOW MUCH FOR JUST THE DING?
CAN'T BREAK UP THE SET.
HAWMART

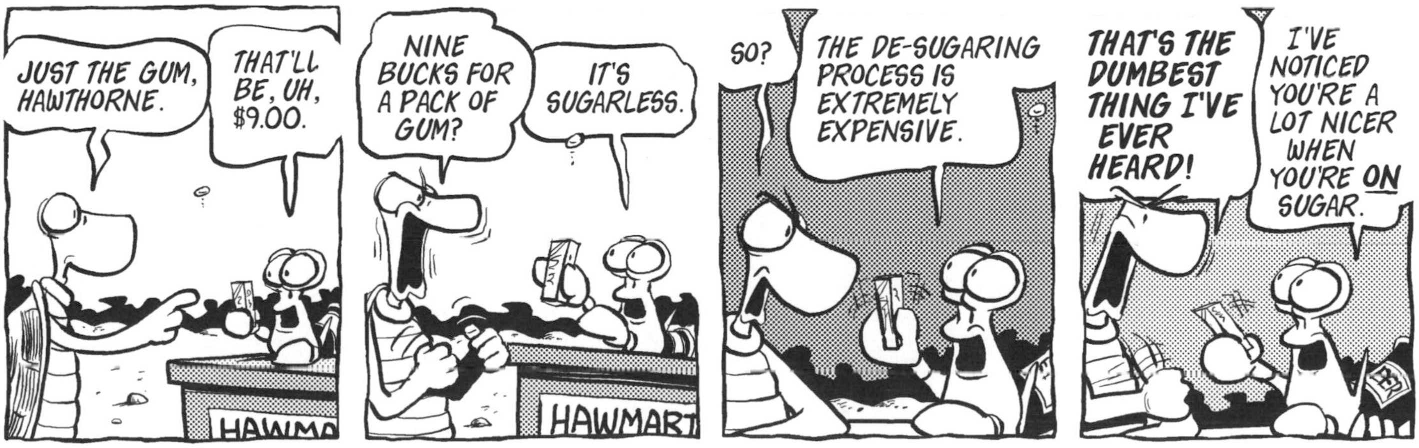
JUST THE GUM, HAWTHORNE.
THAT'LL BE, UH, $9.00.
NINE BUCKS FOR A PACK OF GUM?
IT'S SUGARLESS.
HAWMART
SO?
THE DE-SUGARING PROCESS IS EXTREMELY EXPENSIVE.
THAT'S THE DUMBEST THING I'VE EVER HEARD!
I'VE NOTICED YOU'RE A LOT NICER WHEN YOU'RE ON SUGAR.

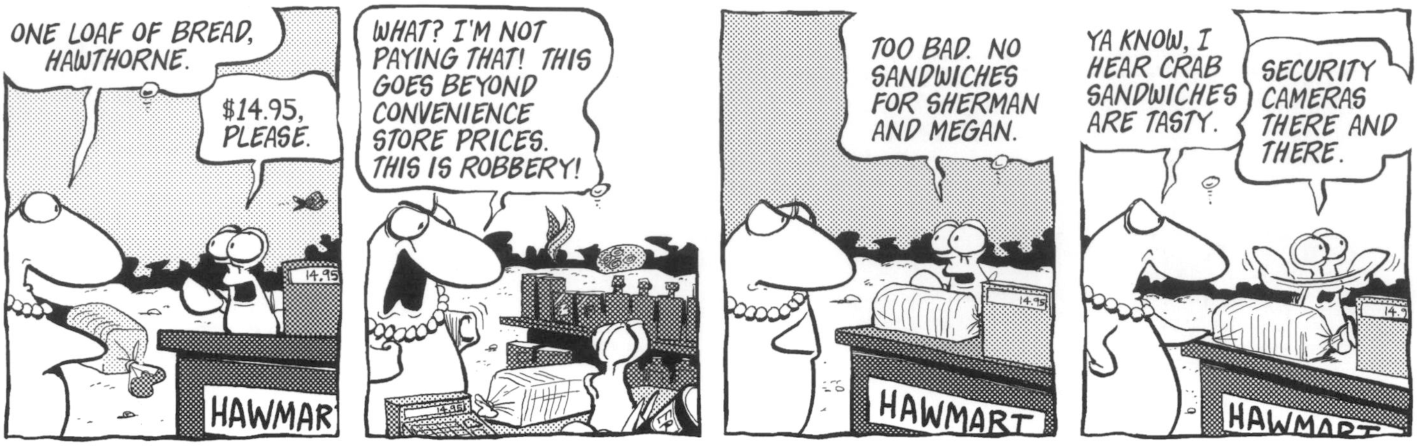
ONE LOAF OF BREAD, HAWTHORNE.
$14.95, PLEASE.
HAWMART
WHAT? I'M NOT PAYING THAT! THIS GOES BEYOND CONVENIENCE STORE PRICES. THIS IS ROBBERY!
TOO BAD. NO SANDWICHES FOR SHERMAN AND MEGAN.
HAWMART
YA KNOW, I HEAR CRAB SANDWICHES ARE TASTY.
SECURITY CAMERAS THERE AND THERE.

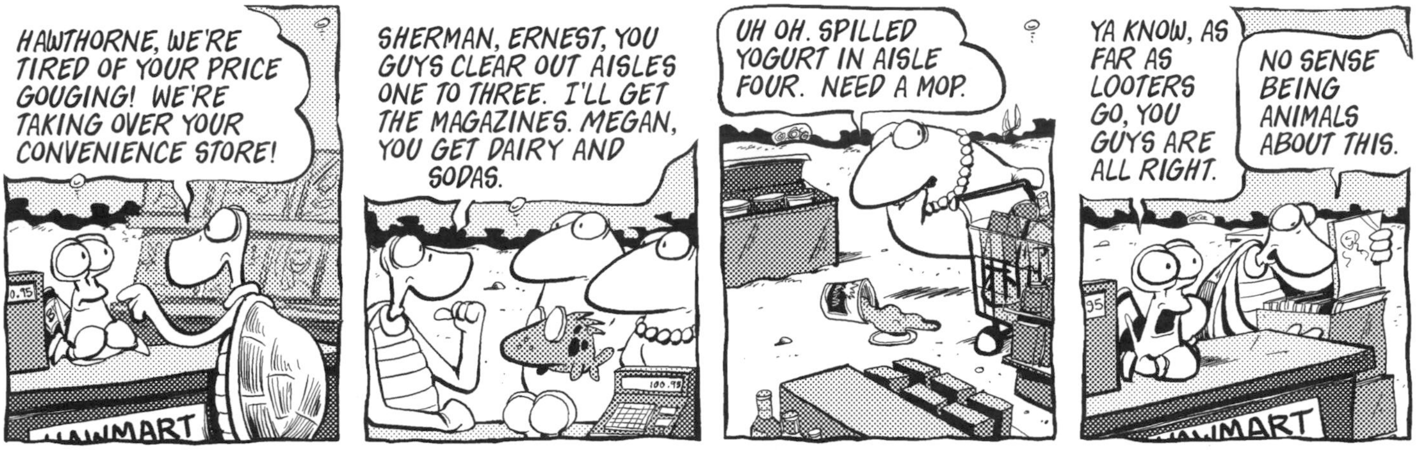
HAWTHORNE, WE'RE TIRED OF YOUR PRICE GOUGING! WE'RE TAKING OVER YOUR CONVENIENCE STORE!
SHERMAN, ERNEST, YOU GUYS CLEAR OUT AISLES ONE TO THREE. I'LL GET THE MAGAZINES. MEGAN, YOU GET DAIRY AND SODAS.
UH OH. SPILLED YOGURT IN AISLE FOUR. NEED A MOP.
YA KNOW, AS FAR AS LOOTERS GO, YOU GUYS ARE ALL RIGHT.
NO SENSE BEING ANIMALS ABOUT THIS.

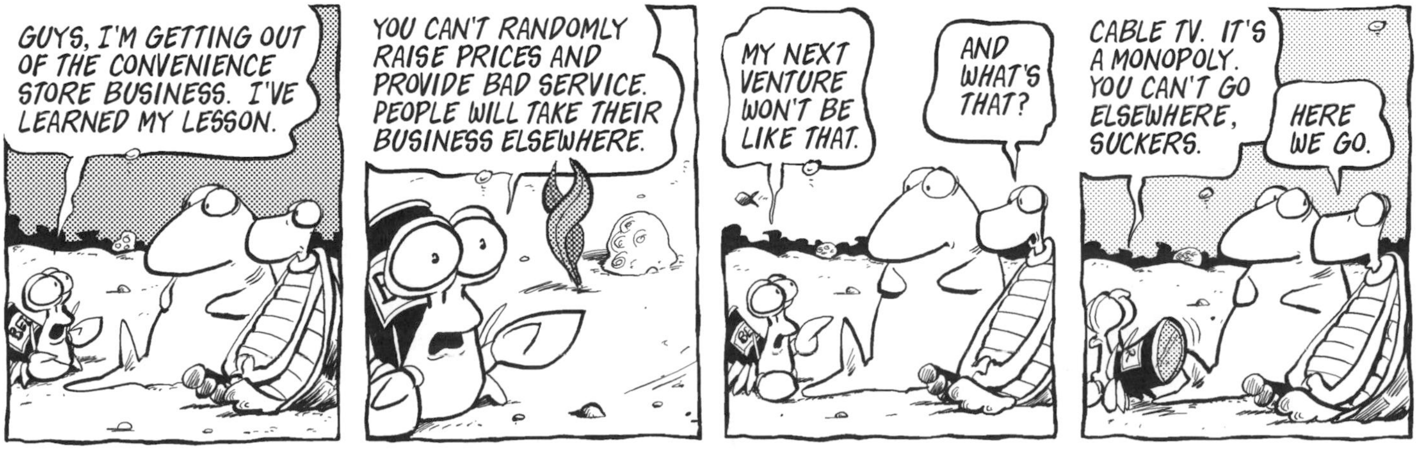
GUYS, I'M GETTING OUT OF THE CONVENIENCE STORE BUSINESS. I'VE LEARNED MY LESSON.
YOU CAN'T RANDOMLY RAISE PRICES AND PROVIDE BAD SERVICE. PEOPLE WILL TAKE THEIR BUSINESS ELSEWHERE.
MY NEXT VENTURE WON'T BE LIKE THAT.
AND WHAT'S THAT?
CABLE TV. IT'S A MONOPOLY. YOU CAN'T GO ELSEWHERE, SUCKERS.
HERE WE GO.

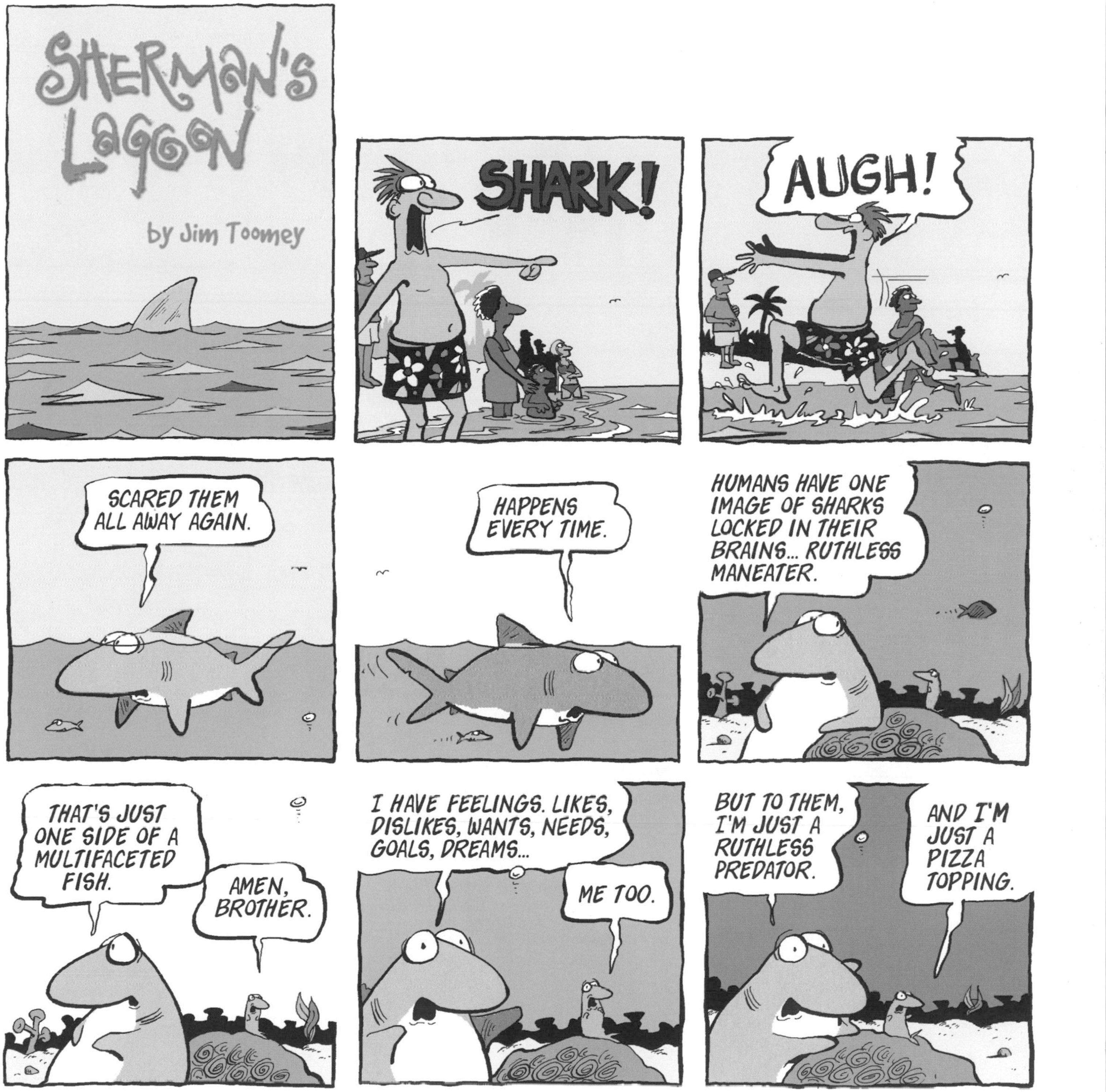
SHERMAN'S LAGOON
by Jim Toomey
SHARK!
AUGH!
SCARED THEM ALL AWAY AGAIN.
HAPPENS EVERY TIME.
HUMANS HAVE ONE IMAGE OF SHARKS LOCKED IN THEIR BRAINS... RUTHLESS MANEATER.
THAT'S JUST ONE SIDE OF A MULTIFACETED FISH.
AMEN, BROTHER.
I HAVE FEELINGS. LIKES, DISLIKES, WANTS, NEEDS, GOALS, DREAMS...
ME TOO.
BUT TO THEM, I'M JUST A RUTHLESS PREDATOR.
AND I'M JUST A PIZZA TOPPING.

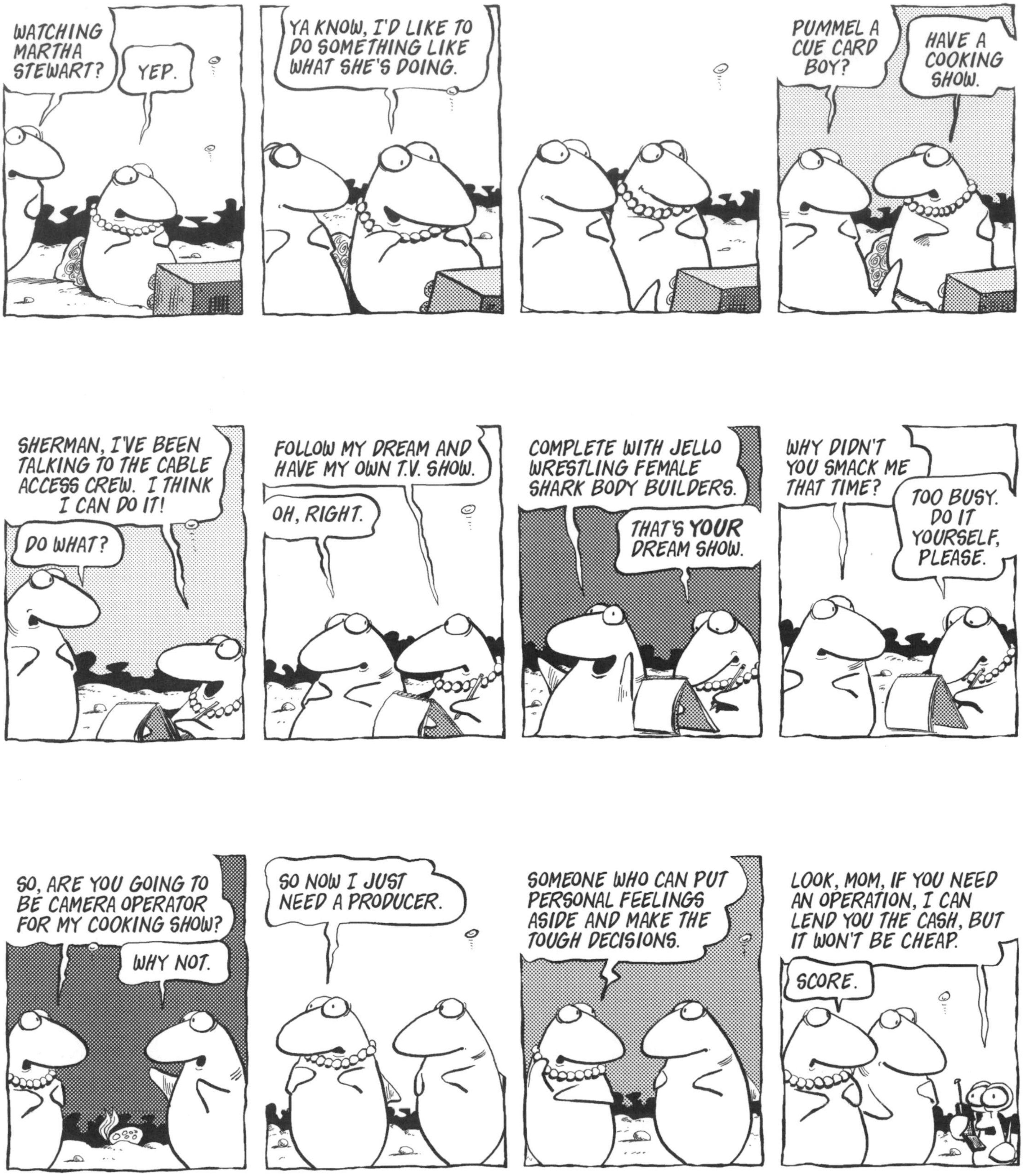

WATCHING MARTHA STEWART?
YEP.
YA KNOW, I'D LIKE TO DO SOMETHING LIKE WHAT SHE'S DOING.
PUMMEL A CUE CARD BOY?
HAVE A COOKING SHOW.
SHERMAN, I'VE BEEN TALKING TO THE CABLE ACCESS CREW. I THINK I CAN DO IT!
DO WHAT?
FOLLOW MY DREAM AND HAVE MY OWN T.V. SHOW.
OH, RIGHT.
COMPLETE WITH JELLO WRESTLING FEMALE SHARK BODY BUILDERS.
THAT'S YOUR DREAM SHOW.
WHY DIDN'T YOU SMACK ME THAT TIME?
TOO BUSY. DO IT YOURSELF, PLEASE.
SO, ARE YOU GOING TO BE CAMERA OPERATOR FOR MY COOKING SHOW?
WHY NOT.
SO NOW I JUST NEED A PRODUCER.
SOMEONE WHO CAN PUT PERSONAL FEELINGS ASIDE AND MAKE THE TOUGH DECISIONS.
LOOK, MOM, IF YOU NEED AN OPERATION, I CAN LEND YOU THE CASH, BUT IT WON'T BE CHEAP.
SCORE.

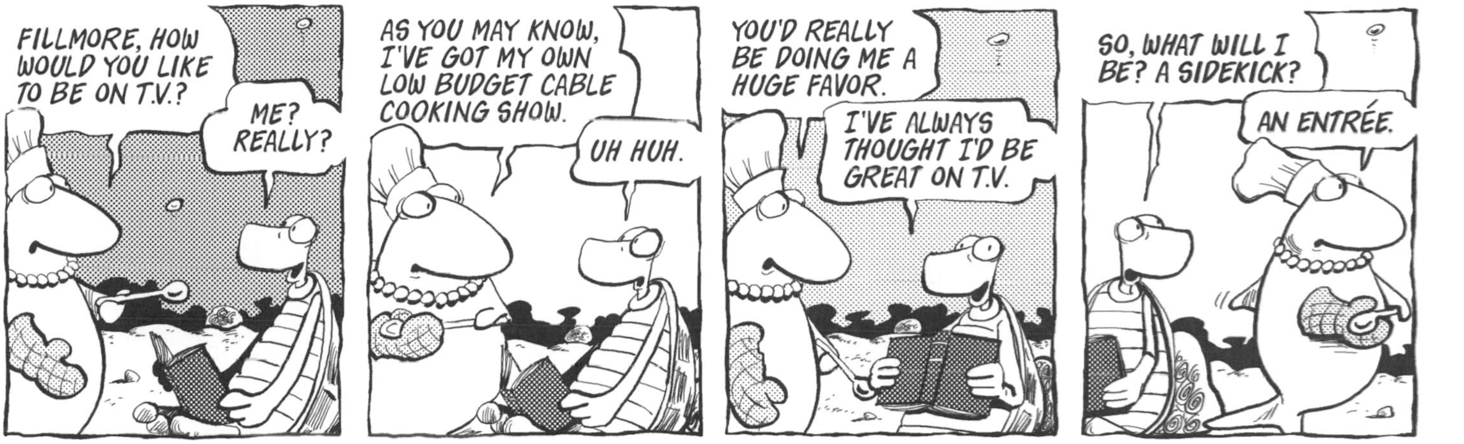
FILLMORE, HOW WOULD YOU LIKE TO BE ON T.V.?
ME? REALLY?
AS YOU MAY KNOW, I'VE GOT MY OWN LOW BUDGET CABLE COOKING SHOW.
UH HUH.
YOU'D REALLY BE DOING ME A HUGE FAVOR.
I'VE ALWAYS THOUGHT I'D BE GREAT ON T.V.
SO, WHAT WILL I BE? A SIDEKICK?
AN ENTRÉE.

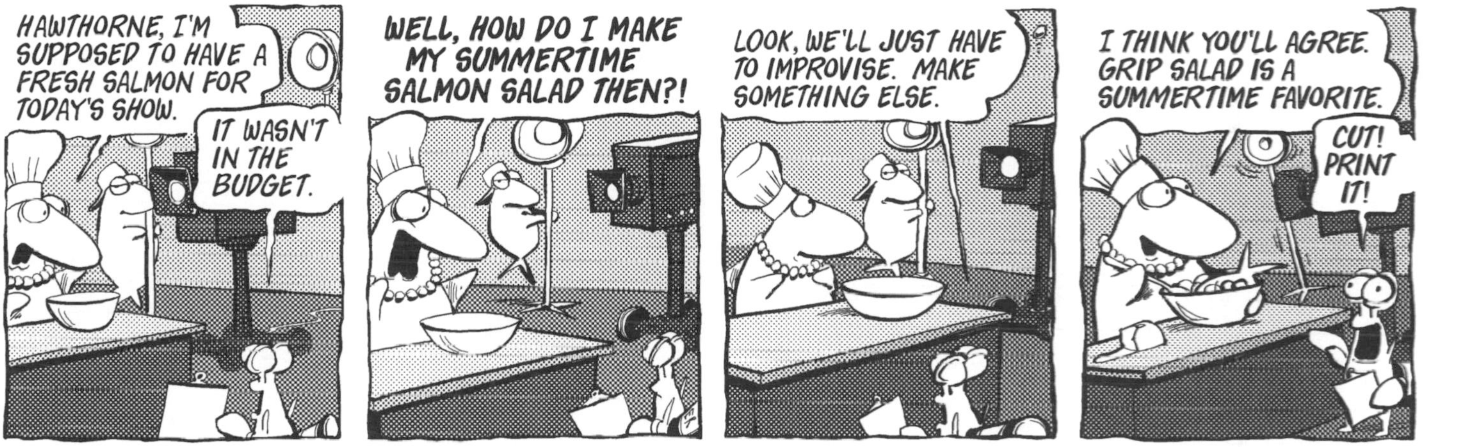
HAWTHORNE, I'M SUPPOSED TO HAVE A FRESH SALMON FOR TODAY'S SHOW.
IT WASN'T IN THE BUDGET.
WELL, HOW DO I MAKE MY SUMMERTIME SALMON SALAD THEN?!
LOOK, WE'LL JUST HAVE TO IMPROVISE. MAKE SOMETHING ELSE.
I THINK YOU'LL AGREE. GRIP SALAD IS A SUMMERTIME FAVORITE.
CUT! PRINT IT!

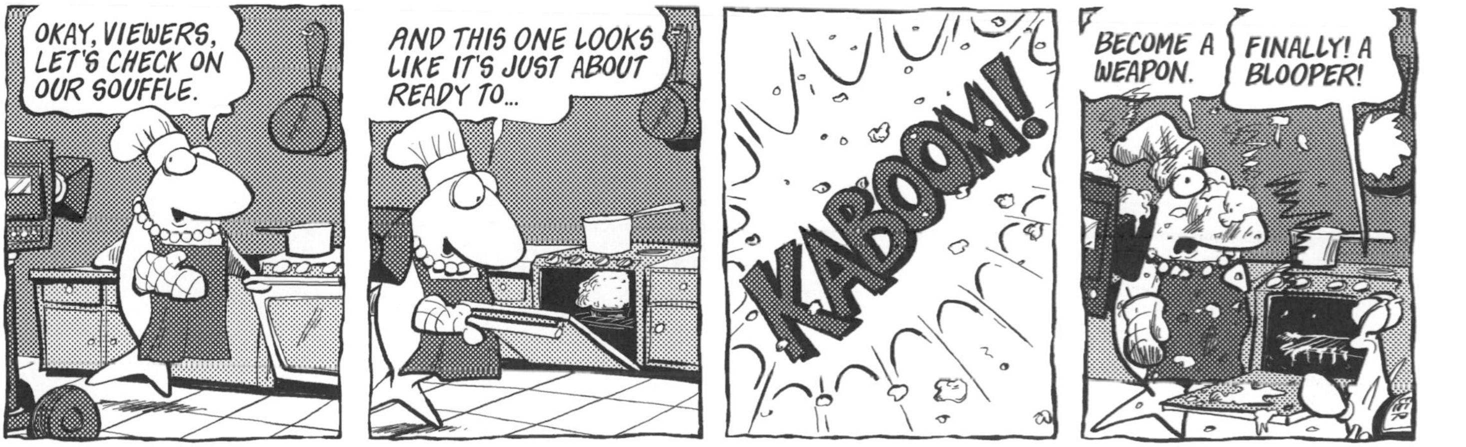
OKAY, VIEWERS, LET'S CHECK ON OUR SOUFFLE.
AND THIS ONE LOOKS LIKE IT'S JUST ABOUT READY TO...
KABOOM!
BECOME A WEAPON.
FINALLY! A BLOOPER!

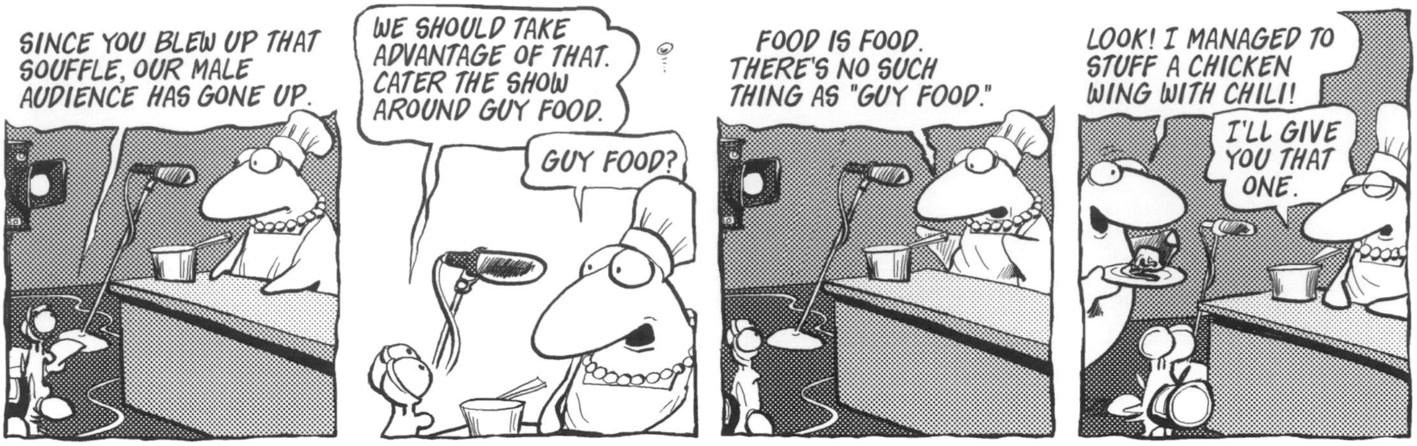
SINCE YOU BLEW UP THAT SOUFFLE, OUR MALE AUDIENCE HAS GONE UP.
WE SHOULD TAKE ADVANTAGE OF THAT. CATER THE SHOW AROUND GUY FOOD.
GUY FOOD?
FOOD IS FOOD. THERE'S NO SUCH THING AS "GUY FOOD."
LOOK! I MANAGED TO STUFF A CHICKEN WING WITH CHILI!
I'LL GIVE YOU THAT ONE.

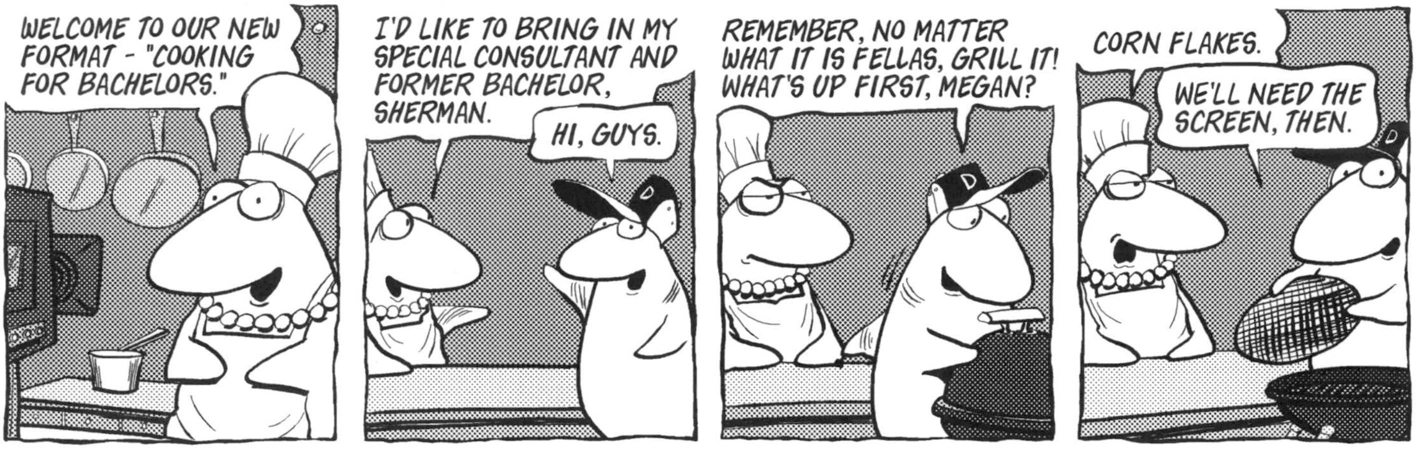
WELCOME TO OUR NEW FORMAT - "COOKING FOR BACHELORS."
I'D LIKE TO BRING IN MY SPECIAL CONSULTANT AND FORMER BACHELOR, SHERMAN.
HI, GUYS.
REMEMBER, NO MATTER WHAT IT IS FELLAS, GRILL IT! WHAT'S UP FIRST, MEGAN?
CORN FLAKES.
WE'LL NEED THE SCREEN, THEN.

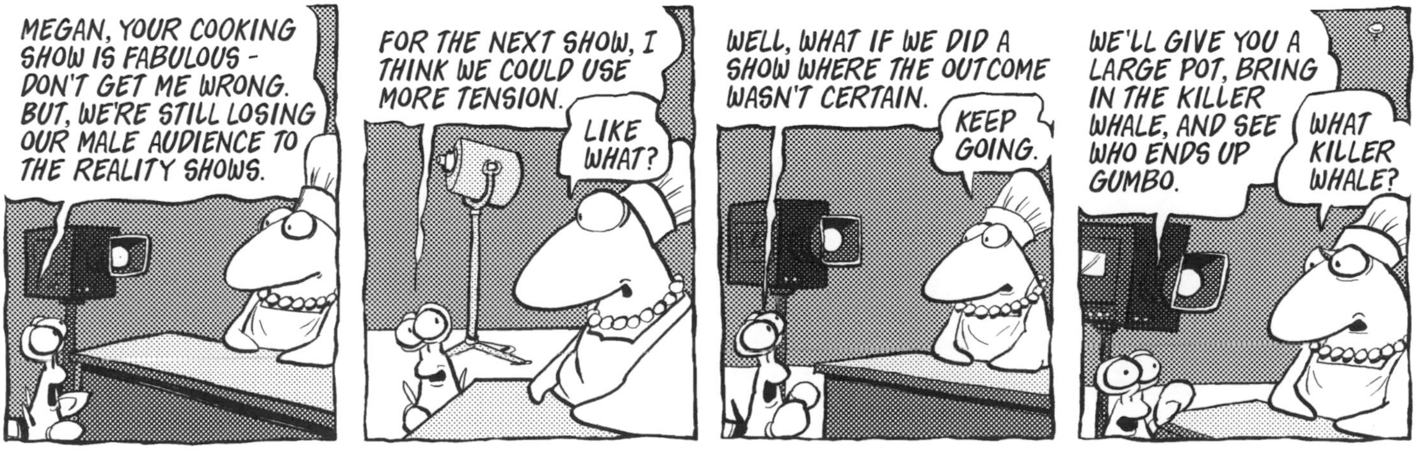
MEGAN, YOUR COOKING SHOW IS FABULOUS - DON'T GET ME WRONG. BUT, WE'RE STILL LOSING OUR MALE AUDIENCE TO THE REALITY SHOWS.
FOR THE NEXT SHOW, I THINK WE COULD USE MORE TENSION.
LIKE WHAT?
WELL, WHAT IF WE DID A SHOW WHERE THE OUTCOME WASN'T CERTAIN.
KEEP GOING.
WE'LL GIVE YOU A LARGE POT, BRING IN THE KILLER WHALE, AND SEE WHO ENDS UP GUMBO.
WHAT KILLER WHALE?

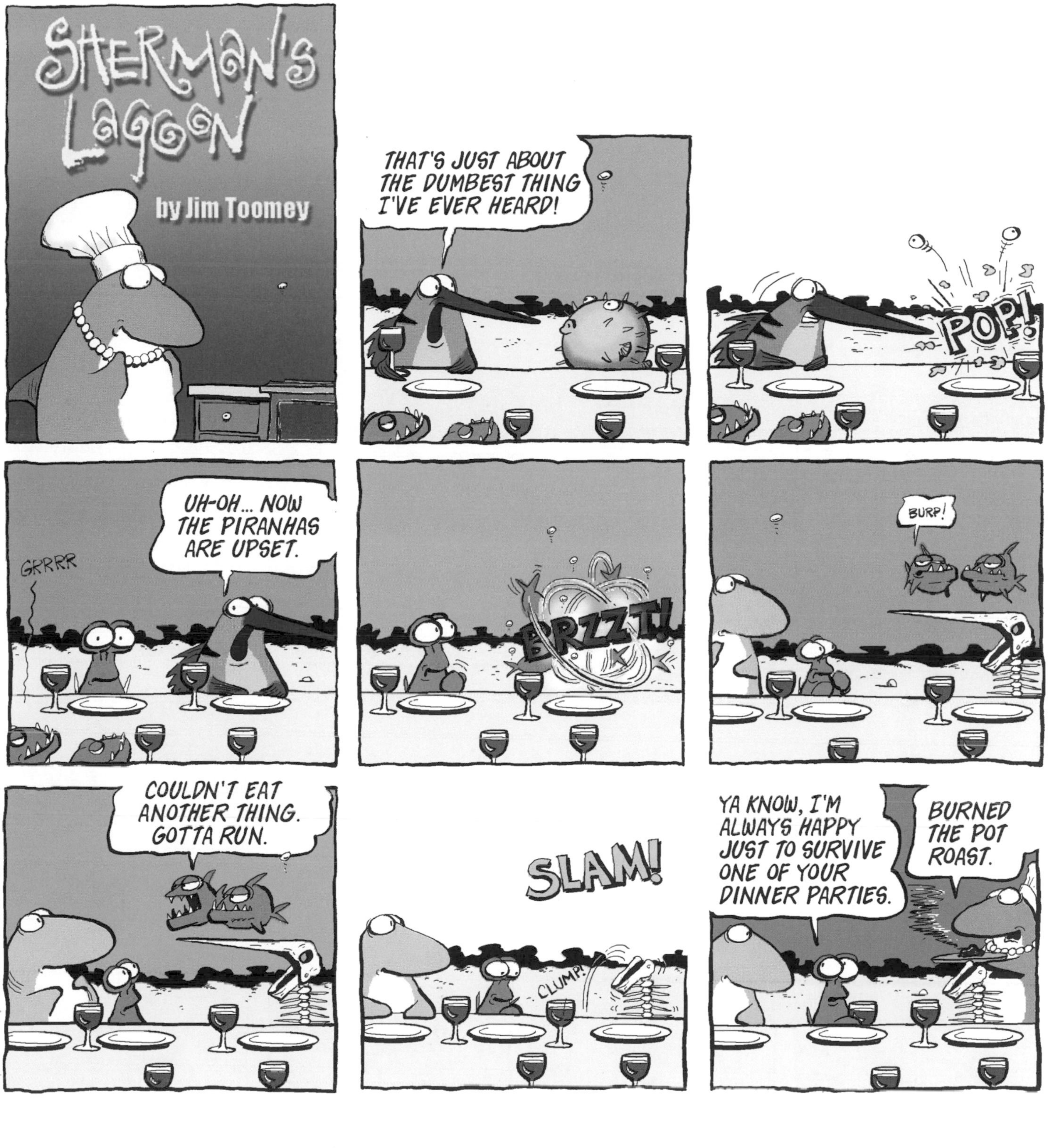
SHERMAN'S LAGOON
by Jim Toomey
THAT'S JUST ABOUT THE DUMBEST THING I'VE EVER HEARD!
POP!
GRRRR
UH-OH... NOW THE PIRANHAS ARE UPSET.
BRZZT!
BURP!
COULDN'T EAT ANOTHER THING. GOTTA RUN.
SLAM!
CLUMP
YA KNOW, I'M ALWAYS HAPPY JUST TO SURVIVE ONE OF YOUR DINNER PARTIES.
BURNED THE POT ROAST.

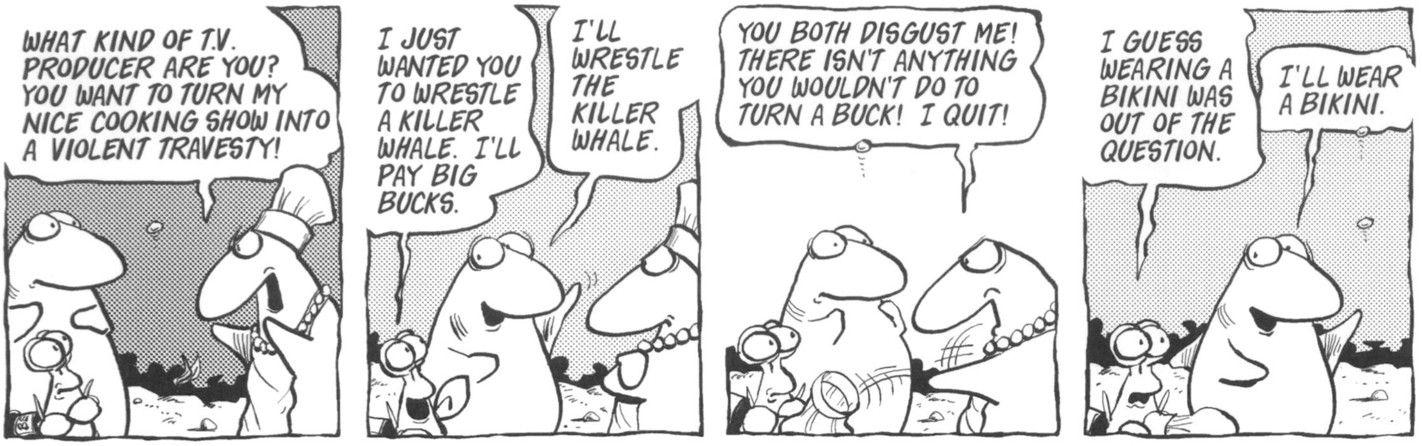
WHAT KIND OF T.V. PRODUCER ARE YOU? YOU WANT TO TURN MY NICE COOKING SHOW INTO A VIOLENT TRAVESTY!
I JUST WANTED YOU TO WRESTLE A KILLER WHALE. I'LL PAY BIG BUCKS.
I'LL WRESTLE THE KILLER WHALE.
YOU BOTH DISGUST ME! THERE ISN'T ANYTHING YOU WOULDN'T DO TO TURN A BUCK! I QUIT!
I GUESS WEARING A BIKINI WAS OUT OF THE QUESTION.
I'LL WEAR A BIKINI.

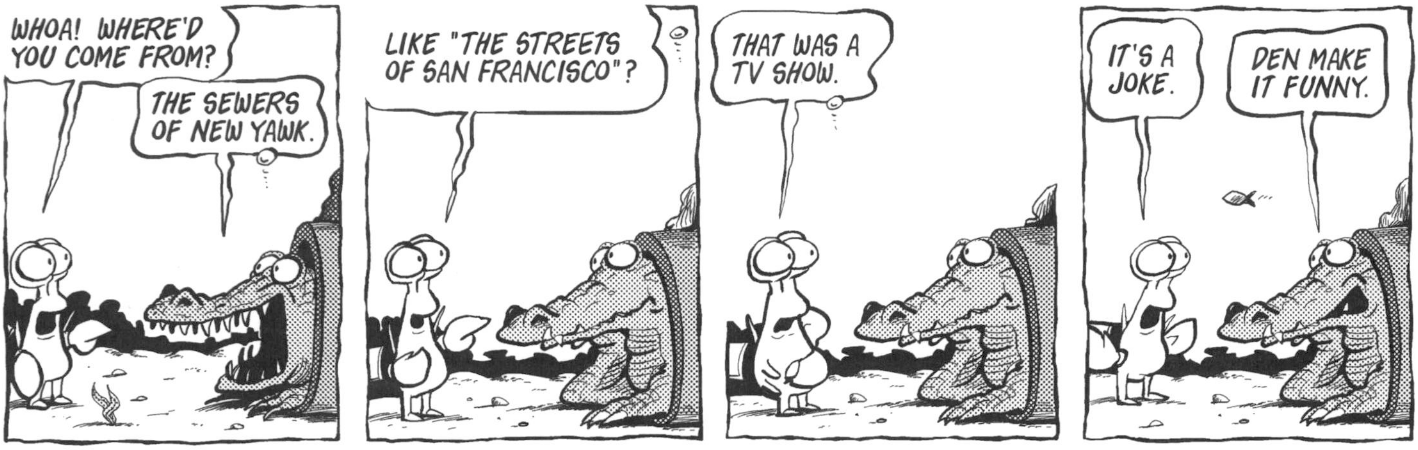
WHOA! WHERE'D YOU COME FROM?
THE SEWERS OF NEW YAWK.
LIKE "THE STREETS OF SAN FRANCISCO"?
THAT WAS A TV SHOW.
IT'S A JOKE.
DEN MAKE IT FUNNY.

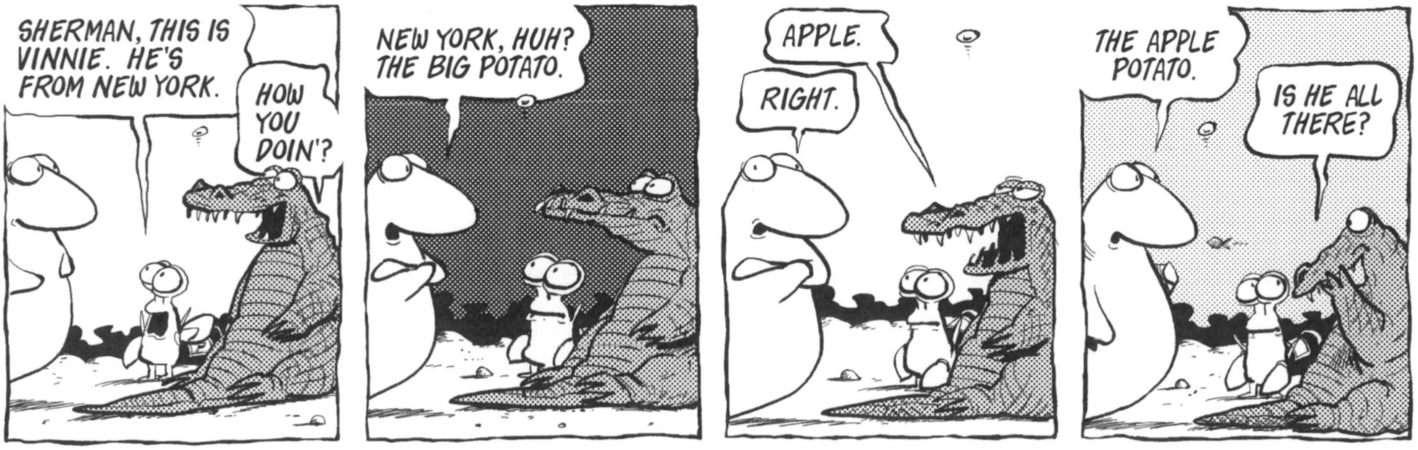
SHERMAN, THIS IS VINNIE. HE'S FROM NEW YORK.
HOW YOU DOIN'?
NEW YORK, HUH? THE BIG POTATO.
APPLE.
RIGHT.
THE APPLE POTATO.
IS HE ALL THERE?

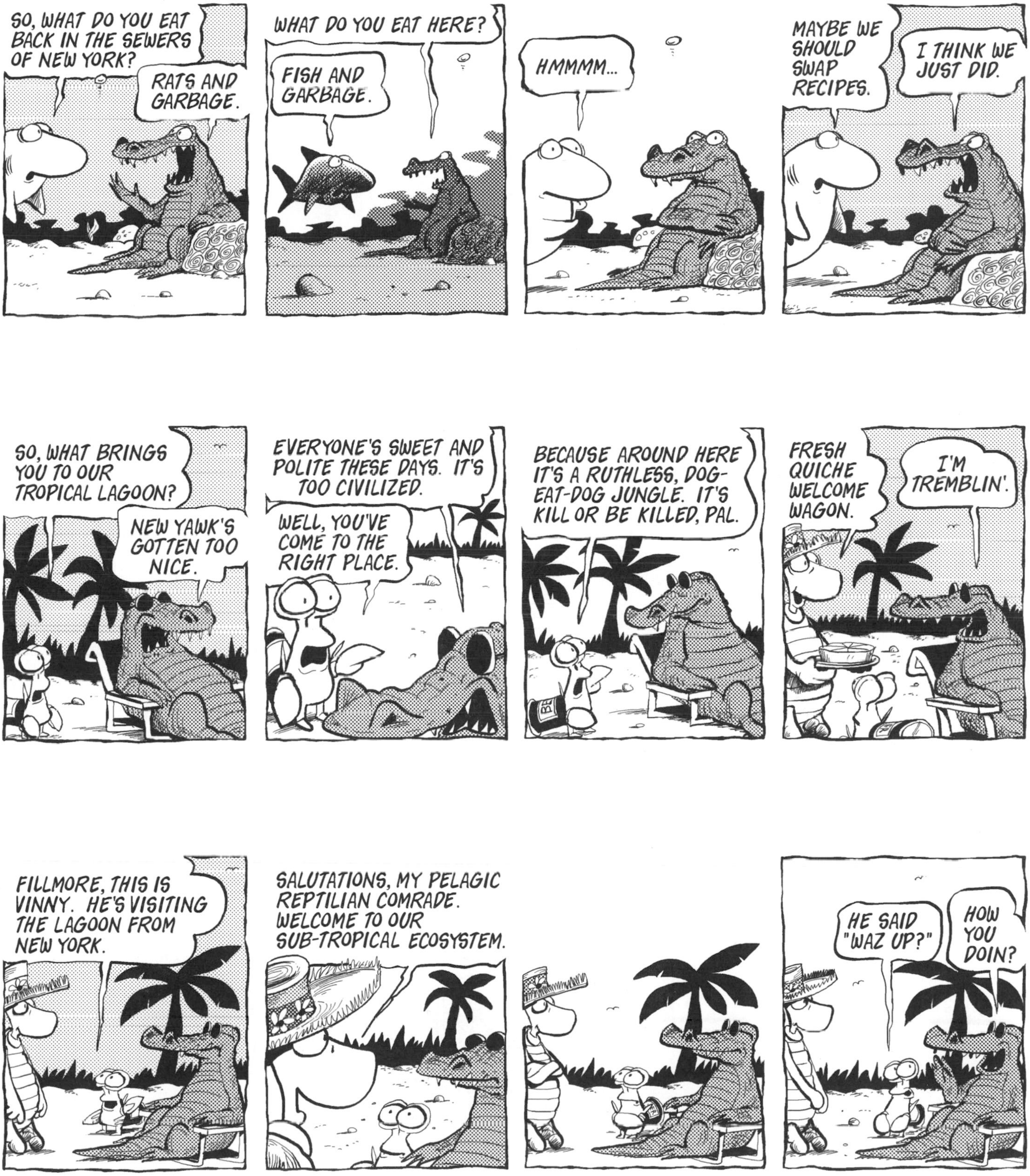
SO, WHAT DO YOU EAT BACK IN THE SEWERS OF NEW YORK?
RATS AND GARBAGE.
WHAT DO YOU EAT HERE?
FISH AND GARBAGE.
HMMMM...
MAYBE WE SHOULD SWAP RECIPES.
I THINK WE JUST DID.
SO, WHAT BRINGS YOU TO OUR TROPICAL LAGOON?
NEW YAWK'S GOTTEN TOO NICE.
EVERYONE'S SWEET AND POLITE THESE DAYS. IT'S TOO CIVILIZED.
WELL, YOU'VE COME TO THE RIGHT PLACE.
BECAUSE AROUND HERE IT'S A RUTHLESS, DOG-EAT-DOG JUNGLE. IT'S KILL OR BE KILLED, PAL.
FRESH QUICHE WELCOME WAGON.
I'M TREMBLIN'.
FILLMORE, THIS IS VINNY. HE'S VISITING THE LAGOON FROM NEW YORK.
SALUTATIONS, MY PELAGIC REPTILIAN COMRADE. WELCOME TO OUR SUB-TROPICAL ECOSYSTEM.
HOW YOU DOIN?
HE SAID "WAZ UP?"

SHERMAN'S LAGOON
by Jim Toomey
HIGH DANGER VOLTAGE
WHY ARE YOU STARING AT THE FRIDGE? YOU USUALLY JUST DIVE RIGHT IN.
IF I TOUCH IT, I'LL GET SHOCKED WITH 25,000 VOLTS OF ELECTRICITY.
WHOA NELLY!
IT'S PART OF MEGAN'S CAMPAIGN TO KEEP ME FROM EATING BETWEEN MEALS.
CRUEL WOMAN.
OH WELL. LET'S SEE HOW BAD THIS REALLY IS.
UMM, I WOULDN'T...
ARRGHH
BRZZZZ
WHAHHHHUGH!!
WE'VE GOT HAM SALAD, JELLO, A SPRITE, AND SOME BRIE.
IT'S MELTED. NICE TOUCH.

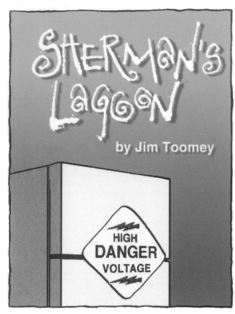

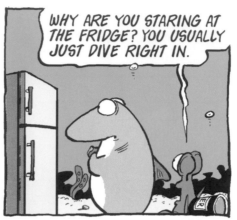

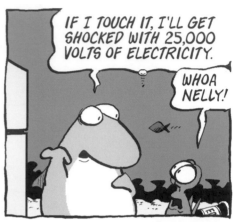

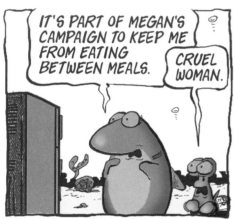

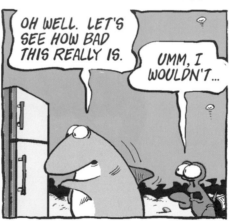

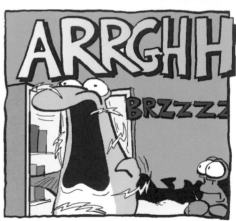

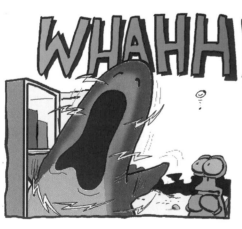

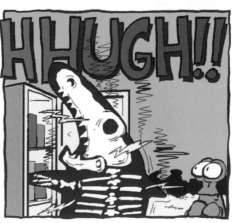

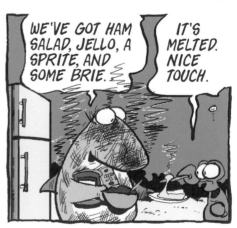

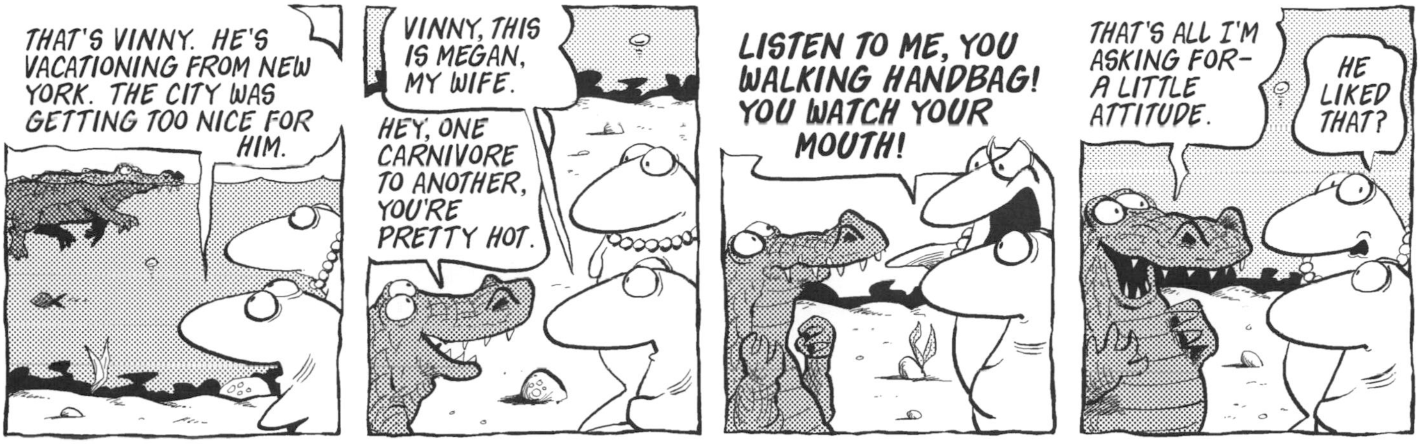
THAT'S VINNY. HE'S VACATIONING FROM NEW YORK. THE CITY WAS GETTING TOO NICE FOR HIM.
VINNY, THIS IS MEGAN, MY WIFE.
HEY, ONE CARNIVORE TO ANOTHER, YOU'RE PRETTY HOT.
LISTEN TO ME, YOU WALKING HANDBAG! YOU WATCH YOUR MOUTH!
THAT'S ALL I'M ASKING FOR– A LITTLE ATTITUDE.
HE LIKED THAT?

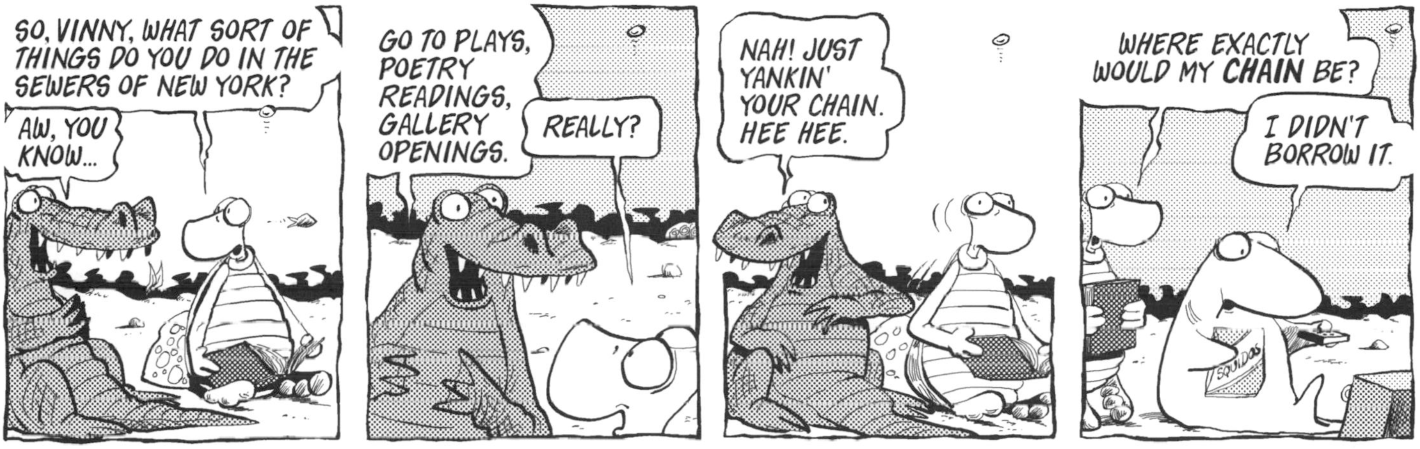
SO, VINNY, WHAT SORT OF THINGS DO YOU DO IN THE SEWERS OF NEW YORK?
AW, YOU KNOW...
GO TO PLAYS, POETRY READINGS, GALLERY OPENINGS.
REALLY?
NAH! JUST YANKIN' YOUR CHAIN. HEE HEE.
WHERE EXACTLY WOULD MY CHAIN BE?
I DIDN'T BORROW IT.

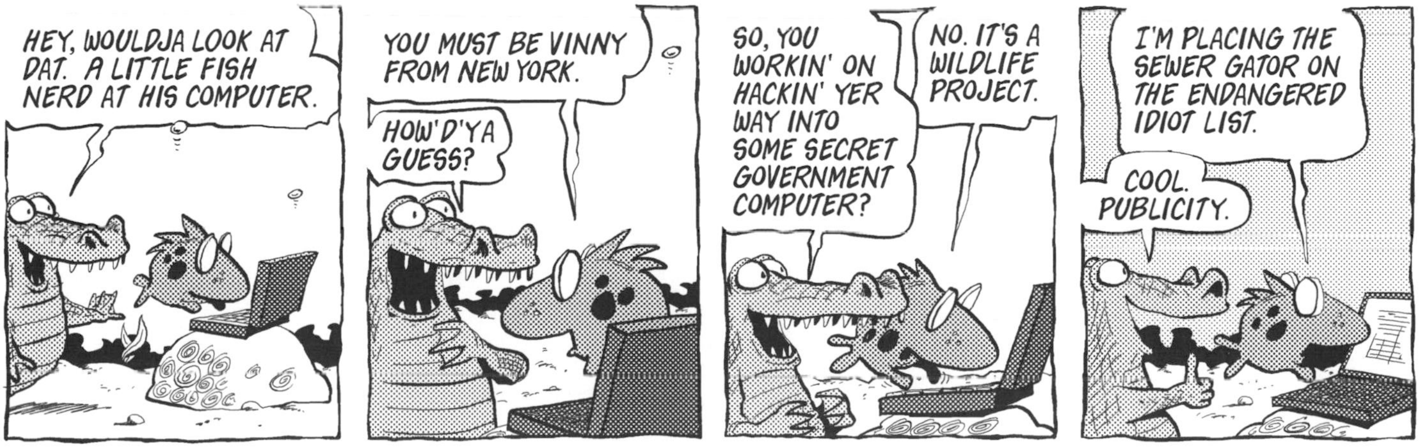
HEY, WOULDJA LOOK AT DAT. A LITTLE FISH NERD AT HIS COMPUTER.
YOU MUST BE VINNY FROM NEW YORK.
HOW'D'YA GUESS?
SO, YOU WORKIN' ON HACKIN' YER WAY INTO SOME SECRET GOVERNMENT COMPUTER?
NO. IT'S A WILDLIFE PROJECT.
I'M PLACING THE SEWER GATOR ON THE ENDANGERED IDIOT LIST.
COOL. PUBLICITY.

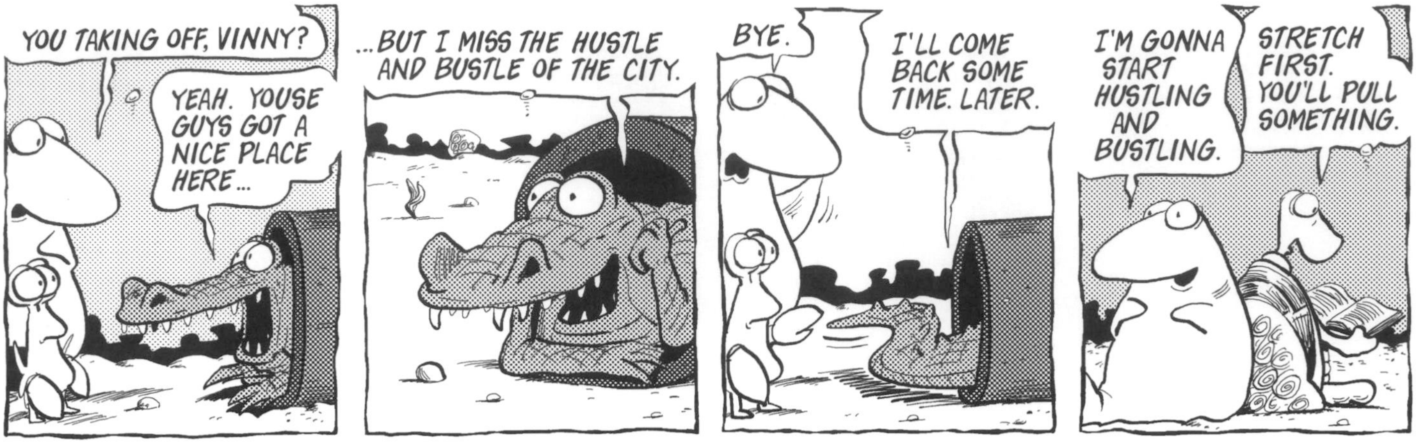
YOU TAKING OFF, VINNY?
YEAH. YOUSE GUYS GOT A NICE PLACE HERE...
...BUT I MISS THE HUSTLE AND BUSTLE OF THE CITY.
BYE.
I'LL COME BACK SOME TIME. LATER.
I'M GONNA START HUSTLING AND BUSTLING.
STRETCH FIRST. YOU'LL PULL SOMETHING.

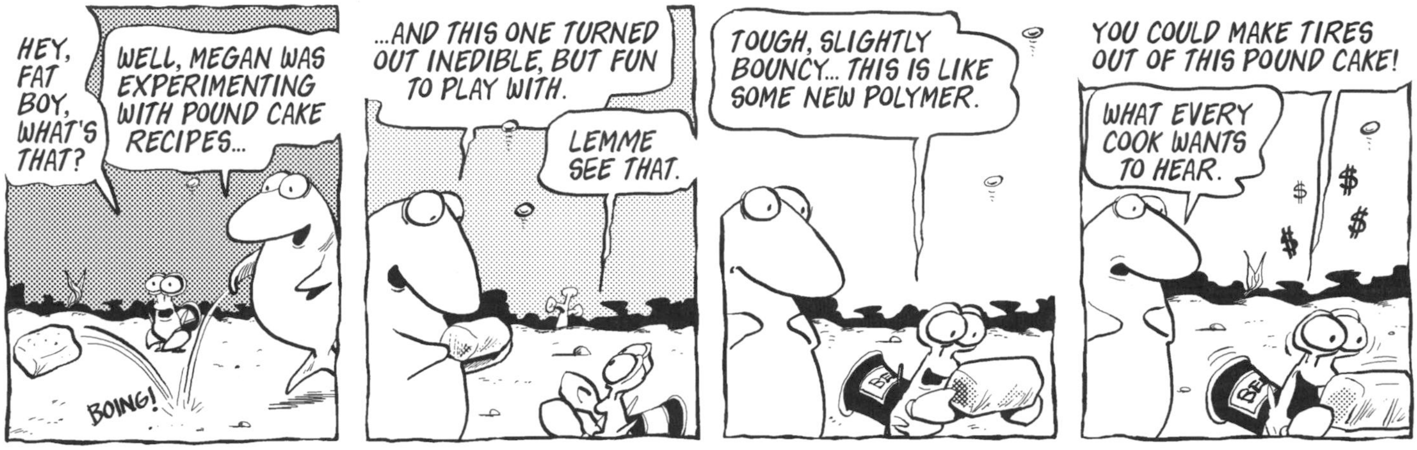
HEY, FAT BOY, WHAT'S THAT?
WELL, MEGAN WAS EXPERIMENTING WITH POUND CAKE RECIPES...
BOING!
...AND THIS ONE TURNED OUT INEDIBLE, BUT FUN TO PLAY WITH.
LEMME SEE THAT.
TOUGH, SLIGHTLY BOUNCY... THIS IS LIKE SOME NEW POLYMER.
YOU COULD MAKE TIRES OUT OF THIS POUND CAKE!
WHAT EVERY COOK WANTS TO HEAR.

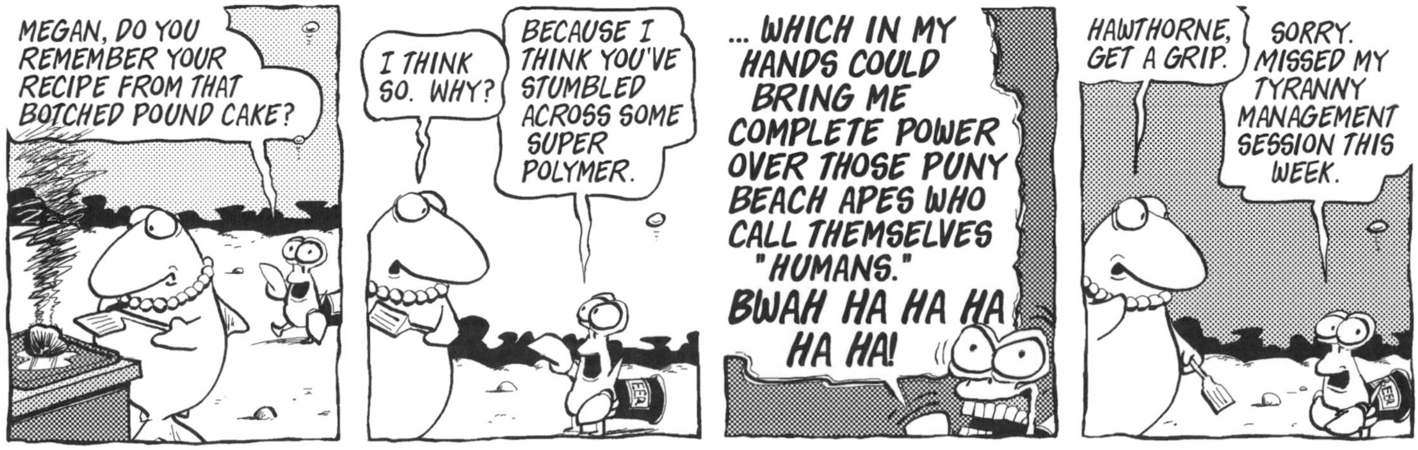
MEGAN, DO YOU REMEMBER YOUR RECIPE FROM THAT BOTCHED POUND CAKE?
I THINK SO. WHY?
BECAUSE I THINK YOU'VE STUMBLED ACROSS SOME SUPER POLYMER.
... WHICH IN MY HANDS COULD BRING ME COMPLETE POWER OVER THOSE PUNY BEACH APES WHO CALL THEMSELVES "HUMANS."
BWAH HA HA HA HA HA!
HAWTHORNE, GET A GRIP.
SORRY. MISSED MY TYRANNY MANAGEMENT SESSION THIS WEEK.

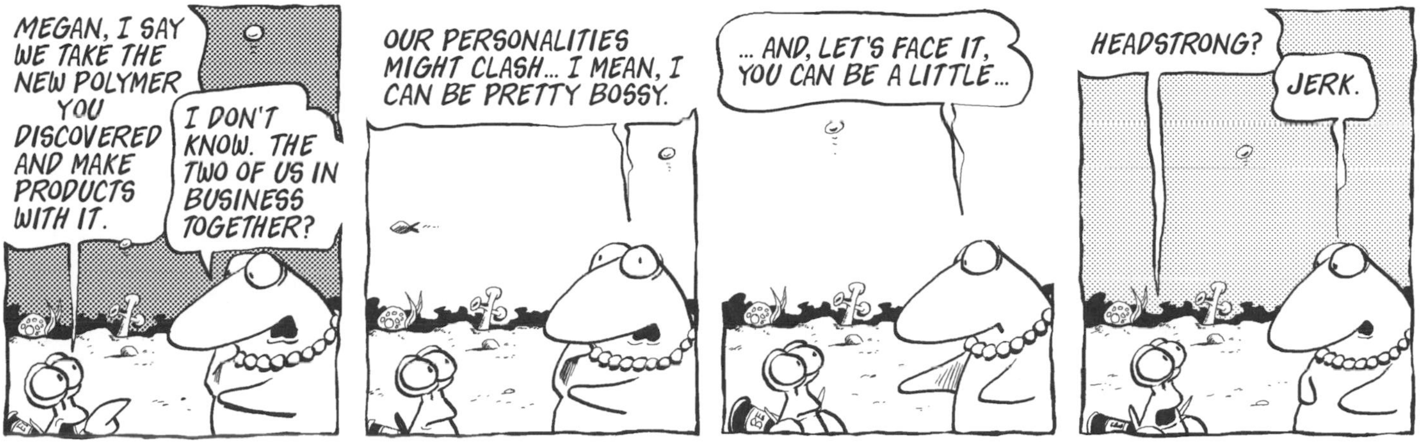
MEGAN, I SAY WE TAKE THE NEW POLYMER YOU DISCOVERED AND MAKE PRODUCTS WITH IT.
I DON'T KNOW. THE TWO OF US IN BUSINESS TOGETHER?
OUR PERSONALITIES MIGHT CLASH... I MEAN, I CAN BE PRETTY BOSSY.
... AND, LET'S FACE IT, YOU CAN BE A LITTLE...
HEADSTRONG?
JERK.

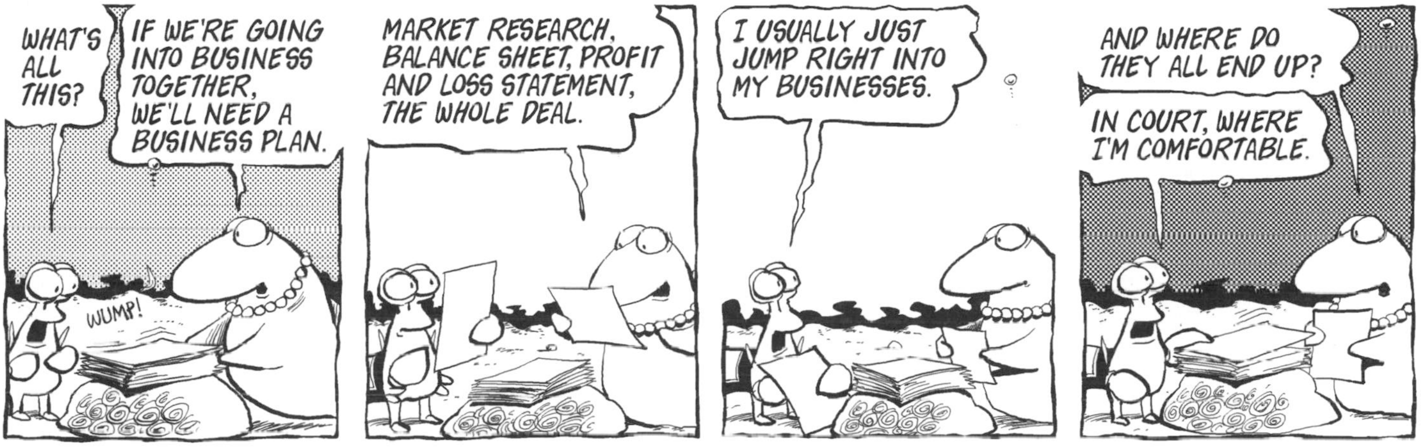
WHAT'S ALL THIS?
IF WE'RE GOING INTO BUSINESS TOGETHER, WE'LL NEED A BUSINESS PLAN.
WUMP!
MARKET RESEARCH, BALANCE SHEET, PROFIT AND LOSS STATEMENT, THE WHOLE DEAL.
I USUALLY JUST JUMP RIGHT INTO MY BUSINESSES.
AND WHERE DO THEY ALL END UP?
IN COURT, WHERE I'M COMFORTABLE.

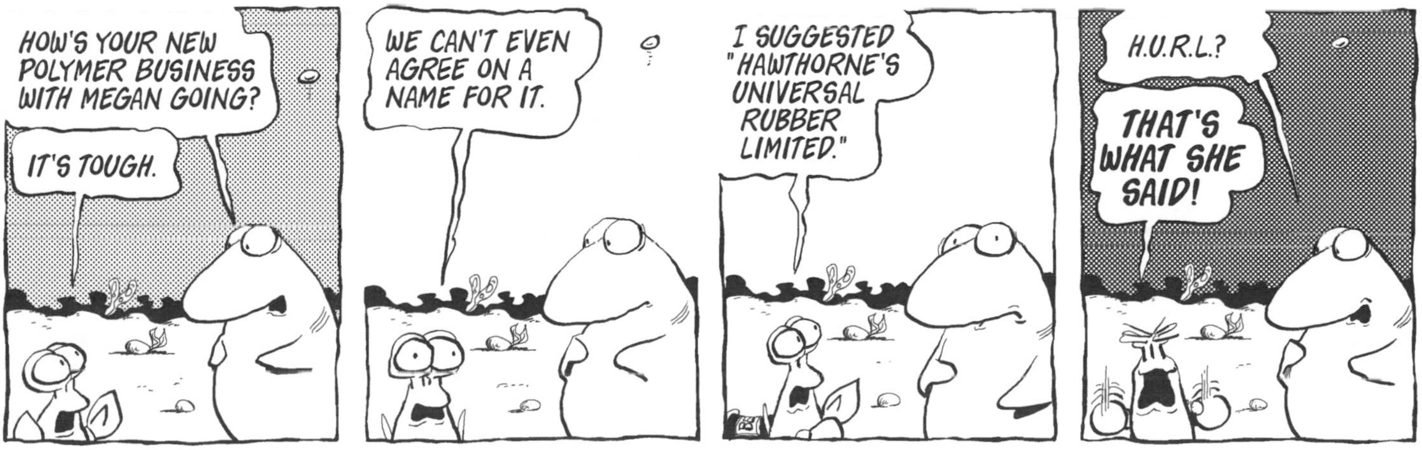
HOW'S YOUR NEW POLYMER BUSINESS WITH MEGAN GOING?
IT'S TOUGH.
WE CAN'T EVEN AGREE ON A NAME FOR IT.
I SUGGESTED "HAWTHORNE'S UNIVERSAL RUBBER LIMITED."
H.U.R.L.?
THAT'S WHAT SHE SAID!

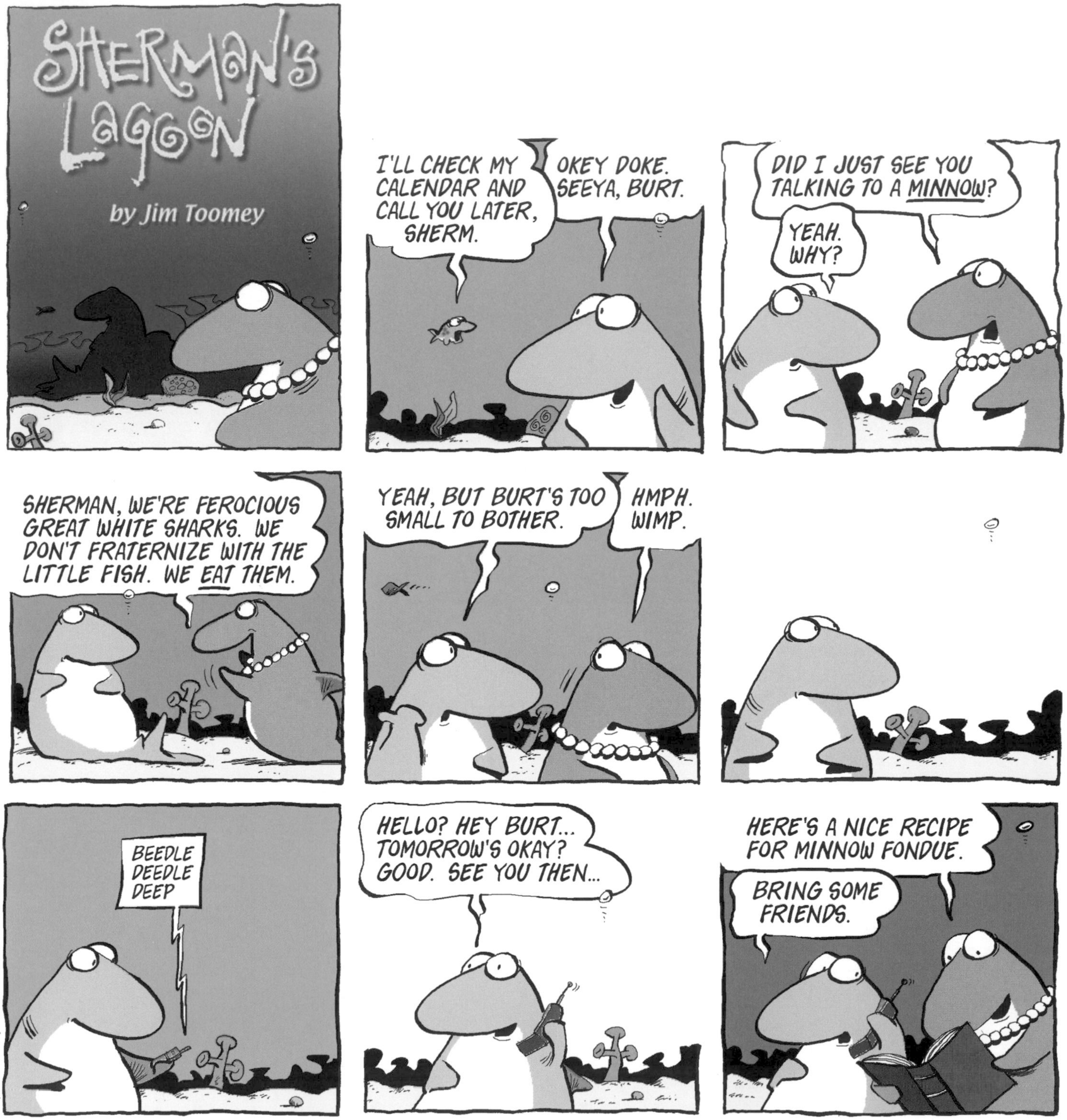
SHERMAN'S LAGOON
by Jim Toomey
I'LL CHECK MY CALENDAR AND CALL YOU LATER, SHERM.
OKEY DOKE. SEEYA, BURT.
DID I JUST SEE YOU TALKING TO A MINNOW?
YEAH. WHY?
SHERMAN, WE'RE FEROCIOUS GREAT WHITE SHARKS. WE DON'T FRATERNIZE WITH THE LITTLE FISH. WE EAT THEM.
YEAH, BUT BURT'S TOO SMALL TO BOTHER.
HMPH. WIMP.
BEEDLE DEEDLE DEEP
HELLO? HEY BURT... TOMORROW'S OKAY? GOOD. SEE YOU THEN...
HERE'S A NICE RECIPE FOR MINNOW FONDUE.
BRING SOME FRIENDS.

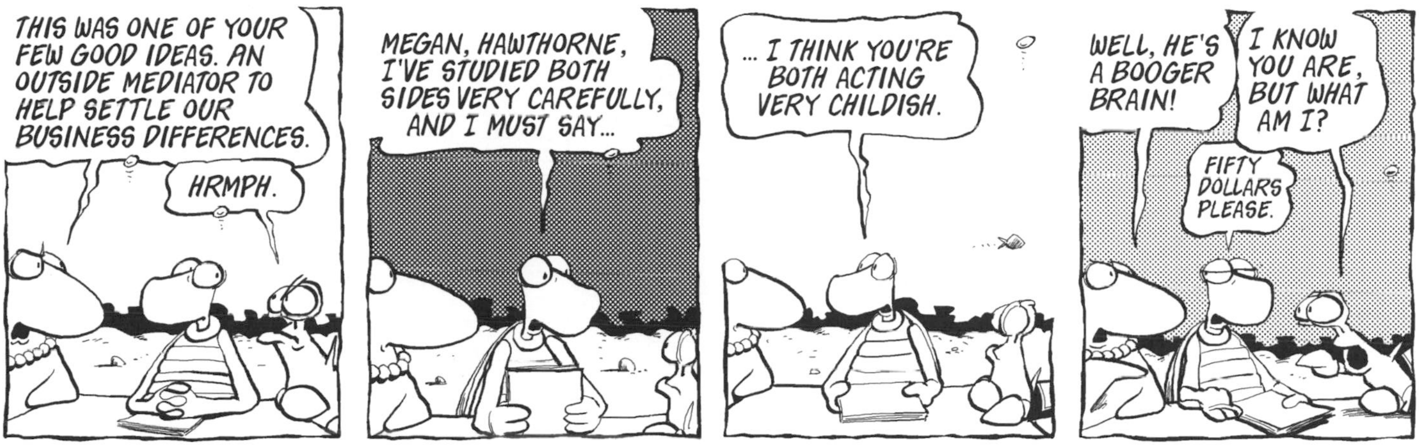
THIS WAS ONE OF YOUR FEW GOOD IDEAS. AN OUTSIDE MEDIATOR TO HELP SETTLE OUR BUSINESS DIFFERENCES.
HRMPH.
MEGAN, HAWTHORNE, I'VE STUDIED BOTH SIDES VERY CAREFULLY, AND I MUST SAY...
... I THINK YOU'RE BOTH ACTING VERY CHILDISH.
WELL, HE'S A BOOGER BRAIN!
I KNOW YOU ARE, BUT WHAT AM I?
FIFTY DOLLARS PLEASE.

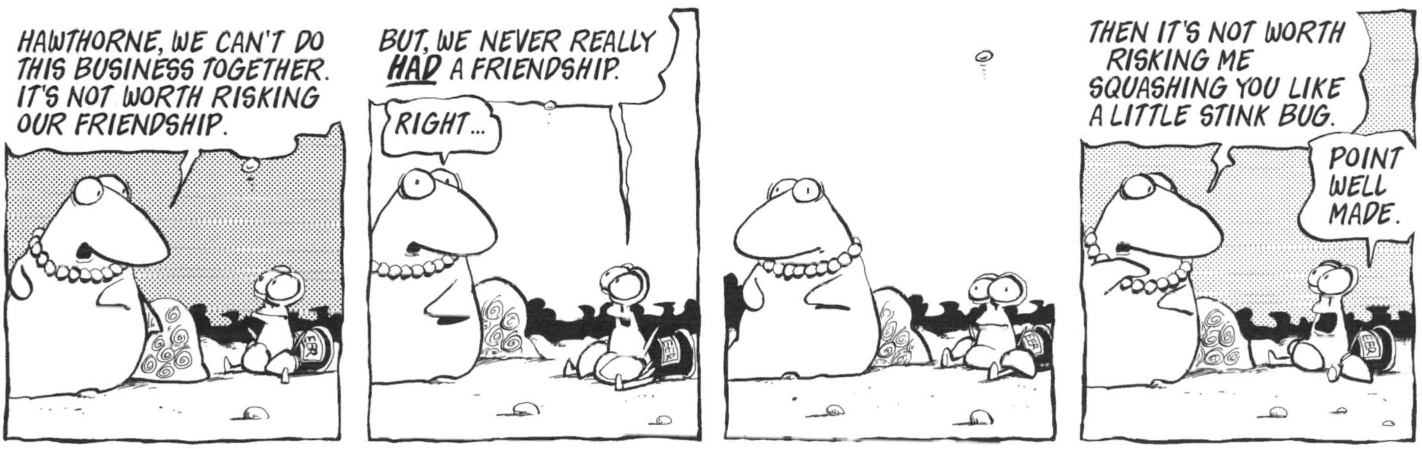
HAWTHORNE, WE CAN'T DO THIS BUSINESS TOGETHER. IT'S NOT WORTH RISKING OUR FRIENDSHIP.
BUT, WE NEVER REALLY HAD A FRIENDSHIP.
RIGHT...
THEN IT'S NOT WORTH RISKING ME SQUASHING YOU LIKE A LITTLE STINK BUG.
POINT WELL MADE.

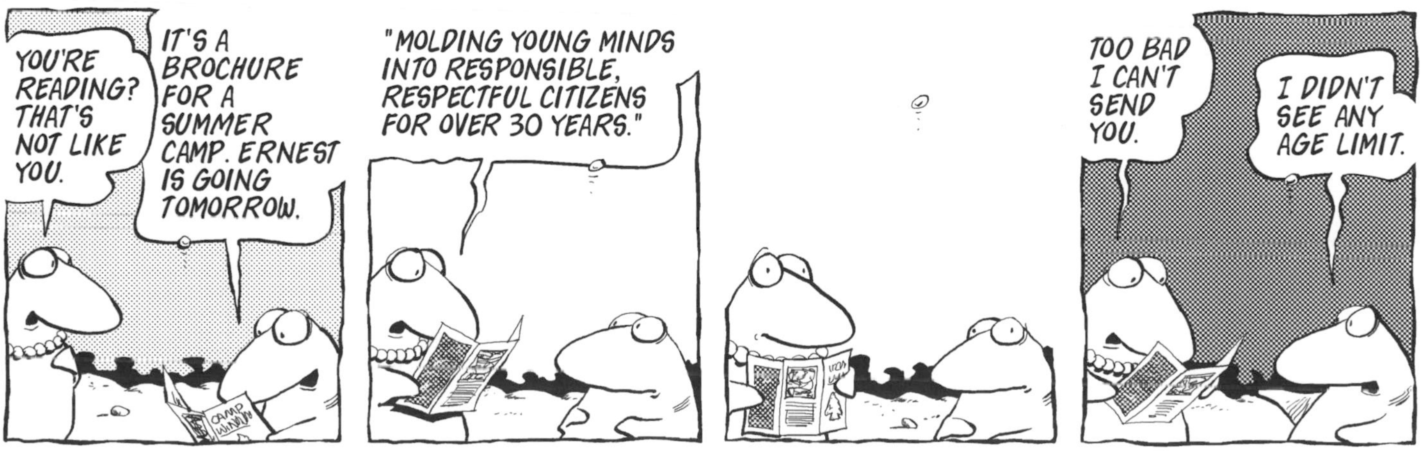
YOU'RE READING? THAT'S NOT LIKE YOU.
IT'S A BROCHURE FOR A SUMMER CAMP. ERNEST IS GOING TOMORROW.
"MOLDING YOUNG MINDS INTO RESPONSIBLE, RESPECTFUL CITIZENS FOR OVER 30 YEARS."
TOO BAD I CAN'T SEND YOU.
I DIDN'T SEE ANY AGE LIMIT.

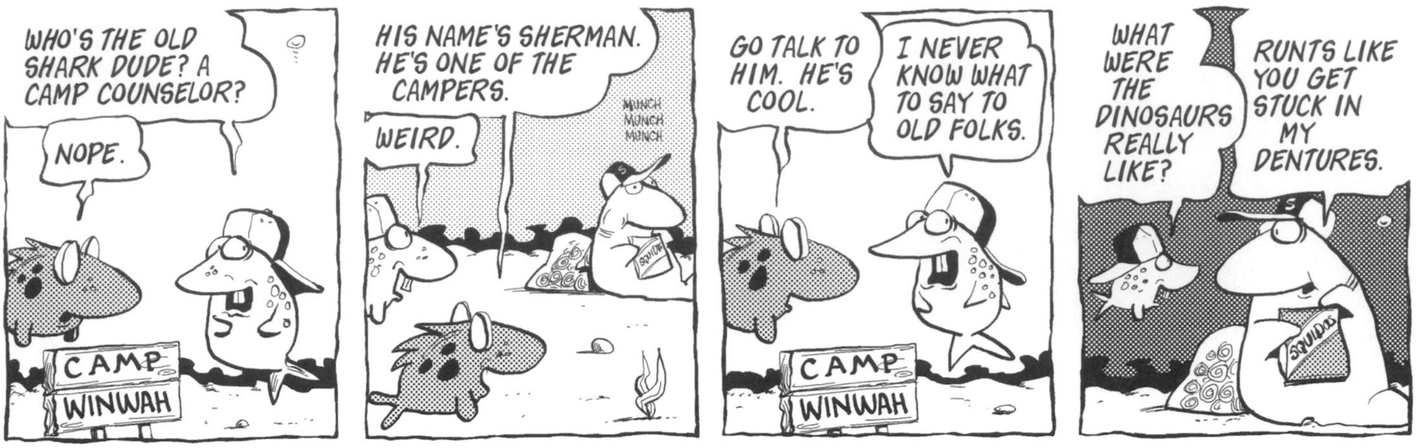
WHO'S THE OLD SHARK DUDE? A CAMP COUNSELOR?
NOPE.
CAMP WINWAH
HIS NAME'S SHERMAN. HE'S ONE OF THE CAMPERS.
WEIRD.
MUNCH MUNCH MUNCH
GO TALK TO HIM. HE'S COOL.
I NEVER KNOW WHAT TO SAY TO OLD FOLKS.
CAMP WINWAH
WHAT WERE THE DINOSAURS REALLY LIKE?
RUNTS LIKE YOU GET STUCK IN MY DENTURES.
SQUIDOS

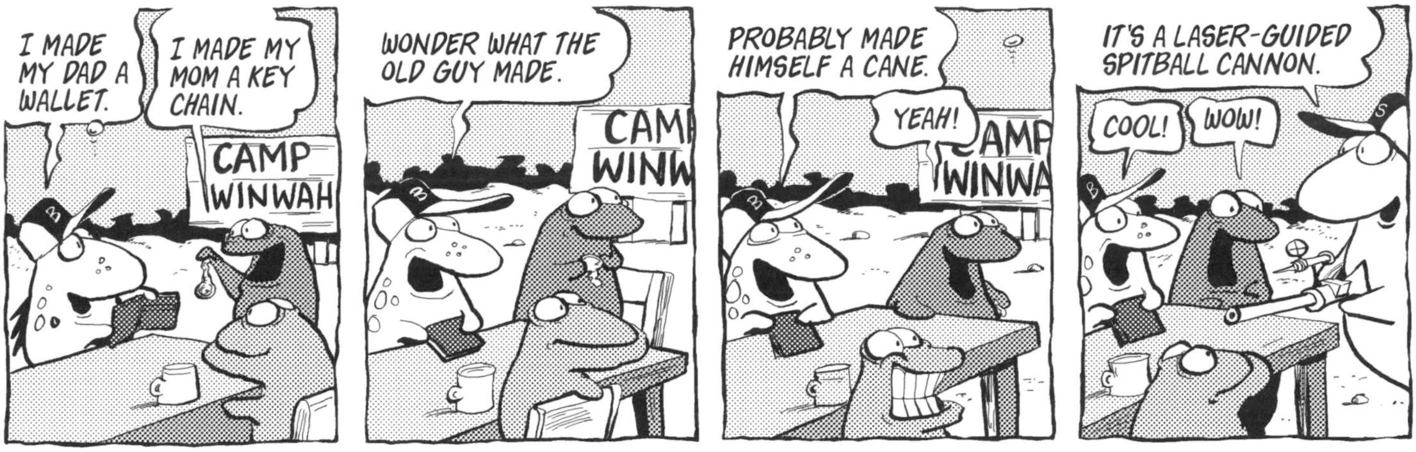
I MADE MY DAD A WALLET.
I MADE MY MOM A KEY CHAIN.
CAMP WINWAH
WONDER WHAT THE OLD GUY MADE.
PROBABLY MADE HIMSELF A CANE.
YEAH!
IT'S A LASER-GUIDED SPITBALL CANNON.
COOL!
WOW!

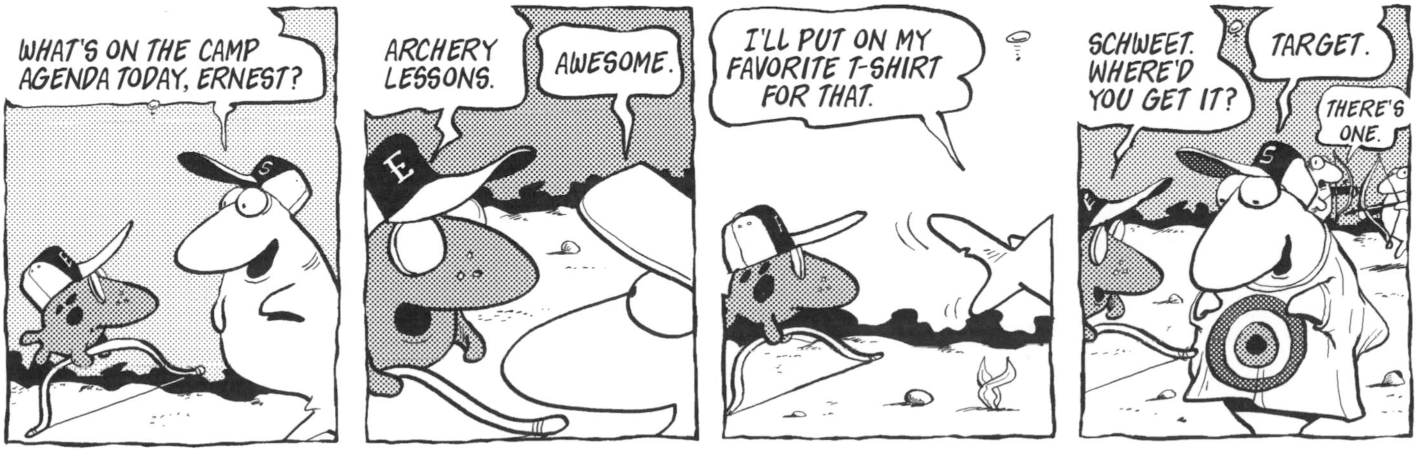
WHAT'S ON THE CAMP AGENDA TODAY, ERNEST?
ARCHERY LESSONS.
AWESOME.
I'LL PUT ON MY FAVORITE T-SHIRT FOR THAT.
SCHWEET. WHERE'D YOU GET IT?
TARGET.
THERE'S ONE.

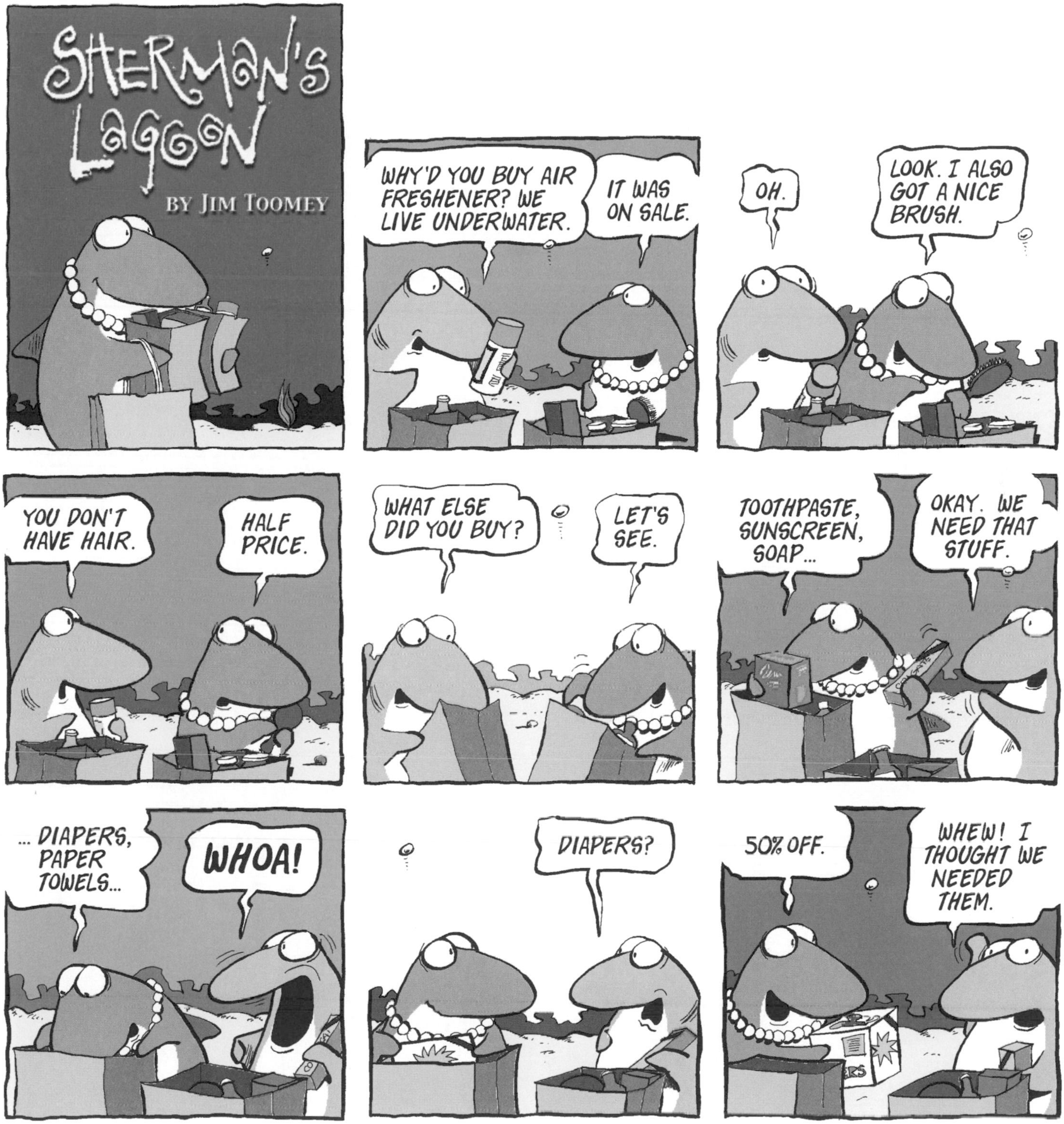
SHERMAN'S LAGOON
BY JIM TOOMEY
WHY'D YOU BUY AIR FRESHENER? WE LIVE UNDERWATER.
IT WAS ON SALE.
OH.
LOOK. I ALSO GOT A NICE BRUSH.
YOU DON'T HAVE HAIR.
HALF PRICE.
WHAT ELSE DID YOU BUY?
LET'S SEE.
TOOTHPASTE, SUNSCREEN, SOAP...
OKAY. WE NEED THAT STUFF.
... DIAPERS, PAPER TOWELS...
WHOA!
DIAPERS?
50% OFF.
WHEW! I THOUGHT WE NEEDED THEM.

IN RETROSPECT, IT WAS PROBABLY A DUMB IDEA WEARING THAT SHIRT TO ARCHERY PRACTICE.

IS HE GOING TO BE OKAY, NURSE?

HE DID TAKE AN ARROW IN THE STOMACH...

IT WAS A MESS, BUT WE MANAGED TO STOP THE HEMORRHAGING.

DID HE LOSE A LOT OF BLOOD?

NOUGAT.

C'MON, SHERMAN! GET A HIT FOR CABIN 3!

YEAH!

CAN THE OLD DUDE PLAY?

ARE YOU KIDDING? HE'S LIKE SAMMY SOSA.

LOOK. HE'S POINTING TOWARD THE FENCE! HE'S CALLING A HOME RUN SHOT!

ACTUALLY, HE'S WAVING OVER THE HOT DOG VENDOR.

YO! TWO HERE!

AND ON QUIET NIGHTS YOU CAN STILL HEAR HIS SCREAM...

OOH...

CAMP WINWAH

WHAT ABOUT THE OLD DUDE. DO YOU HAVE A SCARY STORY?

NOT FOR THESE YOUNG EARS.

AMP NWAH

AW, C'MON, SHERM.

YEAH.

OH, ALRIGHT. BUT BE WARNED, THIS IS SCARY, AND TRUE.

AMP NWAH

THEY CALL HER "MOTHER-IN-LAW."

OOH...

AM NWAH

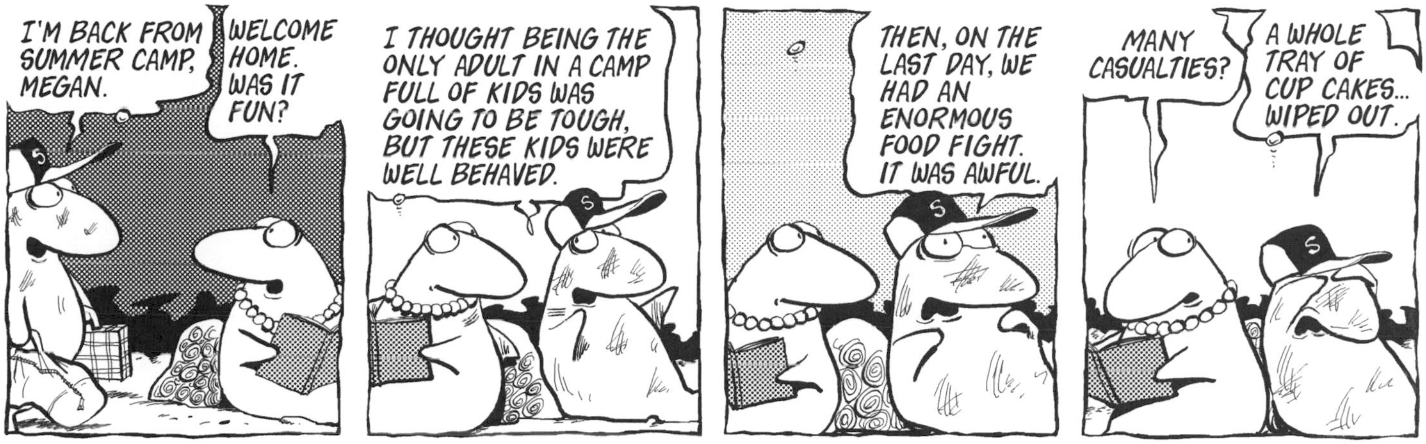
I'M BACK FROM SUMMER CAMP, MEGAN.
WELCOME HOME. WAS IT FUN?
I THOUGHT BEING THE ONLY ADULT IN A CAMP FULL OF KIDS WAS GOING TO BE TOUGH, BUT THESE KIDS WERE WELL BEHAVED.
THEN, ON THE LAST DAY, WE HAD AN ENORMOUS FOOD FIGHT. IT WAS AWFUL.
MANY CASUALTIES?
A WHOLE TRAY OF CUP CAKES... WIPED OUT.

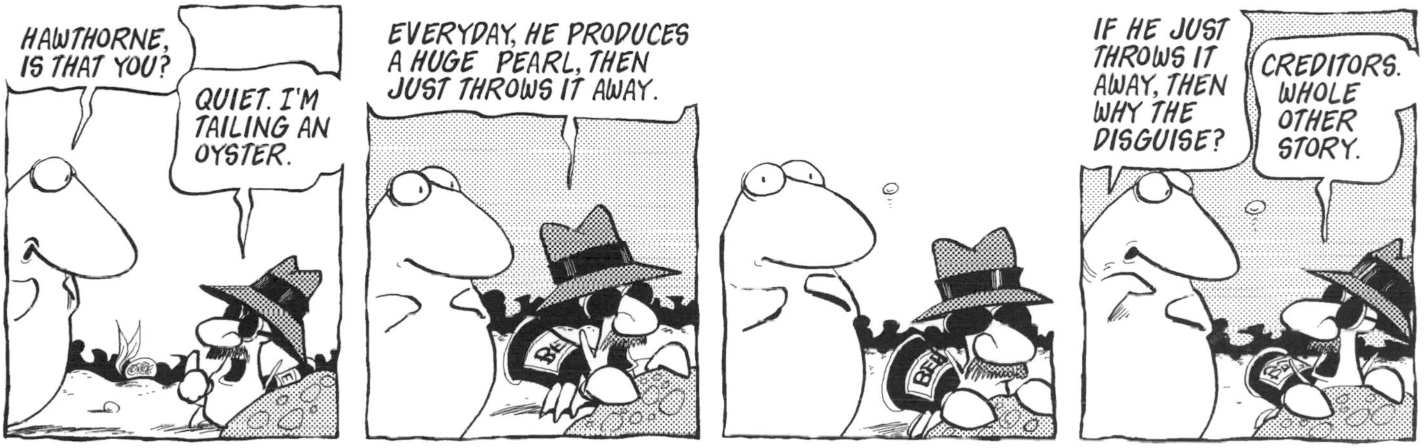
HAWTHORNE, IS THAT YOU?
QUIET. I'M TAILING AN OYSTER.
EVERYDAY, HE PRODUCES A HUGE PEARL, THEN JUST THROWS IT AWAY.
IF HE JUST THROWS IT AWAY, THEN WHY THE DISGUISE?
CREDITORS. WHOLE OTHER STORY.

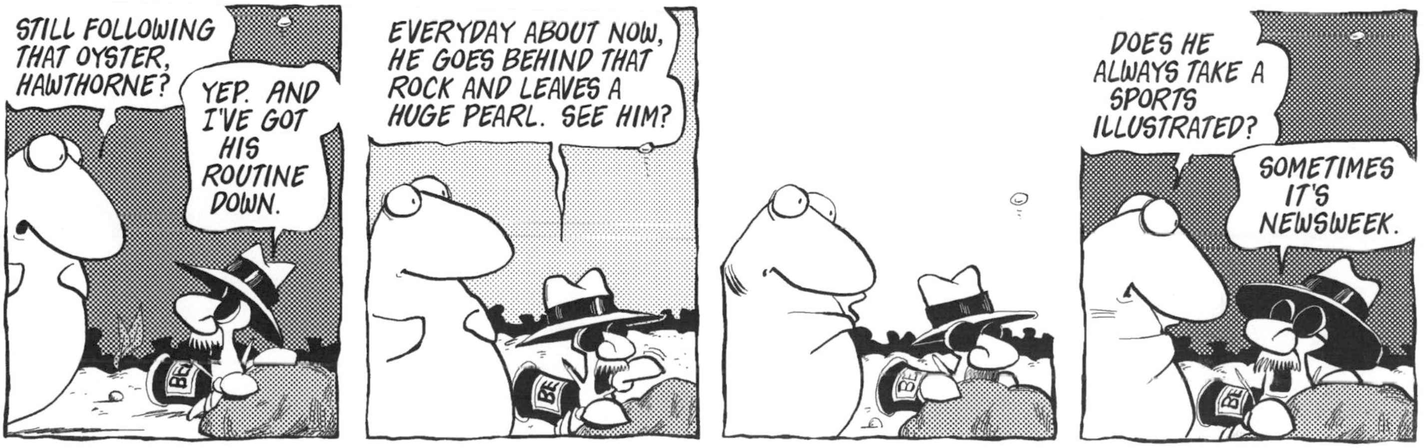
STILL FOLLOWING THAT OYSTER, HAWTHORNE?
YEP. AND I'VE GOT HIS ROUTINE DOWN.
EVERYDAY ABOUT NOW, HE GOES BEHIND THAT ROCK AND LEAVES A HUGE PEARL. SEE HIM?
DOES HE ALWAYS TAKE A SPORTS ILLUSTRATED?
SOMETIMES IT'S NEWSWEEK.

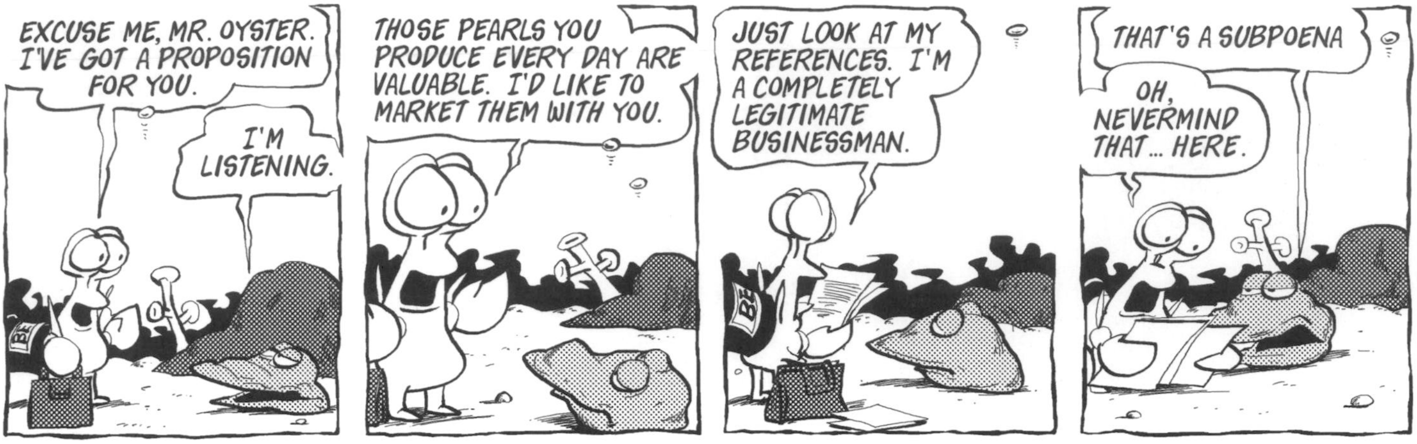
EXCUSE ME, MR. OYSTER. I'VE GOT A PROPOSITION FOR YOU.
I'M LISTENING.
THOSE PEARLS YOU PRODUCE EVERY DAY ARE VALUABLE. I'D LIKE TO MARKET THEM WITH YOU.
JUST LOOK AT MY REFERENCES. I'M A COMPLETELY LEGITIMATE BUSINESSMAN.
THAT'S A SUBPOENA
OH, NEVERMIND THAT... HERE.

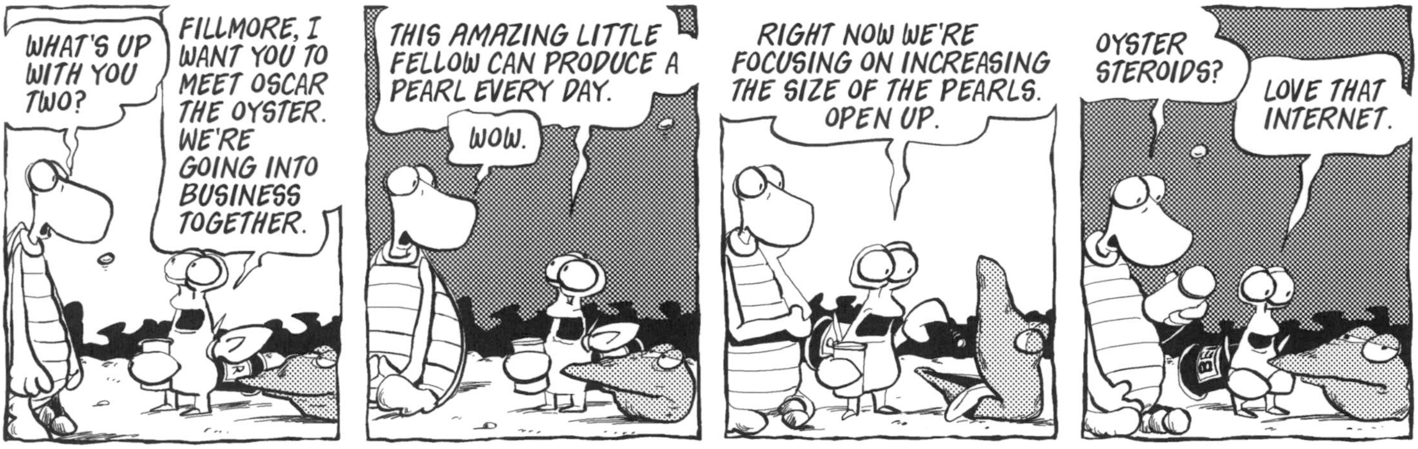
WHAT'S UP WITH YOU TWO?
FILLMORE, I WANT YOU TO MEET OSCAR THE OYSTER. WE'RE GOING INTO BUSINESS TOGETHER.
THIS AMAZING LITTLE FELLOW CAN PRODUCE A PEARL EVERY DAY.
WOW.
RIGHT NOW WE'RE FOCUSING ON INCREASING THE SIZE OF THE PEARLS. OPEN UP.
OYSTER STEROIDS?
LOVE THAT INTERNET.

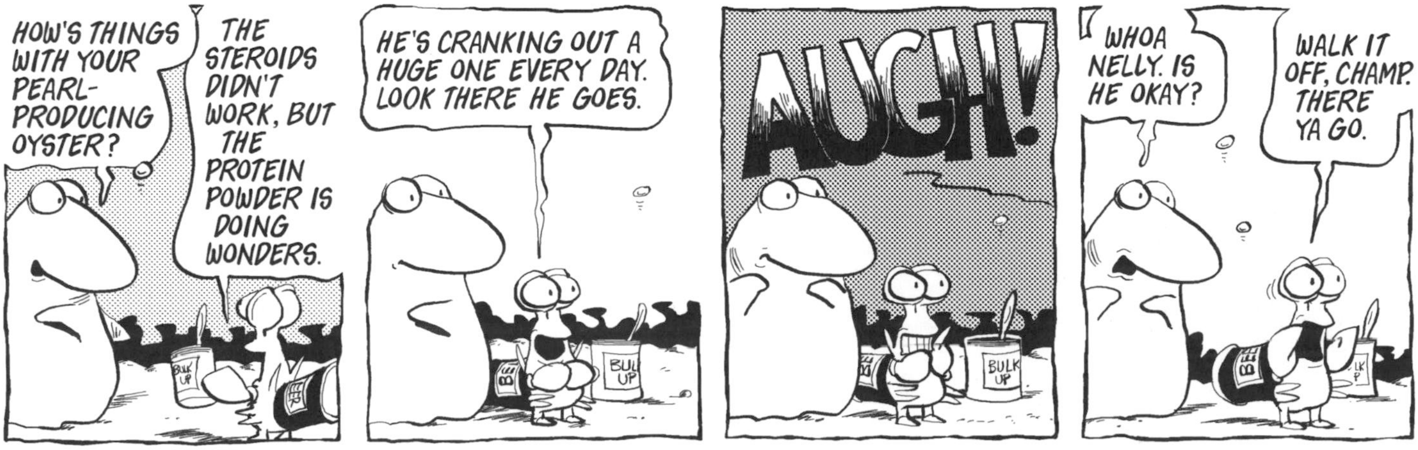
HOW'S THINGS WITH YOUR PEARL-PRODUCING OYSTER?
THE STEROIDS DIDN'T WORK, BUT THE PROTEIN POWDER IS DOING WONDERS.
HE'S CRANKING OUT A HUGE ONE EVERY DAY. LOOK THERE HE GOES.
AUGH!
WHOA NELLY. IS HE OKAY?
WALK IT OFF, CHAMP. THERE YA GO.

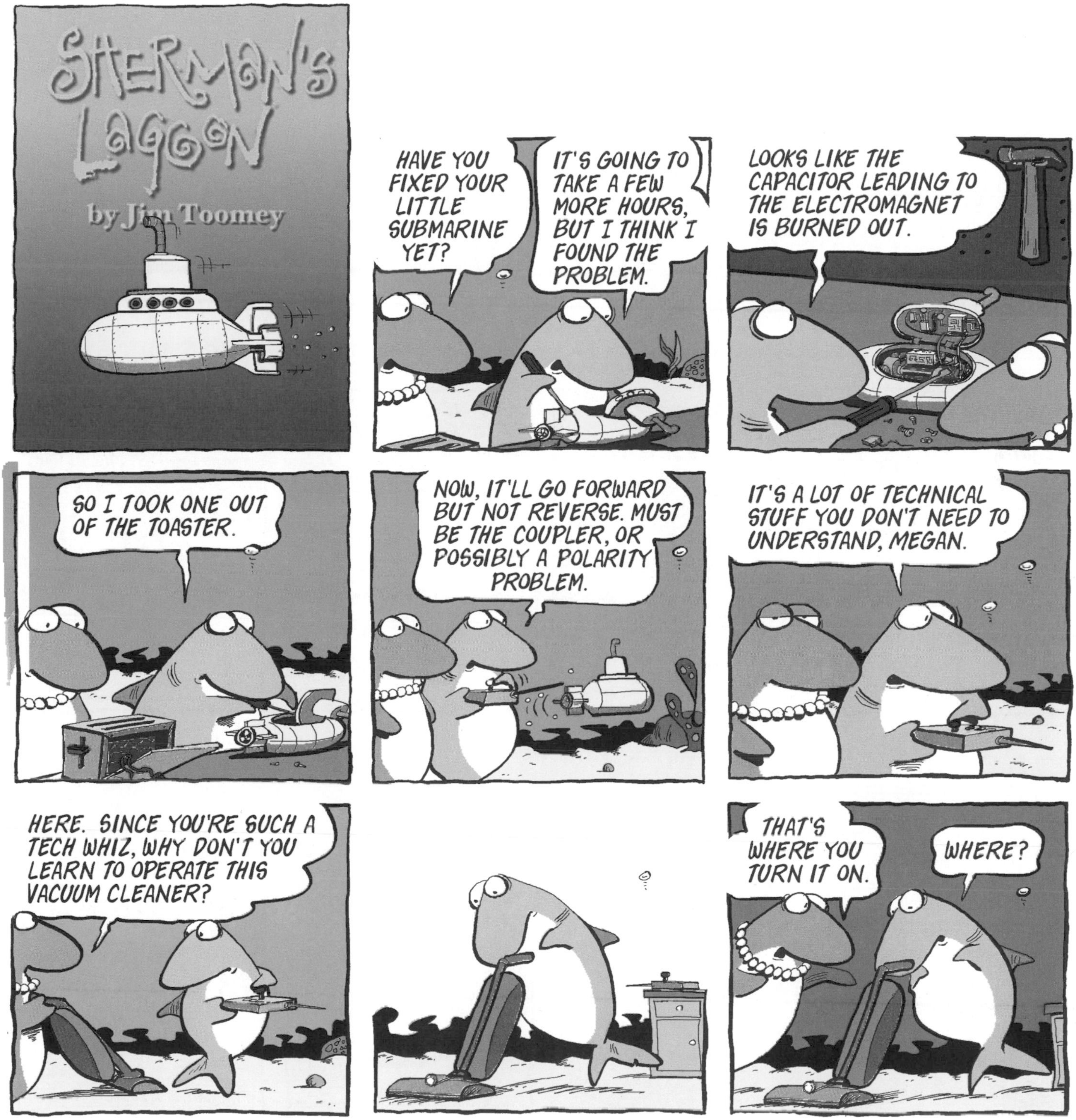
Sherman's Lagoon
by Jim Toomey
HAVE YOU FIXED YOUR LITTLE SUBMARINE YET?
IT'S GOING TO TAKE A FEW MORE HOURS, BUT I THINK I FOUND THE PROBLEM.
LOOKS LIKE THE CAPACITOR LEADING TO THE ELECTROMAGNET IS BURNED OUT.
SO I TOOK ONE OUT OF THE TOASTER.
NOW, IT'LL GO FORWARD BUT NOT REVERSE. MUST BE THE COUPLER, OR POSSIBLY A POLARITY PROBLEM.
IT'S A LOT OF TECHNICAL STUFF YOU DON'T NEED TO UNDERSTAND, MEGAN.
HERE. SINCE YOU'RE SUCH A TECH WHIZ, WHY DON'T YOU LEARN TO OPERATE THIS VACUUM CLEANER?
THAT'S WHERE YOU TURN IT ON.
WHERE?

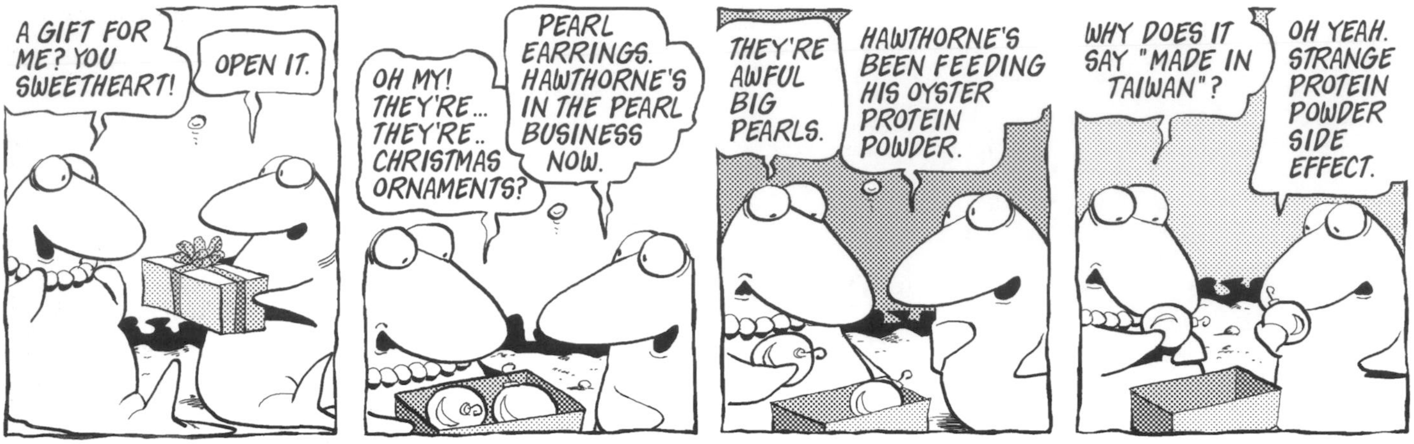
A GIFT FOR ME? YOU SWEETHEART!
OPEN IT.
OH MY! THEY'RE... THEY'RE.. CHRISTMAS ORNAMENTS?
PEARL EARRINGS. HAWTHORNE'S IN THE PEARL BUSINESS NOW.
THEY'RE AWFUL BIG PEARLS.
HAWTHORNE'S BEEN FEEDING HIS OYSTER PROTEIN POWDER.
WHY DOES IT SAY "MADE IN TAIWAN"?
OH YEAH. STRANGE PROTEIN POWDER SIDE EFFECT.

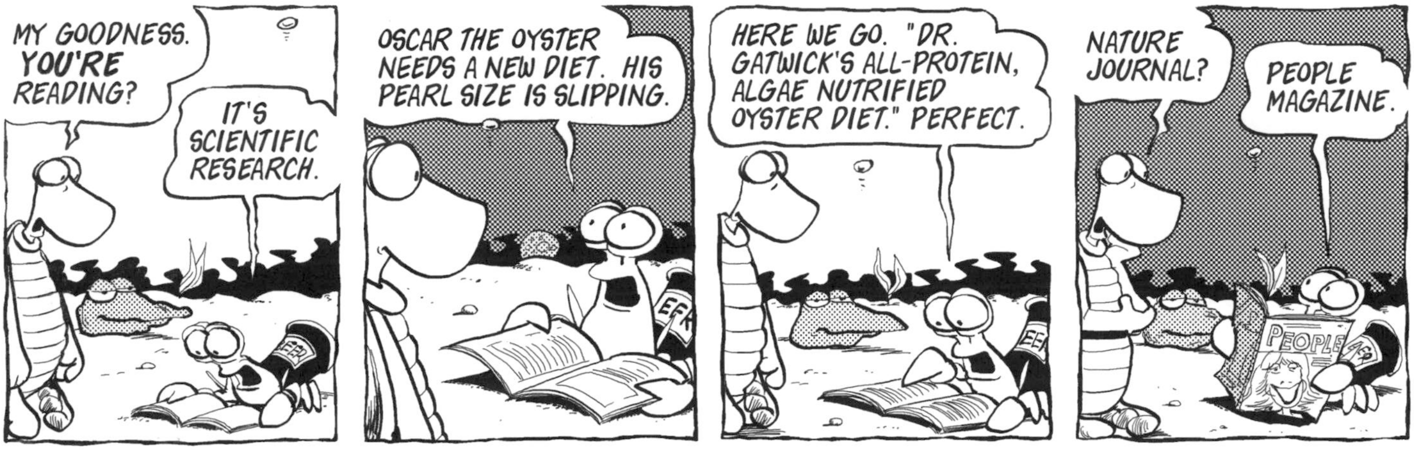
MY GOODNESS. **YOU'RE** READING?
IT'S SCIENTIFIC RESEARCH.
OSCAR THE OYSTER NEEDS A NEW DIET. HIS PEARL SIZE IS SLIPPING.
HERE WE GO. "DR. GATWICK'S ALL-PROTEIN, ALGAE NUTRIFIED OYSTER DIET." PERFECT.
NATURE JOURNAL?
PEOPLE MAGAZINE.
PEOPLE

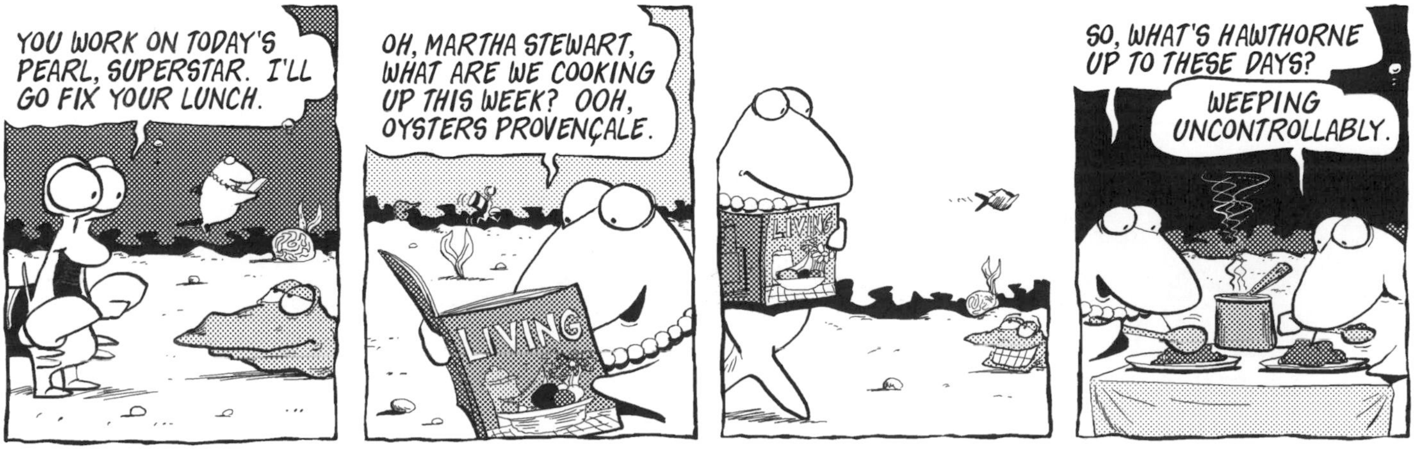
YOU WORK ON TODAY'S PEARL, SUPERSTAR. I'LL GO FIX YOUR LUNCH.
OH, MARTHA STEWART, WHAT ARE WE COOKING UP THIS WEEK? OOH, OYSTERS PROVENÇALE.
LIVING
LIVING
SO, WHAT'S HAWTHORNE UP TO THESE DAYS?
WEEPING UNCONTROLLABLY.

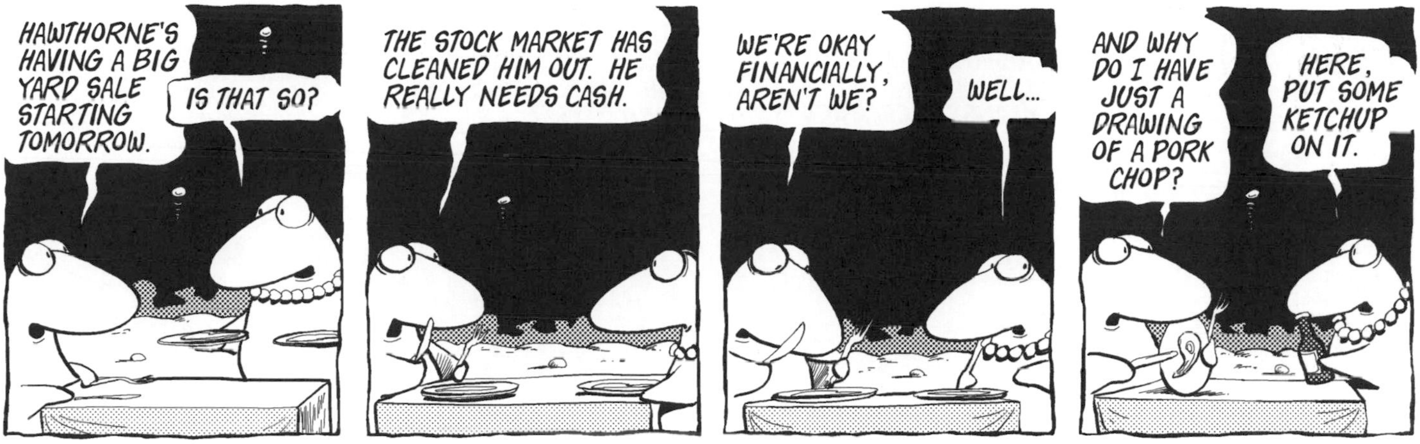
HAWTHORNE'S HAVING A BIG YARD SALE STARTING TOMORROW.
IS THAT SO?
THE STOCK MARKET HAS CLEANED HIM OUT. HE REALLY NEEDS CASH.
WE'RE OKAY FINANCIALLY, AREN'T WE?
WELL...
AND WHY DO I HAVE JUST A DRAWING OF A PORK CHOP?
HERE, PUT SOME KETCHUP ON IT.

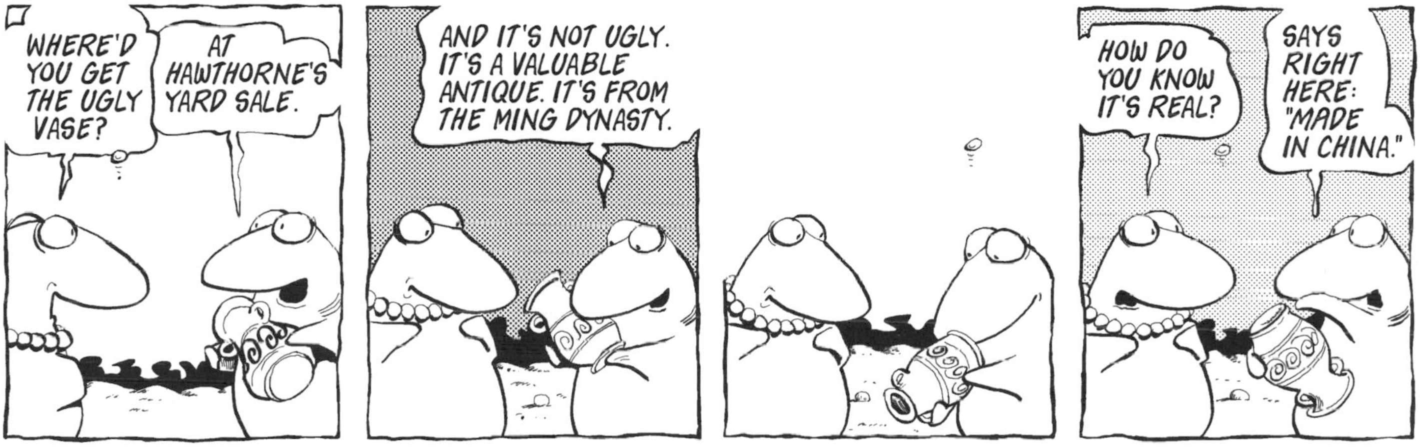
WHERE'D YOU GET THE UGLY VASE?
AT HAWTHORNE'S YARD SALE.
AND IT'S NOT UGLY. IT'S A VALUABLE ANTIQUE. IT'S FROM THE MING DYNASTY.
HOW DO YOU KNOW IT'S REAL?
SAYS RIGHT HERE: "MADE IN CHINA."

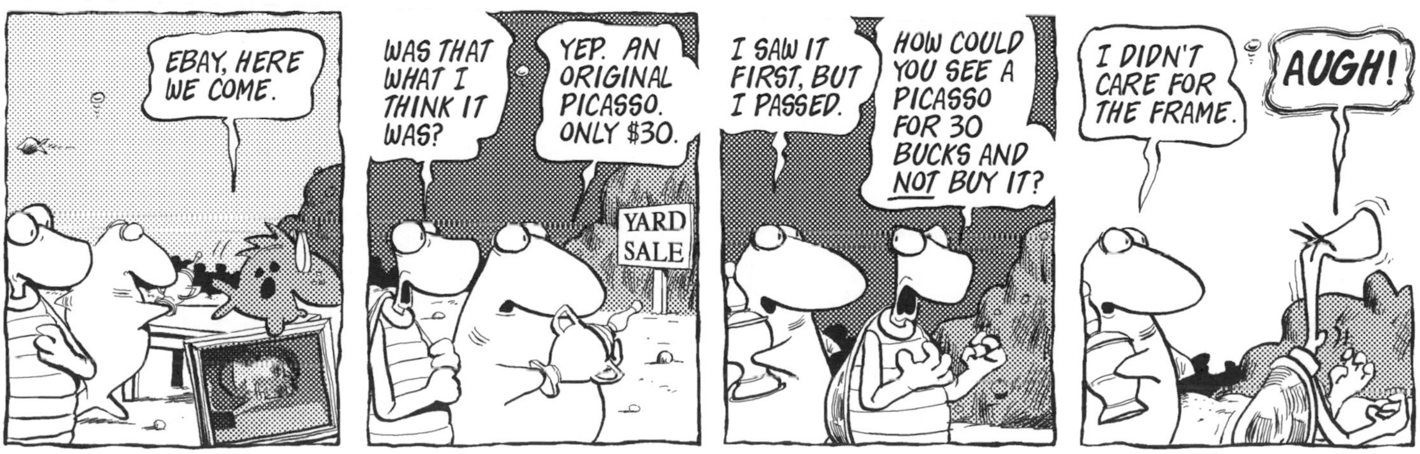
EBAY, HERE WE COME.
WAS THAT WHAT I THINK IT WAS?
YEP. AN ORIGINAL PICASSO. ONLY $30.
YARD SALE
I SAW IT FIRST, BUT I PASSED.
HOW COULD YOU SEE A PICASSO FOR 30 BUCKS AND NOT BUY IT?
I DIDN'T CARE FOR THE FRAME.
AUGH!

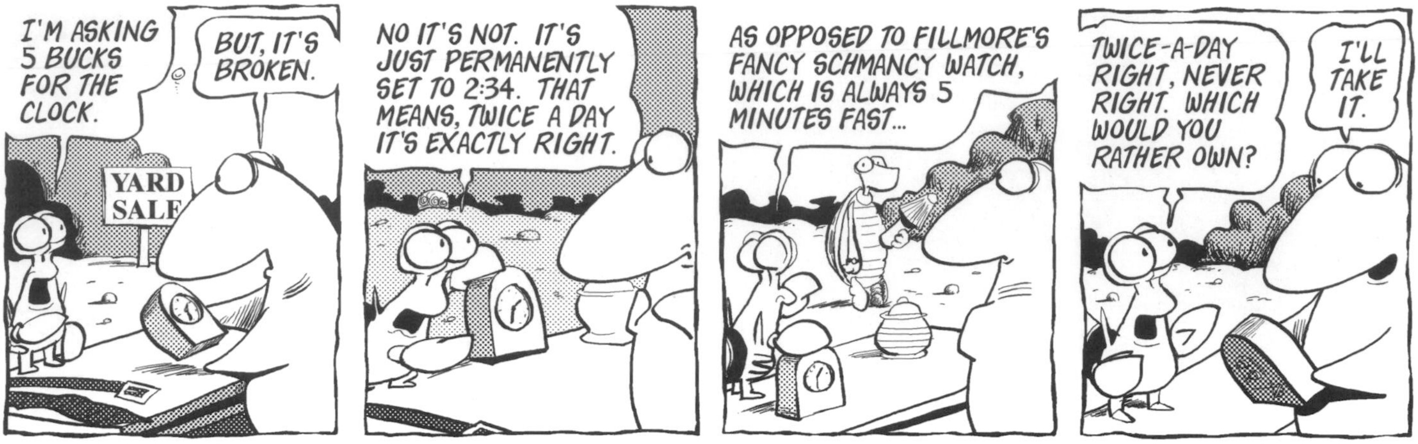
I'M ASKING 5 BUCKS FOR THE CLOCK.
BUT, IT'S BROKEN.
YARD SALE
NO IT'S NOT. IT'S JUST PERMANENTLY SET TO 2:34. THAT MEANS, TWICE A DAY IT'S EXACTLY RIGHT.
AS OPPOSED TO FILLMORE'S FANCY SCHMANCY WATCH, WHICH IS ALWAYS 5 MINUTES FAST...
TWICE-A-DAY RIGHT, NEVER RIGHT. WHICH WOULD YOU RATHER OWN?
I'LL TAKE IT.

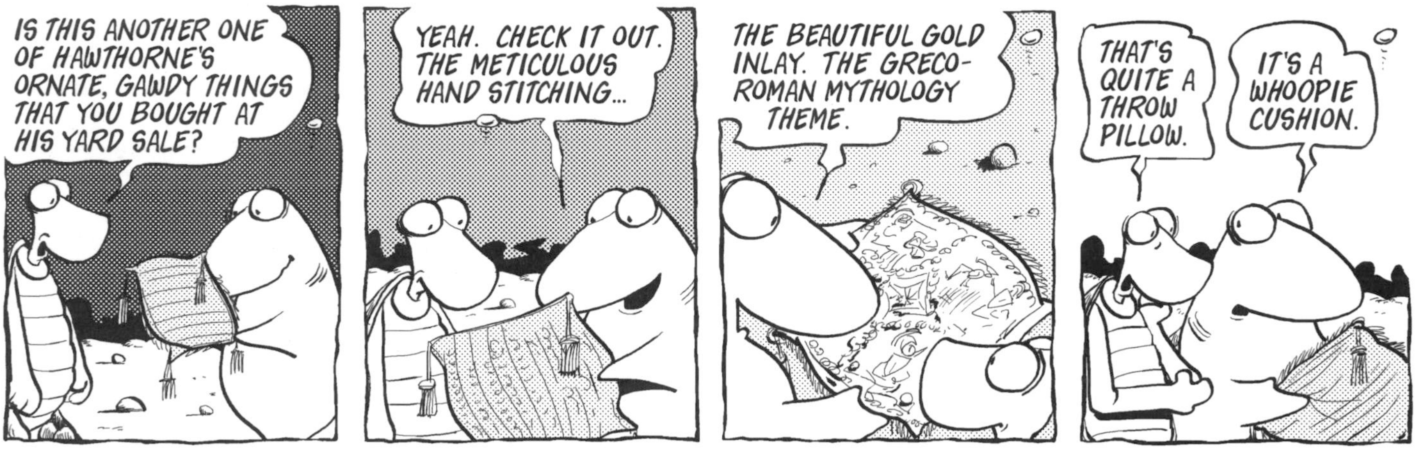
IS THIS ANOTHER ONE OF HAWTHORNE'S ORNATE, GAWDY THINGS THAT YOU BOUGHT AT HIS YARD SALE?
YEAH. CHECK IT OUT. THE METICULOUS HAND STITCHING...
THE BEAUTIFUL GOLD INLAY. THE GRECO-ROMAN MYTHOLOGY THEME.
THAT'S QUITE A THROW PILLOW.
IT'S A WHOOPIE CUSHION.

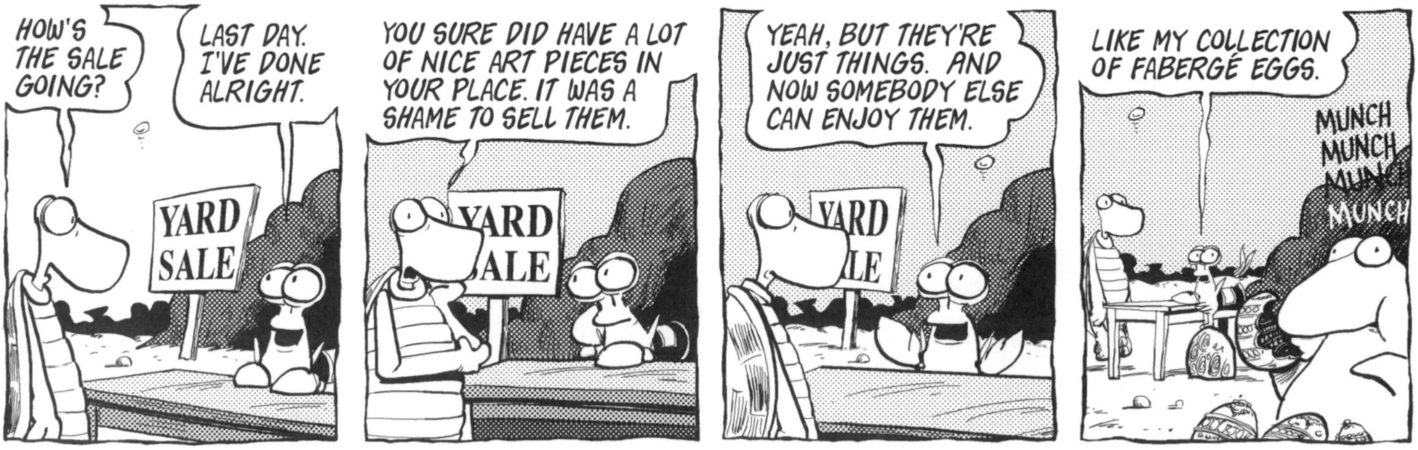
HOW'S THE SALE GOING?
LAST DAY. I'VE DONE ALRIGHT.
YARD SALE
YOU SURE DID HAVE A LOT OF NICE ART PIECES IN YOUR PLACE. IT WAS A SHAME TO SELL THEM.
YEAH, BUT THEY'RE JUST THINGS. AND NOW SOMEBODY ELSE CAN ENJOY THEM.
LIKE MY COLLECTION OF FABERGÉ EGGS.
MUNCH
MUNCH
MUNCH

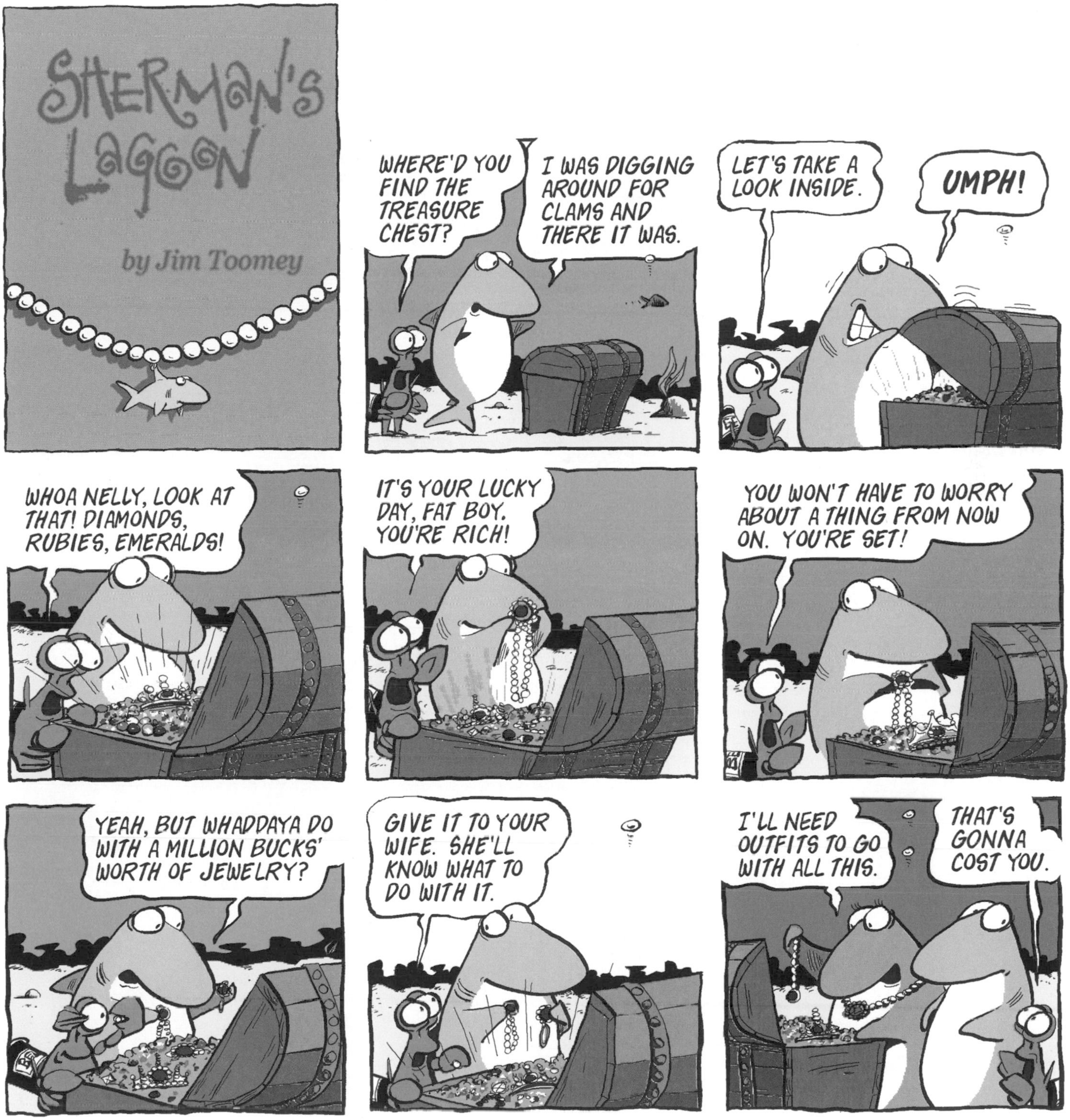
Sherman's Lagoon
by Jim Toomey
WHERE'D YOU FIND THE TREASURE CHEST?
I WAS DIGGING AROUND FOR CLAMS AND THERE IT WAS.
LET'S TAKE A LOOK INSIDE.
UMPH!
WHOA NELLY, LOOK AT THAT! DIAMONDS, RUBIES, EMERALDS!
IT'S YOUR LUCKY DAY, FAT BOY. YOU'RE RICH!
YOU WON'T HAVE TO WORRY ABOUT A THING FROM NOW ON. YOU'RE SET!
YEAH, BUT WHADDAYA DO WITH A MILLION BUCKS' WORTH OF JEWELRY?
GIVE IT TO YOUR WIFE. SHE'LL KNOW WHAT TO DO WITH IT.
I'LL NEED OUTFITS TO GO WITH ALL THIS.
THAT'S GONNA COST YOU.

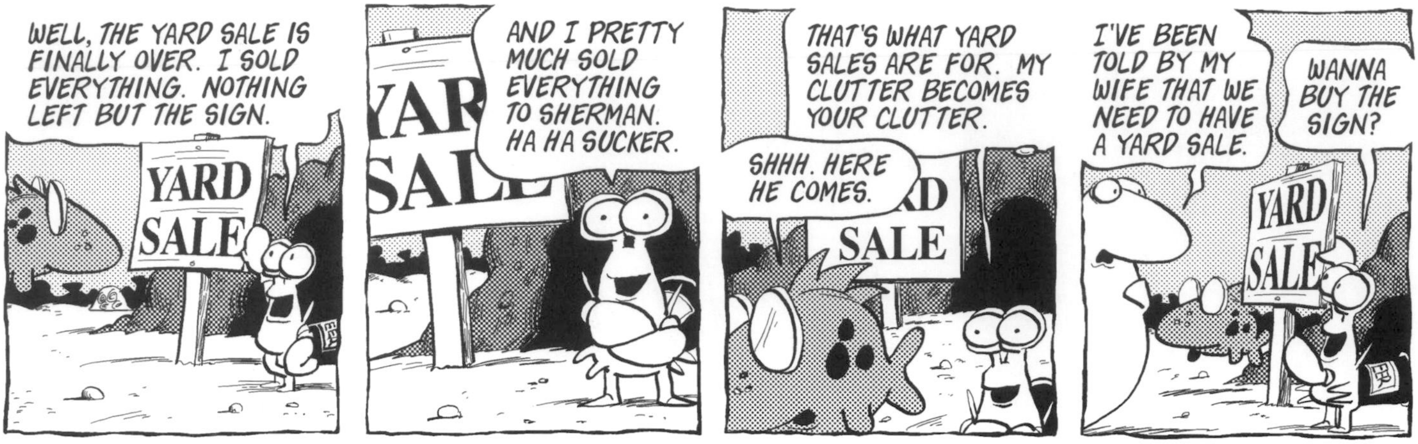
WELL, THE YARD SALE IS FINALLY OVER. I SOLD EVERYTHING. NOTHING LEFT BUT THE SIGN.
YARD SALE
AND I PRETTY MUCH SOLD EVERYTHING TO SHERMAN. HA HA SUCKER.
THAT'S WHAT YARD SALES ARE FOR. MY CLUTTER BECOMES YOUR CLUTTER.
SHHH. HERE HE COMES.
I'VE BEEN TOLD BY MY WIFE THAT WE NEED TO HAVE A YARD SALE.
WANNA BUY THE SIGN?

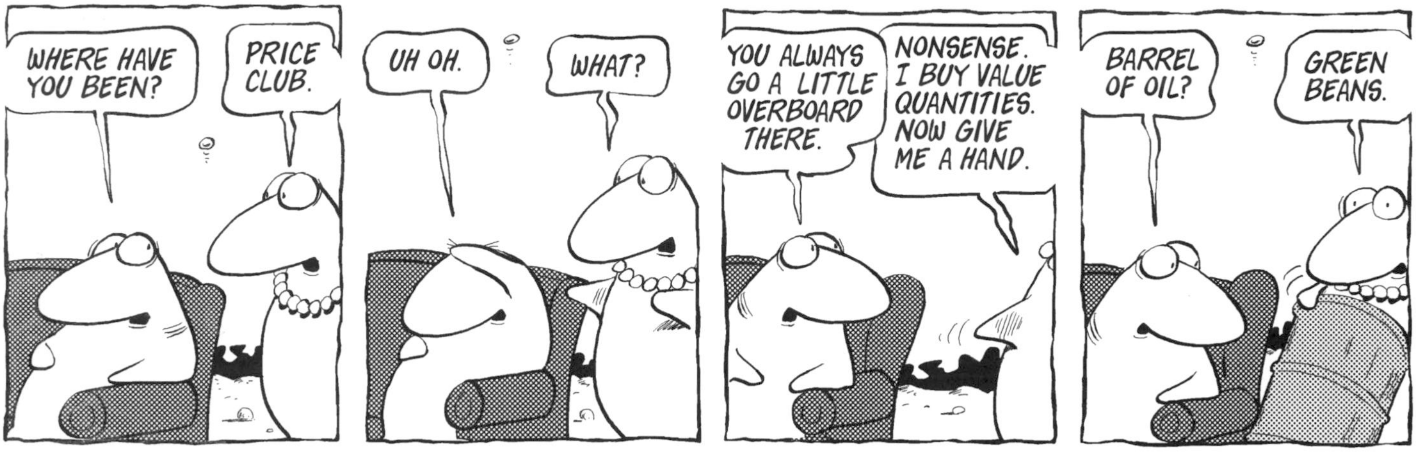
WHERE HAVE YOU BEEN?
PRICE CLUB.
UH OH.
WHAT?
YOU ALWAYS GO A LITTLE OVERBOARD THERE.
NONSENSE. I BUY VALUE QUANTITIES. NOW GIVE ME A HAND.
BARREL OF OIL?
GREEN BEANS.

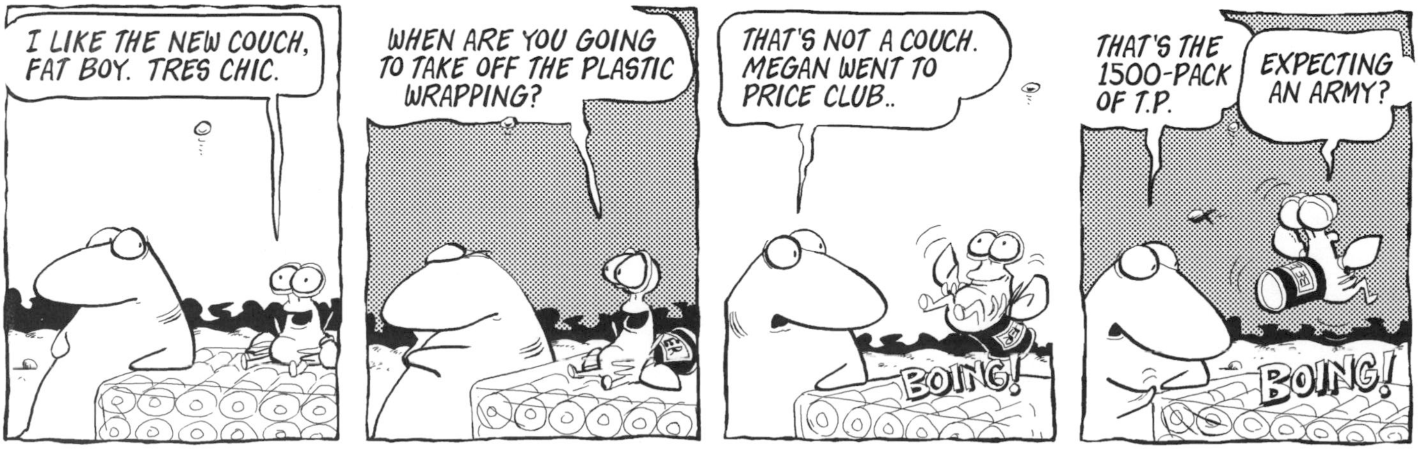
I LIKE THE NEW COUCH, FAT BOY. TRES CHIC.
WHEN ARE YOU GOING TO TAKE OFF THE PLASTIC WRAPPING?
THAT'S NOT A COUCH. MEGAN WENT TO PRICE CLUB..
BOING!
THAT'S THE 1500-PACK OF T.P.
EXPECTING AN ARMY?
BOING!

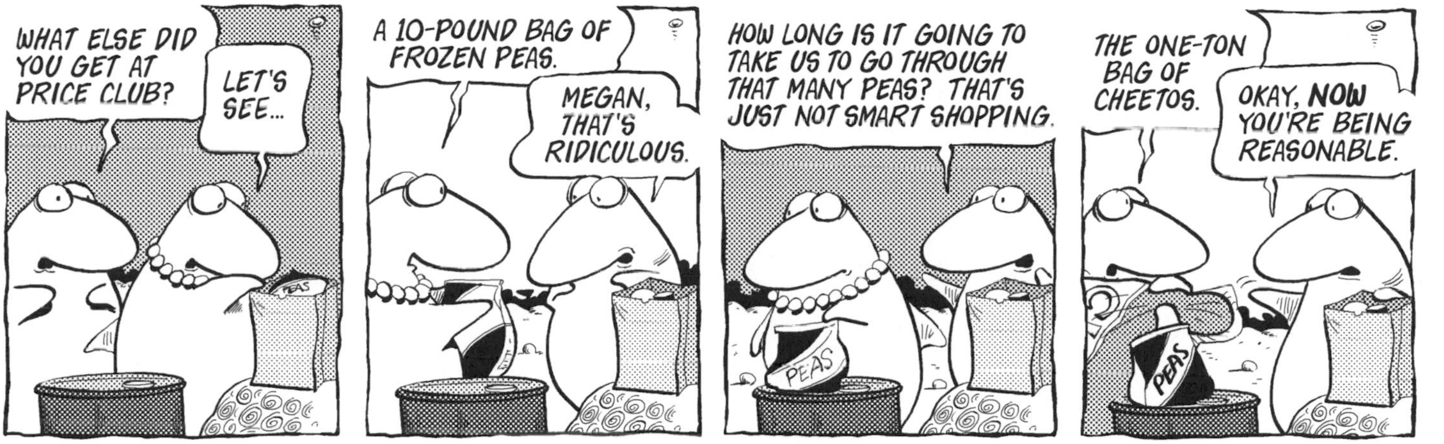
WHAT ELSE DID YOU GET AT PRICE CLUB?
LET'S SEE...
PEAS
A 10-POUND BAG OF FROZEN PEAS.
MEGAN, THAT'S RIDICULOUS.
HOW LONG IS IT GOING TO TAKE US TO GO THROUGH THAT MANY PEAS? THAT'S JUST NOT SMART SHOPPING.
PEAS
THE ONE-TON BAG OF CHEETOS.
OKAY, **NOW** YOU'RE BEING REASONABLE.
PEAS

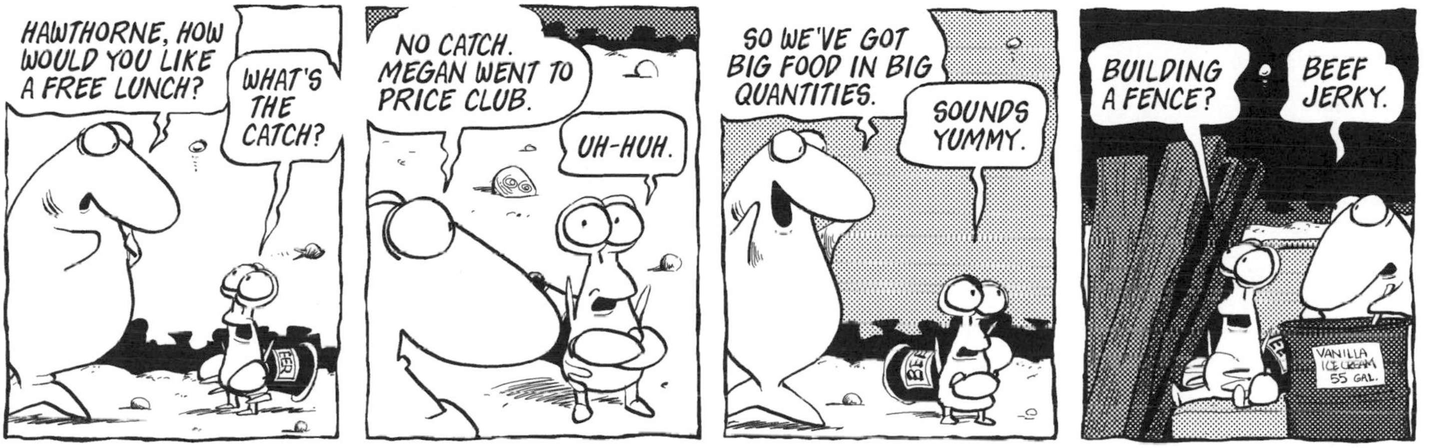
HAWTHORNE, HOW WOULD YOU LIKE A FREE LUNCH?
WHAT'S THE CATCH?
NO CATCH. MEGAN WENT TO PRICE CLUB.
UH-HUH.
SO WE'VE GOT BIG FOOD IN BIG QUANTITIES.
SOUNDS YUMMY.
BUILDING A FENCE?
BEEF JERKY.
VANILLA ICE CREAM 55 GAL.

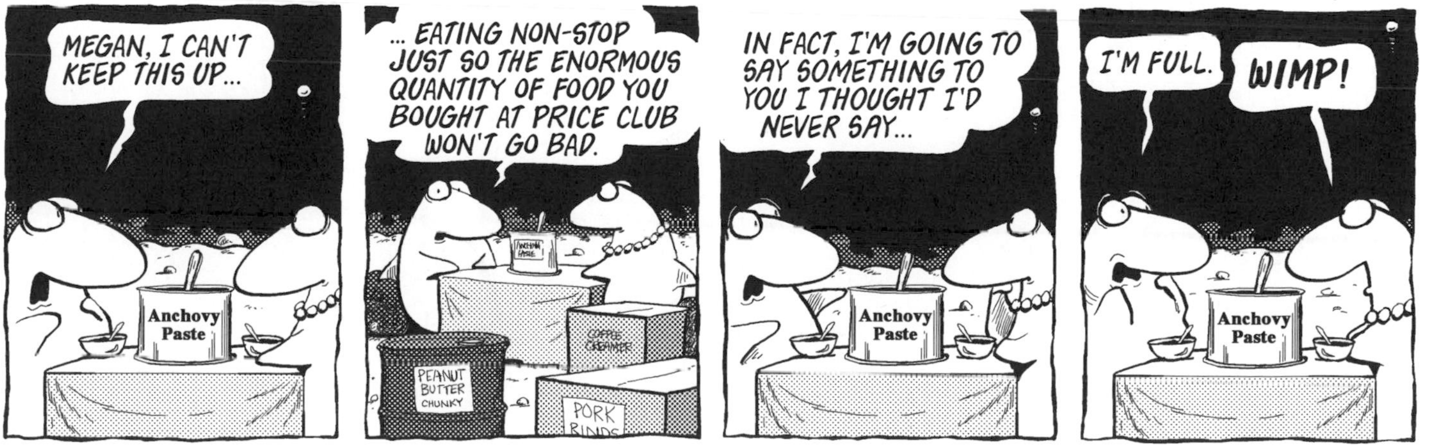
MEGAN, I CAN'T KEEP THIS UP...
Anchovy Paste
... EATING NON-STOP JUST SO THE ENORMOUS QUANTITY OF FOOD YOU BOUGHT AT PRICE CLUB WON'T GO BAD.
PEANUT BUTTER CHUNKY
IN FACT, I'M GOING TO SAY SOMETHING TO YOU I THOUGHT I'D NEVER SAY...
Anchovy Paste
I'M FULL.
WIMP!
Anchovy Paste

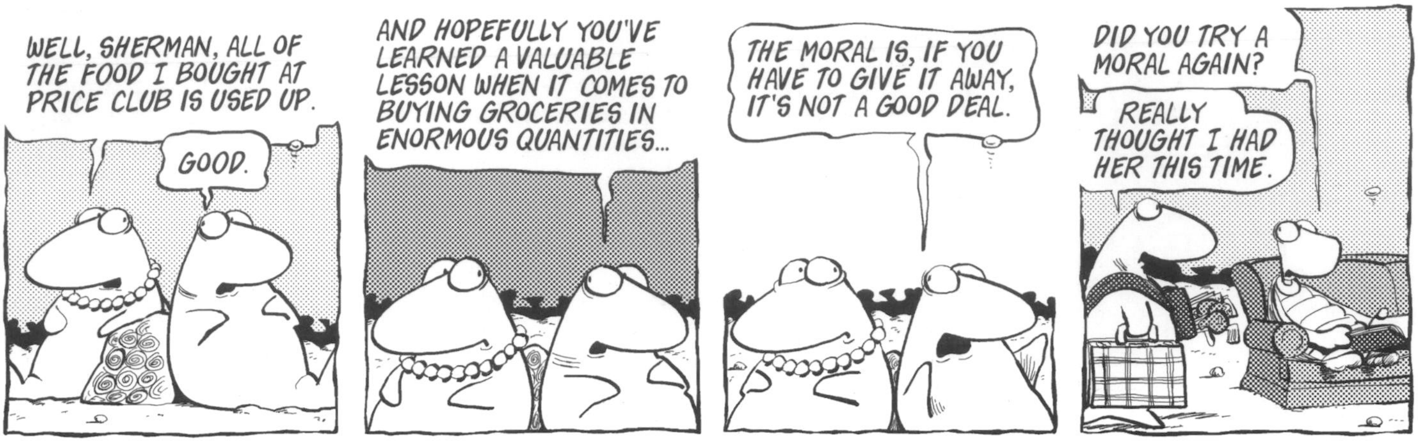
WELL, SHERMAN, ALL OF THE FOOD I BOUGHT AT PRICE CLUB IS USED UP.
GOOD.
AND HOPEFULLY YOU'VE LEARNED A VALUABLE LESSON WHEN IT COMES TO BUYING GROCERIES IN ENORMOUS QUANTITIES...
THE MORAL IS, IF YOU HAVE TO GIVE IT AWAY, IT'S NOT A GOOD DEAL.
DID YOU TRY A MORAL AGAIN?
REALLY THOUGHT I HAD HER THIS TIME.

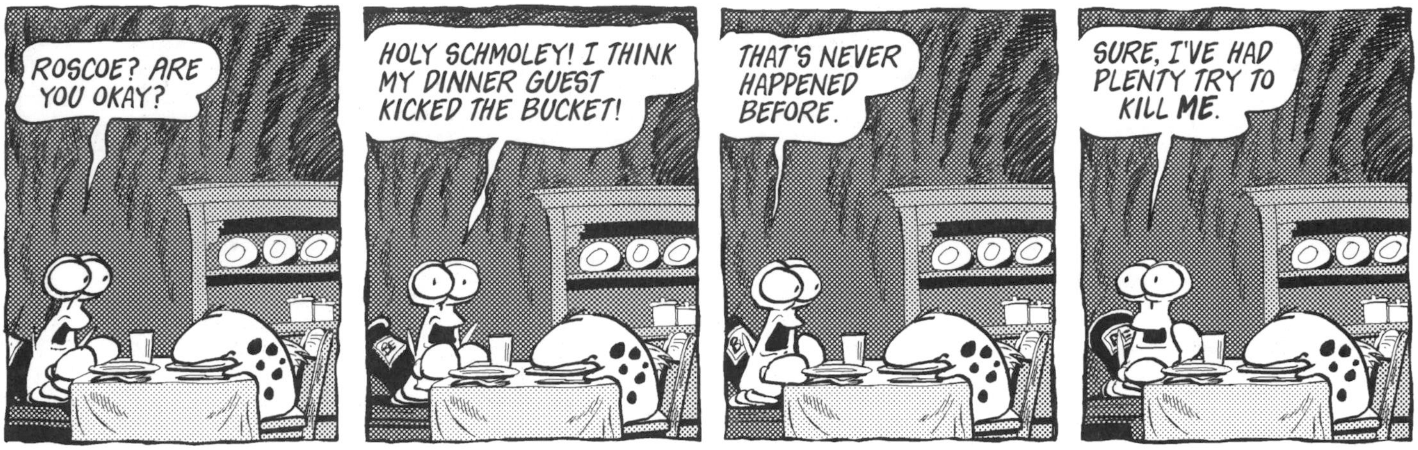
ROSCOE? ARE YOU OKAY?
HOLY SCHMOLEY! I THINK MY DINNER GUEST KICKED THE BUCKET!
THAT'S NEVER HAPPENED BEFORE.
SURE, I'VE HAD PLENTY TRY TO KILL **ME**.

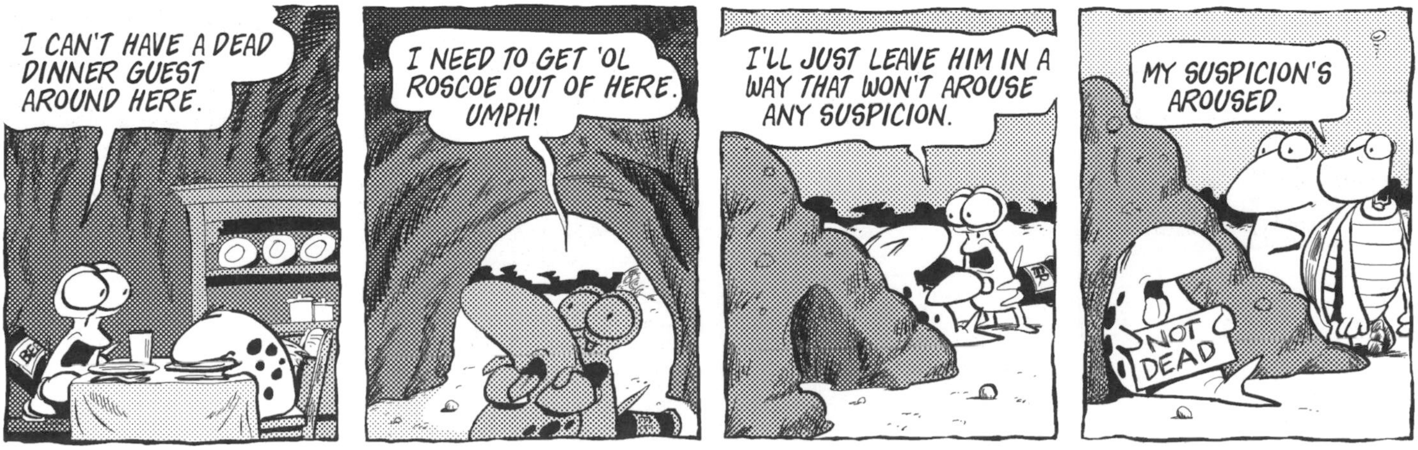
I CAN'T HAVE A DEAD DINNER GUEST AROUND HERE.
I NEED TO GET 'OL ROSCOE OUT OF HERE. UMPH!
I'LL JUST LEAVE HIM IN A WAY THAT WON'T AROUSE ANY SUSPICION.
MY SUSPICION'S AROUSED.
NOT DEAD

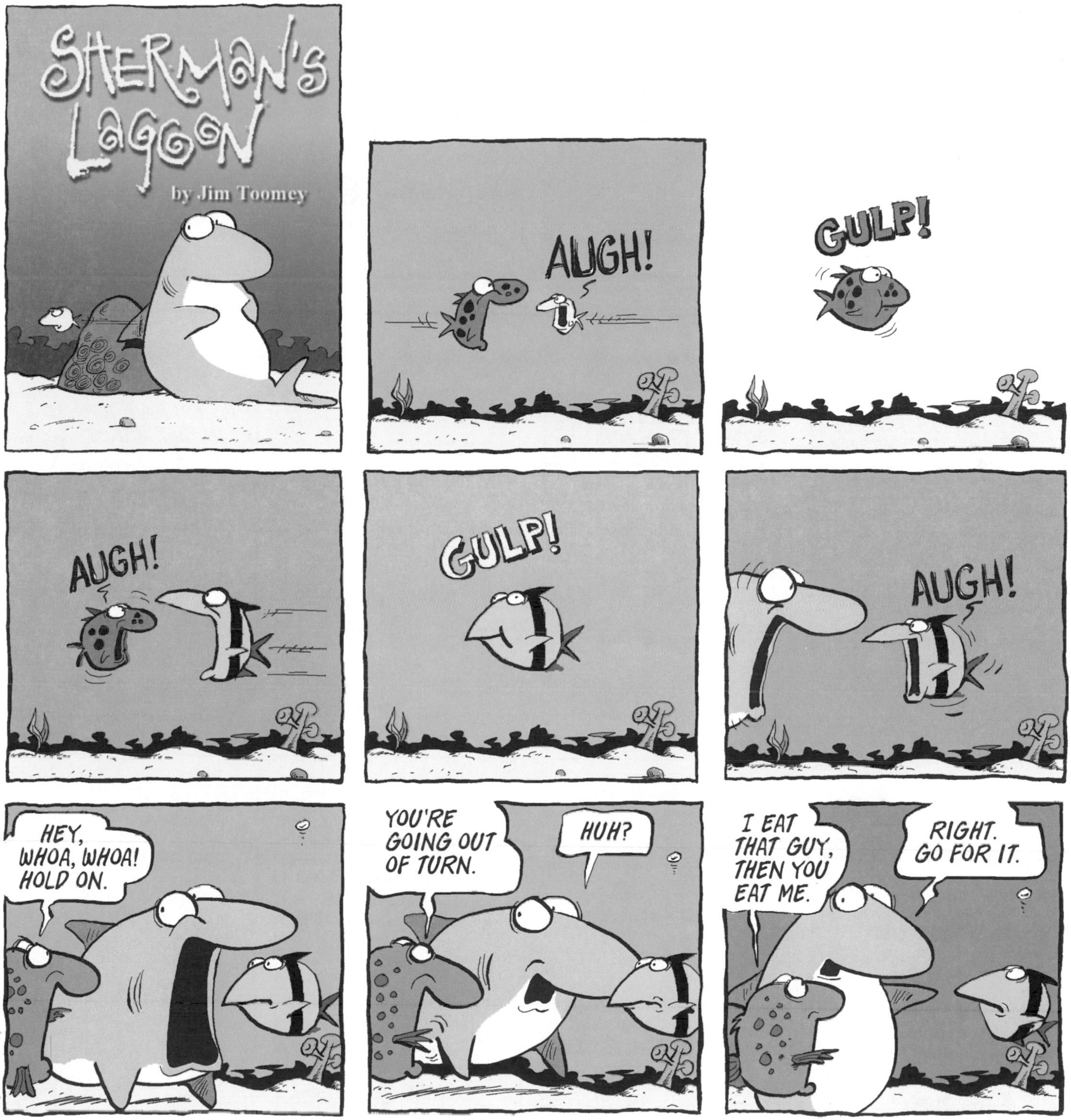
SHERMAN'S LAGOON
by Jim Toomey
AUGH!
GULP!
AUGH!
GULP!
AUGH!
HEY, WHOA, WHOA! HOLD ON.
YOU'RE GOING OUT OF TURN.
HUH?
I EAT THAT GUY, THEN YOU EAT ME.
RIGHT. GO FOR IT.

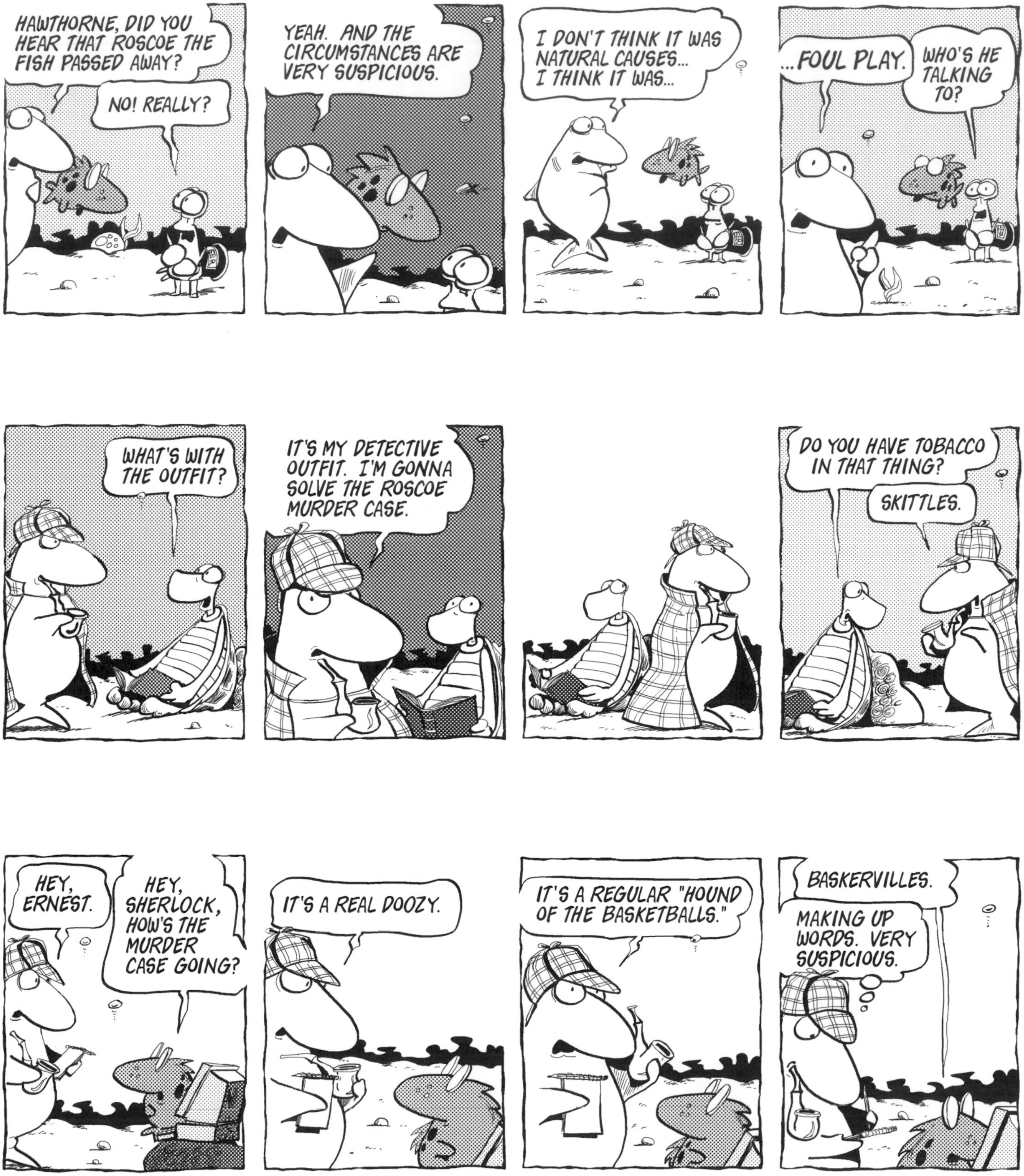

HAWTHORNE, DID YOU HEAR THAT ROSCOE THE FISH PASSED AWAY?
NO! REALLY?
YEAH. AND THE CIRCUMSTANCES ARE VERY SUSPICIOUS.
I DON'T THINK IT WAS NATURAL CAUSES... I THINK IT WAS...
...FOUL PLAY.
WHO'S HE TALKING TO?
WHAT'S WITH THE OUTFIT?
IT'S MY DETECTIVE OUTFIT. I'M GONNA SOLVE THE ROSCOE MURDER CASE.
DO YOU HAVE TOBACCO IN THAT THING?
SKITTLES.
HEY, ERNEST.
HEY, SHERLOCK, HOW'S THE MURDER CASE GOING?
IT'S A REAL DOOZY.
IT'S A REGULAR "HOUND OF THE BASKETBALLS."
BASKERVILLES.
MAKING UP WORDS. VERY SUSPICIOUS.

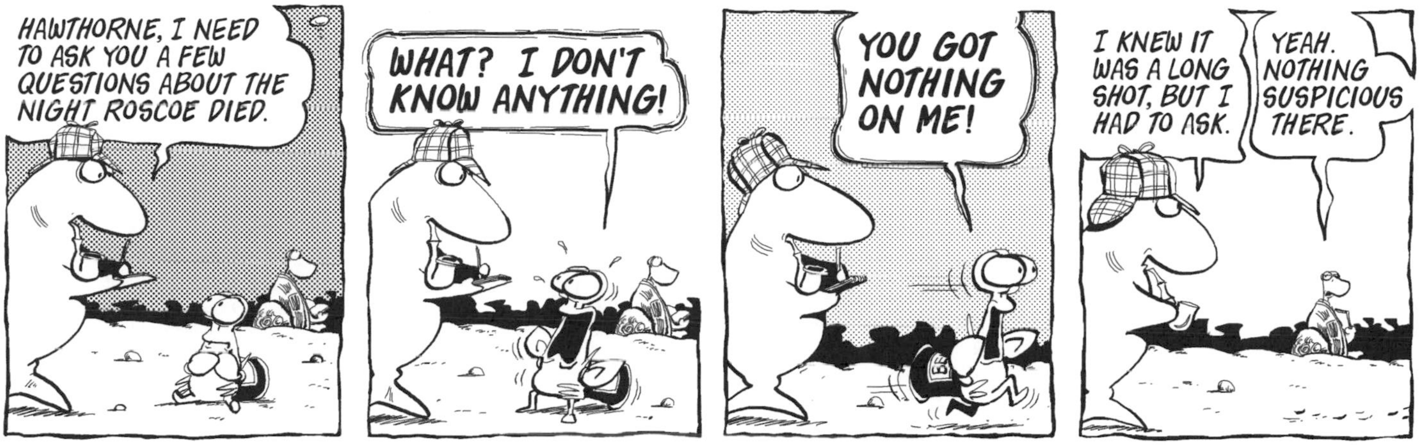
HAWTHORNE, I NEED TO ASK YOU A FEW QUESTIONS ABOUT THE NIGHT ROSCOE DIED.
WHAT? I DON'T KNOW ANYTHING!
YOU GOT NOTHING ON ME!
I KNEW IT WAS A LONG SHOT, BUT I HAD TO ASK.
YEAH. NOTHING SUSPICIOUS THERE.

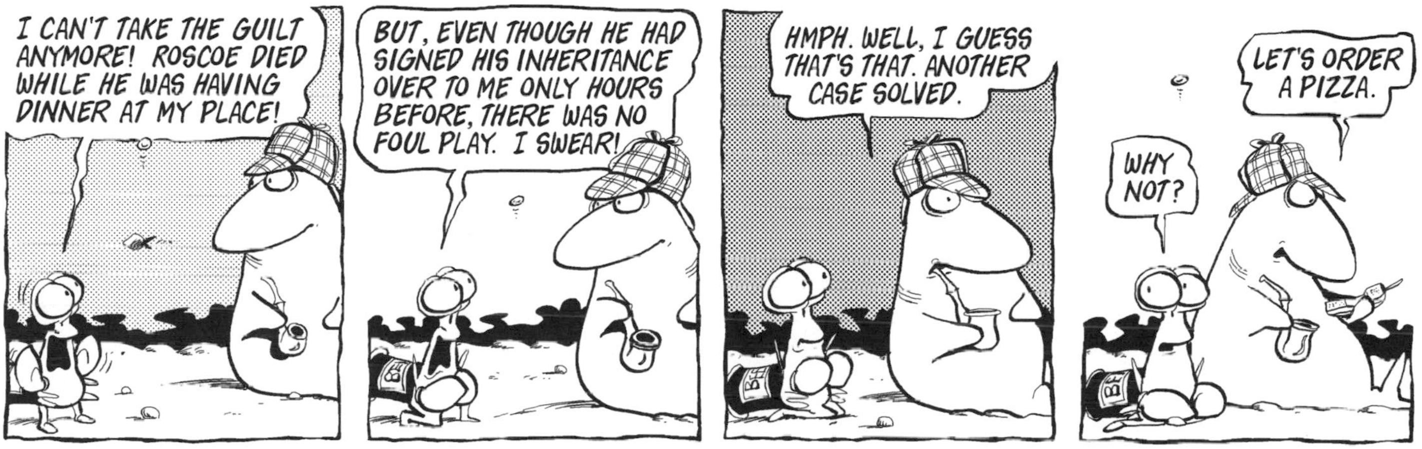
I CAN'T TAKE THE GUILT ANYMORE! ROSCOE DIED WHILE HE WAS HAVING DINNER AT MY PLACE!
BUT, EVEN THOUGH HE HAD SIGNED HIS INHERITANCE OVER TO ME ONLY HOURS BEFORE, THERE WAS NO FOUL PLAY. I SWEAR!
HMPH. WELL, I GUESS THAT'S THAT. ANOTHER CASE SOLVED.
LET'S ORDER A PIZZA.
WHY NOT?

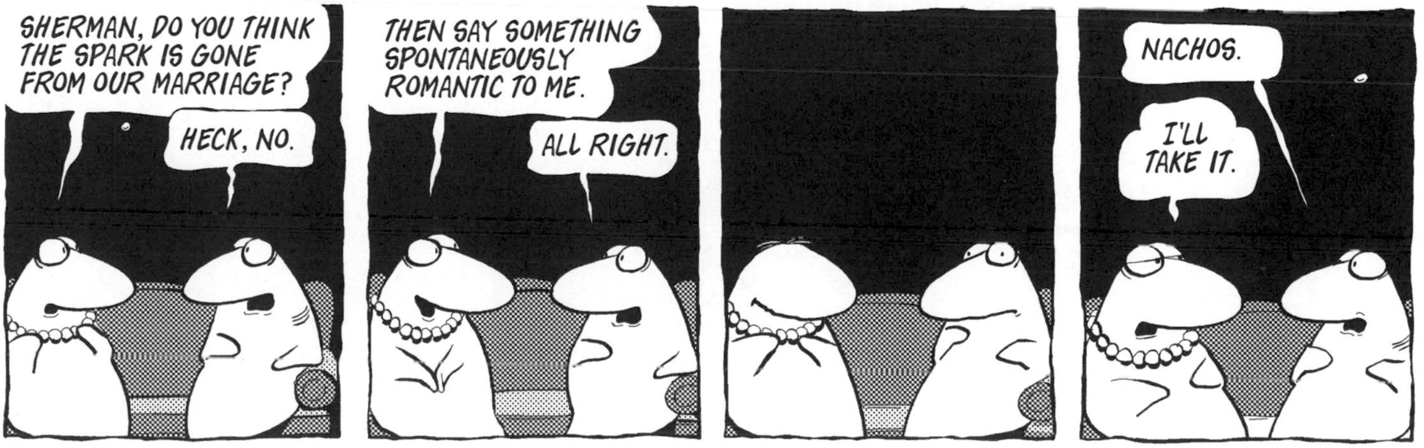
SHERMAN, DO YOU THINK THE SPARK IS GONE FROM OUR MARRIAGE?
HECK, NO.
THEN SAY SOMETHING SPONTANEOUSLY ROMANTIC TO ME.
ALL RIGHT.
NACHOS.
I'LL TAKE IT.

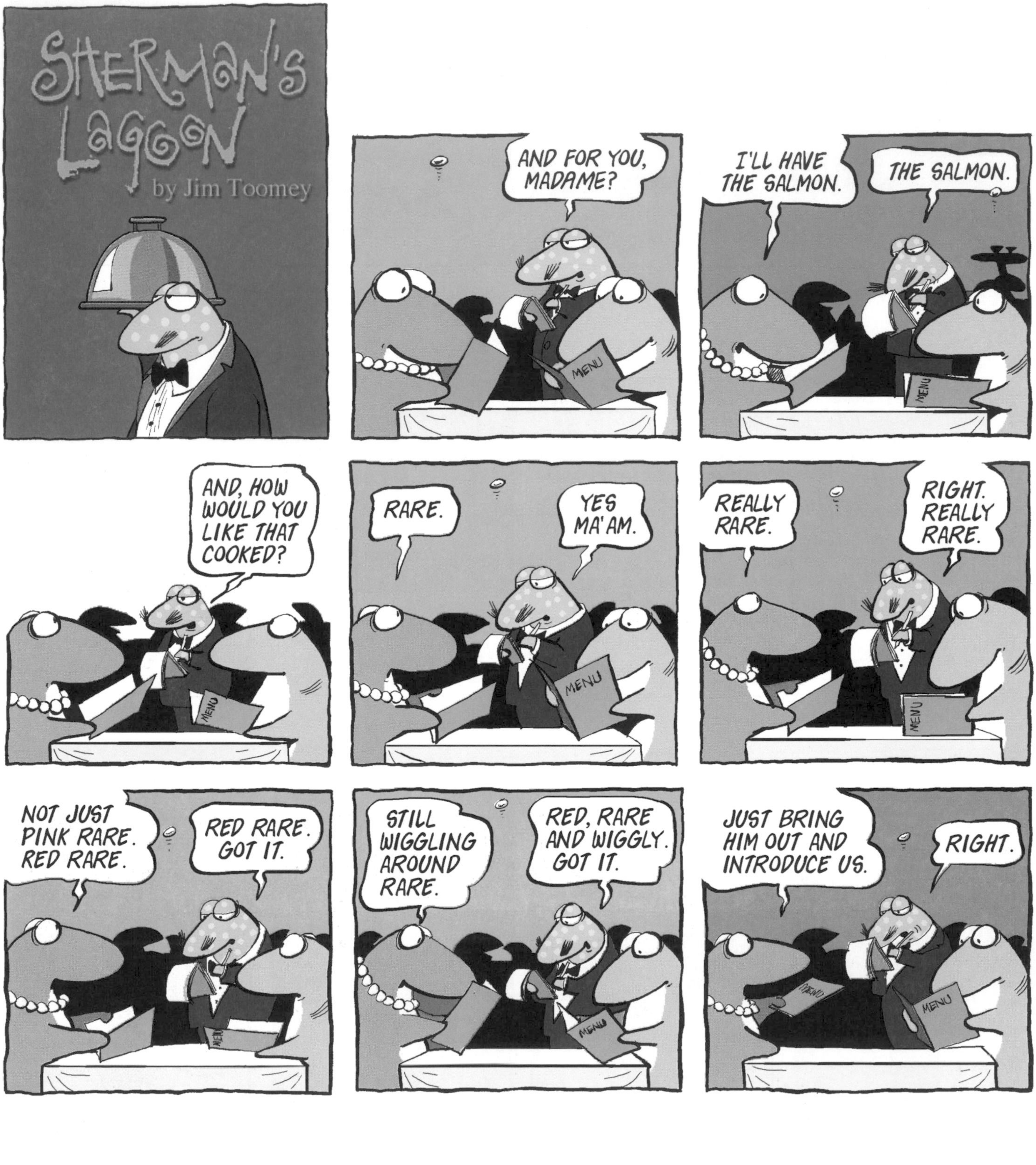
SHERMAN'S LAGOON
by Jim Toomey
AND FOR YOU, MADAME?
I'LL HAVE THE SALMON.
THE SALMON.
MENU
AND, HOW WOULD YOU LIKE THAT COOKED?
RARE.
YES MA'AM.
REALLY RARE.
RIGHT. REALLY RARE.
NOT JUST PINK RARE. RED RARE.
RED RARE. GOT IT.
STILL WIGGLING AROUND RARE.
RED, RARE AND WIGGLY. GOT IT.
JUST BRING HIM OUT AND INTRODUCE US.
RIGHT.

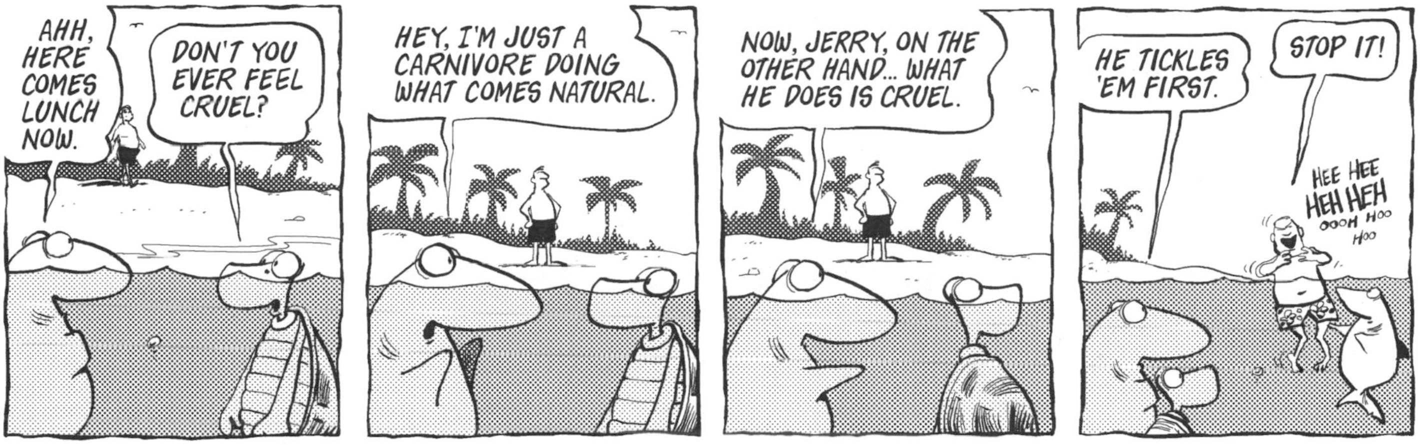
AHH, HERE COMES LUNCH NOW.
DON'T YOU EVER FEEL CRUEL?
HEY, I'M JUST A CARNIVORE DOING WHAT COMES NATURAL.
NOW, JERRY, ON THE OTHER HAND... WHAT HE DOES IS CRUEL.
HE TICKLES 'EM FIRST.
STOP IT!
HEE HEE HEH HEH OOOH HOO HOO

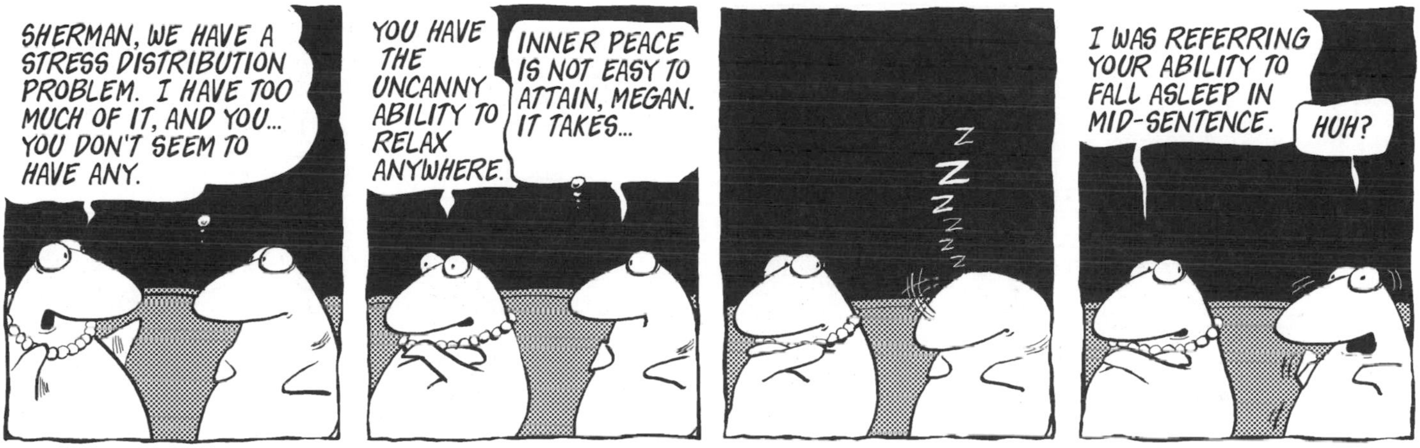
SHERMAN, WE HAVE A STRESS DISTRIBUTION PROBLEM. I HAVE TOO MUCH OF IT, AND YOU... YOU DON'T SEEM TO HAVE ANY.
YOU HAVE THE UNCANNY ABILITY TO RELAX ANYWHERE.
INNER PEACE IS NOT EASY TO ATTAIN, MEGAN. IT TAKES...
Z Z Z Z Z Z
I WAS REFERRING YOUR ABILITY TO FALL ASLEEP IN MID-SENTENCE.
HUH?

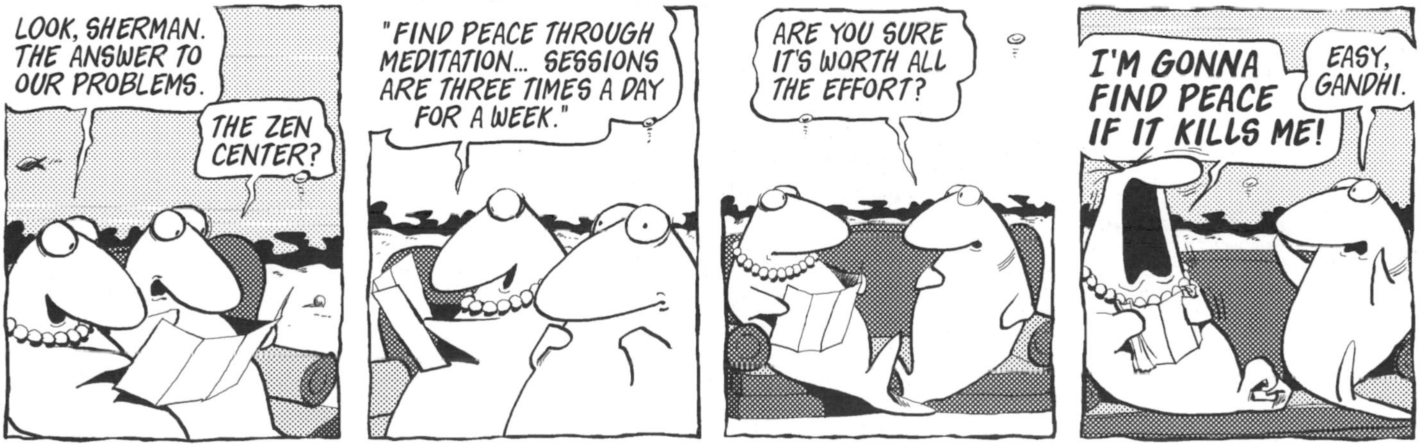
LOOK, SHERMAN. THE ANSWER TO OUR PROBLEMS.
THE ZEN CENTER?
"FIND PEACE THROUGH MEDITATION... SESSIONS ARE THREE TIMES A DAY FOR A WEEK."
ARE YOU SURE IT'S WORTH ALL THE EFFORT?
I'M GONNA FIND PEACE IF IT KILLS ME!
EASY, GANDHI.

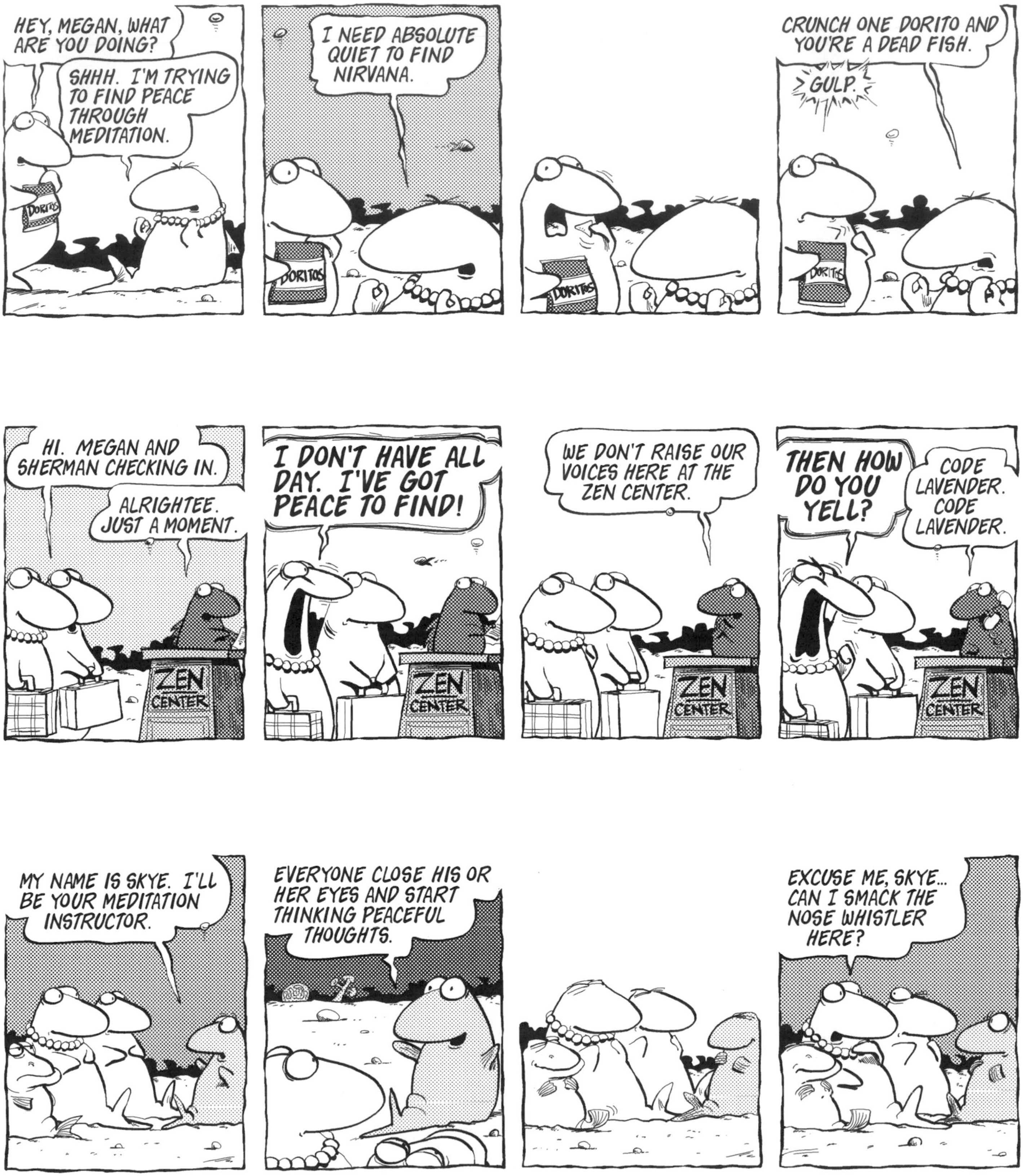
HEY, MEGAN, WHAT ARE YOU DOING?
SHHH. I'M TRYING TO FIND PEACE THROUGH MEDITATION.
I NEED ABSOLUTE QUIET TO FIND NIRVANA.
CRUNCH ONE DORITO AND YOU'RE A DEAD FISH.
GULP.
HI. MEGAN AND SHERMAN CHECKING IN.
ALRIGHTEE. JUST A MOMENT.
I DON'T HAVE ALL DAY. I'VE GOT PEACE TO FIND!
WE DON'T RAISE OUR VOICES HERE AT THE ZEN CENTER.
THEN HOW DO YOU YELL?
CODE LAVENDER. CODE LAVENDER.
ZEN CENTER
MY NAME IS SKYE. I'LL BE YOUR MEDITATION INSTRUCTOR.
EVERYONE CLOSE HIS OR HER EYES AND START THINKING PEACEFUL THOUGHTS.
EXCUSE ME, SKYE... CAN I SMACK THE NOSE WHISTLER HERE?

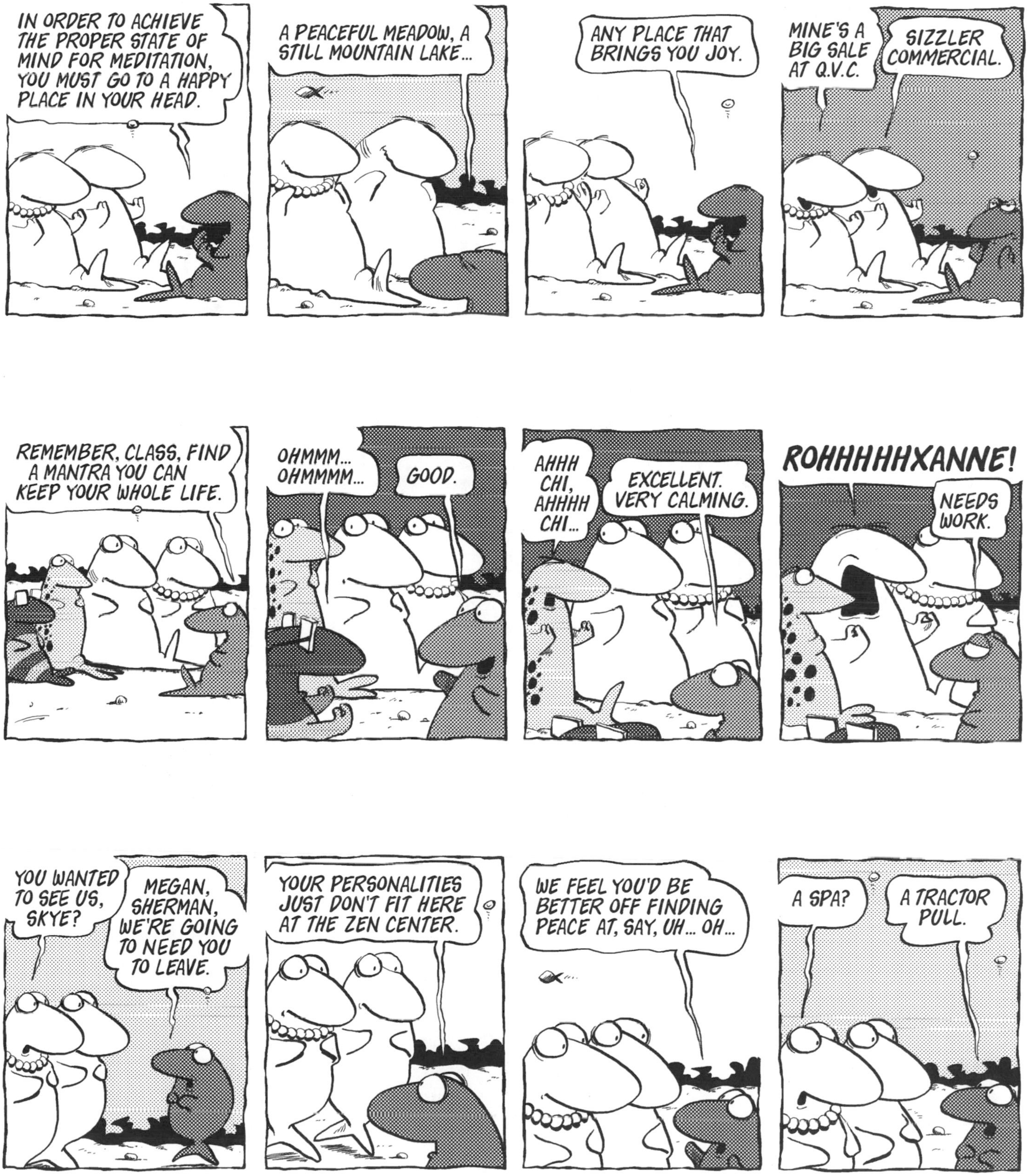
IN ORDER TO ACHIEVE THE PROPER STATE OF MIND FOR MEDITATION, YOU MUST GO TO A HAPPY PLACE IN YOUR HEAD.
A PEACEFUL MEADOW, A STILL MOUNTAIN LAKE...
ANY PLACE THAT BRINGS YOU JOY.
MINE'S A BIG SALE AT Q.V.C.
SIZZLER COMMERCIAL.
REMEMBER, CLASS, FIND A MANTRA YOU CAN KEEP YOUR WHOLE LIFE.
OHMMM... OHMMMM...
GOOD.
AHHH CHI, AHHHH CHI...
EXCELLENT. VERY CALMING.
ROHHHHHXANNE!
NEEDS WORK.
YOU WANTED TO SEE US, SKYE?
MEGAN, SHERMAN, WE'RE GOING TO NEED YOU TO LEAVE.
YOUR PERSONALITIES JUST DON'T FIT HERE AT THE ZEN CENTER.
WE FEEL YOU'D BE BETTER OFF FINDING PEACE AT, SAY, UH... OH...
A SPA?
A TRACTOR PULL.

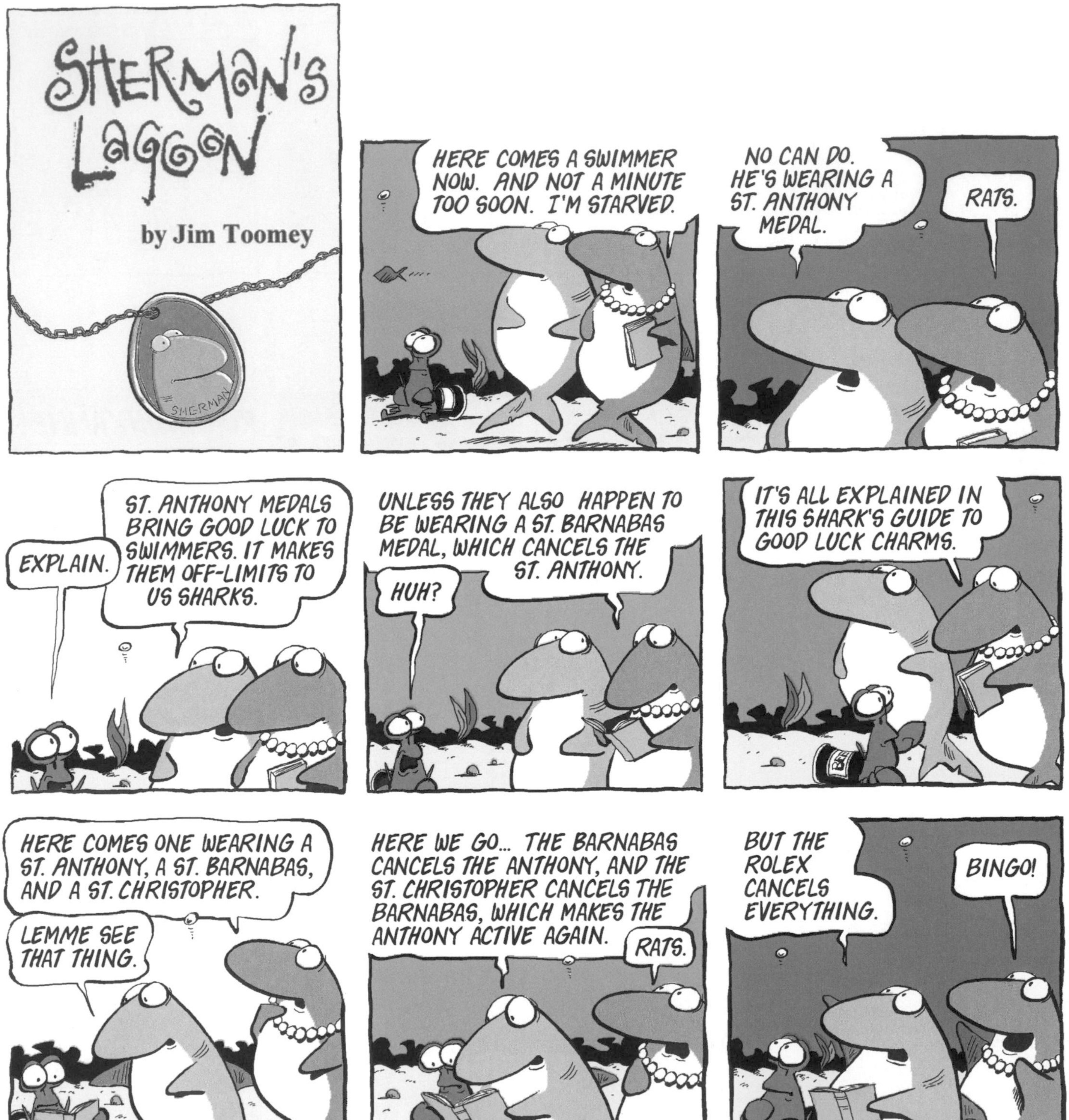
SHERMAN'S LAGOON
by Jim Toomey
SHERMAN
HERE COMES A SWIMMER NOW. AND NOT A MINUTE TOO SOON. I'M STARVED.
NO CAN DO. HE'S WEARING A ST. ANTHONY MEDAL.
RATS.
EXPLAIN.
ST. ANTHONY MEDALS BRING GOOD LUCK TO SWIMMERS. IT MAKES THEM OFF-LIMITS TO US SHARKS.
UNLESS THEY ALSO HAPPEN TO BE WEARING A ST. BARNABAS MEDAL, WHICH CANCELS THE ST. ANTHONY.
HUH?
IT'S ALL EXPLAINED IN THIS SHARK'S GUIDE TO GOOD LUCK CHARMS.
HERE COMES ONE WEARING A ST. ANTHONY, A ST. BARNABAS, AND A ST. CHRISTOPHER.
LEMME SEE THAT THING.
HERE WE GO... THE BARNABAS CANCELS THE ANTHONY, AND THE ST. CHRISTOPHER CANCELS THE BARNABAS, WHICH MAKES THE ANTHONY ACTIVE AGAIN.
RATS.
BUT THE ROLEX CANCELS EVERYTHING.
BINGO!

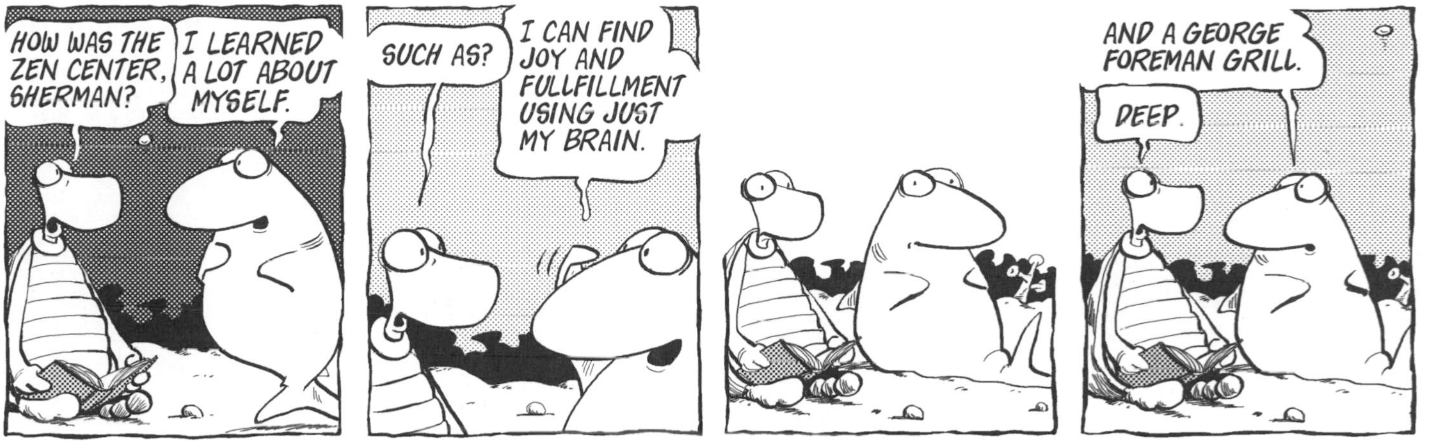
HOW WAS THE ZEN CENTER, SHERMAN?
I LEARNED A LOT ABOUT MYSELF.
SUCH AS?
I CAN FIND JOY AND FULLFILLMENT USING JUST MY BRAIN.
AND A GEORGE FOREMAN GRILL.
DEEP.

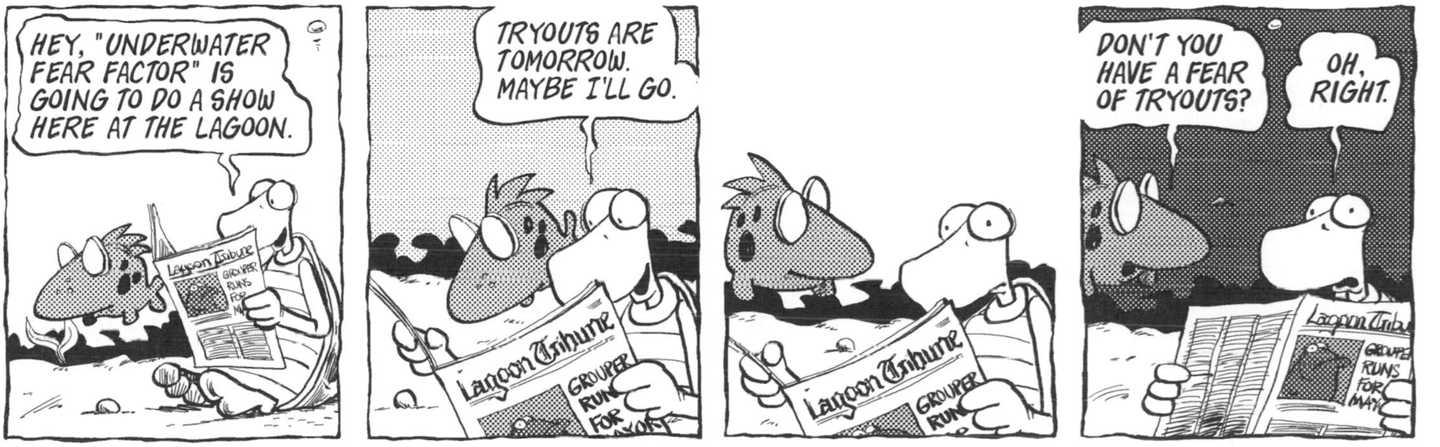
HEY, "UNDERWATER FEAR FACTOR" IS GOING TO DO A SHOW HERE AT THE LAGOON.
TRYOUTS ARE TOMORROW. MAYBE I'LL GO.
DON'T YOU HAVE A FEAR OF TRYOUTS?
OH, RIGHT.
Lagoon Tribune
GROUPER RUNS FOR

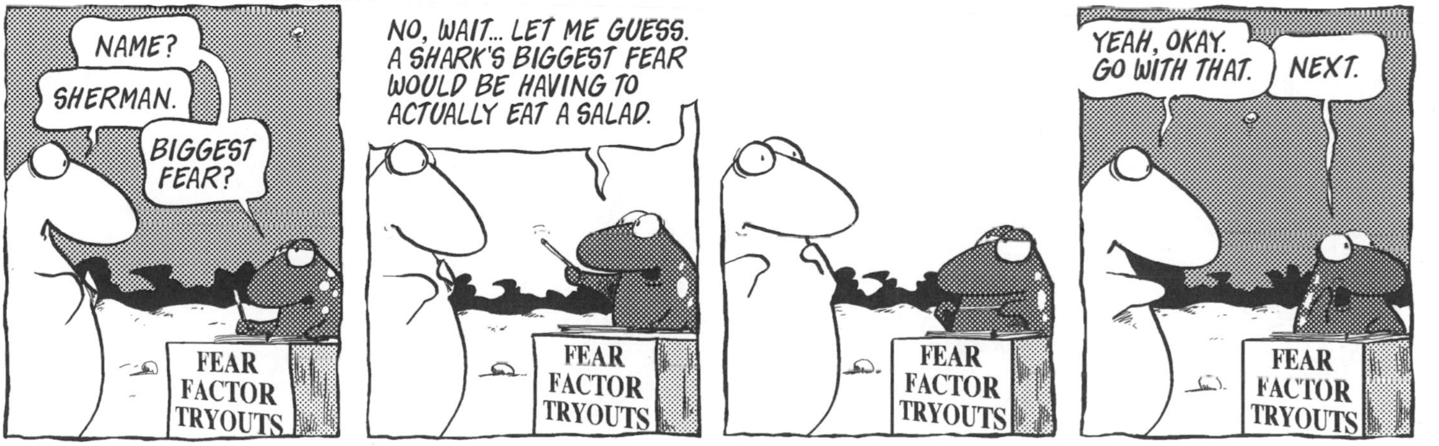
NAME?
SHERMAN.
BIGGEST FEAR?
NO, WAIT... LET ME GUESS. A SHARK'S BIGGEST FEAR WOULD BE HAVING TO ACTUALLY EAT A SALAD.
YEAH, OKAY. GO WITH THAT.
NEXT.
FEAR FACTOR TRYOUTS

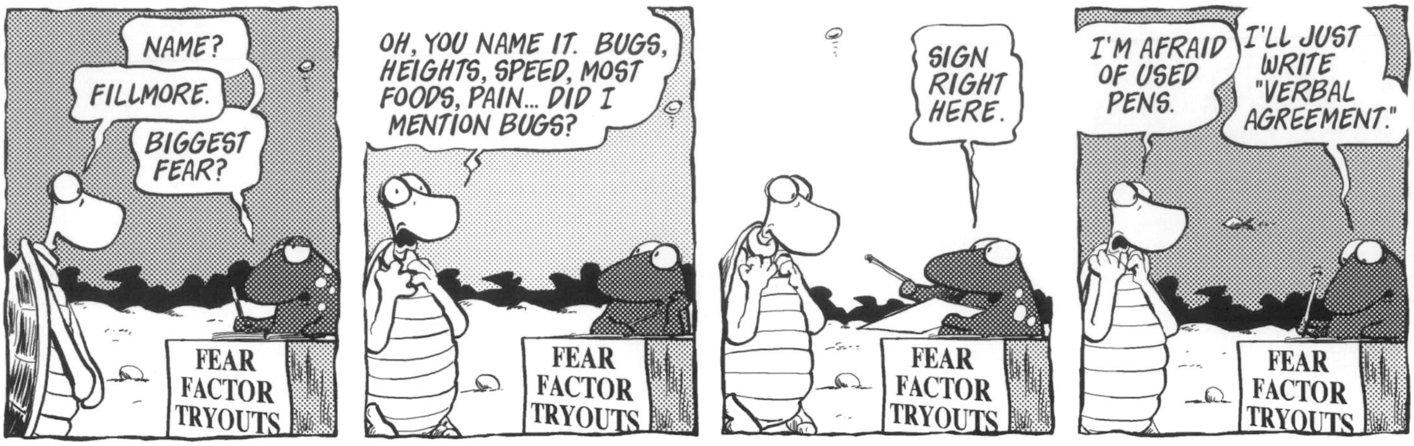
NAME?
FILLMORE.
BIGGEST FEAR?
FEAR FACTOR TRYOUTS
OH, YOU NAME IT. BUGS, HEIGHTS, SPEED, MOST FOODS, PAIN... DID I MENTION BUGS?
FEAR FACTOR TRYOUTS
SIGN RIGHT HERE.
FEAR FACTOR TRYOUTS
I'M AFRAID OF USED PENS.
I'LL JUST WRITE "VERBAL AGREEMENT."
FEAR FACTOR TRYOUTS

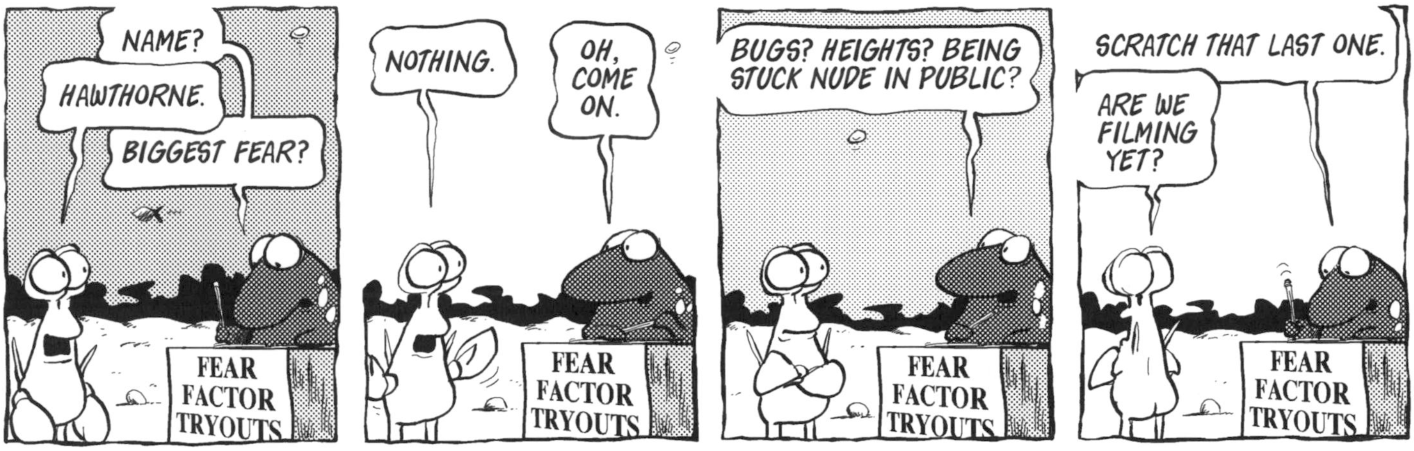
NAME?
HAWTHORNE.
BIGGEST FEAR?
FEAR FACTOR TRYOUTS
NOTHING.
OH, COME ON.
FEAR FACTOR TRYOUTS
BUGS? HEIGHTS? BEING STUCK NUDE IN PUBLIC?
FEAR FACTOR TRYOUTS
SCRATCH THAT LAST ONE.
ARE WE FILMING YET?
FEAR FACTOR TRYOUTS

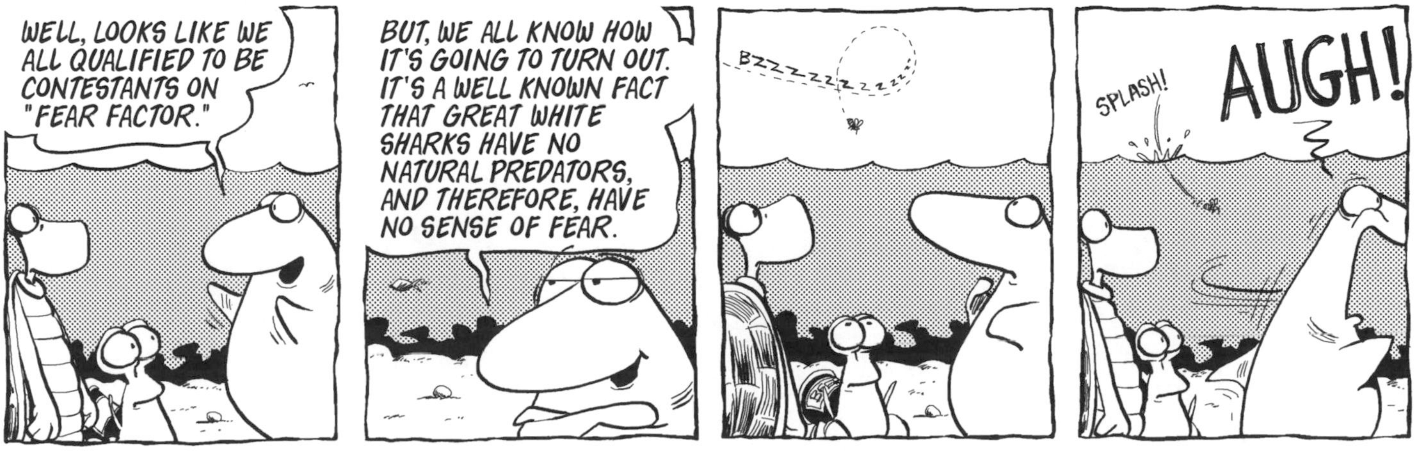
WELL, LOOKS LIKE WE ALL QUALIFIED TO BE CONTESTANTS ON "FEAR FACTOR."
BUT, WE ALL KNOW HOW IT'S GOING TO TURN OUT. IT'S A WELL KNOWN FACT THAT GREAT WHITE SHARKS HAVE NO NATURAL PREDATORS, AND THEREFORE, HAVE NO SENSE OF FEAR.
BZZZZZZZZZZZ
SPLASH!
AUGH!

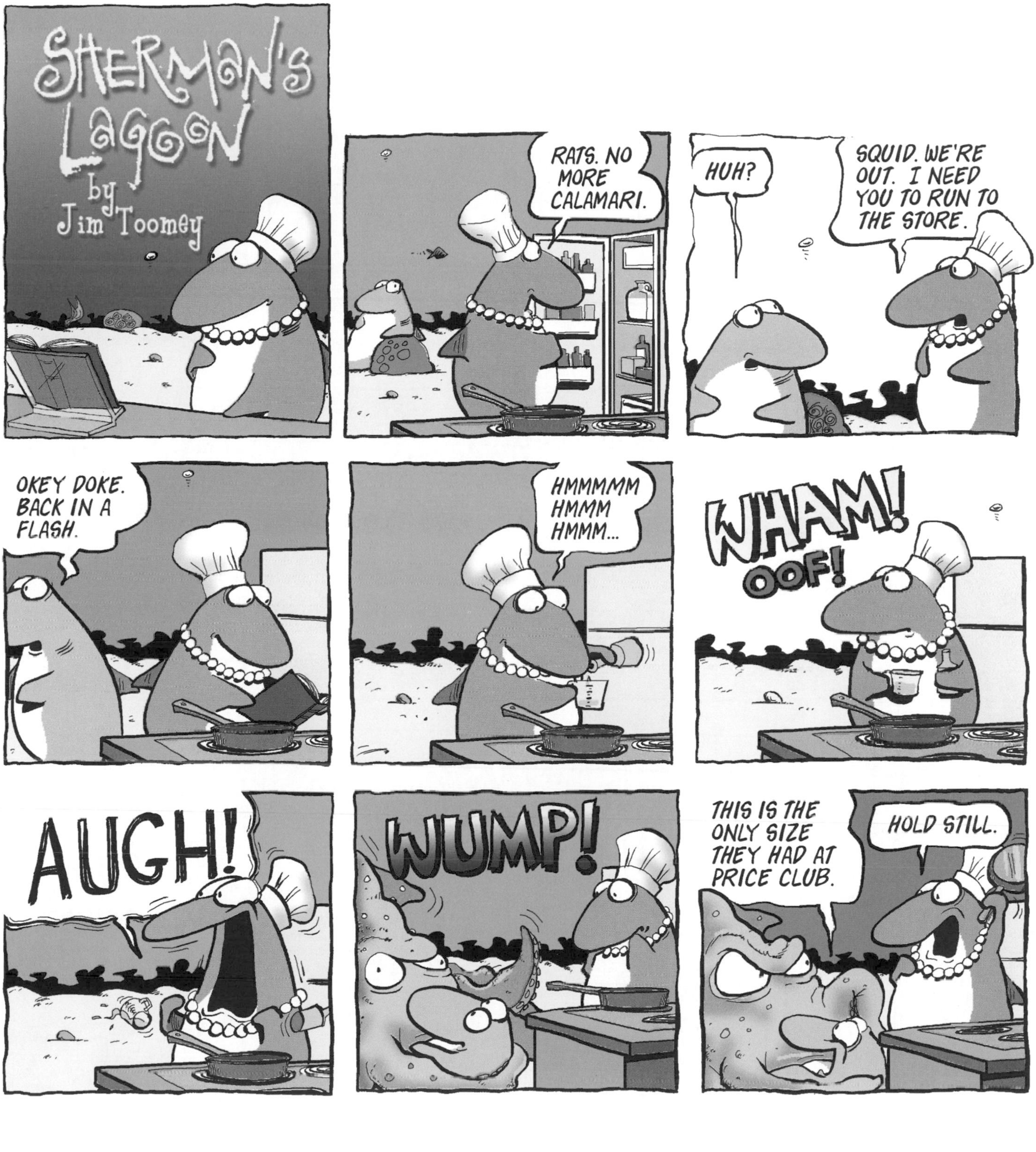
SHERMAN'S LAGOON
by Jim Toomey
RATS. NO MORE CALAMARI.
HUH?
SQUID. WE'RE OUT. I NEED YOU TO RUN TO THE STORE.
OKEY DOKE. BACK IN A FLASH.
HMMMMM HMMM HMMM...
WHAM!
OOF!
AUGH!
WUMP!
THIS IS THE ONLY SIZE THEY HAD AT PRICE CLUB.
HOLD STILL.

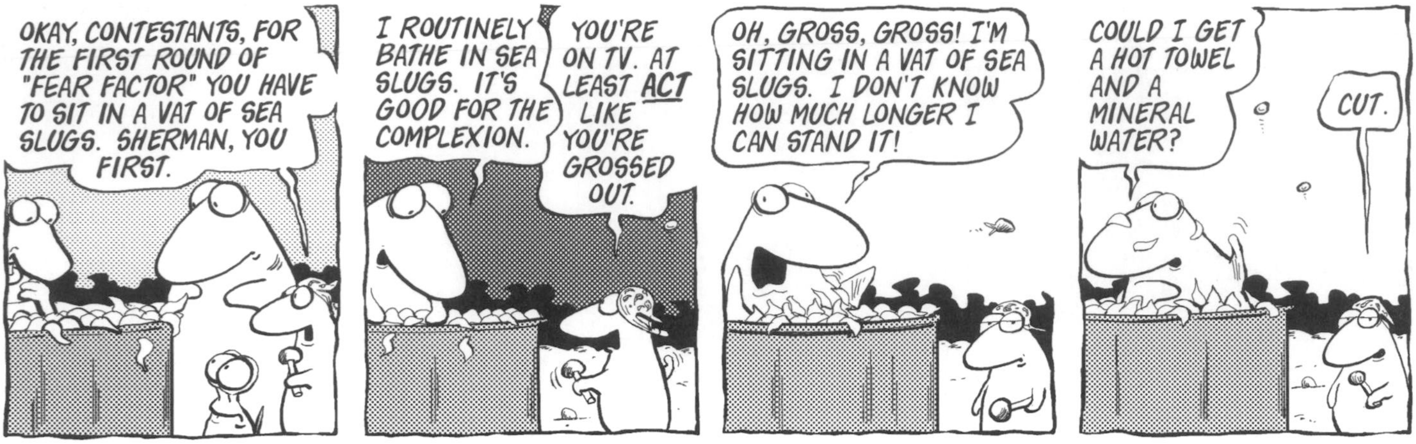
OKAY, CONTESTANTS, FOR THE FIRST ROUND OF "FEAR FACTOR" YOU HAVE TO SIT IN A VAT OF SEA SLUGS. SHERMAN, YOU FIRST.
I ROUTINELY BATHE IN SEA SLUGS. IT'S GOOD FOR THE COMPLEXION.
YOU'RE ON TV. AT LEAST ACT LIKE YOU'RE GROSSED OUT.
OH, GROSS, GROSS! I'M SITTING IN A VAT OF SEA SLUGS. I DON'T KNOW HOW MUCH LONGER I CAN STAND IT!
COULD I GET A HOT TOWEL AND A MINERAL WATER?
CUT.

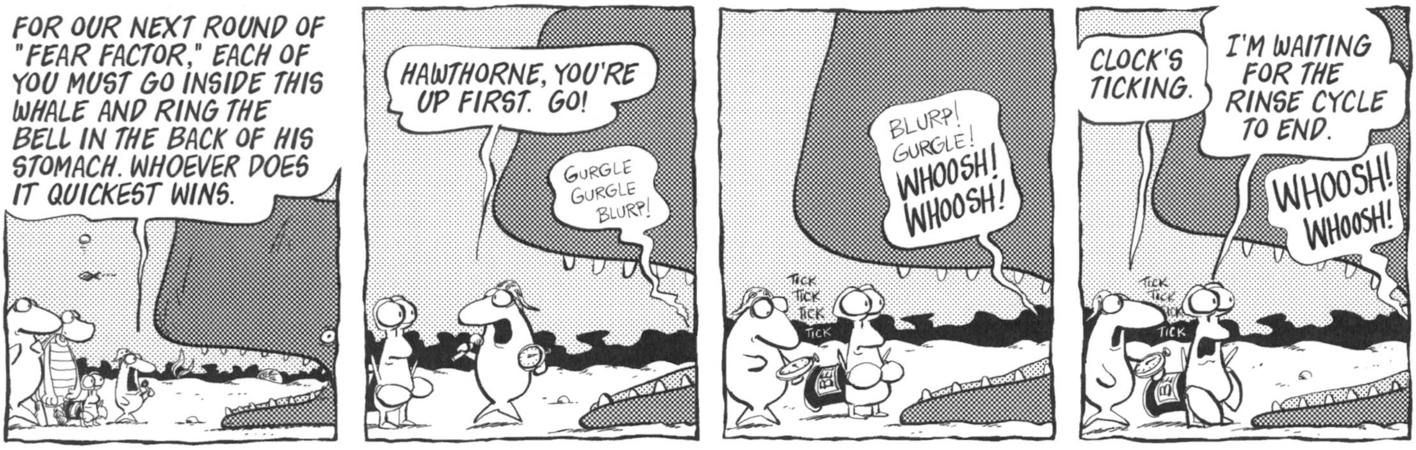
FOR OUR NEXT ROUND OF "FEAR FACTOR," EACH OF YOU MUST GO INSIDE THIS WHALE AND RING THE BELL IN THE BACK OF HIS STOMACH. WHOEVER DOES IT QUICKEST WINS.
HAWTHORNE, YOU'RE UP FIRST. GO!
GURGLE GURGLE BLURP!
TICK TICK TICK TICK
BLURP! GURGLE! WHOOSH! WHOOSH!
CLOCK'S TICKING.
I'M WAITING FOR THE RINSE CYCLE TO END.
WHOOSH! WHOOSH!

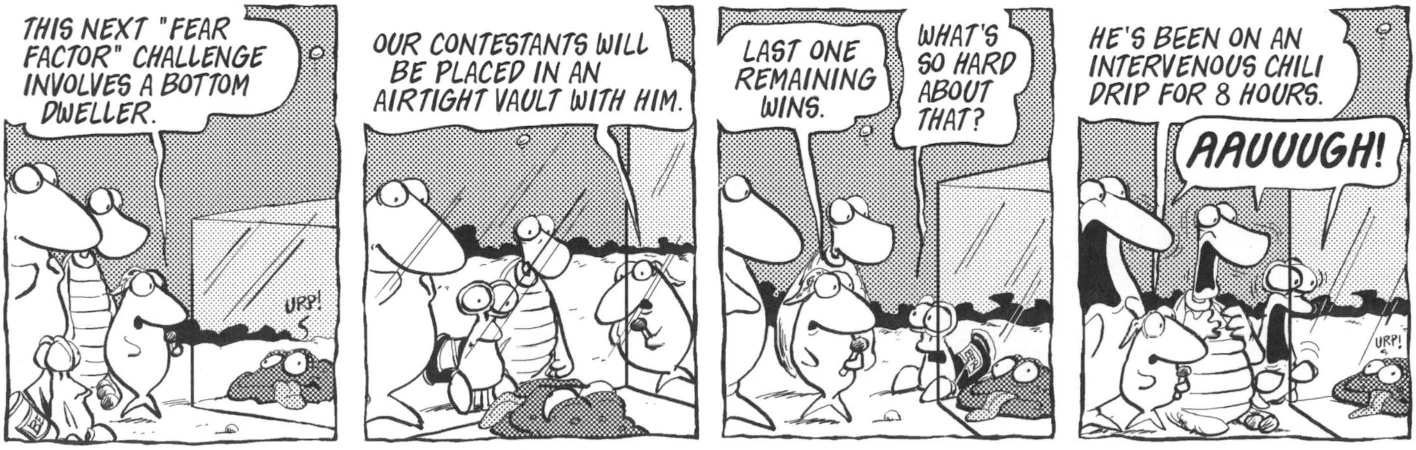
THIS NEXT "FEAR FACTOR" CHALLENGE INVOLVES A BOTTOM DWELLER.
URP!
OUR CONTESTANTS WILL BE PLACED IN AN AIRTIGHT VAULT WITH HIM.
LAST ONE REMAINING WINS.
WHAT'S SO HARD ABOUT THAT?
HE'S BEEN ON AN INTERVENOUS CHILI DRIP FOR 8 HOURS.
AAUUUGH!
URP!

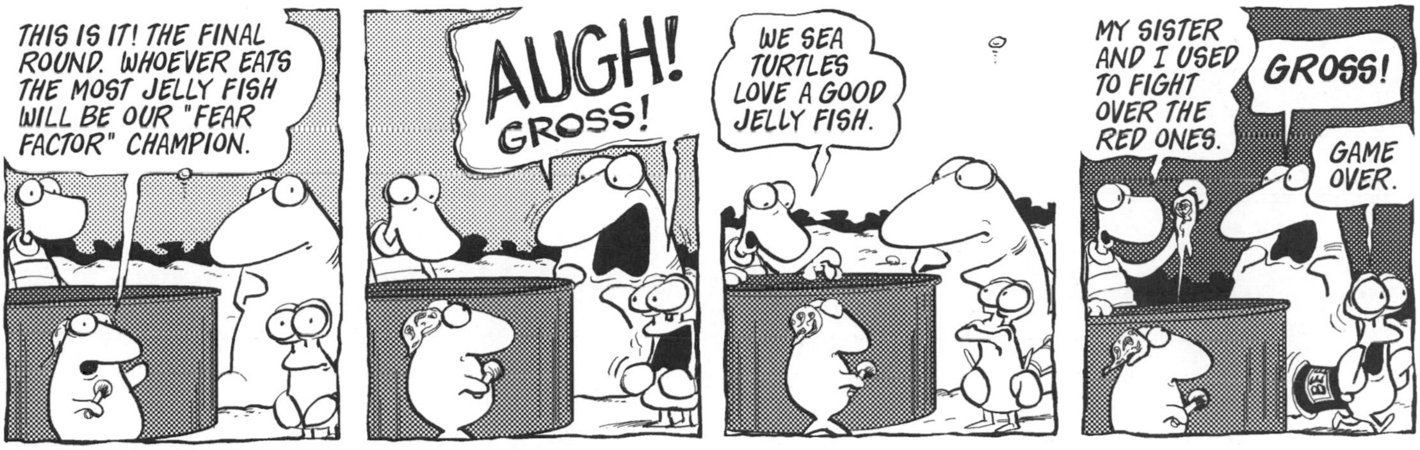
THIS IS IT! THE FINAL ROUND. WHOEVER EATS THE MOST JELLY FISH WILL BE OUR "FEAR FACTOR" CHAMPION.
AUGH! GROSS!
WE SEA TURTLES LOVE A GOOD JELLY FISH.
MY SISTER AND I USED TO FIGHT OVER THE RED ONES.
GROSS!
GAME OVER.

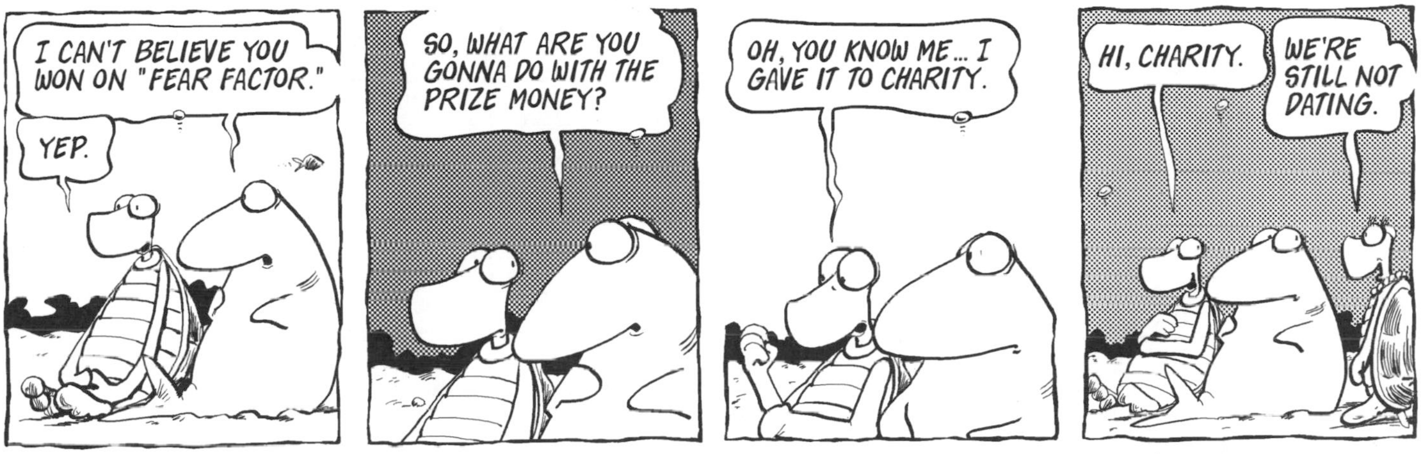
I CAN'T BELIEVE YOU WON ON "FEAR FACTOR."
YEP.
SO, WHAT ARE YOU GONNA DO WITH THE PRIZE MONEY?
OH, YOU KNOW ME... I GAVE IT TO CHARITY.
HI, CHARITY.
WE'RE STILL NOT DATING.

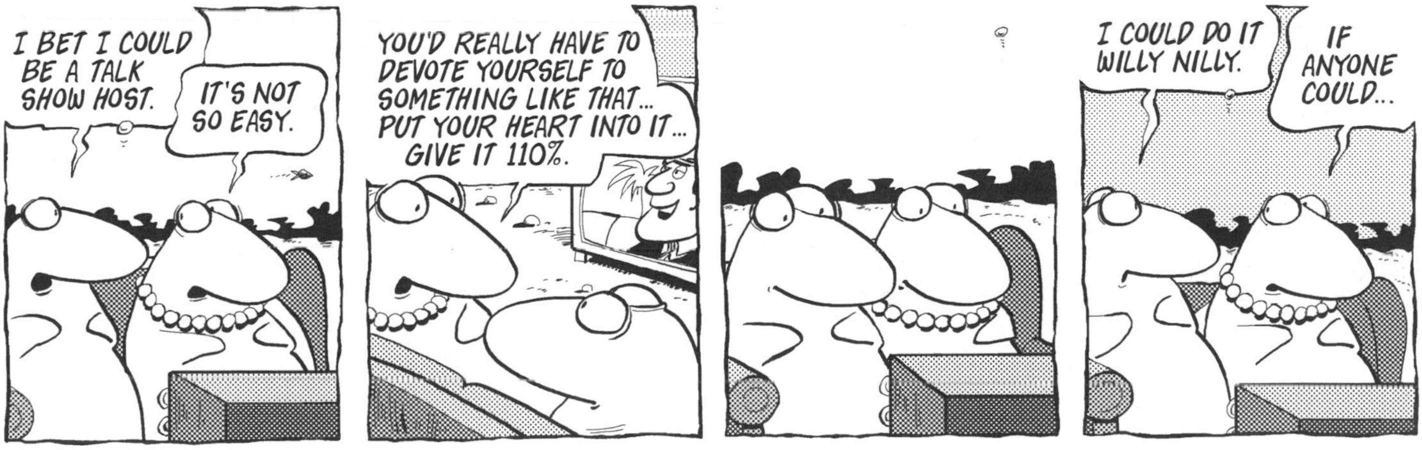
I BET I COULD BE A TALK SHOW HOST.
IT'S NOT SO EASY.
YOU'D REALLY HAVE TO DEVOTE YOURSELF TO SOMETHING LIKE THAT... PUT YOUR HEART INTO IT... GIVE IT 110%.
I COULD DO IT WILLY NILLY.
IF ANYONE COULD...

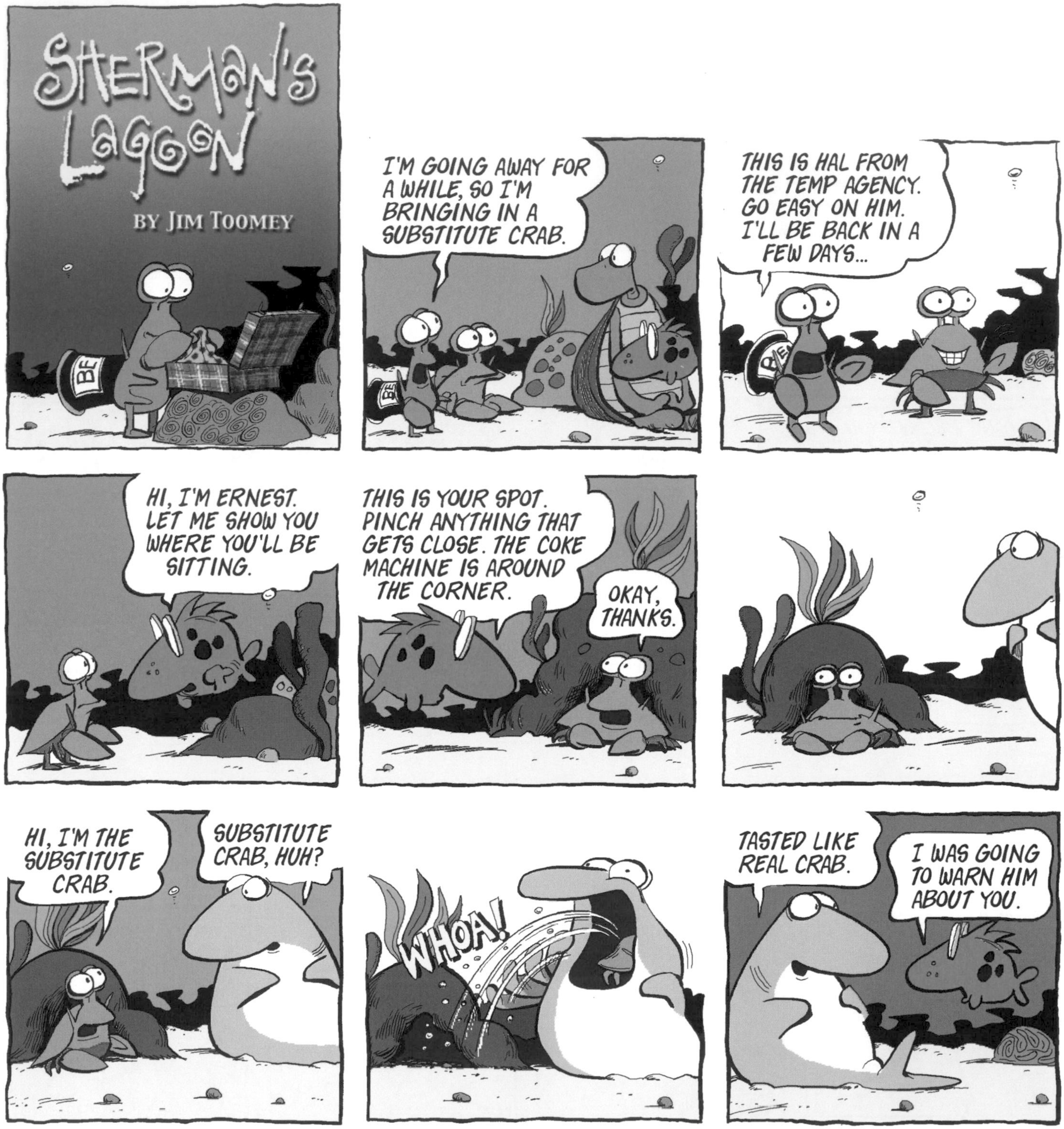
SHERMAN'S LAGOON
BY JIM TOOMEY
I'M GOING AWAY FOR A WHILE, SO I'M BRINGING IN A SUBSTITUTE CRAB.
THIS IS HAL FROM THE TEMP AGENCY. GO EASY ON HIM. I'LL BE BACK IN A FEW DAYS...
HI, I'M ERNEST. LET ME SHOW YOU WHERE YOU'LL BE SITTING.
THIS IS YOUR SPOT. PINCH ANYTHING THAT GETS CLOSE. THE COKE MACHINE IS AROUND THE CORNER.
OKAY, THANKS.
HI, I'M THE SUBSTITUTE CRAB.
SUBSTITUTE CRAB, HUH?
WHOA!
TASTED LIKE REAL CRAB.
I WAS GOING TO WARN HIM ABOUT YOU.

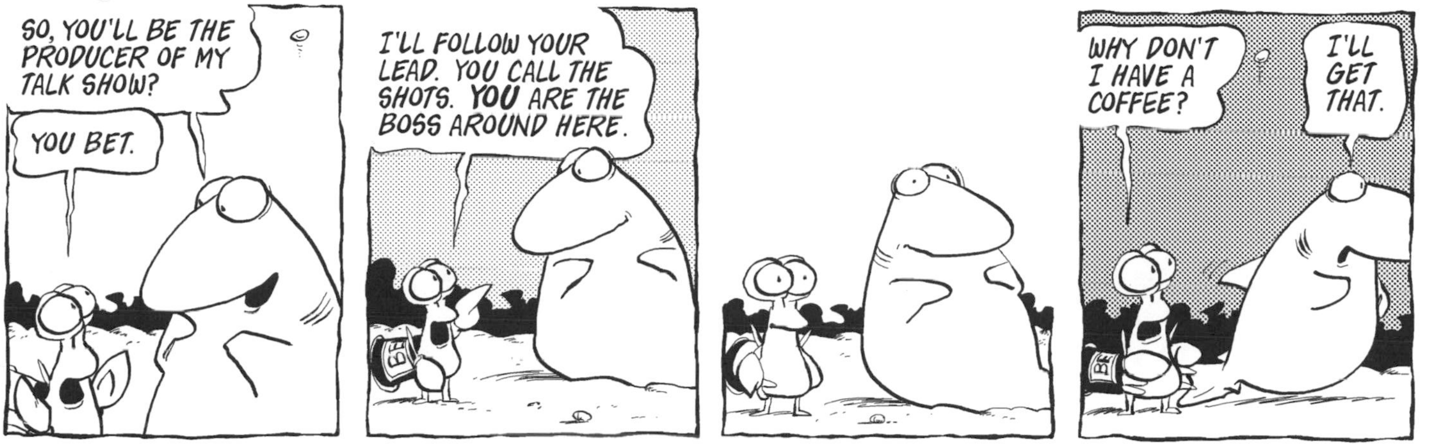
SO, YOU'LL BE THE PRODUCER OF MY TALK SHOW?
YOU BET.
I'LL FOLLOW YOUR LEAD. YOU CALL THE SHOTS. YOU ARE THE BOSS AROUND HERE.
WHY DON'T I HAVE A COFFEE?
I'LL GET THAT.

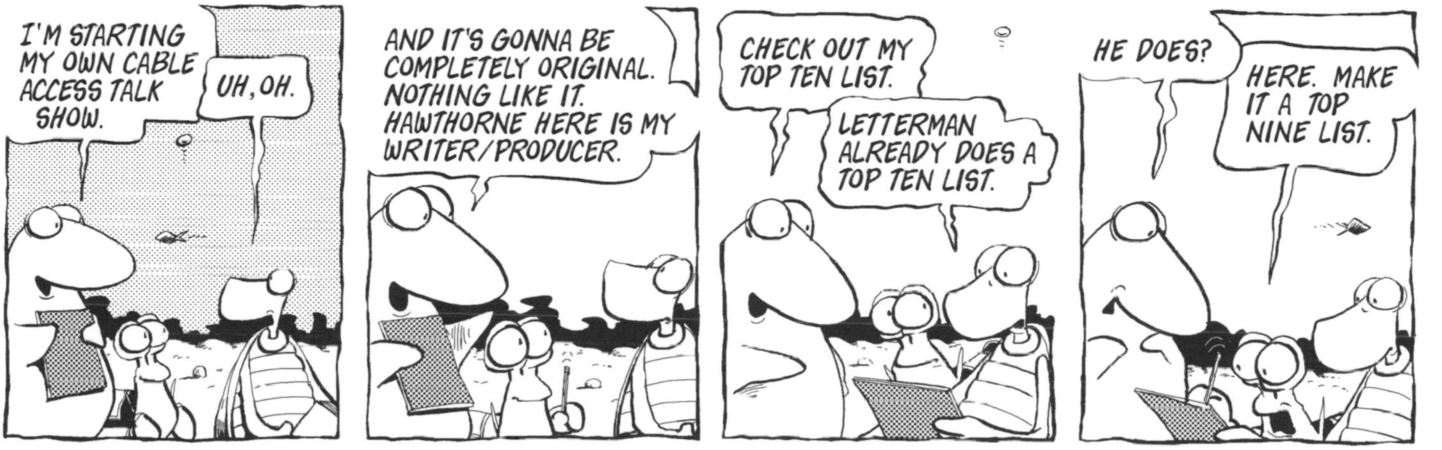
I'M STARTING MY OWN CABLE ACCESS TALK SHOW.
UH, OH.
AND IT'S GONNA BE COMPLETELY ORIGINAL. NOTHING LIKE IT. HAWTHORNE HERE IS MY WRITER/PRODUCER.
CHECK OUT MY TOP TEN LIST.
LETTERMAN ALREADY DOES A TOP TEN LIST.
HE DOES?
HERE. MAKE IT A TOP NINE LIST.

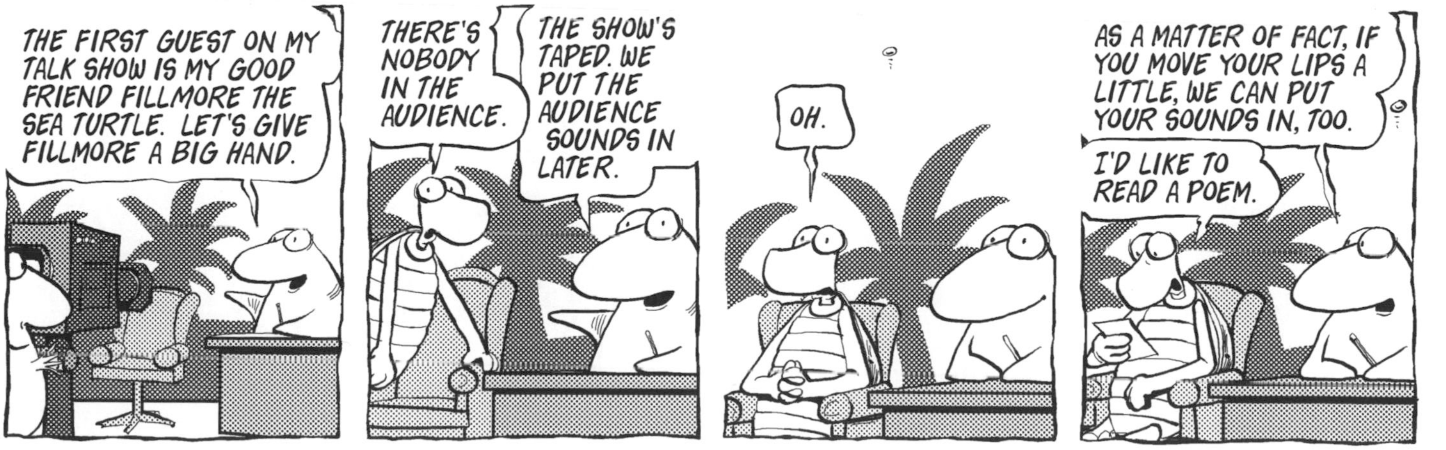
THE FIRST GUEST ON MY TALK SHOW IS MY GOOD FRIEND FILLMORE THE SEA TURTLE. LET'S GIVE FILLMORE A BIG HAND.
THERE'S NOBODY IN THE AUDIENCE.
THE SHOW'S TAPED. WE PUT THE AUDIENCE SOUNDS IN LATER.
OH.
AS A MATTER OF FACT, IF YOU MOVE YOUR LIPS A LITTLE, WE CAN PUT YOUR SOUNDS IN, TOO.
I'D LIKE TO READ A POEM.

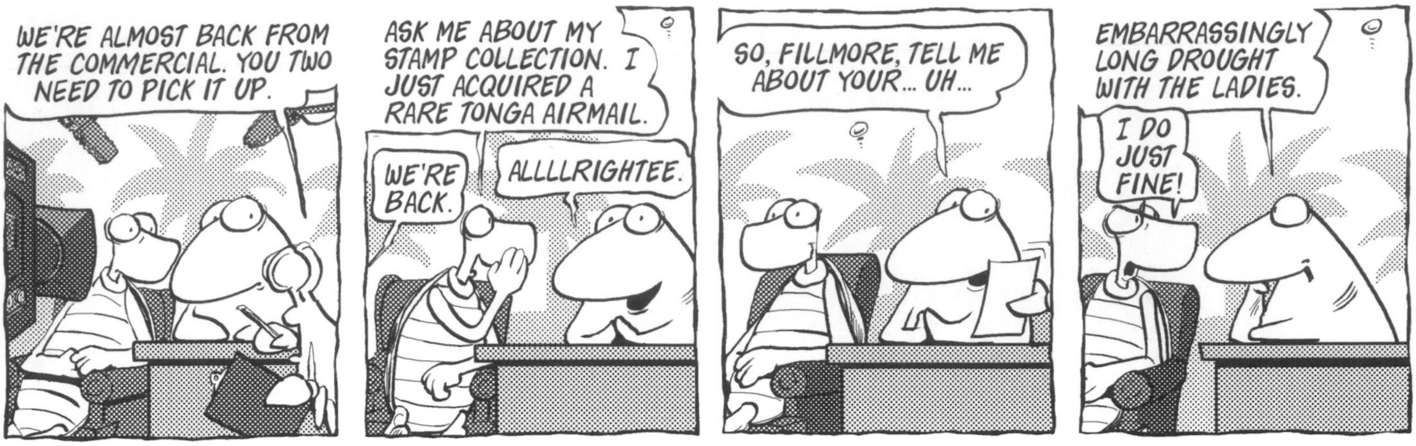
WE'RE ALMOST BACK FROM THE COMMERCIAL. YOU TWO NEED TO PICK IT UP.
ASK ME ABOUT MY STAMP COLLECTION. I JUST ACQUIRED A RARE TONGA AIRMAIL.
WE'RE BACK.
ALLLLRIGHTEE.
SO, FILLMORE, TELL ME ABOUT YOUR... UH...
EMBARRASSINGLY LONG DROUGHT WITH THE LADIES.
I DO JUST FINE!

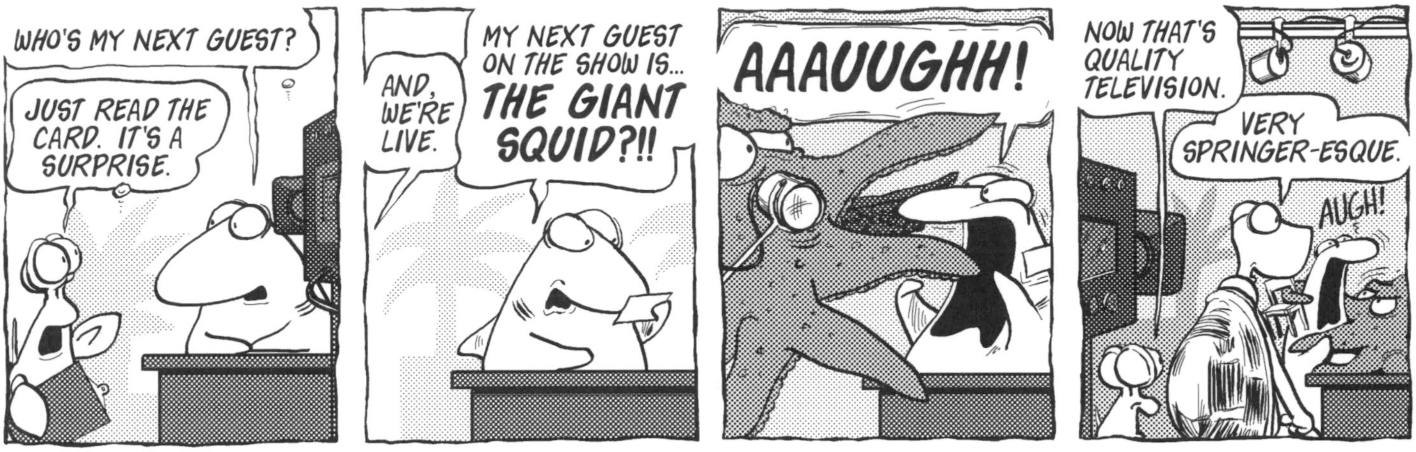
WHO'S MY NEXT GUEST?
JUST READ THE CARD. IT'S A SURPRISE.
AND, WE'RE LIVE.
MY NEXT GUEST ON THE SHOW IS... THE GIANT SQUID?!!
AAAUUGHH!
NOW THAT'S QUALITY TELEVISION.
VERY SPRINGER-ESQUE.
AUGH!

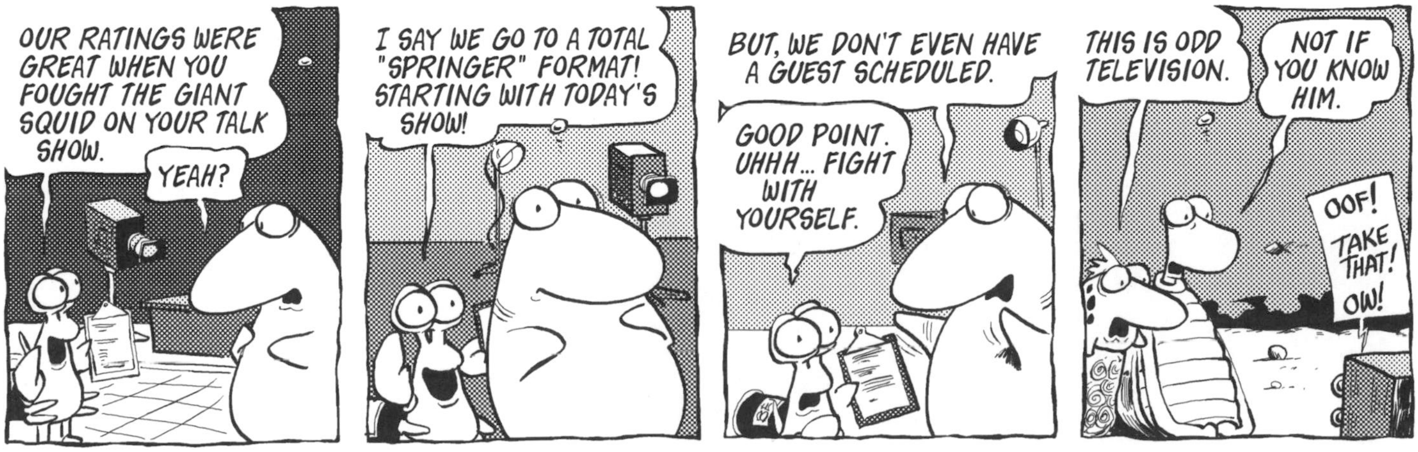
OUR RATINGS WERE GREAT WHEN YOU FOUGHT THE GIANT SQUID ON YOUR TALK SHOW.
YEAH?
I SAY WE GO TO A TOTAL "SPRINGER" FORMAT! STARTING WITH TODAY'S SHOW!
BUT, WE DON'T EVEN HAVE A GUEST SCHEDULED.
GOOD POINT. UHHH... FIGHT WITH YOURSELF.
THIS IS ODD TELEVISION.
NOT IF YOU KNOW HIM.
OOF! TAKE THAT! OW!

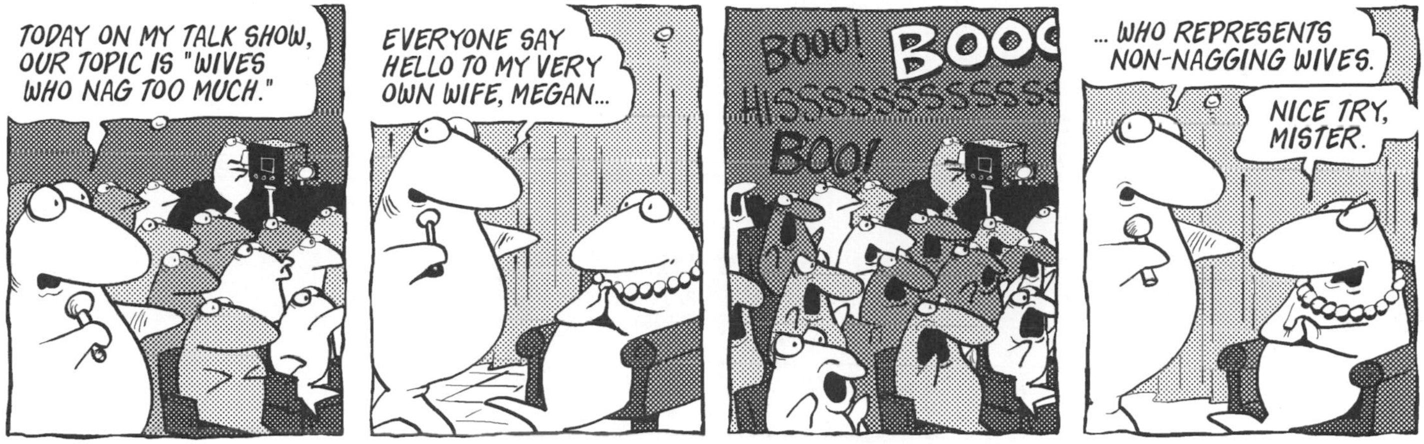
TODAY ON MY TALK SHOW, OUR TOPIC IS "WIVES WHO NAG TOO MUCH."
EVERYONE SAY HELLO TO MY VERY OWN WIFE, MEGAN...
BOOO!
BOO!
... WHO REPRESENTS NON-NAGGING WIVES.
NICE TRY, MISTER.

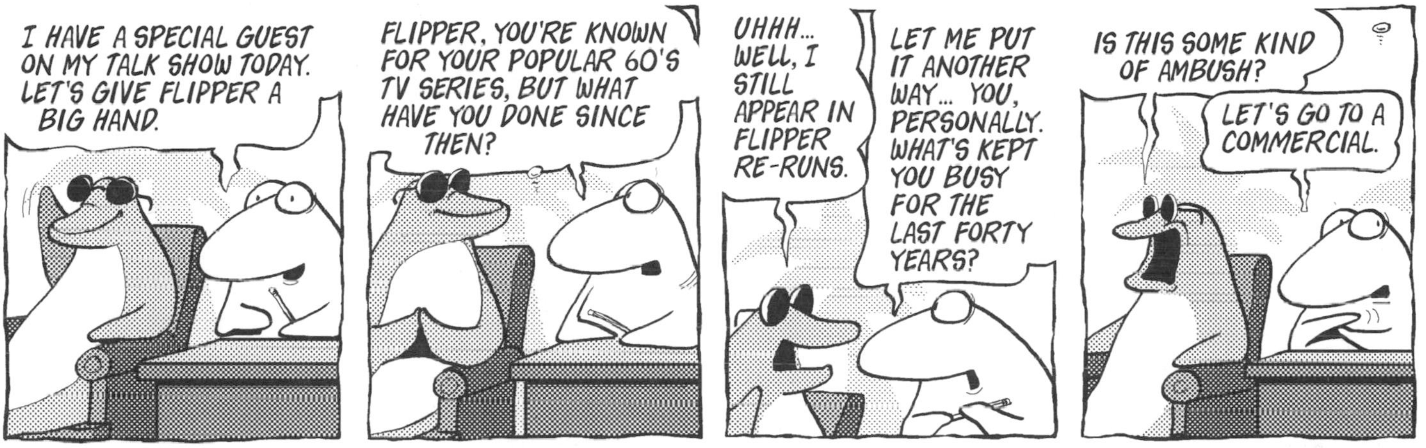
I HAVE A SPECIAL GUEST ON MY TALK SHOW TODAY. LET'S GIVE FLIPPER A BIG HAND.
FLIPPER, YOU'RE KNOWN FOR YOUR POPULAR 60'S TV SERIES, BUT WHAT HAVE YOU DONE SINCE THEN?
UHHH... WELL, I STILL APPEAR IN FLIPPER RE-RUNS.
LET ME PUT IT ANOTHER WAY... YOU, PERSONALLY. WHAT'S KEPT YOU BUSY FOR THE LAST FORTY YEARS?
IS THIS SOME KIND OF AMBUSH?
LET'S GO TO A COMMERCIAL.

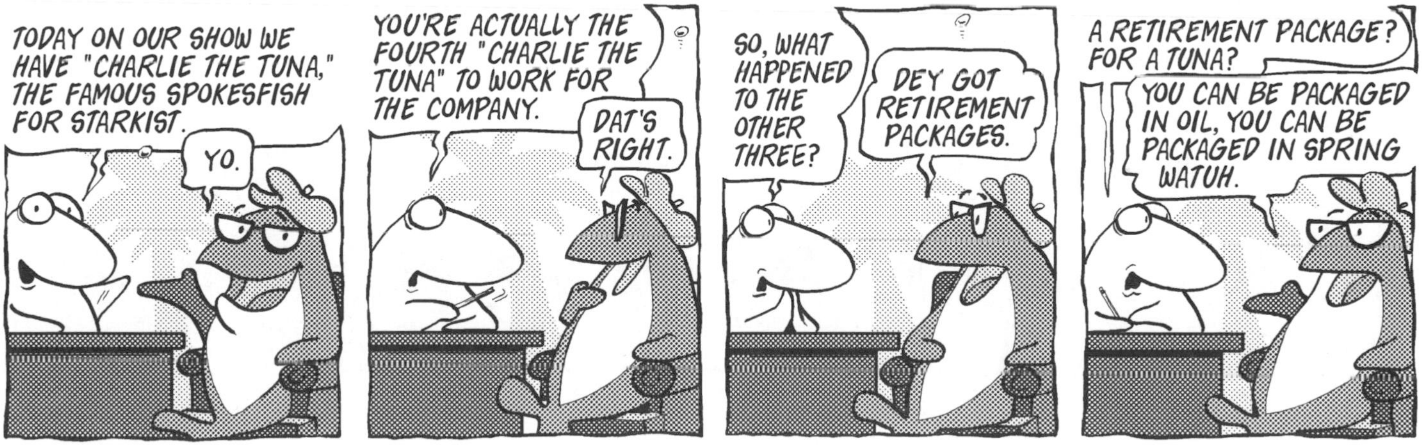
TODAY ON OUR SHOW WE HAVE "CHARLIE THE TUNA," THE FAMOUS SPOKESFISH FOR STARKIST.
YO.
YOU'RE ACTUALLY THE FOURTH "CHARLIE THE TUNA" TO WORK FOR THE COMPANY.
DAT'S RIGHT.
SO, WHAT HAPPENED TO THE OTHER THREE?
DEY GOT RETIREMENT PACKAGES.
A RETIREMENT PACKAGE? FOR A TUNA?
YOU CAN BE PACKAGED IN OIL, YOU CAN BE PACKAGED IN SPRING WATUH.

Sherman's Lagoon

by Jim Toomey

WHY DO YOU EAT ONE GRAPE FROM OVER HERE AND ANOTHER FROM OVER HERE? JUST BREAK OFF A BUNCH AND EAT IT.

SORRY.

YOU LEAVE HALF A PAPER TOWEL ON THE ROLL. WHAT AM I SUPPOSED TO DO WITH THE OTHER HALF?

IT WON'T HAPPEN AGAIN.

HINT: IF YOU EAT A PIECE OF CHOCOLATE, THROW AWAY THE LITTLE WAX PAPER CUP IT CAME IN.

WHAT WAS I THINKING?

YOU KNOW, HAWTHORNE, YOU SHOULD TRY THIS MARRIAGE THING.

IT'LL MAKE A BETTER MAN OUT OF YOU.

I'M GOING TO GO EAT THE MIDDLE OUT OF A WHOLE PACK OF OREOS.

CAN I COME?

108

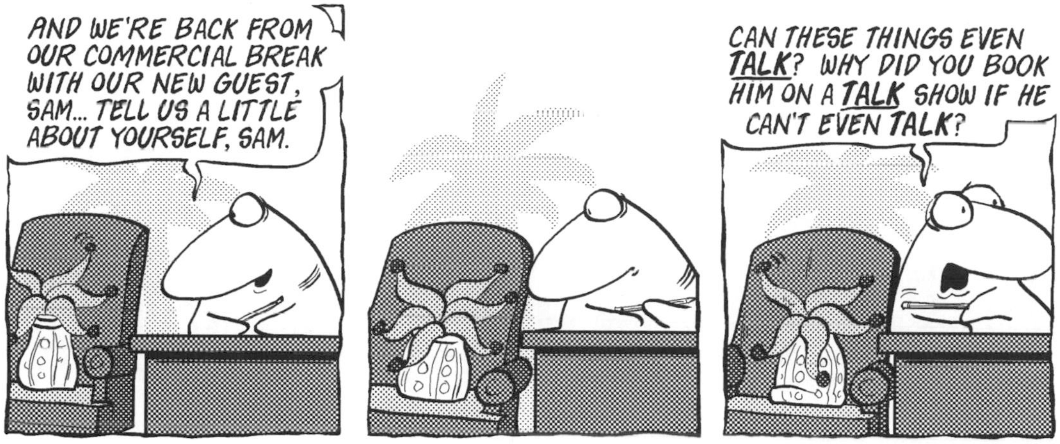
AND WE'RE BACK FROM OUR COMMERCIAL BREAK WITH OUR NEW GUEST, SAM... TELL US A LITTLE ABOUT YOURSELF, SAM.
CAN THESE THINGS EVEN TALK? WHY DID YOU BOOK HIM ON A TALK SHOW IF HE CAN'T EVEN TALK?
OH, GROSS! GET A CLOSE-UP!!
PTUI!
SPLAT

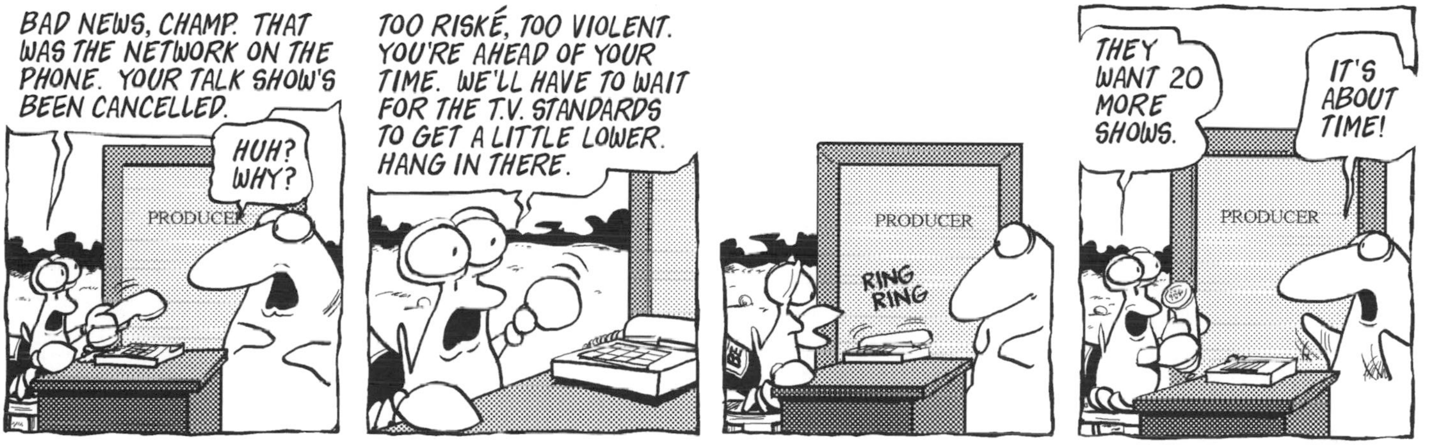
BAD NEWS, CHAMP. THAT WAS THE NETWORK ON THE PHONE. YOUR TALK SHOW'S BEEN CANCELLED.
HUH? WHY?
PRODUCER
TOO RISKÉ, TOO VIOLENT. YOU'RE AHEAD OF YOUR TIME. WE'LL HAVE TO WAIT FOR THE T.V. STANDARDS TO GET A LITTLE LOWER. HANG IN THERE.
PRODUCER
RING RING
THEY WANT 20 MORE SHOWS.
IT'S ABOUT TIME!
PRODUCER

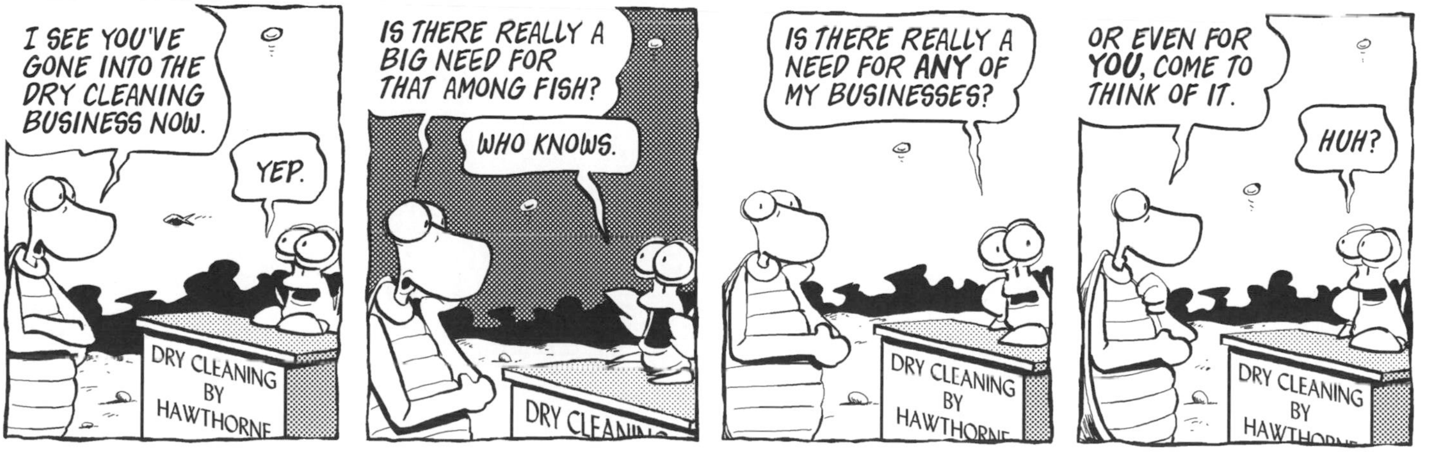
I SEE YOU'VE GONE INTO THE DRY CLEANING BUSINESS NOW.
YEP.
DRY CLEANING BY HAWTHORNE
IS THERE REALLY A BIG NEED FOR THAT AMONG FISH?
WHO KNOWS.
IS THERE REALLY A NEED FOR ANY OF MY BUSINESSES?
DRY CLEANING BY HAWTHORNE
OR EVEN FOR YOU, COME TO THINK OF IT.
HUH?
DRY CLEANING BY HAWTHORNE

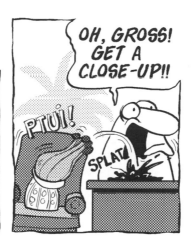

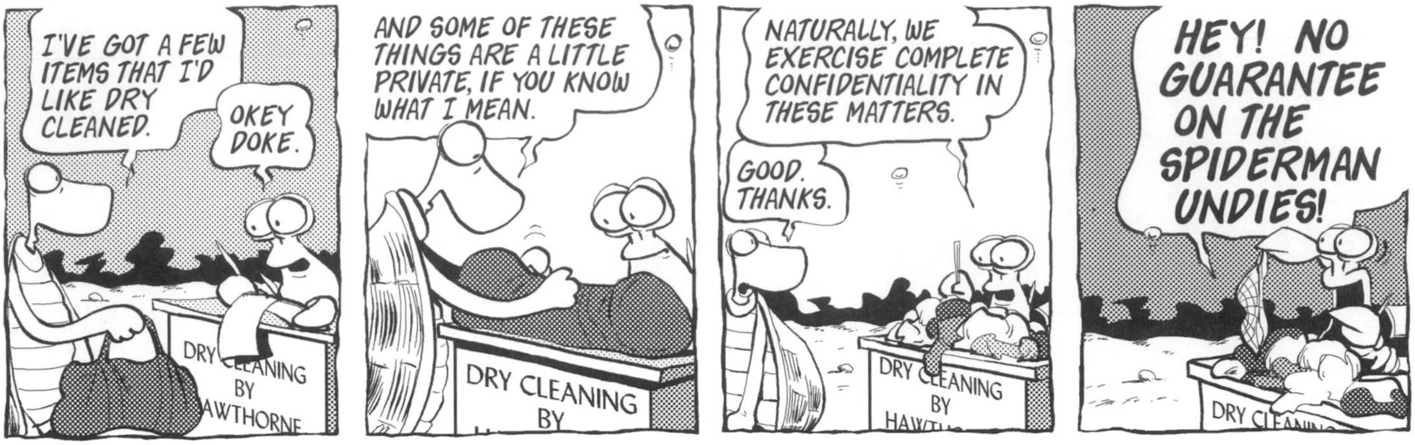
I'VE GOT A FEW ITEMS THAT I'D LIKE DRY CLEANED.
OKEY DOKE.
DRY CLEANING BY HAWTHORNE
AND SOME OF THESE THINGS ARE A LITTLE PRIVATE, IF YOU KNOW WHAT I MEAN.
DRY CLEANING BY
NATURALLY, WE EXERCISE COMPLETE CONFIDENTIALITY IN THESE MATTERS.
GOOD. THANKS.
HEY! NO GUARANTEE ON THE SPIDERMAN UNDIES!

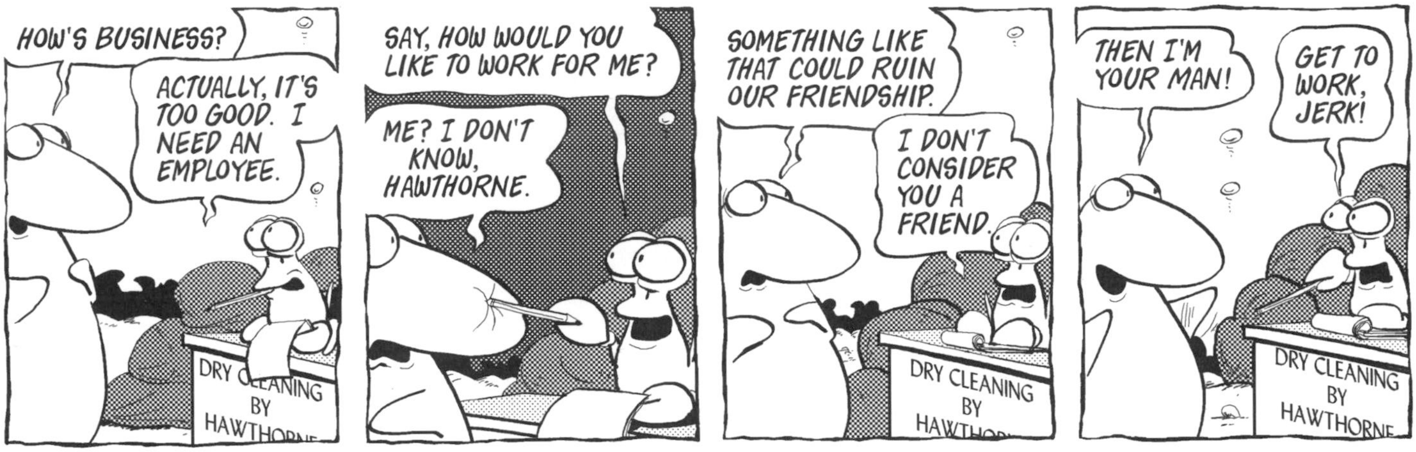
HOW'S BUSINESS?
ACTUALLY, IT'S TOO GOOD. I NEED AN EMPLOYEE.
DRY CLEANING BY
SAY, HOW WOULD YOU LIKE TO WORK FOR ME?
ME? I DON'T KNOW, HAWTHORNE.
SOMETHING LIKE THAT COULD RUIN OUR FRIENDSHIP.
I DON'T CONSIDER YOU A FRIEND.
DRY CLEANING BY
THEN I'M YOUR MAN!
GET TO WORK, JERK!
DRY CLEANING BY HAWTHORNE

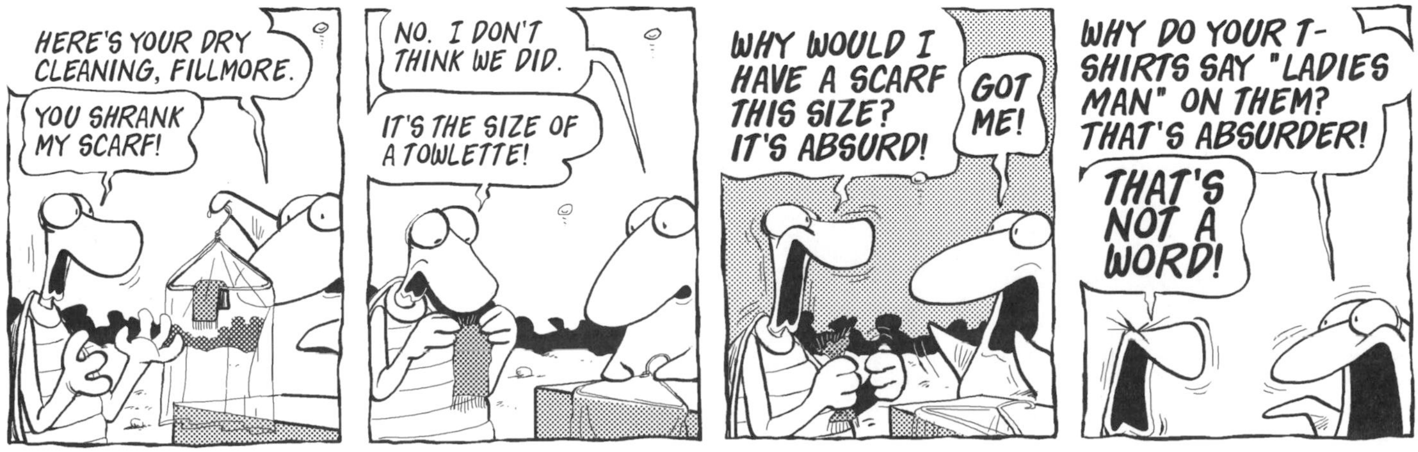
HERE'S YOUR DRY CLEANING, FILLMORE.
YOU SHRANK MY SCARF!
NO. I DON'T THINK WE DID.
IT'S THE SIZE OF A TOWLETTE!
WHY WOULD I HAVE A SCARF THIS SIZE? IT'S ABSURD!
GOT ME!
WHY DO YOUR T-SHIRTS SAY "LADIES MAN" ON THEM? THAT'S ABSURDER!
THAT'S NOT A WORD!

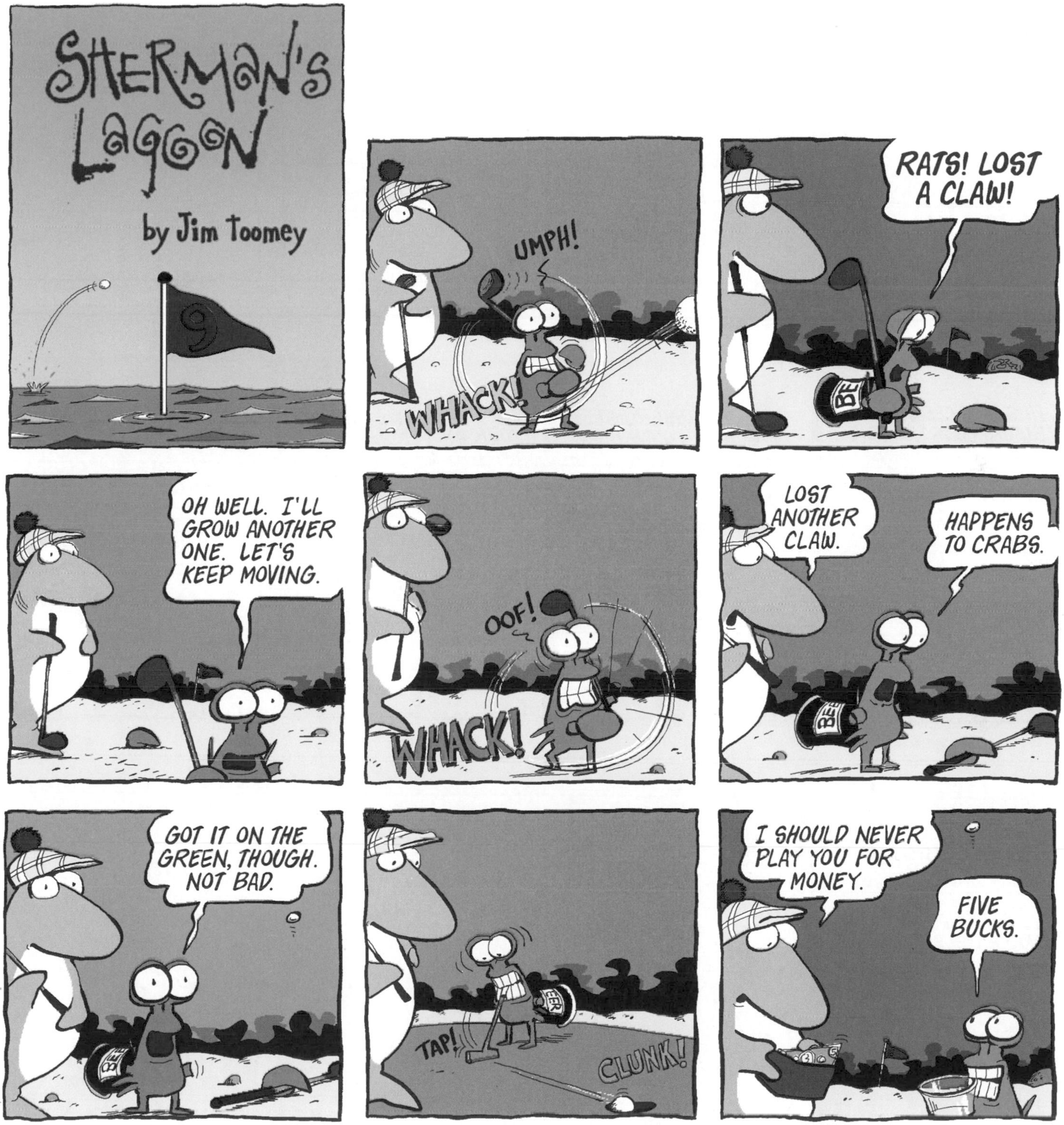

SHERMAN'S LAGOON
by Jim Toomey
UMPH!
WHACK!
RATS! LOST A CLAW!
OH WELL. I'LL GROW ANOTHER ONE. LET'S KEEP MOVING.
OOF!
WHACK!
LOST ANOTHER CLAW.
HAPPENS TO CRABS.
GOT IT ON THE GREEN, THOUGH. NOT BAD.
TAP!
CLUNK!
I SHOULD NEVER PLAY YOU FOR MONEY.
FIVE BUCKS.

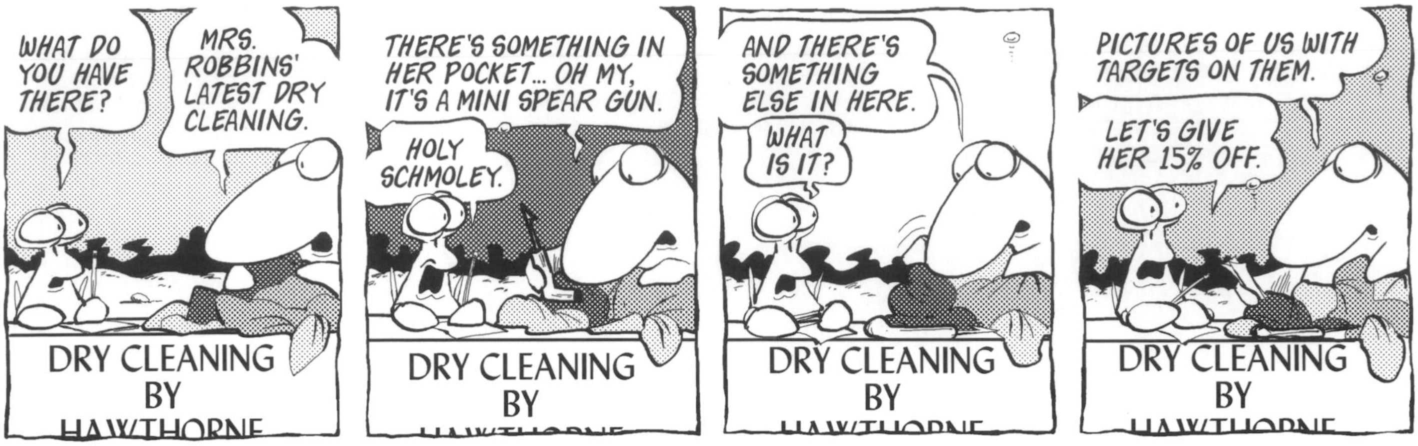
WHAT DO YOU HAVE THERE?
MRS. ROBBINS' LATEST DRY CLEANING.
DRY CLEANING BY
THERE'S SOMETHING IN HER POCKET... OH MY, IT'S A MINI SPEAR GUN.
HOLY SCHMOLEY.
DRY CLEANING BY
AND THERE'S SOMETHING ELSE IN HERE.
WHAT IS IT?
DRY CLEANING BY
PICTURES OF US WITH TARGETS ON THEM.
LET'S GIVE HER 15% OFF.
DRY CLEANING BY

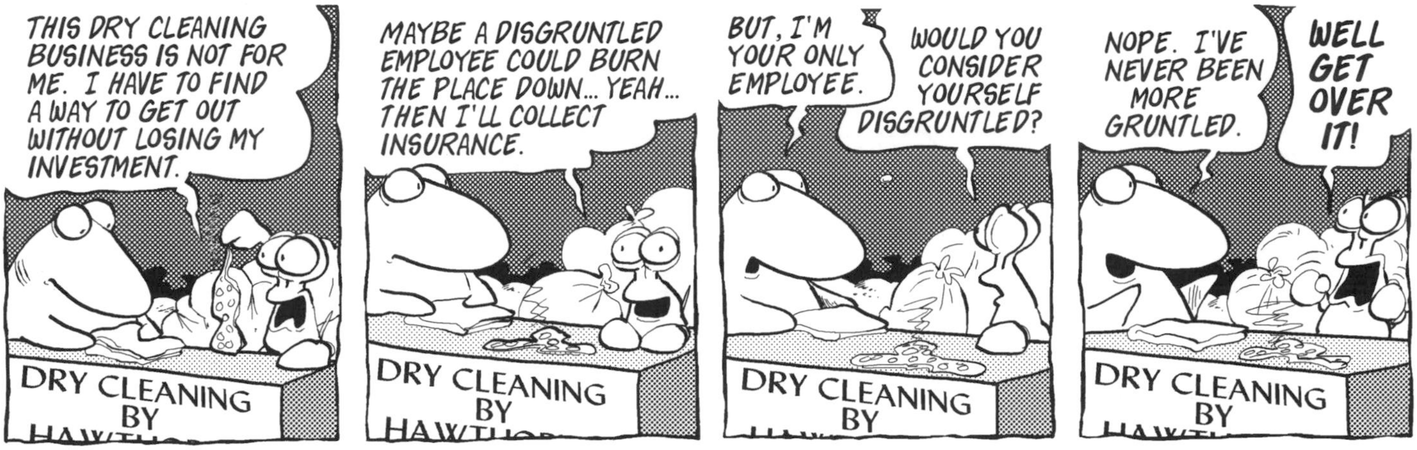
THIS DRY CLEANING BUSINESS IS NOT FOR ME. I HAVE TO FIND A WAY TO GET OUT WITHOUT LOSING MY INVESTMENT.
DRY CLEANING BY
MAYBE A DISGRUNTLED EMPLOYEE COULD BURN THE PLACE DOWN... YEAH... THEN I'LL COLLECT INSURANCE.
DRY CLEANING BY
BUT, I'M YOUR ONLY EMPLOYEE.
WOULD YOU CONSIDER YOURSELF DISGRUNTLED?
DRY CLEANING BY
NOPE. I'VE NEVER BEEN MORE GRUNTLED.
WELL GET OVER IT!
DRY CLEANING BY

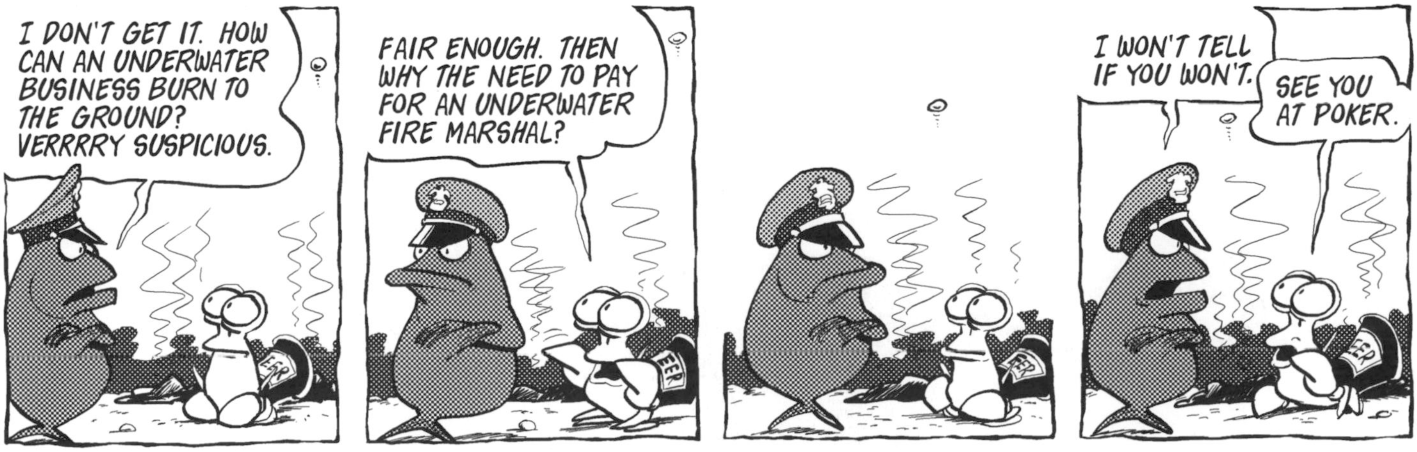
I DON'T GET IT. HOW CAN AN UNDERWATER BUSINESS BURN TO THE GROUND? VERRRRY SUSPICIOUS.
FAIR ENOUGH. THEN WHY THE NEED TO PAY FOR AN UNDERWATER FIRE MARSHAL?
I WON'T TELL IF YOU WON'T.
SEE YOU AT POKER.

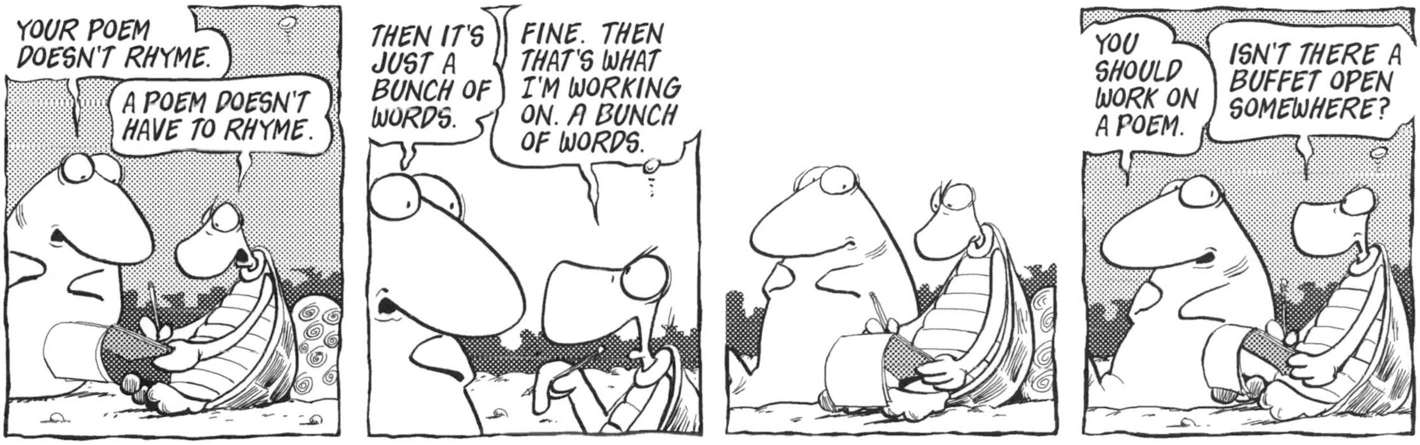
YOUR POEM DOESN'T RHYME.
A POEM DOESN'T HAVE TO RHYME.
THEN IT'S JUST A BUNCH OF WORDS.
FINE. THEN THAT'S WHAT I'M WORKING ON. A BUNCH OF WORDS.
YOU SHOULD WORK ON A POEM.
ISN'T THERE A BUFFET OPEN SOMEWHERE?

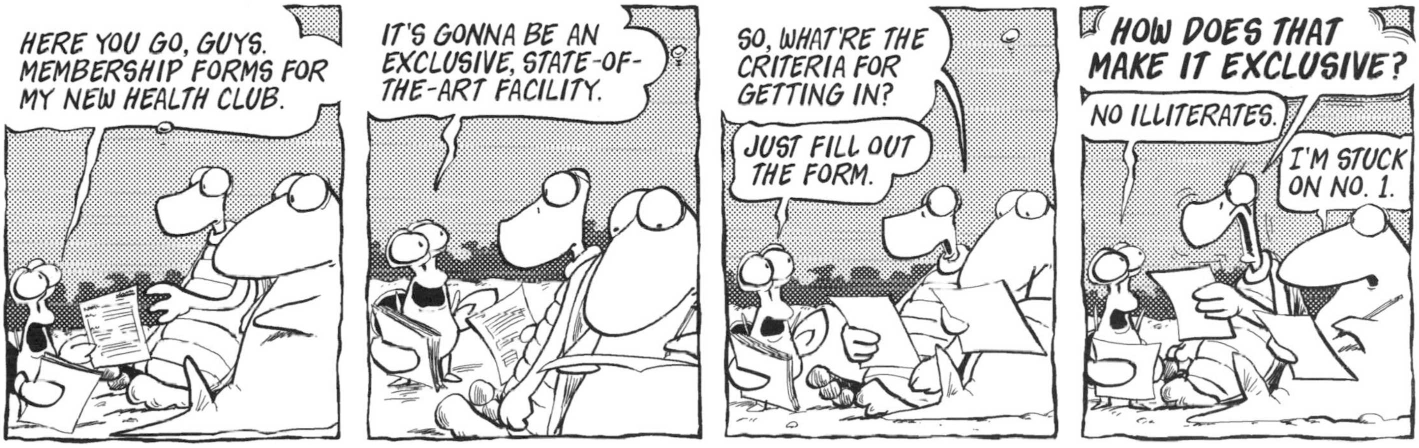
HERE YOU GO, GUYS. MEMBERSHIP FORMS FOR MY NEW HEALTH CLUB.
IT'S GONNA BE AN EXCLUSIVE, STATE-OF-THE-ART FACILITY.
SO, WHAT'RE THE CRITERIA FOR GETTING IN?
JUST FILL OUT THE FORM.
HOW DOES THAT MAKE IT EXCLUSIVE?
NO ILLITERATES.
I'M STUCK ON NO. 1.

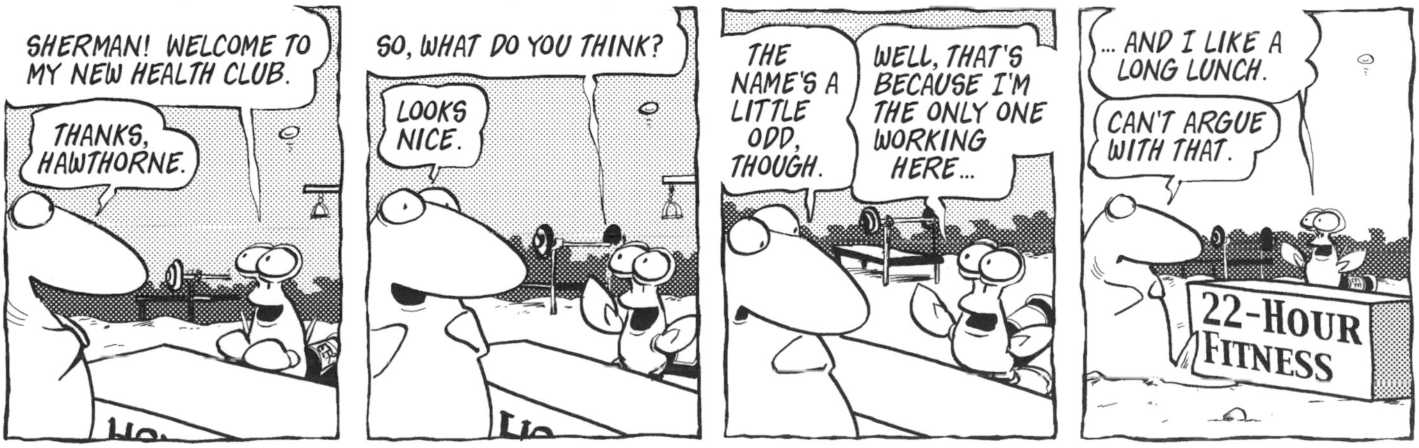
SHERMAN! WELCOME TO MY NEW HEALTH CLUB.
THANKS, HAWTHORNE.
SO, WHAT DO YOU THINK?
LOOKS NICE.
THE NAME'S A LITTLE ODD, THOUGH.
WELL, THAT'S BECAUSE I'M THE ONLY ONE WORKING HERE...
... AND I LIKE A LONG LUNCH.
CAN'T ARGUE WITH THAT.
22-HOUR FITNESS

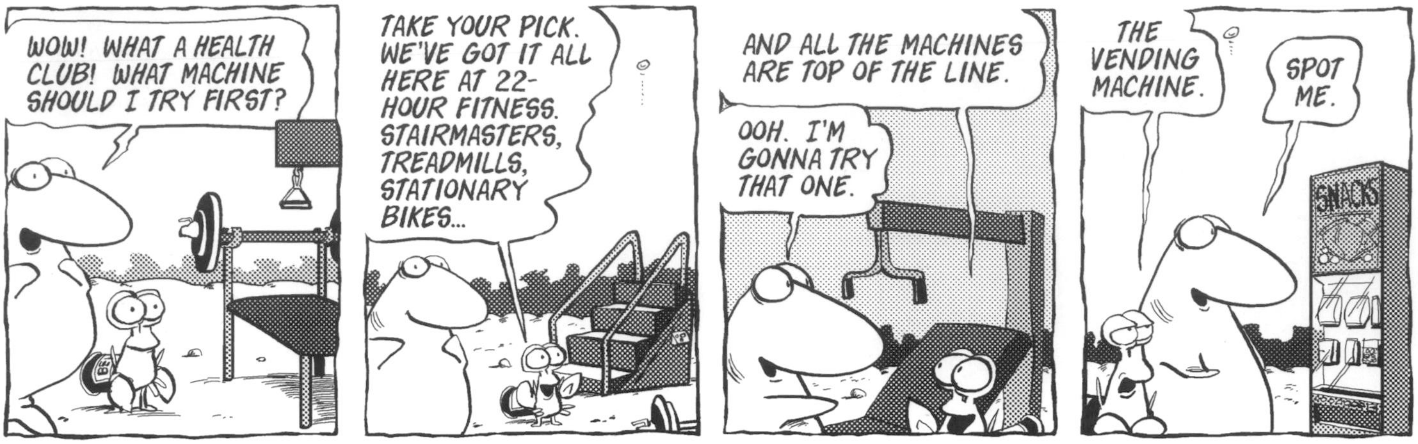
WOW! WHAT A HEALTH CLUB! WHAT MACHINE SHOULD I TRY FIRST?
TAKE YOUR PICK. WE'VE GOT IT ALL HERE AT 22-HOUR FITNESS. STAIRMASTERS, TREADMILLS, STATIONARY BIKES...
AND ALL THE MACHINES ARE TOP OF THE LINE.
OOH. I'M GONNA TRY THAT ONE.
THE VENDING MACHINE.
SPOT ME.
SNACKS

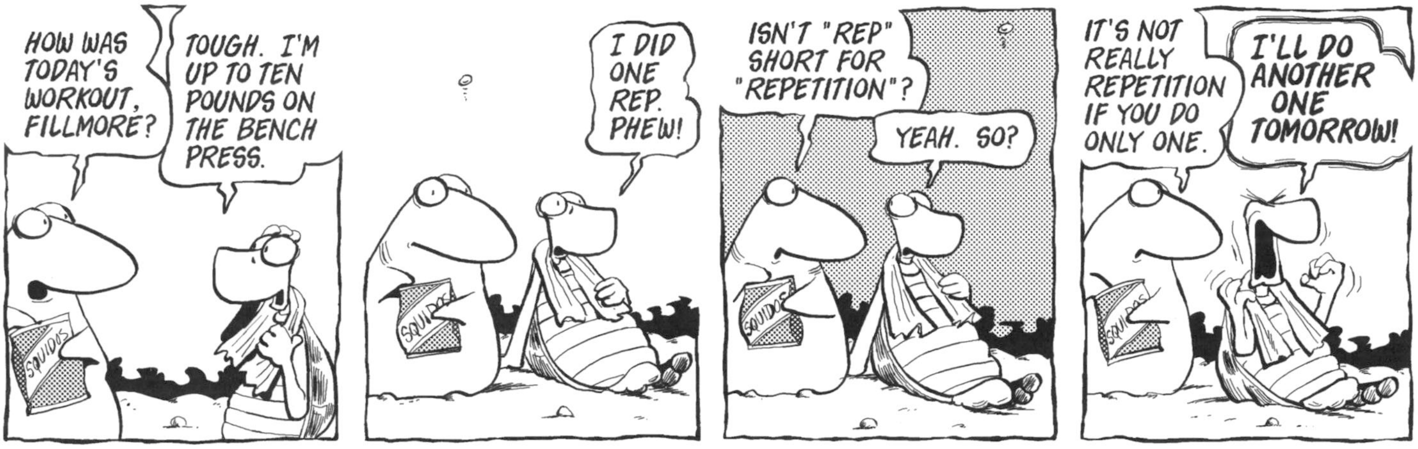
HOW WAS TODAY'S WORKOUT, FILLMORE?
TOUGH. I'M UP TO TEN POUNDS ON THE BENCH PRESS.
I DID ONE REP. PHEW!
ISN'T "REP" SHORT FOR "REPETITION"?
YEAH. SO?
IT'S NOT REALLY REPETITION IF YOU DO ONLY ONE.
I'LL DO ANOTHER ONE TOMORROW!

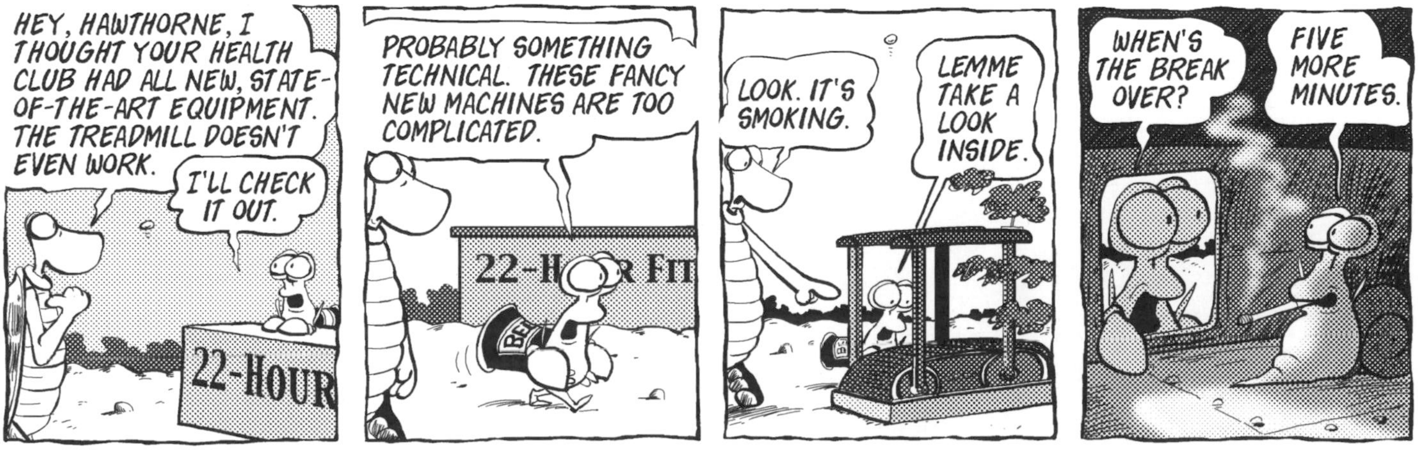
HEY, HAWTHORNE, I THOUGHT YOUR HEALTH CLUB HAD ALL NEW, STATE-OF-THE-ART EQUIPMENT. THE TREADMILL DOESN'T EVEN WORK.
I'LL CHECK IT OUT.
22-HOUR
PROBABLY SOMETHING TECHNICAL. THESE FANCY NEW MACHINES ARE TOO COMPLICATED.
LOOK. IT'S SMOKING.
LEMME TAKE A LOOK INSIDE.
WHEN'S THE BREAK OVER?
FIVE MORE MINUTES.

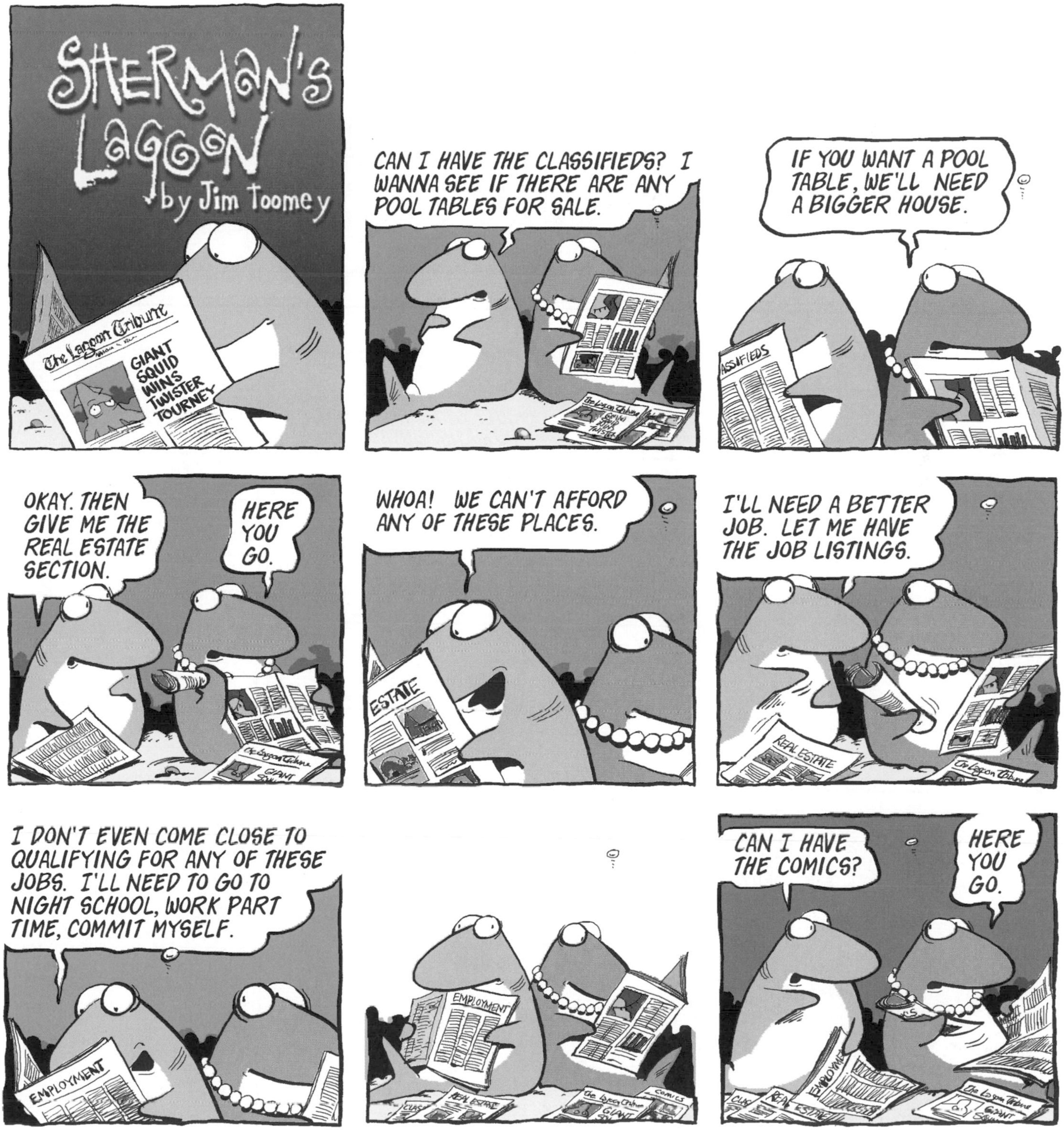
SHERMAN'S LAGOON
by Jim Toomey
The Lagoon Tribune
GIANT SQUID WINS TWISTER TOURNEY
CAN I HAVE THE CLASSIFIEDS? I WANNA SEE IF THERE ARE ANY POOL TABLES FOR SALE.
IF YOU WANT A POOL TABLE, WE'LL NEED A BIGGER HOUSE.
OKAY. THEN GIVE ME THE REAL ESTATE SECTION.
HERE YOU GO.
WHOA! WE CAN'T AFFORD ANY OF THESE PLACES.
ESTATE
I'LL NEED A BETTER JOB. LET ME HAVE THE JOB LISTINGS.
REAL ESTATE
I DON'T EVEN COME CLOSE TO QUALIFYING FOR ANY OF THESE JOBS. I'LL NEED TO GO TO NIGHT SCHOOL, WORK PART TIME, COMMIT MYSELF.
EMPLOYMENT
CAN I HAVE THE COMICS?
HERE YOU GO.
COMICS

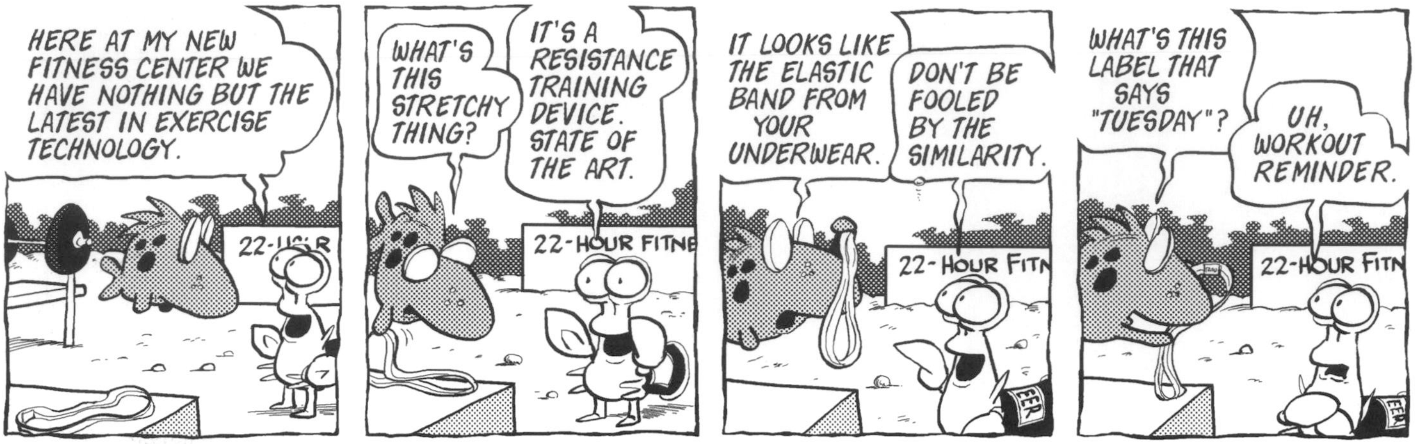
HERE AT MY NEW FITNESS CENTER WE HAVE NOTHING BUT THE LATEST IN EXERCISE TECHNOLOGY.
WHAT'S THIS STRETCHY THING?
IT'S A RESISTANCE TRAINING DEVICE. STATE OF THE ART.
IT LOOKS LIKE THE ELASTIC BAND FROM YOUR UNDERWEAR.
DON'T BE FOOLED BY THE SIMILARITY.
WHAT'S THIS LABEL THAT SAYS "TUESDAY"?
UH, WORKOUT REMINDER.

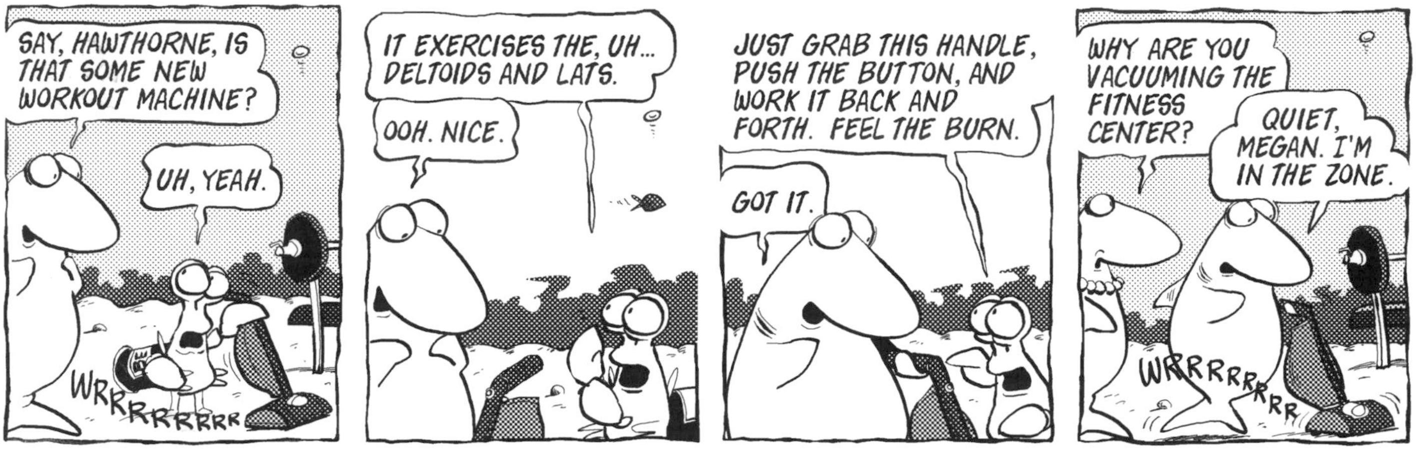
SAY, HAWTHORNE, IS THAT SOME NEW WORKOUT MACHINE?
UH, YEAH.
WRRRRRRRRR
IT EXERCISES THE, UH... DELTOIDS AND LATS.
OOH. NICE.
JUST GRAB THIS HANDLE, PUSH THE BUTTON, AND WORK IT BACK AND FORTH. FEEL THE BURN.
GOT IT.
WHY ARE YOU VACUUMING THE FITNESS CENTER?
QUIET, MEGAN. I'M IN THE ZONE.
WRRRRRRRRR

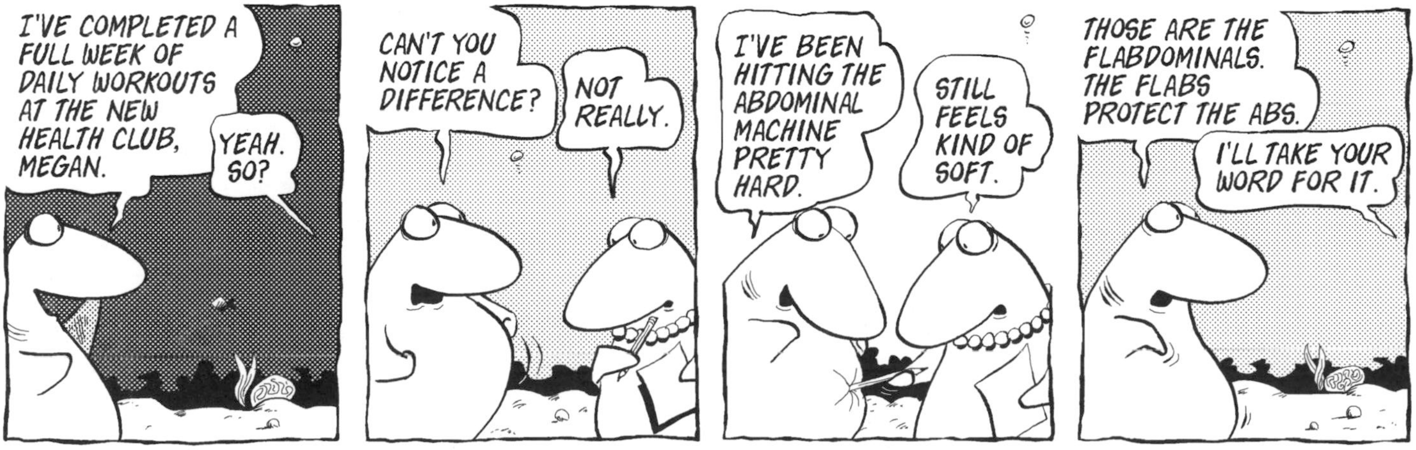
I'VE COMPLETED A FULL WEEK OF DAILY WORKOUTS AT THE NEW HEALTH CLUB, MEGAN.
YEAH. SO?
CAN'T YOU NOTICE A DIFFERENCE?
NOT REALLY.
I'VE BEEN HITTING THE ABDOMINAL MACHINE PRETTY HARD.
STILL FEELS KIND OF SOFT.
THOSE ARE THE FLABDOMINALS. THE FLABS PROTECT THE ABS.
I'LL TAKE YOUR WORD FOR IT.

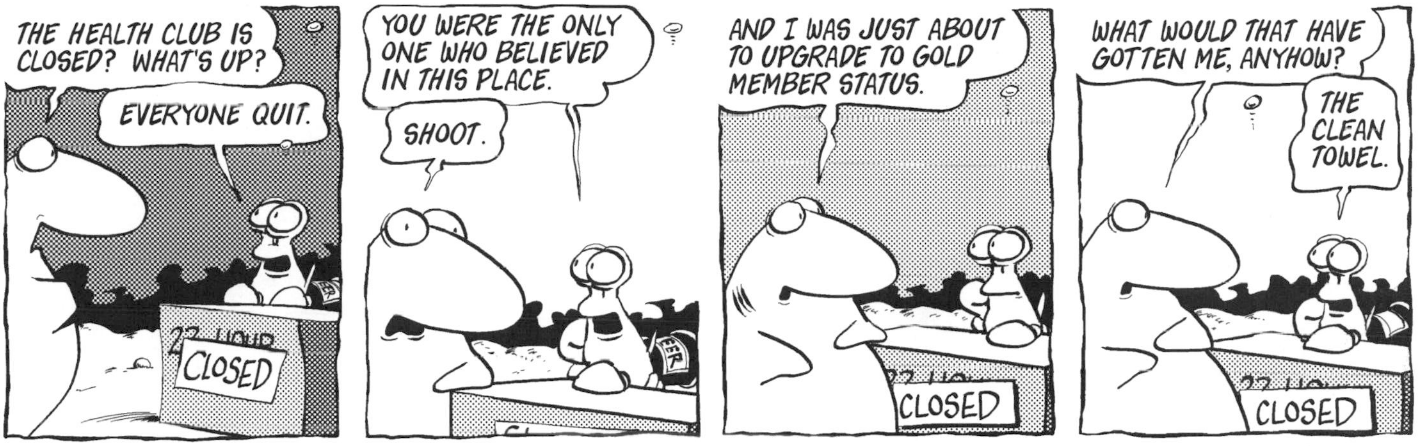
THE HEALTH CLUB IS CLOSED? WHAT'S UP?
EVERYONE QUIT.
CLOSED
YOU WERE THE ONLY ONE WHO BELIEVED IN THIS PLACE.
SHOOT.
AND I WAS JUST ABOUT TO UPGRADE TO GOLD MEMBER STATUS.
CLOSED
WHAT WOULD THAT HAVE GOTTEN ME, ANYHOW?
THE CLEAN TOWEL.
CLOSED

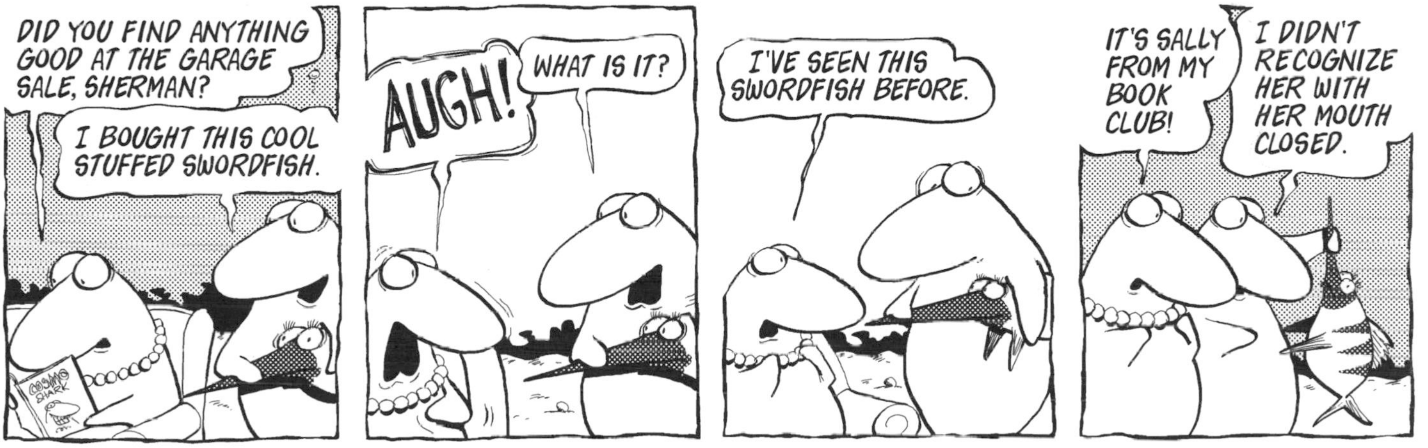
DID YOU FIND ANYTHING GOOD AT THE GARAGE SALE, SHERMAN?
I BOUGHT THIS COOL STUFFED SWORDFISH.
AUGH!
WHAT IS IT?
I'VE SEEN THIS SWORDFISH BEFORE.
IT'S SALLY FROM MY BOOK CLUB!
I DIDN'T RECOGNIZE HER WITH HER MOUTH CLOSED.

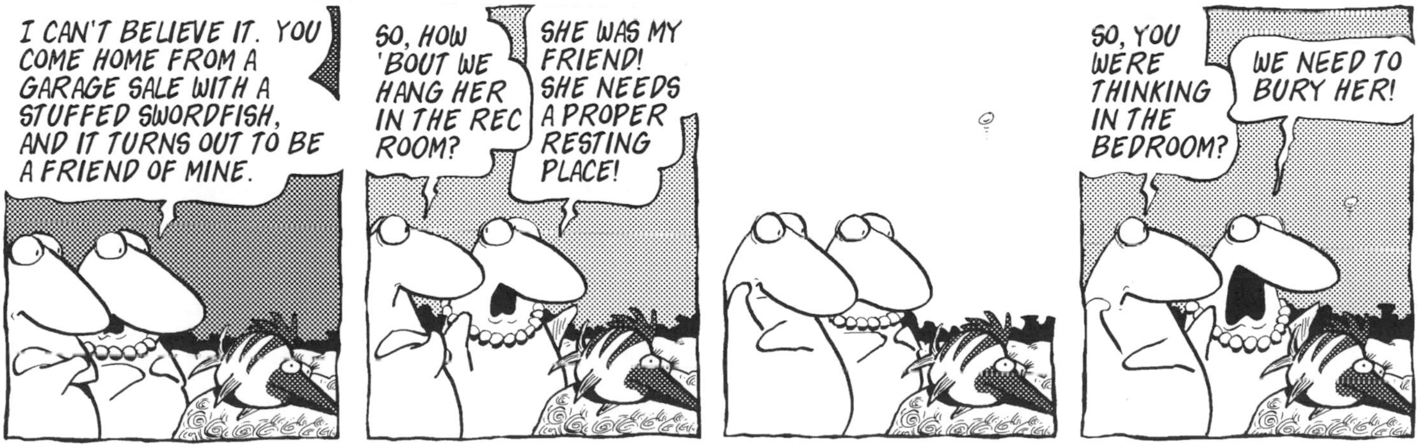
I CAN'T BELIEVE IT. YOU COME HOME FROM A GARAGE SALE WITH A STUFFED SWORDFISH, AND IT TURNS OUT TO BE A FRIEND OF MINE.
SO, HOW 'BOUT WE HANG HER IN THE REC ROOM?
SHE WAS MY FRIEND! SHE NEEDS A PROPER RESTING PLACE!
SO, YOU WERE THINKING IN THE BEDROOM?
WE NEED TO BURY HER!

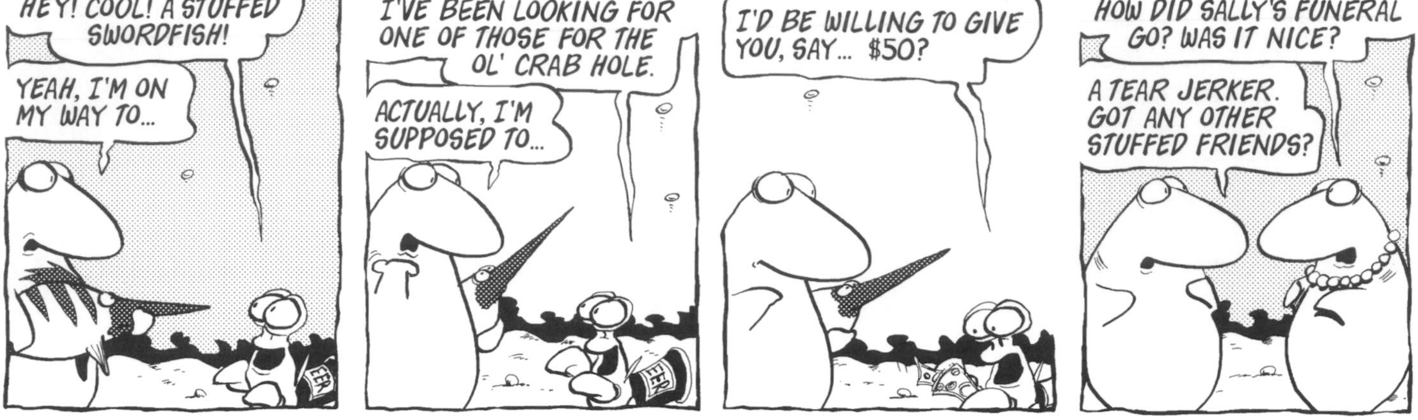
HEY! COOL! A STUFFED SWORDFISH!
YEAH, I'M ON MY WAY TO...
I'VE BEEN LOOKING FOR ONE OF THOSE FOR THE OL' CRAB HOLE.
ACTUALLY, I'M SUPPOSED TO...
BEER
I'D BE WILLING TO GIVE YOU, SAY... $50?
HOW DID SALLY'S FUNERAL GO? WAS IT NICE?
A TEAR JERKER. GOT ANY OTHER STUFFED FRIENDS?

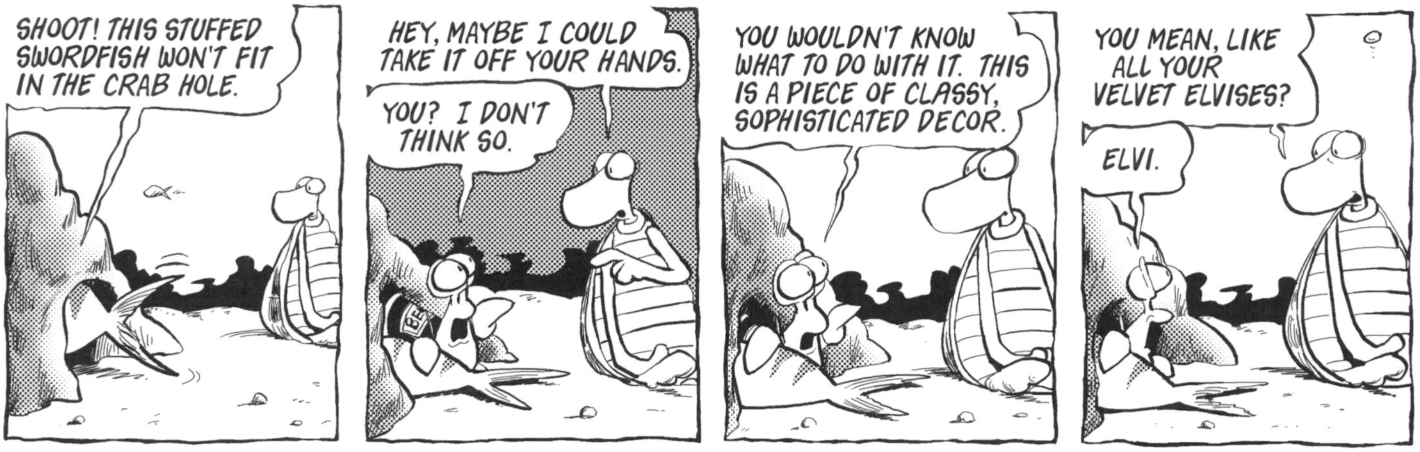
SHOOT! THIS STUFFED SWORDFISH WON'T FIT IN THE CRAB HOLE.
HEY, MAYBE I COULD TAKE IT OFF YOUR HANDS.
YOU? I DON'T THINK SO.
YOU WOULDN'T KNOW WHAT TO DO WITH IT. THIS IS A PIECE OF CLASSY, SOPHISTICATED DECOR.
YOU MEAN, LIKE ALL YOUR VELVET ELVISES?
ELVI.

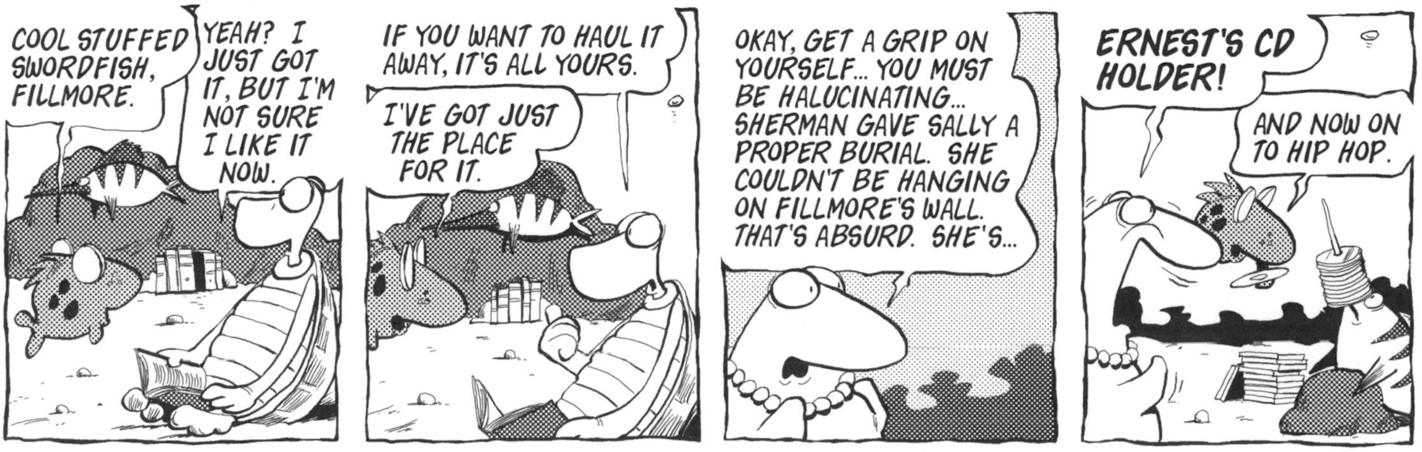
COOL STUFFED SWORDFISH, FILLMORE.
YEAH? I JUST GOT IT, BUT I'M NOT SURE I LIKE IT NOW.
IF YOU WANT TO HAUL IT AWAY, IT'S ALL YOURS.
I'VE GOT JUST THE PLACE FOR IT.
OKAY, GET A GRIP ON YOURSELF... YOU MUST BE HALUCINATING... SHERMAN GAVE SALLY A PROPER BURIAL. SHE COULDN'T BE HANGING ON FILLMORE'S WALL. THAT'S ABSURD. SHE'S...
ERNEST'S CD HOLDER!
AND NOW ON TO HIP HOP.

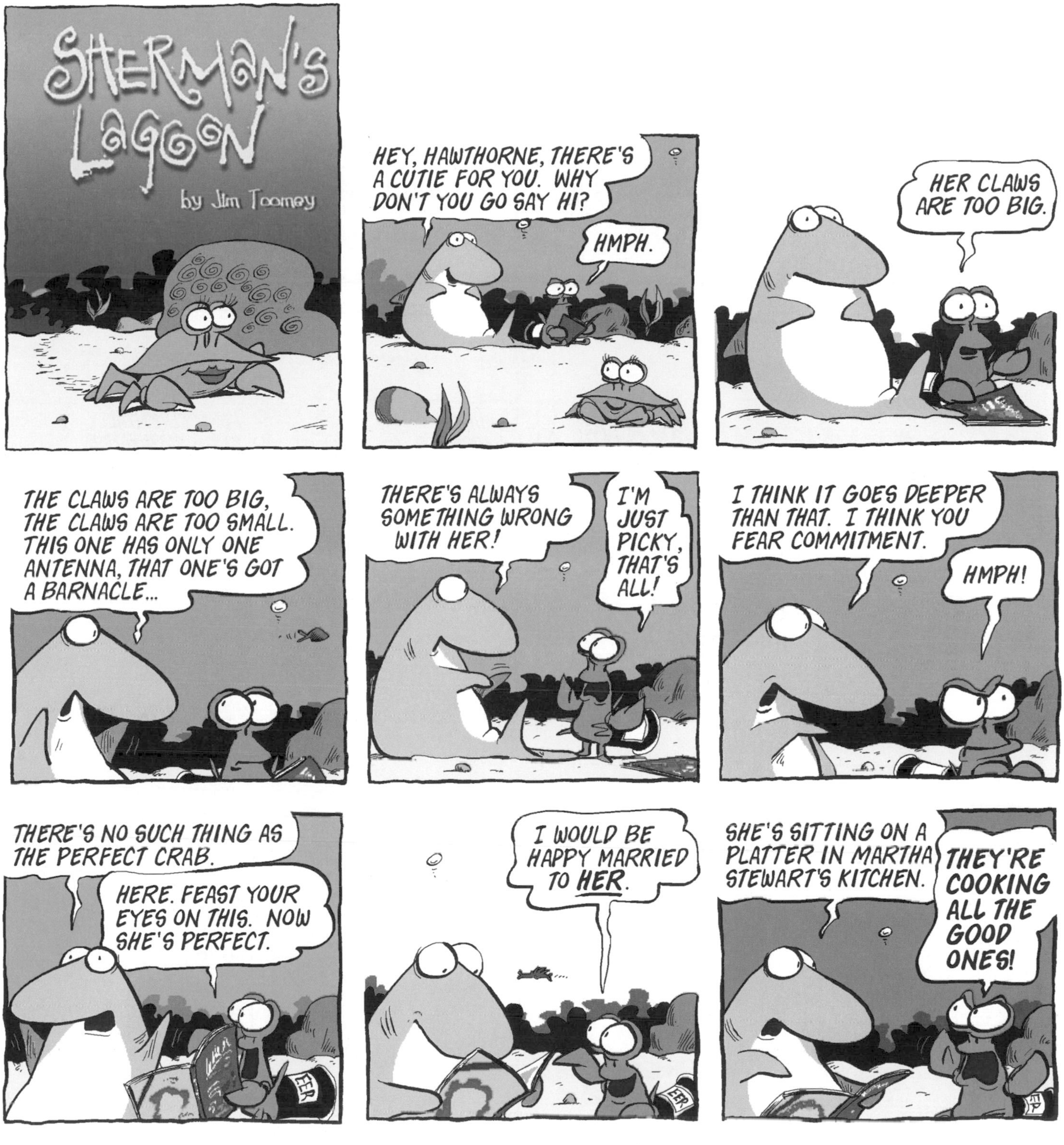
SHERMAN'S LAGOON
by Jim Toomey
HEY, HAWTHORNE, THERE'S A CUTIE FOR YOU. WHY DON'T YOU GO SAY HI?
HMPH.
HER CLAWS ARE TOO BIG.
THE CLAWS ARE TOO BIG, THE CLAWS ARE TOO SMALL. THIS ONE HAS ONLY ONE ANTENNA, THAT ONE'S GOT A BARNACLE...
THERE'S ALWAYS SOMETHING WRONG WITH HER!
I'M JUST PICKY, THAT'S ALL!
I THINK IT GOES DEEPER THAN THAT. I THINK YOU FEAR COMMITMENT.
HMPH!
THERE'S NO SUCH THING AS THE PERFECT CRAB.
HERE. FEAST YOUR EYES ON THIS. NOW SHE'S PERFECT.
I WOULD BE HAPPY MARRIED TO HER.
SHE'S SITTING ON A PLATTER IN MARTHA STEWART'S KITCHEN.
THEY'RE COOKING ALL THE GOOD ONES!

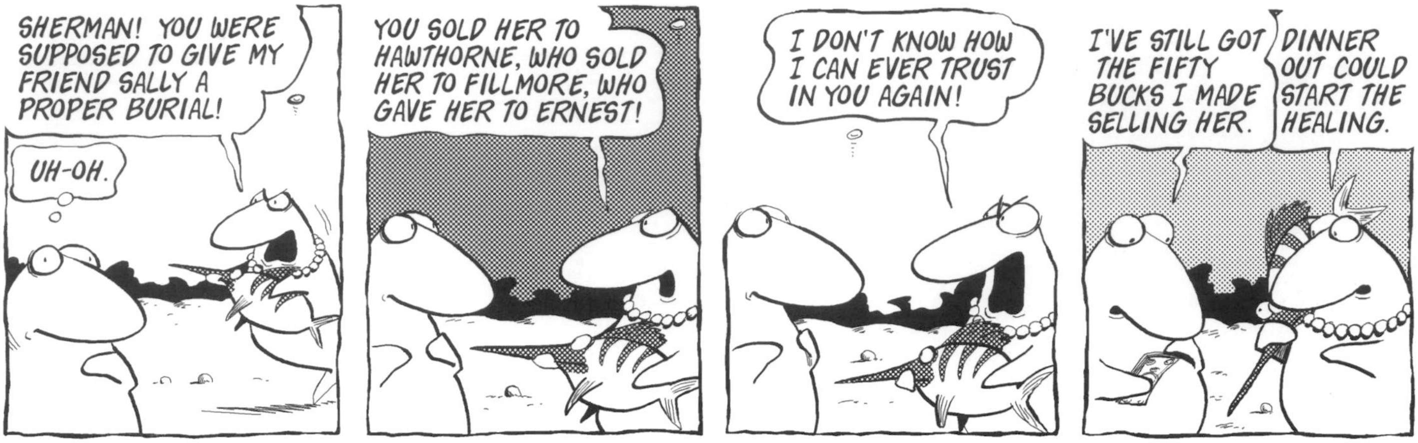
SHERMAN! YOU WERE SUPPOSED TO GIVE MY FRIEND SALLY A PROPER BURIAL!
UH-OH.
YOU SOLD HER TO HAWTHORNE, WHO SOLD HER TO FILLMORE, WHO GAVE HER TO ERNEST!
I DON'T KNOW HOW I CAN EVER TRUST IN YOU AGAIN!
I'VE STILL GOT THE FIFTY BUCKS I MADE SELLING HER.
DINNER OUT COULD START THE HEALING.

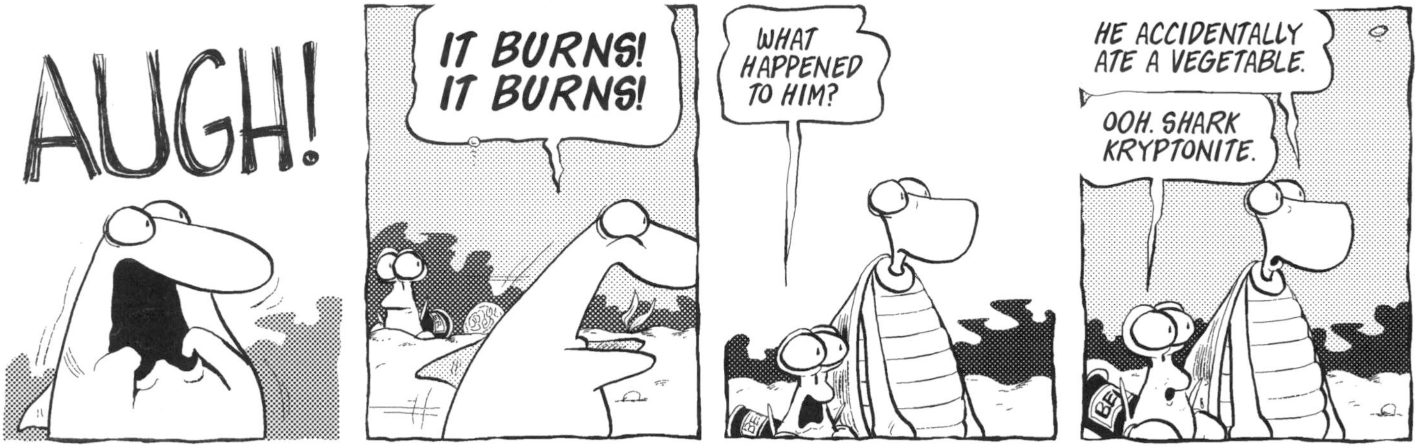
AUGH!
IT BURNS! IT BURNS!
WHAT HAPPENED TO HIM?
HE ACCIDENTALLY ATE A VEGETABLE.
OOH. SHARK KRYPTONITE.

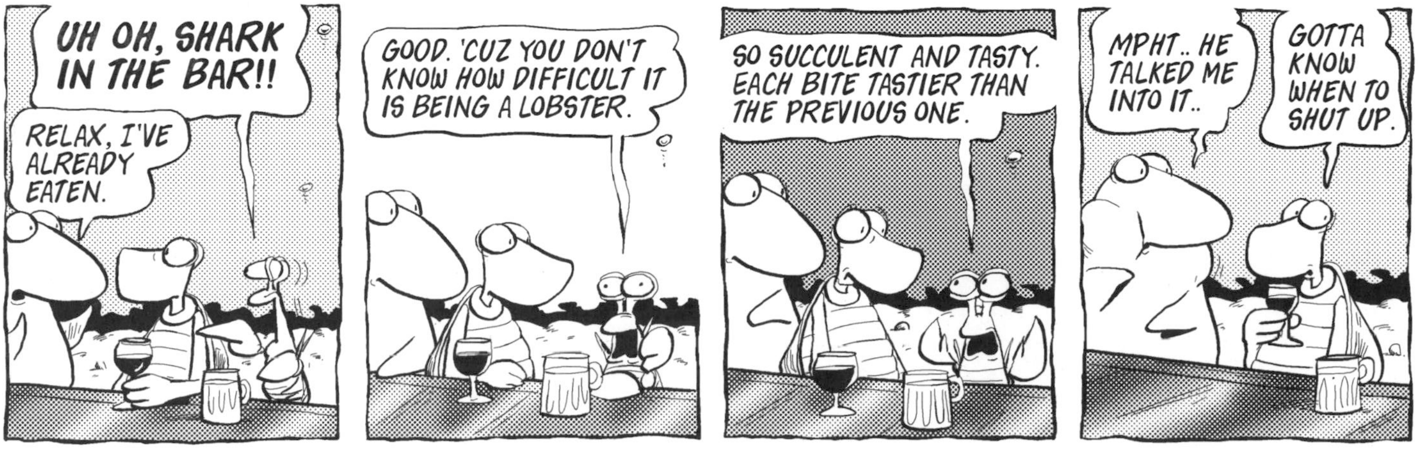
UH OH, SHARK IN THE BAR!!
RELAX, I'VE ALREADY EATEN.
GOOD. 'CUZ YOU DON'T KNOW HOW DIFFICULT IT IS BEING A LOBSTER.
SO SUCCULENT AND TASTY. EACH BITE TASTIER THAN THE PREVIOUS ONE.
MPHT.. HE TALKED ME INTO IT..
GOTTA KNOW WHEN TO SHUT UP.

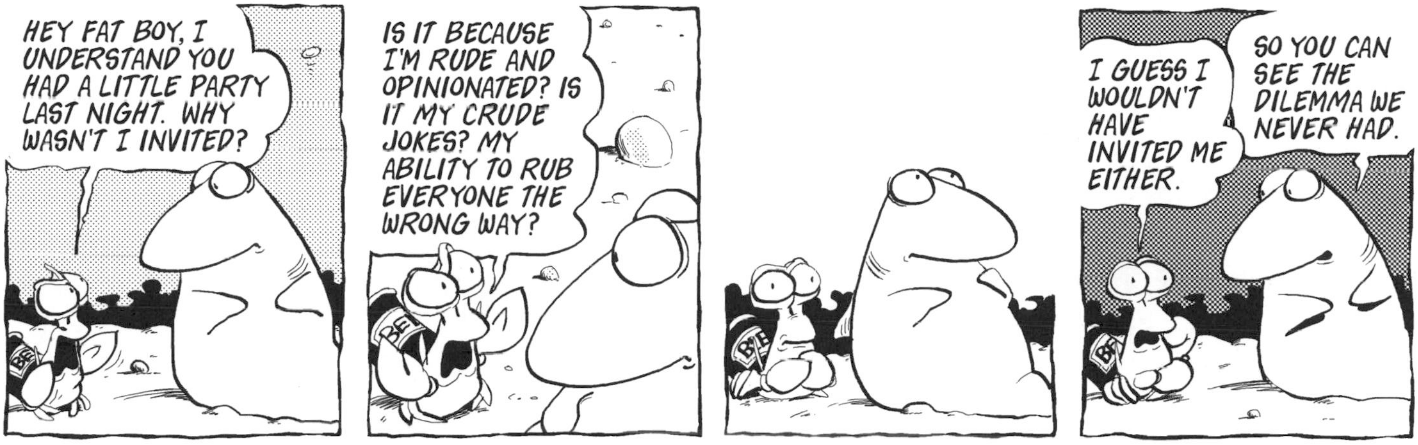
HEY FAT BOY, I UNDERSTAND YOU HAD A LITTLE PARTY LAST NIGHT. WHY WASN'T I INVITED?
IS IT BECAUSE I'M RUDE AND OPINIONATED? IS IT MY CRUDE JOKES? MY ABILITY TO RUB EVERYONE THE WRONG WAY?
I GUESS I WOULDN'T HAVE INVITED ME EITHER.
SO YOU CAN SEE THE DILEMMA WE NEVER HAD.

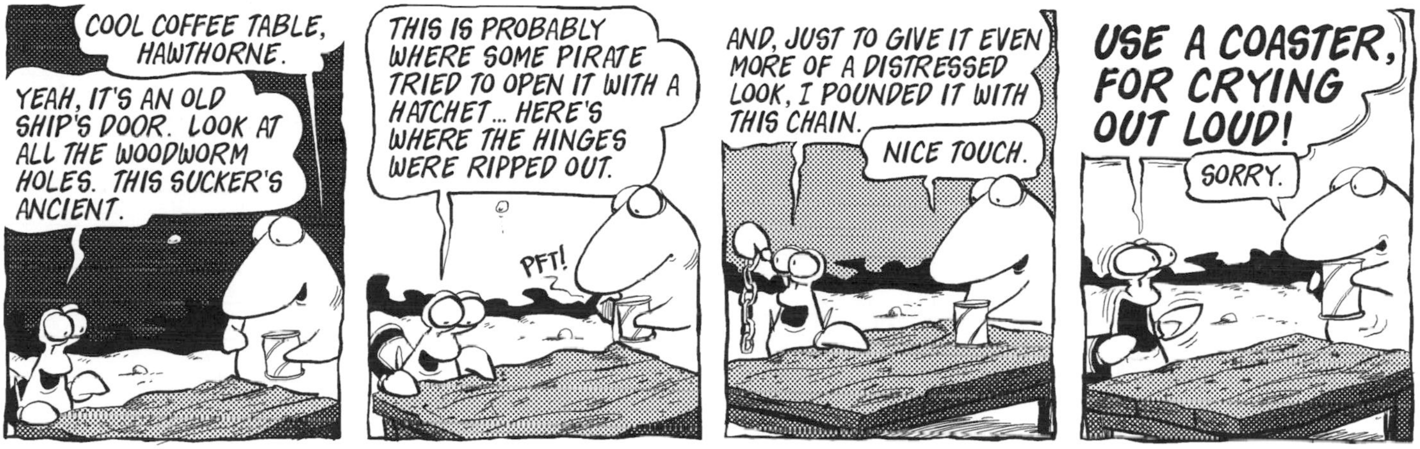
COOL COFFEE TABLE, HAWTHORNE.
YEAH, IT'S AN OLD SHIP'S DOOR. LOOK AT ALL THE WOODWORM HOLES. THIS SUCKER'S ANCIENT.
THIS IS PROBABLY WHERE SOME PIRATE TRIED TO OPEN IT WITH A HATCHET... HERE'S WHERE THE HINGES WERE RIPPED OUT.
PFT!
AND, JUST TO GIVE IT EVEN MORE OF A DISTRESSED LOOK, I POUNDED IT WITH THIS CHAIN.
NICE TOUCH.
USE A COASTER, FOR CRYING OUT LOUD!
SORRY.

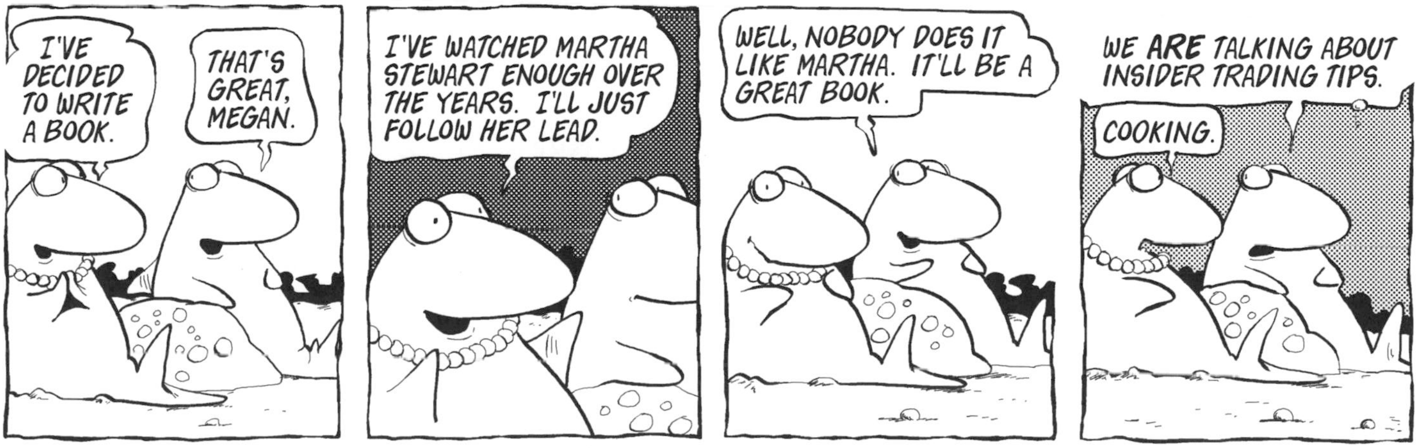
I'VE DECIDED TO WRITE A BOOK.
THAT'S GREAT, MEGAN.
I'VE WATCHED MARTHA STEWART ENOUGH OVER THE YEARS. I'LL JUST FOLLOW HER LEAD.
WELL, NOBODY DOES IT LIKE MARTHA. IT'LL BE A GREAT BOOK.
WE ARE TALKING ABOUT INSIDER TRADING TIPS.
COOKING.

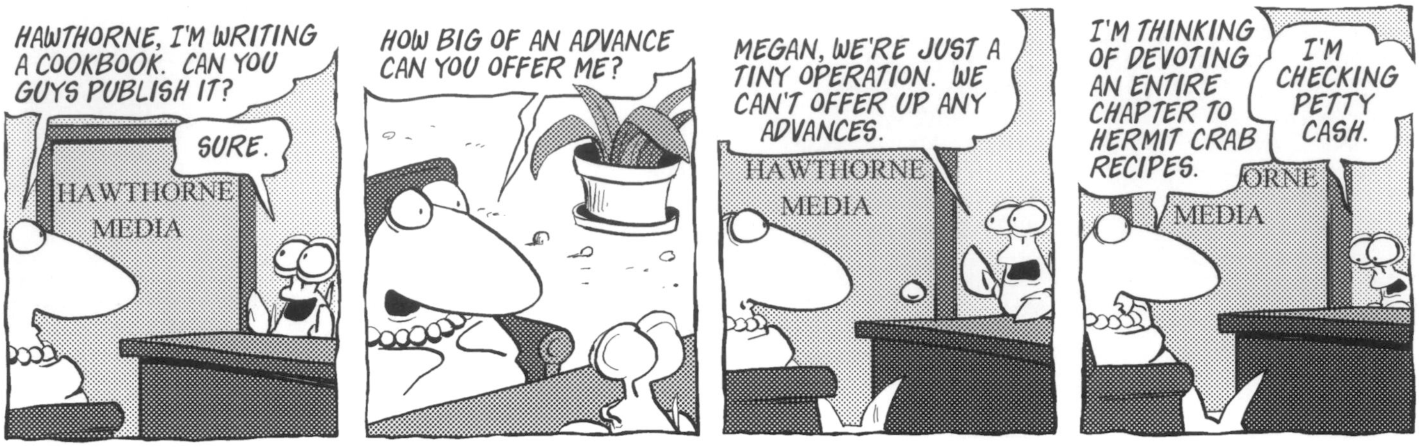
HAWTHORNE, I'M WRITING A COOKBOOK. CAN YOU GUYS PUBLISH IT?
SURE.
HAWTHORNE MEDIA
HOW BIG OF AN ADVANCE CAN YOU OFFER ME?
MEGAN, WE'RE JUST A TINY OPERATION. WE CAN'T OFFER UP ANY ADVANCES.
HAWTHORNE MEDIA
I'M THINKING OF DEVOTING AN ENTIRE CHAPTER TO HERMIT CRAB RECIPES.
I'M CHECKING PETTY CASH.

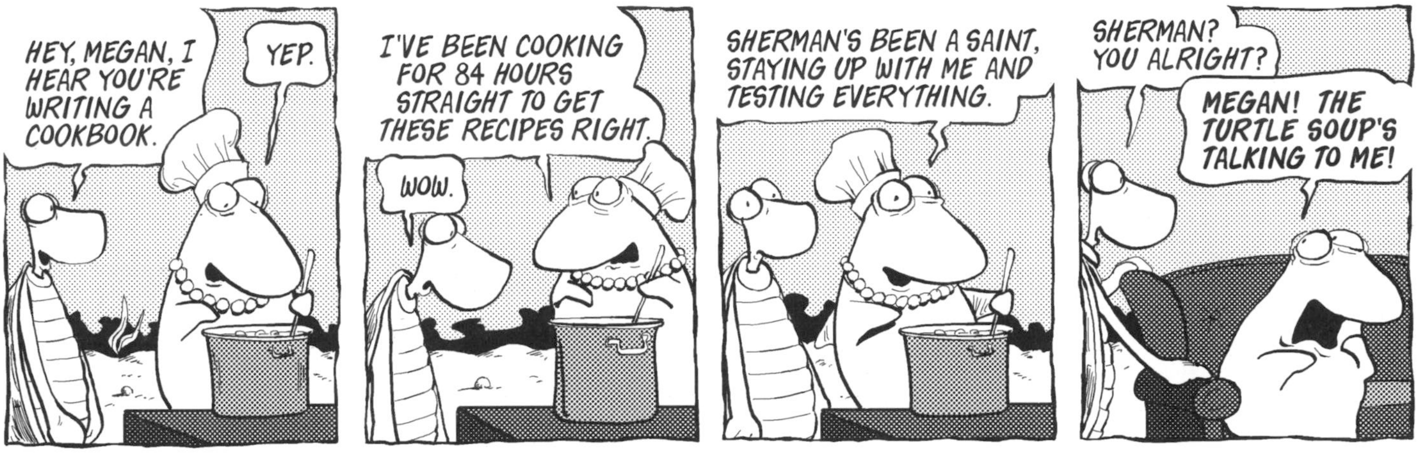
HEY, MEGAN, I HEAR YOU'RE WRITING A COOKBOOK.
YEP.
I'VE BEEN COOKING FOR 84 HOURS STRAIGHT TO GET THESE RECIPES RIGHT.
WOW.
SHERMAN'S BEEN A SAINT, STAYING UP WITH ME AND TESTING EVERYTHING.
SHERMAN? YOU ALRIGHT?
MEGAN! THE TURTLE SOUP'S TALKING TO ME!

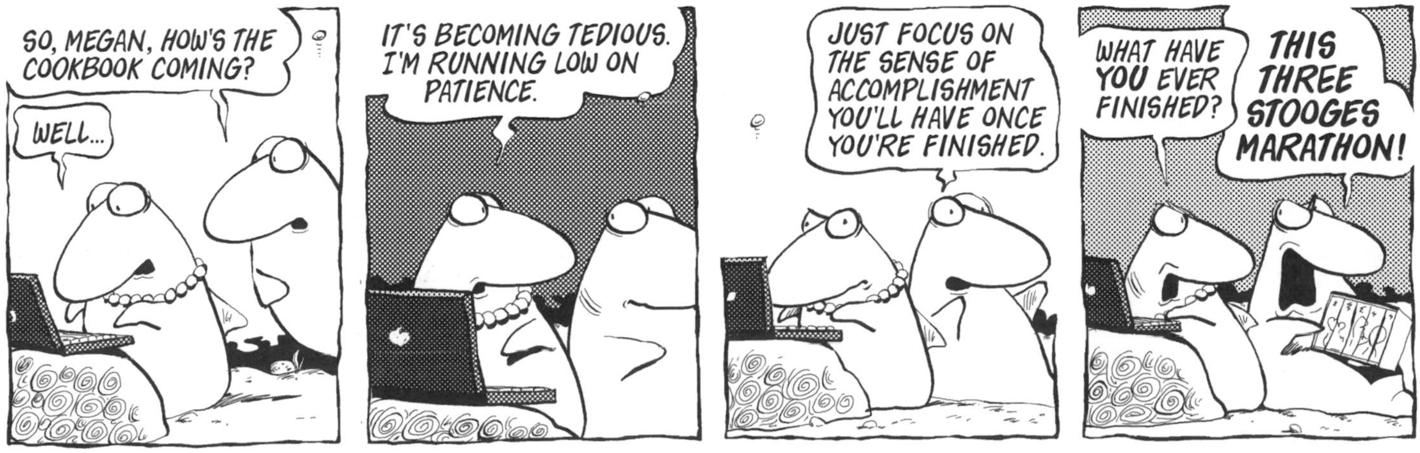
SO, MEGAN, HOW'S THE COOKBOOK COMING?
WELL...
IT'S BECOMING TEDIOUS. I'M RUNNING LOW ON PATIENCE.
JUST FOCUS ON THE SENSE OF ACCOMPLISHMENT YOU'LL HAVE ONCE YOU'RE FINISHED.
WHAT HAVE YOU EVER FINISHED?
THIS THREE STOOGES MARATHON!

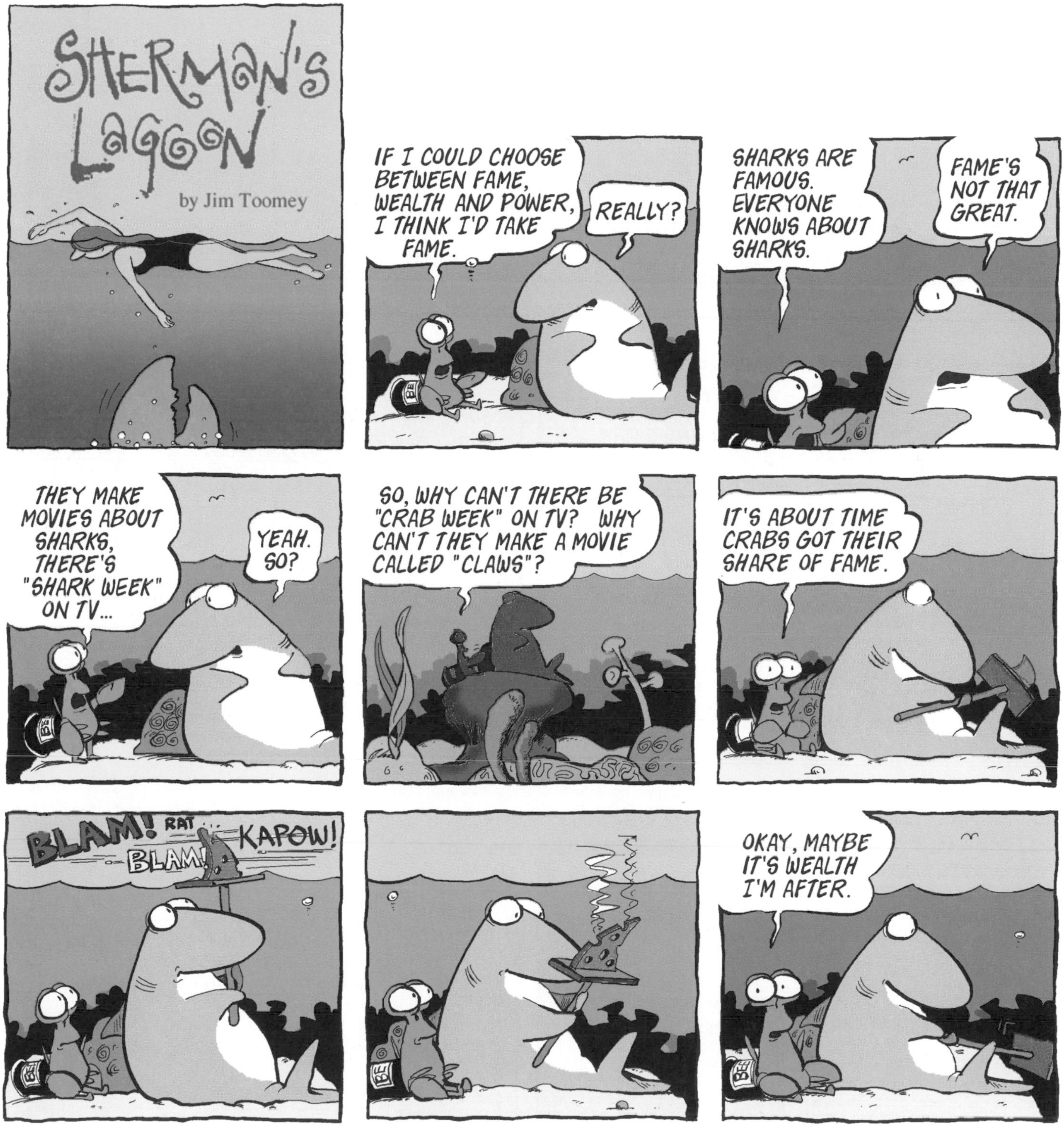
SHERMAN'S LAGOON
by Jim Toomey
IF I COULD CHOOSE BETWEEN FAME, WEALTH AND POWER, I THINK I'D TAKE FAME.
REALLY?
SHARKS ARE FAMOUS. EVERYONE KNOWS ABOUT SHARKS.
FAME'S NOT THAT GREAT.
THEY MAKE MOVIES ABOUT SHARKS, THERE'S "SHARK WEEK" ON TV...
YEAH. SO?
SO, WHY CAN'T THERE BE "CRAB WEEK" ON TV? WHY CAN'T THEY MAKE A MOVIE CALLED "CLAWS"?
IT'S ABOUT TIME CRABS GOT THEIR SHARE OF FAME.
BLAM! RAT BLAM! KAPOW!
OKAY, MAYBE IT'S WEALTH I'M AFTER.

MEGAN, WE'RE ALMOST READY TO GO TO PRINT WITH YOUR COOKBOOK.

GREAT.

Hawt Media Enterprises

President/CEO/CFO

YOU'RE SURE ALL THESE RECIPES ARE LEGITIMATE?

OF COURSE!

Hawt Media Enterprises

President/CEO/CFO

ARE YOU IMPLYING THAT I GOT LAZY AND FILLED UP PAGES JUST TO MEET MY DEADLINE?

WELL...

Hawthorne Media Enterprises

President/CEO/CFO

...THIS RECIPE IS IDENTICAL TO THE ONE ON THE BOX OF CAPTAIN CRUNCH.

THEY GOT IT FROM ME!

Hawthorne Media Enterprises

President/CEO/CFO

MEGAN, I'M HAVING TROUBLE WITH YOUR "BEANS AND FRANKS" RECIPE.

BOOK SIGNING

OH MY. EVERY SELF-RESPECTING SHARK SHOULD KNOW HOW TO MAKE THAT.

I MANAGED TO FIND BEANS EASILY ENOUGH.

BUT I CAN'T FIND 3 HAIRLESS BEACH APES NAMED "FRANK."

THAT CAN BE TRICKY.

BOOK SIGNING

THERE'S AN EASIER VERSION ON PAGE 27.

"BEANS AND STEVES"?

BOOK SIGNING

YOU WANTED TO SEE ME?

MEGAN, WE HAVE TO PULL YOUR COOKBOOK.

Ha Media Enterprises

President/CEO/CFO

TOO MANY COMPLAINTS ABOUT YOUR RECIPES. "UNSOPHISTICATED... SIMPLISTIC.... TOO FATTENING... JUST PLAIN WEIRD..."

President/CEO/CFO

DID YOU TRY ANY OF THEM?

I TRIED YOUR "SUGAR SPRINKLED ON A STICK OF BUTTER," AND I MUST SAY, IT WAS ADDICTING.

Hawthor Media Enterpri

President/CEO/CFO

AND, WHILE I PERSONALLY AM A FAN OF YOUR WORK...

WHAT ARE YOU HIDING BACK THERE?

Hawthorne Media Enterprises

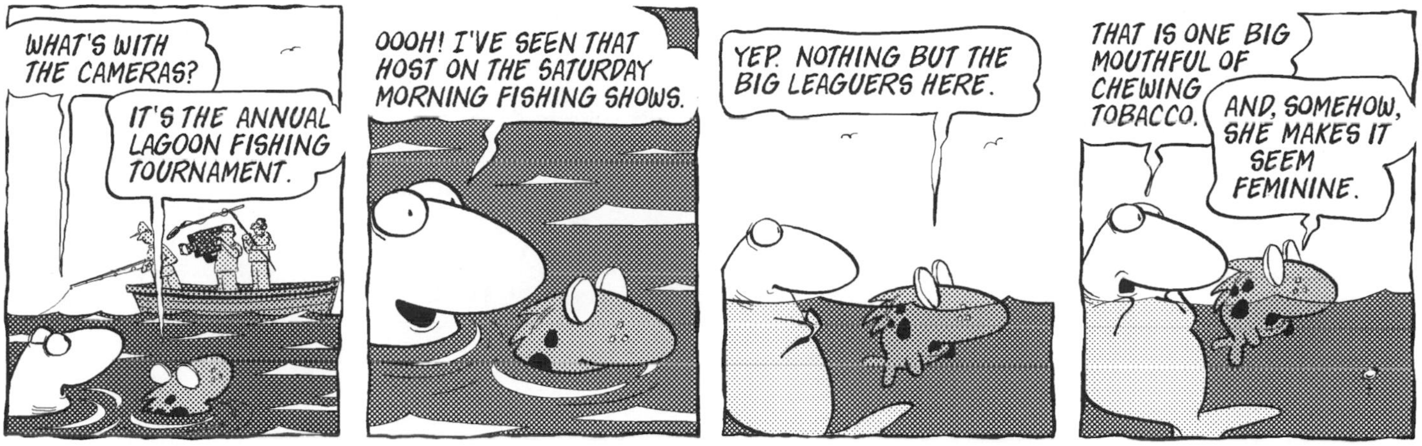
WHAT'S WITH THE CAMERAS?
IT'S THE ANNUAL LAGOON FISHING TOURNAMENT.
OOOH! I'VE SEEN THAT HOST ON THE SATURDAY MORNING FISHING SHOWS.
YEP. NOTHING BUT THE BIG LEAGUERS HERE.
THAT IS ONE BIG MOUTHFUL OF CHEWING TOBACCO.
AND, SOMEHOW, SHE MAKES IT SEEM FEMININE.

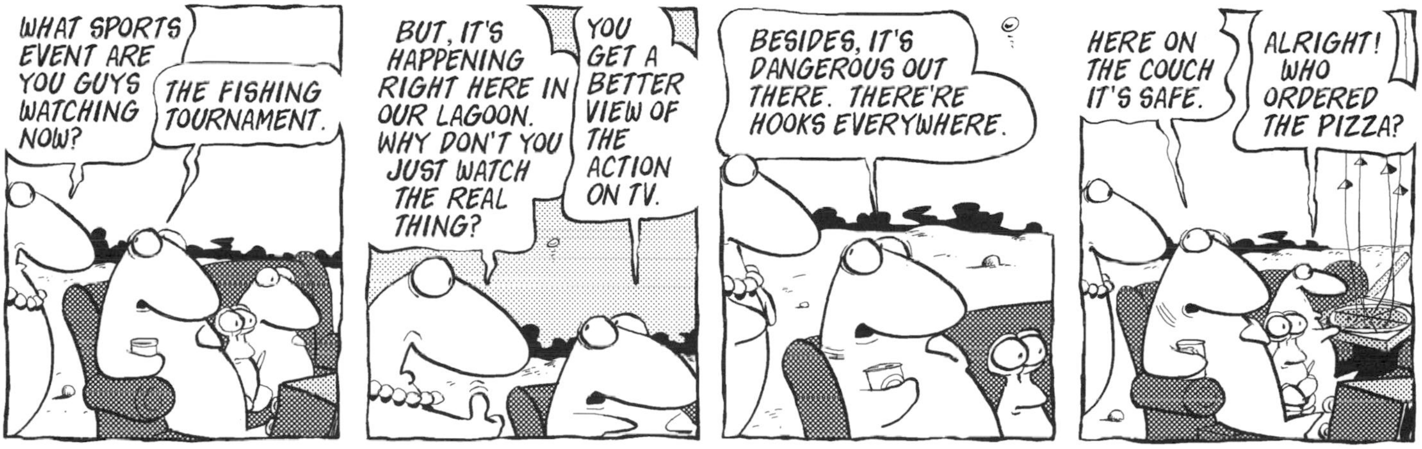
WHAT SPORTS EVENT ARE YOU GUYS WATCHING NOW?
THE FISHING TOURNAMENT.
BUT, IT'S HAPPENING RIGHT HERE IN OUR LAGOON. WHY DON'T YOU JUST WATCH THE REAL THING?
YOU GET A BETTER VIEW OF THE ACTION ON TV.
BESIDES, IT'S DANGEROUS OUT THERE. THERE'RE HOOKS EVERYWHERE.
HERE ON THE COUCH IT'S SAFE.
ALRIGHT! WHO ORDERED THE PIZZA?

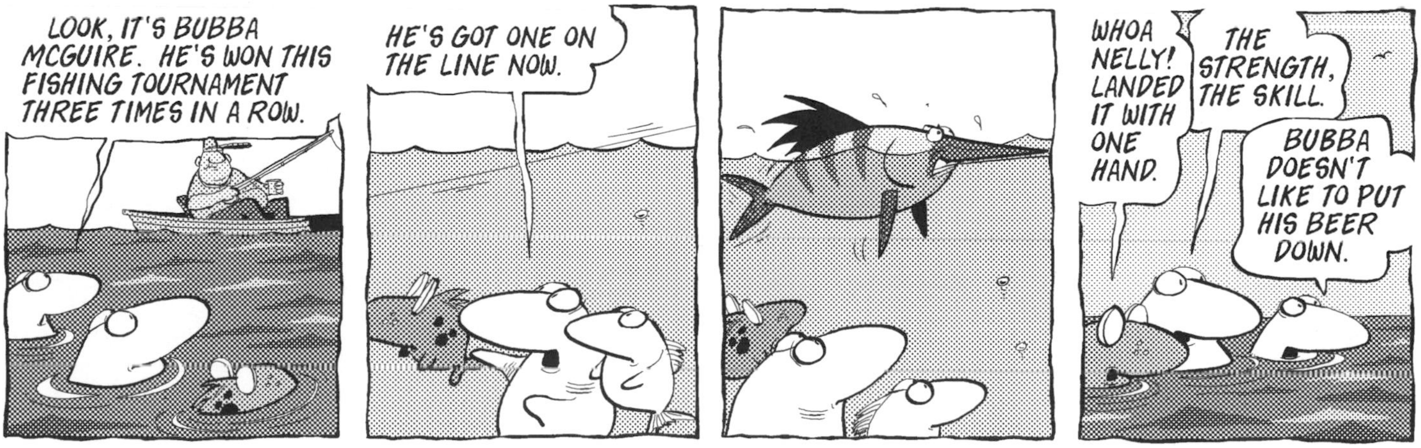
LOOK, IT'S BUBBA MCGUIRE. HE'S WON THIS FISHING TOURNAMENT THREE TIMES IN A ROW.
HE'S GOT ONE ON THE LINE NOW.
WHOA NELLY! LANDED IT WITH ONE HAND.
THE STRENGTH, THE SKILL.
BUBBA DOESN'T LIKE TO PUT HIS BEER DOWN.

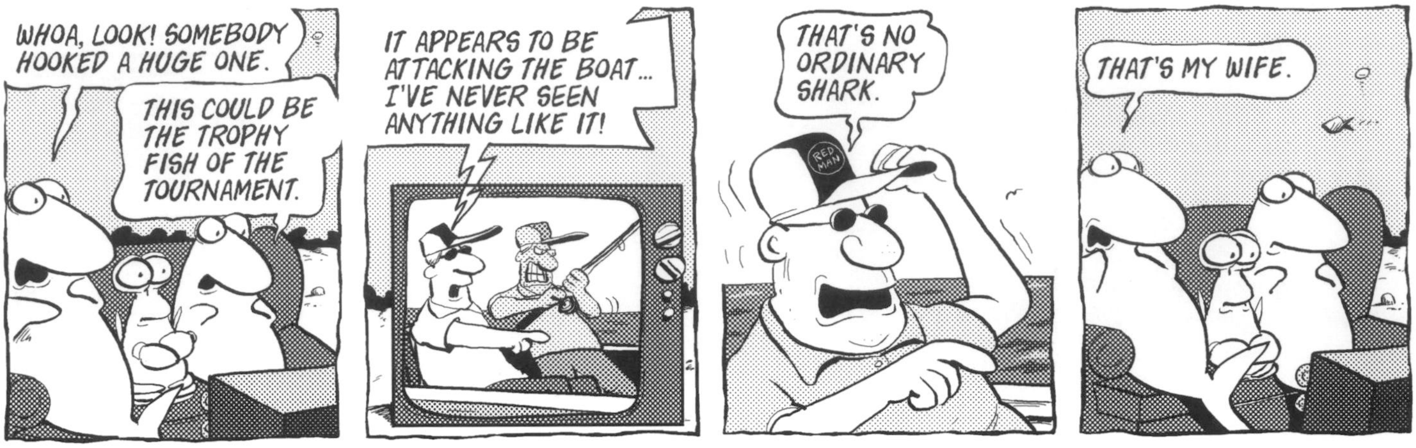
WHOA, LOOK! SOMEBODY HOOKED A HUGE ONE.
THIS COULD BE THE TROPHY FISH OF THE TOURNAMENT.
IT APPEARS TO BE ATTACKING THE BOAT... I'VE NEVER SEEN ANYTHING LIKE IT!
THAT'S NO ORDINARY SHARK.
RED MAN
THAT'S MY WIFE.

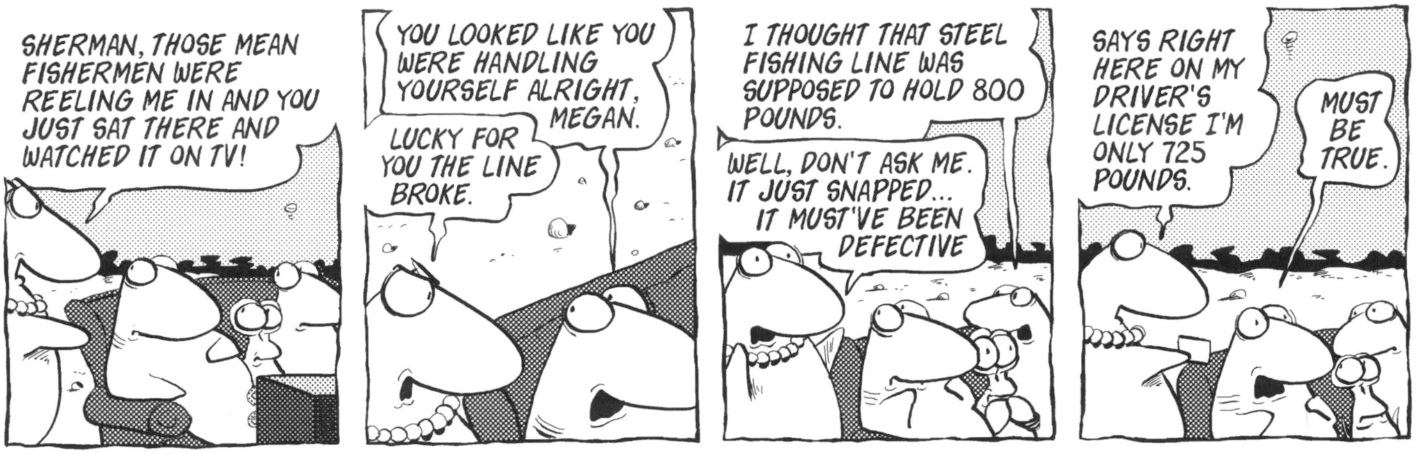
SHERMAN, THOSE MEAN FISHERMEN WERE REELING ME IN AND YOU JUST SAT THERE AND WATCHED IT ON TV!
YOU LOOKED LIKE YOU WERE HANDLING YOURSELF ALRIGHT, MEGAN.
LUCKY FOR YOU THE LINE BROKE.
I THOUGHT THAT STEEL FISHING LINE WAS SUPPOSED TO HOLD 800 POUNDS.
WELL, DON'T ASK ME. IT JUST SNAPPED... IT MUST'VE BEEN DEFECTIVE
SAYS RIGHT HERE ON MY DRIVER'S LICENSE I'M ONLY 725 POUNDS.
MUST BE TRUE.

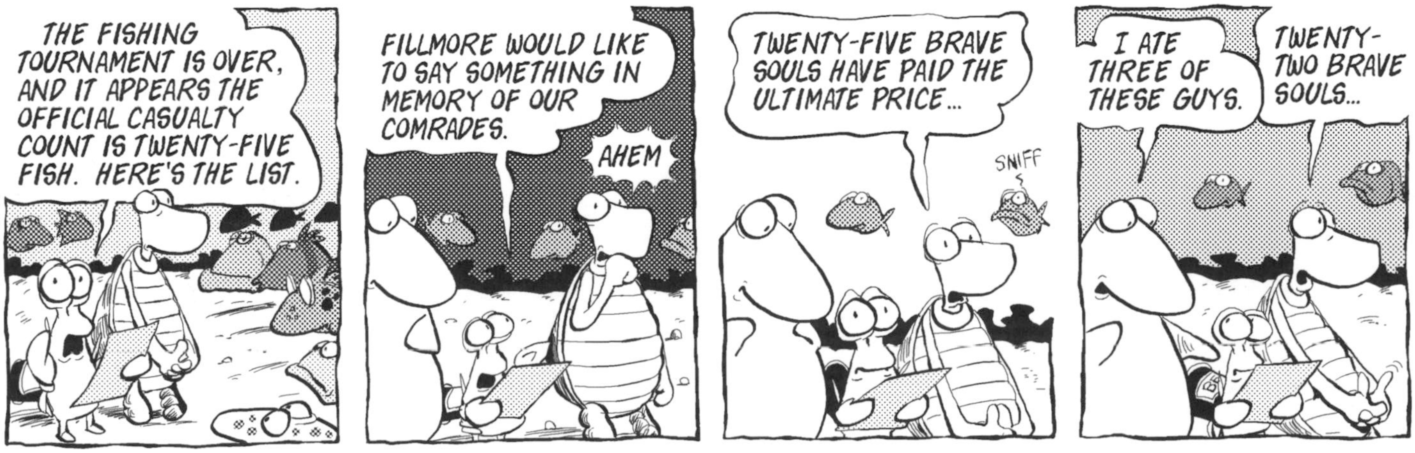
THE FISHING TOURNAMENT IS OVER, AND IT APPEARS THE OFFICIAL CASUALTY COUNT IS TWENTY-FIVE FISH. HERE'S THE LIST.
FILLMORE WOULD LIKE TO SAY SOMETHING IN MEMORY OF OUR COMRADES.
AHEM
TWENTY-FIVE BRAVE SOULS HAVE PAID THE ULTIMATE PRICE...
SNIFF
I ATE THREE OF THESE GUYS.
TWENTY-TWO BRAVE SOULS...

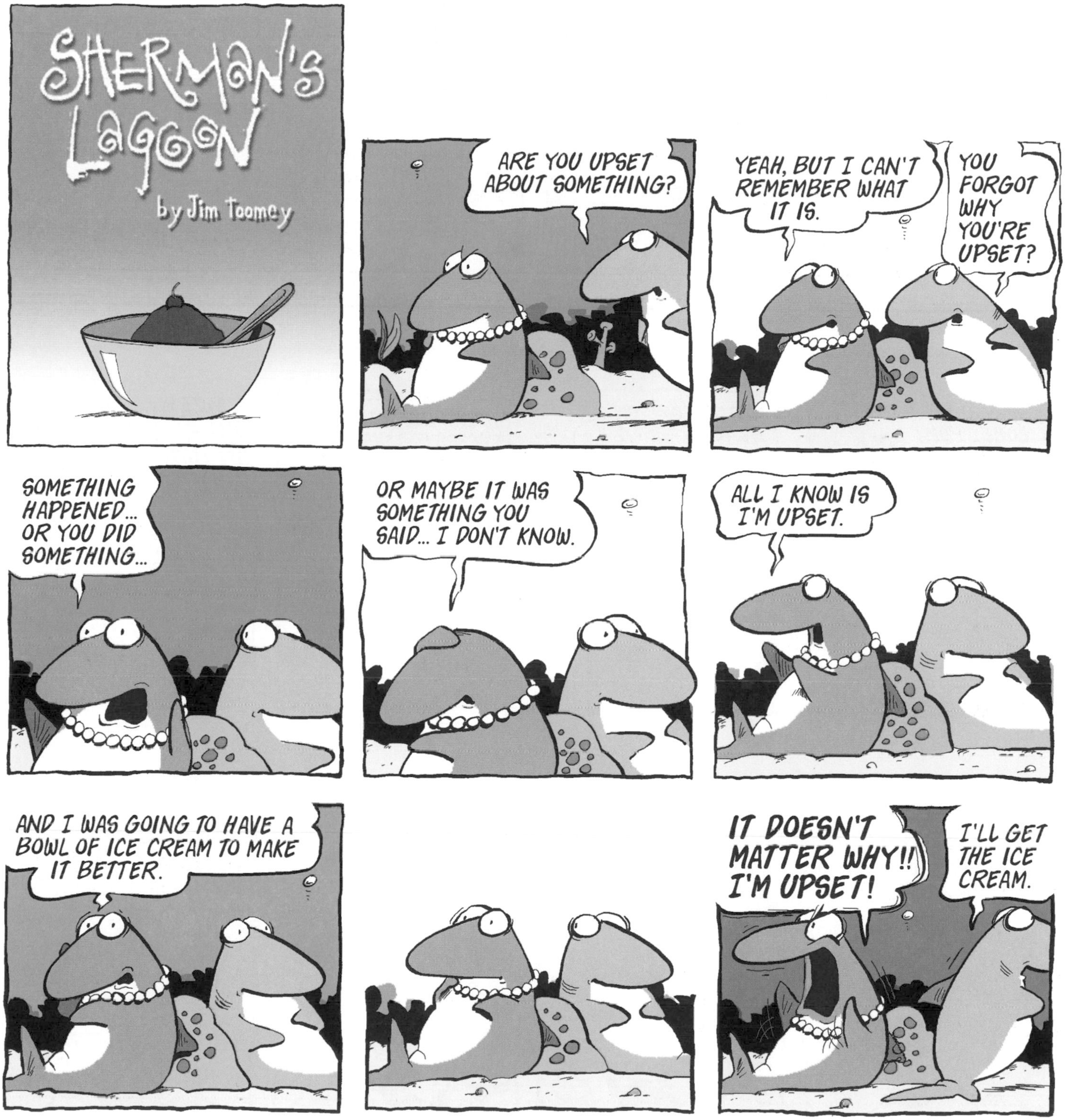
SHERMAN'S LAGOON
by Jim Toomey
ARE YOU UPSET ABOUT SOMETHING?
YEAH, BUT I CAN'T REMEMBER WHAT IT IS.
YOU FORGOT WHY YOU'RE UPSET?
SOMETHING HAPPENED... OR YOU DID SOMETHING...
OR MAYBE IT WAS SOMETHING YOU SAID... I DON'T KNOW.
ALL I KNOW IS I'M UPSET.
AND I WAS GOING TO HAVE A BOWL OF ICE CREAM TO MAKE IT BETTER.
IT DOESN'T MATTER WHY!! I'M UPSET!
I'LL GET THE ICE CREAM.

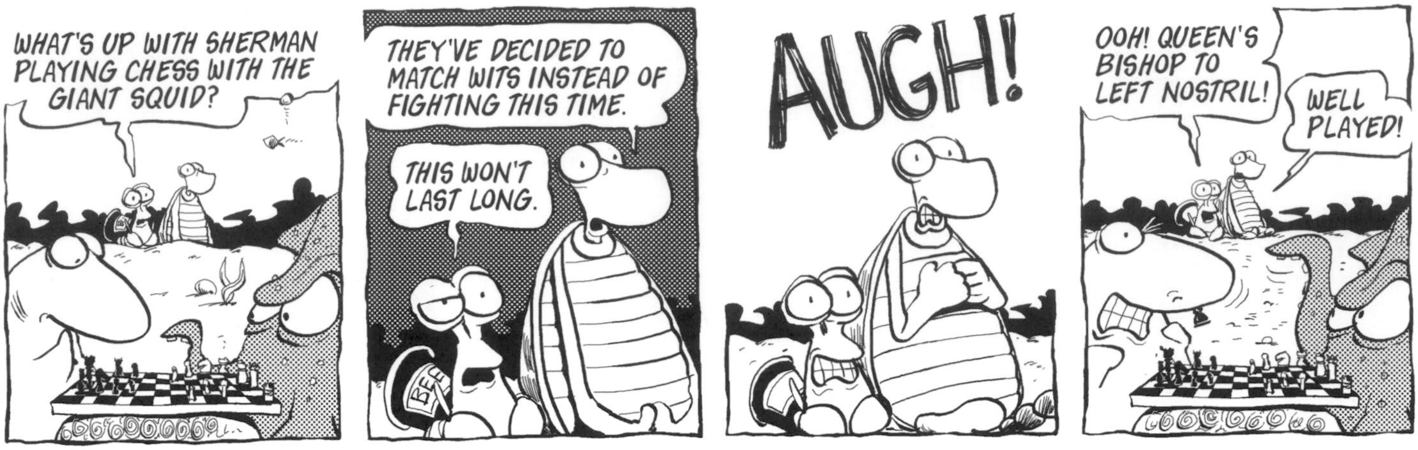
WHAT'S UP WITH SHERMAN PLAYING CHESS WITH THE GIANT SQUID?
THEY'VE DECIDED TO MATCH WITS INSTEAD OF FIGHTING THIS TIME.
THIS WON'T LAST LONG.
AUGH!
OOH! QUEEN'S BISHOP TO LEFT NOSTRIL!
WELL PLAYED!

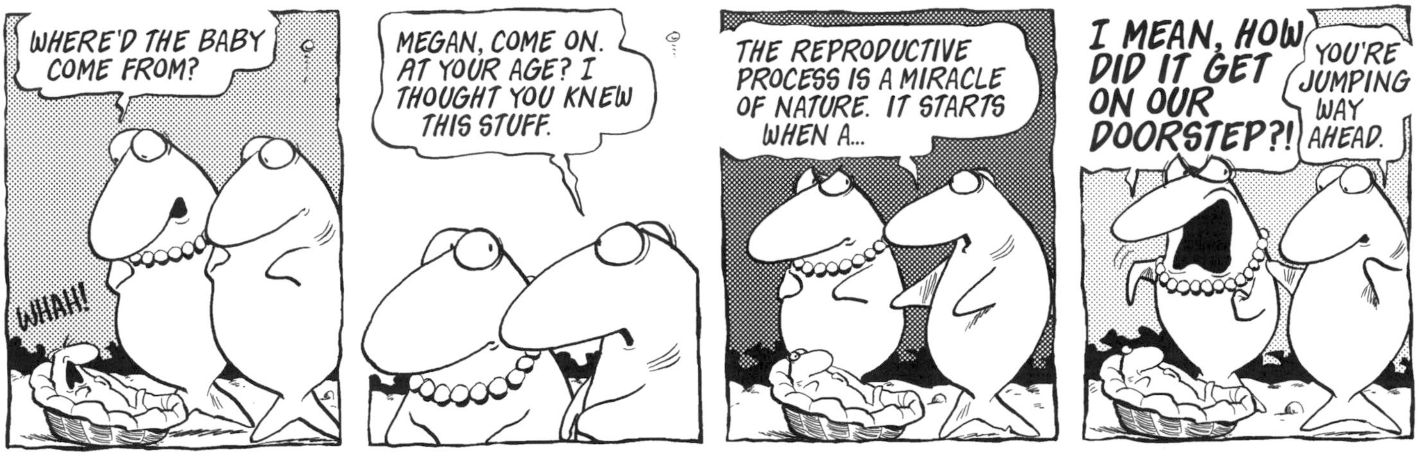
WHERE'D THE BABY COME FROM?
WHAH!
MEGAN, COME ON. AT YOUR AGE? I THOUGHT YOU KNEW THIS STUFF.
THE REPRODUCTIVE PROCESS IS A MIRACLE OF NATURE. IT STARTS WHEN A...
I MEAN, HOW DID IT GET ON OUR DOORSTEP?!
YOU'RE JUMPING WAY AHEAD.

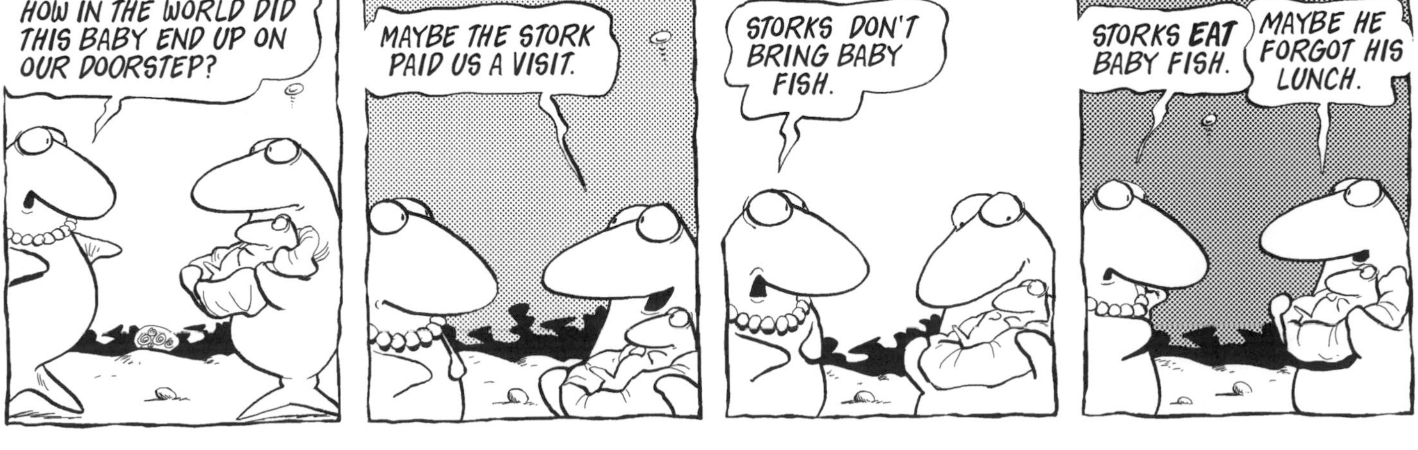
HOW IN THE WORLD DID THIS BABY END UP ON OUR DOORSTEP?
MAYBE THE STORK PAID US A VISIT.
STORKS DON'T BRING BABY FISH.
STORKS EAT BABY FISH.
MAYBE HE FORGOT HIS LUNCH.

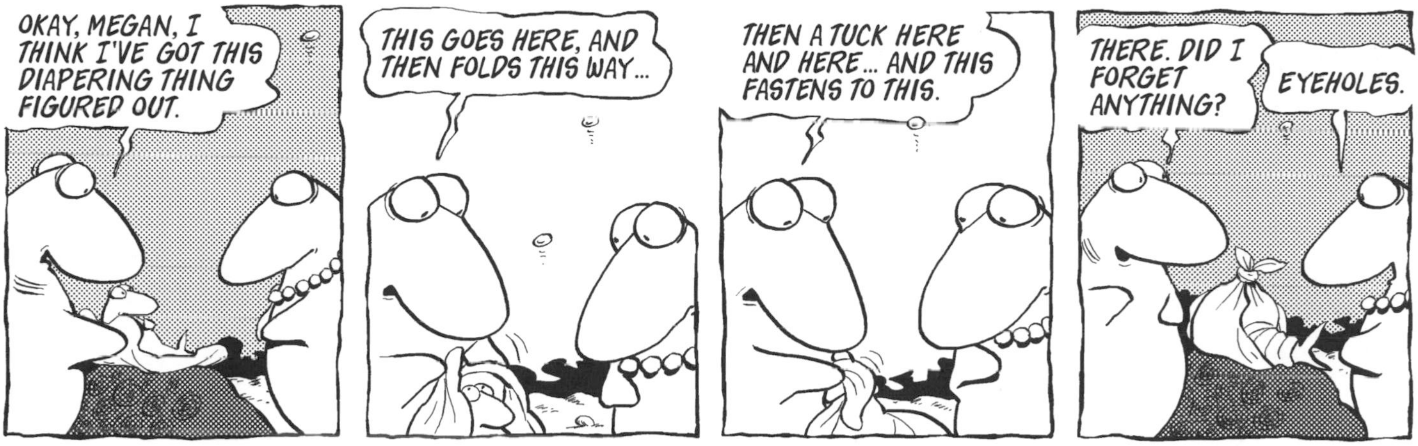
OKAY, MEGAN, I THINK I'VE GOT THIS DIAPERING THING FIGURED OUT.
THIS GOES HERE, AND THEN FOLDS THIS WAY...
THEN A TUCK HERE AND HERE... AND THIS FASTENS TO THIS.
THERE. DID I FORGET ANYTHING?
EYEHOLES.

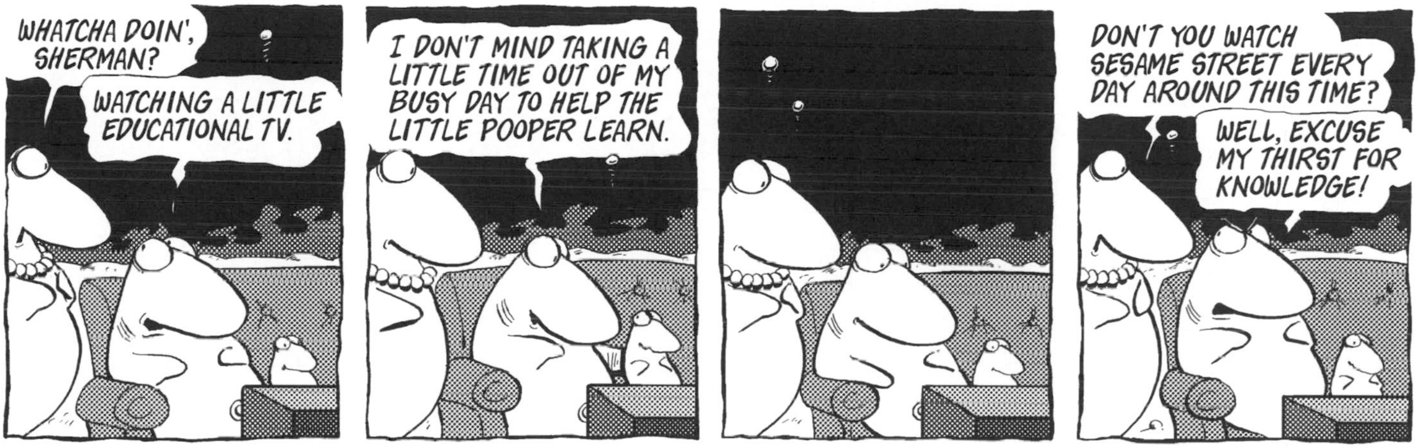
WHATCHA DOIN', SHERMAN?
WATCHING A LITTLE EDUCATIONAL TV.
I DON'T MIND TAKING A LITTLE TIME OUT OF MY BUSY DAY TO HELP THE LITTLE POOPER LEARN.
DON'T YOU WATCH SESAME STREET EVERY DAY AROUND THIS TIME?
WELL, EXCUSE MY THIRST FOR KNOWLEDGE!

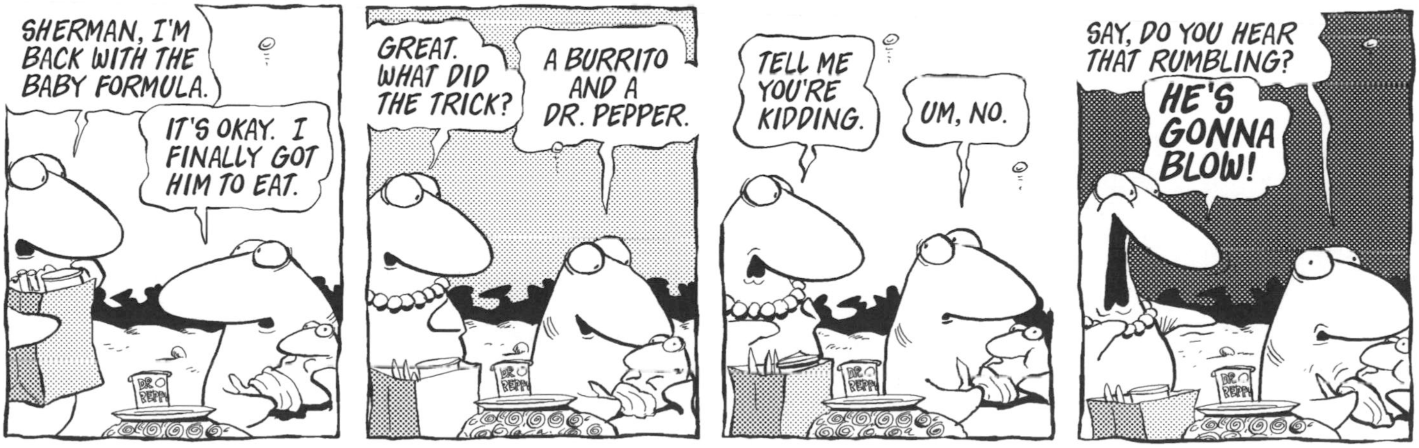
SHERMAN, I'M BACK WITH THE BABY FORMULA.
IT'S OKAY. I FINALLY GOT HIM TO EAT.
GREAT. WHAT DID THE TRICK?
A BURRITO AND A DR. PEPPER.
TELL ME YOU'RE KIDDING.
UM, NO.
SAY, DO YOU HEAR THAT RUMBLING?
HE'S GONNA BLOW!

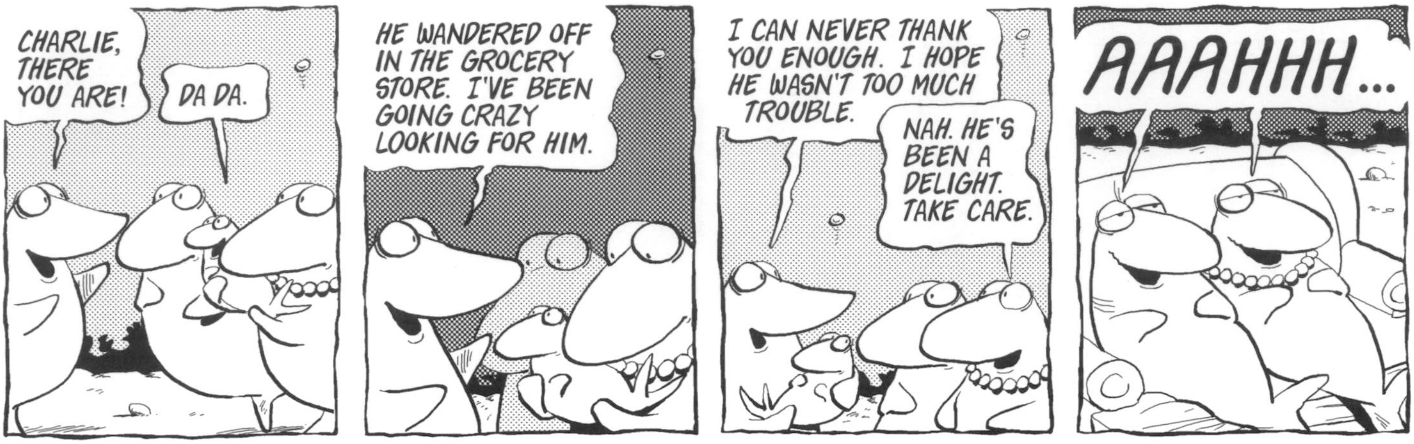
CHARLIE, THERE YOU ARE!
DA DA.
HE WANDERED OFF IN THE GROCERY STORE. I'VE BEEN GOING CRAZY LOOKING FOR HIM.
I CAN NEVER THANK YOU ENOUGH. I HOPE HE WASN'T TOO MUCH TROUBLE.
NAH. HE'S BEEN A DELIGHT. TAKE CARE.
AAAHHH...

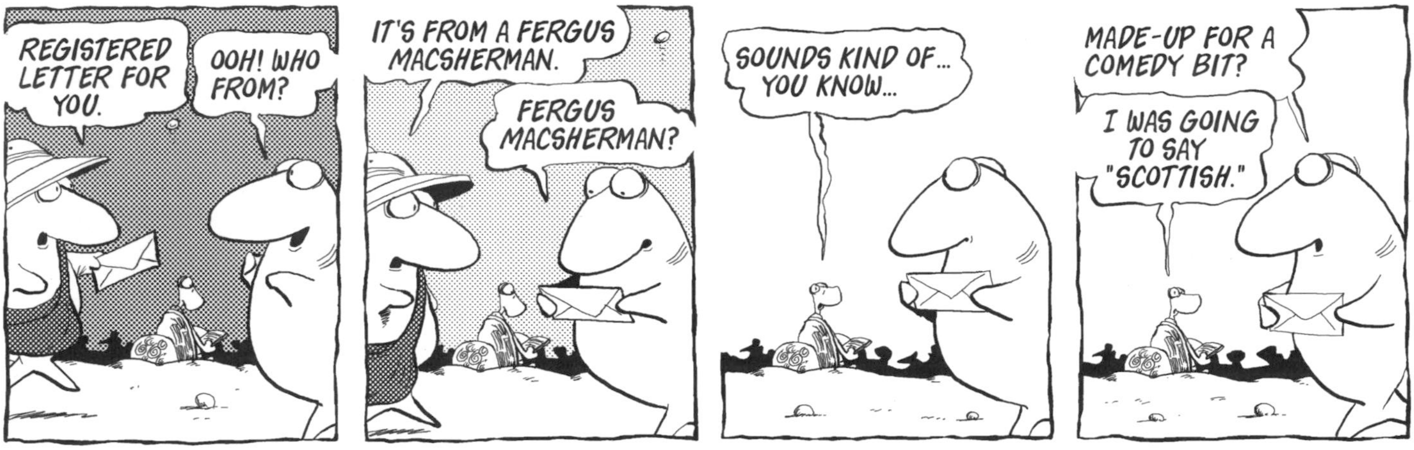
REGISTERED LETTER FOR YOU.
OOH! WHO FROM?
IT'S FROM A FERGUS MACSHERMAN.
FERGUS MACSHERMAN?
SOUNDS KIND OF... YOU KNOW...
MADE-UP FOR A COMEDY BIT?
I WAS GOING TO SAY "SCOTTISH."

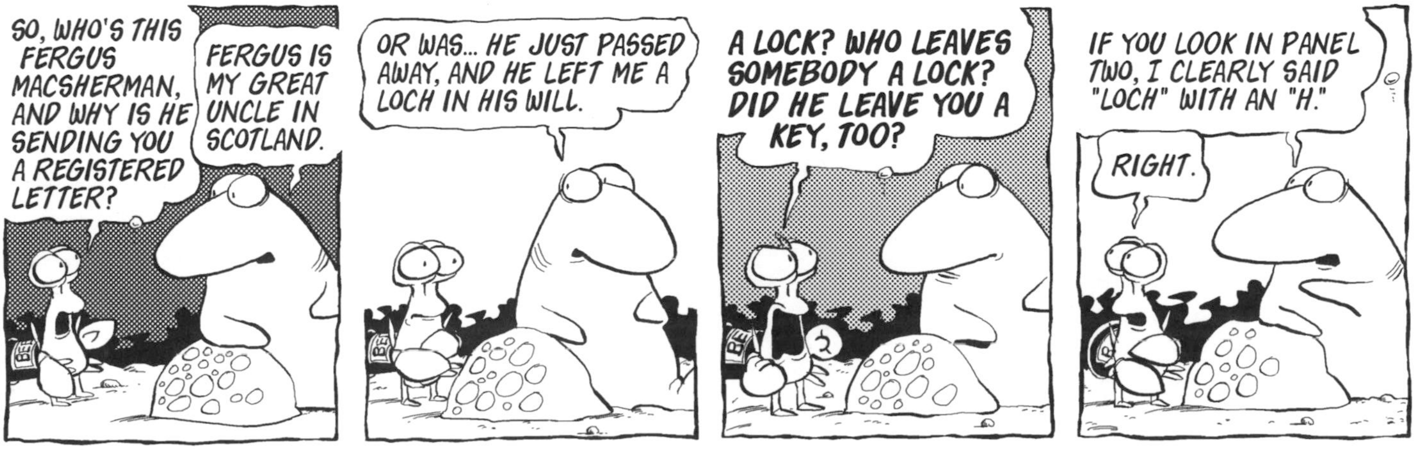
SO, WHO'S THIS FERGUS MACSHERMAN, AND WHY IS HE SENDING YOU A REGISTERED LETTER?
FERGUS IS MY GREAT UNCLE IN SCOTLAND.
OR WAS... HE JUST PASSED AWAY, AND HE LEFT ME A LOCH IN HIS WILL.
A LOCK? WHO LEAVES SOMEBODY A LOCK? DID HE LEAVE YOU A KEY, TOO?
IF YOU LOOK IN PANEL TWO, I CLEARLY SAID "LOCH" WITH AN "H."
RIGHT.

SHERMAN'S LAGOON

by Jim Toomey

HAWTHORNE, CAN YOU DO US A FAVOR?

SURE.

NOBODY SEEMS TO WANT TO GO SWIMMING TODAY, AND IT'S WELL PAST LUNCH. CAN YOU CRAWL UP ON THE BEACH AND PUT THIS LASSO AROUND SOMEBODY'S ANKLE?

WE'LL DO THE REST.

ANYBODY IN PARTICULAR?

NOPE. YOU DECIDE.

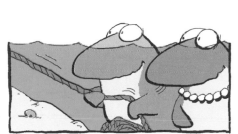

LET'S GIVE HIM A SHORTER ROPE NEXT TIME.

HE JUST GOT ON A BUS!

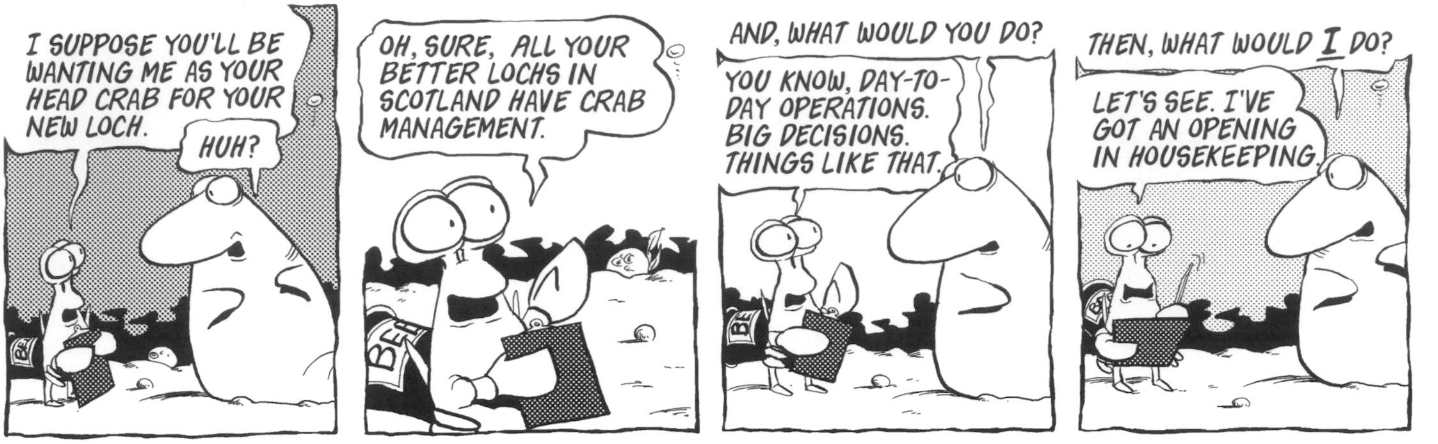
I SUPPOSE YOU'LL BE WANTING ME AS YOUR HEAD CRAB FOR YOUR NEW LOCH.
HUH?
OH, SURE, ALL YOUR BETTER LOCHS IN SCOTLAND HAVE CRAB MANAGEMENT.
AND, WHAT WOULD YOU DO?
YOU KNOW, DAY-TO-DAY OPERATIONS. BIG DECISIONS. THINGS LIKE THAT.
THEN, WHAT WOULD I DO?
LET'S SEE. I'VE GOT AN OPENING IN HOUSEKEEPING.

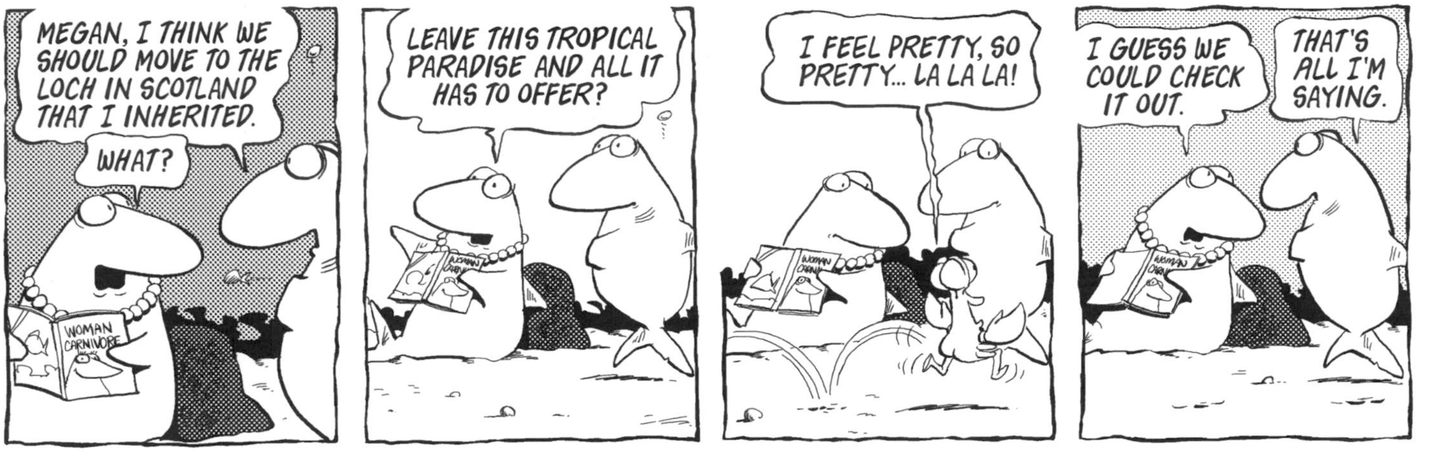
MEGAN, I THINK WE SHOULD MOVE TO THE LOCH IN SCOTLAND THAT I INHERITED.
WHAT?
WOMAN CARNIVORE
LEAVE THIS TROPICAL PARADISE AND ALL IT HAS TO OFFER?
I FEEL PRETTY, SO PRETTY... LA LA LA!
I GUESS WE COULD CHECK IT OUT.
THAT'S ALL I'M SAYING.

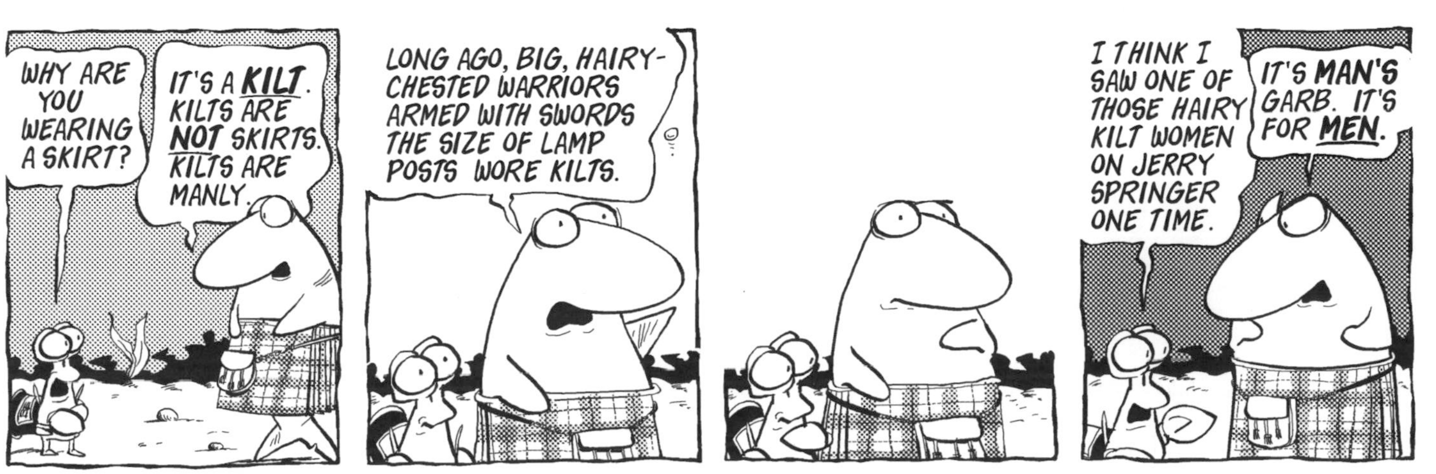
WHY ARE YOU WEARING A SKIRT?
IT'S A KILT. KILTS ARE NOT SKIRTS. KILTS ARE MANLY.
LONG AGO, BIG, HAIRY-CHESTED WARRIORS ARMED WITH SWORDS THE SIZE OF LAMP POSTS WORE KILTS.
I THINK I SAW ONE OF THOSE HAIRY KILT WOMEN ON JERRY SPRINGER ONE TIME.
IT'S MAN'S GARB. IT'S FOR MEN.

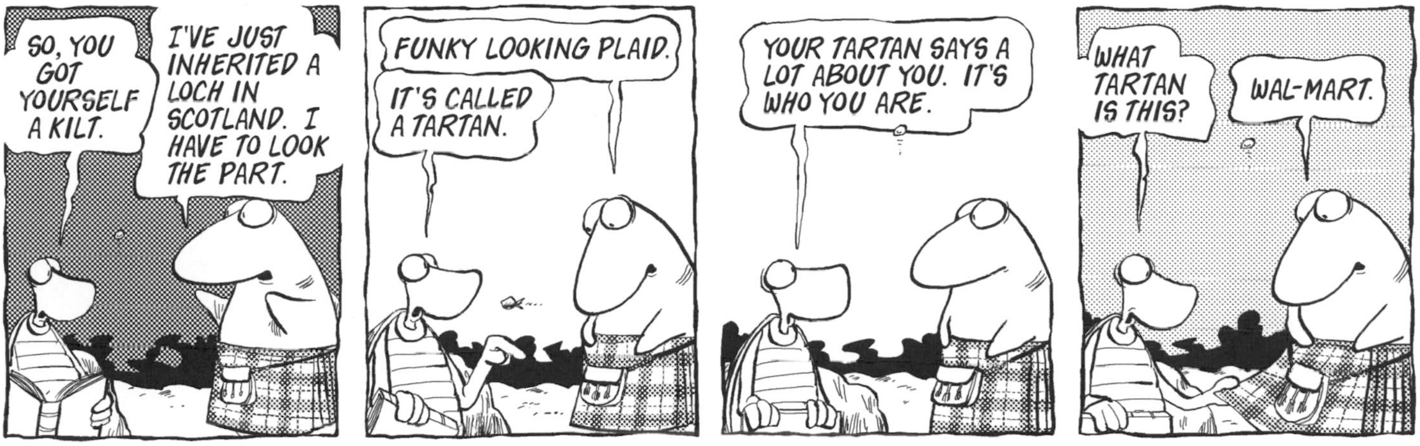
SO, YOU GOT YOURSELF A KILT.
I'VE JUST INHERITED A LOCH IN SCOTLAND. I HAVE TO LOOK THE PART.
FUNKY LOOKING PLAID.
IT'S CALLED A TARTAN.
YOUR TARTAN SAYS A LOT ABOUT YOU. IT'S WHO YOU ARE.
WHAT TARTAN IS THIS?
WAL-MART.

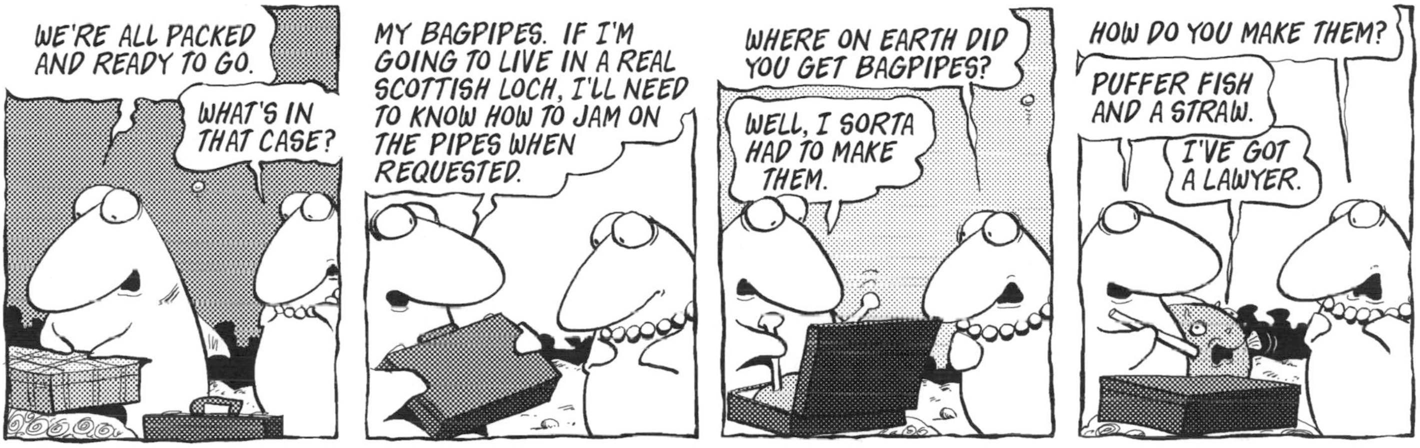
WE'RE ALL PACKED AND READY TO GO.
WHAT'S IN THAT CASE?
MY BAGPIPES. IF I'M GOING TO LIVE IN A REAL SCOTTISH LOCH, I'LL NEED TO KNOW HOW TO JAM ON THE PIPES WHEN REQUESTED.
WHERE ON EARTH DID YOU GET BAGPIPES?
WELL, I SORTA HAD TO MAKE THEM.
HOW DO YOU MAKE THEM?
PUFFER FISH AND A STRAW.
I'VE GOT A LAWYER.

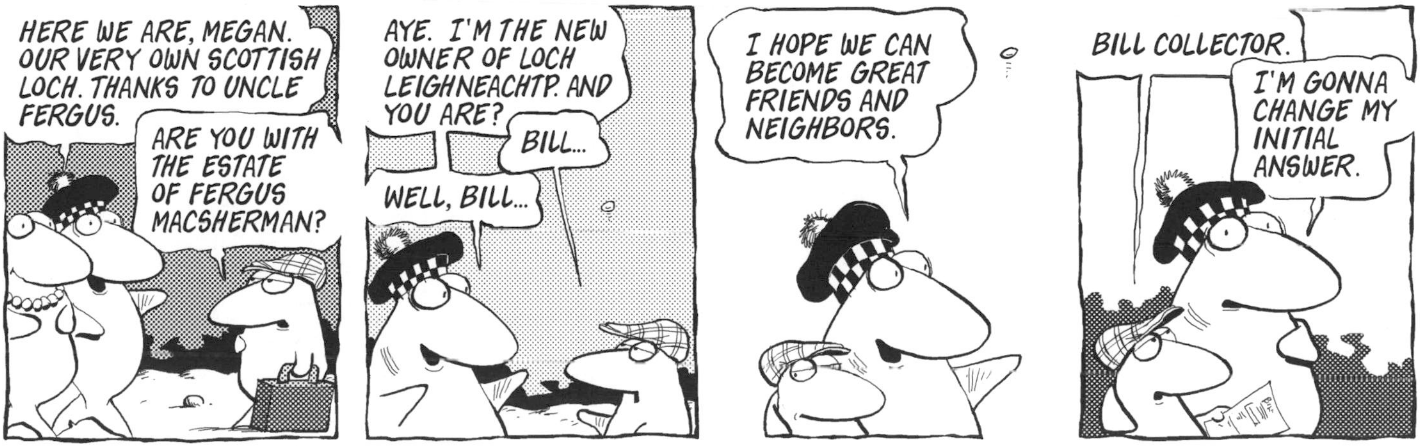
HERE WE ARE, MEGAN. OUR VERY OWN SCOTTISH LOCH. THANKS TO UNCLE FERGUS.
ARE YOU WITH THE ESTATE OF FERGUS MACSHERMAN?
AYE. I'M THE NEW OWNER OF LOCH LEIGHNEACHTP. AND YOU ARE?
BILL...
WELL, BILL...
I HOPE WE CAN BECOME GREAT FRIENDS AND NEIGHBORS.
BILL COLLECTOR.
I'M GONNA CHANGE MY INITIAL ANSWER.

SHERMAN'S LAGOON
by Jim Toomey
I'M GOING TOPSIDE. NEED ANYTHING?
I WROTE IT DOWN.
PETS
HEY! GET OUT OF HERE!
BEEEEEEEEP!
HERE'S YOUR GOLDFISH.
I MEANT THE LITTLE CRACKERS.

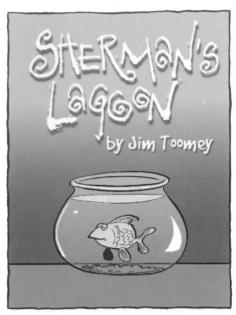

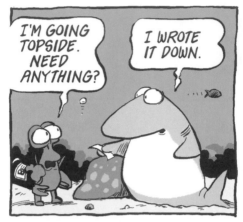

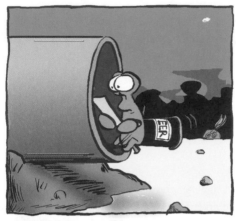

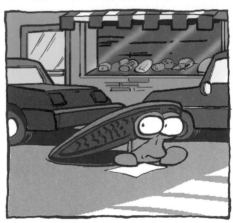

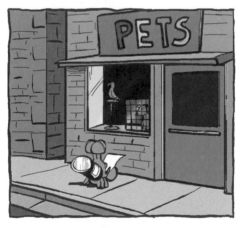

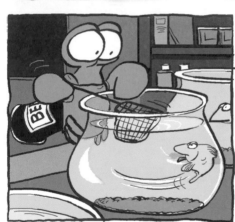

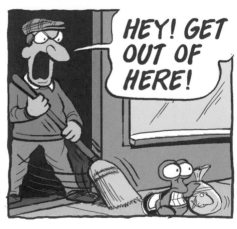

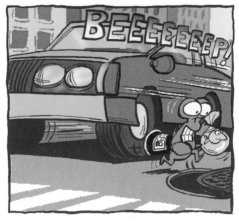

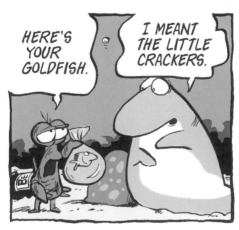

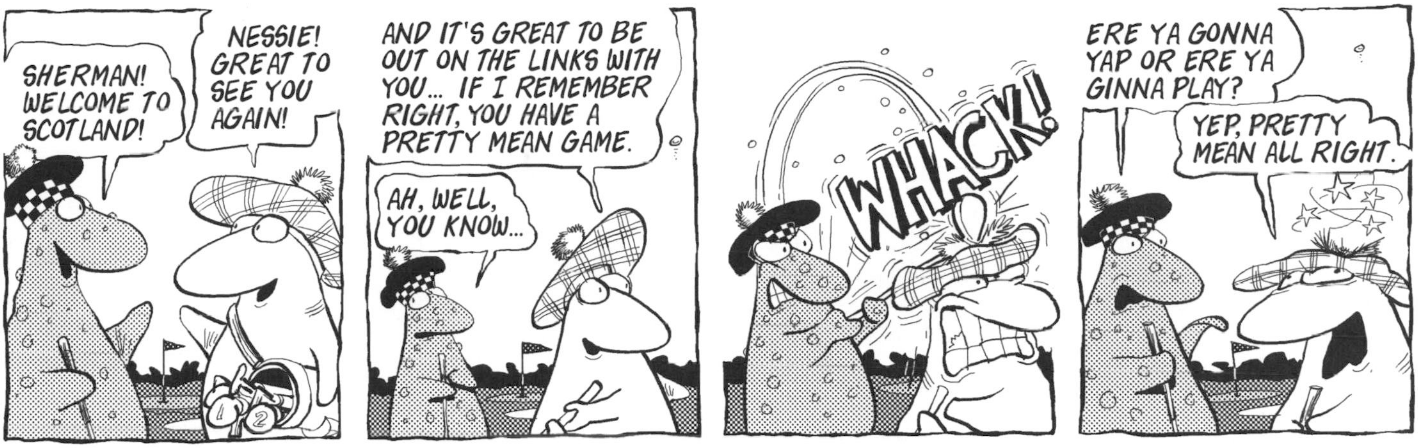
SHERMAN! WELCOME TO SCOTLAND!
NESSIE! GREAT TO SEE YOU AGAIN!
AND IT'S GREAT TO BE OUT ON THE LINKS WITH YOU... IF I REMEMBER RIGHT, YOU HAVE A PRETTY MEAN GAME.
AH, WELL, YOU KNOW...
WHACK!
ERE YA GONNA YAP OR ERE YA GINNA PLAY?
YEP, PRETTY MEAN ALL RIGHT.

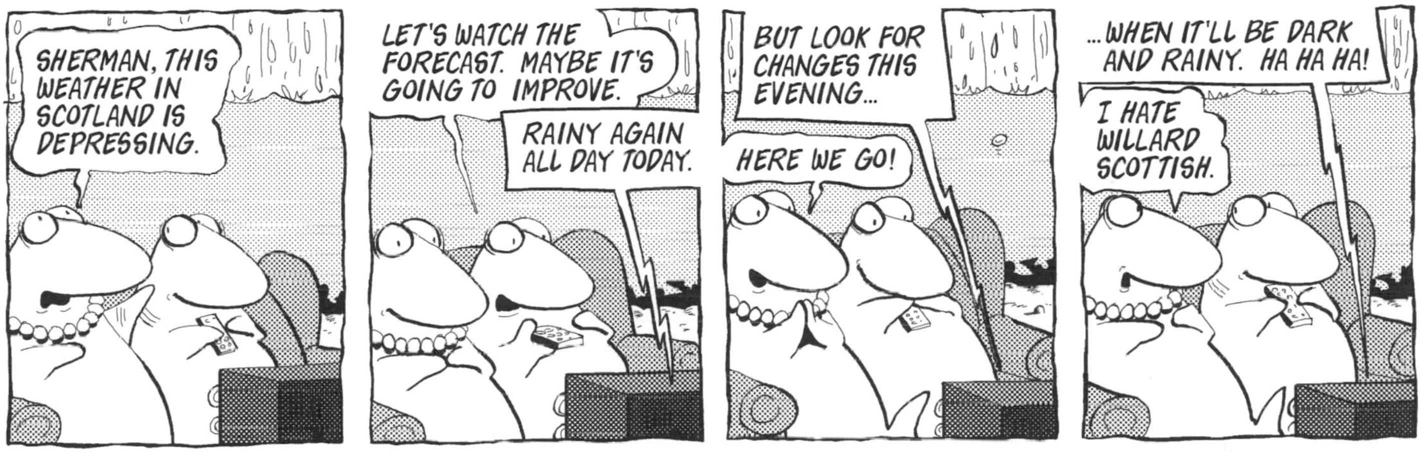
SHERMAN, THIS WEATHER IN SCOTLAND IS DEPRESSING.
LET'S WATCH THE FORECAST. MAYBE IT'S GOING TO IMPROVE.
RAINY AGAIN ALL DAY TODAY.
BUT LOOK FOR CHANGES THIS EVENING...
HERE WE GO!
...WHEN IT'LL BE DARK AND RAINY. HA HA HA!
I HATE WILLARD SCOTTISH.

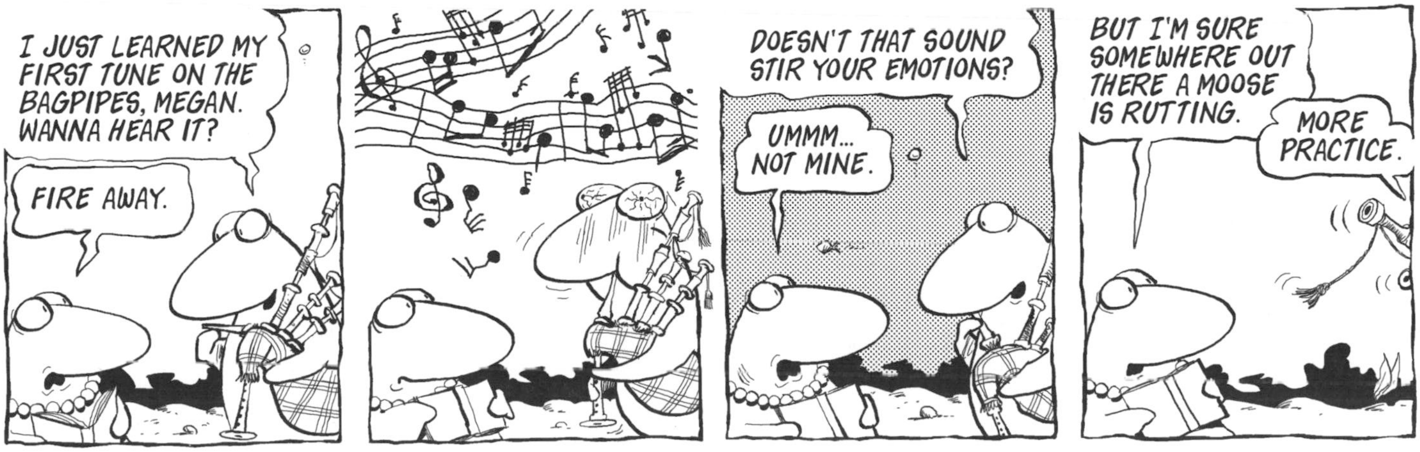
I JUST LEARNED MY FIRST TUNE ON THE BAGPIPES, MEGAN. WANNA HEAR IT?
FIRE AWAY.
DOESN'T THAT SOUND STIR YOUR EMOTIONS?
UMMM... NOT MINE.
BUT I'M SURE SOMEWHERE OUT THERE A MOOSE IS RUTTING.
MORE PRACTICE.

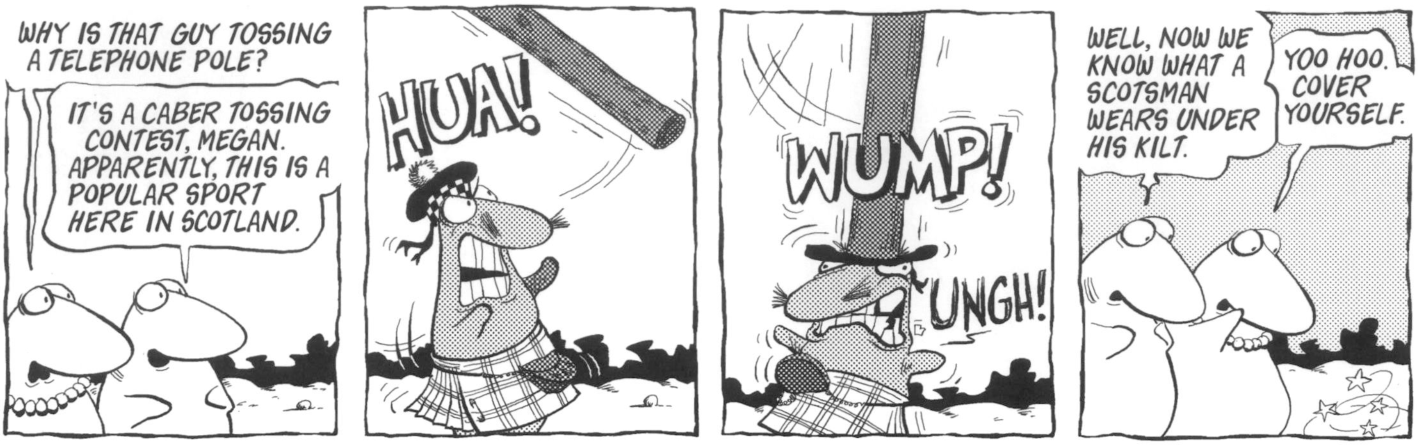
WHY IS THAT GUY TOSSING A TELEPHONE POLE?
IT'S A CABER TOSSING CONTEST, MEGAN. APPARENTLY, THIS IS A POPULAR SPORT HERE IN SCOTLAND.
HUA!
WUMP!
UNGH!
WELL, NOW WE KNOW WHAT A SCOTSMAN WEARS UNDER HIS KILT.
YOO HOO. COVER YOURSELF.

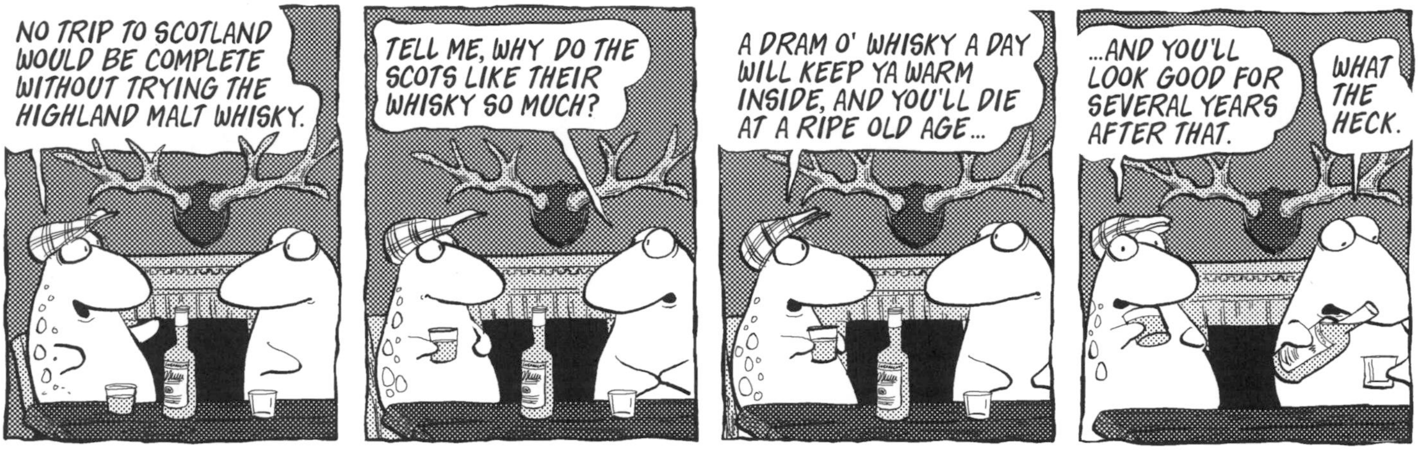
NO TRIP TO SCOTLAND WOULD BE COMPLETE WITHOUT TRYING THE HIGHLAND MALT WHISKY.
TELL ME, WHY DO THE SCOTS LIKE THEIR WHISKY SO MUCH?
A DRAM O' WHISKY A DAY WILL KEEP YA WARM INSIDE, AND YOU'LL DIE AT A RIPE OLD AGE...
...AND YOU'LL LOOK GOOD FOR SEVERAL YEARS AFTER THAT.
WHAT THE HECK.

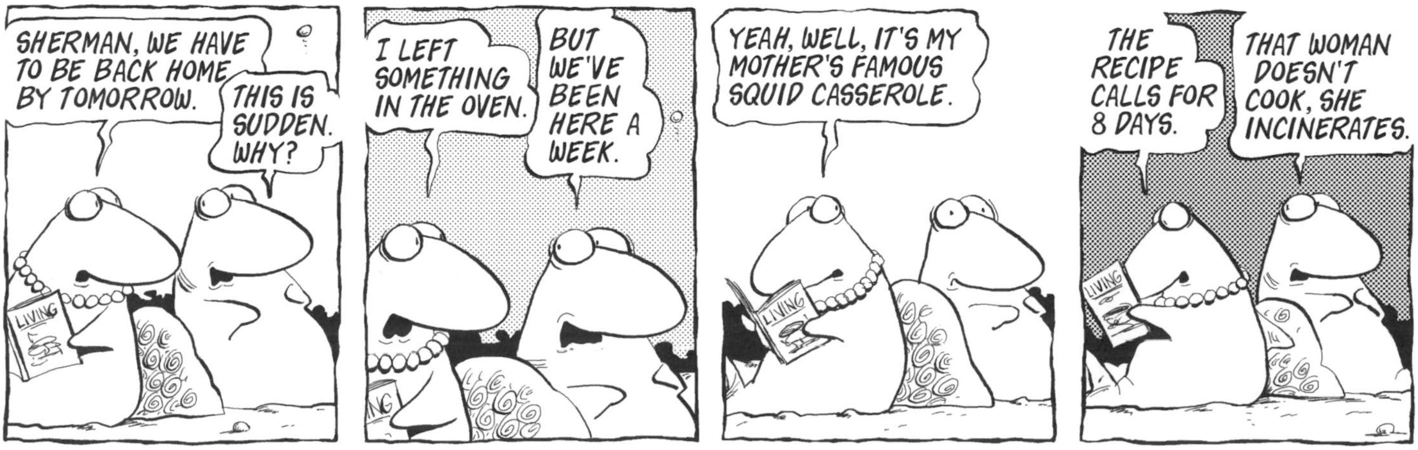
SHERMAN, WE HAVE TO BE BACK HOME BY TOMORROW.
THIS IS SUDDEN. WHY?
I LEFT SOMETHING IN THE OVEN.
BUT WE'VE BEEN HERE A WEEK.
YEAH, WELL, IT'S MY MOTHER'S FAMOUS SQUID CASSEROLE.
THE RECIPE CALLS FOR 8 DAYS.
THAT WOMAN DOESN'T COOK, SHE INCINERATES.

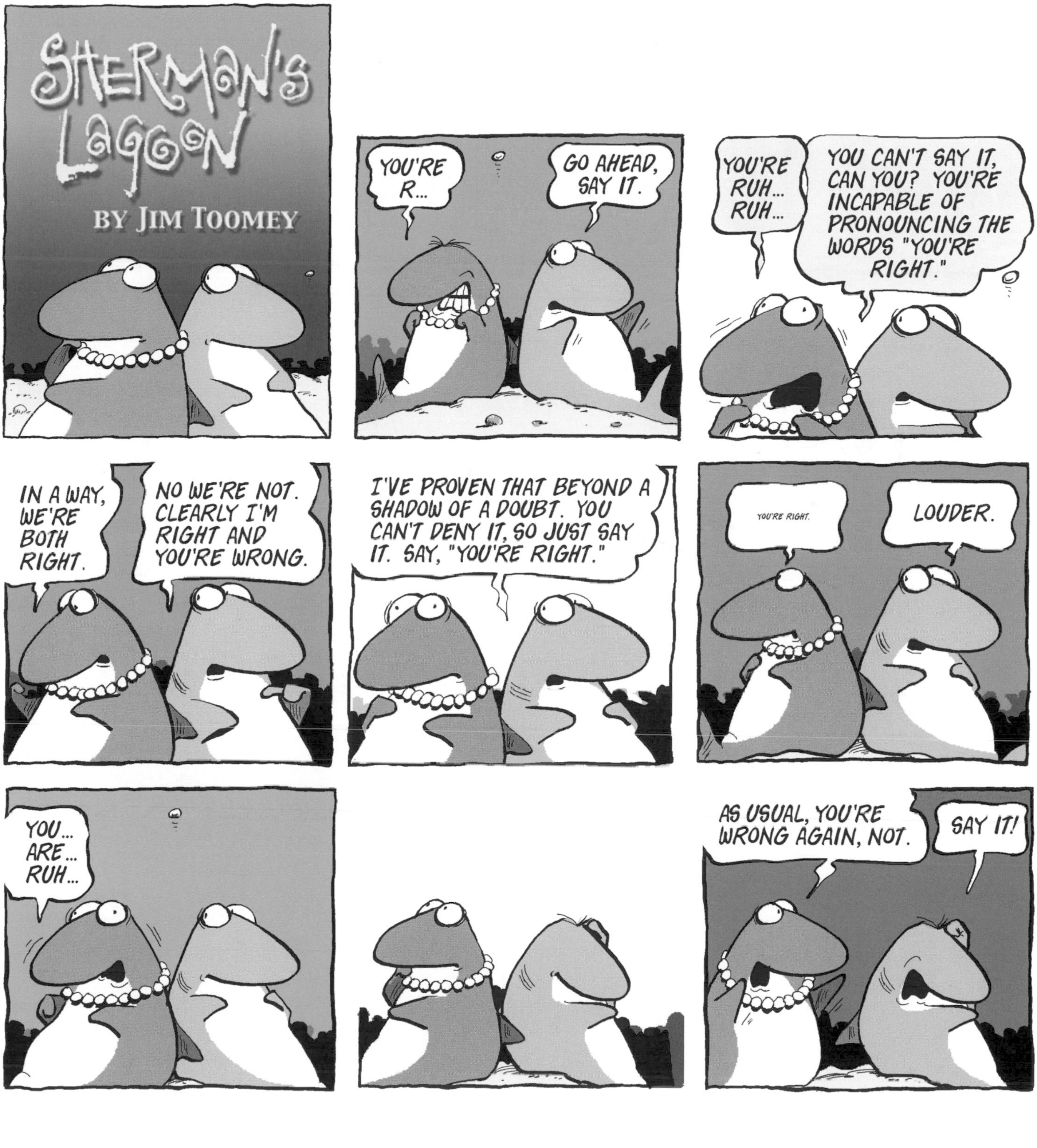
SHERMAN'S LAGOON
BY JIM TOOMEY
YOU'RE R...
GO AHEAD, SAY IT.
YOU'RE RUH... RUH...
YOU CAN'T SAY IT, CAN YOU? YOU'RE INCAPABLE OF PRONOUNCING THE WORDS "YOU'RE RIGHT."
IN A WAY, WE'RE BOTH RIGHT.
NO WE'RE NOT. CLEARLY I'M RIGHT AND YOU'RE WRONG.
I'VE PROVEN THAT BEYOND A SHADOW OF A DOUBT. YOU CAN'T DENY IT, SO JUST SAY IT. SAY, "YOU'RE RIGHT."
YOU'RE RIGHT.
LOUDER.
YOU... ARE... RUH...
AS USUAL, YOU'RE WRONG AGAIN, NOT.
SAY IT!

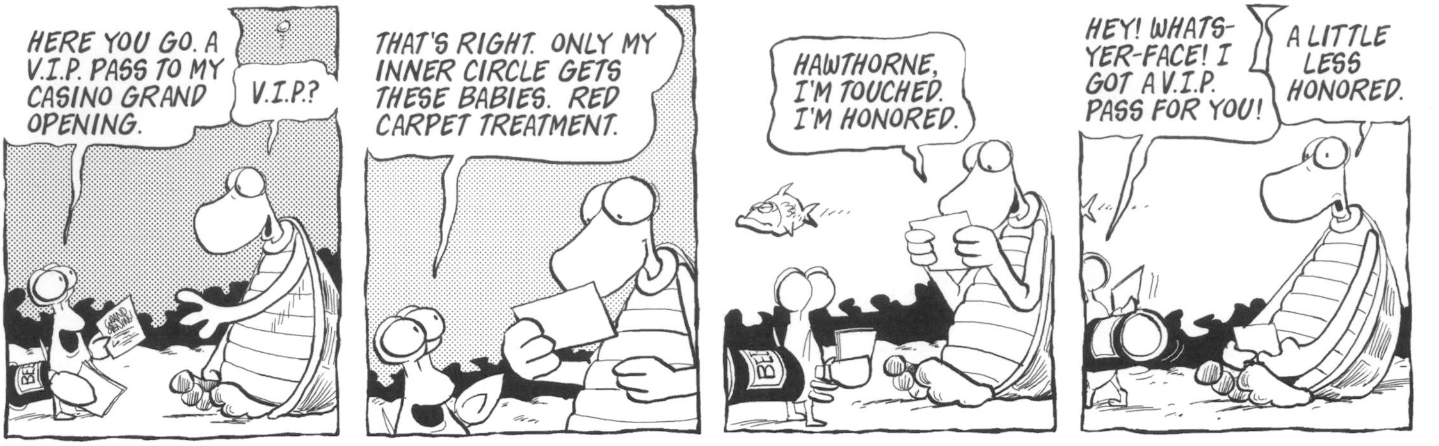

HERE YOU GO. A V.I.P. PASS TO MY CASINO GRAND OPENING.
V.I.P.?
THAT'S RIGHT. ONLY MY INNER CIRCLE GETS THESE BABIES. RED CARPET TREATMENT.
HAWTHORNE, I'M TOUCHED. I'M HONORED.
HEY! WHATS-YER-FACE! I GOT A V.I.P. PASS FOR YOU!
A LITTLE LESS HONORED.

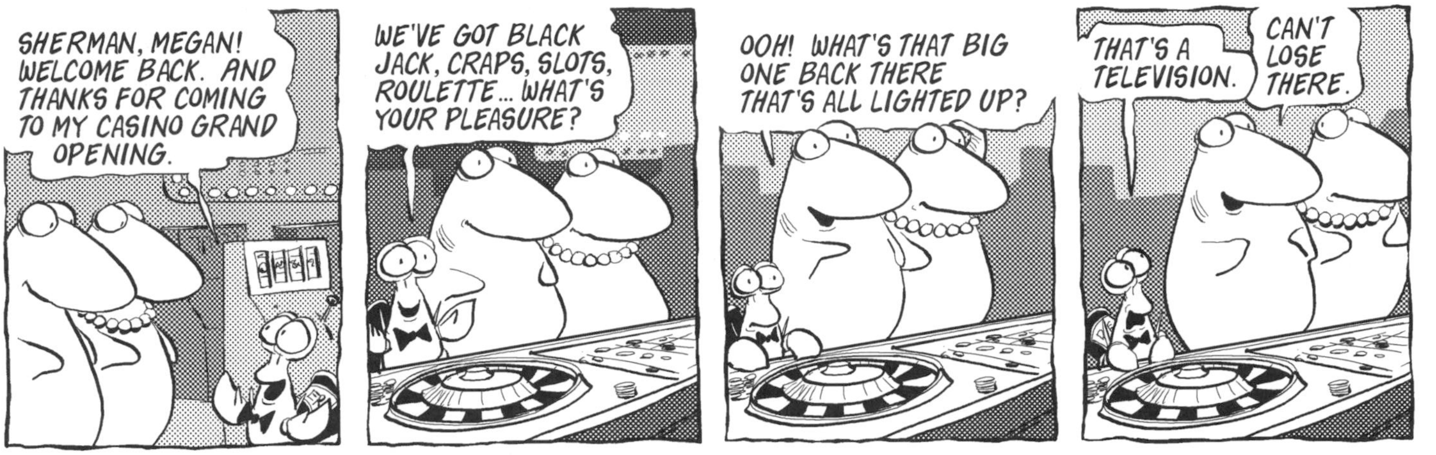

SHERMAN, MEGAN! WELCOME BACK. AND THANKS FOR COMING TO MY CASINO GRAND OPENING.
WE'VE GOT BLACK JACK, CRAPS, SLOTS, ROULETTE... WHAT'S YOUR PLEASURE?
OOH! WHAT'S THAT BIG ONE BACK THERE THAT'S ALL LIGHTED UP?
THAT'S A TELEVISION.
CAN'T LOSE THERE.

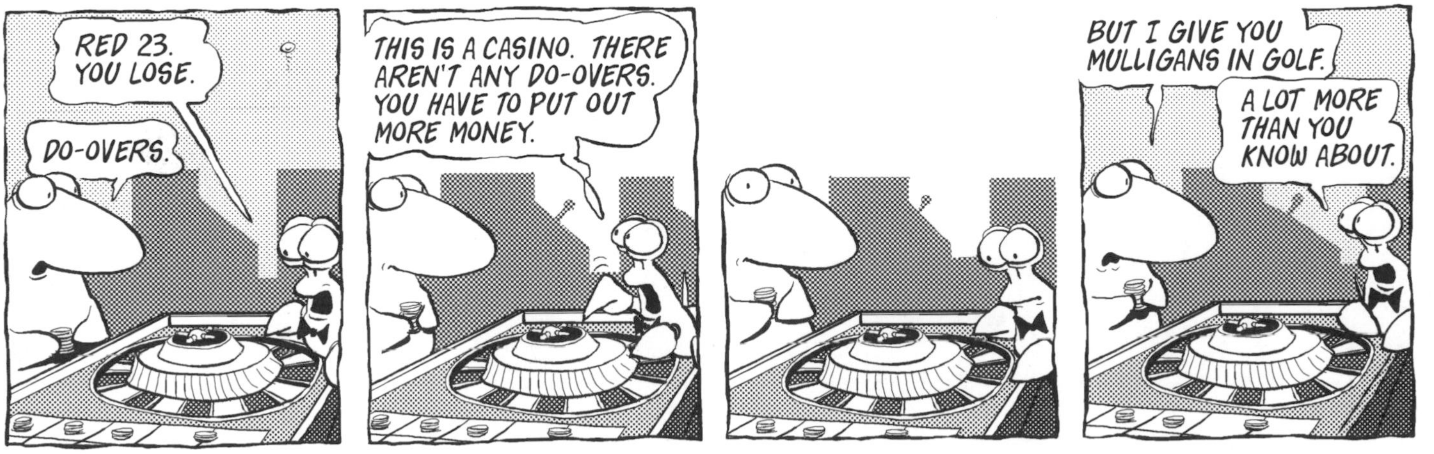

RED 23. YOU LOSE.
DO-OVERS.
THIS IS A CASINO. THERE AREN'T ANY DO-OVERS. YOU HAVE TO PUT OUT MORE MONEY.
BUT I GIVE YOU MULLIGANS IN GOLF.
A LOT MORE THAN YOU KNOW ABOUT.

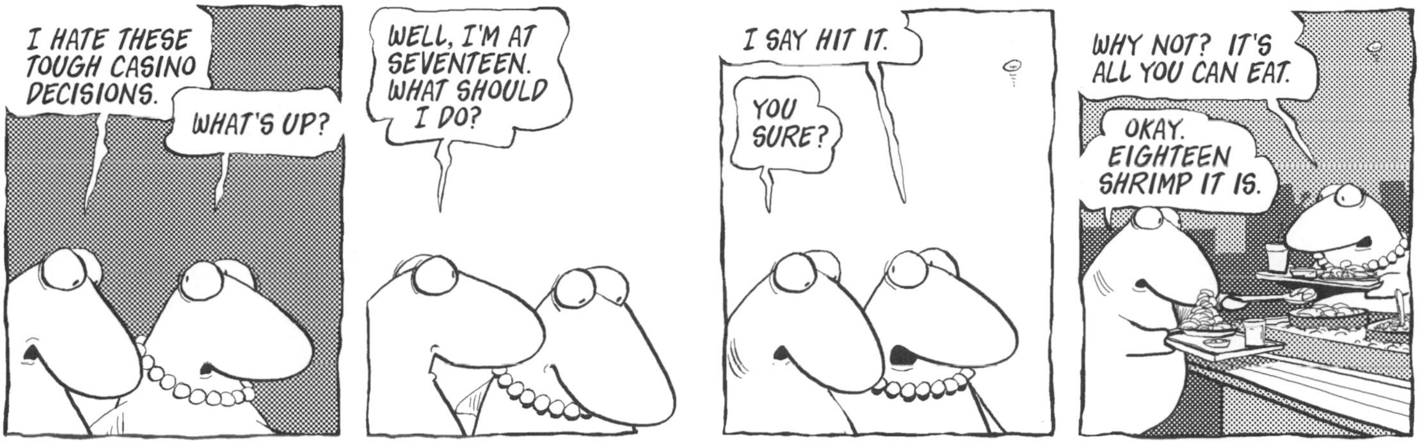
I HATE THESE TOUGH CASINO DECISIONS.
WHAT'S UP?
WELL, I'M AT SEVENTEEN. WHAT SHOULD I DO?
I SAY HIT IT.
YOU SURE?
WHY NOT? IT'S ALL YOU CAN EAT.
OKAY. EIGHTEEN SHRIMP IT IS.

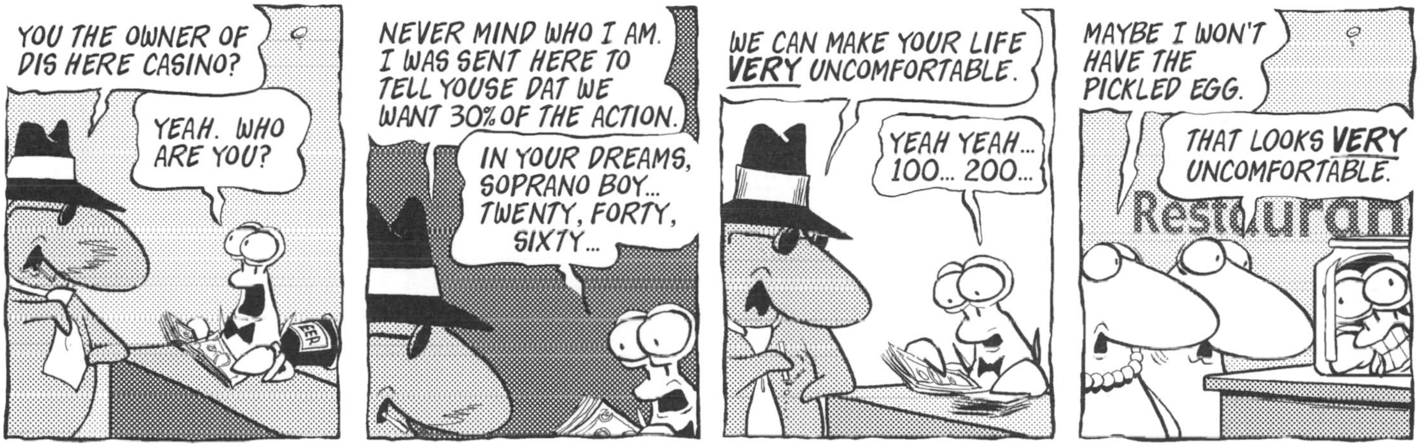
YOU THE OWNER OF DIS HERE CASINO?
YEAH. WHO ARE YOU?
NEVER MIND WHO I AM. I WAS SENT HERE TO TELL YOUSE DAT WE WANT 30% OF THE ACTION.
IN YOUR DREAMS, SOPRANO BOY... TWENTY, FORTY, SIXTY...
WE CAN MAKE YOUR LIFE VERY UNCOMFORTABLE.
YEAH YEAH... 100... 200...
MAYBE I WON'T HAVE THE PICKLED EGG.
THAT LOOKS VERY UNCOMFORTABLE.
Restauran

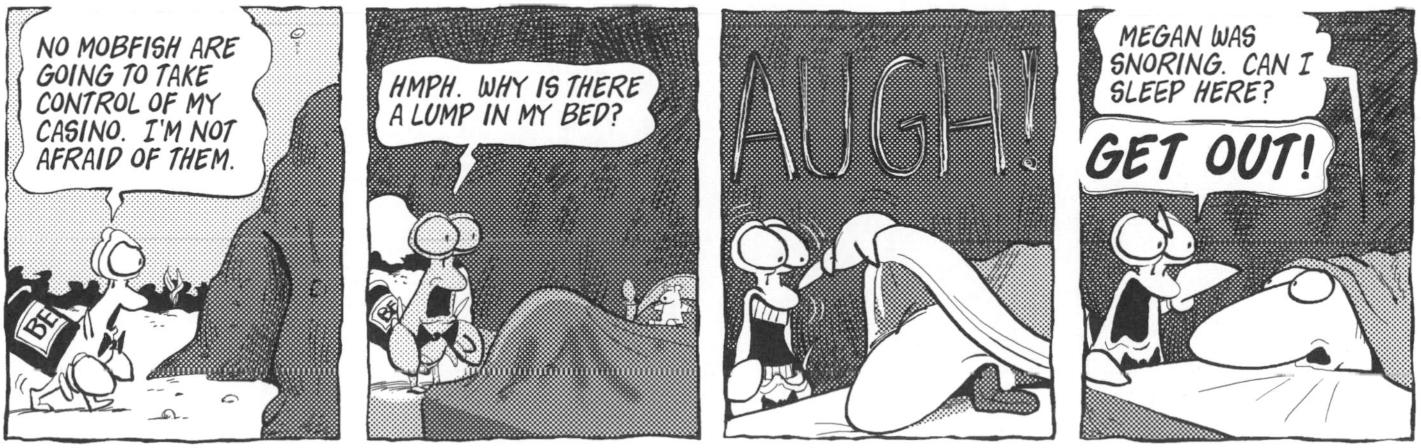
NO MOBFISH ARE GOING TO TAKE CONTROL OF MY CASINO. I'M NOT AFRAID OF THEM.
HMPH. WHY IS THERE A LUMP IN MY BED?
AUGH!
MEGAN WAS SNORING. CAN I SLEEP HERE?
GET OUT!

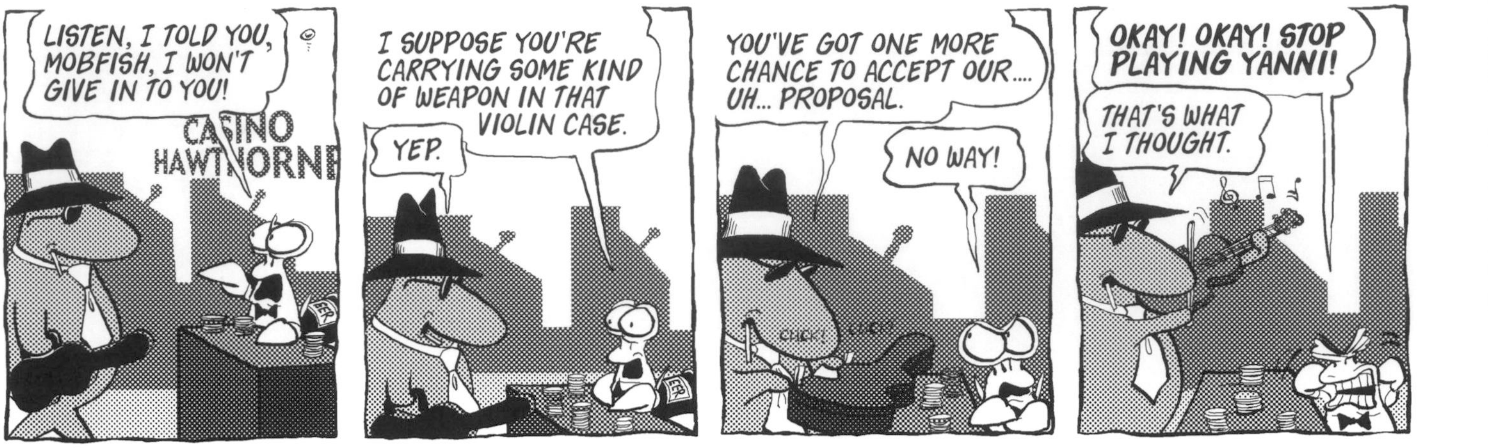
LISTEN, I TOLD YOU, MOBFISH, I WON'T GIVE IN TO YOU!
CASINO HAWTHORNE
I SUPPOSE YOU'RE CARRYING SOME KIND OF WEAPON IN THAT VIOLIN CASE.
YEP.
YOU'VE GOT ONE MORE CHANCE TO ACCEPT OUR.... UH... PROPOSAL.
NO WAY!
OKAY! OKAY! STOP PLAYING YANNI!
THAT'S WHAT I THOUGHT.

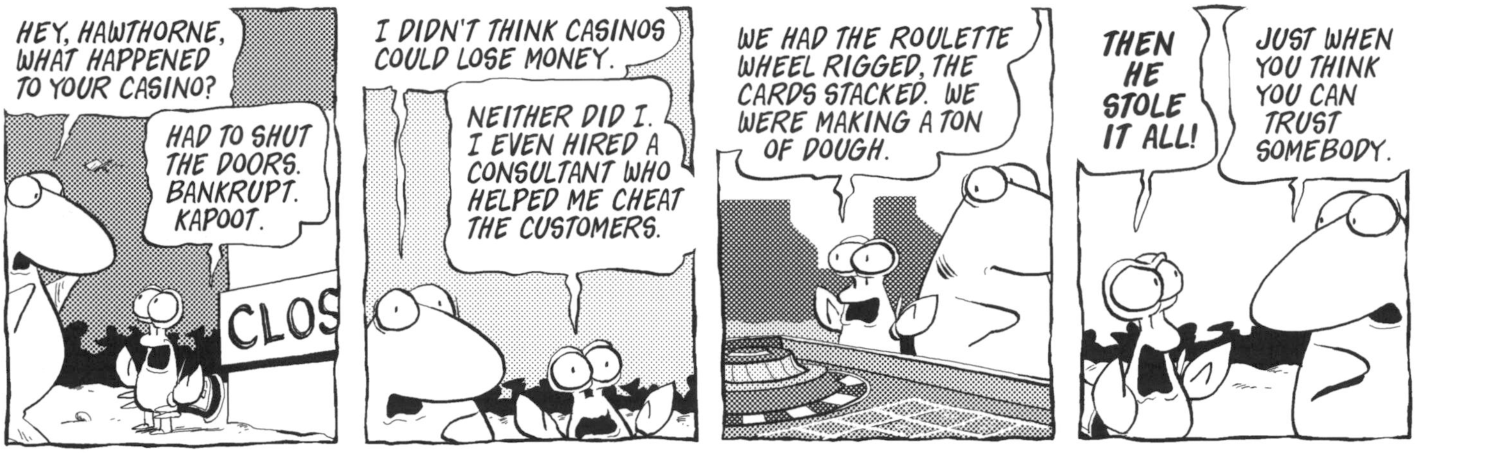
HEY, HAWTHORNE, WHAT HAPPENED TO YOUR CASINO?
HAD TO SHUT THE DOORS. BANKRUPT. KAPOOT.
CLOS
I DIDN'T THINK CASINOS COULD LOSE MONEY.
NEITHER DID I. I EVEN HIRED A CONSULTANT WHO HELPED ME CHEAT THE CUSTOMERS.
WE HAD THE ROULETTE WHEEL RIGGED, THE CARDS STACKED. WE WERE MAKING A TON OF DOUGH.
THEN HE STOLE IT ALL!
JUST WHEN YOU THINK YOU CAN TRUST SOMEBODY.

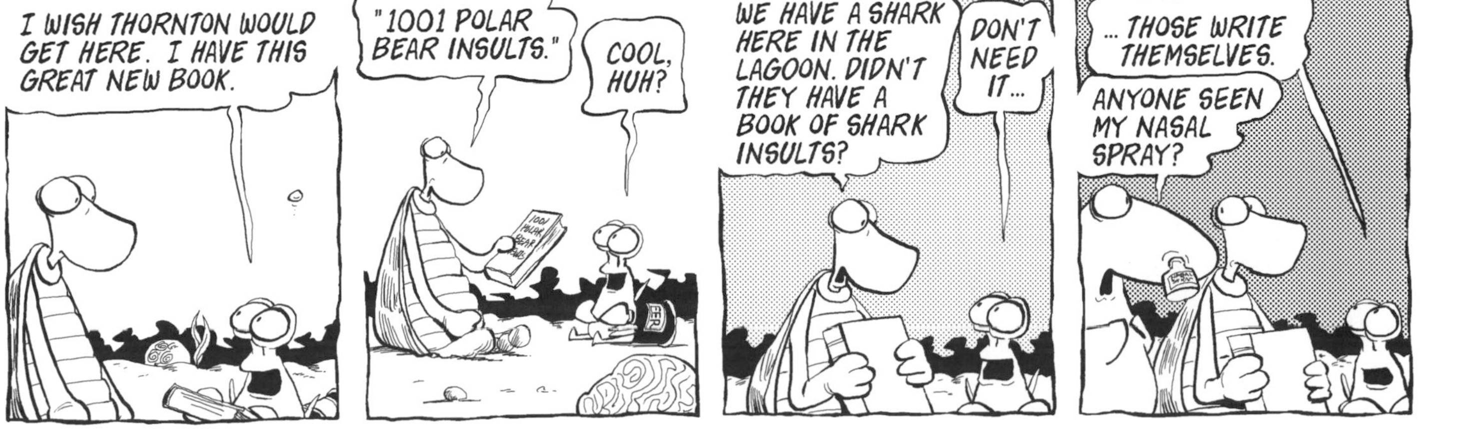
I WISH THORNTON WOULD GET HERE. I HAVE THIS GREAT NEW BOOK.
"1001 POLAR BEAR INSULTS."
COOL, HUH?
WE HAVE A SHARK HERE IN THE LAGOON. DIDN'T THEY HAVE A BOOK OF SHARK INSULTS?
DON'T NEED IT...
... THOSE WRITE THEMSELVES.
ANYONE SEEN MY NASAL SPRAY?

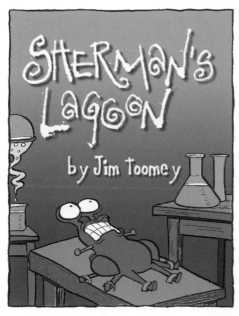

SHERMAN'S LAGOON

by Jim Toomey

WHOA NELLY, HAWTHORNE. THIS LOOKS LIKE A MAJOR PROJECT.

I AM CREATING FRANKENCRAB.

FRANKEN-WHO?

A SUPERIOR LIFE FORM MADE FROM VARIOUS CRAB PARTS I HAVE COLLECTED IN MY LAB.

ONCE I HAVE PERFECTED FRANKENCRAB I WILL TURN MY GENIUS TOWARD CREATING A CRAB ARMY THAT WILL RULE THE PLANET!

BWA-HA HA HA HA!

LET 'ER RIP!!

BRRZZZT!

RATS! WHAT DID I DO WRONG? THE BOOK SAYS 2000 VOLTS FOR 30 SECONDS.

KETCHUP CAN SAVE THIS.

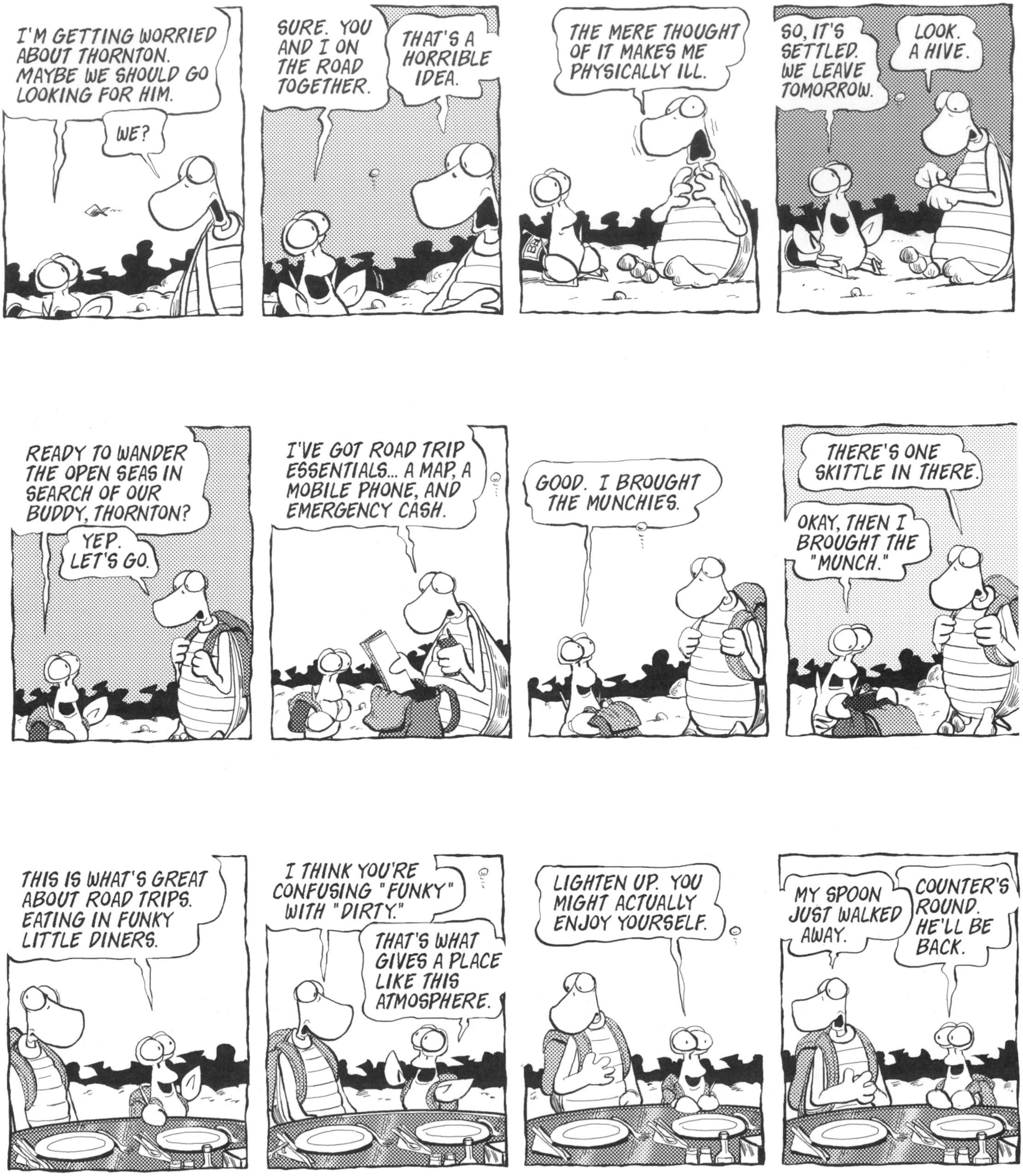
I'M GETTING WORRIED ABOUT THORNTON. MAYBE WE SHOULD GO LOOKING FOR HIM.
WE?
SURE. YOU AND I ON THE ROAD TOGETHER.
THAT'S A HORRIBLE IDEA.
THE MERE THOUGHT OF IT MAKES ME PHYSICALLY ILL.
SO, IT'S SETTLED. WE LEAVE TOMORROW.
LOOK. A HIVE.
READY TO WANDER THE OPEN SEAS IN SEARCH OF OUR BUDDY, THORNTON?
YEP. LET'S GO.
I'VE GOT ROAD TRIP ESSENTIALS... A MAP, A MOBILE PHONE, AND EMERGENCY CASH.
GOOD. I BROUGHT THE MUNCHIES.
THERE'S ONE SKITTLE IN THERE.
OKAY, THEN I BROUGHT THE "MUNCH."
THIS IS WHAT'S GREAT ABOUT ROAD TRIPS. EATING IN FUNKY LITTLE DINERS.
I THINK YOU'RE CONFUSING "FUNKY" WITH "DIRTY."
THAT'S WHAT GIVES A PLACE LIKE THIS ATMOSPHERE.
LIGHTEN UP. YOU MIGHT ACTUALLY ENJOY YOURSELF.
MY SPOON JUST WALKED AWAY.
COUNTER'S ROUND. HE'LL BE BACK.

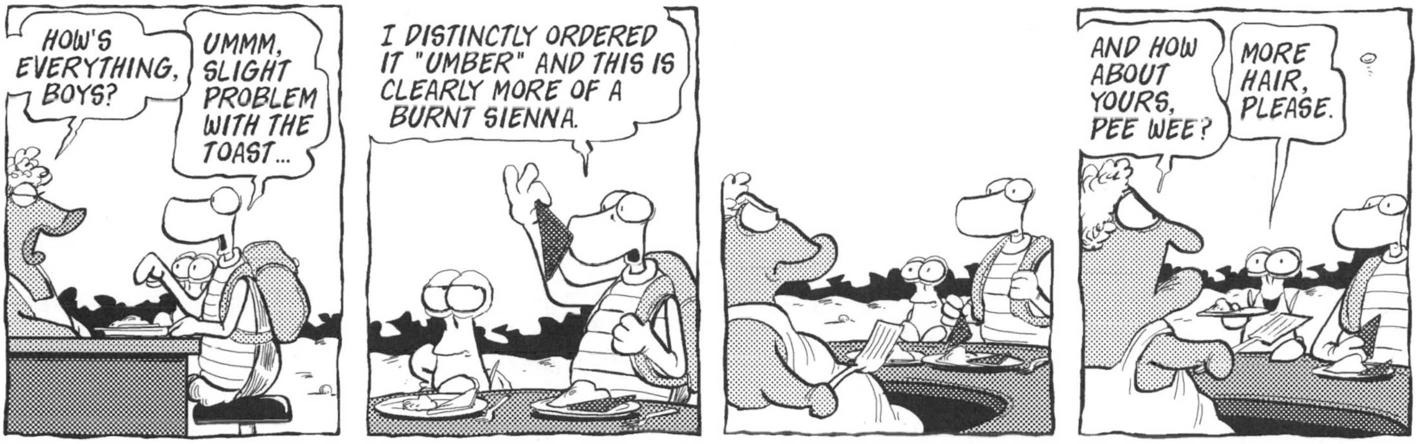
HOW'S EVERYTHING, BOYS?
UMMM, SLIGHT PROBLEM WITH THE TOAST...
I DISTINCTLY ORDERED IT "UMBER" AND THIS IS CLEARLY MORE OF A BURNT SIENNA.
AND HOW ABOUT YOURS, PEE WEE?
MORE HAIR, PLEASE.

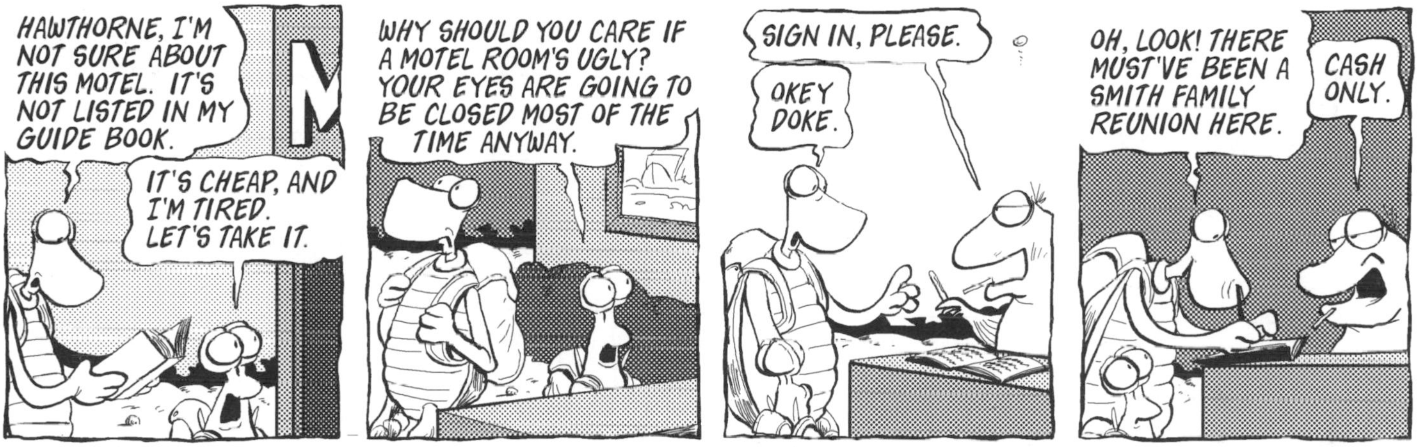
HAWTHORNE, I'M NOT SURE ABOUT THIS MOTEL. IT'S NOT LISTED IN MY GUIDE BOOK.
IT'S CHEAP, AND I'M TIRED. LET'S TAKE IT.
WHY SHOULD YOU CARE IF A MOTEL ROOM'S UGLY? YOUR EYES ARE GOING TO BE CLOSED MOST OF THE TIME ANYWAY.
SIGN IN, PLEASE.
OKEY DOKE.
OH, LOOK! THERE MUST'VE BEEN A SMITH FAMILY REUNION HERE.
CASH ONLY.

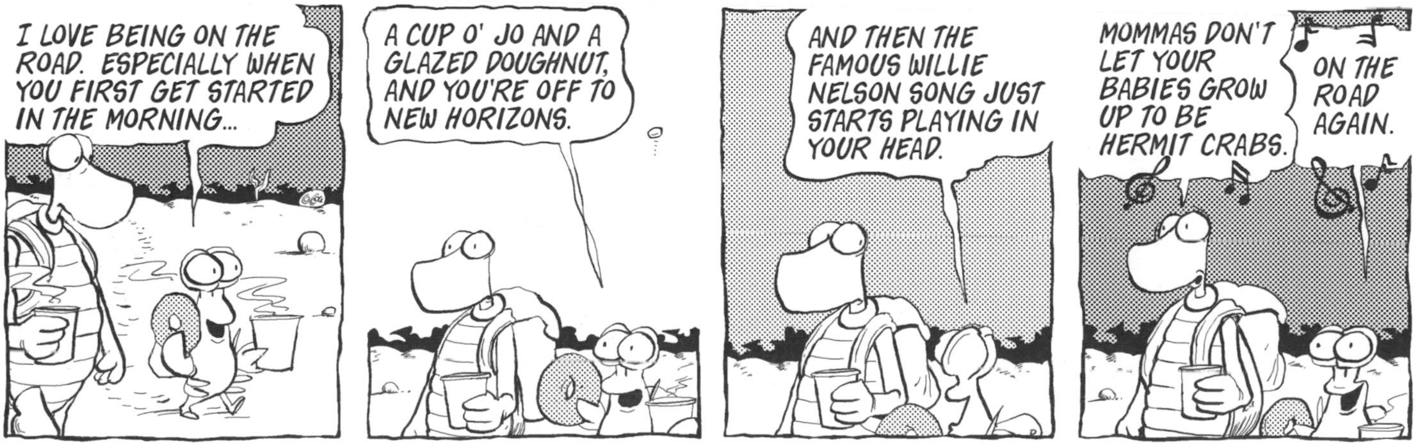
I LOVE BEING ON THE ROAD. ESPECIALLY WHEN YOU FIRST GET STARTED IN THE MORNING...
A CUP O' JO AND A GLAZED DOUGHNUT, AND YOU'RE OFF TO NEW HORIZONS.
AND THEN THE FAMOUS WILLIE NELSON SONG JUST STARTS PLAYING IN YOUR HEAD.
MOMMAS DON'T LET YOUR BABIES GROW UP TO BE HERMIT CRABS.
ON THE ROAD AGAIN.

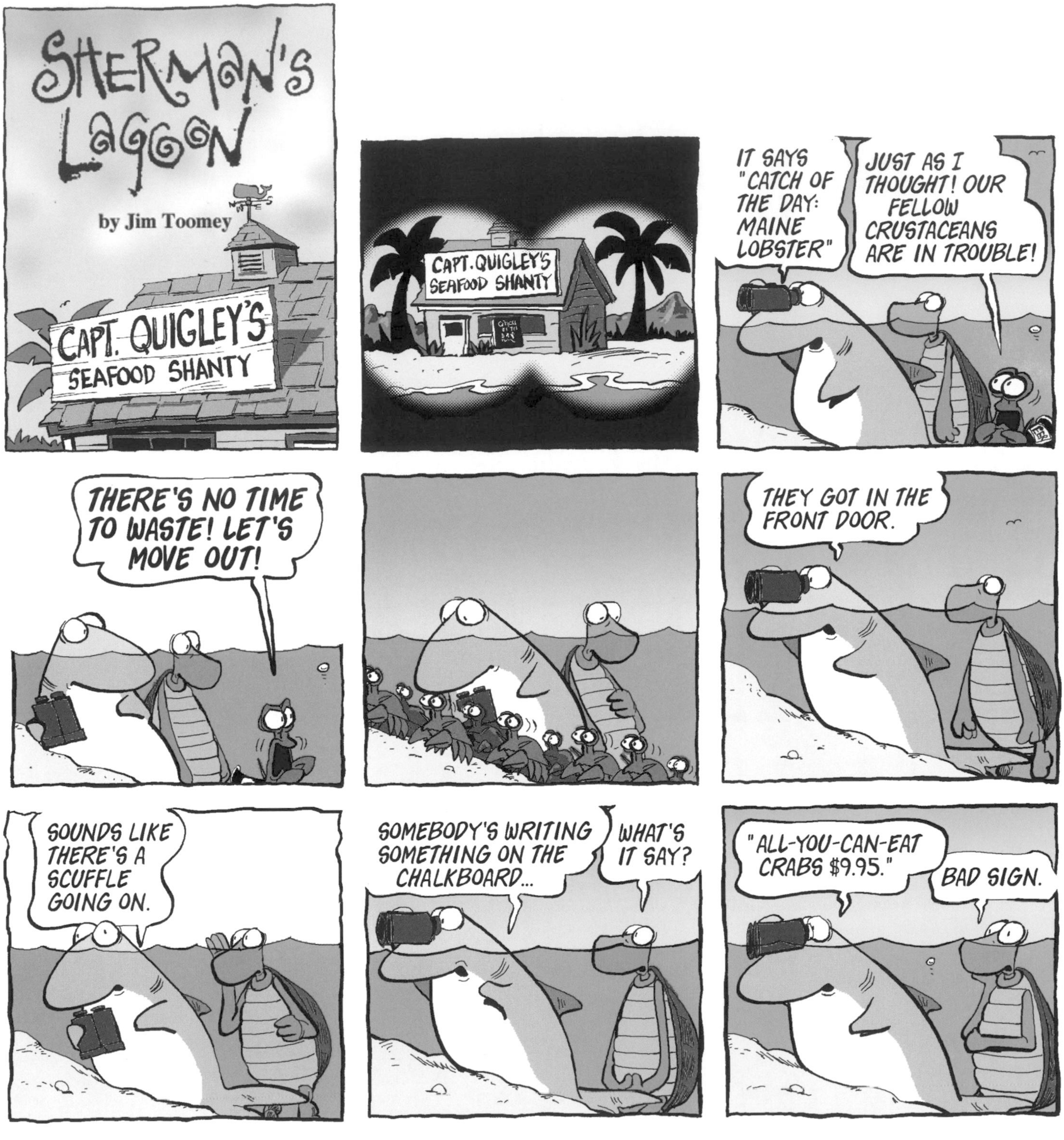
SHERMAN'S LAGOON
by Jim Toomey
CAPT. QUIGLEY'S SEAFOOD SHANTY
CAPT. QUIGLEY'S SEAFOOD SHANTY
IT SAYS "CATCH OF THE DAY: MAINE LOBSTER"
JUST AS I THOUGHT! OUR FELLOW CRUSTACEANS ARE IN TROUBLE!
THERE'S NO TIME TO WASTE! LET'S MOVE OUT!
THEY GOT IN THE FRONT DOOR.
SOUNDS LIKE THERE'S A SCUFFLE GOING ON.
SOMEBODY'S WRITING SOMETHING ON THE CHALKBOARD...
WHAT'S IT SAY?
"ALL-YOU-CAN-EAT CRABS $9.95."
BAD SIGN.

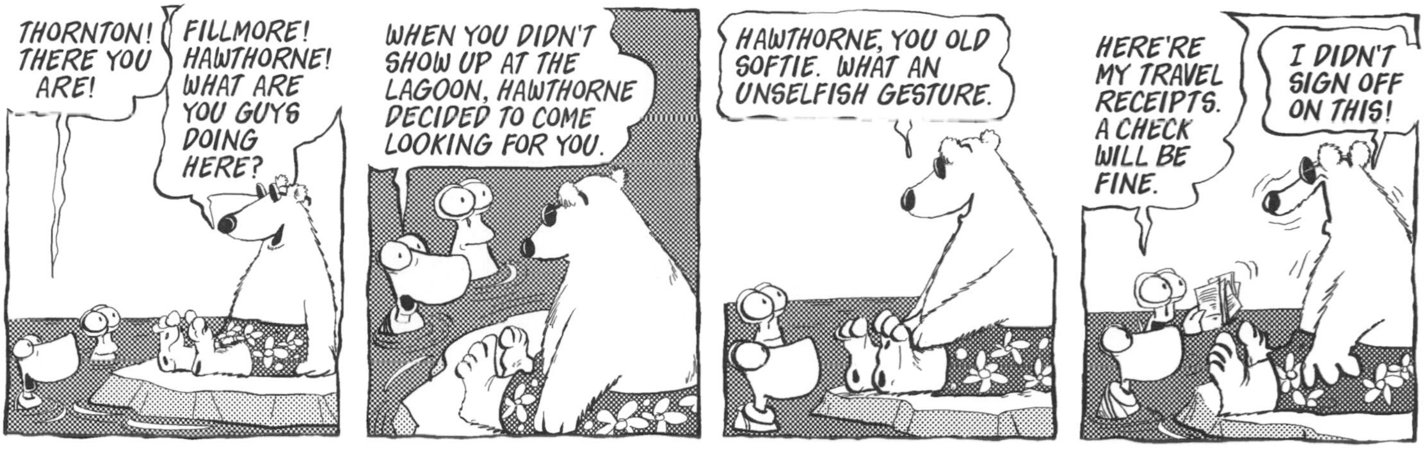
THORNTON! THERE YOU ARE!
FILLMORE! HAWTHORNE! WHAT ARE YOU GUYS DOING HERE?
WHEN YOU DIDN'T SHOW UP AT THE LAGOON, HAWTHORNE DECIDED TO COME LOOKING FOR YOU.
HAWTHORNE, YOU OLD SOFTIE. WHAT AN UNSELFISH GESTURE.
HERE'RE MY TRAVEL RECEIPTS. A CHECK WILL BE FINE.
I DIDN'T SIGN OFF ON THIS!

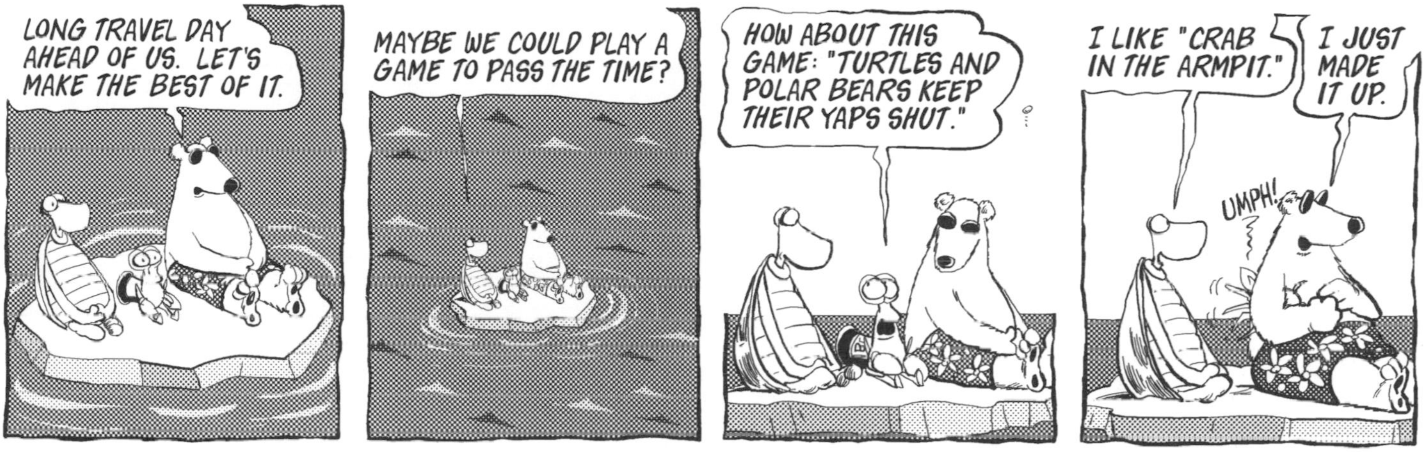
LONG TRAVEL DAY AHEAD OF US. LET'S MAKE THE BEST OF IT.
MAYBE WE COULD PLAY A GAME TO PASS THE TIME?
HOW ABOUT THIS GAME: "TURTLES AND POLAR BEARS KEEP THEIR YAPS SHUT."
I LIKE "CRAB IN THE ARMPIT."
UMPH!
I JUST MADE IT UP.

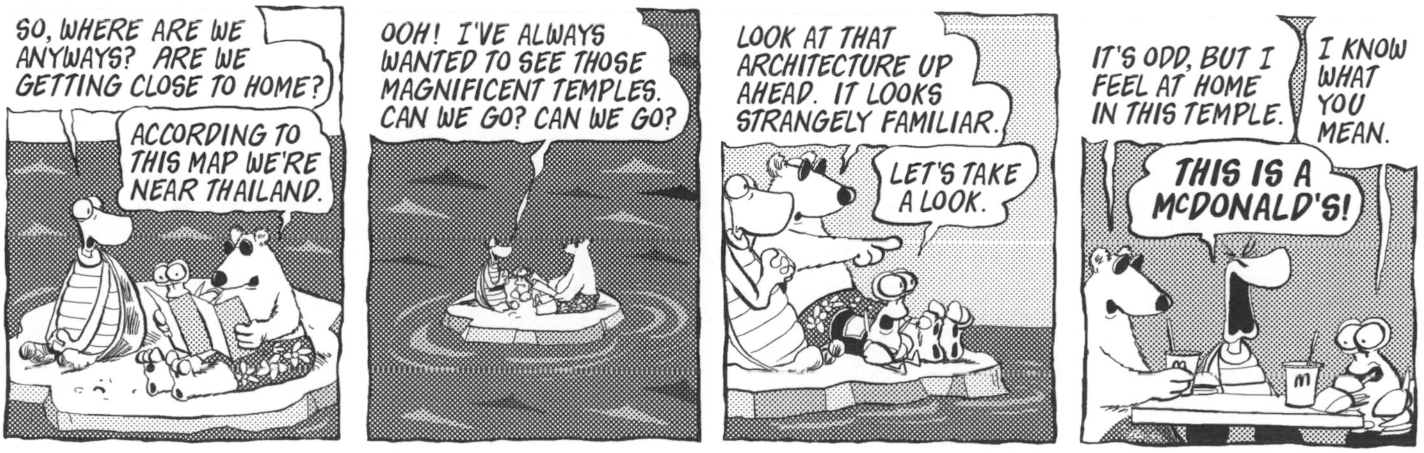
SO, WHERE ARE WE ANYWAYS? ARE WE GETTING CLOSE TO HOME?
ACCORDING TO THIS MAP WE'RE NEAR THAILAND.
OOH! I'VE ALWAYS WANTED TO SEE THOSE MAGNIFICENT TEMPLES. CAN WE GO? CAN WE GO?
LOOK AT THAT ARCHITECTURE UP AHEAD. IT LOOKS STRANGELY FAMILIAR.
LET'S TAKE A LOOK.
IT'S ODD, BUT I FEEL AT HOME IN THIS TEMPLE.
I KNOW WHAT YOU MEAN.
THIS IS A McDONALD'S!

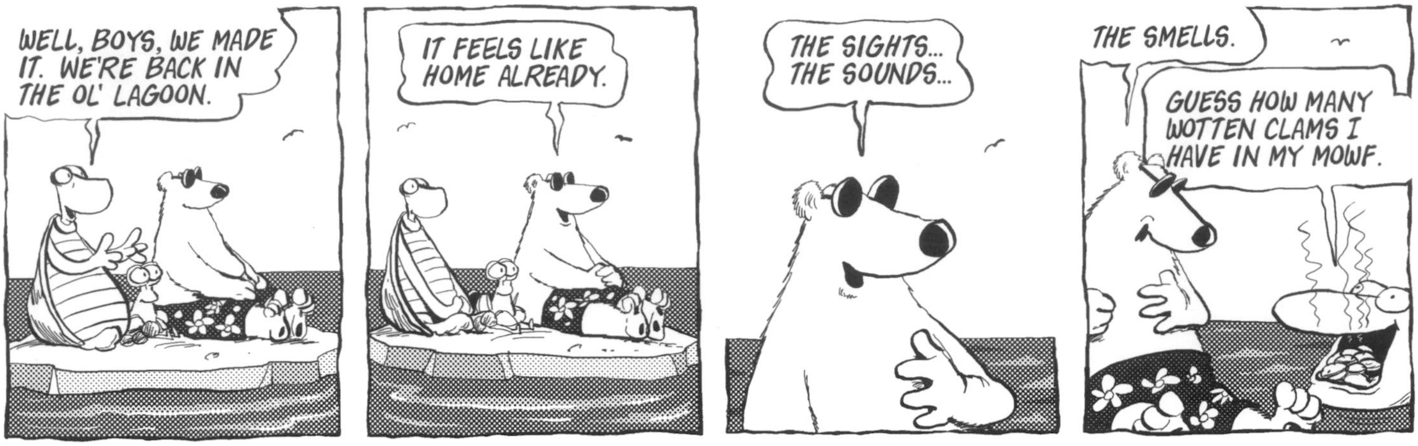
WELL, BOYS, WE MADE IT. WE'RE BACK IN THE OL' LAGOON.
IT FEELS LIKE HOME ALREADY.
THE SIGHTS... THE SOUNDS...
THE SMELLS.
GUESS HOW MANY WOTTEN CLAMS I HAVE IN MY MOWF.

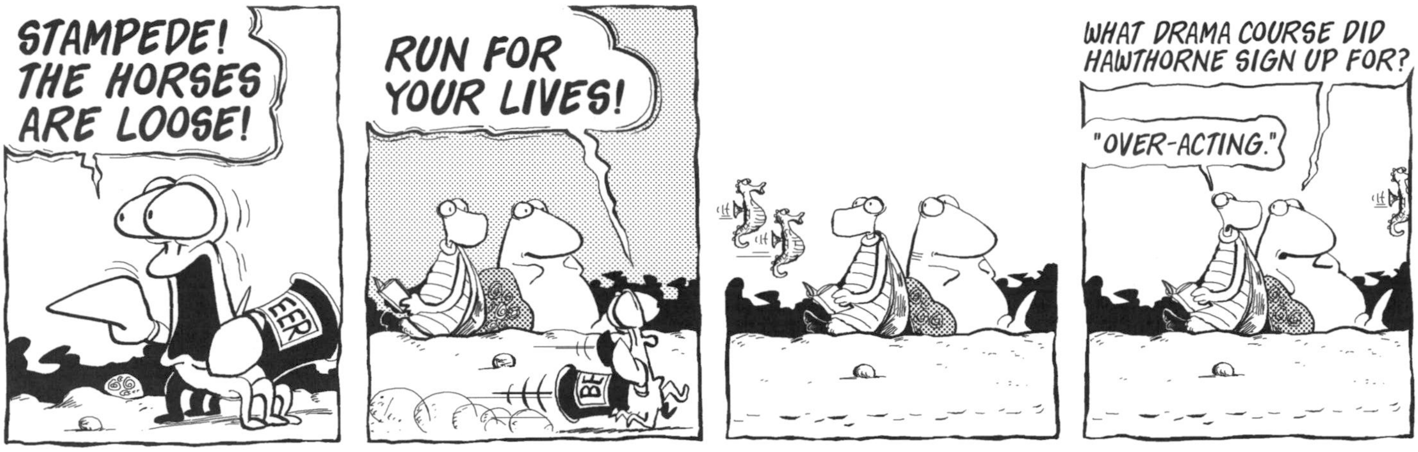
STAMPEDE! THE HORSES ARE LOOSE!
RUN FOR YOUR LIVES!
WHAT DRAMA COURSE DID HAWTHORNE SIGN UP FOR?
"OVER-ACTING."

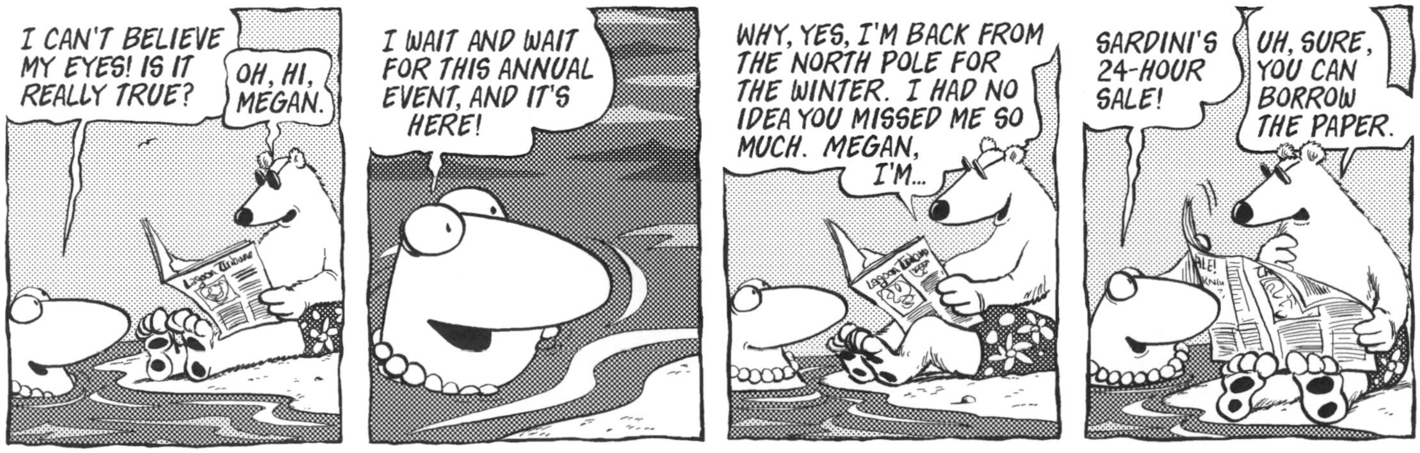
I CAN'T BELIEVE MY EYES! IS IT REALLY TRUE?
OH, HI, MEGAN.
I WAIT AND WAIT FOR THIS ANNUAL EVENT, AND IT'S HERE!
WHY, YES, I'M BACK FROM THE NORTH POLE FOR THE WINTER. I HAD NO IDEA YOU MISSED ME SO MUCH. MEGAN, I'M...
SARDINI'S 24-HOUR SALE!
UH, SURE, YOU CAN BORROW THE PAPER.

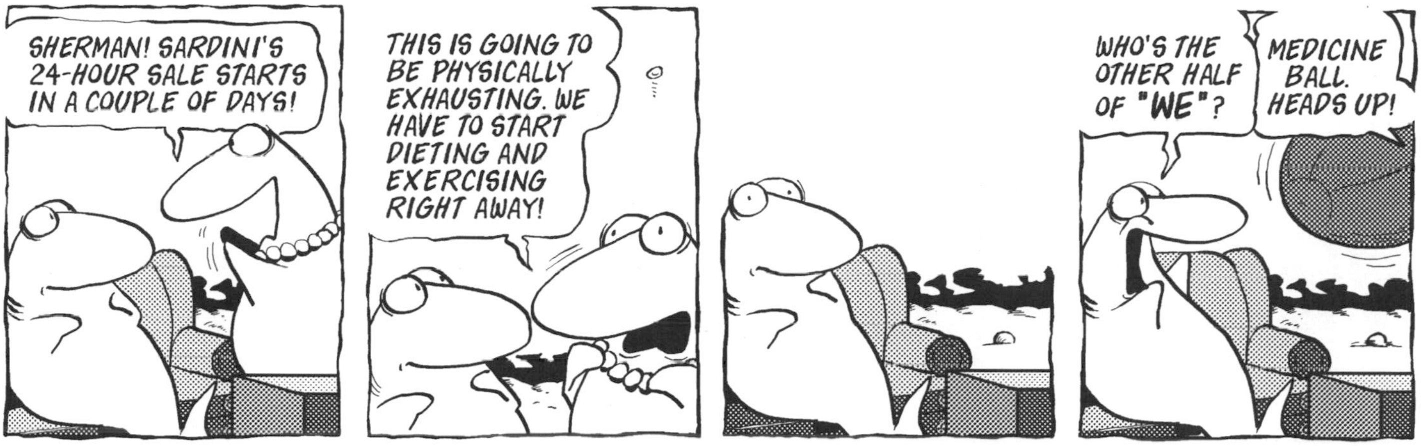
SHERMAN! SARDINI'S 24-HOUR SALE STARTS IN A COUPLE OF DAYS!
THIS IS GOING TO BE PHYSICALLY EXHAUSTING. WE HAVE TO START DIETING AND EXERCISING RIGHT AWAY!
WHO'S THE OTHER HALF OF "WE"?
MEDICINE BALL. HEADS UP!

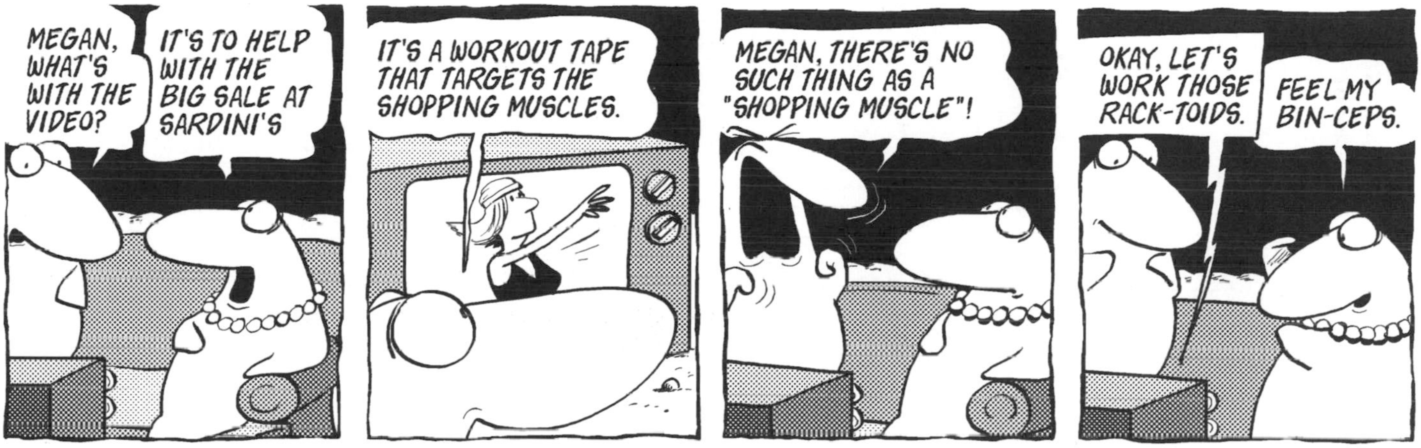
MEGAN, WHAT'S WITH THE VIDEO?
IT'S TO HELP WITH THE BIG SALE AT SARDINI'S
IT'S A WORKOUT TAPE THAT TARGETS THE SHOPPING MUSCLES.
MEGAN, THERE'S NO SUCH THING AS A "SHOPPING MUSCLE"!
OKAY, LET'S WORK THOSE RACK-TOIDS.
FEEL MY BIN-CEPS.

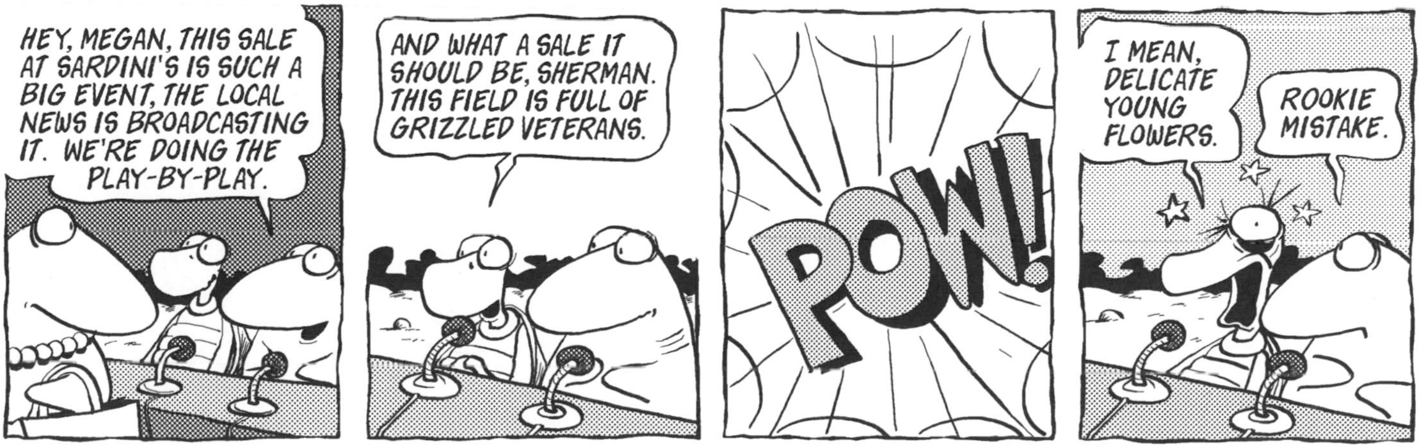
HEY, MEGAN, THIS SALE AT SARDINI'S IS SUCH A BIG EVENT, THE LOCAL NEWS IS BROADCASTING IT. WE'RE DOING THE PLAY-BY-PLAY.
AND WHAT A SALE IT SHOULD BE, SHERMAN. THIS FIELD IS FULL OF GRIZZLED VETERANS.
POW!!
I MEAN, DELICATE YOUNG FLOWERS.
ROOKIE MISTAKE.

SHERMAN'S LAGOON
by Jim Toomey
I WISH WE WEREN'T FISH. THERE ARE SUCH LIMITED SHOPPING OPPORTUNITIES FOR FISH.
IF WE WERE HUMANS, BOY, THE PLACES I'D GO.
OR HOW ABOUT AIR-BREATHING SHARKS WITH LEGS?
I GUESS THAT WOULD WORK, TOO.
WHAT A DIFFERENT PLANET IT WOULD BE.
IMAGINE A 20-FOOT-LONG CARNIVORE STALKING THE COUNTRYSIDE.
PEOPLE WOULD SCREAM AND RUN AWAY. WE'D DOMINATE.
WE'D ROAM THE EARTH WREAKING HAVOC EVERYWHERE WE WENT... LAND SHARK, BEWARE.
IMAGINE THAT.
I'D WREAK HAVOC IN FERRAGAMO SHOES.
WHATEVER.

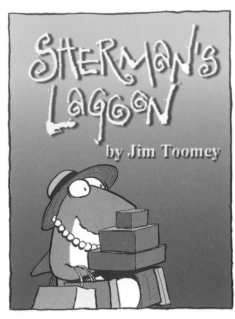

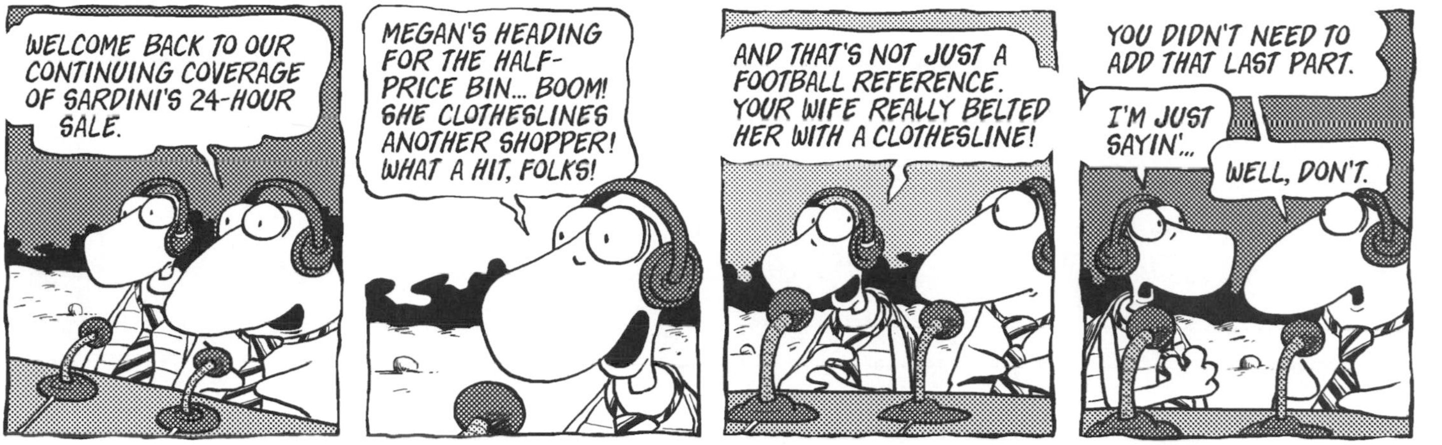
WELCOME BACK TO OUR CONTINUING COVERAGE OF SARDINI'S 24-HOUR SALE.
MEGAN'S HEADING FOR THE HALF-PRICE BIN... BOOM! SHE CLOTHESLINES ANOTHER SHOPPER! WHAT A HIT, FOLKS!
AND THAT'S NOT JUST A FOOTBALL REFERENCE. YOUR WIFE REALLY BELTED HER WITH A CLOTHESLINE!
YOU DIDN'T NEED TO ADD THAT LAST PART.
I'M JUST SAYIN'...
WELL, DON'T.

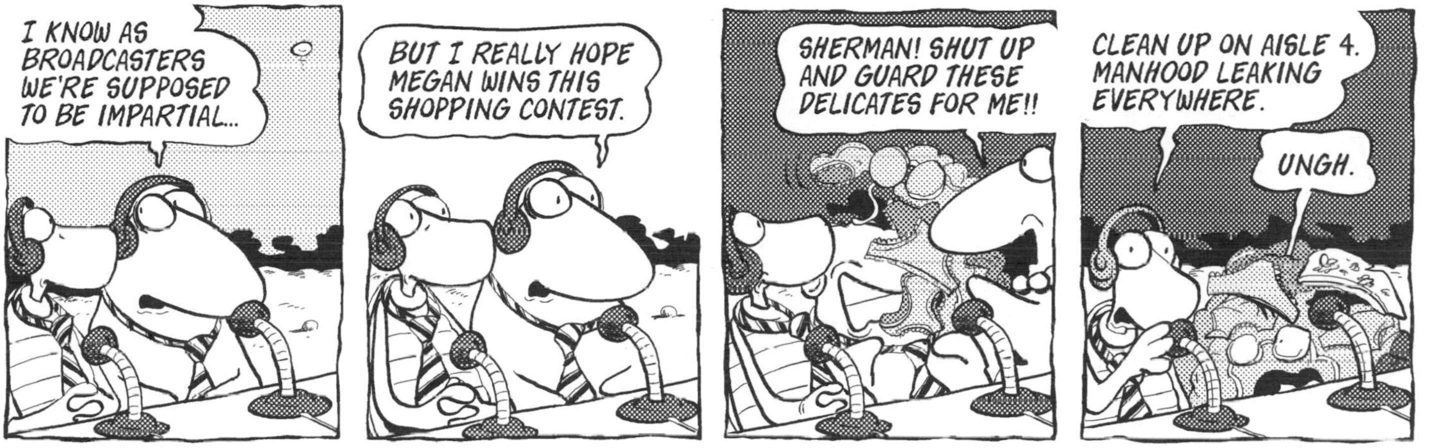
I KNOW AS BROADCASTERS WE'RE SUPPOSED TO BE IMPARTIAL...
BUT I REALLY HOPE MEGAN WINS THIS SHOPPING CONTEST.
SHERMAN! SHUT UP AND GUARD THESE DELICATES FOR ME!!
CLEAN UP ON AISLE 4. MANHOOD LEAKING EVERYWHERE.
UNGH.

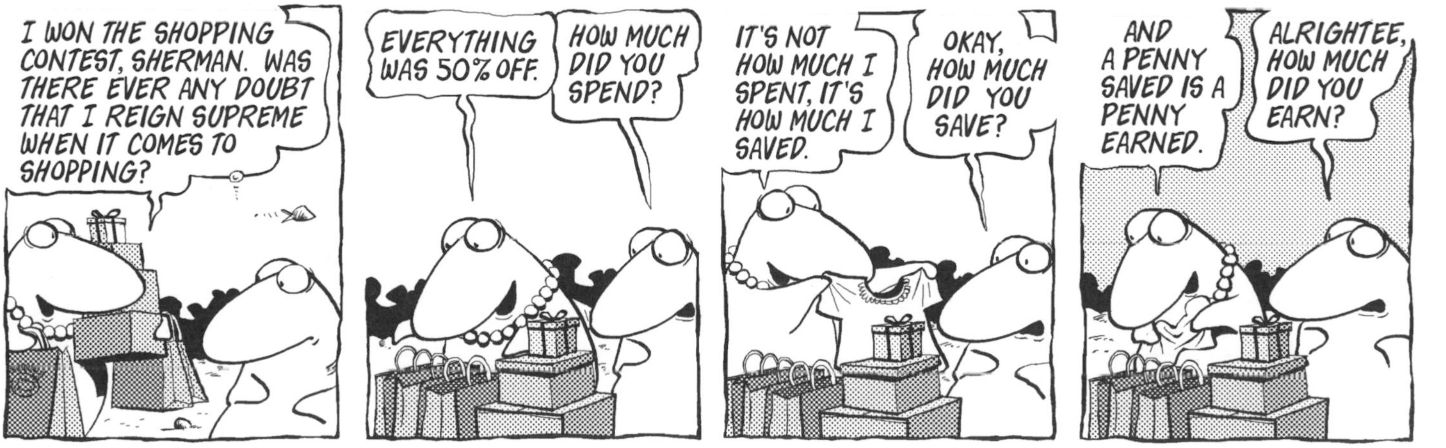
I WON THE SHOPPING CONTEST, SHERMAN. WAS THERE EVER ANY DOUBT THAT I REIGN SUPREME WHEN IT COMES TO SHOPPING?
EVERYTHING WAS 50% OFF.
HOW MUCH DID YOU SPEND?
IT'S NOT HOW MUCH I SPENT, IT'S HOW MUCH I SAVED.
OKAY, HOW MUCH DID YOU SAVE?
AND A PENNY SAVED IS A PENNY EARNED.
ALRIGHTEE, HOW MUCH DID YOU EARN?

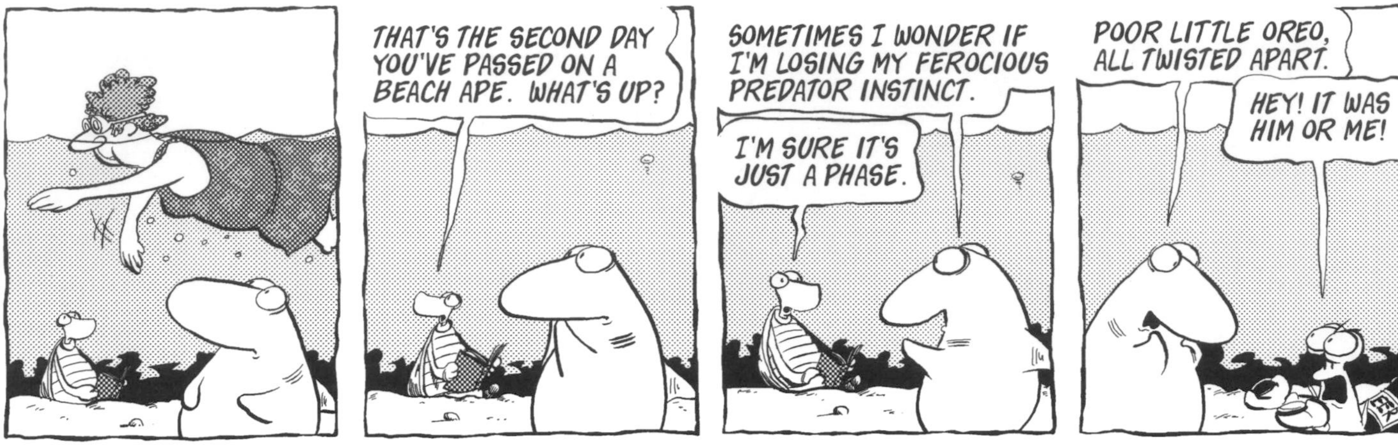
THAT'S THE SECOND DAY YOU'VE PASSED ON A BEACH APE. WHAT'S UP?
SOMETIMES I WONDER IF I'M LOSING MY FEROCIOUS PREDATOR INSTINCT.
I'M SURE IT'S JUST A PHASE.
POOR LITTLE OREO, ALL TWISTED APART.
HEY! IT WAS HIM OR ME!

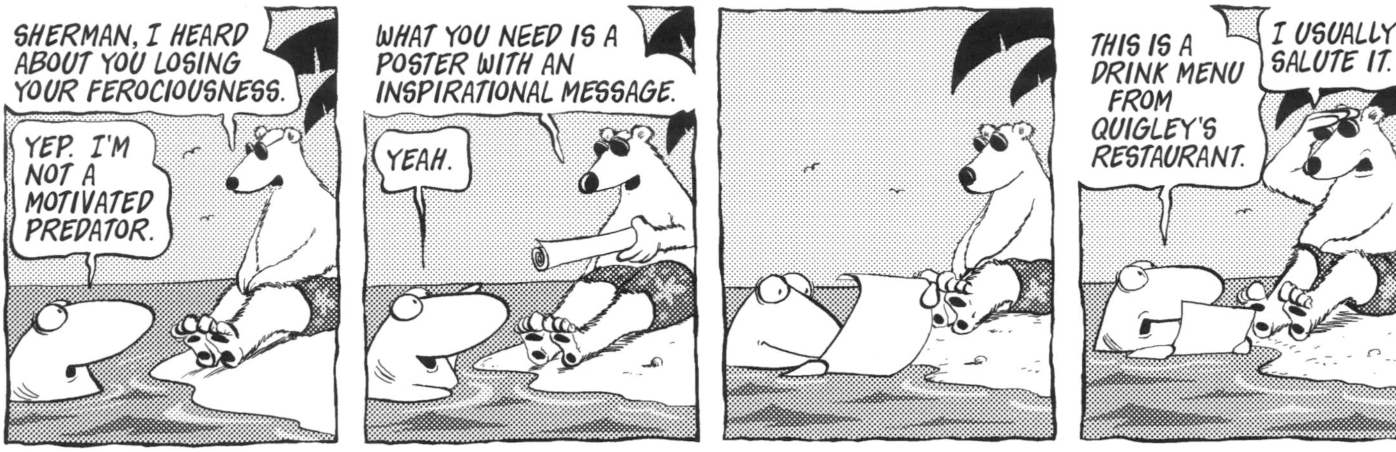
SHERMAN, I HEARD ABOUT YOU LOSING YOUR FEROCIOUSNESS.
YEP. I'M NOT A MOTIVATED PREDATOR.
WHAT YOU NEED IS A POSTER WITH AN INSPIRATIONAL MESSAGE.
YEAH.
THIS IS A DRINK MENU FROM QUIGLEY'S RESTAURANT.
I USUALLY SALUTE IT.

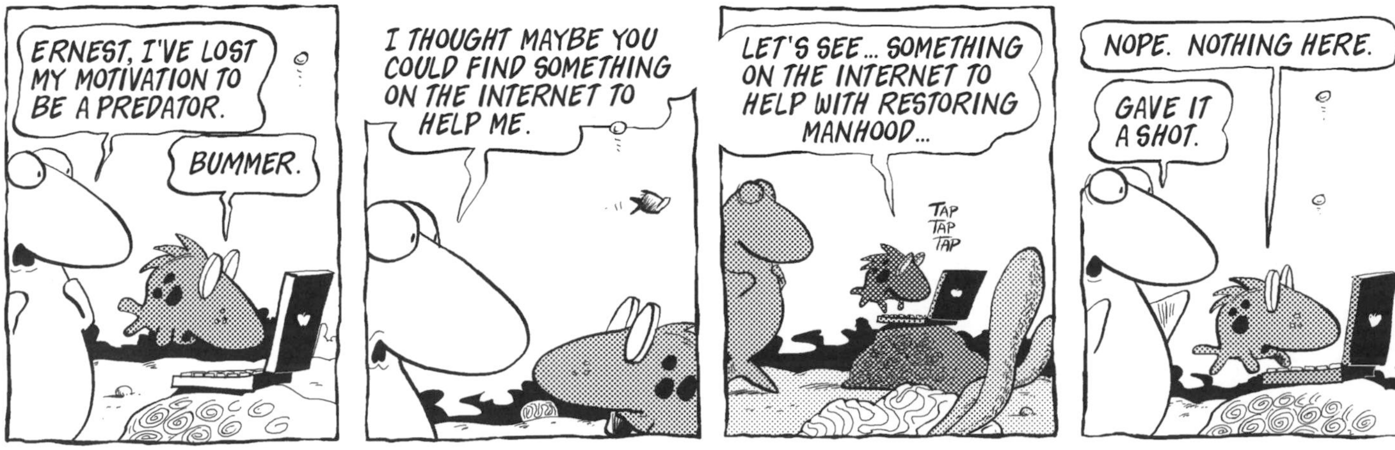
ERNEST, I'VE LOST MY MOTIVATION TO BE A PREDATOR.
BUMMER.
I THOUGHT MAYBE YOU COULD FIND SOMETHING ON THE INTERNET TO HELP ME.
LET'S SEE... SOMETHING ON THE INTERNET TO HELP WITH RESTORING MANHOOD...
TAP
TAP
TAP
NOPE. NOTHING HERE.
GAVE IT A SHOT.

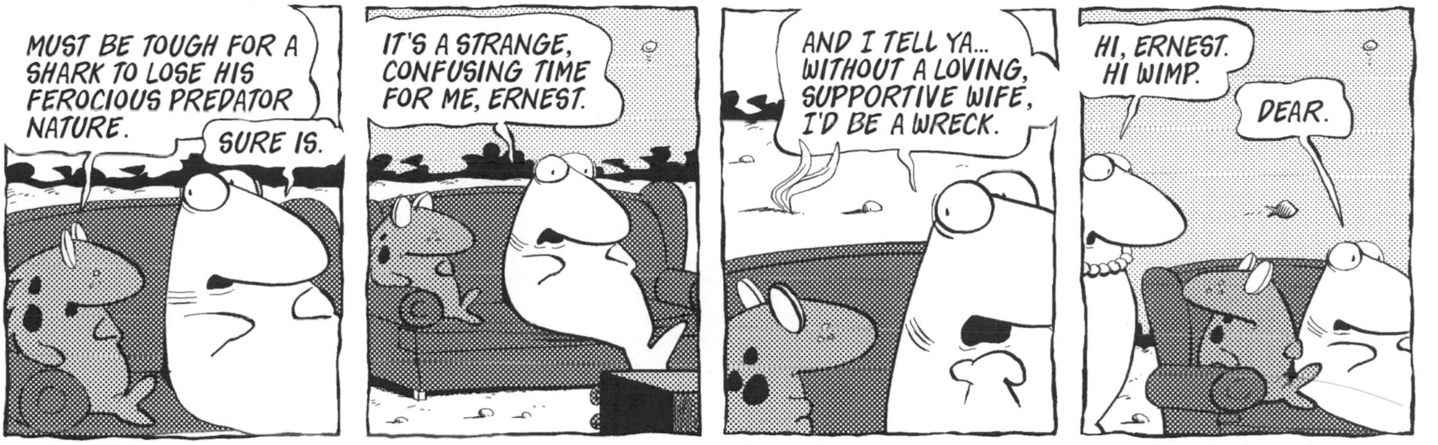
MUST BE TOUGH FOR A SHARK TO LOSE HIS FEROCIOUS PREDATOR NATURE.
SURE IS.
IT'S A STRANGE, CONFUSING TIME FOR ME, ERNEST.
AND I TELL YA... WITHOUT A LOVING, SUPPORTIVE WIFE, I'D BE A WRECK.
HI, ERNEST. HI WIMP.
DEAR.

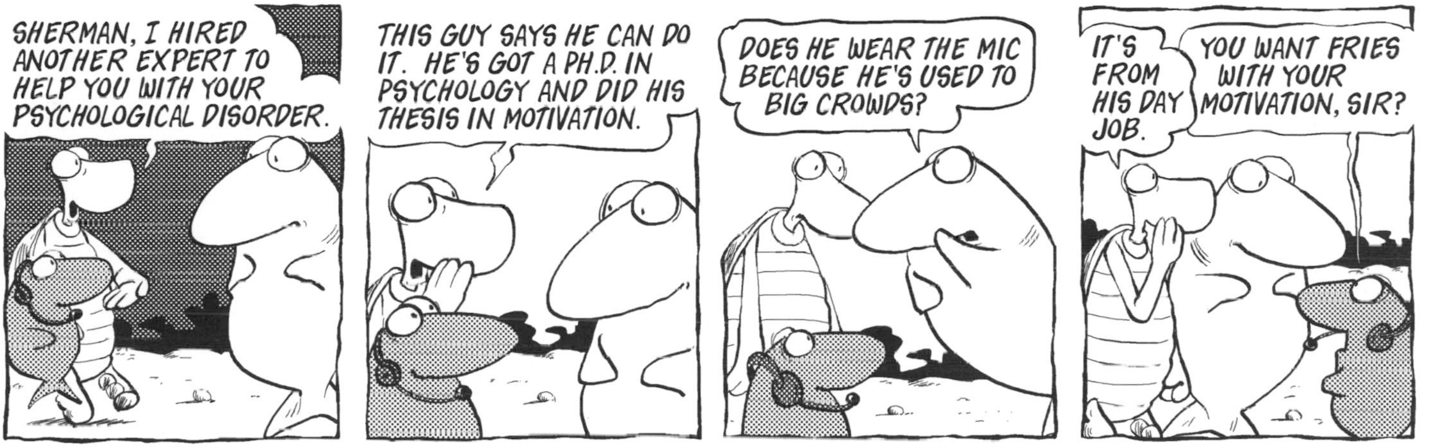
SHERMAN, I HIRED ANOTHER EXPERT TO HELP YOU WITH YOUR PSYCHOLOGICAL DISORDER.
THIS GUY SAYS HE CAN DO IT. HE'S GOT A PH.D. IN PSYCHOLOGY AND DID HIS THESIS IN MOTIVATION.
DOES HE WEAR THE MIC BECAUSE HE'S USED TO BIG CROWDS?
IT'S FROM HIS DAY JOB.
YOU WANT FRIES WITH YOUR MOTIVATION, SIR?

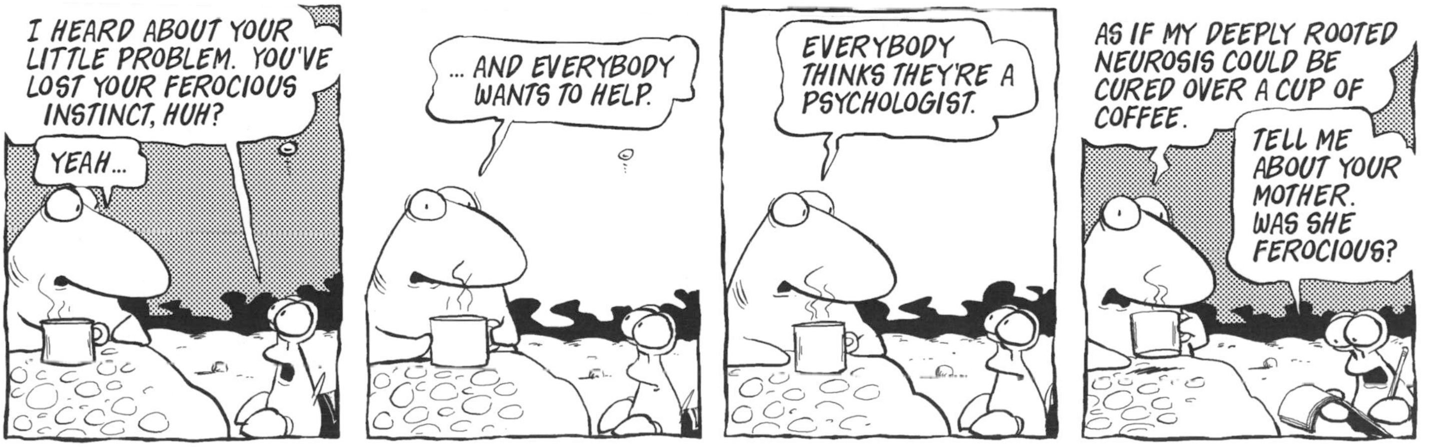
I HEARD ABOUT YOUR LITTLE PROBLEM. YOU'VE LOST YOUR FEROCIOUS INSTINCT, HUH?
YEAH...
... AND EVERYBODY WANTS TO HELP.
EVERYBODY THINKS THEY'RE A PSYCHOLOGIST.
AS IF MY DEEPLY ROOTED NEUROSIS COULD BE CURED OVER A CUP OF COFFEE.
TELL ME ABOUT YOUR MOTHER. WAS SHE FEROCIOUS?

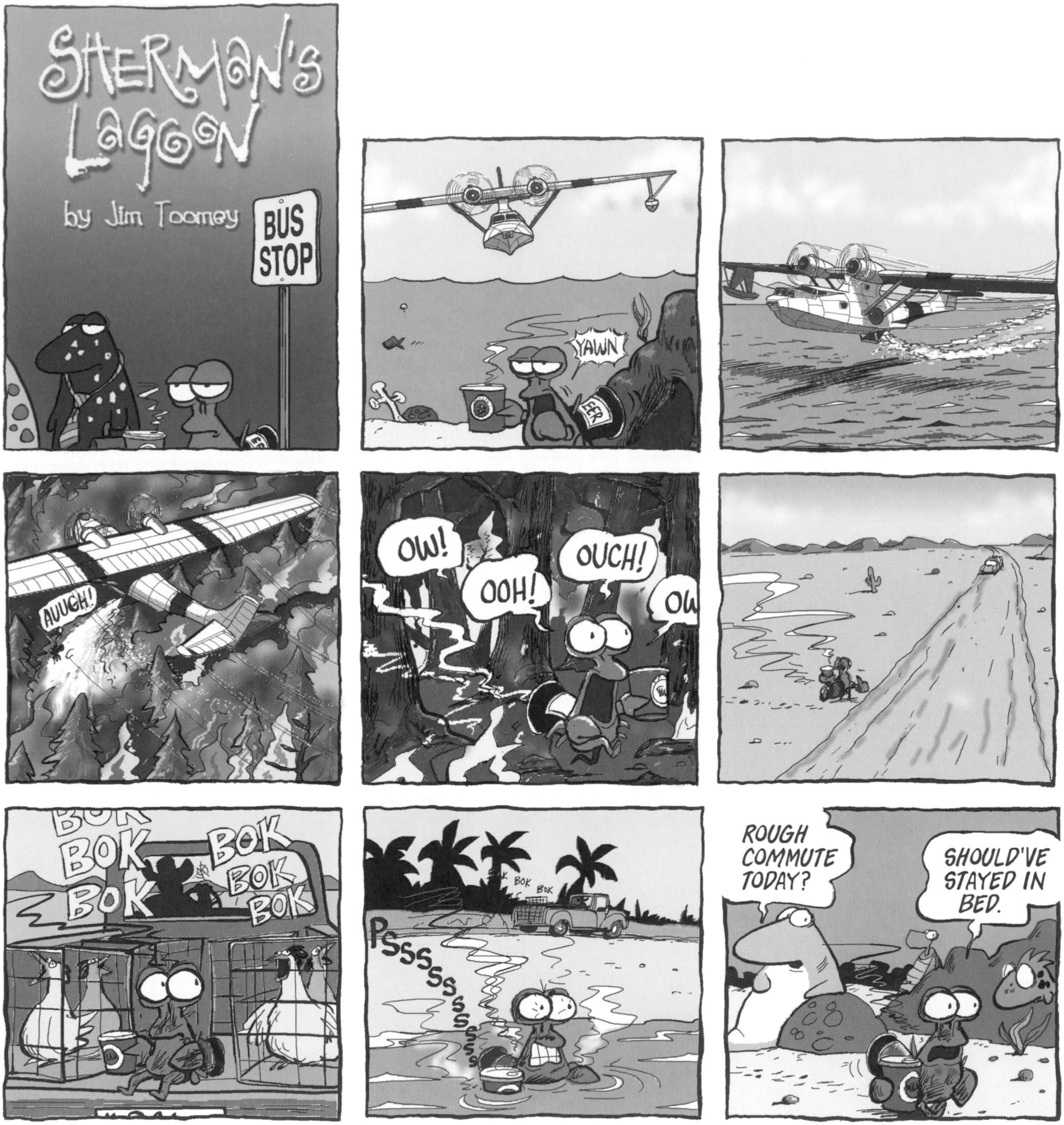
SHERMAN'S LAGOON
by Jim Toomey
BUS STOP
YAWN
AUUGH!
OW!
OOH!
OUCH!
OW
BOK
BOK
BOK
BOK
BOK
BOK
BOK BOK
PSSSSSSSSS
ROUGH COMMUTE TODAY?
SHOULD'VE STAYED IN BED.

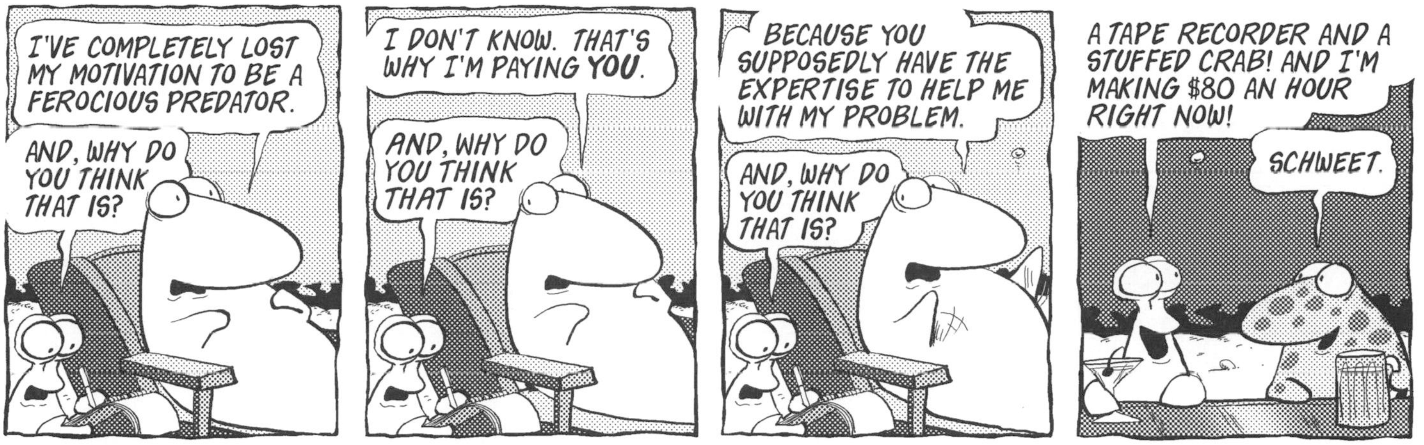
I'VE COMPLETELY LOST MY MOTIVATION TO BE A FEROCIOUS PREDATOR.
AND, WHY DO YOU THINK THAT IS?
I DON'T KNOW. THAT'S WHY I'M PAYING **YOU**.
AND, WHY DO YOU THINK THAT IS?
BECAUSE YOU SUPPOSEDLY HAVE THE EXPERTISE TO HELP ME WITH MY PROBLEM.
AND, WHY DO YOU THINK THAT IS?
A TAPE RECORDER AND A STUFFED CRAB! AND I'M MAKING $80 AN HOUR RIGHT NOW!
SCHWEET.

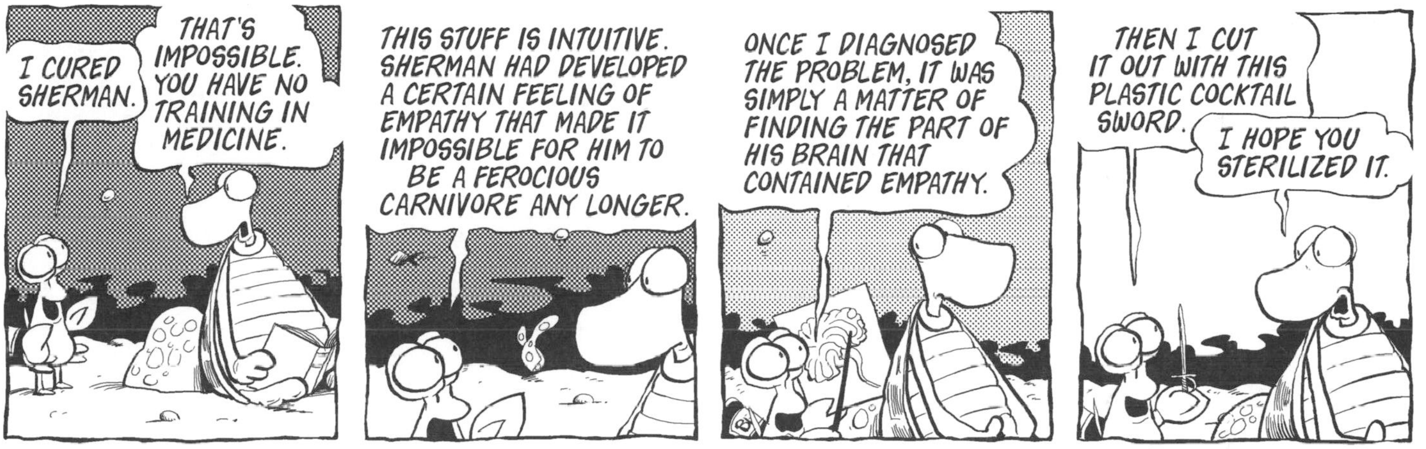
I CURED SHERMAN.
THAT'S IMPOSSIBLE. YOU HAVE NO TRAINING IN MEDICINE.
THIS STUFF IS INTUITIVE. SHERMAN HAD DEVELOPED A CERTAIN FEELING OF EMPATHY THAT MADE IT IMPOSSIBLE FOR HIM TO BE A FEROCIOUS CARNIVORE ANY LONGER.
ONCE I DIAGNOSED THE PROBLEM, IT WAS SIMPLY A MATTER OF FINDING THE PART OF HIS BRAIN THAT CONTAINED EMPATHY.
THEN I CUT IT OUT WITH THIS PLASTIC COCKTAIL SWORD.
I HOPE YOU STERILIZED IT.

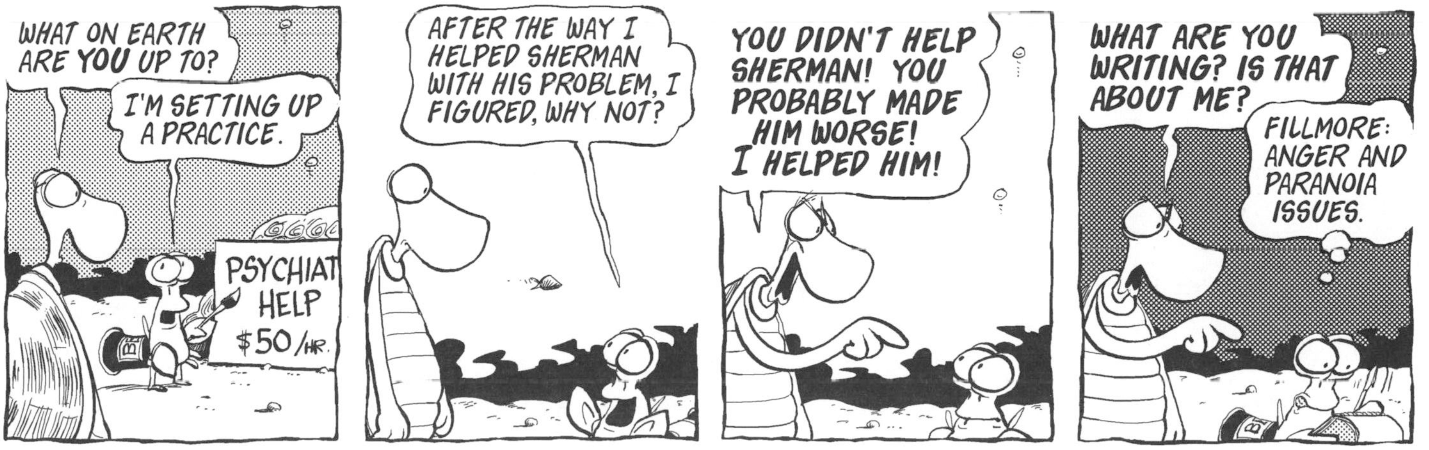
WHAT ON EARTH ARE **YOU** UP TO?
I'M SETTING UP A PRACTICE.
PSYCHIAT HELP $50/HR.
AFTER THE WAY I HELPED SHERMAN WITH HIS PROBLEM, I FIGURED, WHY NOT?
YOU DIDN'T HELP SHERMAN! YOU PROBABLY MADE HIM WORSE! I HELPED HIM!
WHAT ARE YOU WRITING? IS THAT ABOUT ME?
FILLMORE: ANGER AND PARANOIA ISSUES.

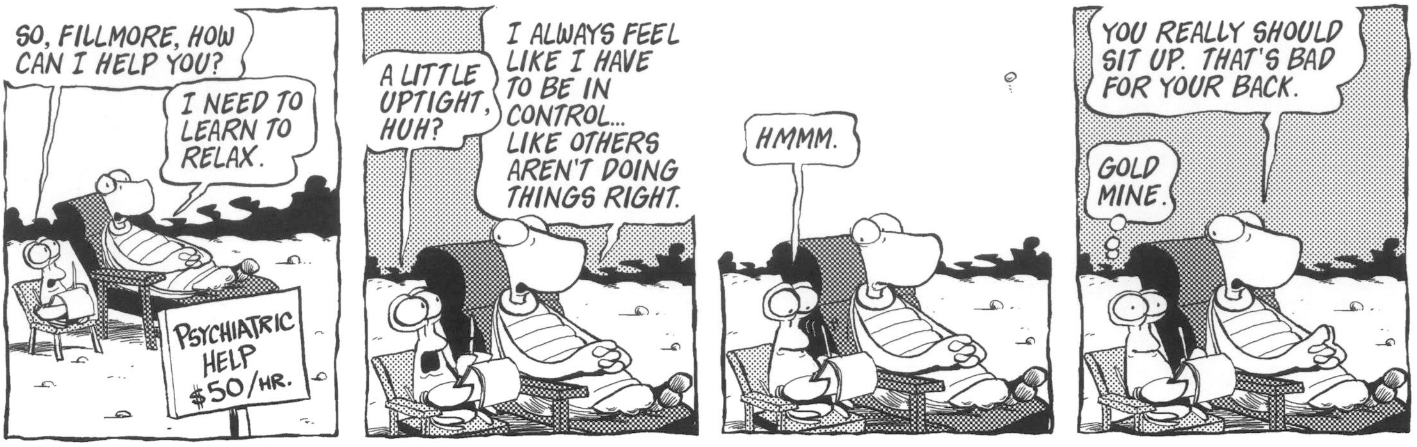
SO, FILLMORE, HOW CAN I HELP YOU?
I NEED TO LEARN TO RELAX.
PSYCHIATRIC HELP $50/HR.
A LITTLE UPTIGHT, HUH?
I ALWAYS FEEL LIKE I HAVE TO BE IN CONTROL... LIKE OTHERS AREN'T DOING THINGS RIGHT.
HMMM.
YOU REALLY SHOULD SIT UP. THAT'S BAD FOR YOUR BACK.
GOLD MINE.

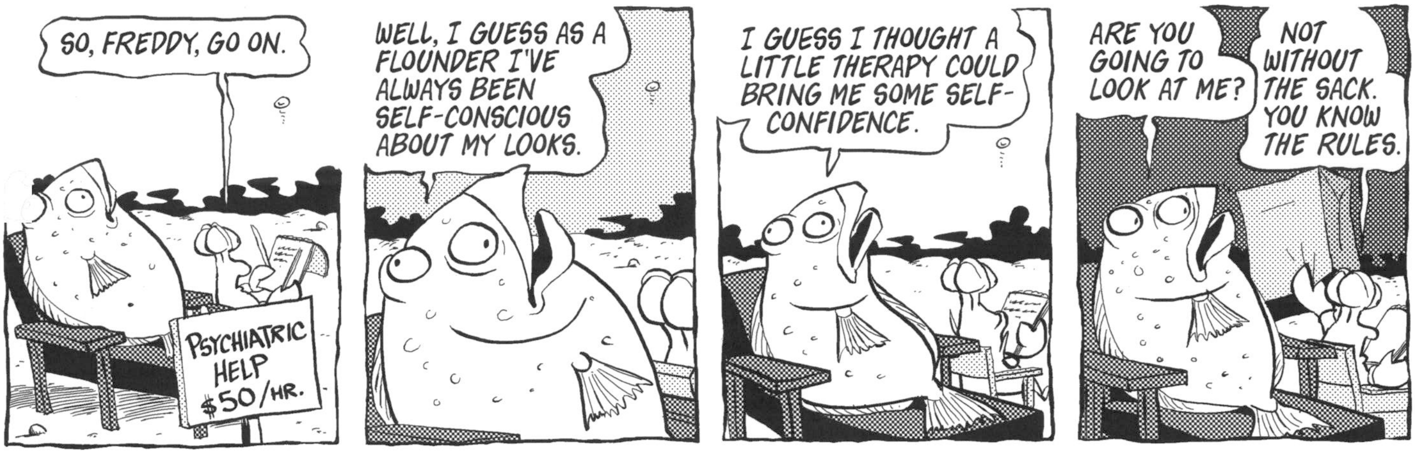
SO, FREDDY, GO ON.
PSYCHIATRIC HELP $50/HR.
WELL, I GUESS AS A FLOUNDER I'VE ALWAYS BEEN SELF-CONSCIOUS ABOUT MY LOOKS.
I GUESS I THOUGHT A LITTLE THERAPY COULD BRING ME SOME SELF-CONFIDENCE.
ARE YOU GOING TO LOOK AT ME?
NOT WITHOUT THE SACK. YOU KNOW THE RULES.

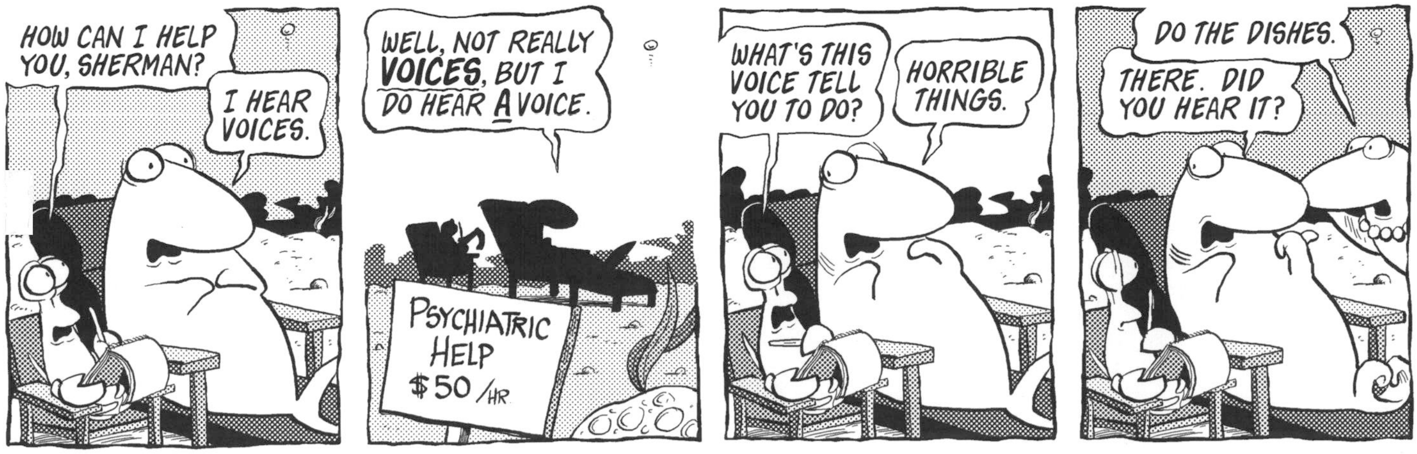
HOW CAN I HELP YOU, SHERMAN?
I HEAR VOICES.
WELL, NOT REALLY VOICES, BUT I DO HEAR A VOICE.
PSYCHIATRIC HELP $50/HR
WHAT'S THIS VOICE TELL YOU TO DO?
HORRIBLE THINGS.
DO THE DISHES.
THERE. DID YOU HEAR IT?

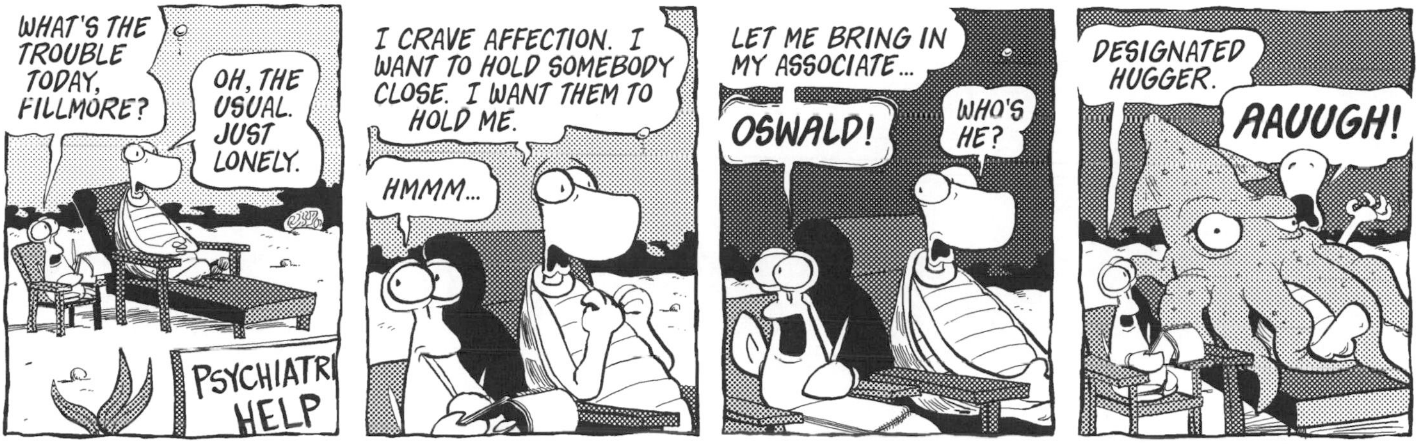
WHAT'S THE TROUBLE TODAY, FILLMORE?
OH, THE USUAL. JUST LONELY.
PSYCHIATRI HELP
I CRAVE AFFECTION. I WANT TO HOLD SOMEBODY CLOSE. I WANT THEM TO HOLD ME.
HMMM...
LET ME BRING IN MY ASSOCIATE...
OSWALD!
WHO'S HE?
DESIGNATED HUGGER.
AAUUGH!

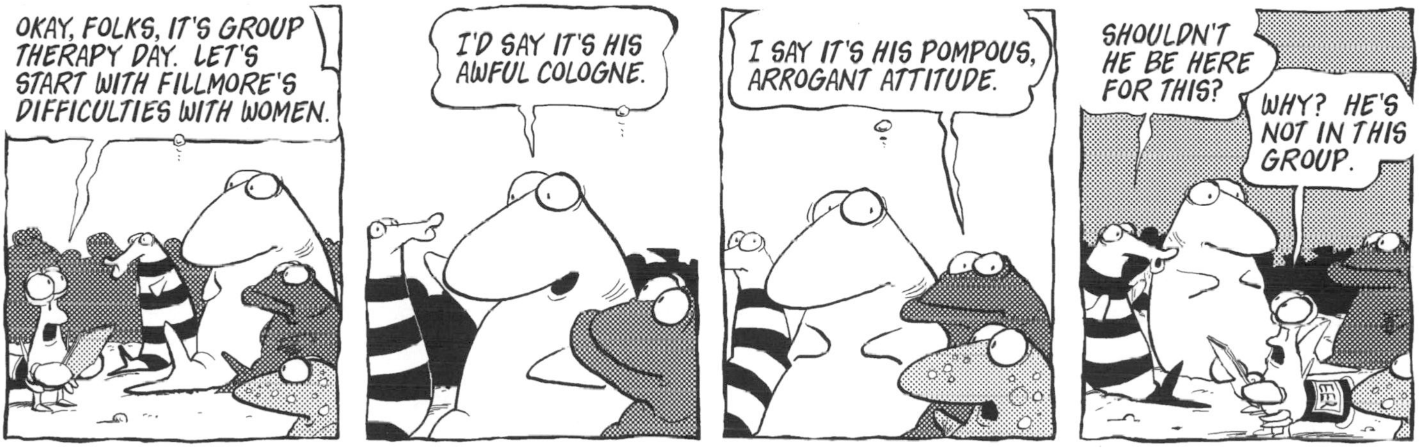
OKAY, FOLKS, IT'S GROUP THERAPY DAY. LET'S START WITH FILLMORE'S DIFFICULTIES WITH WOMEN.
I'D SAY IT'S HIS AWFUL COLOGNE.
I SAY IT'S HIS POMPOUS, ARROGANT ATTITUDE.
SHOULDN'T HE BE HERE FOR THIS?
WHY? HE'S NOT IN THIS GROUP.

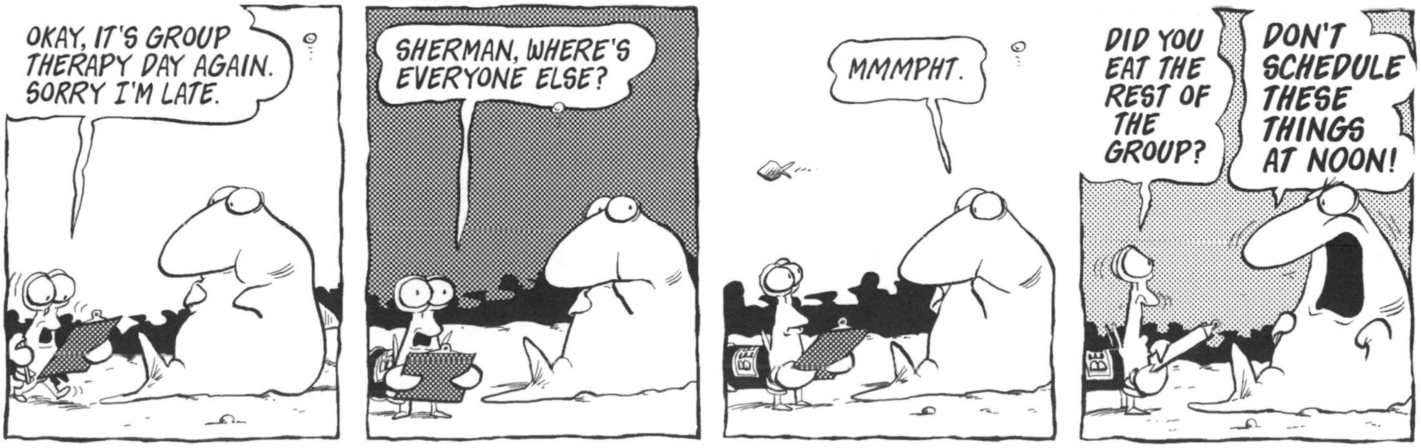
OKAY, IT'S GROUP THERAPY DAY AGAIN. SORRY I'M LATE.
SHERMAN, WHERE'S EVERYONE ELSE?
MMMPHT.
DID YOU EAT THE REST OF THE GROUP?
DON'T SCHEDULE THESE THINGS AT NOON!

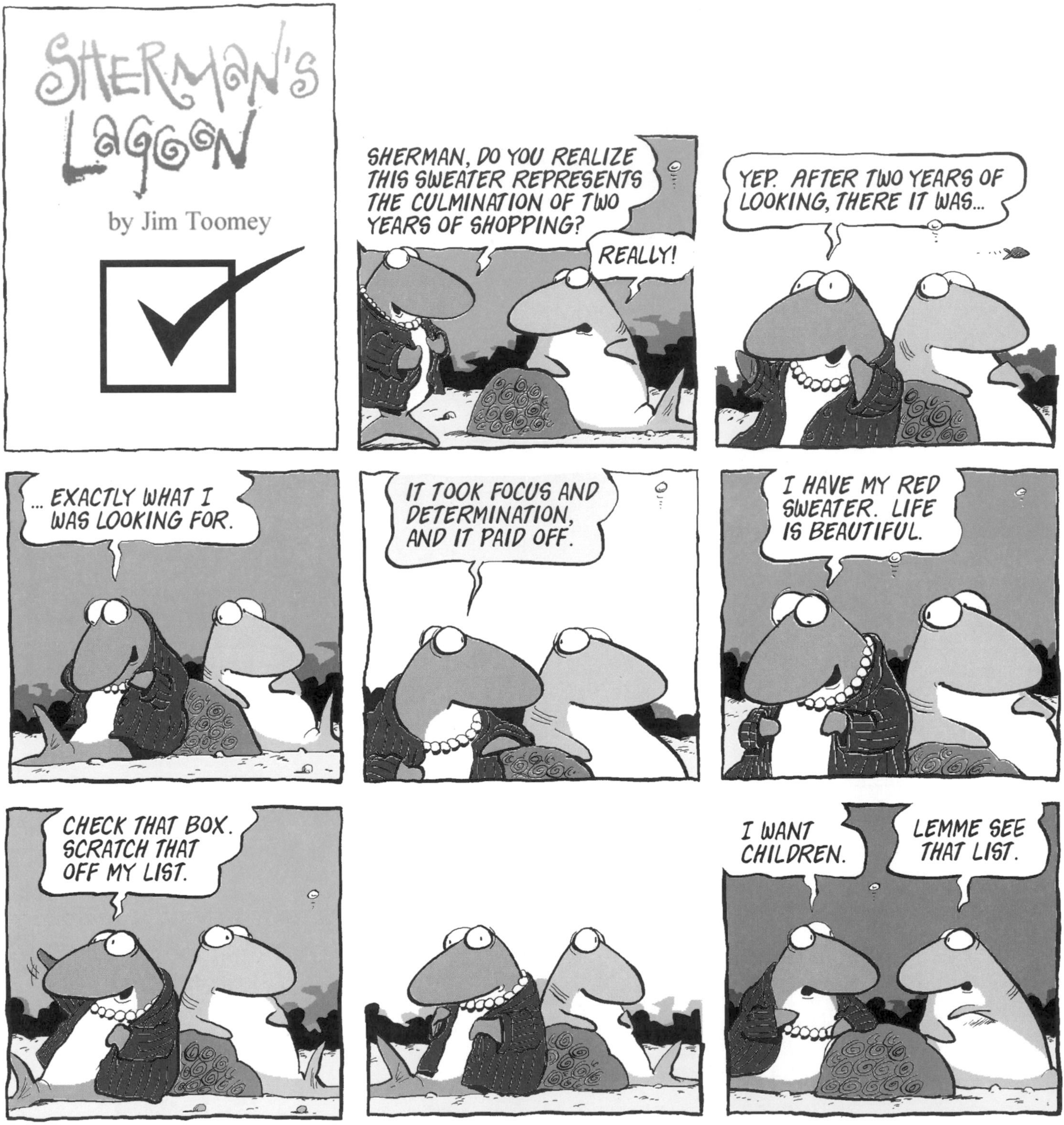
SHERMAN'S LAGOON
by Jim Toomey
SHERMAN, DO YOU REALIZE THIS SWEATER REPRESENTS THE CULMINATION OF TWO YEARS OF SHOPPING?
REALLY!
YEP. AFTER TWO YEARS OF LOOKING, THERE IT WAS...
... EXACTLY WHAT I WAS LOOKING FOR.
IT TOOK FOCUS AND DETERMINATION, AND IT PAID OFF.
I HAVE MY RED SWEATER. LIFE IS BEAUTIFUL.
CHECK THAT BOX. SCRATCH THAT OFF MY LIST.
I WANT CHILDREN.
LEMME SEE THAT LIST.

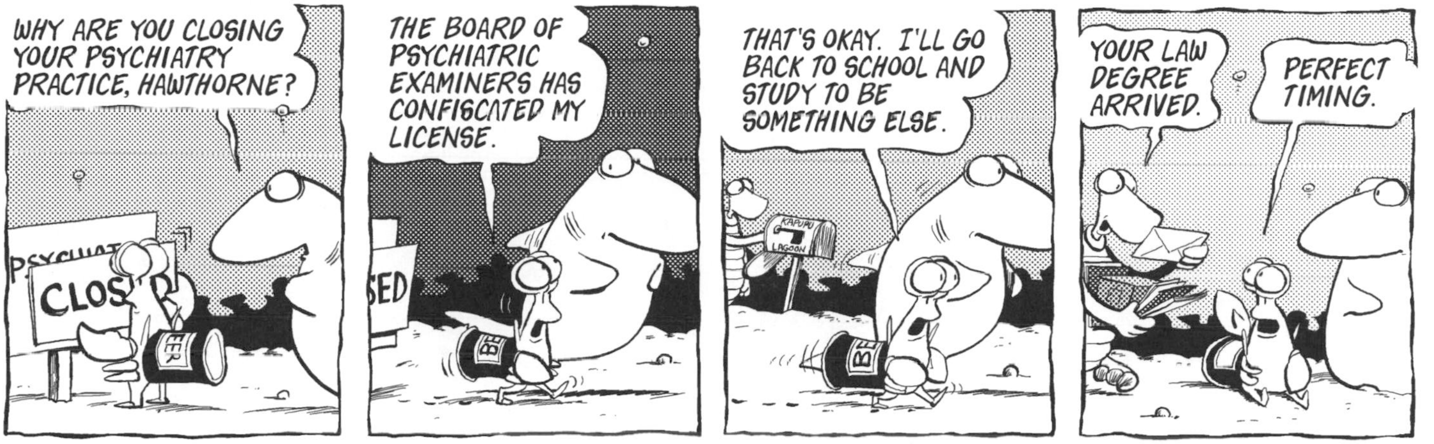
WHY ARE YOU CLOSING YOUR PSYCHIATRY PRACTICE, HAWTHORNE?
THE BOARD OF PSYCHIATRIC EXAMINERS HAS CONFISCATED MY LICENSE.
THAT'S OKAY. I'LL GO BACK TO SCHOOL AND STUDY TO BE SOMETHING ELSE.
YOUR LAW DEGREE ARRIVED.
PERFECT TIMING.

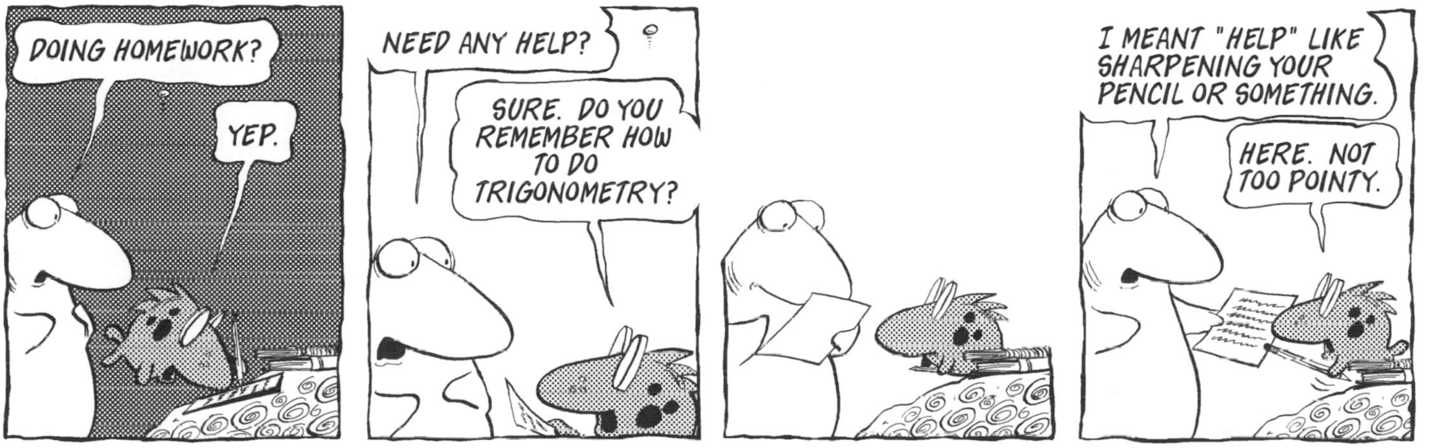
DOING HOMEWORK?
YEP.
NEED ANY HELP?
SURE. DO YOU REMEMBER HOW TO DO TRIGONOMETRY?
I MEANT "HELP" LIKE SHARPENING YOUR PENCIL OR SOMETHING.
HERE. NOT TOO POINTY.

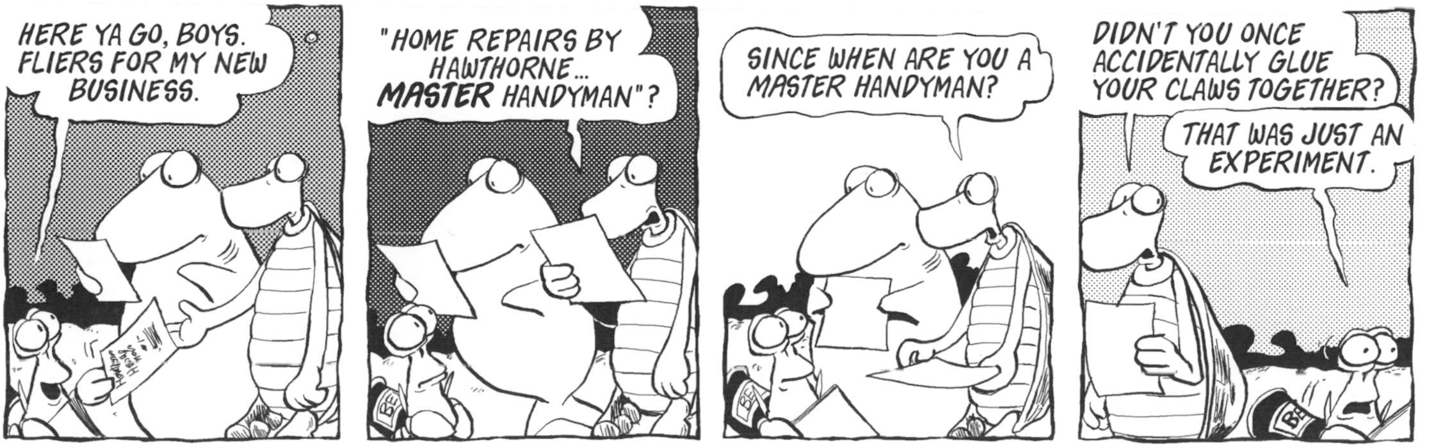
HERE YA GO, BOYS. FLIERS FOR MY NEW BUSINESS.
"HOME REPAIRS BY HAWTHORNE... MASTER HANDYMAN"?
SINCE WHEN ARE YOU A MASTER HANDYMAN?
DIDN'T YOU ONCE ACCIDENTALLY GLUE YOUR CLAWS TOGETHER?
THAT WAS JUST AN EXPERIMENT.

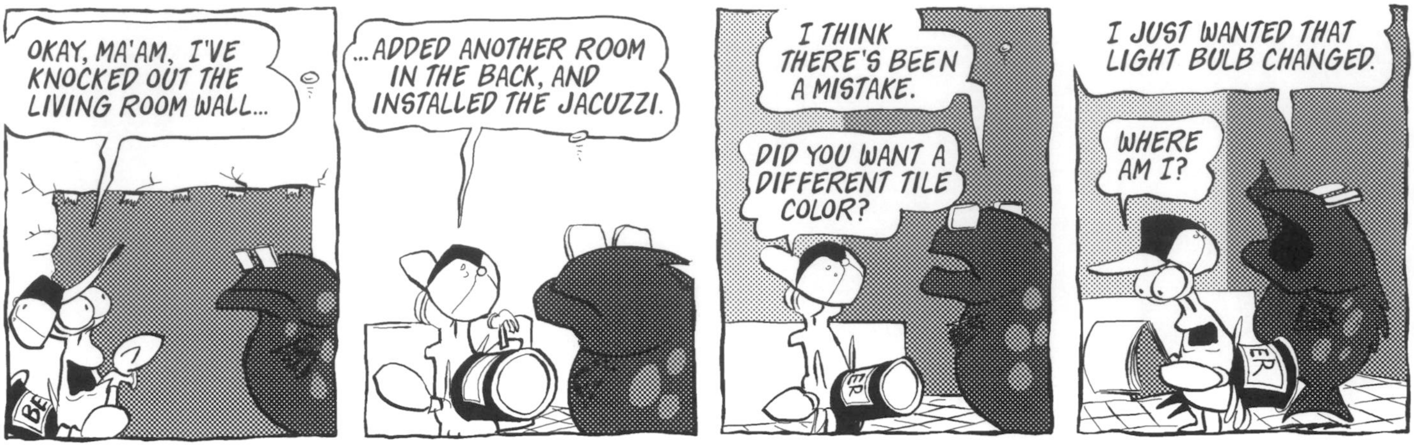
OKAY, MA'AM, I'VE KNOCKED OUT THE LIVING ROOM WALL...
...ADDED ANOTHER ROOM IN THE BACK, AND INSTALLED THE JACUZZI.
I THINK THERE'S BEEN A MISTAKE.
DID YOU WANT A DIFFERENT TILE COLOR?
I JUST WANTED THAT LIGHT BULB CHANGED.
WHERE AM I?

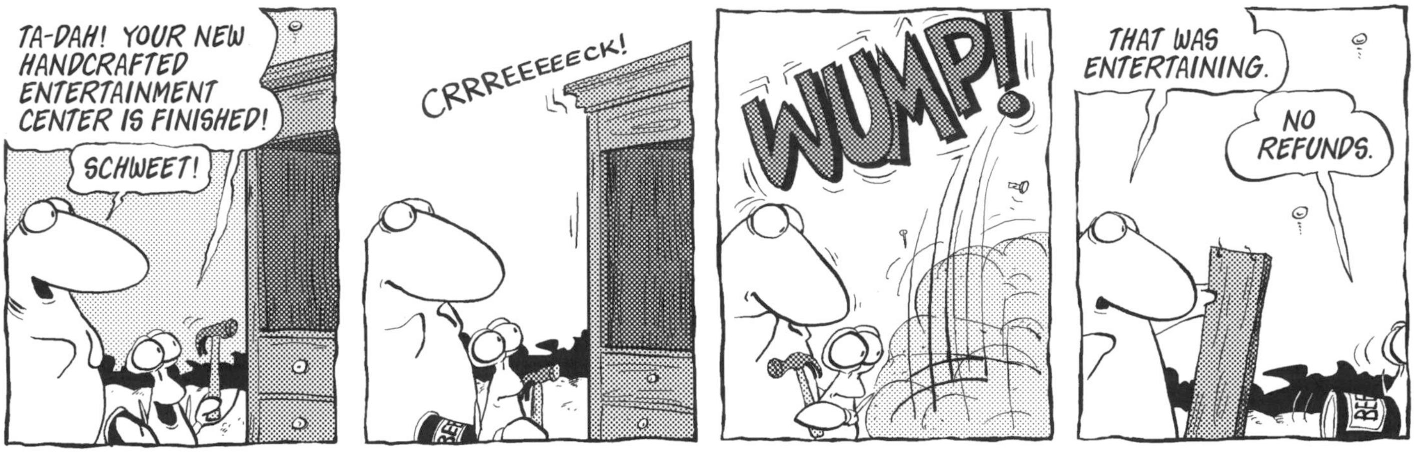
TA-DAH! YOUR NEW HANDCRAFTED ENTERTAINMENT CENTER IS FINISHED!
SCHWEET!
CRRREEEEEECK!
WUMP!
THAT WAS ENTERTAINING.
NO REFUNDS.

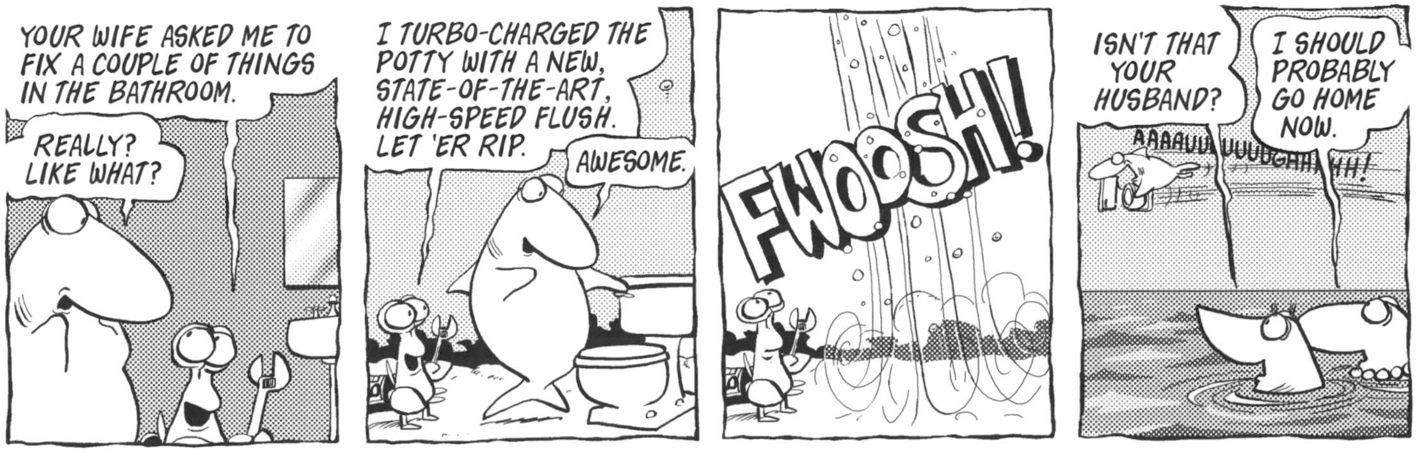
YOUR WIFE ASKED ME TO FIX A COUPLE OF THINGS IN THE BATHROOM.
REALLY? LIKE WHAT?
I TURBO-CHARGED THE POTTY WITH A NEW, STATE-OF-THE-ART, HIGH-SPEED FLUSH. LET 'ER RIP.
AWESOME.
FWOOSH!
ISN'T THAT YOUR HUSBAND?
I SHOULD PROBABLY GO HOME NOW.

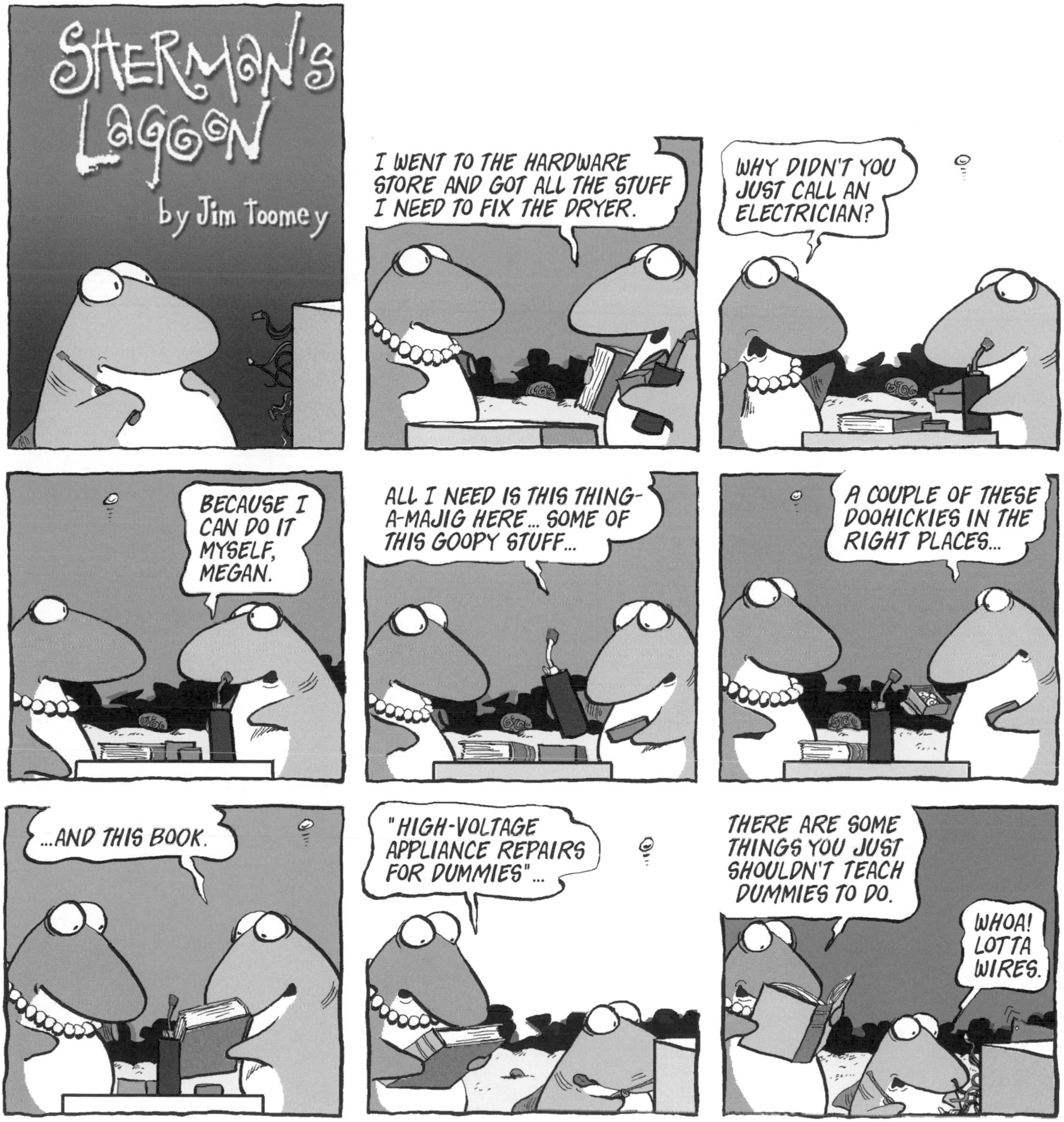

SHERMAN'S LAGOON
by Jim Toomey
I WENT TO THE HARDWARE STORE AND GOT ALL THE STUFF I NEED TO FIX THE DRYER.
WHY DIDN'T YOU JUST CALL AN ELECTRICIAN?
BECAUSE I CAN DO IT MYSELF, MEGAN.
ALL I NEED IS THIS THING-A-MAJIG HERE... SOME OF THIS GOOPY STUFF...
A COUPLE OF THESE DOOHICKIES IN THE RIGHT PLACES...
...AND THIS BOOK.
"HIGH-VOLTAGE APPLIANCE REPAIRS FOR DUMMIES"...
THERE ARE SOME THINGS YOU JUST SHOULDN'T TEACH DUMMIES TO DO.
WHOA! LOTTA WIRES.

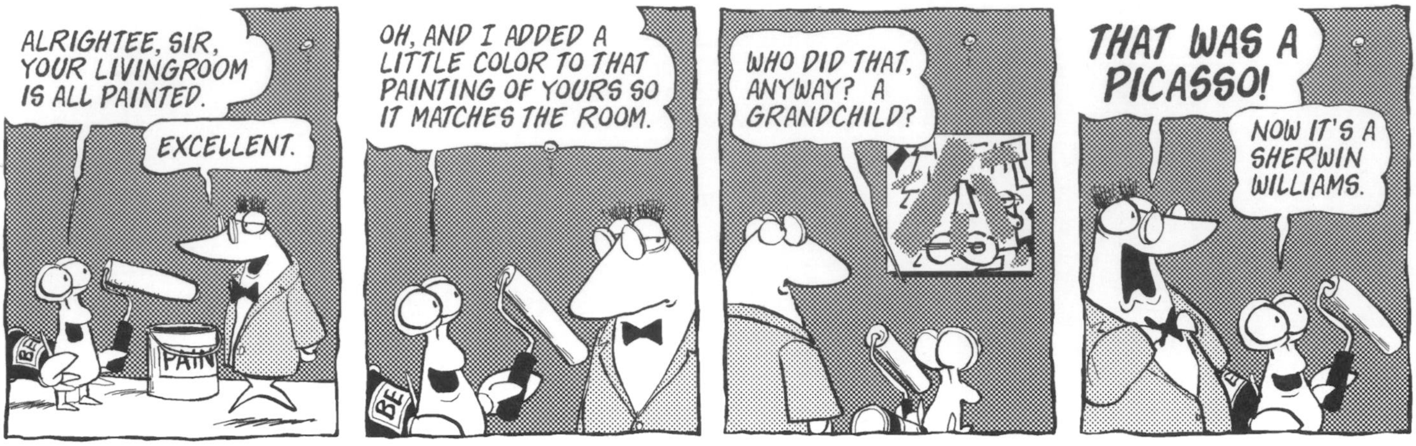
ALRIGHTEE, SIR, YOUR LIVINGROOM IS ALL PAINTED.
EXCELLENT.
PAIN
OH, AND I ADDED A LITTLE COLOR TO THAT PAINTING OF YOURS SO IT MATCHES THE ROOM.
WHO DID THAT, ANYWAY? A GRANDCHILD?
THAT WAS A PICASSO!
NOW IT'S A SHERWIN WILLIAMS.

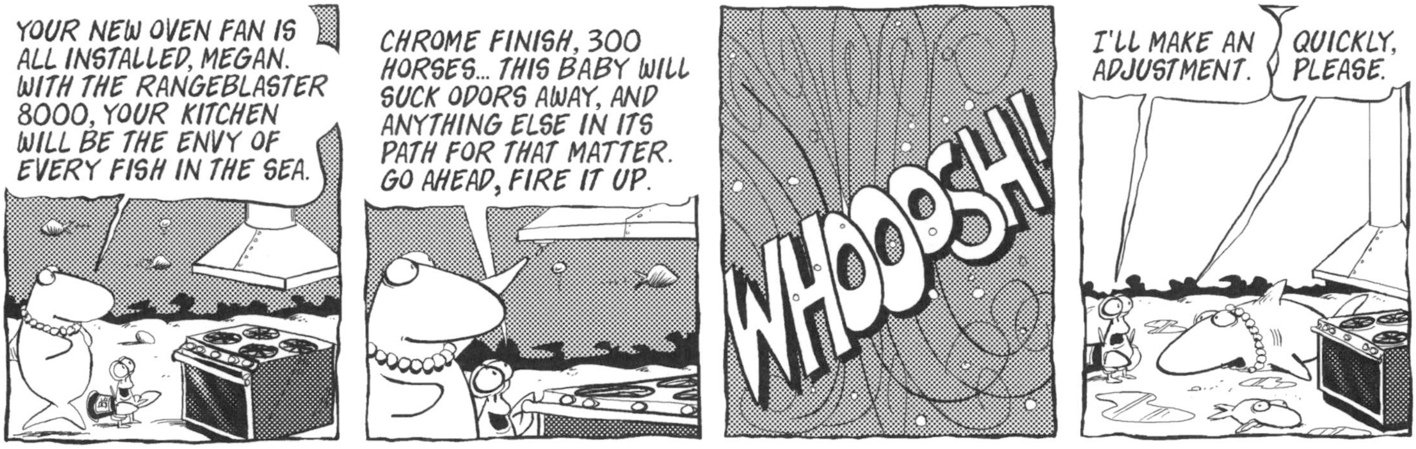
YOUR NEW OVEN FAN IS ALL INSTALLED, MEGAN. WITH THE RANGEBLASTER 8000, YOUR KITCHEN WILL BE THE ENVY OF EVERY FISH IN THE SEA.
CHROME FINISH, 300 HORSES... THIS BABY WILL SUCK ODORS AWAY, AND ANYTHING ELSE IN ITS PATH FOR THAT MATTER. GO AHEAD, FIRE IT UP.
WHOOOSH!
I'LL MAKE AN ADJUSTMENT.
QUICKLY, PLEASE.

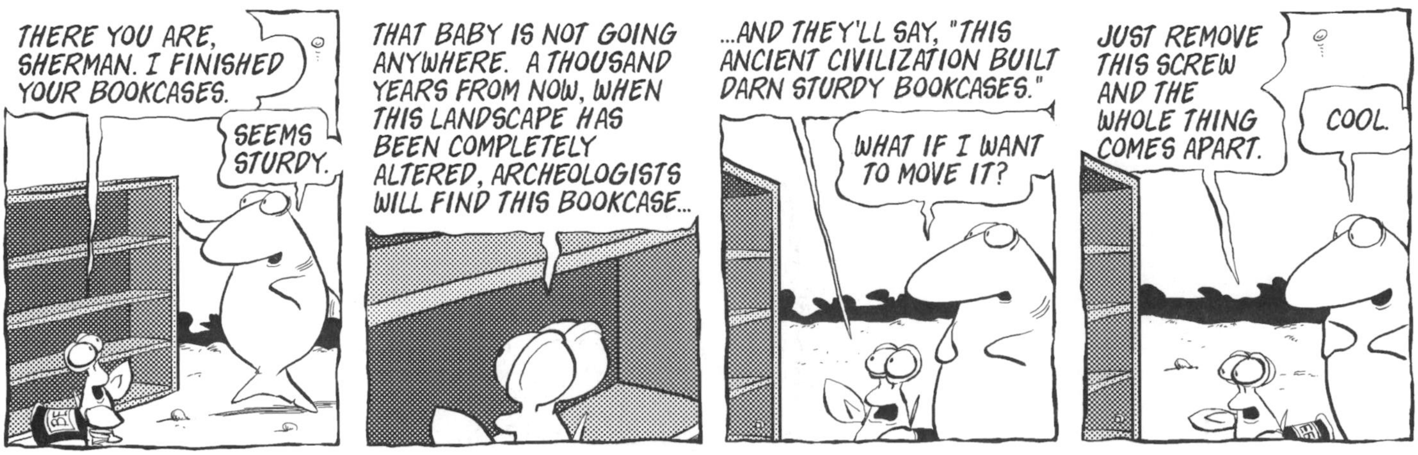
THERE YOU ARE, SHERMAN. I FINISHED YOUR BOOKCASES.
SEEMS STURDY.
THAT BABY IS NOT GOING ANYWHERE. A THOUSAND YEARS FROM NOW, WHEN THIS LANDSCAPE HAS BEEN COMPLETELY ALTERED, ARCHEOLOGISTS WILL FIND THIS BOOKCASE...
...AND THEY'LL SAY, "THIS ANCIENT CIVILIZATION BUILT DARN STURDY BOOKCASES."
WHAT IF I WANT TO MOVE IT?
JUST REMOVE THIS SCREW AND THE WHOLE THING COMES APART.
COOL.

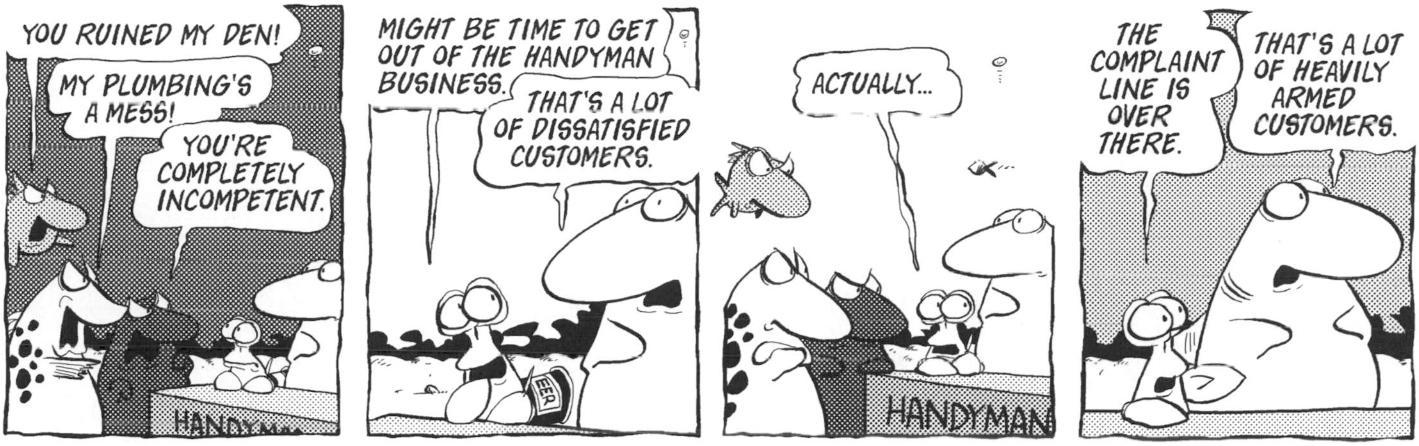
YOU RUINED MY DEN!
MY PLUMBING'S A MESS!
YOU'RE COMPLETELY INCOMPETENT.
HANDYMAN
MIGHT BE TIME TO GET OUT OF THE HANDYMAN BUSINESS.
THAT'S A LOT OF DISSATISFIED CUSTOMERS.
ACTUALLY...
HANDYMAN
THE COMPLAINT LINE IS OVER THERE.
THAT'S A LOT OF HEAVILY ARMED CUSTOMERS.

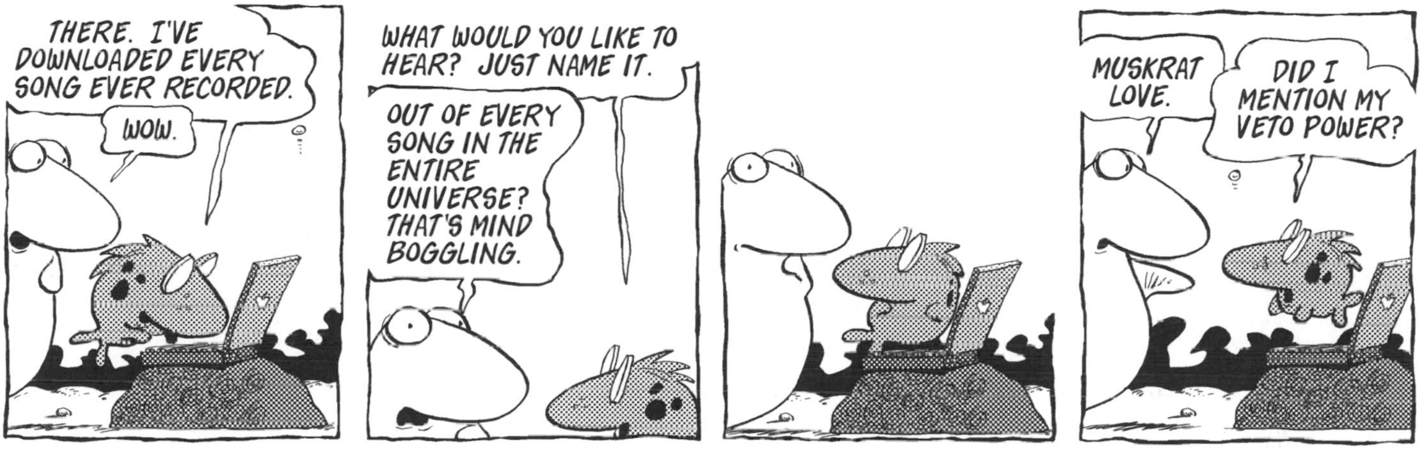
THERE. I'VE DOWNLOADED EVERY SONG EVER RECORDED.
WOW.
WHAT WOULD YOU LIKE TO HEAR? JUST NAME IT.
OUT OF EVERY SONG IN THE ENTIRE UNIVERSE? THAT'S MIND BOGGLING.
MUSKRAT LOVE.
DID I MENTION MY VETO POWER?

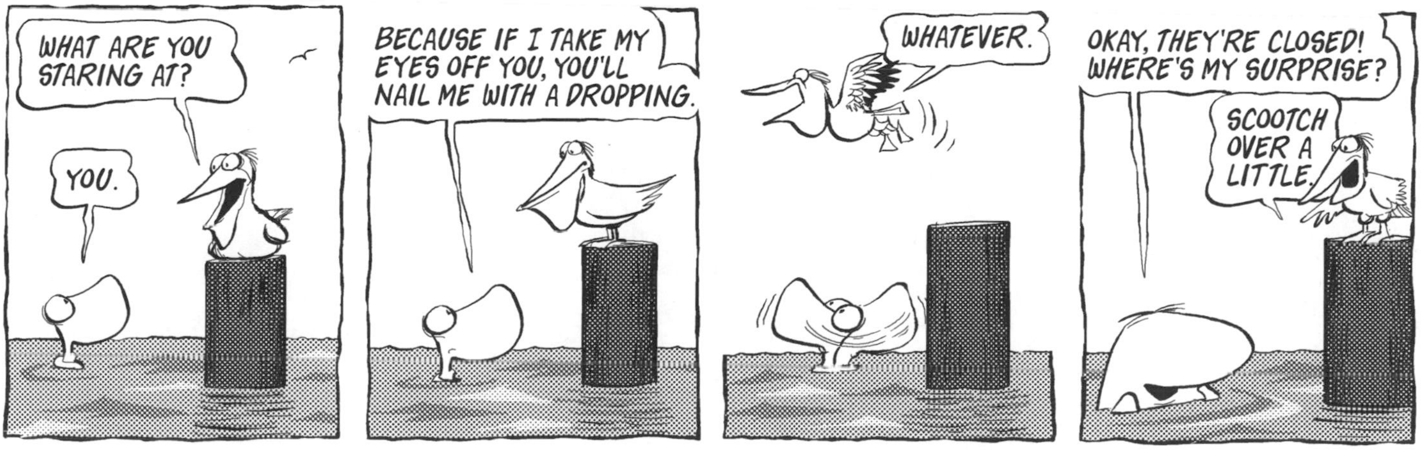
WHAT ARE YOU STARING AT?
YOU.
BECAUSE IF I TAKE MY EYES OFF YOU, YOU'LL NAIL ME WITH A DROPPING.
WHATEVER.
OKAY, THEY'RE CLOSED! WHERE'S MY SURPRISE?
SCOOTCH OVER A LITTLE.

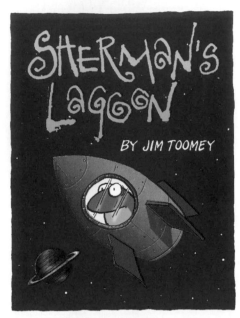

SHERMAN'S LAGOON

BY JIM TOOMEY

YOU'RE ABOUT TO WITNESS SOMETHING HISTORIC. I'M GOING TO BE THE FIRST FISH IN OUTER SPACE.

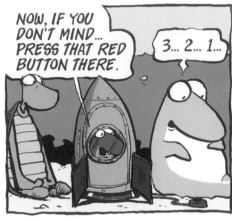

NOW, IF YOU DON'T MIND... PRESS THAT RED BUTTON THERE.

3... 2... 1...

WE HAVE LIFTOFF.

WHOOSH!

WHAM!

WELL, HE DIDN'T MAKE IT TO OUTER SPACE...

... BUT HE'S THE FIRST FISH IN A KFC.

THAT'S HISTORIC.

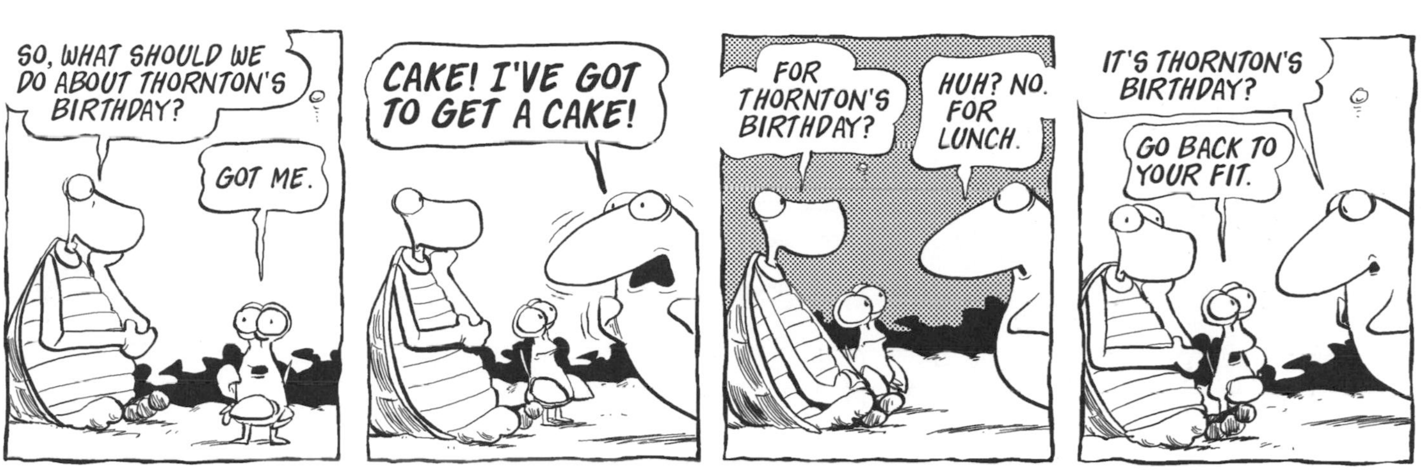
SO, WHAT SHOULD WE DO ABOUT THORNTON'S BIRTHDAY?
GOT ME.
CAKE! I'VE GOT TO GET A CAKE!
FOR THORNTON'S BIRTHDAY?
HUH? NO. FOR LUNCH.
IT'S THORNTON'S BIRTHDAY?
GO BACK TO YOUR FIT.

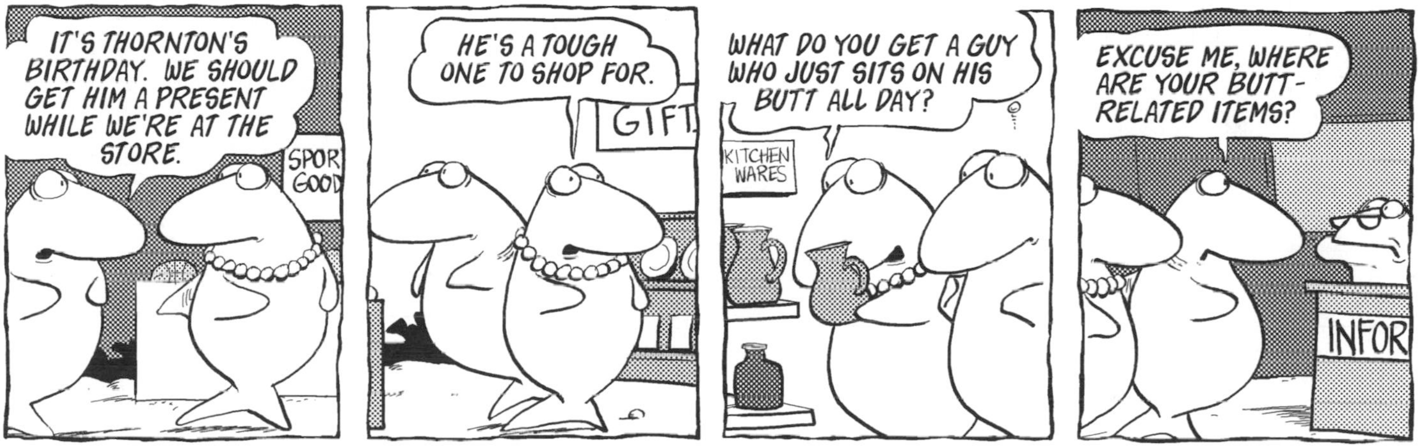
IT'S THORNTON'S BIRTHDAY. WE SHOULD GET HIM A PRESENT WHILE WE'RE AT THE STORE.
SPOR
GOOD
HE'S A TOUGH ONE TO SHOP FOR.
GIFT
WHAT DO YOU GET A GUY WHO JUST SITS ON HIS BUTT ALL DAY?
KITCHEN WARES
EXCUSE ME, WHERE ARE YOUR BUTT-RELATED ITEMS?
INFOR

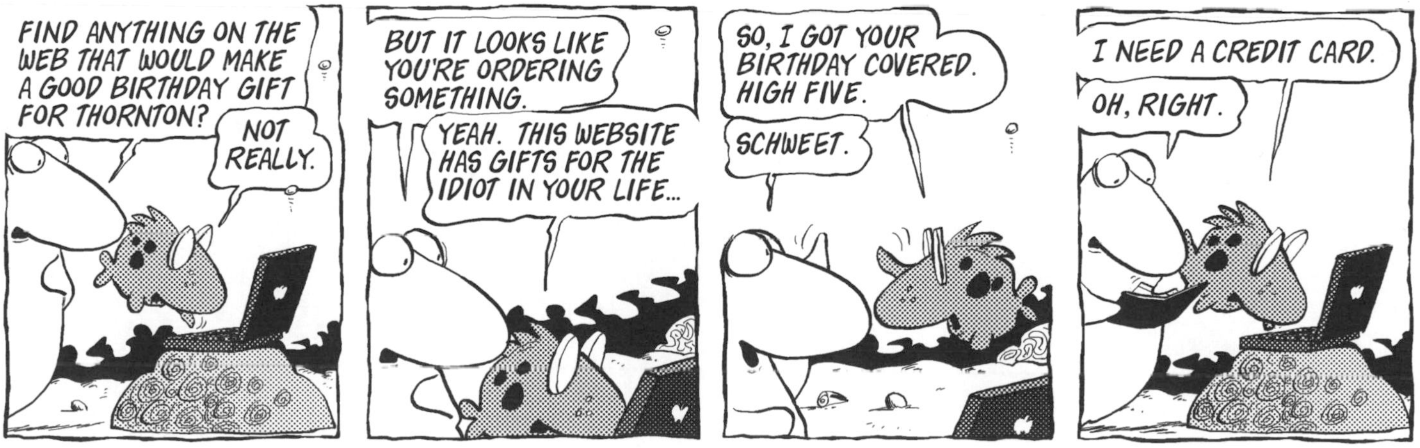
FIND ANYTHING ON THE WEB THAT WOULD MAKE A GOOD BIRTHDAY GIFT FOR THORNTON?
NOT REALLY.
BUT IT LOOKS LIKE YOU'RE ORDERING SOMETHING.
YEAH. THIS WEBSITE HAS GIFTS FOR THE IDIOT IN YOUR LIFE...
SO, I GOT YOUR BIRTHDAY COVERED. HIGH FIVE.
SCHWEET.
I NEED A CREDIT CARD.
OH, RIGHT.

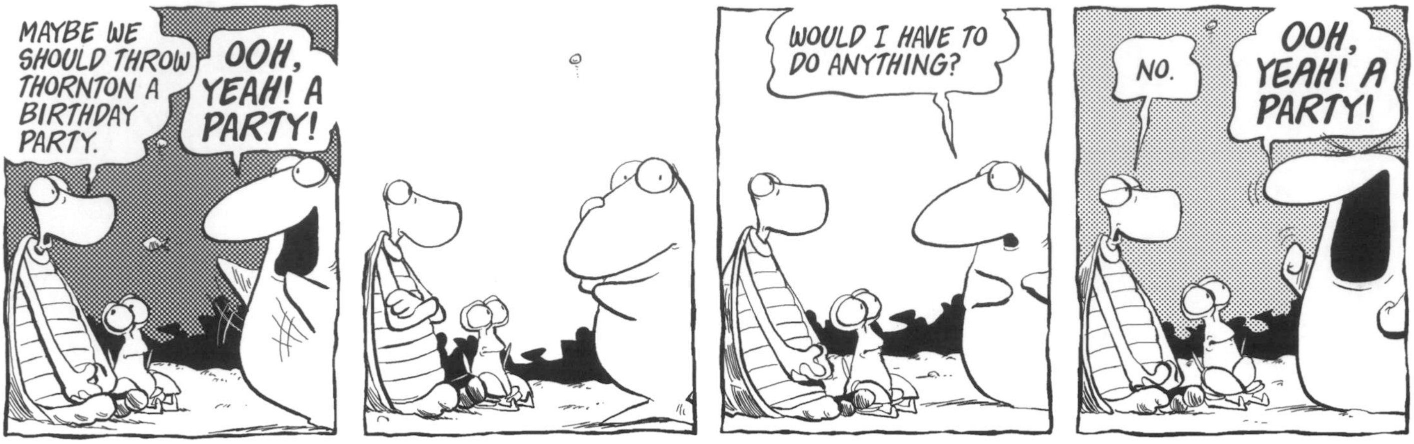
MAYBE WE SHOULD THROW THORNTON A BIRTHDAY PARTY.
OOH, YEAH! A PARTY!
WOULD I HAVE TO DO ANYTHING?
NO.
OOH, YEAH! A PARTY!

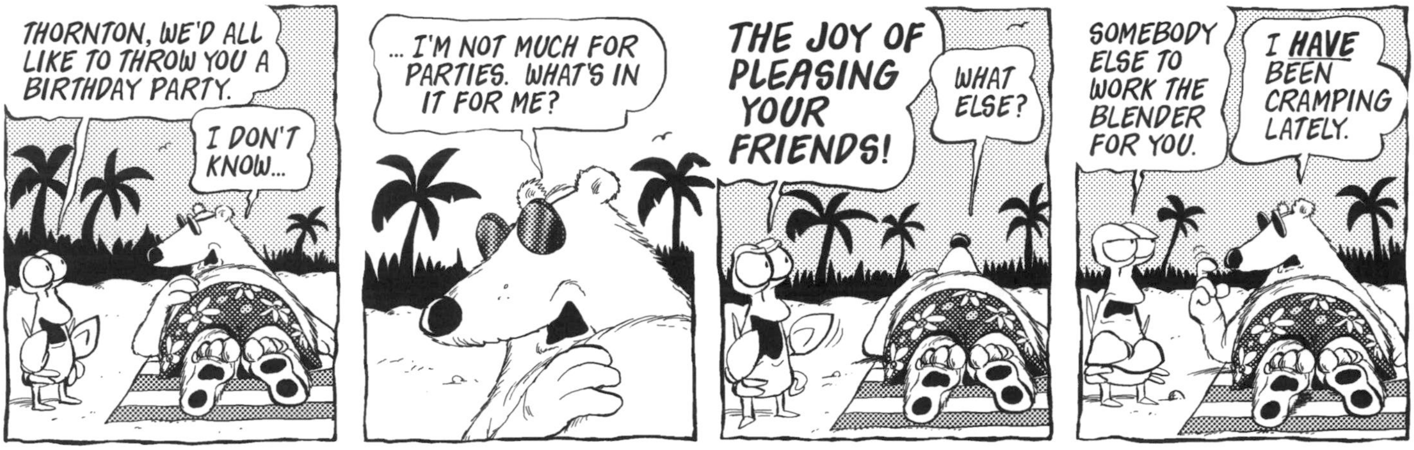
THORNTON, WE'D ALL LIKE TO THROW YOU A BIRTHDAY PARTY.
I DON'T KNOW...
... I'M NOT MUCH FOR PARTIES. WHAT'S IN IT FOR ME?
THE JOY OF PLEASING YOUR FRIENDS!
WHAT ELSE?
SOMEBODY ELSE TO WORK THE BLENDER FOR YOU.
I HAVE BEEN CRAMPING LATELY.

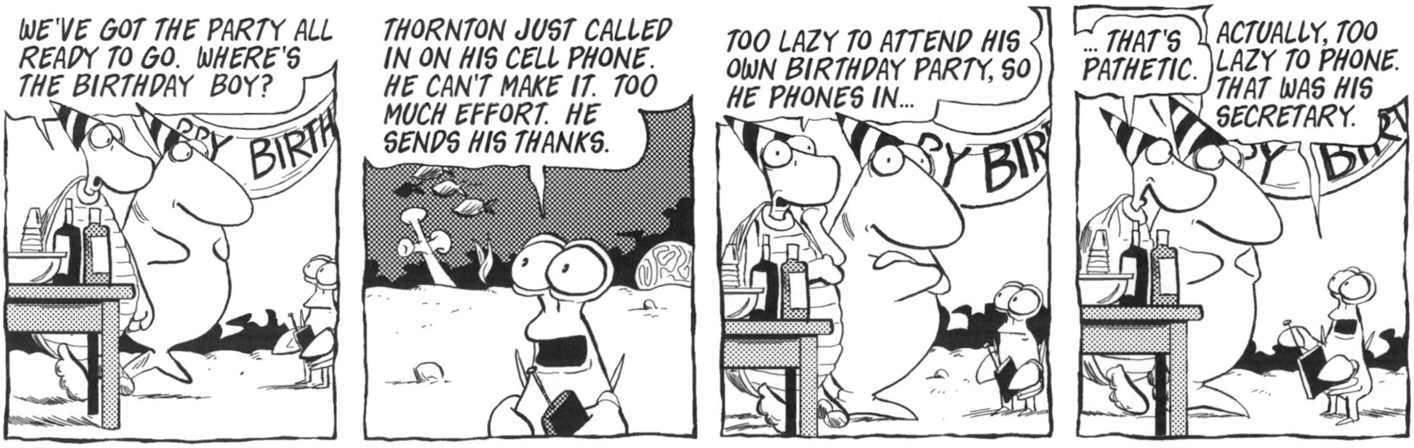
WE'VE GOT THE PARTY ALL READY TO GO. WHERE'S THE BIRTHDAY BOY?
THORNTON JUST CALLED IN ON HIS CELL PHONE. HE CAN'T MAKE IT. TOO MUCH EFFORT. HE SENDS HIS THANKS.
TOO LAZY TO ATTEND HIS OWN BIRTHDAY PARTY, SO HE PHONES IN...
... THAT'S PATHETIC.
ACTUALLY, TOO LAZY TO PHONE. THAT WAS HIS SECRETARY.

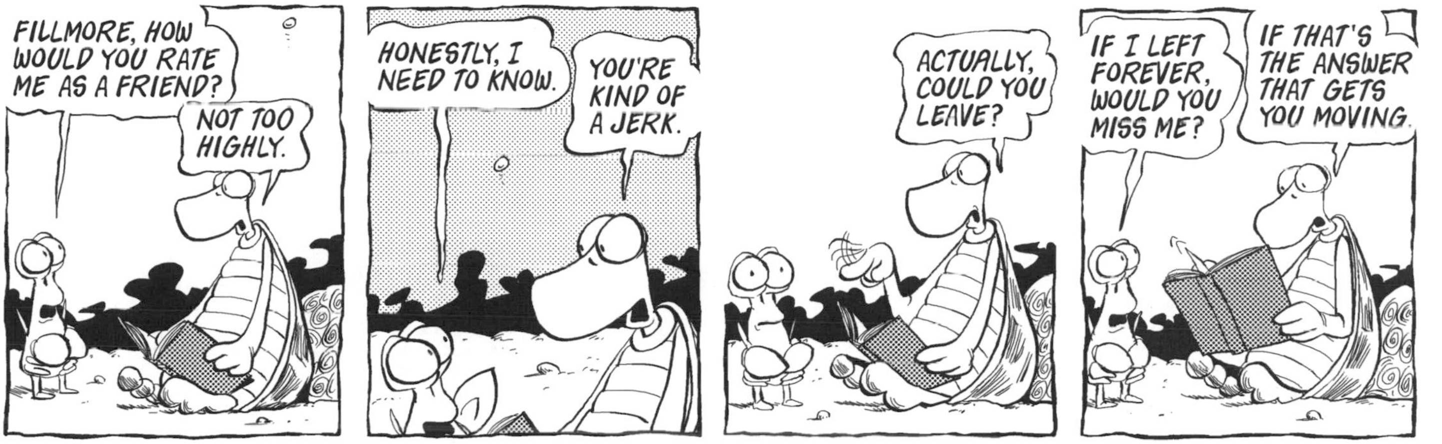
FILLMORE, HOW WOULD YOU RATE ME AS A FRIEND?
NOT TOO HIGHLY.
HONESTLY, I NEED TO KNOW.
YOU'RE KIND OF A JERK.
ACTUALLY, COULD YOU LEAVE?
IF I LEFT FOREVER, WOULD YOU MISS ME?
IF THAT'S THE ANSWER THAT GETS YOU MOVING.

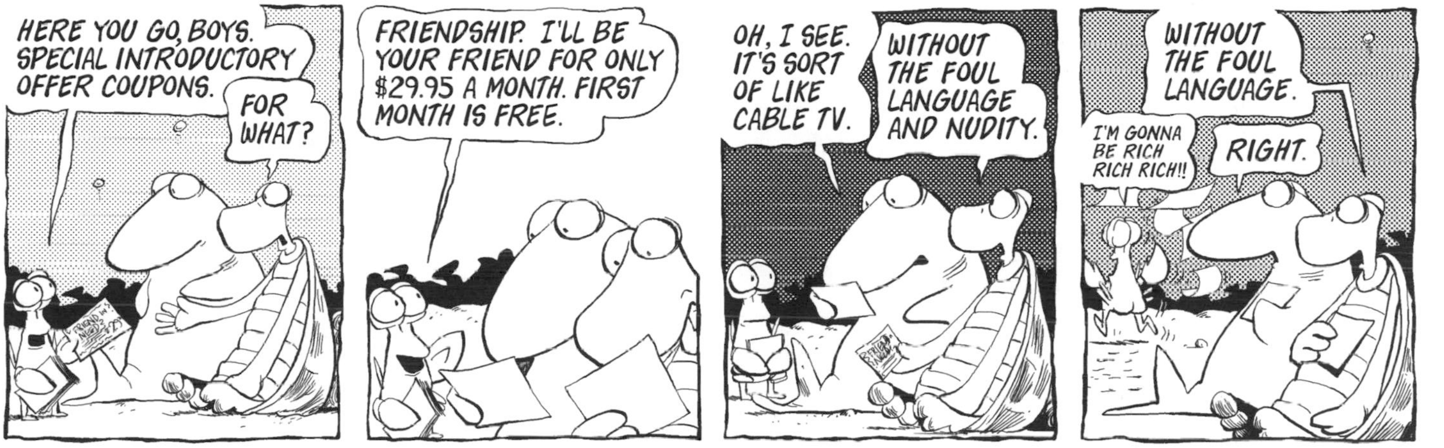
HERE YOU GO, BOYS. SPECIAL INTRODUCTORY OFFER COUPONS.
FOR WHAT?
FRIENDSHIP. I'LL BE YOUR FRIEND FOR ONLY $29.95 A MONTH. FIRST MONTH IS FREE.
OH, I SEE. IT'S SORT OF LIKE CABLE TV.
WITHOUT THE FOUL LANGUAGE AND NUDITY.
WITHOUT THE FOUL LANGUAGE.
I'M GONNA BE RICH RICH RICH!!
RIGHT.

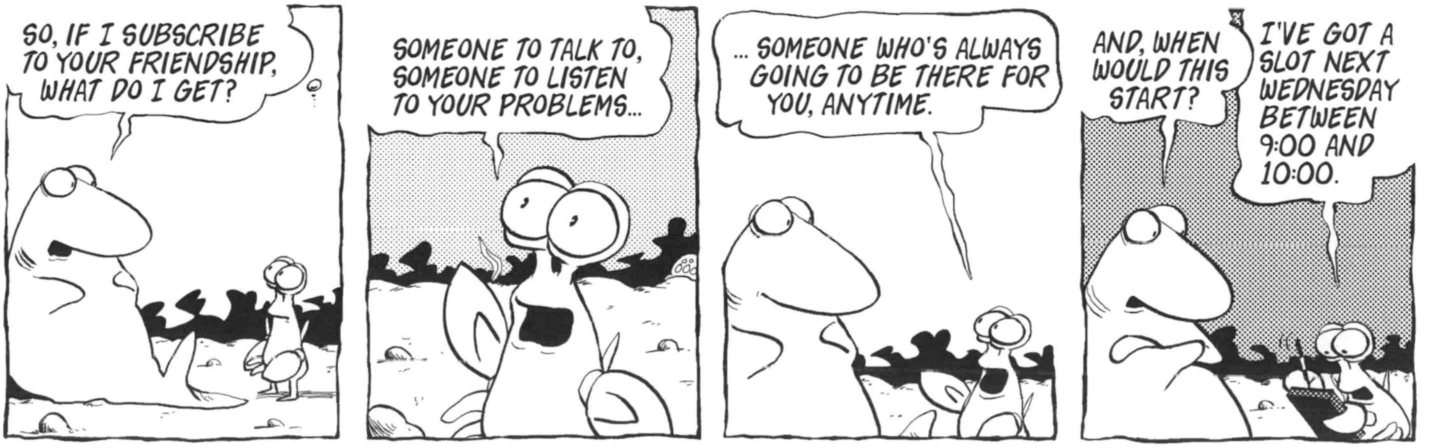
SO, IF I SUBSCRIBE TO YOUR FRIENDSHIP, WHAT DO I GET?
SOMEONE TO TALK TO, SOMEONE TO LISTEN TO YOUR PROBLEMS...
... SOMEONE WHO'S ALWAYS GOING TO BE THERE FOR YOU, ANYTIME.
AND, WHEN WOULD THIS START?
I'VE GOT A SLOT NEXT WEDNESDAY BETWEEN 9:00 AND 10:00.

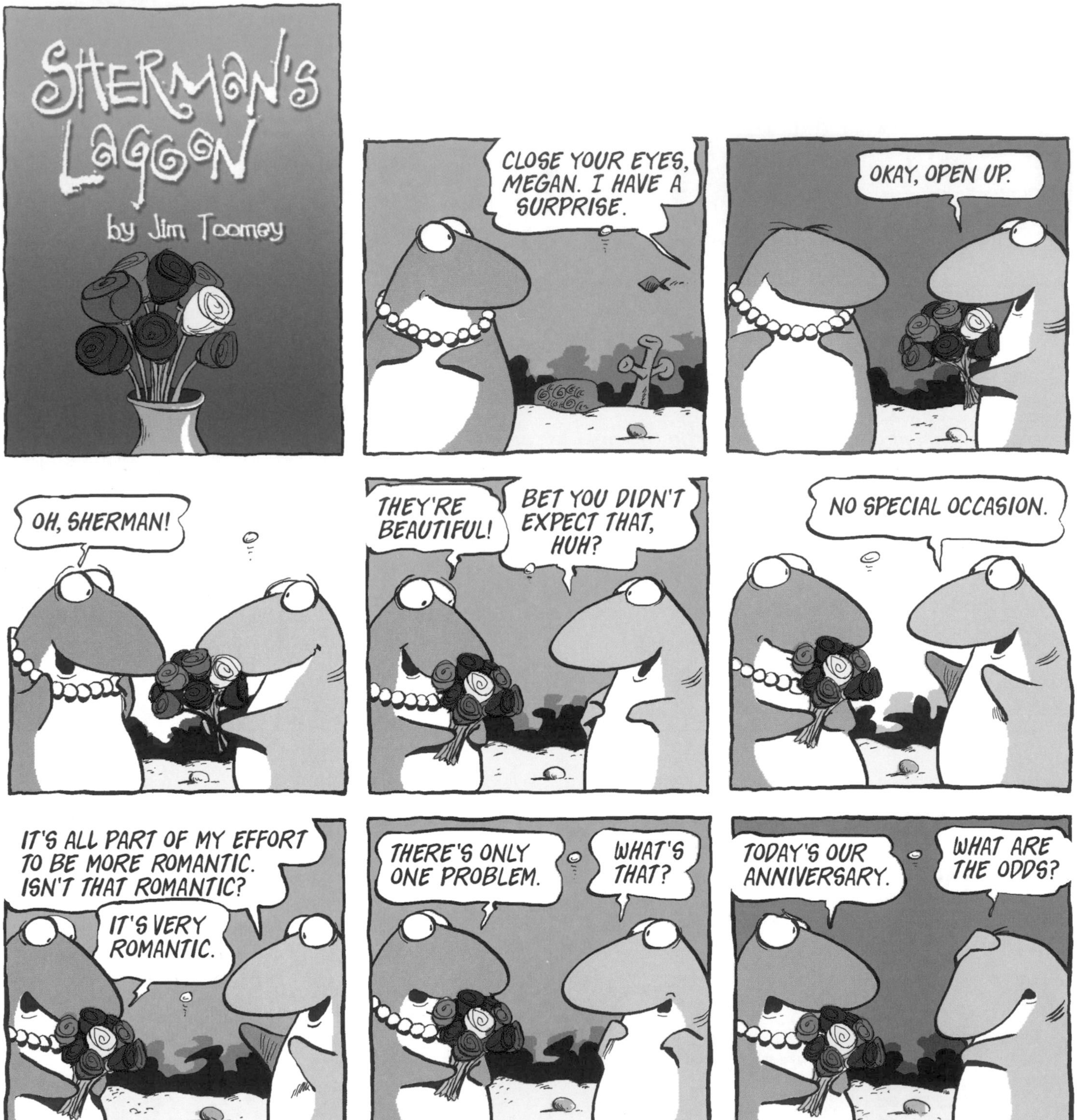
SHERMAN'S LAGOON
by Jim Toomey
CLOSE YOUR EYES, MEGAN. I HAVE A SURPRISE.
OKAY, OPEN UP.
OH, SHERMAN!
THEY'RE BEAUTIFUL!
BET YOU DIDN'T EXPECT THAT, HUH?
NO SPECIAL OCCASION.
IT'S ALL PART OF MY EFFORT TO BE MORE ROMANTIC. ISN'T THAT ROMANTIC?
IT'S VERY ROMANTIC.
THERE'S ONLY ONE PROBLEM.
WHAT'S THAT?
TODAY'S OUR ANNIVERSARY.
WHAT ARE THE ODDS?

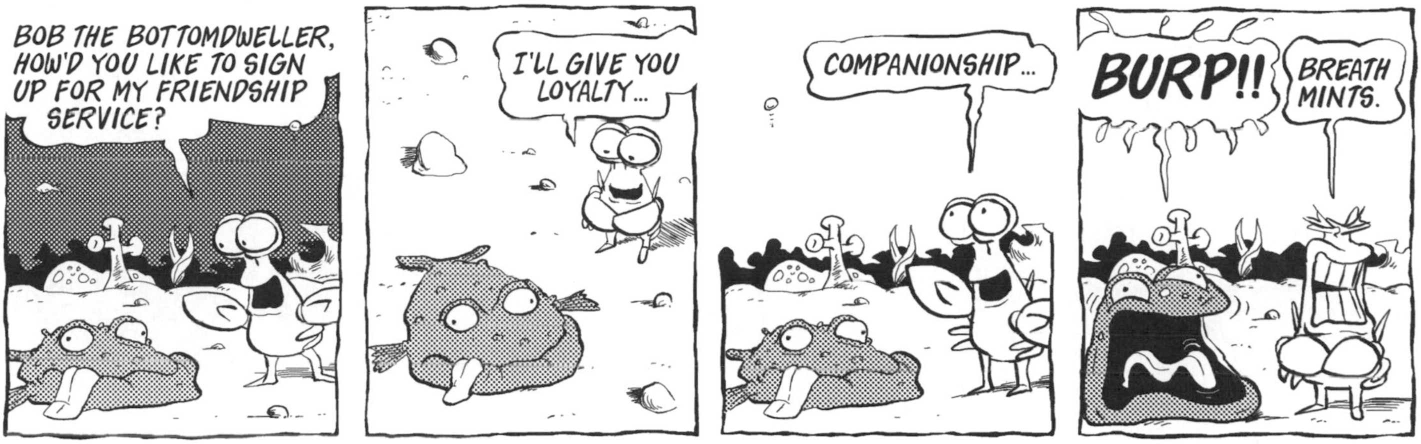
BOB THE BOTTOMDWELLER, HOW'D YOU LIKE TO SIGN UP FOR MY FRIENDSHIP SERVICE?
I'LL GIVE YOU LOYALTY...
COMPANIONSHIP...
BURP!!
BREATH MINTS.

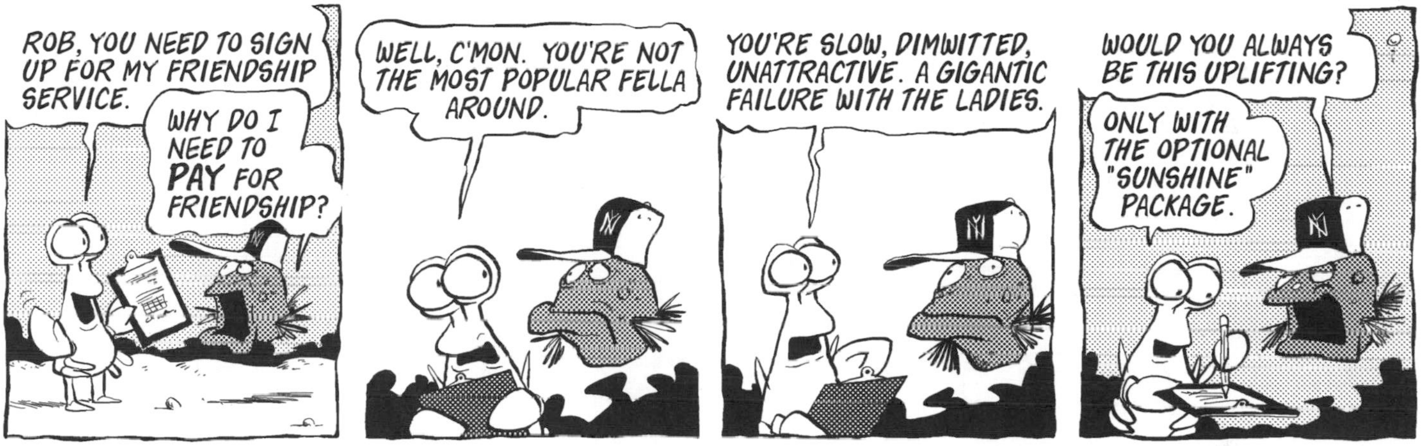
ROB, YOU NEED TO SIGN UP FOR MY FRIENDSHIP SERVICE.
WHY DO I NEED TO PAY FOR FRIENDSHIP?
WELL, C'MON. YOU'RE NOT THE MOST POPULAR FELLA AROUND.
YOU'RE SLOW, DIMWITTED, UNATTRACTIVE. A GIGANTIC FAILURE WITH THE LADIES.
WOULD YOU ALWAYS BE THIS UPLIFTING?
ONLY WITH THE OPTIONAL "SUNSHINE" PACKAGE.

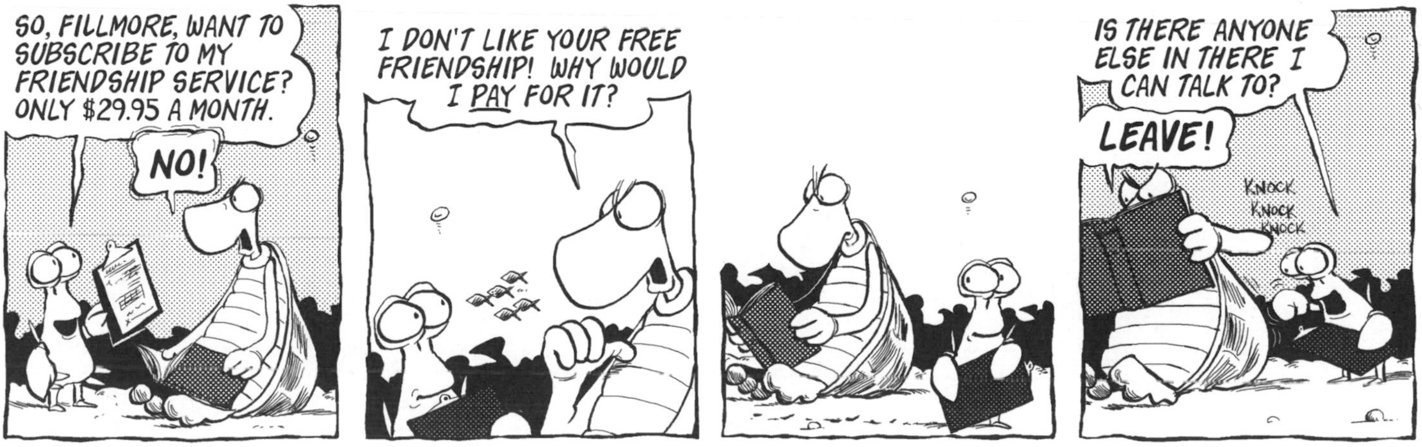
SO, FILLMORE, WANT TO SUBSCRIBE TO MY FRIENDSHIP SERVICE? ONLY $29.95 A MONTH.
NO!
I DON'T LIKE YOUR FREE FRIENDSHIP! WHY WOULD I PAY FOR IT?
IS THERE ANYONE ELSE IN THERE I CAN TALK TO?
LEAVE!
KNOCK KNOCK KNOCK

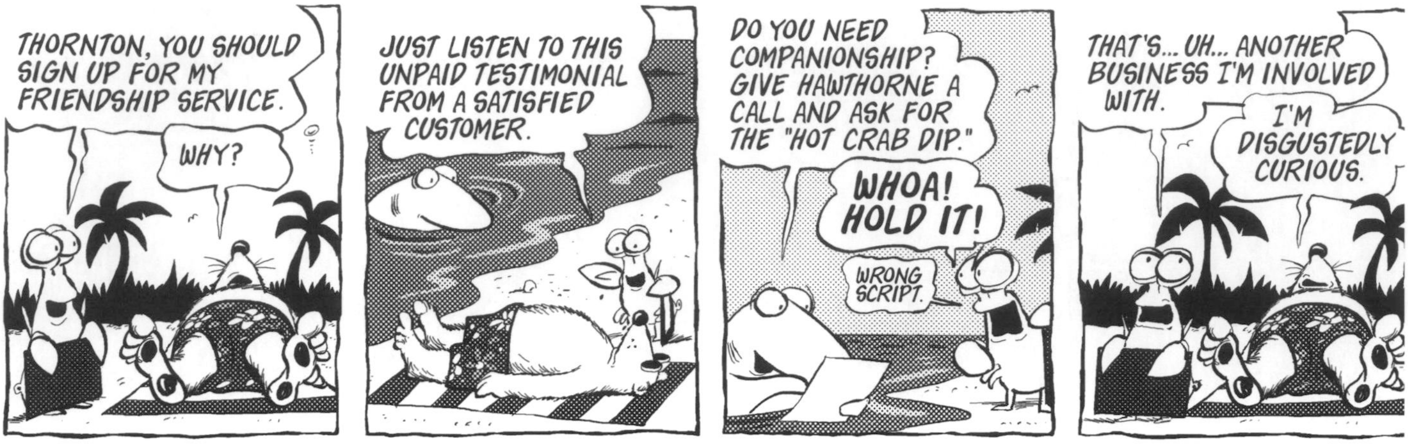
THORNTON, YOU SHOULD SIGN UP FOR MY FRIENDSHIP SERVICE.
WHY?
JUST LISTEN TO THIS UNPAID TESTIMONIAL FROM A SATISFIED CUSTOMER.
DO YOU NEED COMPANIONSHIP? GIVE HAWTHORNE A CALL AND ASK FOR THE "HOT CRAB DIP."
WHOA! HOLD IT!
WRONG SCRIPT.
THAT'S... UH... ANOTHER BUSINESS I'M INVOLVED WITH.
I'M DISGUSTEDLY CURIOUS.

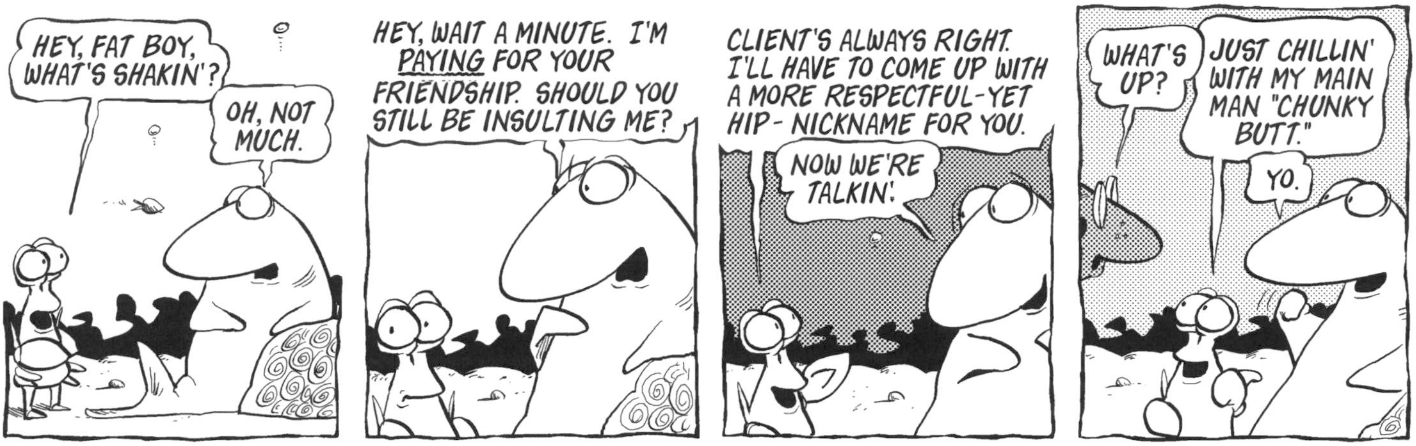
HEY, FAT BOY, WHAT'S SHAKIN'?
OH, NOT MUCH.
HEY, WAIT A MINUTE. I'M PAYING FOR YOUR FRIENDSHIP. SHOULD YOU STILL BE INSULTING ME?
CLIENT'S ALWAYS RIGHT. I'LL HAVE TO COME UP WITH A MORE RESPECTFUL-YET HIP- NICKNAME FOR YOU.
NOW WE'RE TALKIN'.
WHAT'S UP?
JUST CHILLIN' WITH MY MAIN MAN "CHUNKY BUTT."
YO.

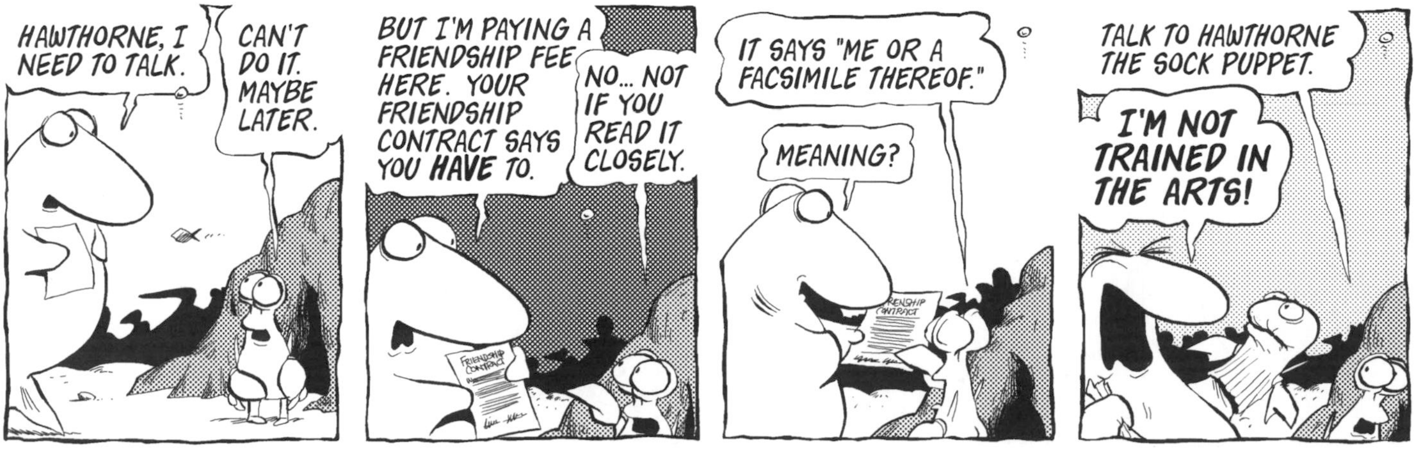
HAWTHORNE, I NEED TO TALK.
CAN'T DO IT. MAYBE LATER.
BUT I'M PAYING A FRIENDSHIP FEE HERE. YOUR FRIENDSHIP CONTRACT SAYS YOU HAVE TO.
NO... NOT IF YOU READ IT CLOSELY.
FRIENDSHIP CONTRACT
IT SAYS "ME OR A FACSIMILE THEREOF."
MEANING?
TALK TO HAWTHORNE THE SOCK PUPPET.
I'M NOT TRAINED IN THE ARTS!

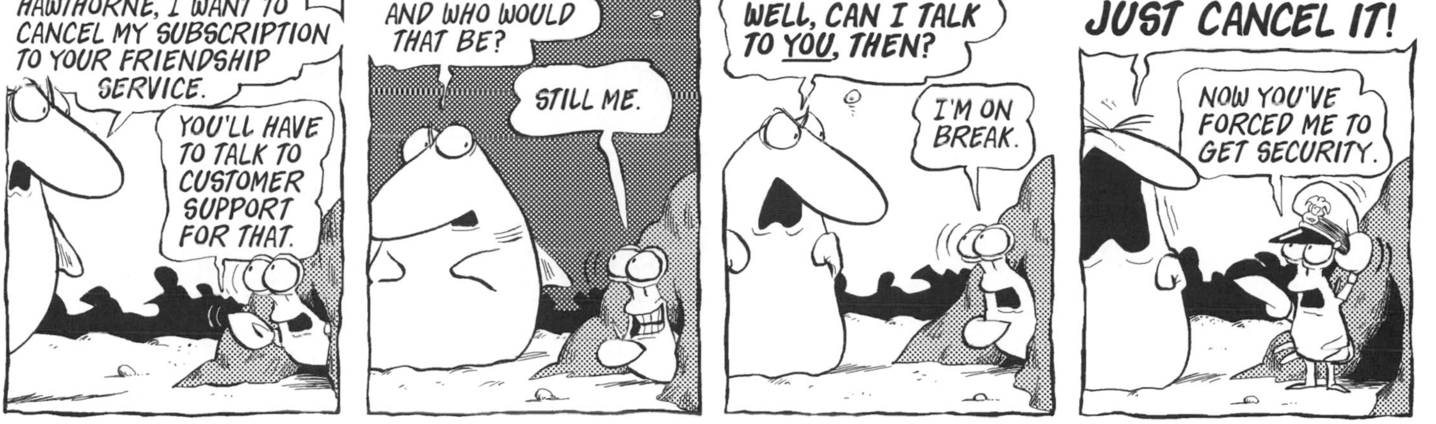
HAWTHORNE, I WANT TO CANCEL MY SUBSCRIPTION TO YOUR FRIENDSHIP SERVICE.
YOU'LL HAVE TO TALK TO CUSTOMER SUPPORT FOR THAT.
AND WHO WOULD THAT BE?
STILL ME.
WELL, CAN I TALK TO YOU, THEN?
I'M ON BREAK.
JUST CANCEL IT!
NOW YOU'VE FORCED ME TO GET SECURITY.

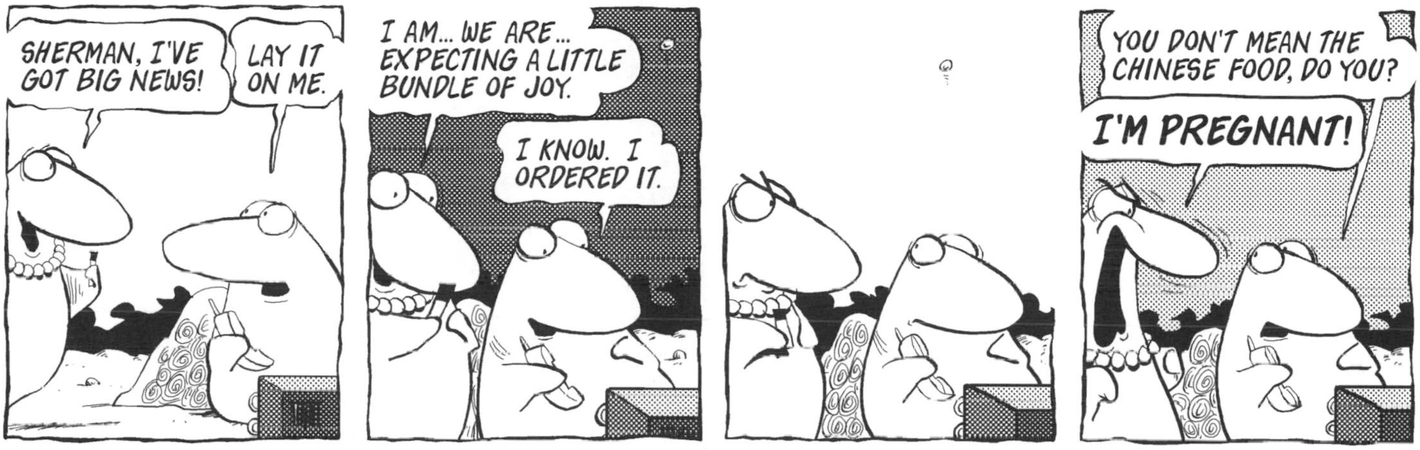
SHERMAN, I'VE GOT BIG NEWS!
LAY IT ON ME.
I AM... WE ARE... EXPECTING A LITTLE BUNDLE OF JOY.
I KNOW. I ORDERED IT.
YOU DON'T MEAN THE CHINESE FOOD, DO YOU?
I'M PREGNANT!

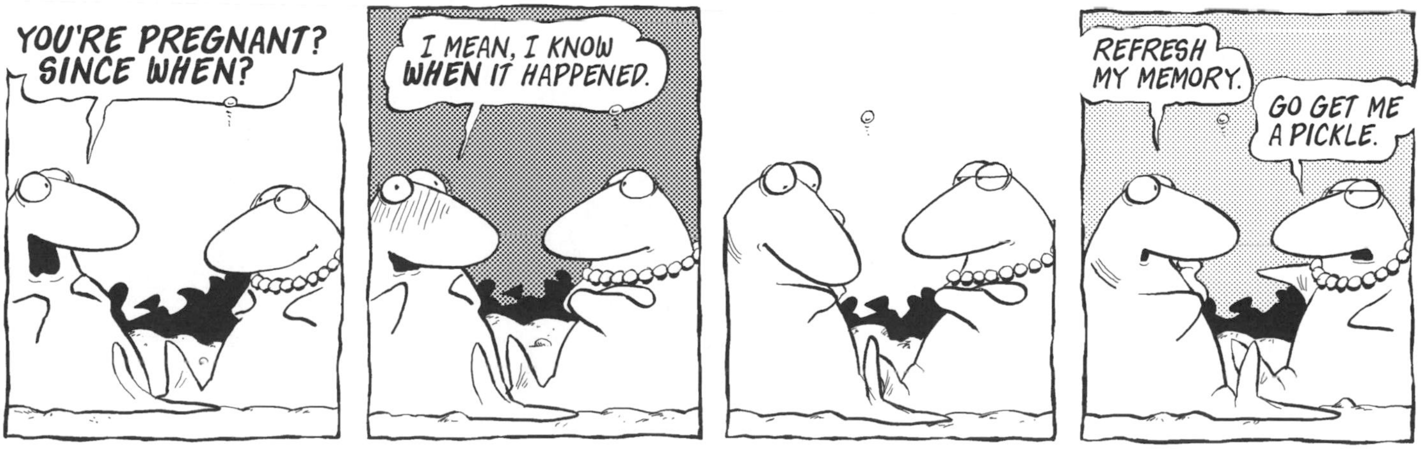
YOU'RE PREGNANT? SINCE WHEN?
I MEAN, I KNOW WHEN IT HAPPENED.
REFRESH MY MEMORY.
GO GET ME A PICKLE.

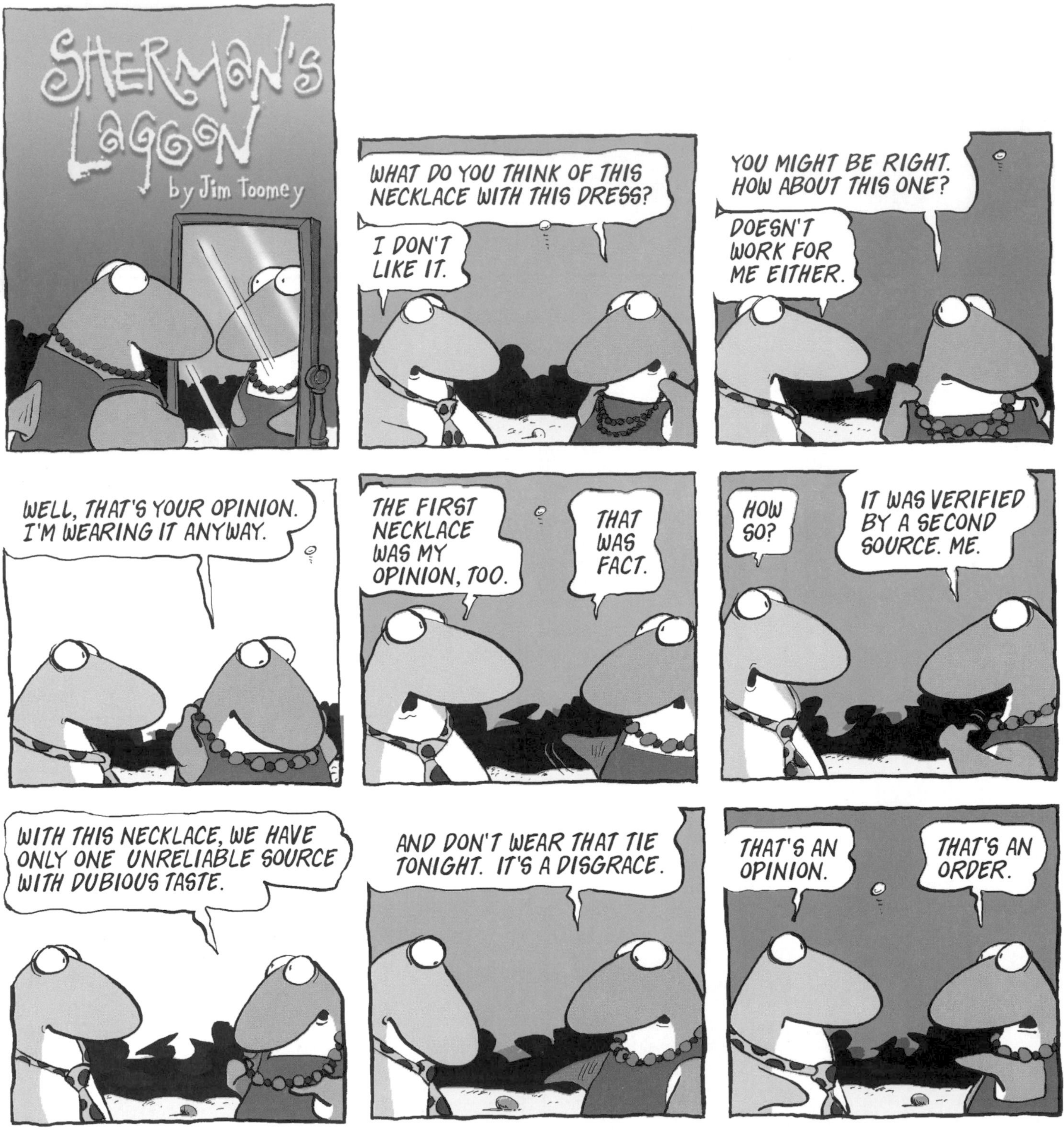
SHERMAN'S LAGOON
by Jim Toomey
WHAT DO YOU THINK OF THIS NECKLACE WITH THIS DRESS?
I DON'T LIKE IT.
YOU MIGHT BE RIGHT. HOW ABOUT THIS ONE?
DOESN'T WORK FOR ME EITHER.
WELL, THAT'S YOUR OPINION. I'M WEARING IT ANYWAY.
THE FIRST NECKLACE WAS MY OPINION, TOO.
THAT WAS FACT.
HOW SO?
IT WAS VERIFIED BY A SECOND SOURCE. ME.
WITH THIS NECKLACE, WE HAVE ONLY ONE UNRELIABLE SOURCE WITH DUBIOUS TASTE.
AND DON'T WEAR THAT TIE TONIGHT. IT'S A DISGRACE.
THAT'S AN OPINION.
THAT'S AN ORDER.

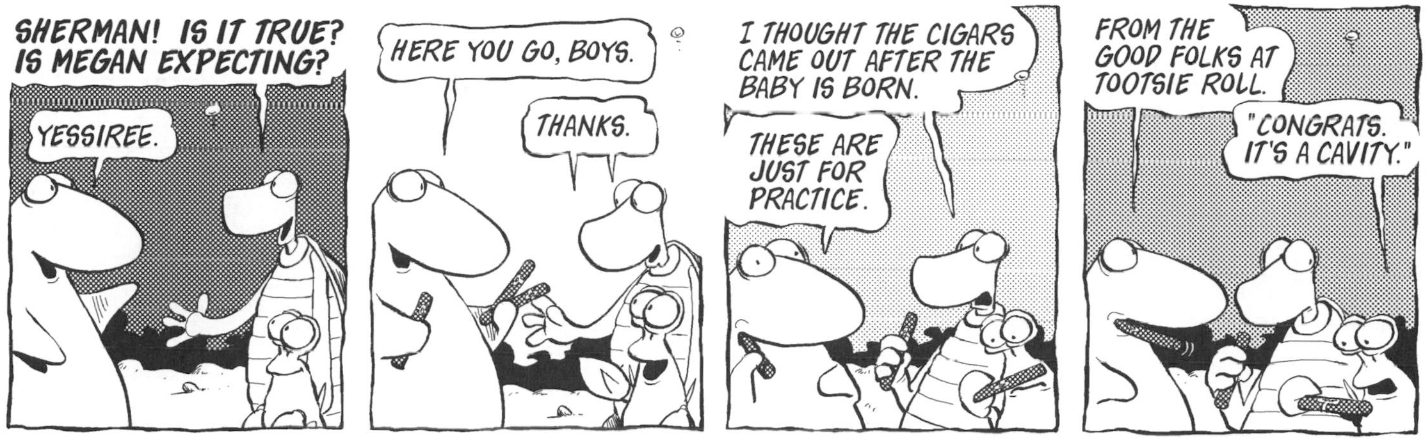
SHERMAN! IS IT TRUE? IS MEGAN EXPECTING?
YESSIREE.
HERE YOU GO, BOYS.
THANKS.
I THOUGHT THE CIGARS CAME OUT AFTER THE BABY IS BORN.
THESE ARE JUST FOR PRACTICE.
FROM THE GOOD FOLKS AT TOOTSIE ROLL.
"CONGRATS. IT'S A CAVITY."

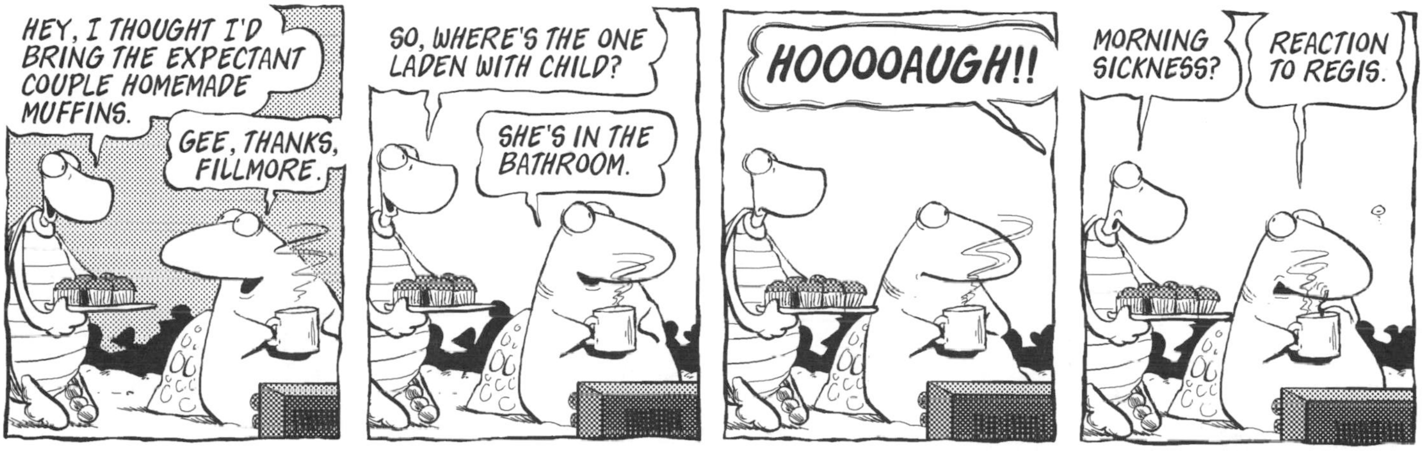
HEY, I THOUGHT I'D BRING THE EXPECTANT COUPLE HOMEMADE MUFFINS.
GEE, THANKS, FILLMORE.
SO, WHERE'S THE ONE LADEN WITH CHILD?
SHE'S IN THE BATHROOM.
HOOOOAUGH!!
MORNING SICKNESS?
REACTION TO REGIS.

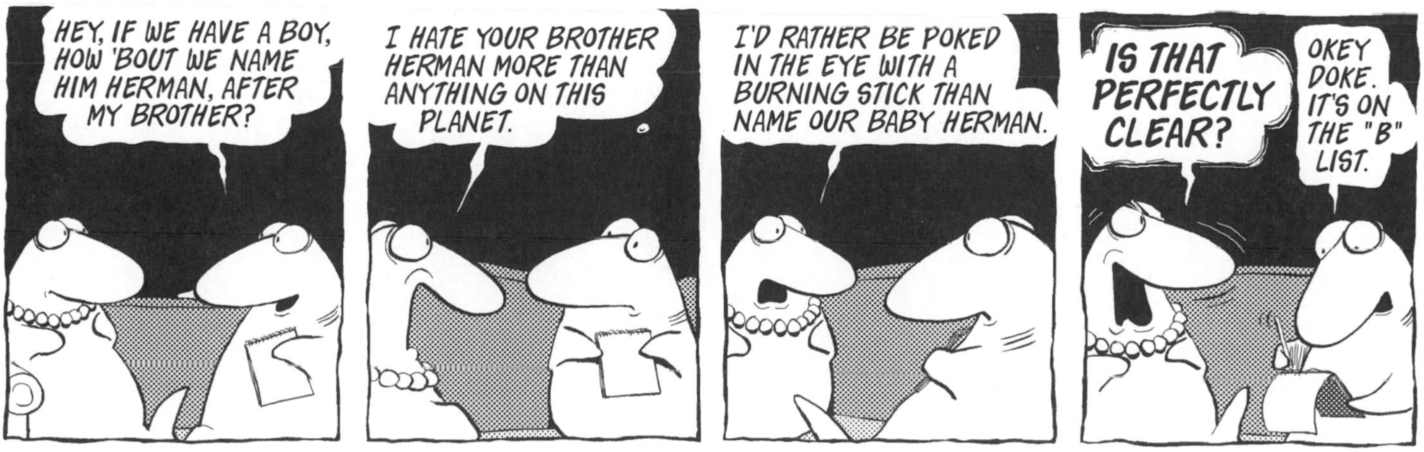
HEY, IF WE HAVE A BOY, HOW 'BOUT WE NAME HIM HERMAN, AFTER MY BROTHER?
I HATE YOUR BROTHER HERMAN MORE THAN ANYTHING ON THIS PLANET.
I'D RATHER BE POKED IN THE EYE WITH A BURNING STICK THAN NAME OUR BABY HERMAN.
IS THAT PERFECTLY CLEAR?
OKEY DOKE. IT'S ON THE "B" LIST.

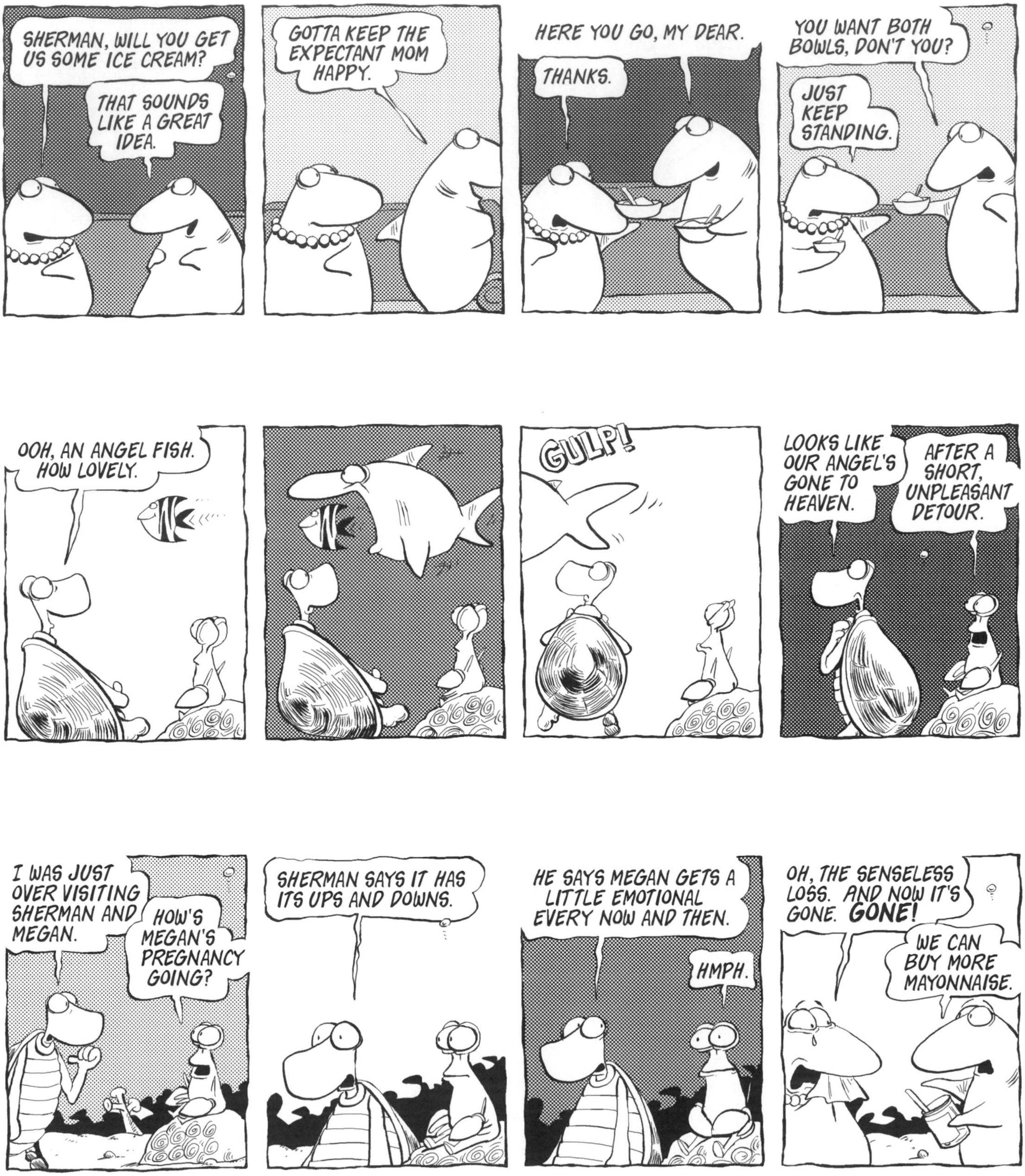
SHERMAN, WILL YOU GET US SOME ICE CREAM?
THAT SOUNDS LIKE A GREAT IDEA.
GOTTA KEEP THE EXPECTANT MOM HAPPY.
HERE YOU GO, MY DEAR.
THANKS.
YOU WANT BOTH BOWLS, DON'T YOU?
JUST KEEP STANDING.
OOH, AN ANGEL FISH. HOW LOVELY.
GULP!
LOOKS LIKE OUR ANGEL'S GONE TO HEAVEN.
AFTER A SHORT, UNPLEASANT DETOUR.
I WAS JUST OVER VISITING SHERMAN AND MEGAN.
HOW'S MEGAN'S PREGNANCY GOING?
SHERMAN SAYS IT HAS ITS UPS AND DOWNS.
HE SAYS MEGAN GETS A LITTLE EMOTIONAL EVERY NOW AND THEN.
HMPH.
OH, THE SENSELESS LOSS. AND NOW IT'S GONE. GONE!
WE CAN BUY MORE MAYONNAISE.

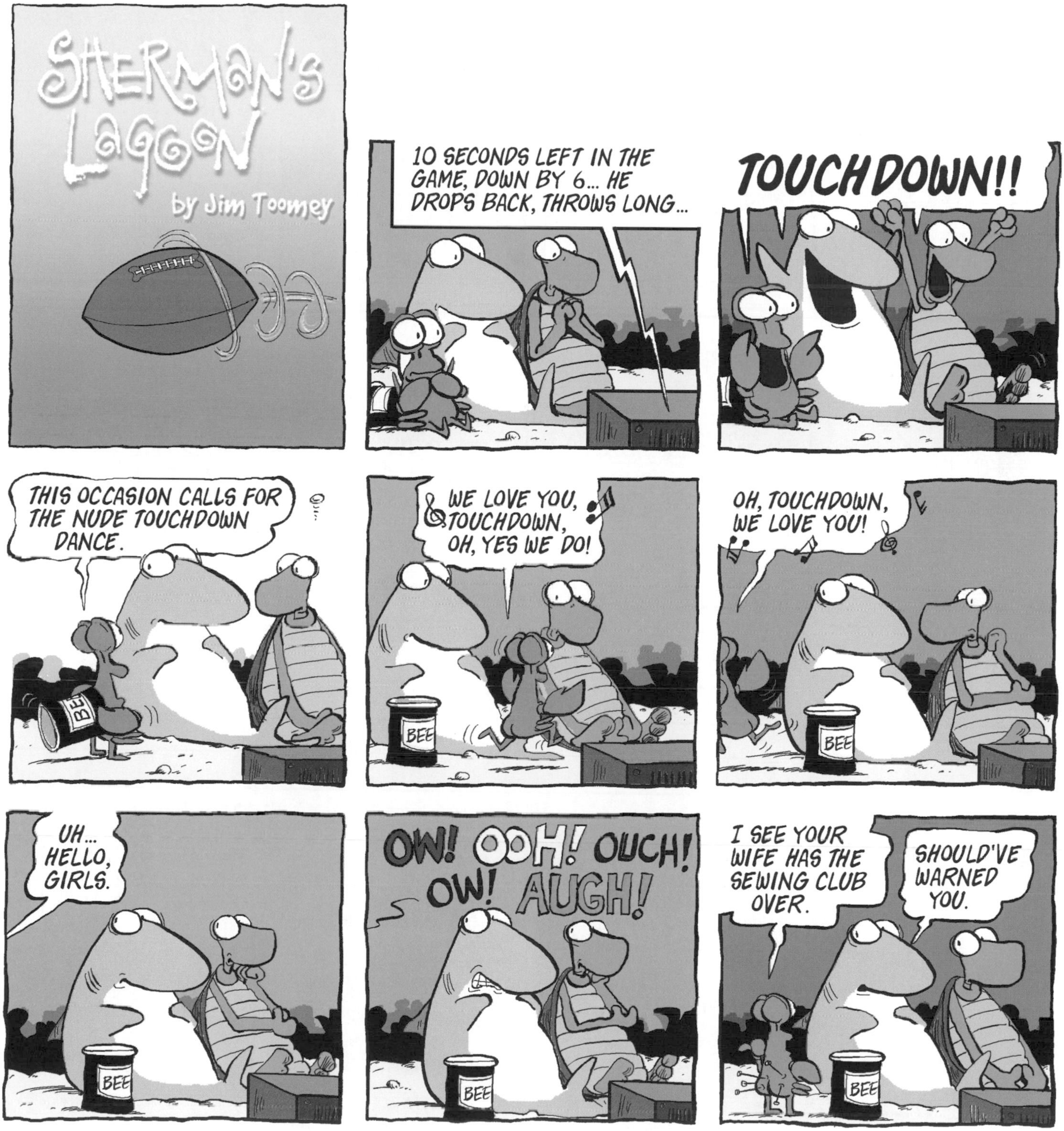
Sherman's Lagoon
by Jim Toomey
10 SECONDS LEFT IN THE GAME, DOWN BY 6... HE DROPS BACK, THROWS LONG...
TOUCHDOWN!!
THIS OCCASION CALLS FOR THE NUDE TOUCHDOWN DANCE.
BEE
WE LOVE YOU, TOUCHDOWN, OH, YES WE DO!
BEE
OH, TOUCHDOWN, WE LOVE YOU!
BEE
UH... HELLO, GIRLS.
BEE
OW! OOH! OUCH! OW! AUGH!
BEE
I SEE YOUR WIFE HAS THE SEWING CLUB OVER.
SHOULD'VE WARNED YOU.
BEE

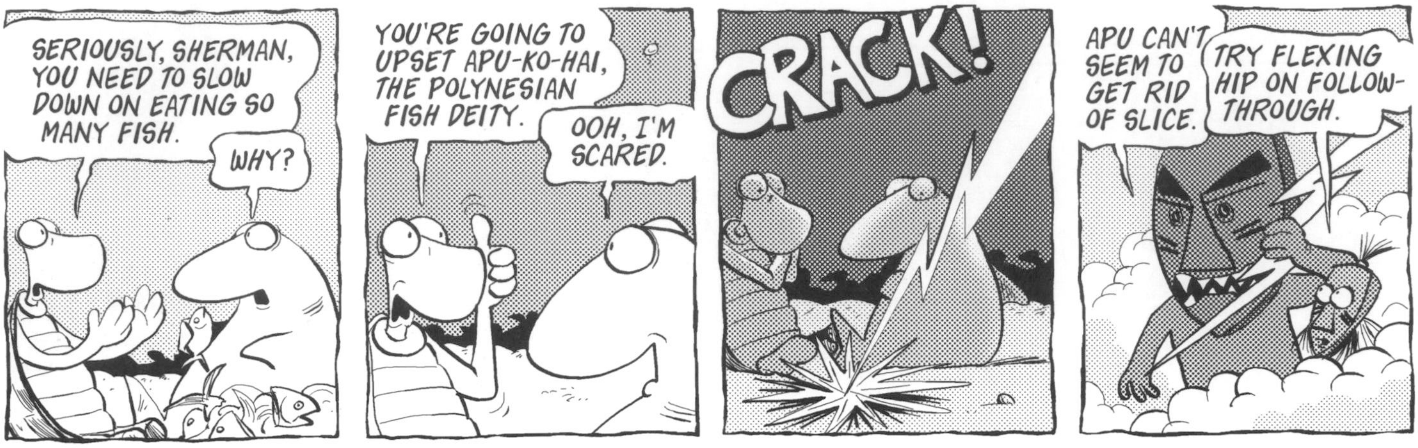
SERIOUSLY, SHERMAN, YOU NEED TO SLOW DOWN ON EATING SO MANY FISH.
WHY?
YOU'RE GOING TO UPSET APU-KO-HAI, THE POLYNESIAN FISH DEITY.
OOH, I'M SCARED.
CRACK!
APU CAN'T SEEM TO GET RID OF SLICE.
TRY FLEXING HIP ON FOLLOW-THROUGH.

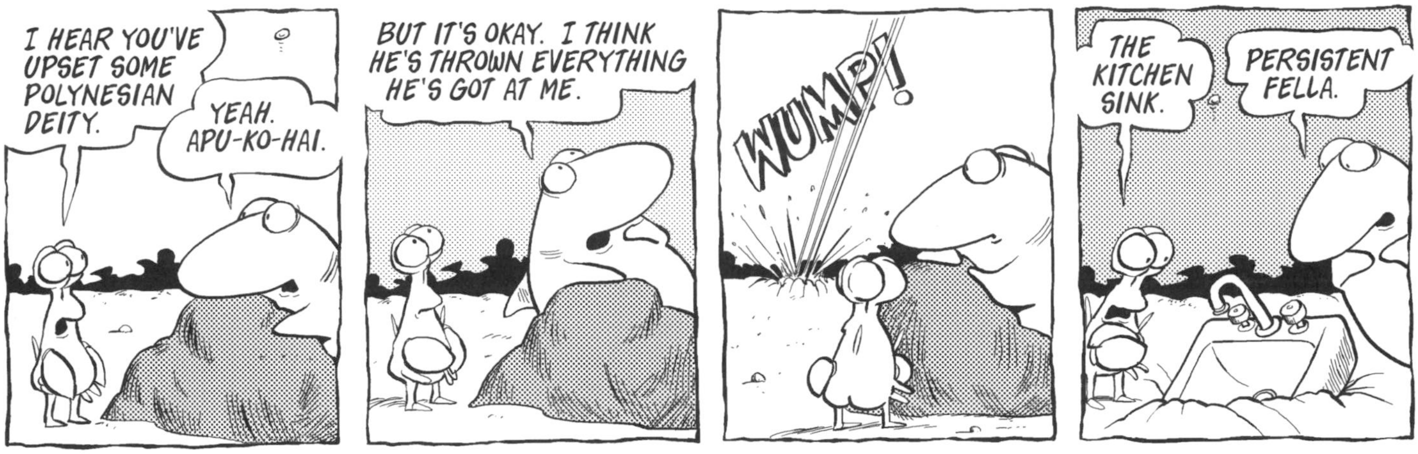
I HEAR YOU'VE UPSET SOME POLYNESIAN DEITY.
YEAH. APU-KO-HAI.
BUT IT'S OKAY. I THINK HE'S THROWN EVERYTHING HE'S GOT AT ME.
WUMP!
THE KITCHEN SINK.
PERSISTENT FELLA.

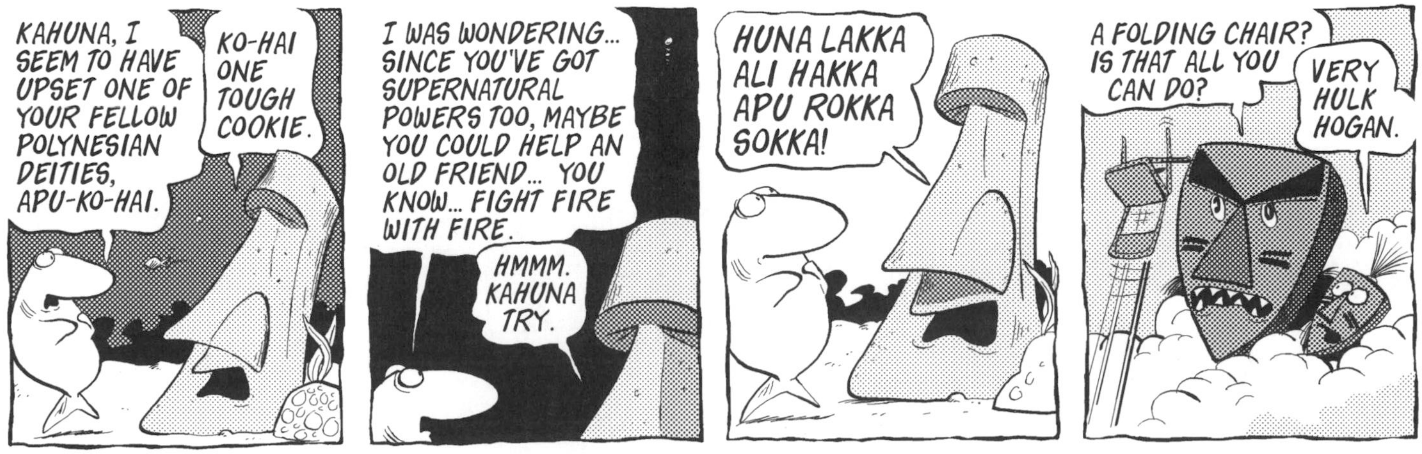
KAHUNA, I SEEM TO HAVE UPSET ONE OF YOUR FELLOW POLYNESIAN DEITIES, APU-KO-HAI.
KO-HAI ONE TOUGH COOKIE.
I WAS WONDERING... SINCE YOU'VE GOT SUPERNATURAL POWERS TOO, MAYBE YOU COULD HELP AN OLD FRIEND... YOU KNOW... FIGHT FIRE WITH FIRE.
HMMM. KAHUNA TRY.
HUNA LAKKA ALI HAKKA APU ROKKA SOKKA!
A FOLDING CHAIR? IS THAT ALL YOU CAN DO?
VERY HULK HOGAN.

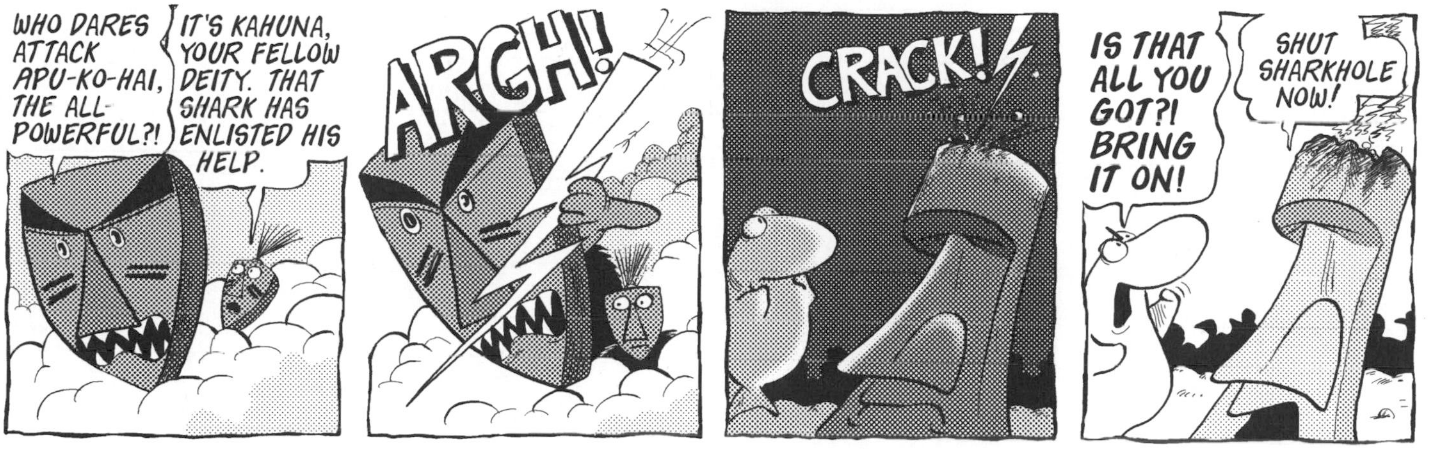
WHO DARES ATTACK APU-KO-HAI, THE ALL-POWERFUL?!
IT'S KAHUNA, YOUR FELLOW DEITY. THAT SHARK HAS ENLISTED HIS HELP.
ARGH!
CRACK!
IS THAT ALL YOU GOT?! BRING IT ON!
SHUT SHARKHOLE NOW!

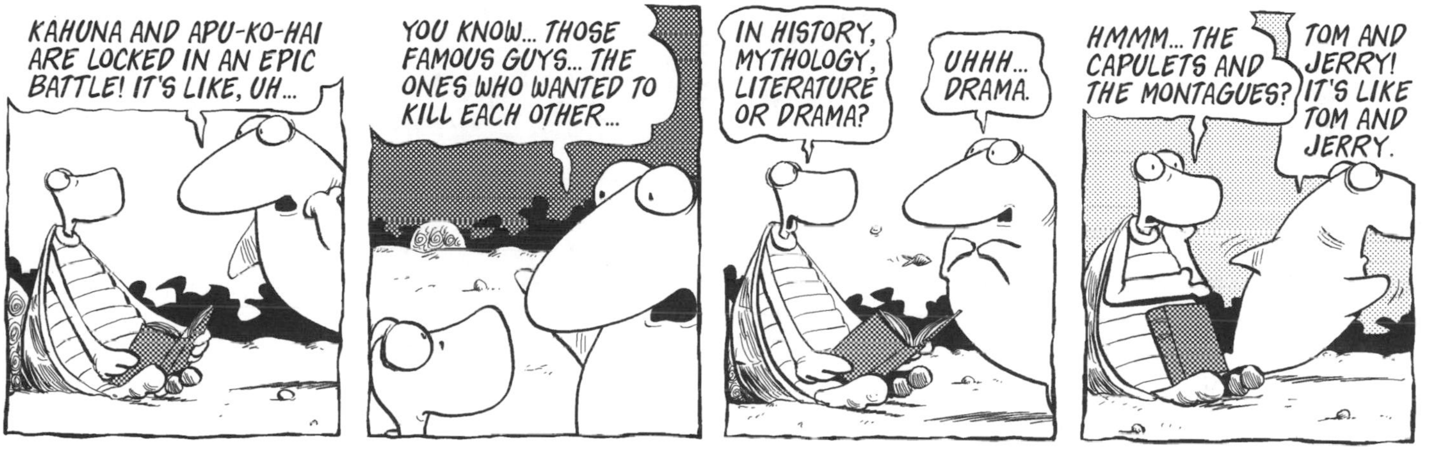
KAHUNA AND APU-KO-HAI ARE LOCKED IN AN EPIC BATTLE! IT'S LIKE, UH...
YOU KNOW... THOSE FAMOUS GUYS... THE ONES WHO WANTED TO KILL EACH OTHER...
IN HISTORY, MYTHOLOGY, LITERATURE OR DRAMA?
UHHH... DRAMA.
HMMM... THE CAPULETS AND THE MONTAGUES?
TOM AND JERRY! IT'S LIKE TOM AND JERRY.

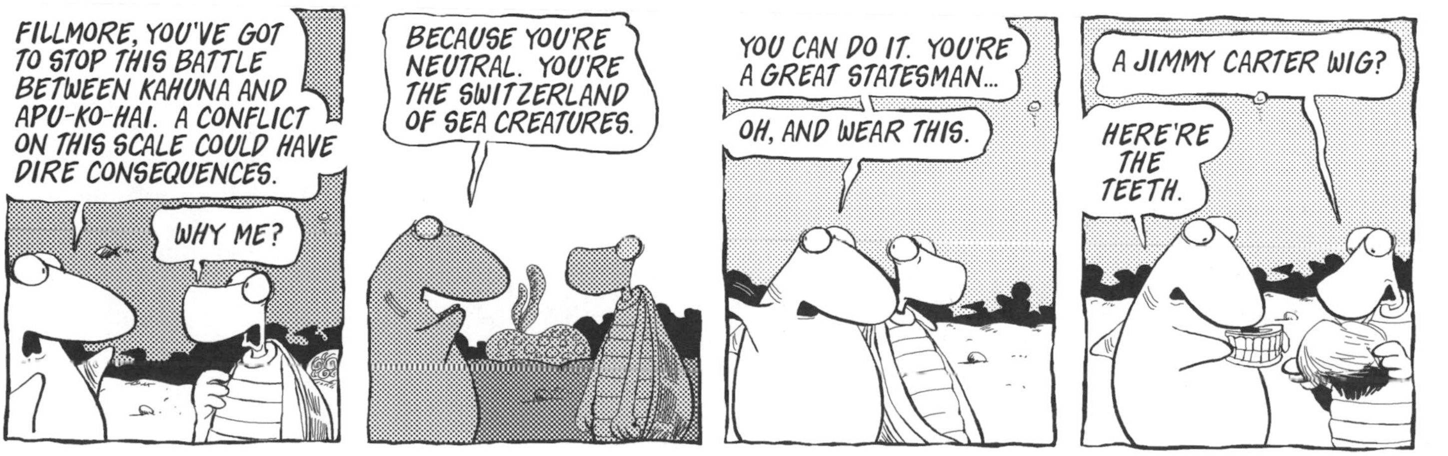
FILLMORE, YOU'VE GOT TO STOP THIS BATTLE BETWEEN KAHUNA AND APU-KO-HAI. A CONFLICT ON THIS SCALE COULD HAVE DIRE CONSEQUENCES.
WHY ME?
BECAUSE YOU'RE NEUTRAL. YOU'RE THE SWITZERLAND OF SEA CREATURES.
YOU CAN DO IT. YOU'RE A GREAT STATESMAN...
OH, AND WEAR THIS.
A JIMMY CARTER WIG?
HERE'RE THE TEETH.

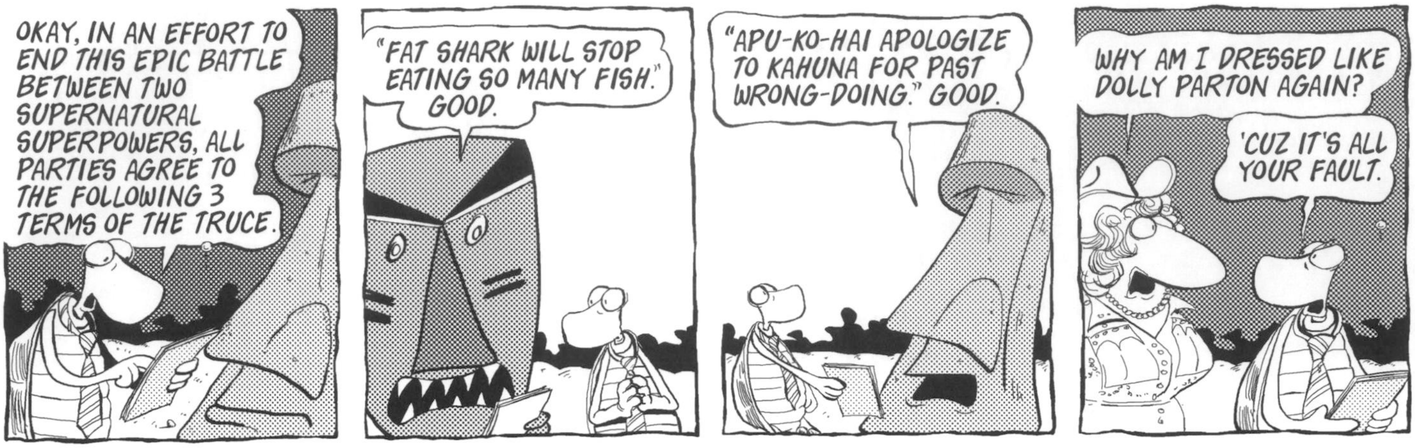
OKAY, IN AN EFFORT TO END THIS EPIC BATTLE BETWEEN TWO SUPERNATURAL SUPERPOWERS, ALL PARTIES AGREE TO THE FOLLOWING 3 TERMS OF THE TRUCE.
"FAT SHARK WILL STOP EATING SO MANY FISH." GOOD.
"APU-KO-HAI APOLOGIZE TO KAHUNA FOR PAST WRONG-DOING." GOOD.
WHY AM I DRESSED LIKE DOLLY PARTON AGAIN?
'CUZ IT'S ALL YOUR FAULT.

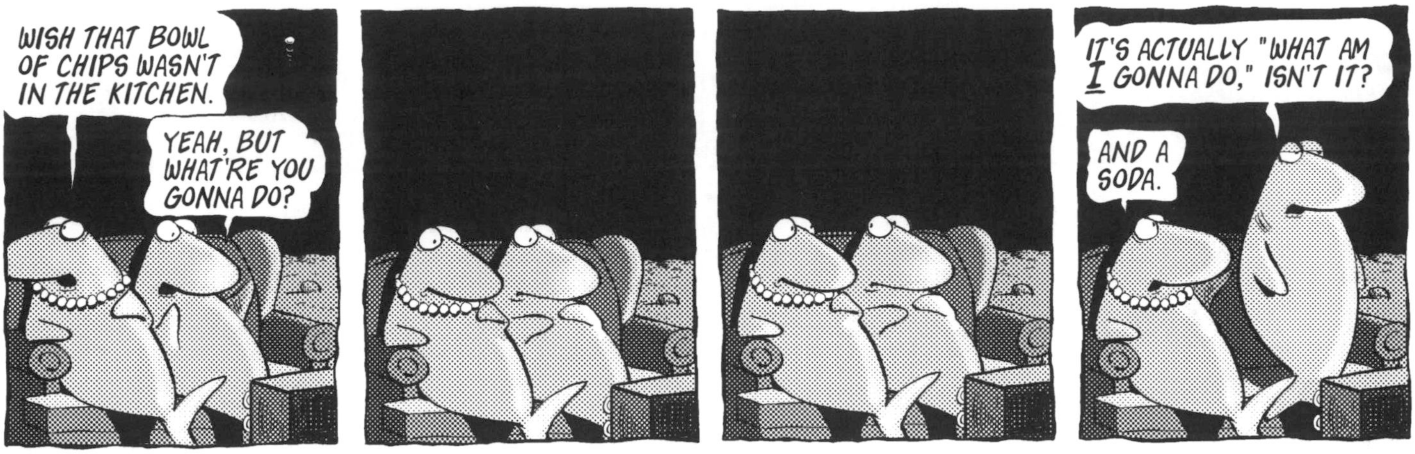
WISH THAT BOWL OF CHIPS WASN'T IN THE KITCHEN.
YEAH, BUT WHAT'RE YOU GONNA DO?
IT'S ACTUALLY "WHAT AM I GONNA DO," ISN'T IT?
AND A SODA.

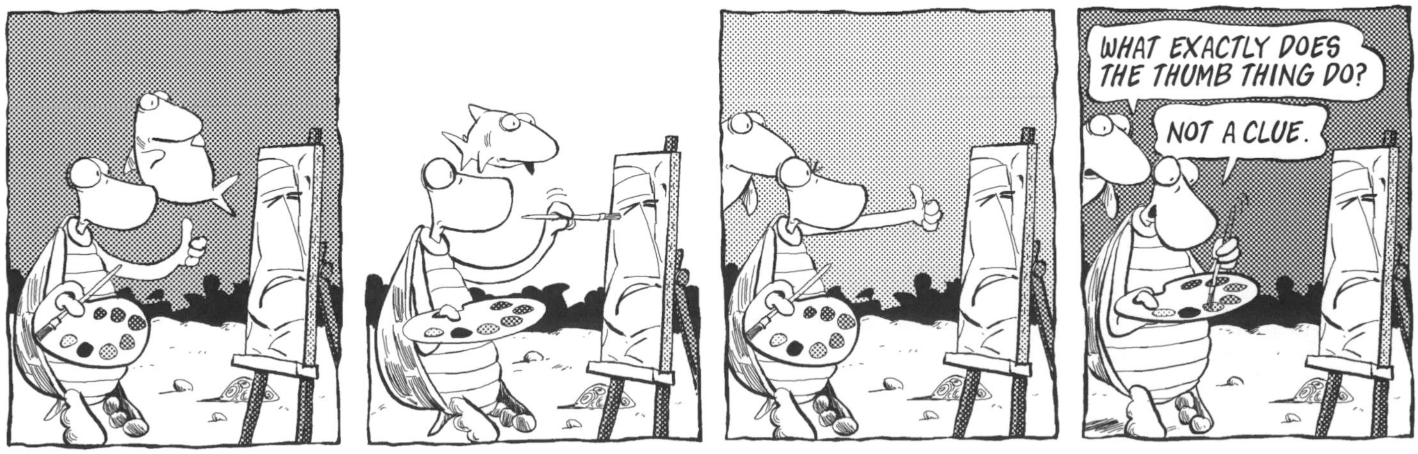
WHAT EXACTLY DOES THE THUMB THING DO?
NOT A CLUE.

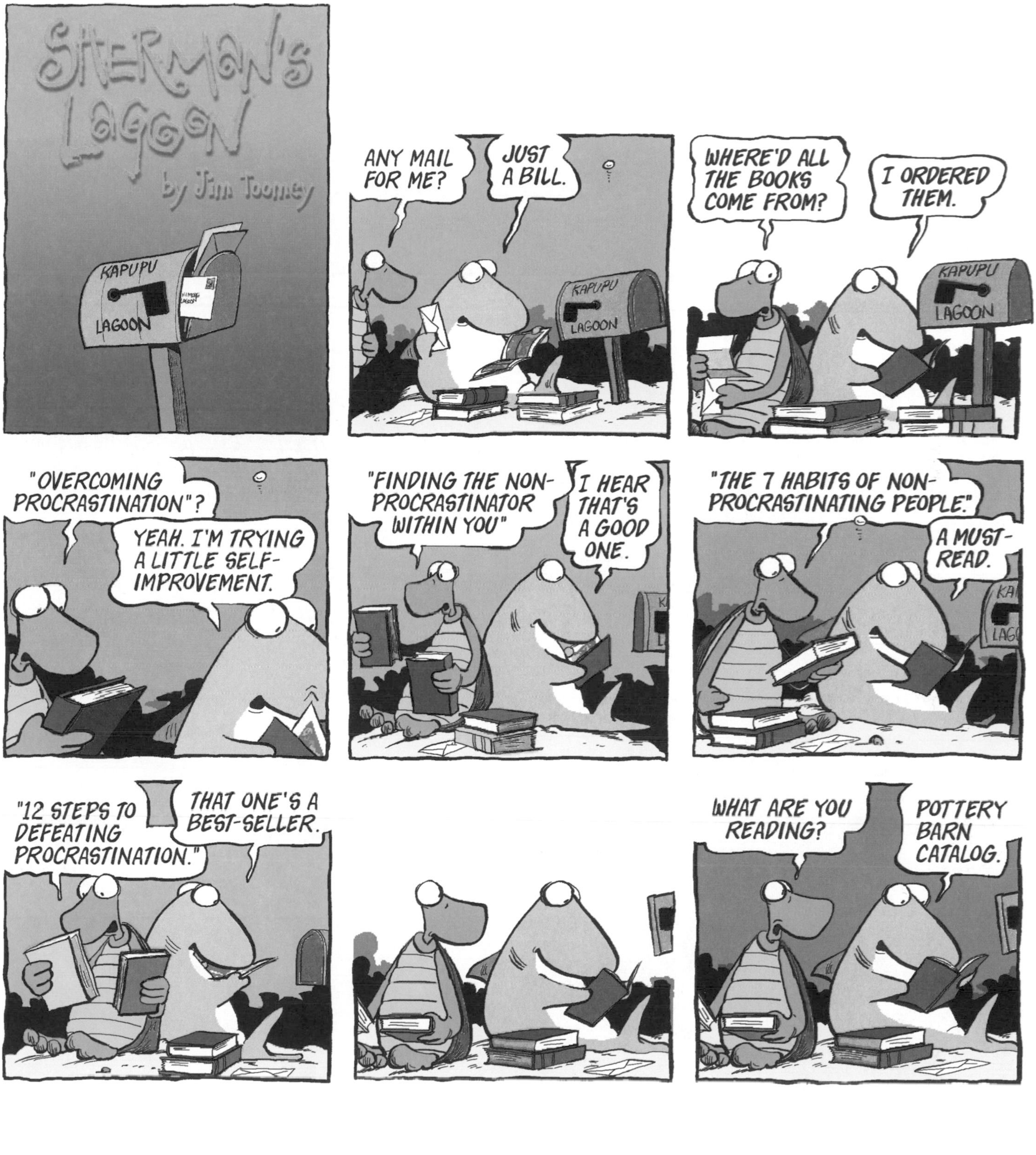
SHERMAN'S LAGOON
by Jim Toomey
KAPUPU
LAGOON
ANY MAIL FOR ME?
JUST A BILL.
KAPUPU
LAGOON
WHERE'D ALL THE BOOKS COME FROM?
I ORDERED THEM.
KAPUPU
LAGOON
"OVERCOMING PROCRASTINATION"?
YEAH. I'M TRYING A LITTLE SELF-IMPROVEMENT.
"FINDING THE NON-PROCRASTINATOR WITHIN YOU"
I HEAR THAT'S A GOOD ONE.
"THE 7 HABITS OF NON-PROCRASTINATING PEOPLE."
A MUST-READ.
"12 STEPS TO DEFEATING PROCRASTINATION."
THAT ONE'S A BEST-SELLER.
WHAT ARE YOU READING?
POTTERY BARN CATALOG.

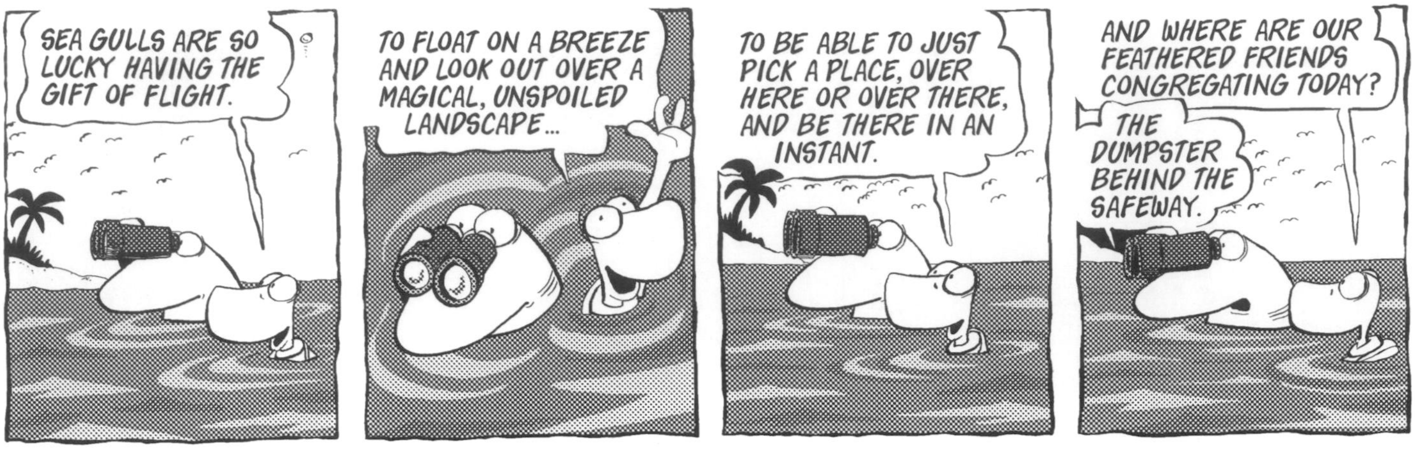
SEA GULLS ARE SO LUCKY HAVING THE GIFT OF FLIGHT.
TO FLOAT ON A BREEZE AND LOOK OUT OVER A MAGICAL, UNSPOILED LANDSCAPE...
TO BE ABLE TO JUST PICK A PLACE, OVER HERE OR OVER THERE, AND BE THERE IN AN INSTANT.
AND WHERE ARE OUR FEATHERED FRIENDS CONGREGATING TODAY?
THE DUMPSTER BEHIND THE SAFEWAY.

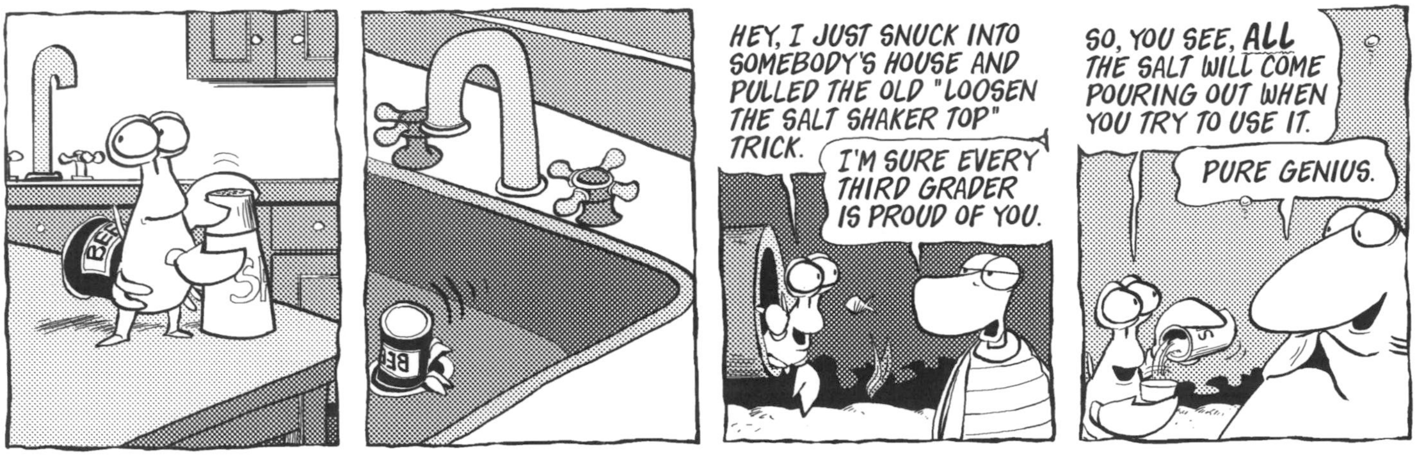
HEY, I JUST SNUCK INTO SOMEBODY'S HOUSE AND PULLED THE OLD "LOOSEN THE SALT SHAKER TOP" TRICK.
I'M SURE EVERY THIRD GRADER IS PROUD OF YOU.
SO, YOU SEE, ALL THE SALT WILL COME POURING OUT WHEN YOU TRY TO USE IT.
PURE GENIUS.

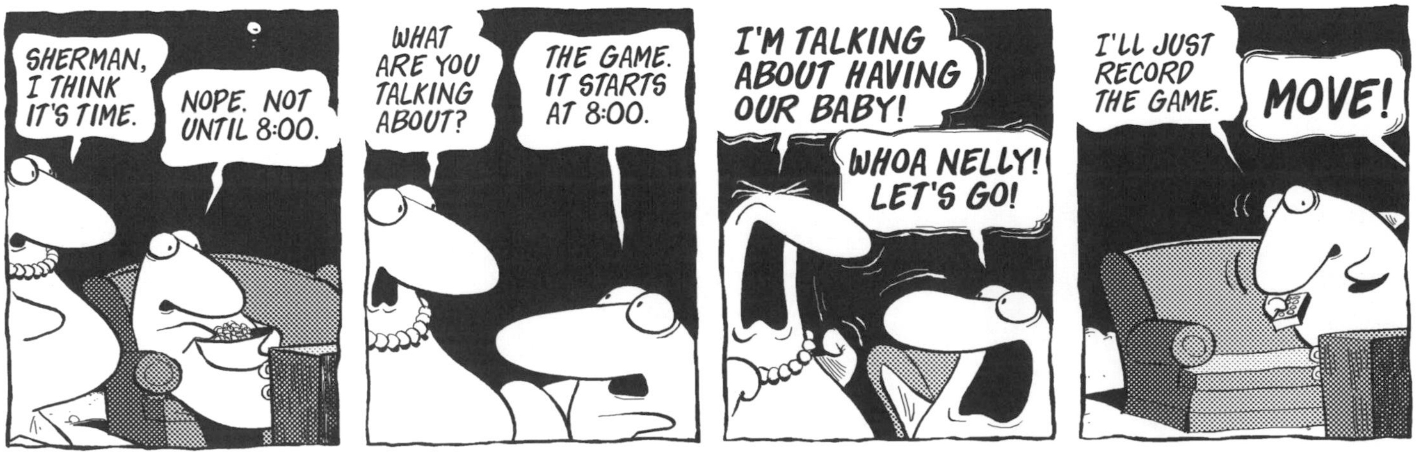
SHERMAN, I THINK IT'S TIME.
NOPE. NOT UNTIL 8:00.
WHAT ARE YOU TALKING ABOUT?
THE GAME. IT STARTS AT 8:00.
I'M TALKING ABOUT HAVING OUR BABY!
WHOA NELLY! LET'S GO!
I'LL JUST RECORD THE GAME.
MOVE!

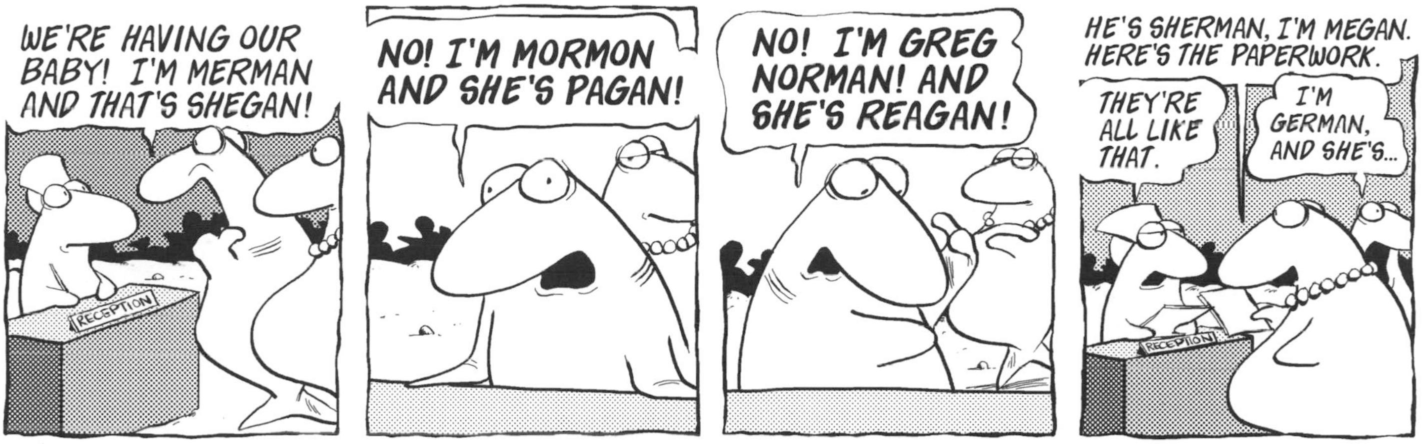
WE'RE HAVING OUR BABY! I'M MERMAN AND THAT'S SHEGAN!
RECEPTION
NO! I'M MORMON AND SHE'S PAGAN!
NO! I'M GREG NORMAN! AND SHE'S REAGAN!
HE'S SHERMAN, I'M MEGAN. HERE'S THE PAPERWORK.
THEY'RE ALL LIKE THAT.
I'M GERMAN, AND SHE'S...
RECEPTION

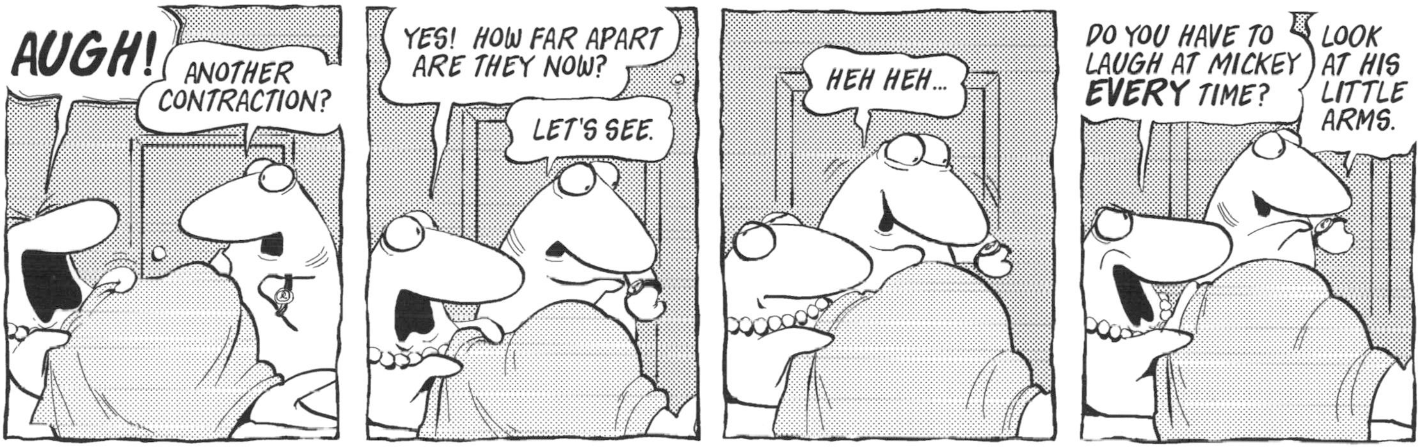
AUGH!
ANOTHER CONTRACTION?
YES! HOW FAR APART ARE THEY NOW?
LET'S SEE.
HEH HEH...
DO YOU HAVE TO LAUGH AT MICKEY EVERY TIME?
LOOK AT HIS LITTLE ARMS.

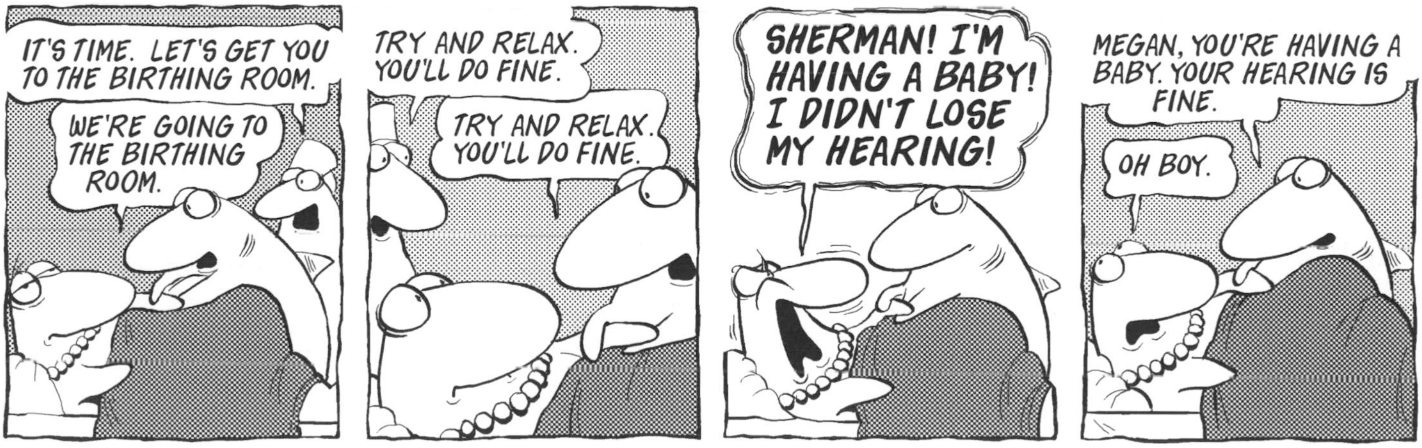
IT'S TIME. LET'S GET YOU TO THE BIRTHING ROOM.
WE'RE GOING TO THE BIRTHING ROOM.
TRY AND RELAX. YOU'LL DO FINE.
TRY AND RELAX. YOU'LL DO FINE.
SHERMAN! I'M HAVING A BABY! I DIDN'T LOSE MY HEARING!
MEGAN, YOU'RE HAVING A BABY. YOUR HEARING IS FINE.
OH BOY.

SHERMAN'S LAGOON
by Jim Toomey
1 2
4 5
RING! RING!
HELLO?
WHOA, WHOA! STOP RIGHT THERE!
I THOUGHT WE WERE ON THE "DO NOT CALL" LIST.
YEAH, WELL, SORRY, NOT INTERESTED.
GOODBYE.
I HATE THAT.
WHAT?
WHEN TELEMARKETERS CALL IN THE MIDDLE OF DINNER.
THAT WAS YOUR MOTHER.

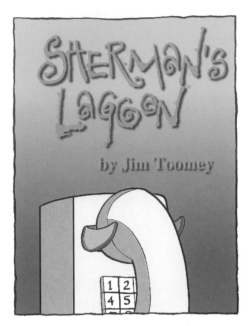

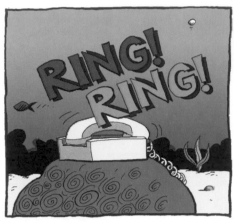

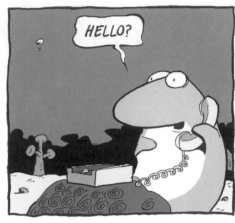

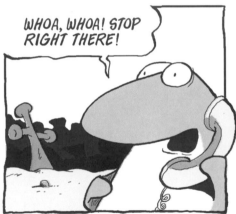

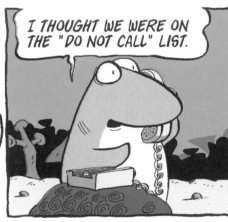

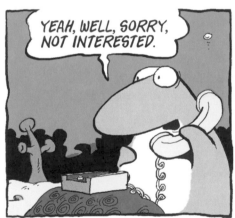

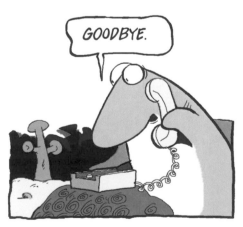

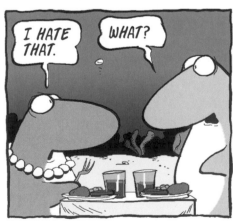

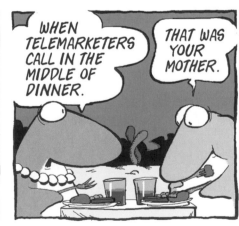

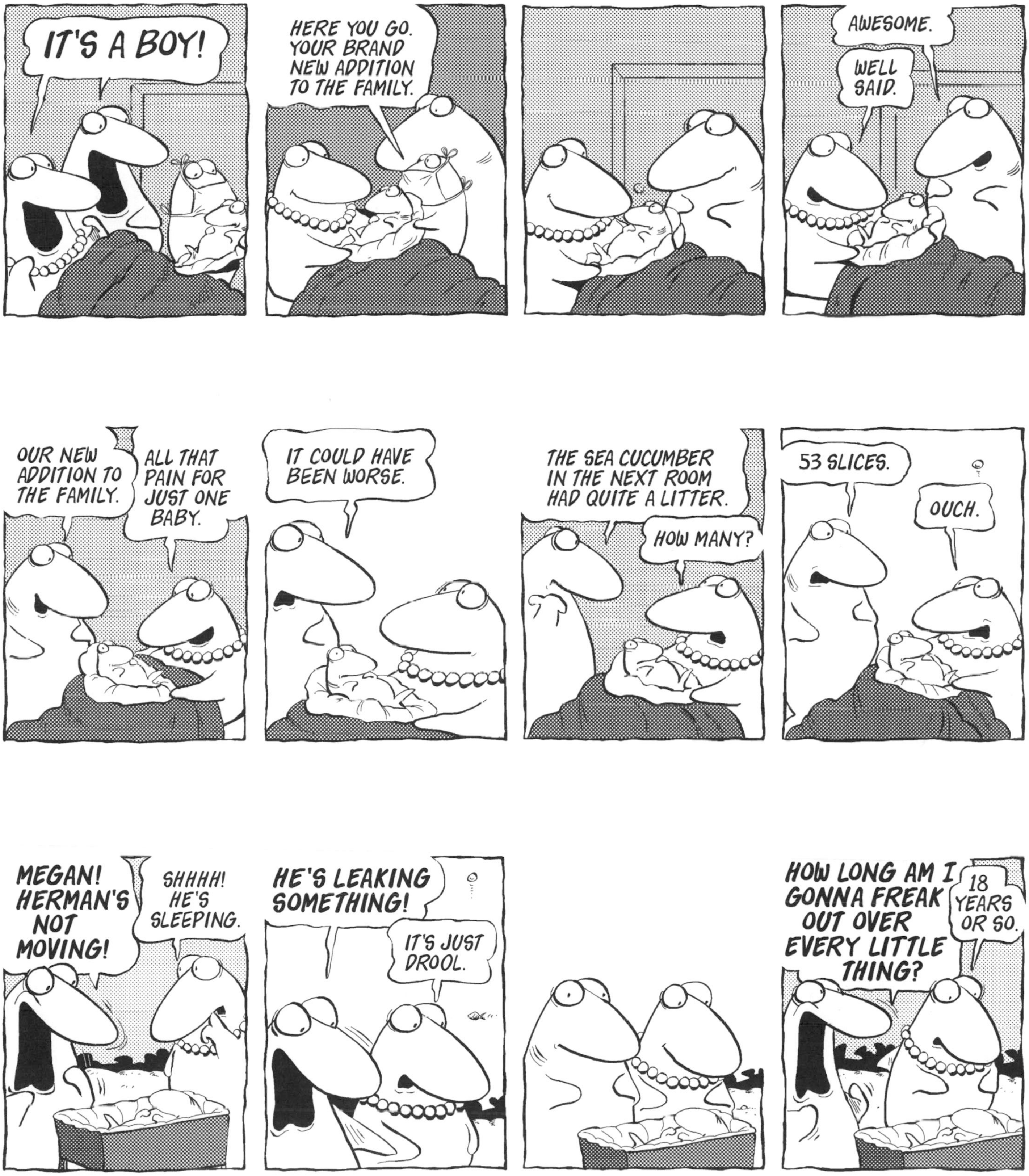

IT'S A BOY!
HERE YOU GO. YOUR BRAND NEW ADDITION TO THE FAMILY.
AWESOME.
WELL SAID.
OUR NEW ADDITION TO THE FAMILY.
ALL THAT PAIN FOR JUST ONE BABY.
IT COULD HAVE BEEN WORSE.
THE SEA CUCUMBER IN THE NEXT ROOM HAD QUITE A LITTER.
HOW MANY?
53 SLICES.
OUCH.
MEGAN! HERMAN'S NOT MOVING!
SHHHH! HE'S SLEEPING.
HE'S LEAKING SOMETHING!
IT'S JUST DROOL.
HOW LONG AM I GONNA FREAK OUT OVER EVERY LITTLE THING?
18 YEARS OR SO.

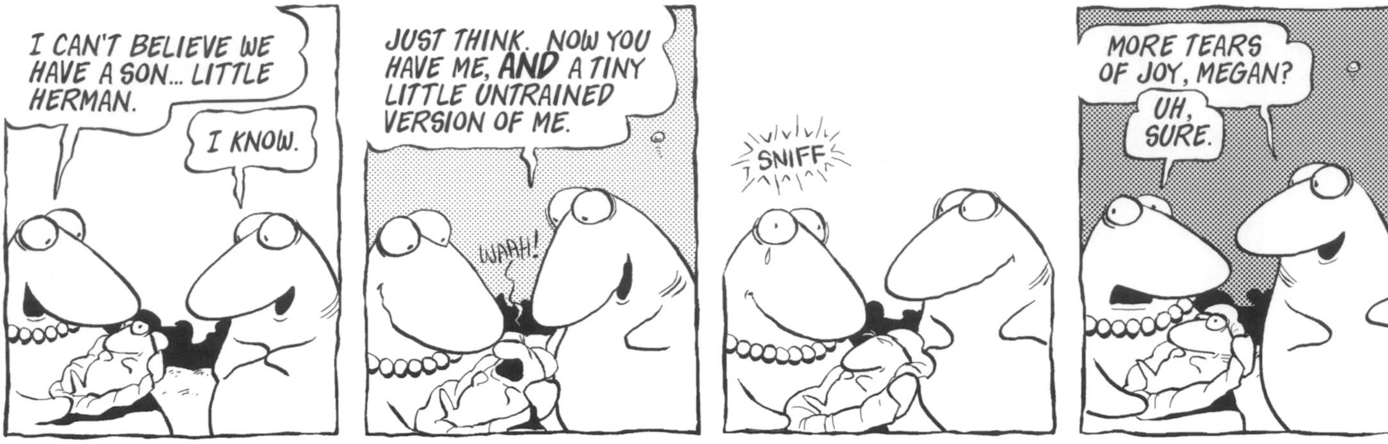
I CAN'T BELIEVE WE HAVE A SON... LITTLE HERMAN.
I KNOW.
JUST THINK. NOW YOU HAVE ME, AND A TINY LITTLE UNTRAINED VERSION OF ME.
WAAH!
SNIFF
MORE TEARS OF JOY, MEGAN?
UH, SURE.

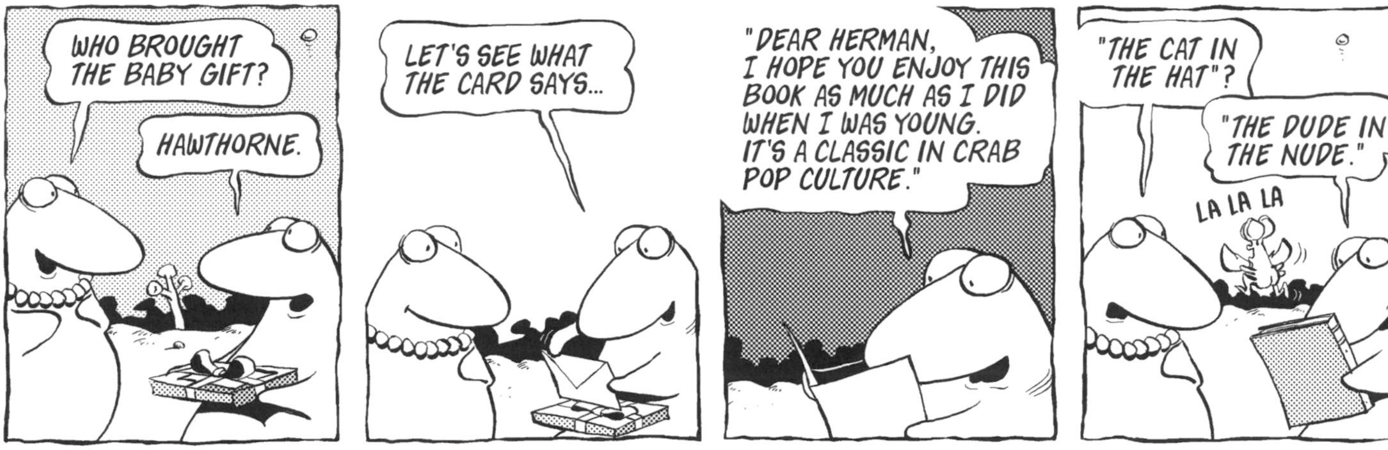
WHO BROUGHT THE BABY GIFT?
HAWTHORNE.
LET'S SEE WHAT THE CARD SAYS...
"DEAR HERMAN, I HOPE YOU ENJOY THIS BOOK AS MUCH AS I DID WHEN I WAS YOUNG. IT'S A CLASSIC IN CRAB POP CULTURE."
"THE CAT IN THE HAT"?
"THE DUDE IN THE NUDE."
LA LA LA

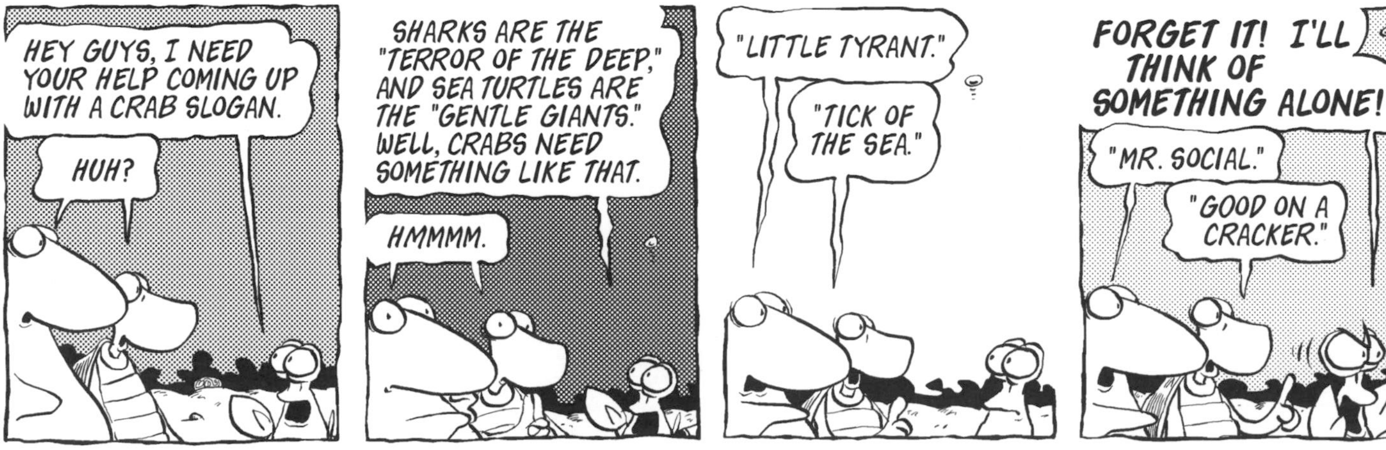
HEY GUYS, I NEED YOUR HELP COMING UP WITH A CRAB SLOGAN.
HUH?
SHARKS ARE THE "TERROR OF THE DEEP," AND SEA TURTLES ARE THE "GENTLE GIANTS." WELL, CRABS NEED SOMETHING LIKE THAT.
HMMMM.
"LITTLE TYRANT."
"TICK OF THE SEA."
FORGET IT! I'LL THINK OF SOMETHING ALONE!
"MR. SOCIAL."
"GOOD ON A CRACKER."

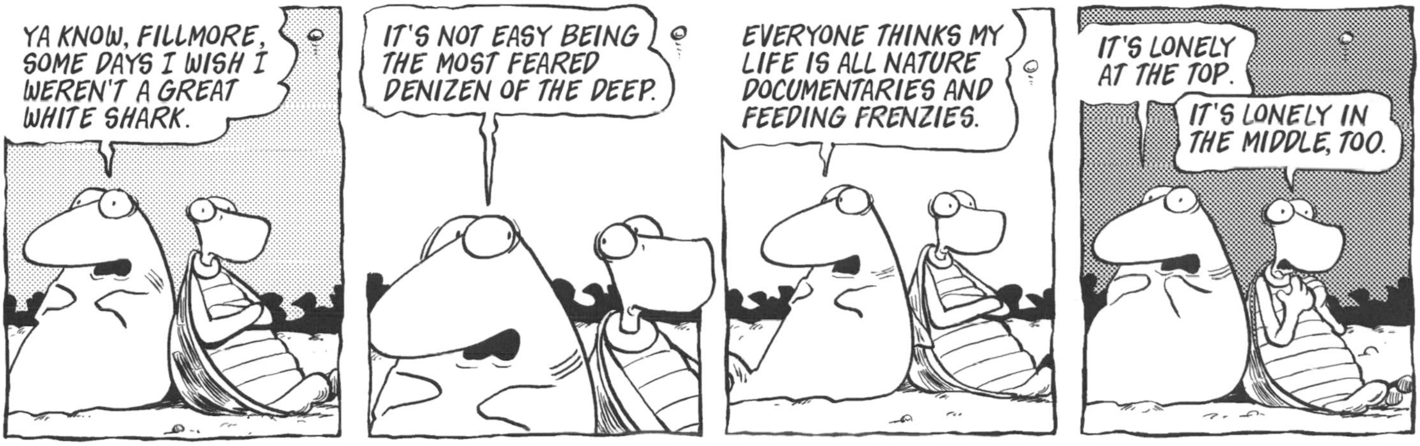
YA KNOW, FILLMORE, SOME DAYS I WISH I WEREN'T A GREAT WHITE SHARK.
IT'S NOT EASY BEING THE MOST FEARED DENIZEN OF THE DEEP.
EVERYONE THINKS MY LIFE IS ALL NATURE DOCUMENTARIES AND FEEDING FRENZIES.
IT'S LONELY AT THE TOP.
IT'S LONELY IN THE MIDDLE, TOO.

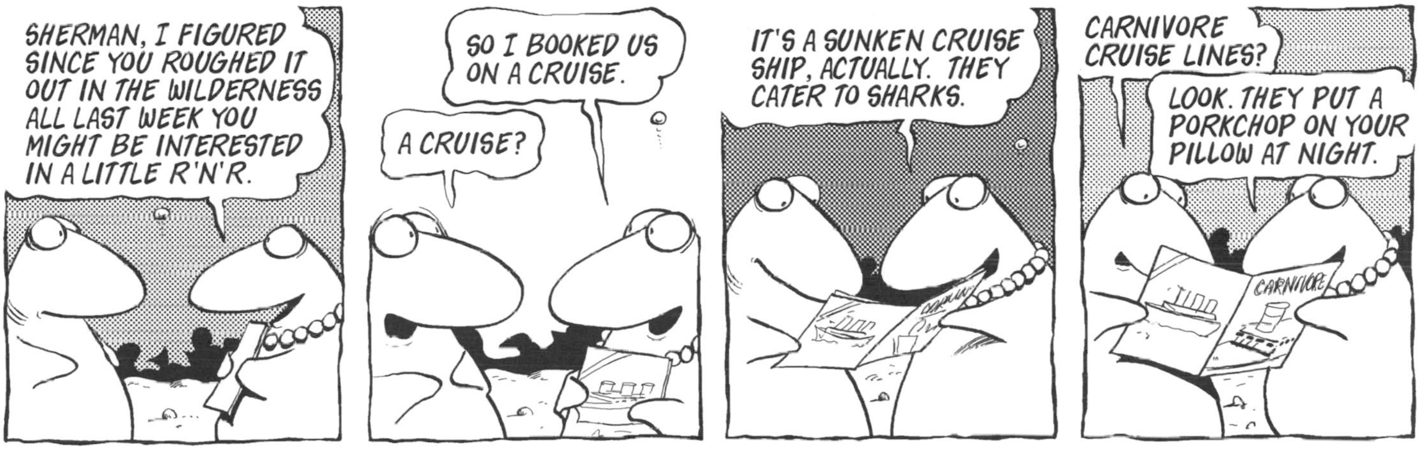
SHERMAN, I FIGURED SINCE YOU ROUGHED IT OUT IN THE WILDERNESS ALL LAST WEEK YOU MIGHT BE INTERESTED IN A LITTLE R'N'R.
SO I BOOKED US ON A CRUISE.
A CRUISE?
IT'S A SUNKEN CRUISE SHIP, ACTUALLY. THEY CATER TO SHARKS.
CARNIVORE CRUISE LINES?
LOOK. THEY PUT A PORKCHOP ON YOUR PILLOW AT NIGHT.

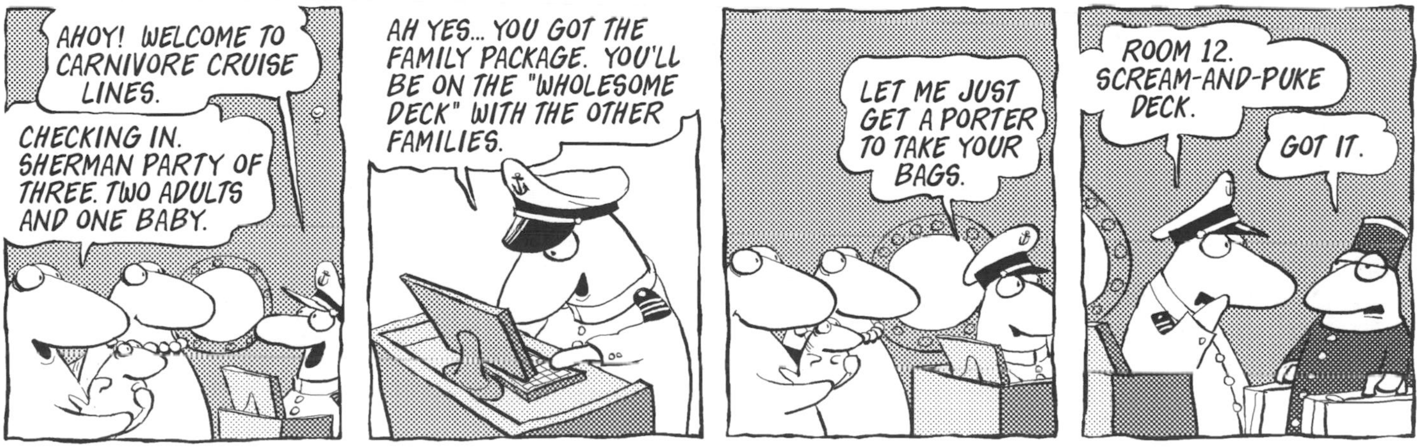
AHOY! WELCOME TO CARNIVORE CRUISE LINES.
CHECKING IN. SHERMAN PARTY OF THREE. TWO ADULTS AND ONE BABY.
AH YES... YOU GOT THE FAMILY PACKAGE. YOU'LL BE ON THE "WHOLESOME DECK" WITH THE OTHER FAMILIES.
LET ME JUST GET A PORTER TO TAKE YOUR BAGS.
ROOM 12. SCREAM-AND-PUKE DECK.
GOT IT.

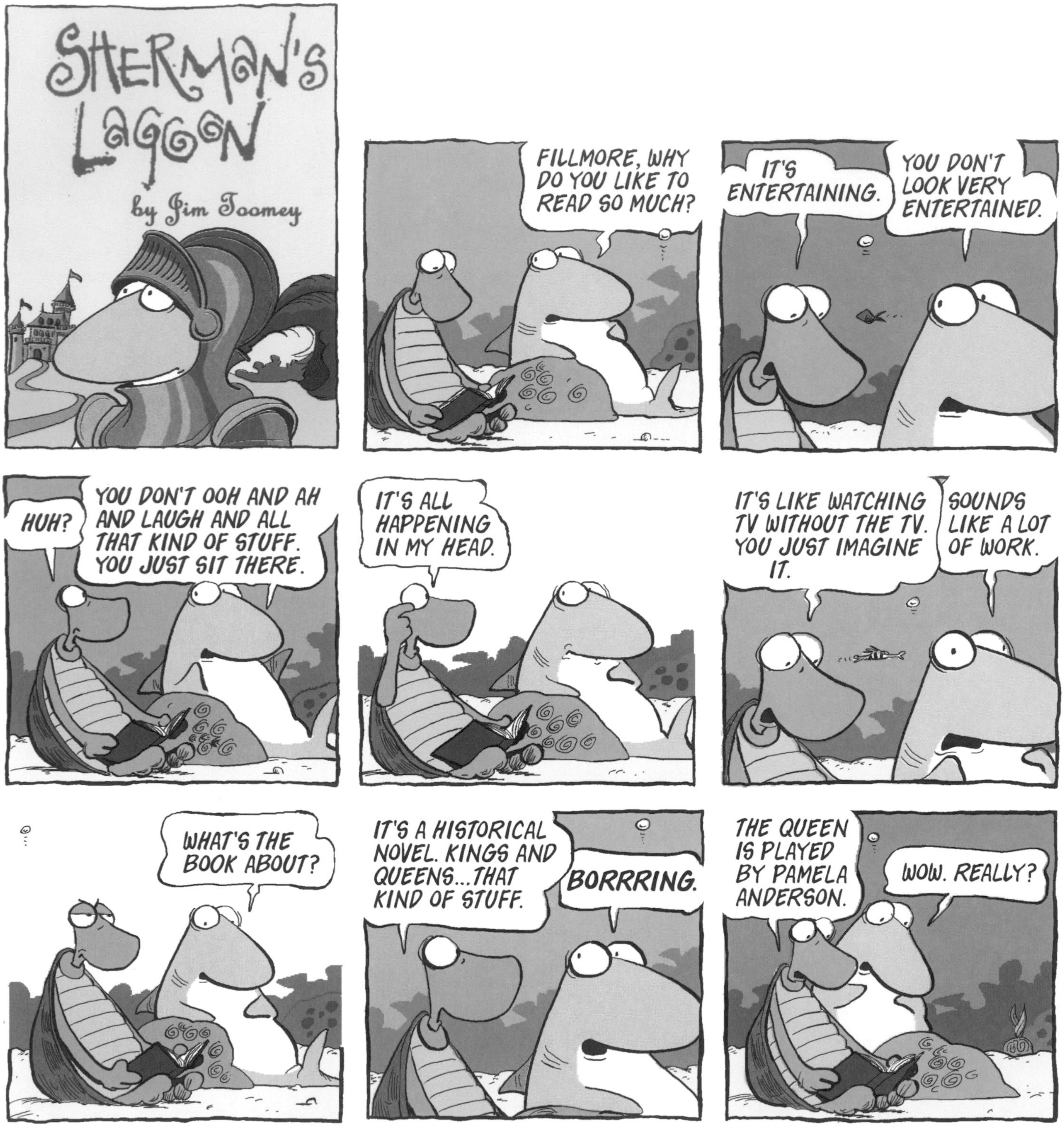
SHERMAN'S LAGOON
by Jim Toomey
FILLMORE, WHY DO YOU LIKE TO READ SO MUCH?
IT'S ENTERTAINING.
YOU DON'T LOOK VERY ENTERTAINED.
HUH?
YOU DON'T OOH AND AH AND LAUGH AND ALL THAT KIND OF STUFF. YOU JUST SIT THERE.
IT'S ALL HAPPENING IN MY HEAD.
IT'S LIKE WATCHING TV WITHOUT THE TV. YOU JUST IMAGINE IT.
SOUNDS LIKE A LOT OF WORK.
WHAT'S THE BOOK ABOUT?
IT'S A HISTORICAL NOVEL. KINGS AND QUEENS...THAT KIND OF STUFF.
BORRRING.
THE QUEEN IS PLAYED BY PAMELA ANDERSON.
WOW. REALLY?

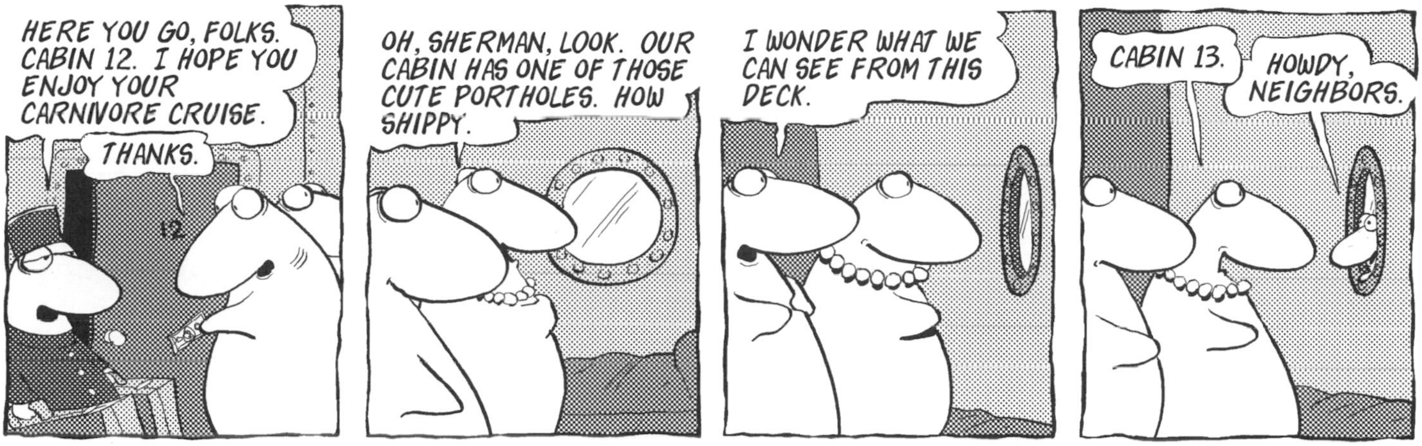
HERE YOU GO, FOLKS. CABIN 12. I HOPE YOU ENJOY YOUR CARNIVORE CRUISE.
THANKS.
12
OH, SHERMAN, LOOK. OUR CABIN HAS ONE OF THOSE CUTE PORTHOLES. HOW SHIPPY.
I WONDER WHAT WE CAN SEE FROM THIS DECK.
CABIN 13.
HOWDY, NEIGHBORS.

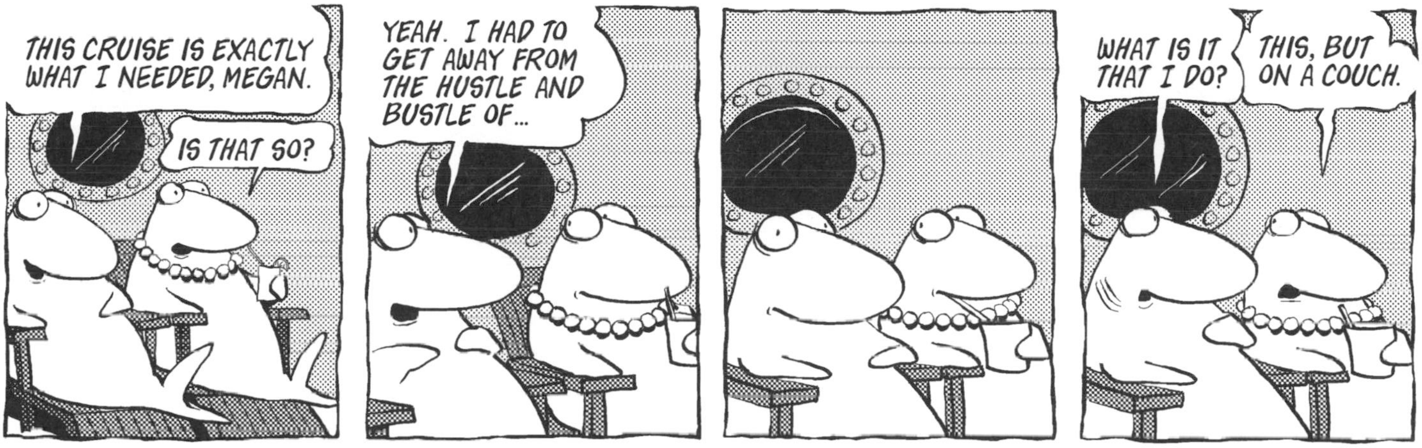
THIS CRUISE IS EXACTLY WHAT I NEEDED, MEGAN.
IS THAT SO?
YEAH. I HAD TO GET AWAY FROM THE HUSTLE AND BUSTLE OF...
WHAT IS IT THAT I DO?
THIS, BUT ON A COUCH.

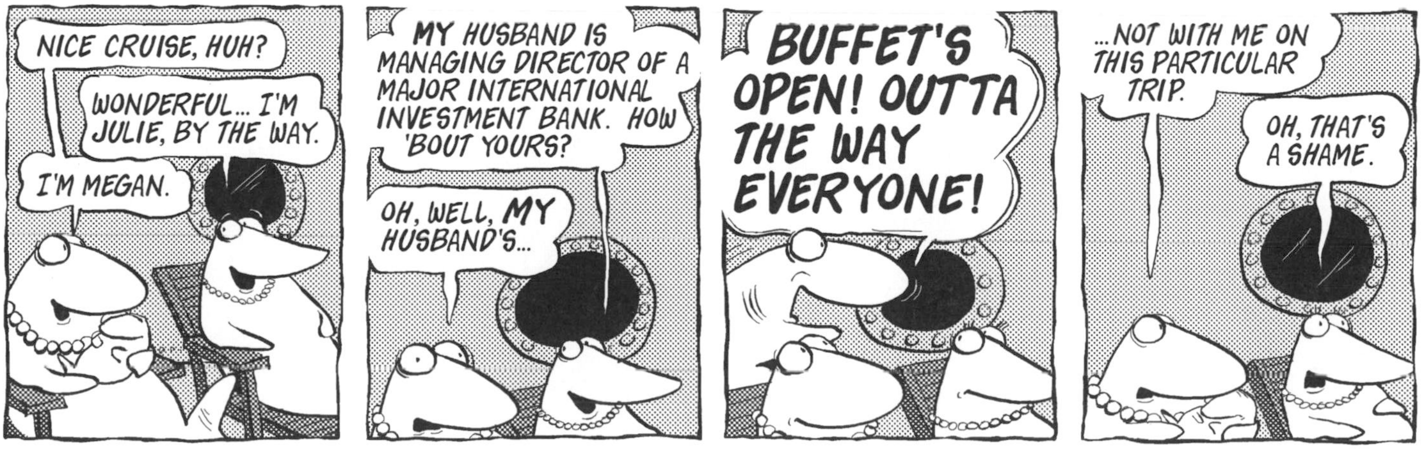
NICE CRUISE, HUH?
WONDERFUL... I'M JULIE, BY THE WAY.
I'M MEGAN.
MY HUSBAND IS MANAGING DIRECTOR OF A MAJOR INTERNATIONAL INVESTMENT BANK. HOW 'BOUT YOURS?
OH, WELL, MY HUSBAND'S...
BUFFET'S OPEN! OUTTA THE WAY EVERYONE!
...NOT WITH ME ON THIS PARTICULAR TRIP.
OH, THAT'S A SHAME.

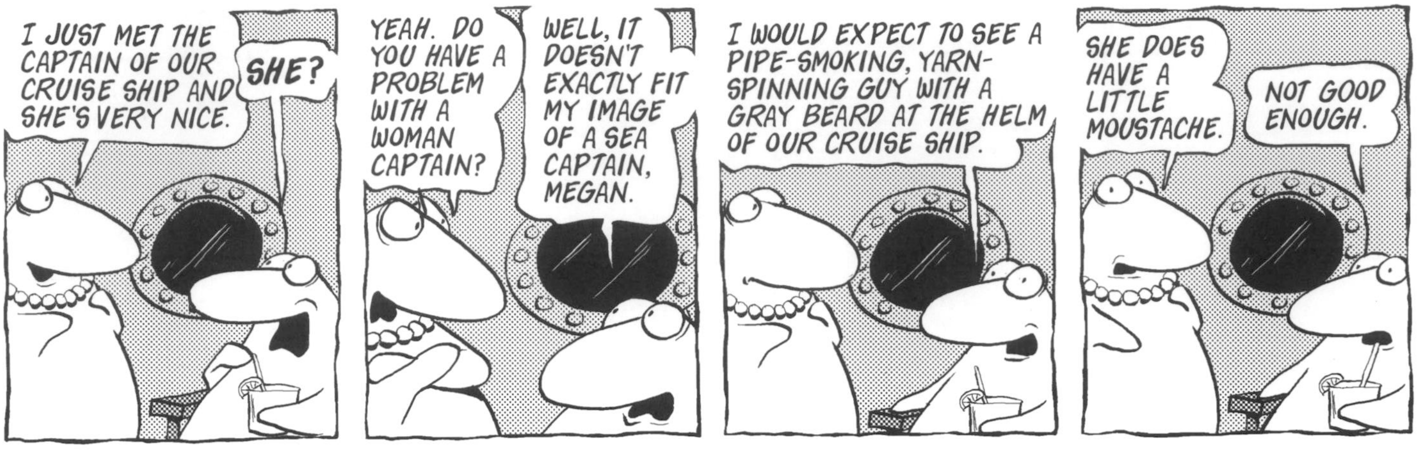
I JUST MET THE CAPTAIN OF OUR CRUISE SHIP AND SHE'S VERY NICE.
SHE?
YEAH. DO YOU HAVE A PROBLEM WITH A WOMAN CAPTAIN?
WELL, IT DOESN'T EXACTLY FIT MY IMAGE OF A SEA CAPTAIN, MEGAN.
I WOULD EXPECT TO SEE A PIPE-SMOKING, YARN-SPINNING GUY WITH A GRAY BEARD AT THE HELM OF OUR CRUISE SHIP.
SHE DOES HAVE A LITTLE MOUSTACHE.
NOT GOOD ENOUGH.

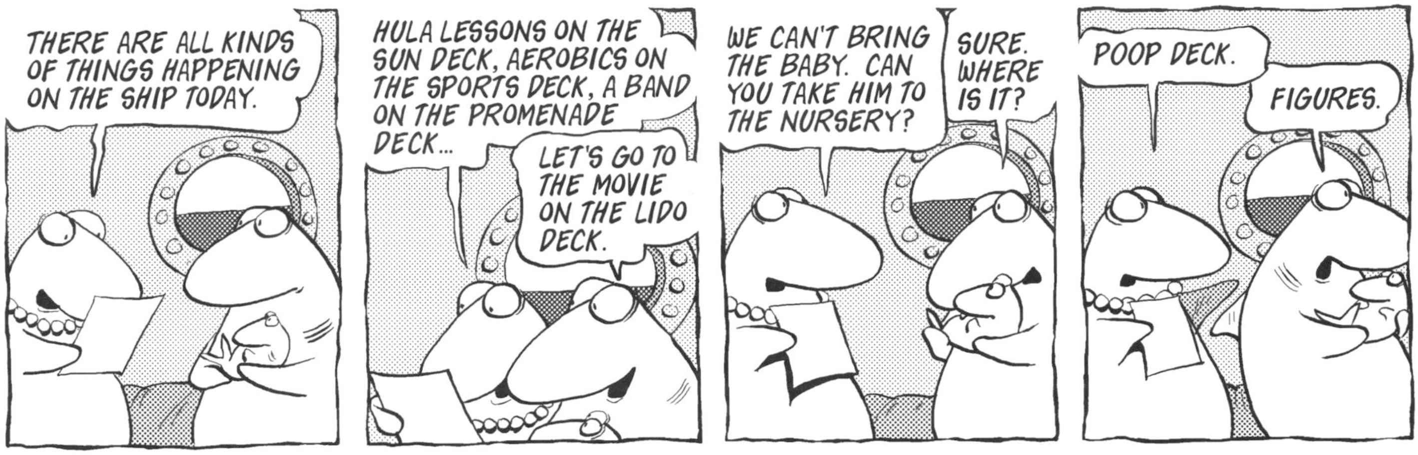
THERE ARE ALL KINDS OF THINGS HAPPENING ON THE SHIP TODAY.
HULA LESSONS ON THE SUN DECK, AEROBICS ON THE SPORTS DECK, A BAND ON THE PROMENADE DECK...
LET'S GO TO THE MOVIE ON THE LIDO DECK.
WE CAN'T BRING THE BABY. CAN YOU TAKE HIM TO THE NURSERY?
SURE. WHERE IS IT?
POOP DECK.
FIGURES.

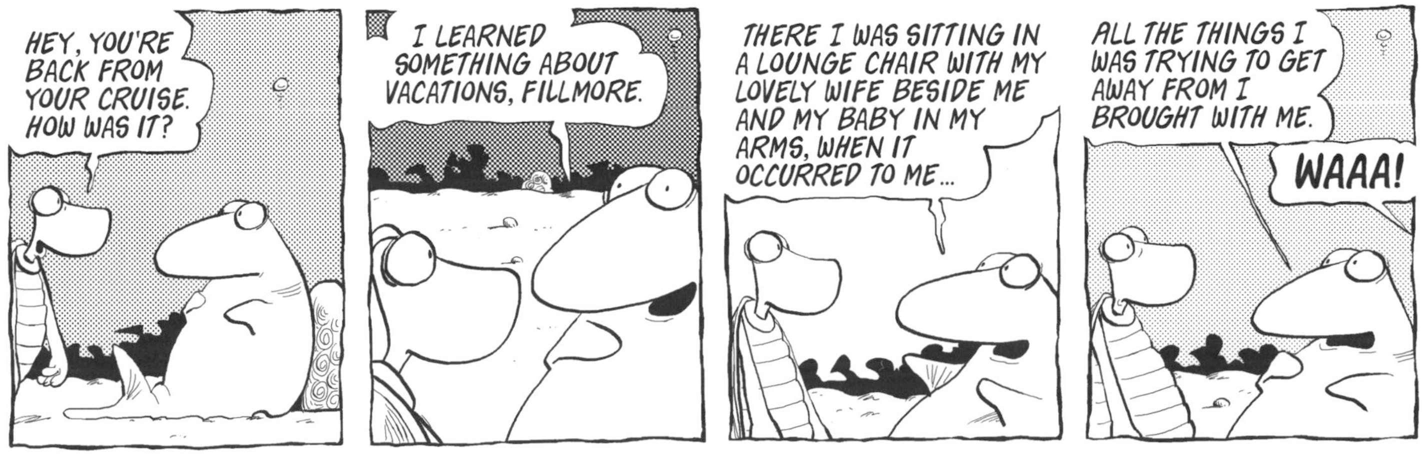
HEY, YOU'RE BACK FROM YOUR CRUISE. HOW WAS IT?
I LEARNED SOMETHING ABOUT VACATIONS, FILLMORE.
THERE I WAS SITTING IN A LOUNGE CHAIR WITH MY LOVELY WIFE BESIDE ME AND MY BABY IN MY ARMS, WHEN IT OCCURRED TO ME...
ALL THE THINGS I WAS TRYING TO GET AWAY FROM I BROUGHT WITH ME.
WAAA!

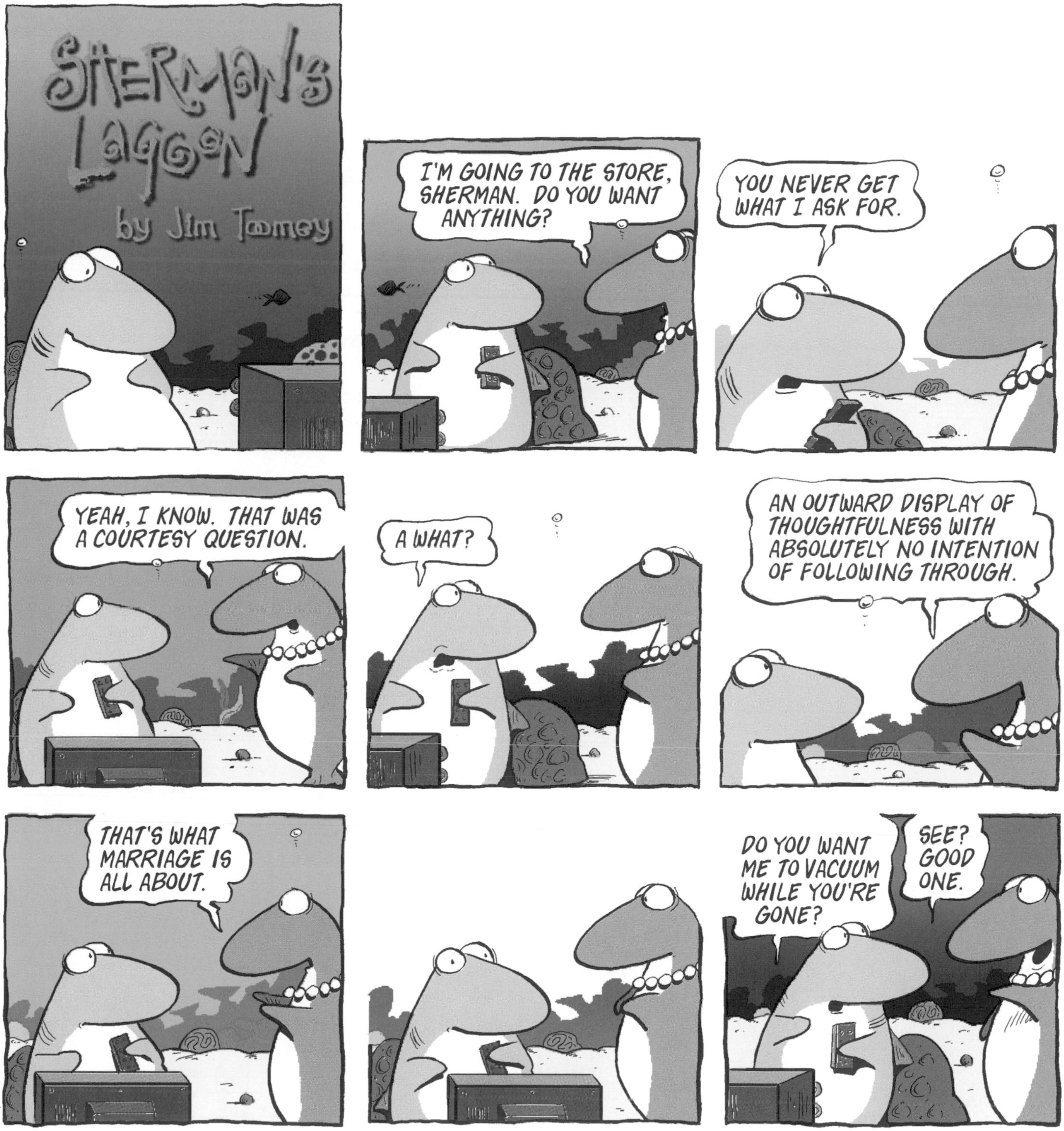
SHERMAN'S LAGOON
by Jim Toomey
I'M GOING TO THE STORE, SHERMAN. DO YOU WANT ANYTHING?
YOU NEVER GET WHAT I ASK FOR.
YEAH, I KNOW. THAT WAS A COURTESY QUESTION.
A WHAT?
AN OUTWARD DISPLAY OF THOUGHTFULNESS WITH ABSOLUTELY NO INTENTION OF FOLLOWING THROUGH.
THAT'S WHAT MARRIAGE IS ALL ABOUT.
DO YOU WANT ME TO VACUUM WHILE YOU'RE GONE?
SEE? GOOD ONE.

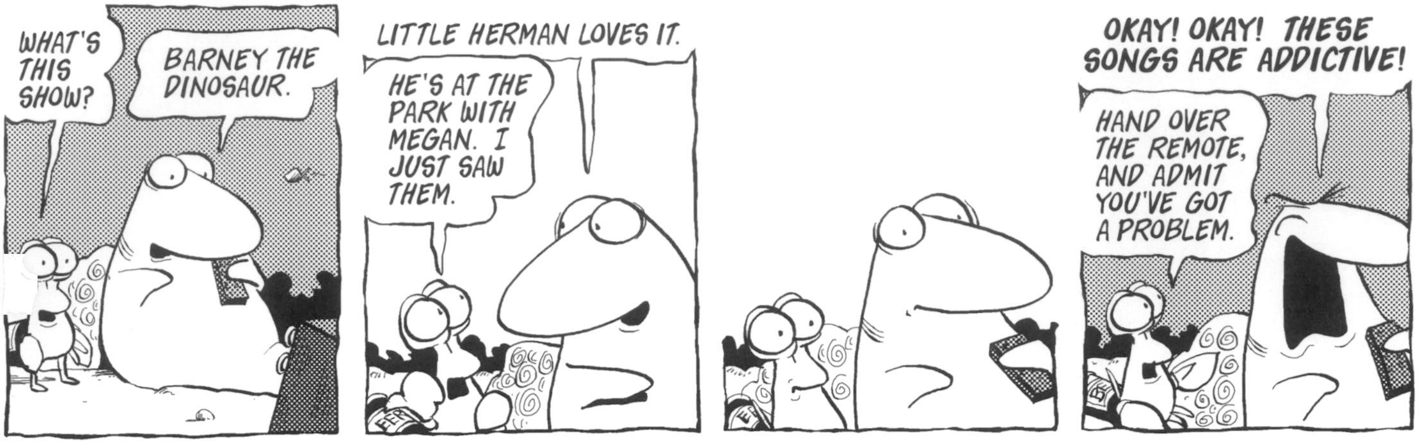
WHAT'S THIS SHOW?
BARNEY THE DINOSAUR.
LITTLE HERMAN LOVES IT.
HE'S AT THE PARK WITH MEGAN. I JUST SAW THEM.
OKAY! OKAY! THESE SONGS ARE ADDICTIVE!
HAND OVER THE REMOTE, AND ADMIT YOU'VE GOT A PROBLEM.

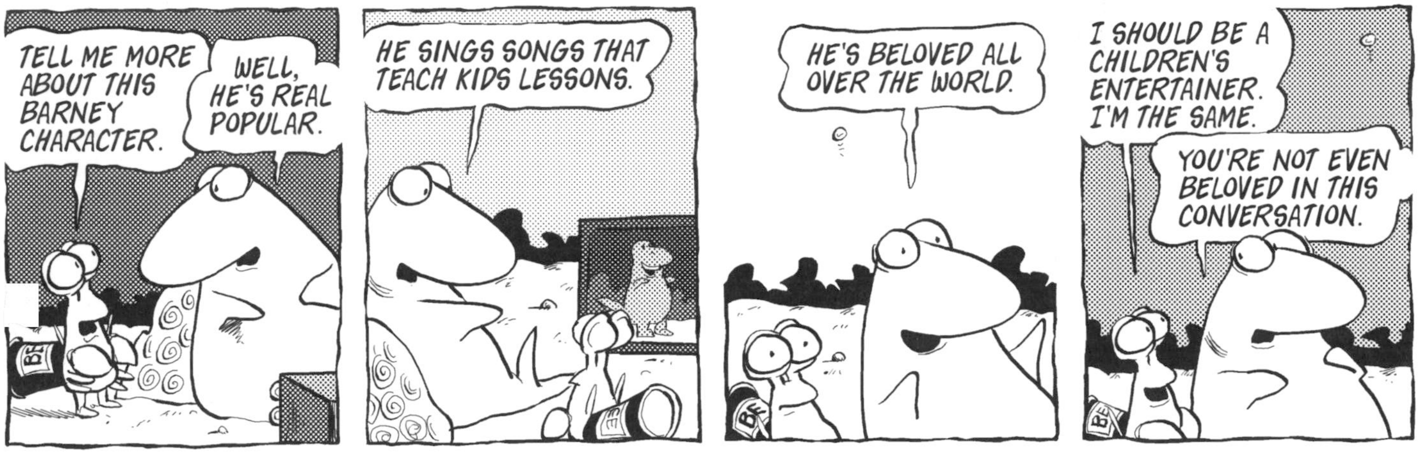
TELL ME MORE ABOUT THIS BARNEY CHARACTER.
WELL, HE'S REAL POPULAR.
HE SINGS SONGS THAT TEACH KIDS LESSONS.
HE'S BELOVED ALL OVER THE WORLD.
I SHOULD BE A CHILDREN'S ENTERTAINER. I'M THE SAME.
YOU'RE NOT EVEN BELOVED IN THIS CONVERSATION.

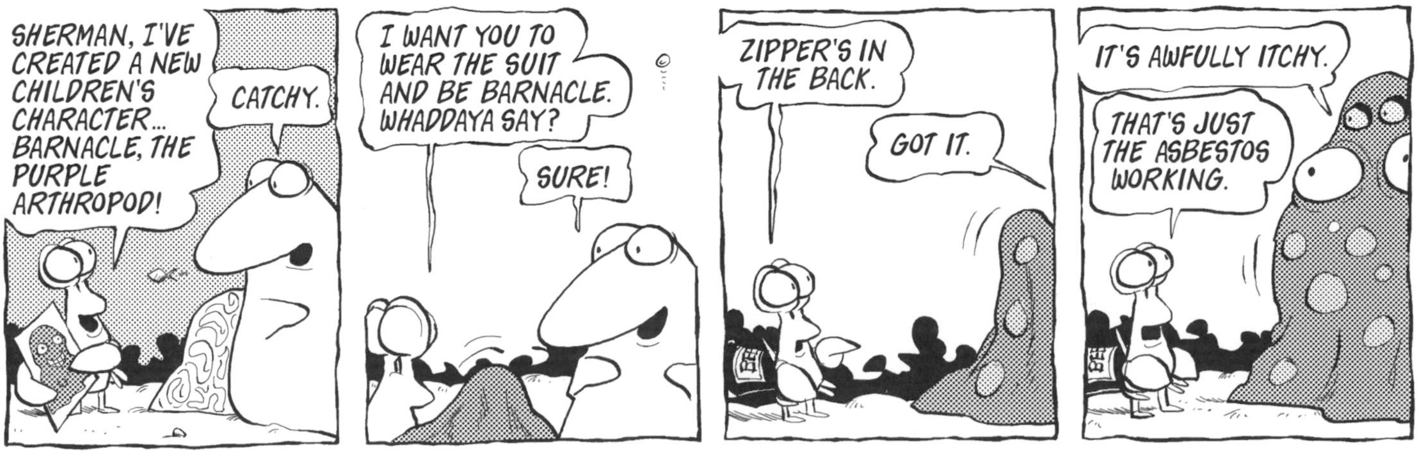
SHERMAN, I'VE CREATED A NEW CHILDREN'S CHARACTER... BARNACLE, THE PURPLE ARTHROPOD!
CATCHY.
I WANT YOU TO WEAR THE SUIT AND BE BARNACLE. WHADDAYA SAY?
SURE!
ZIPPER'S IN THE BACK.
GOT IT.
IT'S AWFULLY ITCHY.
THAT'S JUST THE ASBESTOS WORKING.

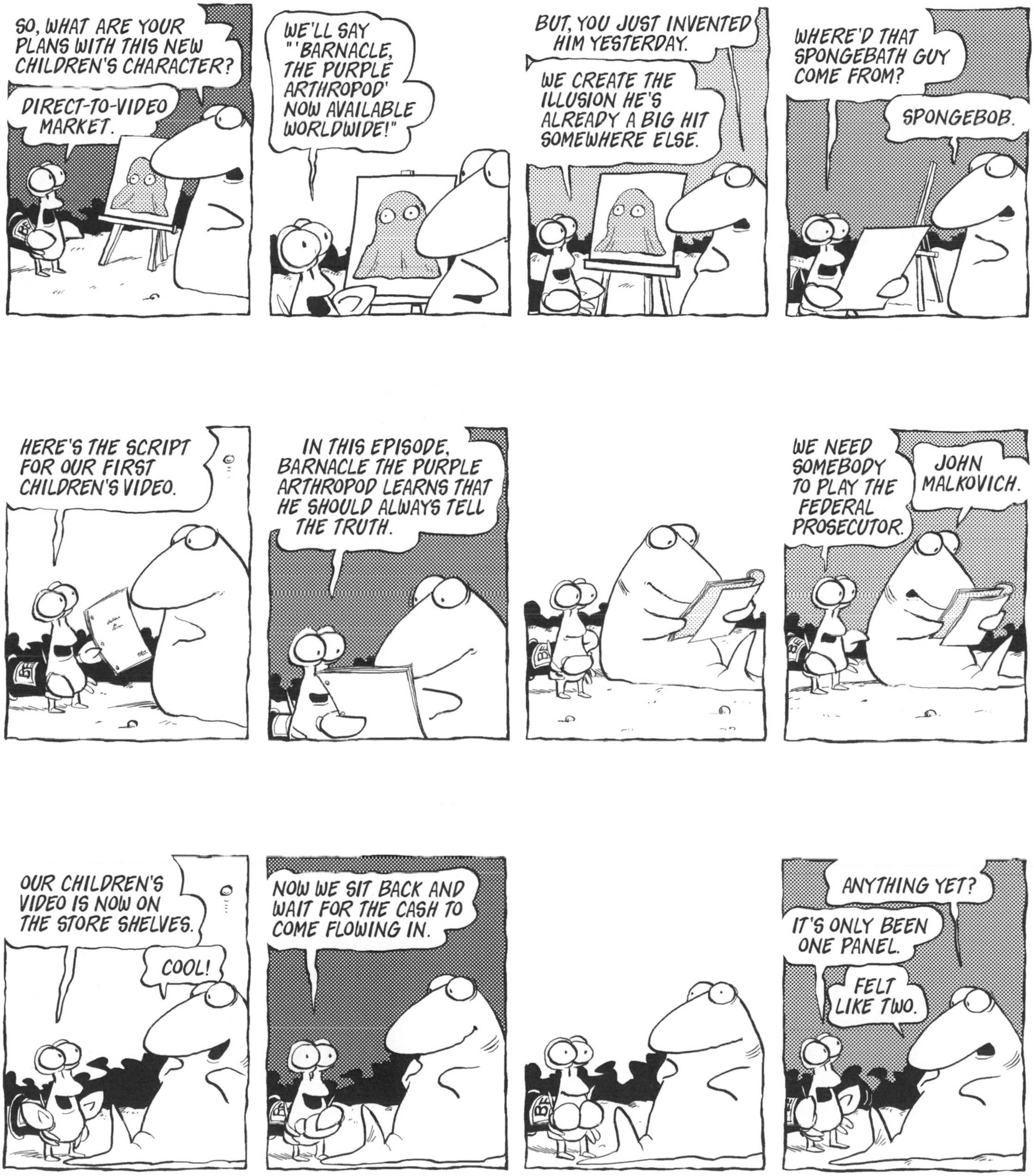
SO, WHAT ARE YOUR PLANS WITH THIS NEW CHILDREN'S CHARACTER?
DIRECT-TO-VIDEO MARKET.
WE'LL SAY "'BARNACLE, THE PURPLE ARTHROPOD' NOW AVAILABLE WORLDWIDE!"
BUT, YOU JUST INVENTED HIM YESTERDAY.
WE CREATE THE ILLUSION HE'S ALREADY A BIG HIT SOMEWHERE ELSE.
WHERE'D THAT SPONGEBATH GUY COME FROM?
SPONGEBOB.
HERE'S THE SCRIPT FOR OUR FIRST CHILDREN'S VIDEO.
IN THIS EPISODE, BARNACLE THE PURPLE ARTHROPOD LEARNS THAT HE SHOULD ALWAYS TELL THE TRUTH.
WE NEED SOMEBODY TO PLAY THE FEDERAL PROSECUTOR.
JOHN MALKOVICH.
OUR CHILDREN'S VIDEO IS NOW ON THE STORE SHELVES.
COOL!
NOW WE SIT BACK AND WAIT FOR THE CASH TO COME FLOWING IN.
ANYTHING YET?
IT'S ONLY BEEN ONE PANEL.
FELT LIKE TWO.

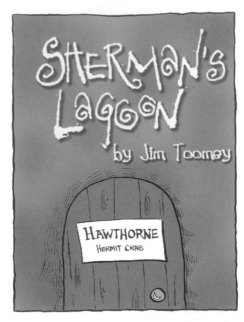

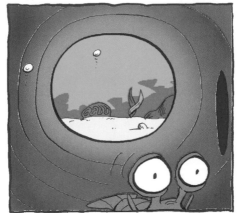

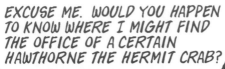

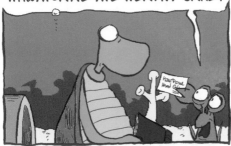

SHERMAN'S LAGOON
by Jim Toomey
HAWTHORNE
HERMIT CRAB
EXCUSE ME. WOULD YOU HAPPEN TO KNOW WHERE I MIGHT FIND THE OFFICE OF A CERTAIN HAWTHORNE THE HERMIT CRAB?
DOWN THE HALL, THIRD LEFT.
THANKS.
AAUGH!
I THINK I HIT THE LADIES' ROOM.
ONE MORE DOWN.

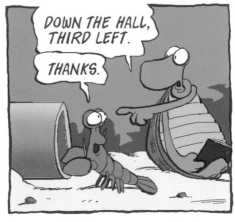

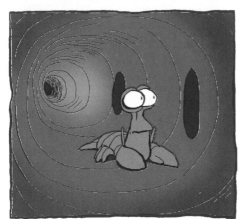

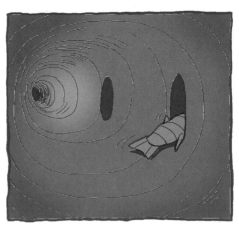

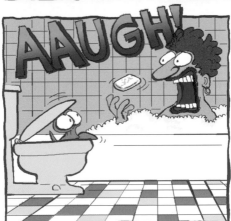

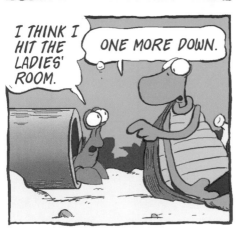

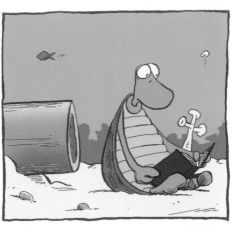

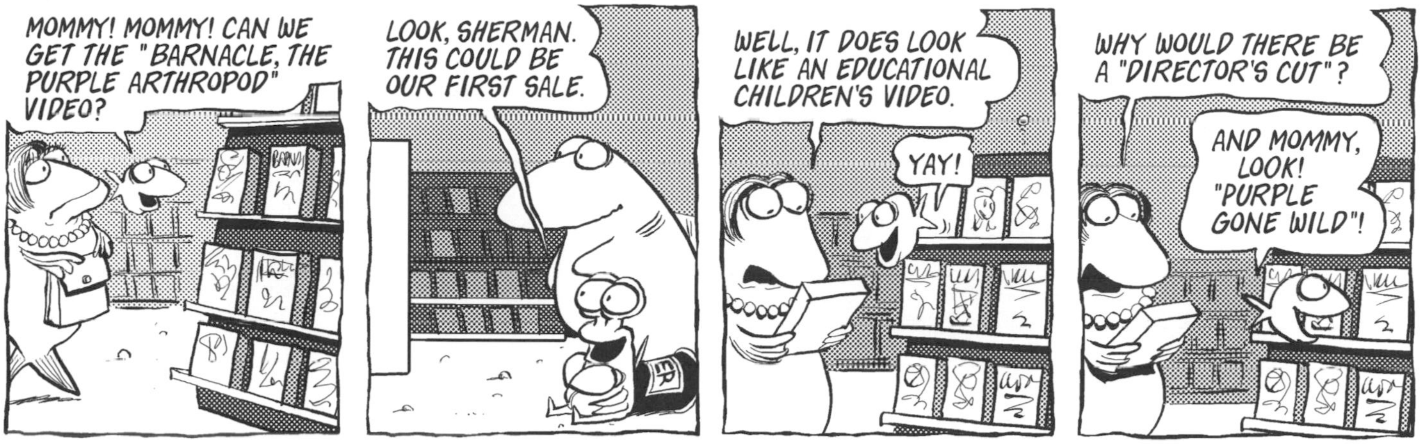
MOMMY! MOMMY! CAN WE GET THE "BARNACLE, THE PURPLE ARTHROPOD" VIDEO?
LOOK, SHERMAN. THIS COULD BE OUR FIRST SALE.
WELL, IT DOES LOOK LIKE AN EDUCATIONAL CHILDREN'S VIDEO.
YAY!
WHY WOULD THERE BE A "DIRECTOR'S CUT"?
AND MOMMY, LOOK! "PURPLE GONE WILD"!

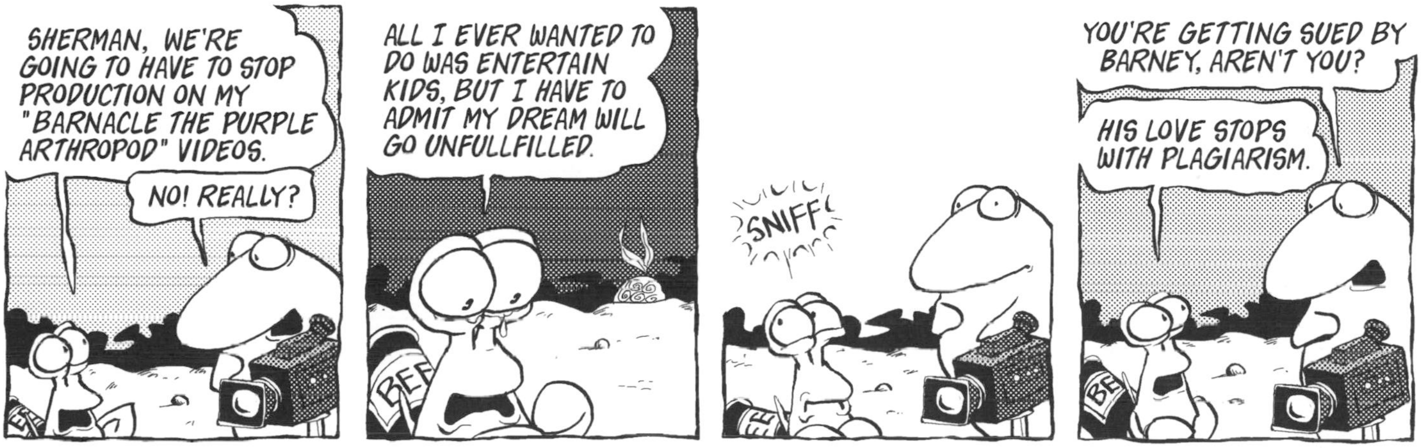
SHERMAN, WE'RE GOING TO HAVE TO STOP PRODUCTION ON MY "BARNACLE THE PURPLE ARTHROPOD" VIDEOS.
NO! REALLY?
ALL I EVER WANTED TO DO WAS ENTERTAIN KIDS, BUT I HAVE TO ADMIT MY DREAM WILL GO UNFULLFILLED.
SNIFF
YOU'RE GETTING SUED BY BARNEY, AREN'T YOU?
HIS LOVE STOPS WITH PLAGIARISM.

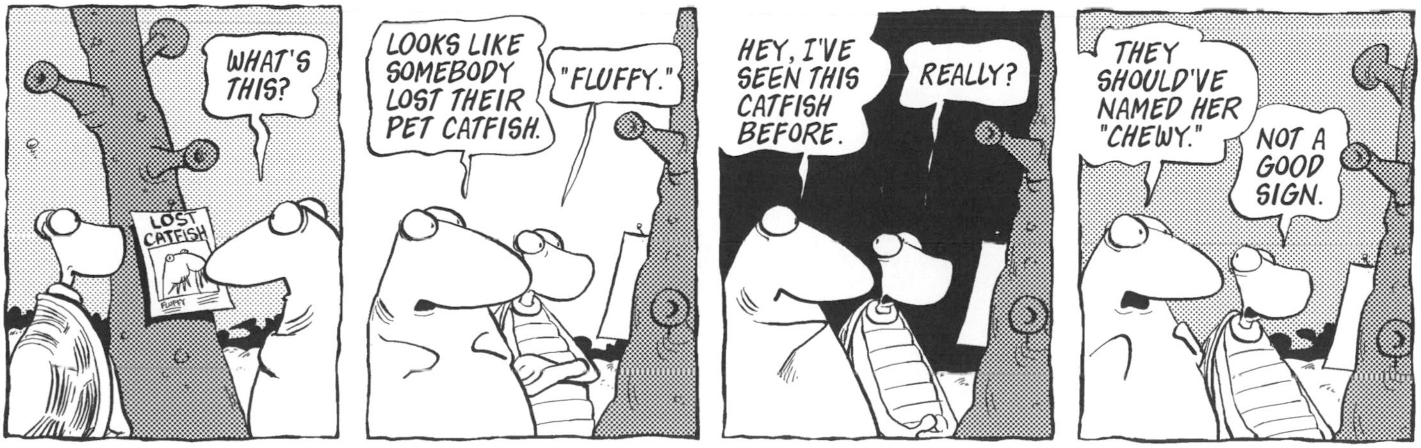
WHAT'S THIS?
LOST CATFISH
LOOKS LIKE SOMEBODY LOST THEIR PET CATFISH.
"FLUFFY."
HEY, I'VE SEEN THIS CATFISH BEFORE.
REALLY?
THEY SHOULD'VE NAMED HER "CHEWY."
NOT A GOOD SIGN.

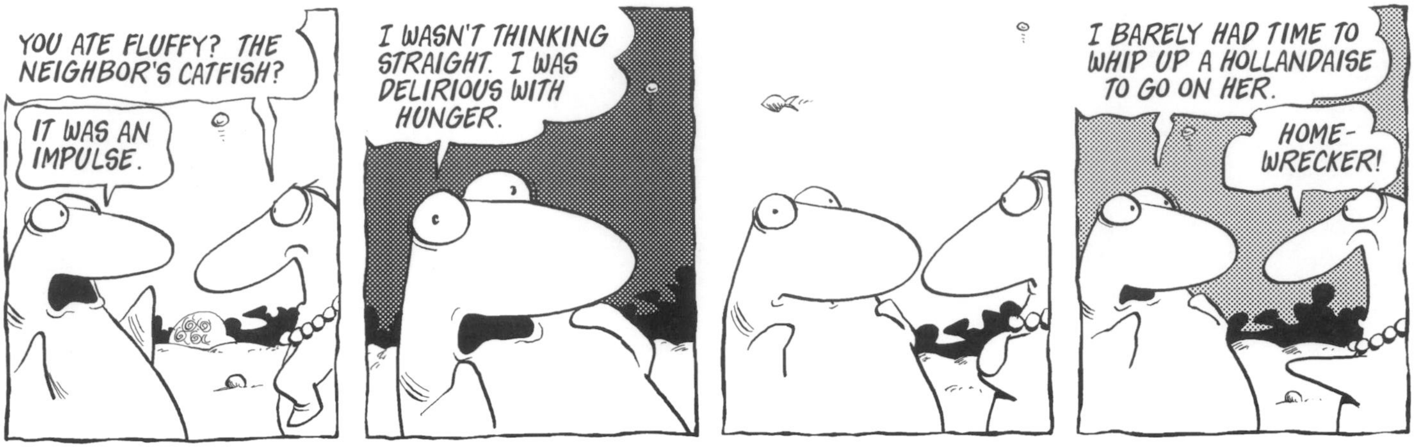
YOU ATE FLUFFY? THE NEIGHBOR'S CATFISH?
IT WAS AN IMPULSE.
I WASN'T THINKING STRAIGHT. I WAS DELIRIOUS WITH HUNGER.
I BARELY HAD TIME TO WHIP UP A HOLLANDAISE TO GO ON HER.
HOME-WRECKER!

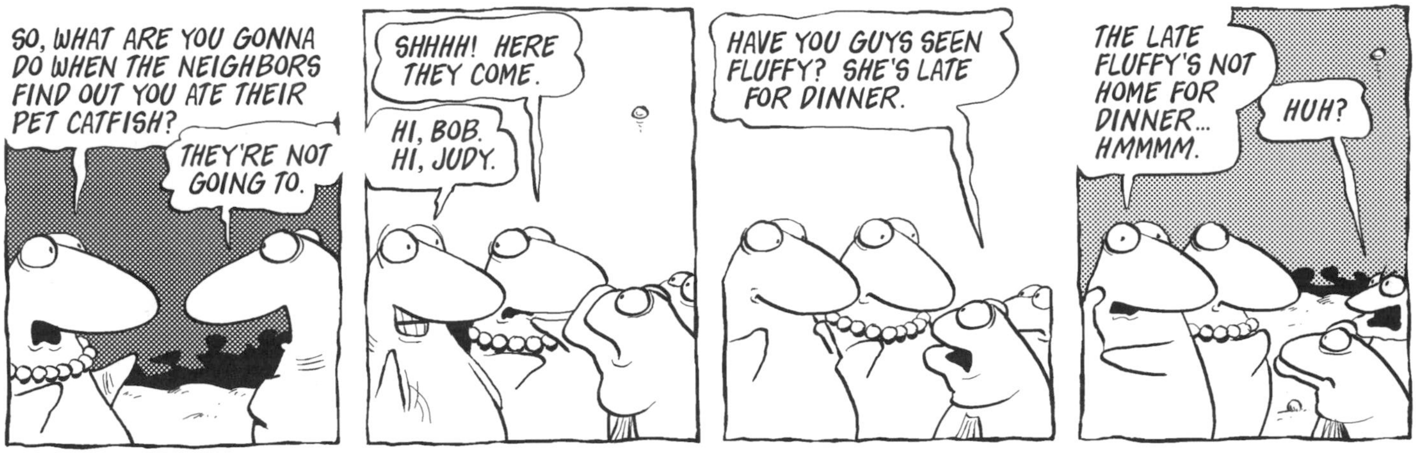
SO, WHAT ARE YOU GONNA DO WHEN THE NEIGHBORS FIND OUT YOU ATE THEIR PET CATFISH?
THEY'RE NOT GOING TO.
SHHHH! HERE THEY COME.
HI, BOB. HI, JUDY.
HAVE YOU GUYS SEEN FLUFFY? SHE'S LATE FOR DINNER.
THE LATE FLUFFY'S NOT HOME FOR DINNER... HMMMM.
HUH?

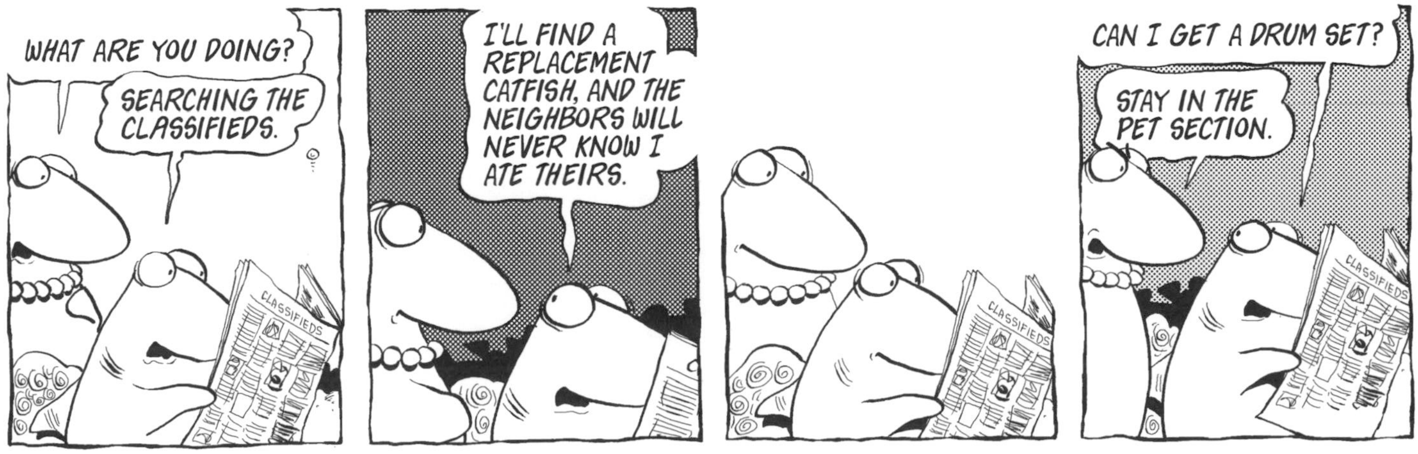
WHAT ARE YOU DOING?
SEARCHING THE CLASSIFIEDS.
I'LL FIND A REPLACEMENT CATFISH, AND THE NEIGHBORS WILL NEVER KNOW I ATE THEIRS.
CAN I GET A DRUM SET?
STAY IN THE PET SECTION.

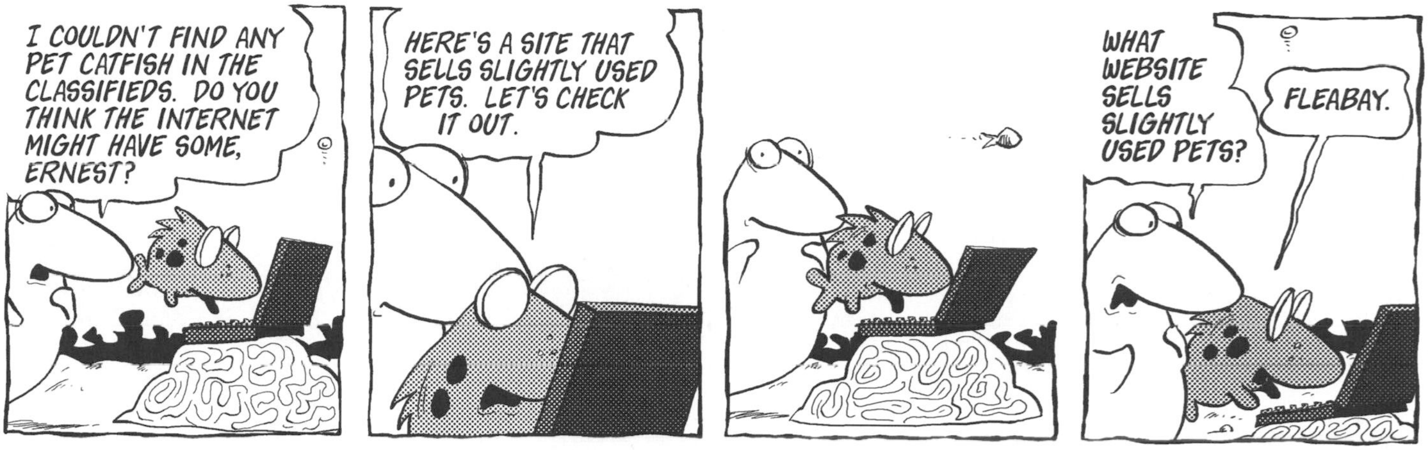
I COULDN'T FIND ANY PET CATFISH IN THE CLASSIFIEDS. DO YOU THINK THE INTERNET MIGHT HAVE SOME, ERNEST?
HERE'S A SITE THAT SELLS SLIGHTLY USED PETS. LET'S CHECK IT OUT.
WHAT WEBSITE SELLS SLIGHTLY USED PETS?
FLEABAY.

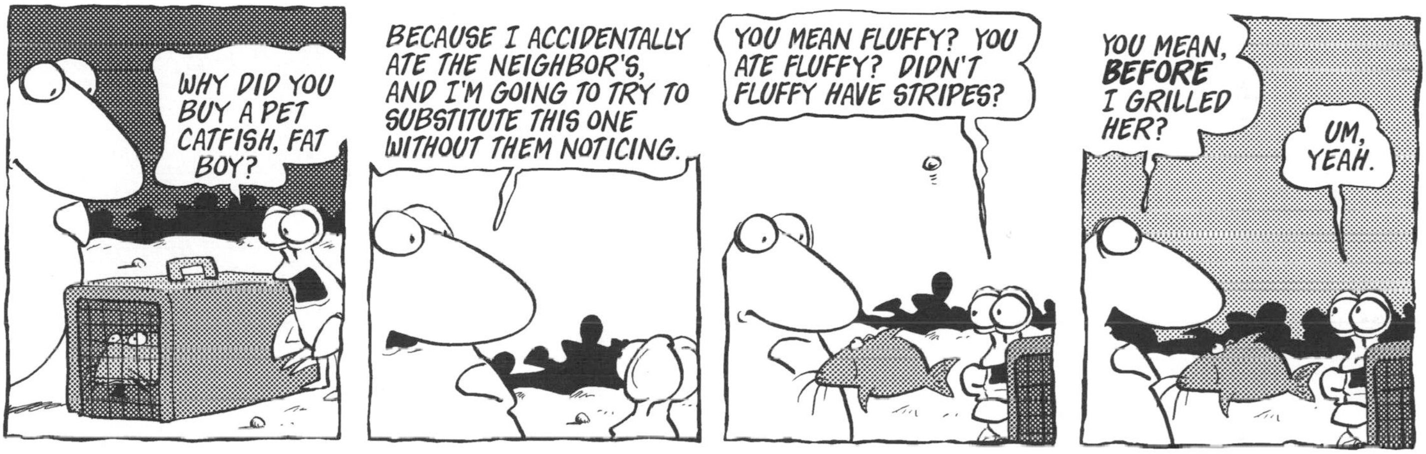
WHY DID YOU BUY A PET CATFISH, FAT BOY?
BECAUSE I ACCIDENTALLY ATE THE NEIGHBOR'S, AND I'M GOING TO TRY TO SUBSTITUTE THIS ONE WITHOUT THEM NOTICING.
YOU MEAN FLUFFY? YOU ATE FLUFFY? DIDN'T FLUFFY HAVE STRIPES?
YOU MEAN, **BEFORE** I GRILLED HER?
UM, YEAH.

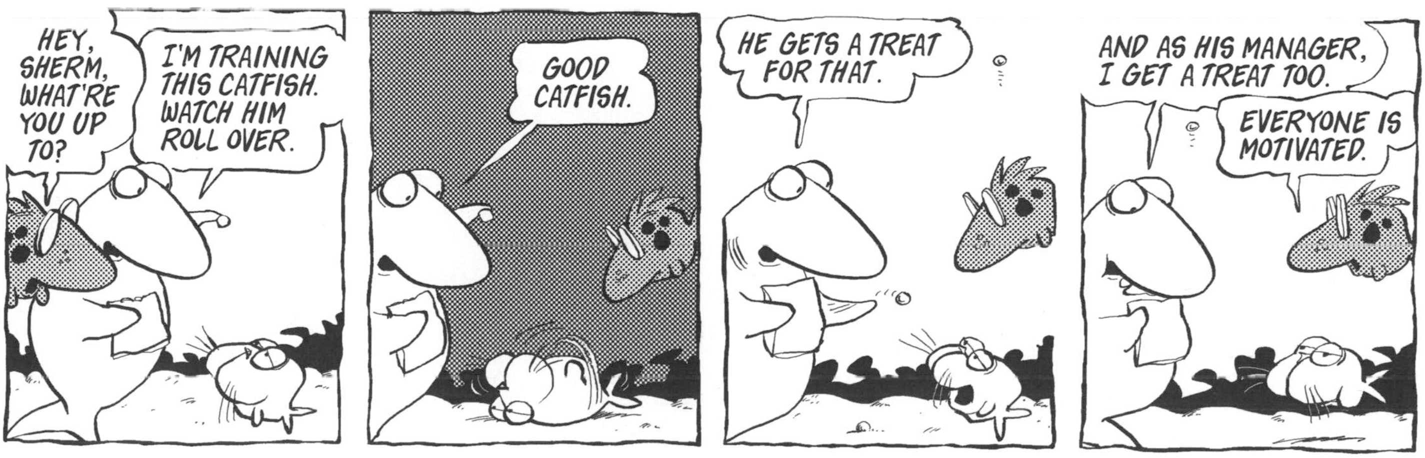
HEY, SHERM, WHAT'RE YOU UP TO?
I'M TRAINING THIS CATFISH. WATCH HIM ROLL OVER.
GOOD CATFISH.
HE GETS A TREAT FOR THAT.
AND AS HIS MANAGER, I GET A TREAT TOO.
EVERYONE IS MOTIVATED.

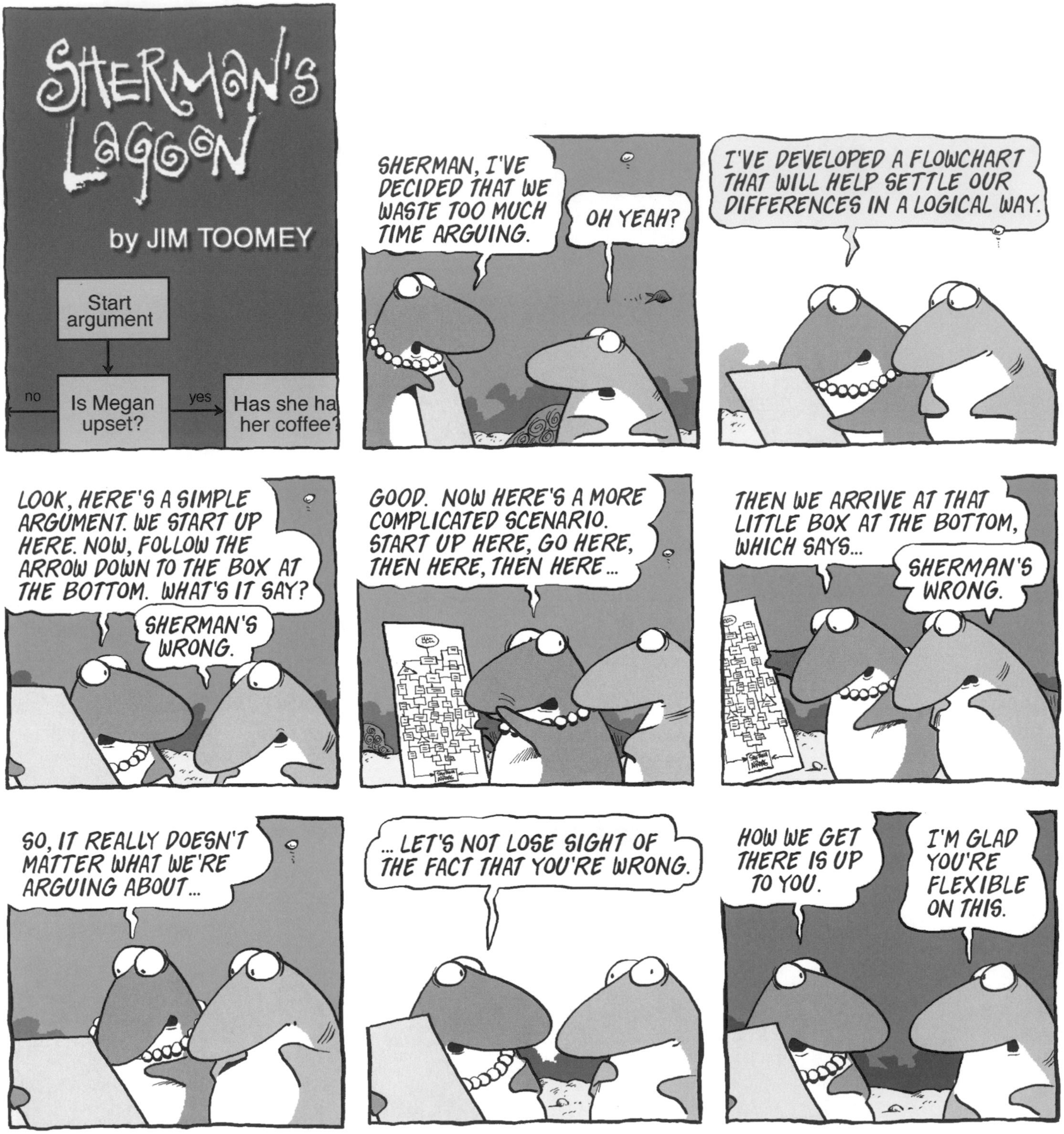
SHERMAN'S LAGOON
by JIM TOOMEY
Start argument
no
Is Megan upset?
yes
Has she ha her coffee?
SHERMAN, I'VE DECIDED THAT WE WASTE TOO MUCH TIME ARGUING.
OH YEAH?
I'VE DEVELOPED A FLOWCHART THAT WILL HELP SETTLE OUR DIFFERENCES IN A LOGICAL WAY.
LOOK, HERE'S A SIMPLE ARGUMENT. WE START UP HERE. NOW, FOLLOW THE ARROW DOWN TO THE BOX AT THE BOTTOM. WHAT'S IT SAY?
SHERMAN'S WRONG.
GOOD. NOW HERE'S A MORE COMPLICATED SCENARIO. START UP HERE, GO HERE, THEN HERE, THEN HERE...
THEN WE ARRIVE AT THAT LITTLE BOX AT THE BOTTOM, WHICH SAYS...
SHERMAN'S WRONG.
SO, IT REALLY DOESN'T MATTER WHAT WE'RE ARGUING ABOUT...
... LET'S NOT LOSE SIGHT OF THE FACT THAT YOU'RE WRONG.
HOW WE GET THERE IS UP TO YOU.
I'M GLAD YOU'RE FLEXIBLE ON THIS.

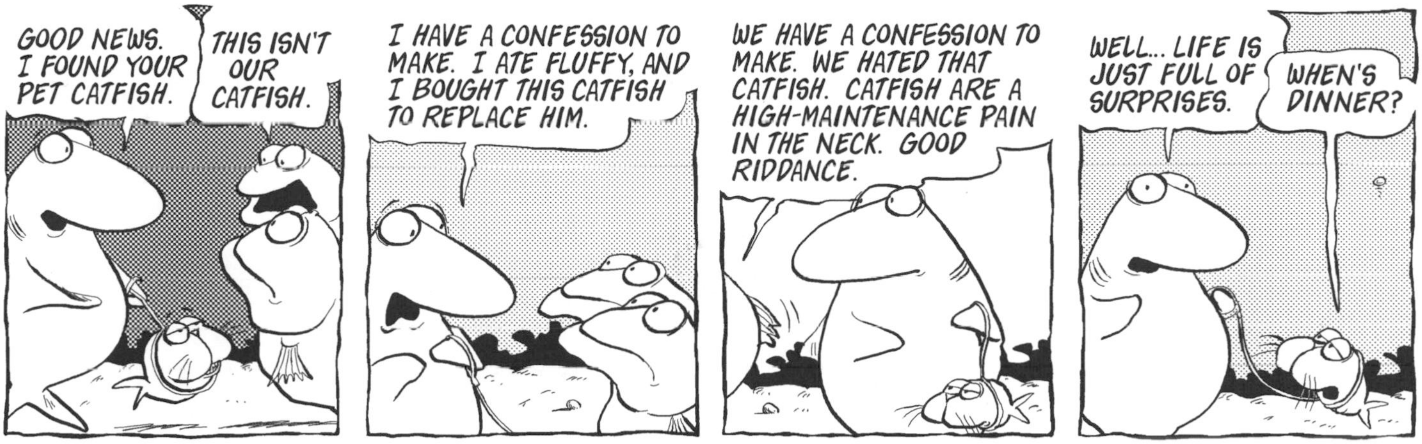
GOOD NEWS. I FOUND YOUR PET CATFISH.
THIS ISN'T OUR CATFISH.
I HAVE A CONFESSION TO MAKE. I ATE FLUFFY, AND I BOUGHT THIS CATFISH TO REPLACE HIM.
WE HAVE A CONFESSION TO MAKE. WE HATED THAT CATFISH. CATFISH ARE A HIGH-MAINTENANCE PAIN IN THE NECK. GOOD RIDDANCE.
WELL... LIFE IS JUST FULL OF SURPRISES.
WHEN'S DINNER?

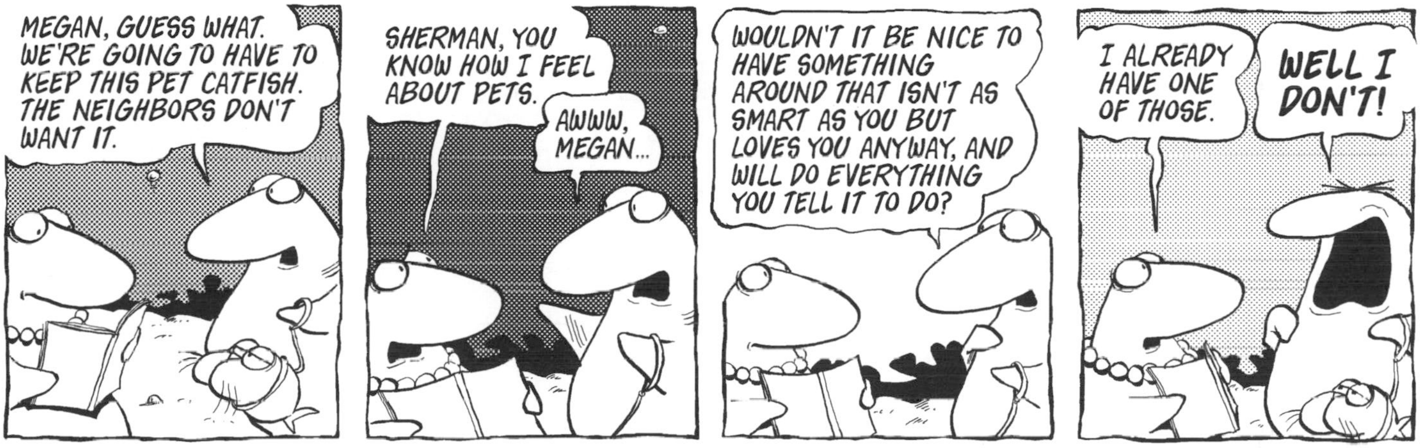
MEGAN, GUESS WHAT. WE'RE GOING TO HAVE TO KEEP THIS PET CATFISH. THE NEIGHBORS DON'T WANT IT.
SHERMAN, YOU KNOW HOW I FEEL ABOUT PETS.
AWWW, MEGAN...
WOULDN'T IT BE NICE TO HAVE SOMETHING AROUND THAT ISN'T AS SMART AS YOU BUT LOVES YOU ANYWAY, AND WILL DO EVERYTHING YOU TELL IT TO DO?
I ALREADY HAVE ONE OF THOSE.
WELL I DON'T!

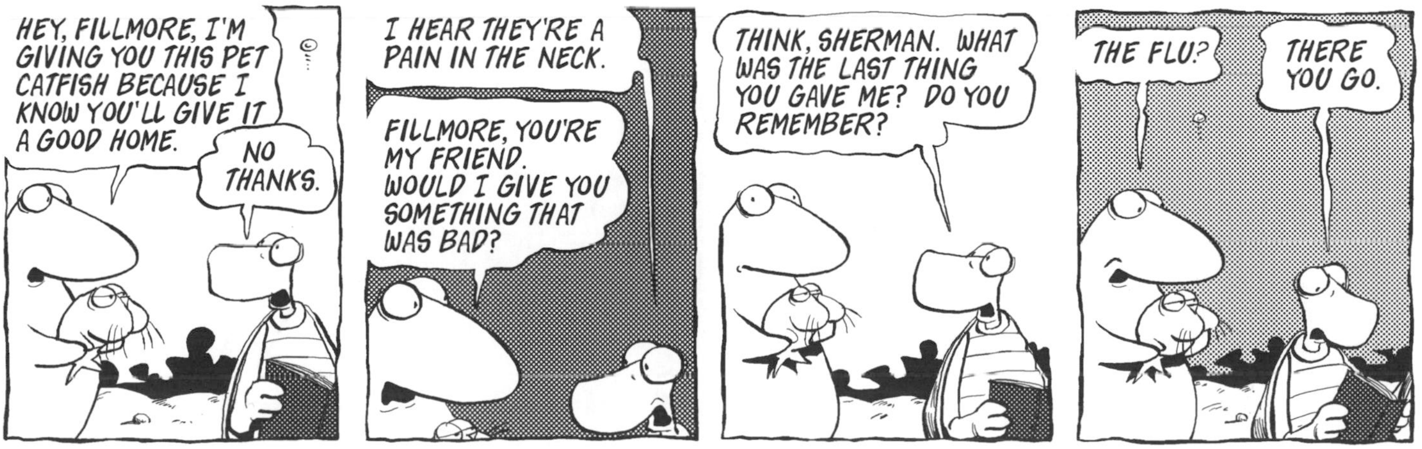
HEY, FILLMORE, I'M GIVING YOU THIS PET CATFISH BECAUSE I KNOW YOU'LL GIVE IT A GOOD HOME.
NO THANKS.
I HEAR THEY'RE A PAIN IN THE NECK.
FILLMORE, YOU'RE MY FRIEND. WOULD I GIVE YOU SOMETHING THAT WAS BAD?
THINK, SHERMAN. WHAT WAS THE LAST THING YOU GAVE ME? DO YOU REMEMBER?
THE FLU?
THERE YOU GO.

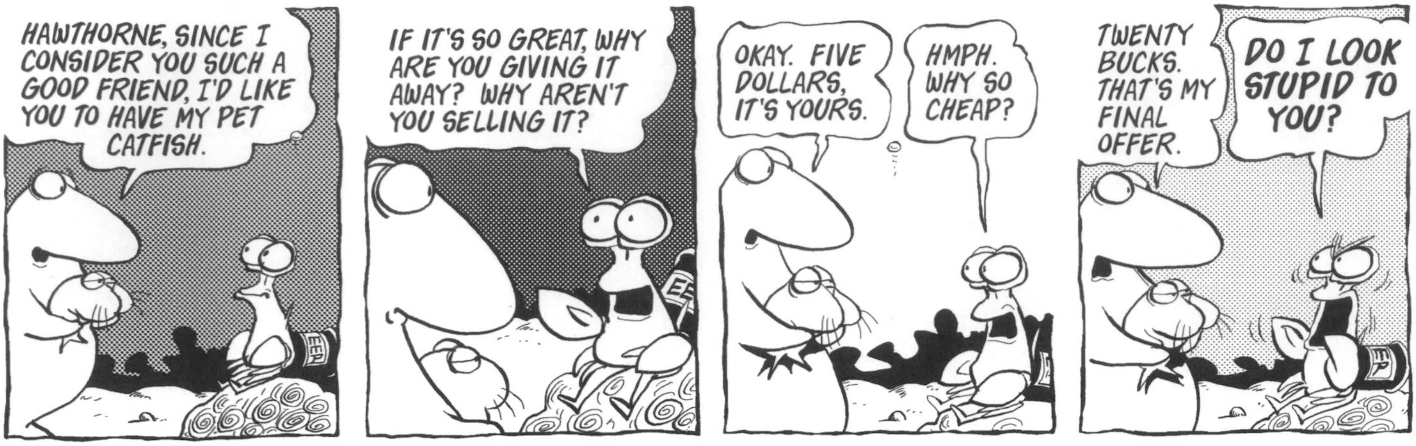
HAWTHORNE, SINCE I CONSIDER YOU SUCH A GOOD FRIEND, I'D LIKE YOU TO HAVE MY PET CATFISH.
IF IT'S SO GREAT, WHY ARE YOU GIVING IT AWAY? WHY AREN'T YOU SELLING IT?
OKAY. FIVE DOLLARS, IT'S YOURS.
HMPH. WHY SO CHEAP?
TWENTY BUCKS. THAT'S MY FINAL OFFER.
DO I LOOK STUPID TO YOU?

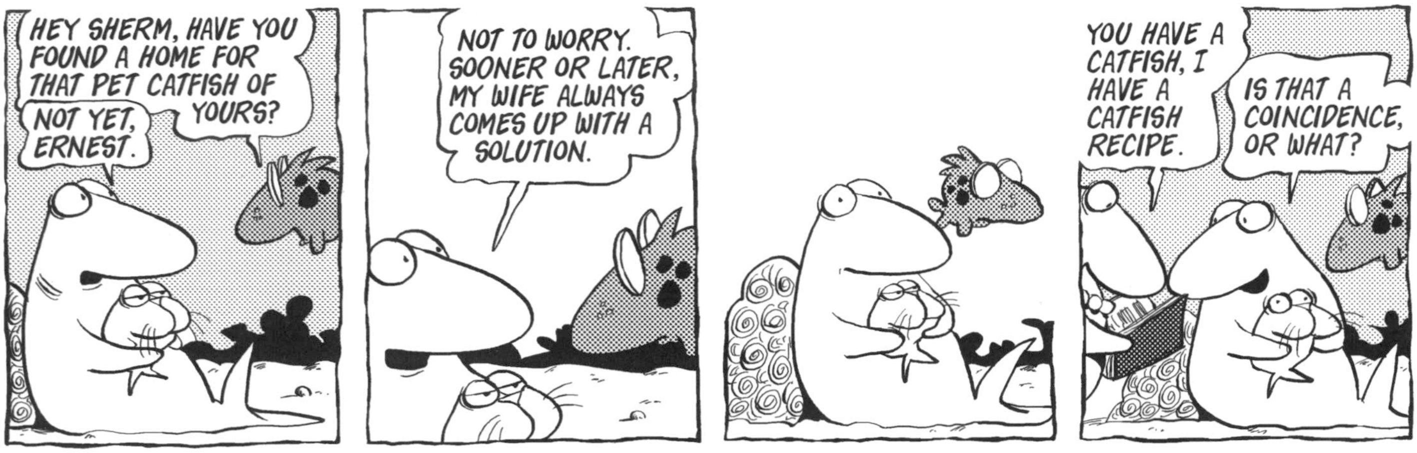
HEY SHERM, HAVE YOU FOUND A HOME FOR THAT PET CATFISH OF YOURS?
NOT YET, ERNEST.
NOT TO WORRY. SOONER OR LATER, MY WIFE ALWAYS COMES UP WITH A SOLUTION.
YOU HAVE A CATFISH, I HAVE A CATFISH RECIPE.
IS THAT A COINCIDENCE, OR WHAT?

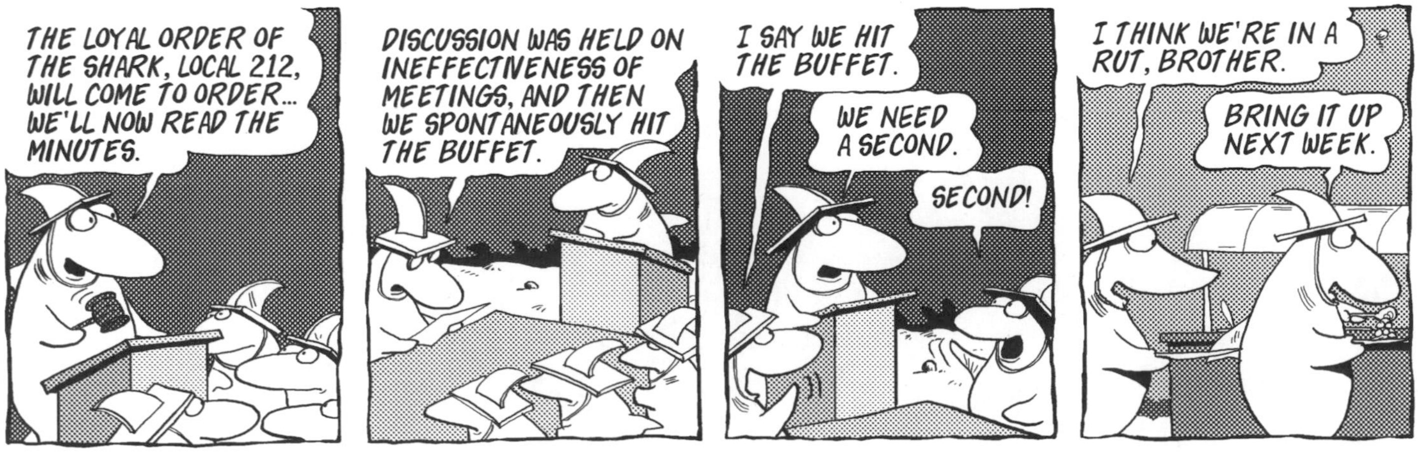
THE LOYAL ORDER OF THE SHARK, LOCAL 212, WILL COME TO ORDER... WE'LL NOW READ THE MINUTES.
DISCUSSION WAS HELD ON INEFFECTIVENESS OF MEETINGS, AND THEN WE SPONTANEOUSLY HIT THE BUFFET.
I SAY WE HIT THE BUFFET.
WE NEED A SECOND.
SECOND!
I THINK WE'RE IN A RUT, BROTHER.
BRING IT UP NEXT WEEK.

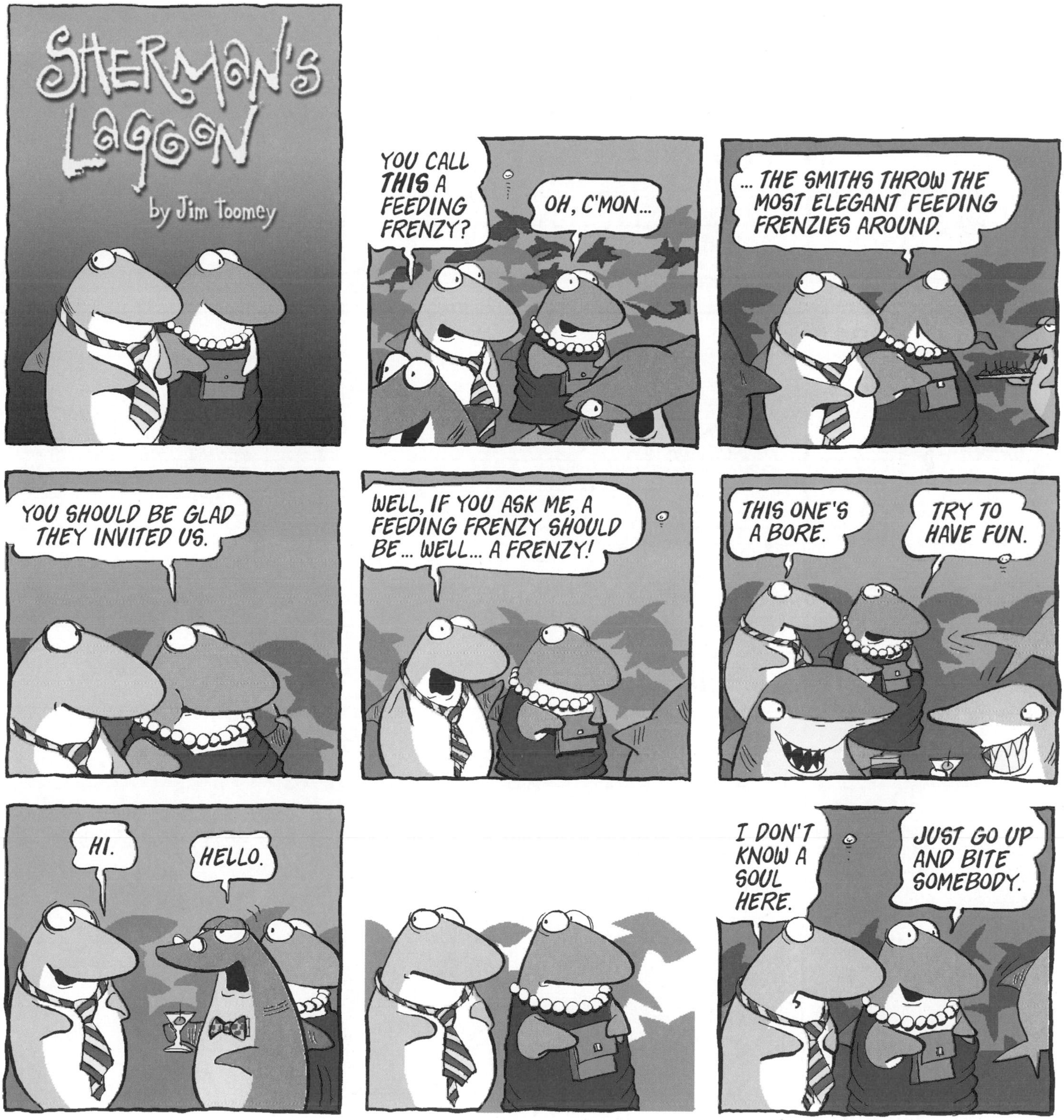

SHERMAN'S LAGOON
by Jim Toomey
YOU CALL THIS A FEEDING FRENZY?
OH, C'MON...
... THE SMITHS THROW THE MOST ELEGANT FEEDING FRENZIES AROUND.
YOU SHOULD BE GLAD THEY INVITED US.
WELL, IF YOU ASK ME, A FEEDING FRENZY SHOULD BE... WELL... A FRENZY!
THIS ONE'S A BORE.
TRY TO HAVE FUN.
HI.
HELLO.
I DON'T KNOW A SOUL HERE.
JUST GO UP AND BITE SOMEBODY.

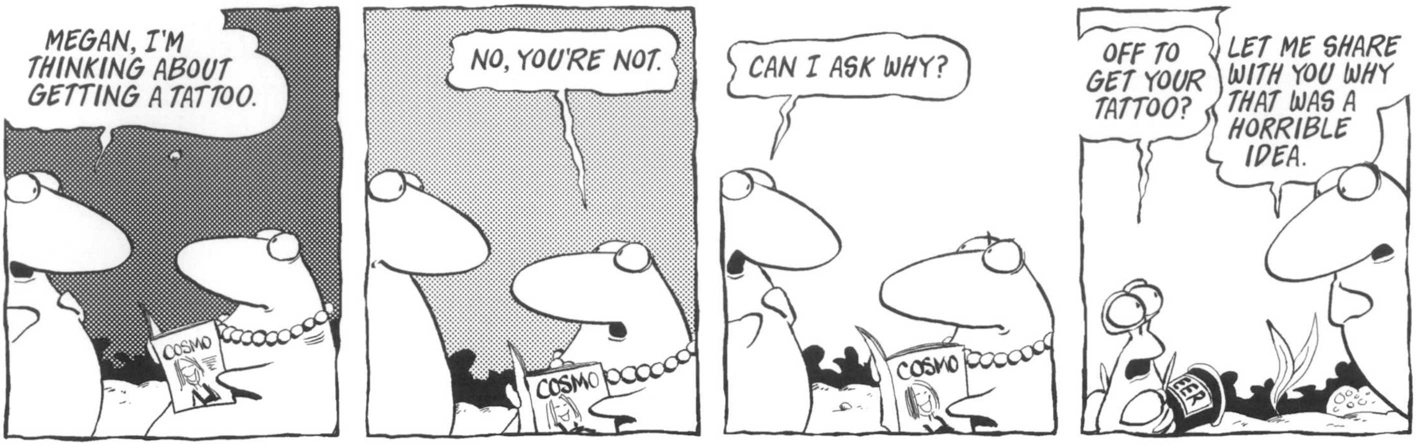
MEGAN, I'M THINKING ABOUT GETTING A TATTOO.
COSMO
NO, YOU'RE NOT.
COSMO
CAN I ASK WHY?
COSMO
OFF TO GET YOUR TATTOO?
LET ME SHARE WITH YOU WHY THAT WAS A HORRIBLE IDEA.

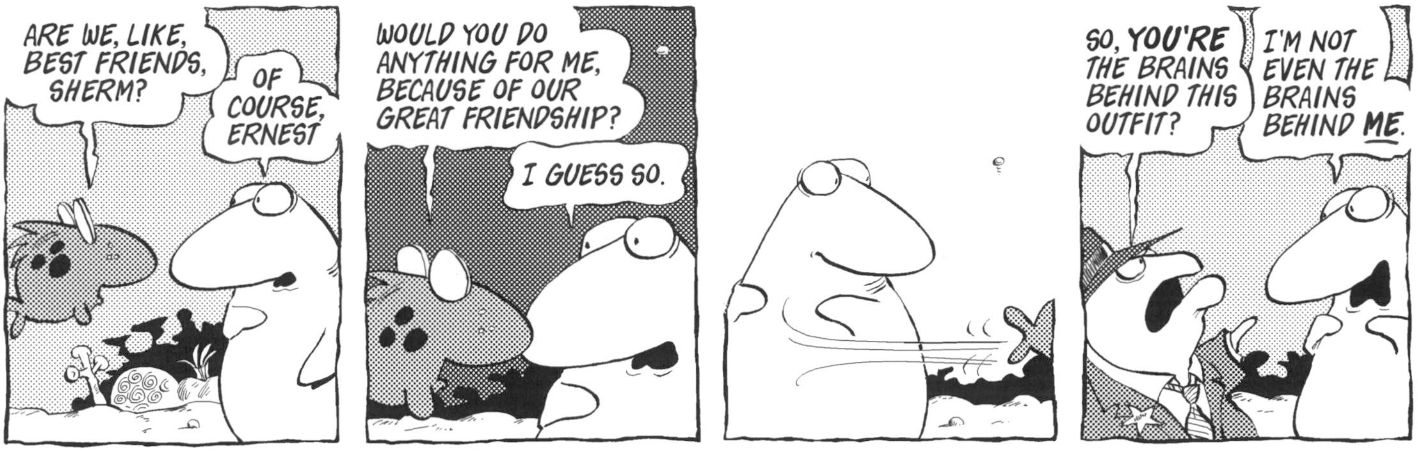
ARE WE, LIKE, BEST FRIENDS, SHERM?
OF COURSE, ERNEST
WOULD YOU DO ANYTHING FOR ME, BECAUSE OF OUR GREAT FRIENDSHIP?
I GUESS SO.
SO, YOU'RE THE BRAINS BEHIND THIS OUTFIT?
I'M NOT EVEN THE BRAINS BEHIND ME.

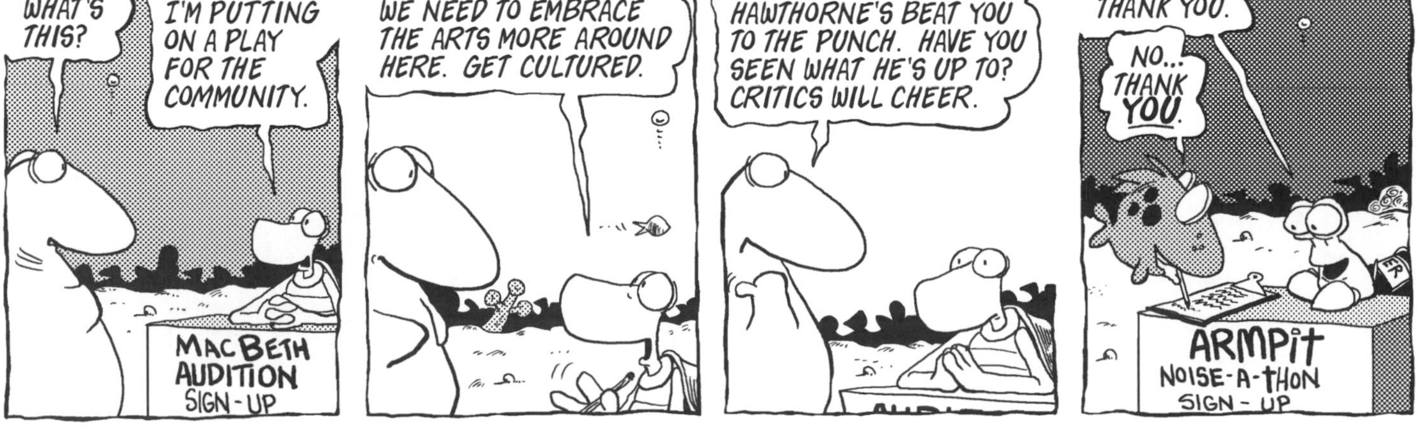
WHAT'S THIS?
I'M PUTTING ON A PLAY FOR THE COMMUNITY.
MAC BETH AUDITION SIGN-UP
WE NEED TO EMBRACE THE ARTS MORE AROUND HERE. GET CULTURED.
HAWTHORNE'S BEAT YOU TO THE PUNCH. HAVE YOU SEEN WHAT HE'S UP TO? CRITICS WILL CHEER.
THANK YOU.
NO... THANK YOU.
ARMPIT NOISE-A-THON SIGN-UP

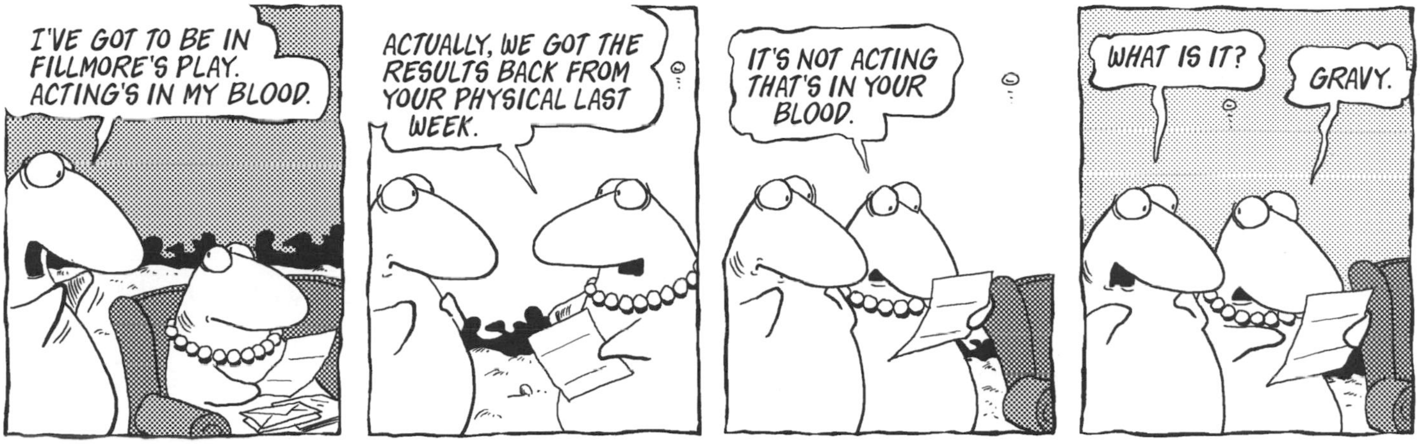
I'VE GOT TO BE IN FILLMORE'S PLAY. ACTING'S IN MY BLOOD.
ACTUALLY, WE GOT THE RESULTS BACK FROM YOUR PHYSICAL LAST WEEK.
IT'S NOT ACTING THAT'S IN YOUR BLOOD.
WHAT IS IT?
GRAVY.

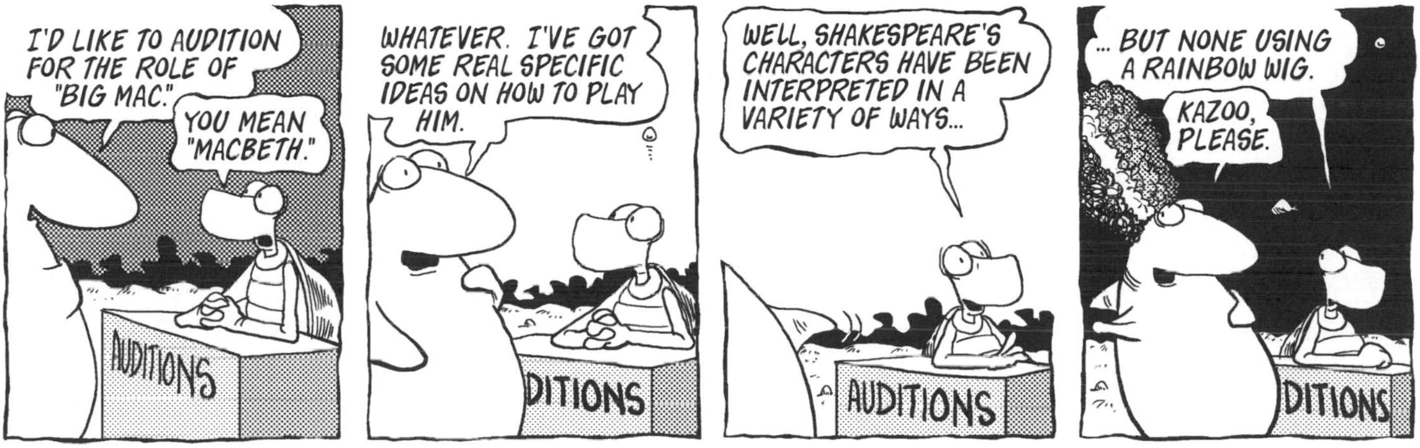
I'D LIKE TO AUDITION FOR THE ROLE OF "BIG MAC."
YOU MEAN "MACBETH."
AUDITIONS
WHATEVER. I'VE GOT SOME REAL SPECIFIC IDEAS ON HOW TO PLAY HIM.
DITIONS
WELL, SHAKESPEARE'S CHARACTERS HAVE BEEN INTERPRETED IN A VARIETY OF WAYS...
AUDITIONS
... BUT NONE USING A RAINBOW WIG.
KAZOO, PLEASE.
DITIONS

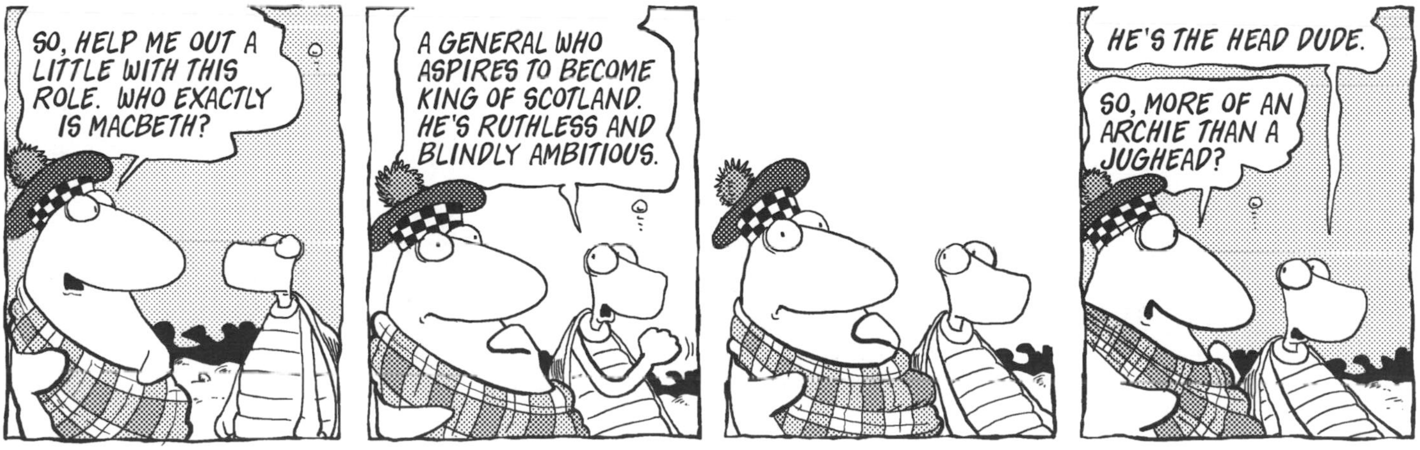
SO, HELP ME OUT A LITTLE WITH THIS ROLE. WHO EXACTLY IS MACBETH?
A GENERAL WHO ASPIRES TO BECOME KING OF SCOTLAND. HE'S RUTHLESS AND BLINDLY AMBITIOUS.
HE'S THE HEAD DUDE.
SO, MORE OF AN ARCHIE THAN A JUGHEAD?

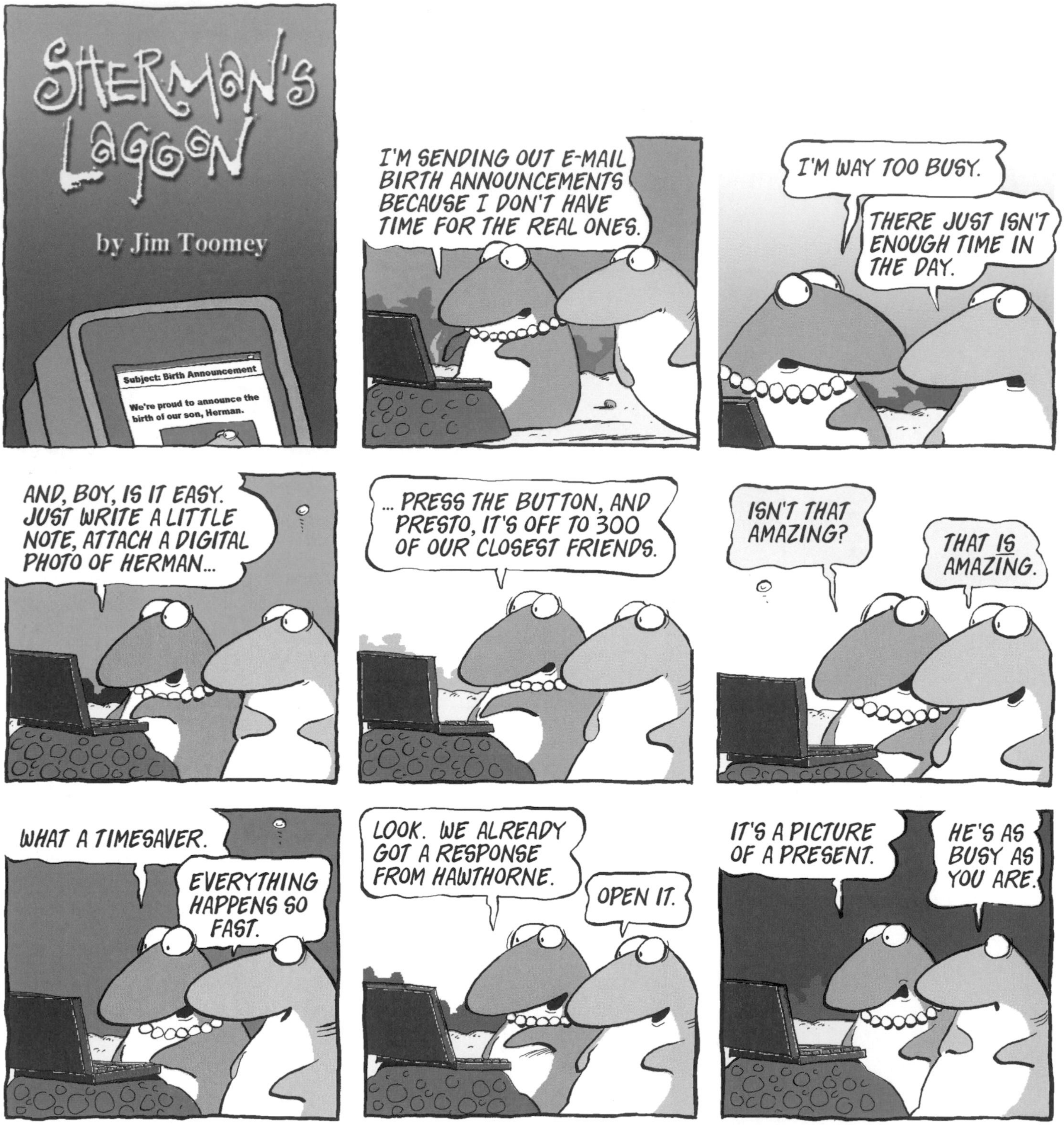

SHERMAN'S LAGOON
by Jim Toomey
Subject: Birth Announcement
We're proud to announce the birth of our son, Herman.
I'M SENDING OUT E-MAIL BIRTH ANNOUNCEMENTS BECAUSE I DON'T HAVE TIME FOR THE REAL ONES.
I'M WAY TOO BUSY.
THERE JUST ISN'T ENOUGH TIME IN THE DAY.
AND, BOY, IS IT EASY. JUST WRITE A LITTLE NOTE, ATTACH A DIGITAL PHOTO OF HERMAN...
... PRESS THE BUTTON, AND PRESTO, IT'S OFF TO 300 OF OUR CLOSEST FRIENDS.
ISN'T THAT AMAZING?
THAT IS AMAZING.
WHAT A TIMESAVER.
EVERYTHING HAPPENS SO FAST.
LOOK. WE ALREADY GOT A RESPONSE FROM HAWTHORNE.
OPEN IT.
IT'S A PICTURE OF A PRESENT.
HE'S AS BUSY AS YOU ARE.

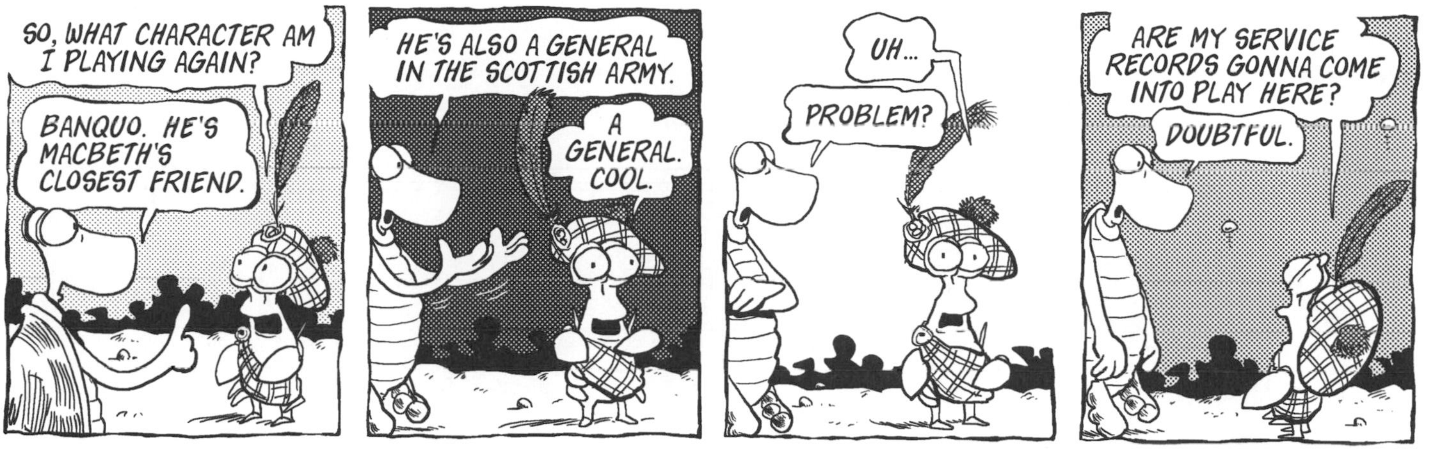
SO, WHAT CHARACTER AM I PLAYING AGAIN?
BANQUO. HE'S MACBETH'S CLOSEST FRIEND.
HE'S ALSO A GENERAL IN THE SCOTTISH ARMY.
A GENERAL. COOL.
UH...
PROBLEM?
ARE MY SERVICE RECORDS GONNA COME INTO PLAY HERE?
DOUBTFUL.

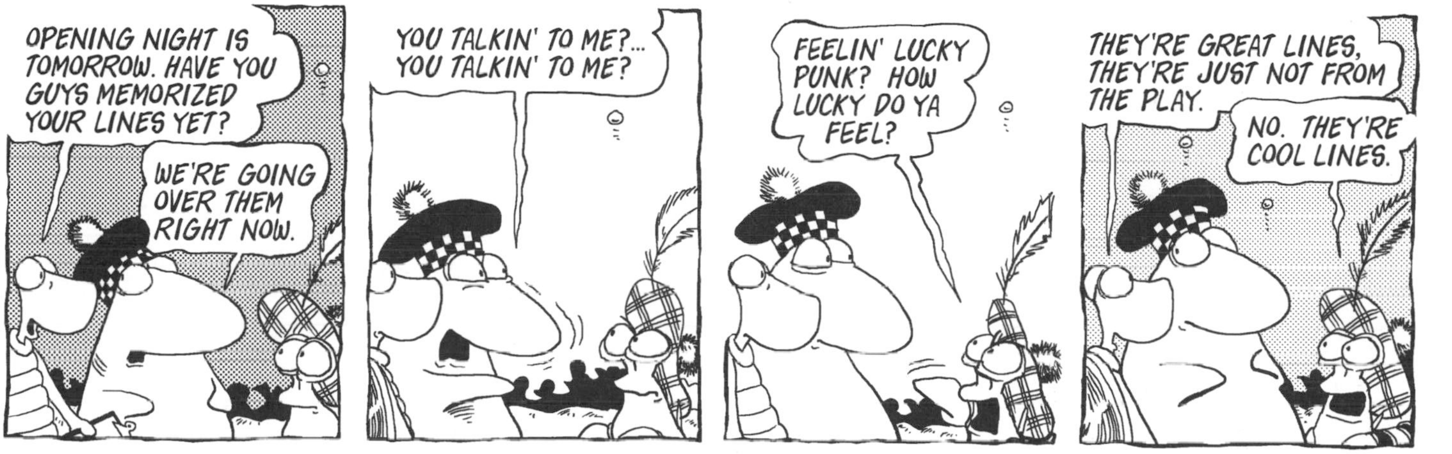
OPENING NIGHT IS TOMORROW. HAVE YOU GUYS MEMORIZED YOUR LINES YET?
WE'RE GOING OVER THEM RIGHT NOW.
YOU TALKIN' TO ME?... YOU TALKIN' TO ME?
FEELIN' LUCKY PUNK? HOW LUCKY DO YA FEEL?
THEY'RE GREAT LINES, THEY'RE JUST NOT FROM THE PLAY.
NO. THEY'RE COOL LINES.

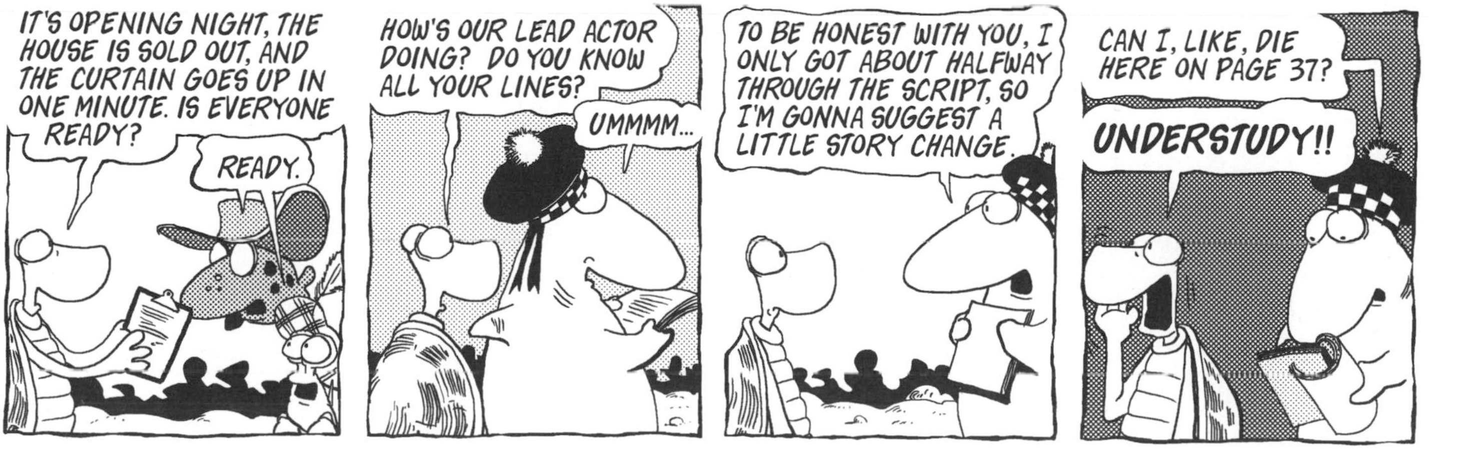
IT'S OPENING NIGHT, THE HOUSE IS SOLD OUT, AND THE CURTAIN GOES UP IN ONE MINUTE. IS EVERYONE READY?
READY.
HOW'S OUR LEAD ACTOR DOING? DO YOU KNOW ALL YOUR LINES?
UMMMM...
TO BE HONEST WITH YOU, I ONLY GOT ABOUT HALFWAY THROUGH THE SCRIPT, SO I'M GONNA SUGGEST A LITTLE STORY CHANGE.
CAN I, LIKE, DIE HERE ON PAGE 37?
UNDERSTUDY!!

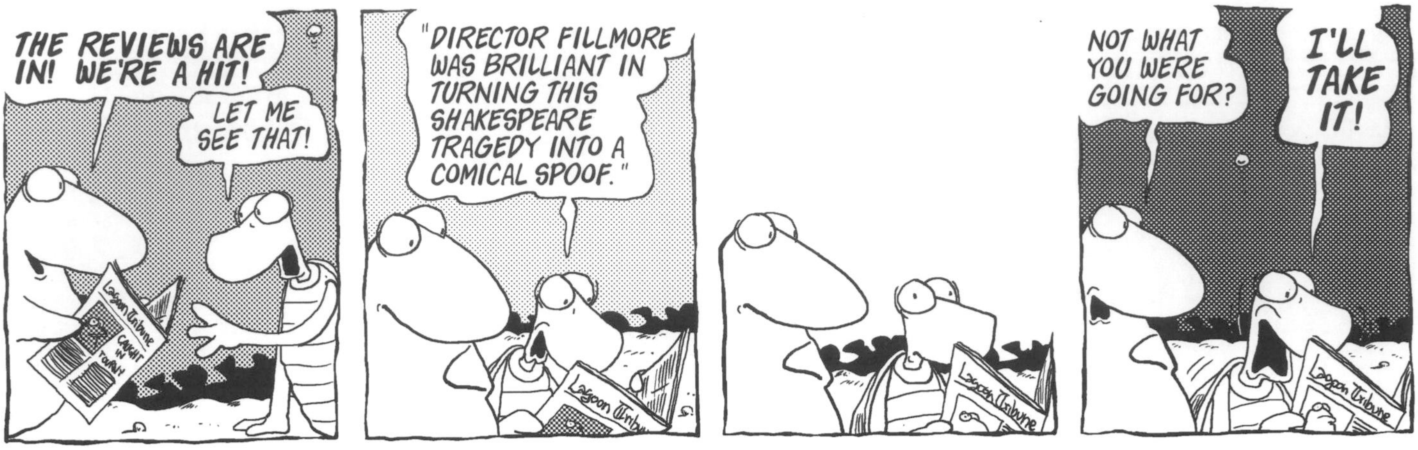
THE REVIEWS ARE IN! WE'RE A HIT!
LET ME SEE THAT!
"DIRECTOR FILLMORE WAS BRILLIANT IN TURNING THIS SHAKESPEARE TRAGEDY INTO A COMICAL SPOOF."
NOT WHAT YOU WERE GOING FOR?
I'LL TAKE IT!

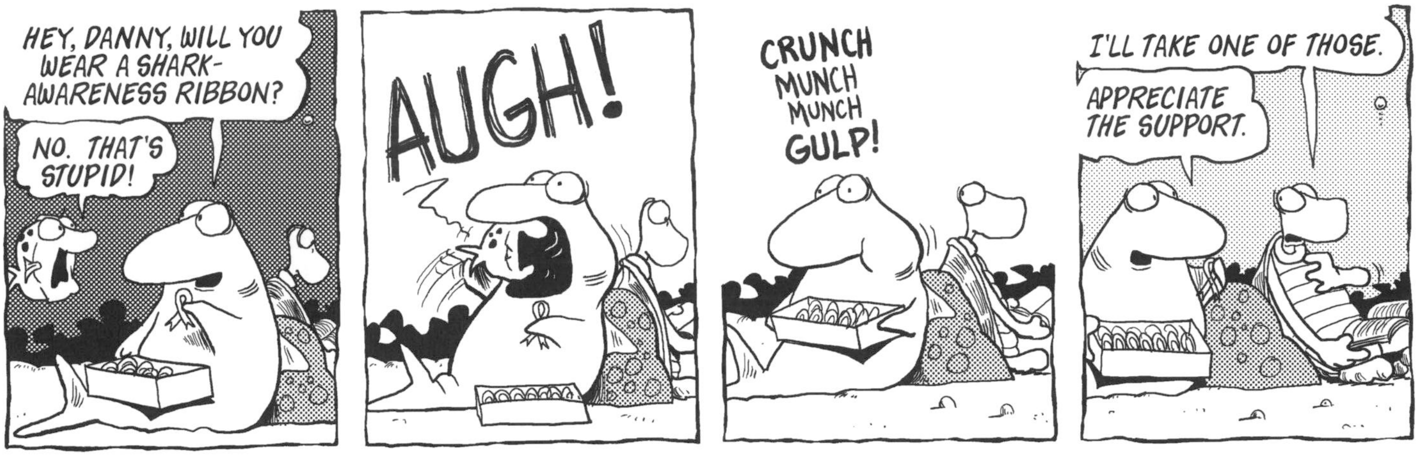
HEY, DANNY, WILL YOU WEAR A SHARK-AWARENESS RIBBON?
NO. THAT'S STUPID!
AUGH!
CRUNCH MUNCH MUNCH GULP!
I'LL TAKE ONE OF THOSE.
APPRECIATE THE SUPPORT.

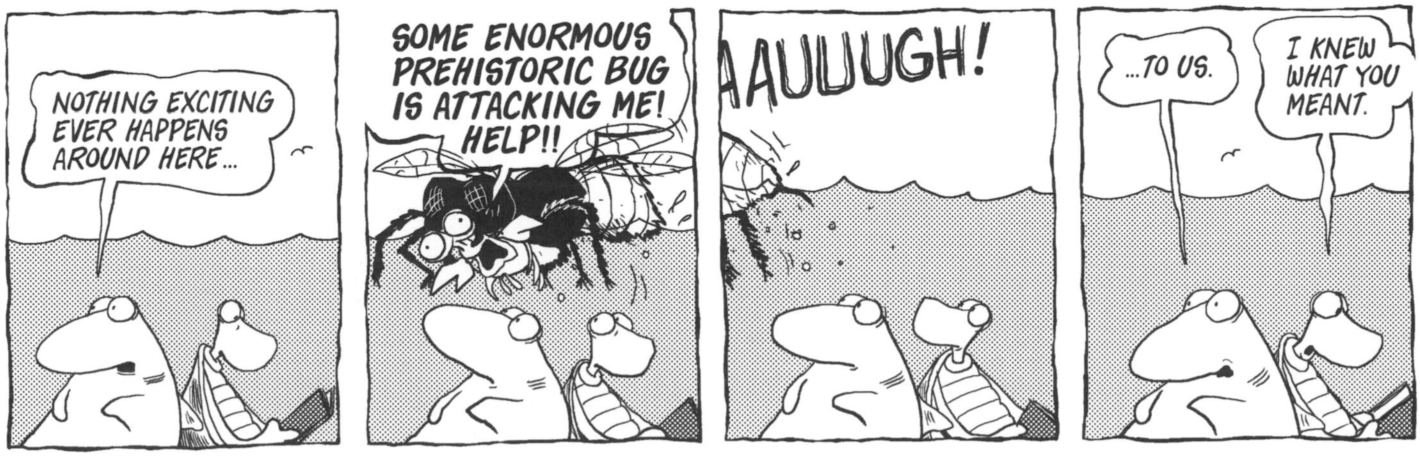
NOTHING EXCITING EVER HAPPENS AROUND HERE...
SOME ENORMOUS PREHISTORIC BUG IS ATTACKING ME! HELP!!
AAUUUUGH!
...TO US.
I KNEW WHAT YOU MEANT.

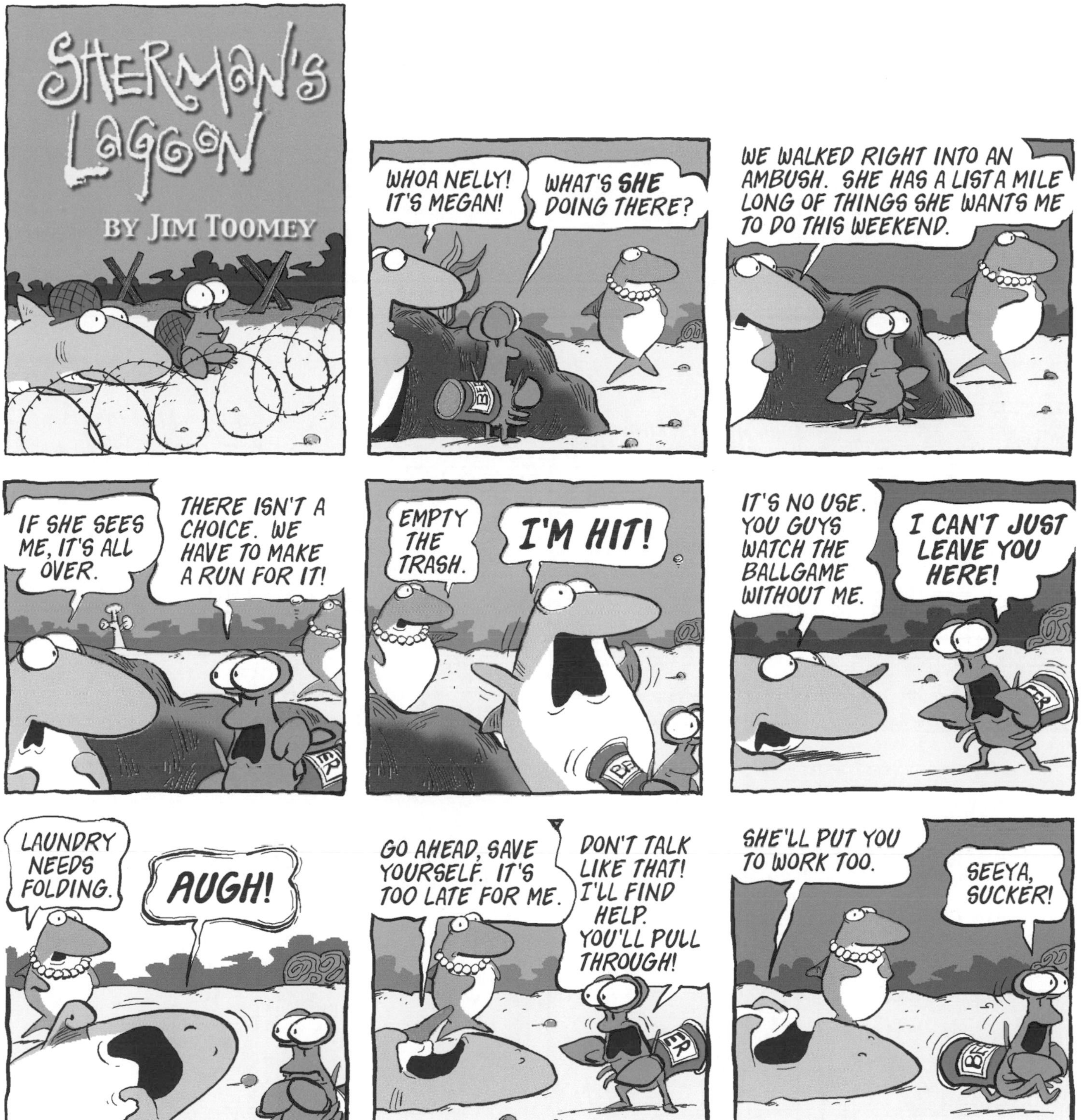

SHERMAN'S LAGOON
BY JIM TOOMEY
WHOA NELLY! IT'S MEGAN!
WHAT'S SHE DOING THERE?
WE WALKED RIGHT INTO AN AMBUSH. SHE HAS A LIST A MILE LONG OF THINGS SHE WANTS ME TO DO THIS WEEKEND.
IF SHE SEES ME, IT'S ALL OVER.
THERE ISN'T A CHOICE. WE HAVE TO MAKE A RUN FOR IT!
EMPTY THE TRASH.
I'M HIT!
IT'S NO USE. YOU GUYS WATCH THE BALLGAME WITHOUT ME.
I CAN'T JUST LEAVE YOU HERE!
LAUNDRY NEEDS FOLDING.
AUGH!
GO AHEAD, SAVE YOURSELF. IT'S TOO LATE FOR ME.
DON'T TALK LIKE THAT! I'LL FIND HELP. YOU'LL PULL THROUGH!
SHE'LL PUT YOU TO WORK TOO.
SEEYA, SUCKER!

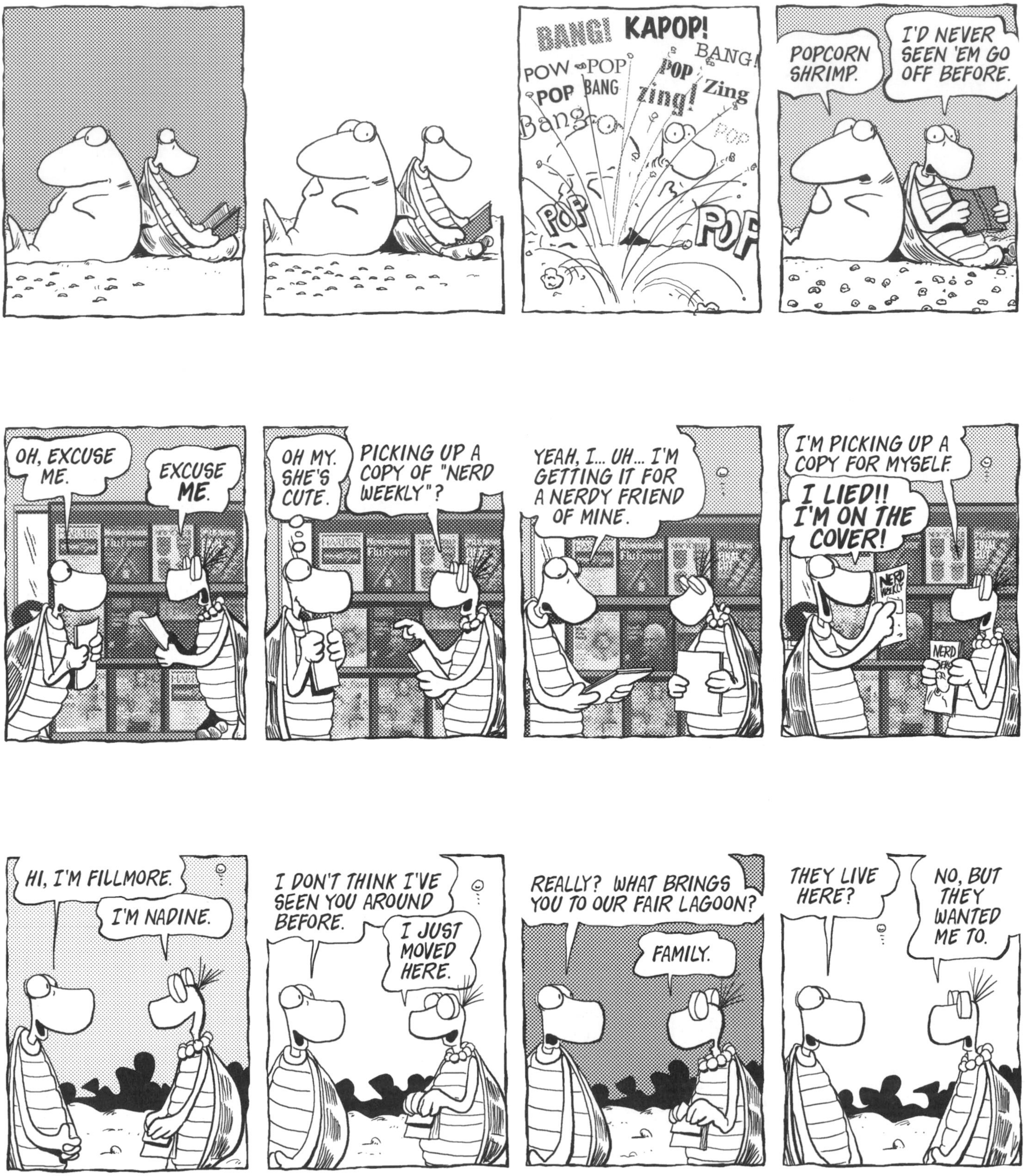
BANG! KAPOP!
POW POP BANG!
POP BANG POP Zing
zing! Zing
Bang POP
POP POP
POPCORN SHRIMP.
I'D NEVER SEEN 'EM GO OFF BEFORE.
OH, EXCUSE ME.
EXCUSE ME.
OH MY. SHE'S CUTE.
PICKING UP A COPY OF "NERD WEEKLY"?
YEAH, I... UH... I'M GETTING IT FOR A NERDY FRIEND OF MINE.
I'M PICKING UP A COPY FOR MYSELF.
I LIED!! I'M ON THE COVER!
NERD WEEKLY
NERD
HI, I'M FILLMORE.
I'M NADINE.
I DON'T THINK I'VE SEEN YOU AROUND BEFORE.
I JUST MOVED HERE.
REALLY? WHAT BRINGS YOU TO OUR FAIR LAGOON?
FAMILY.
THEY LIVE HERE?
NO, BUT THEY WANTED ME TO.

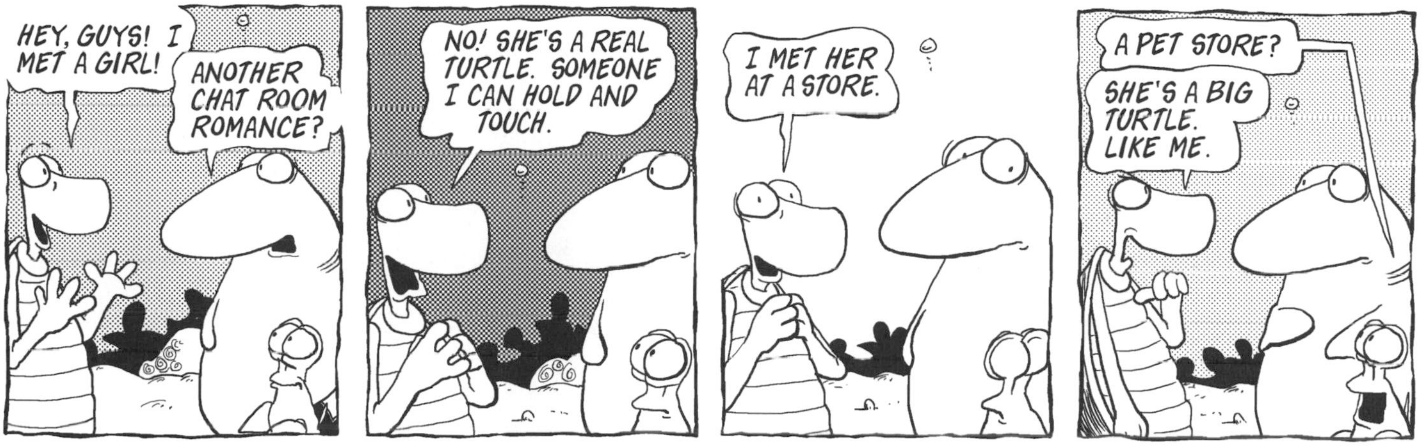
HEY, GUYS! I MET A GIRL!
ANOTHER CHAT ROOM ROMANCE?
NO! SHE'S A REAL TURTLE. SOMEONE I CAN HOLD AND TOUCH.
I MET HER AT A STORE.
A PET STORE?
SHE'S A BIG TURTLE. LIKE ME.

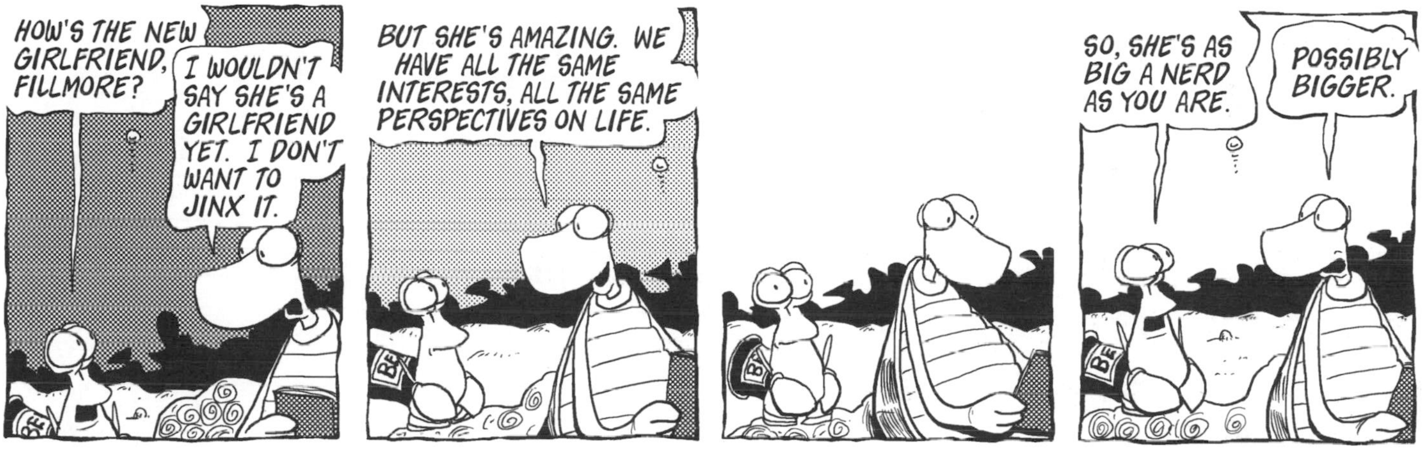
HOW'S THE NEW GIRLFRIEND, FILLMORE?
I WOULDN'T SAY SHE'S A GIRLFRIEND YET. I DON'T WANT TO JINX IT.
BUT SHE'S AMAZING. WE HAVE ALL THE SAME INTERESTS, ALL THE SAME PERSPECTIVES ON LIFE.
SO, SHE'S AS BIG A NERD AS YOU ARE.
POSSIBLY BIGGER.

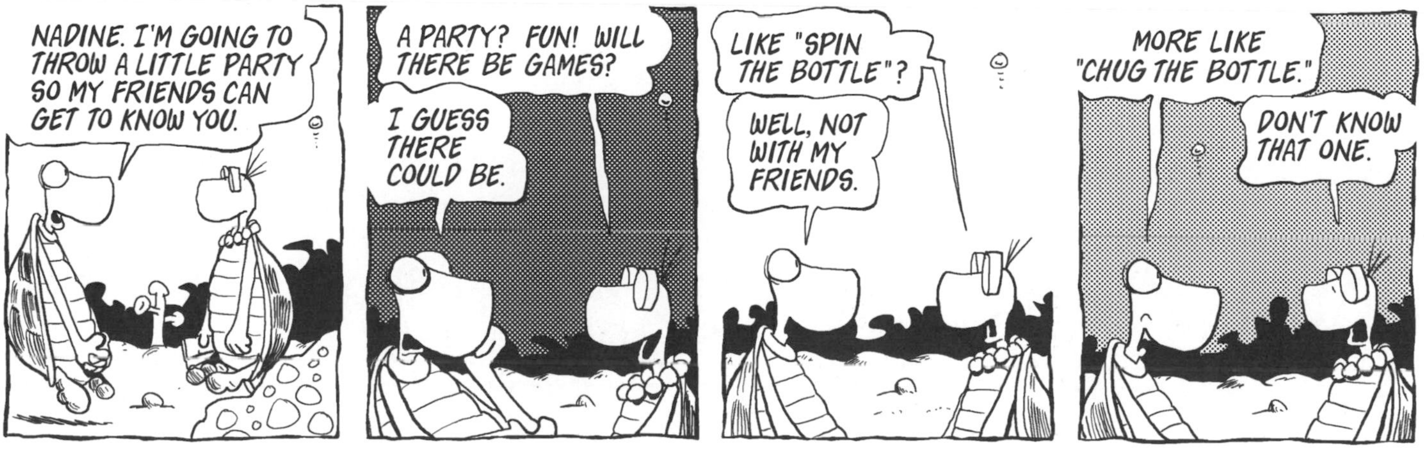
NADINE. I'M GOING TO THROW A LITTLE PARTY SO MY FRIENDS CAN GET TO KNOW YOU.
A PARTY? FUN! WILL THERE BE GAMES?
I GUESS THERE COULD BE.
LIKE "SPIN THE BOTTLE"?
WELL, NOT WITH MY FRIENDS.
MORE LIKE "CHUG THE BOTTLE."
DON'T KNOW THAT ONE.

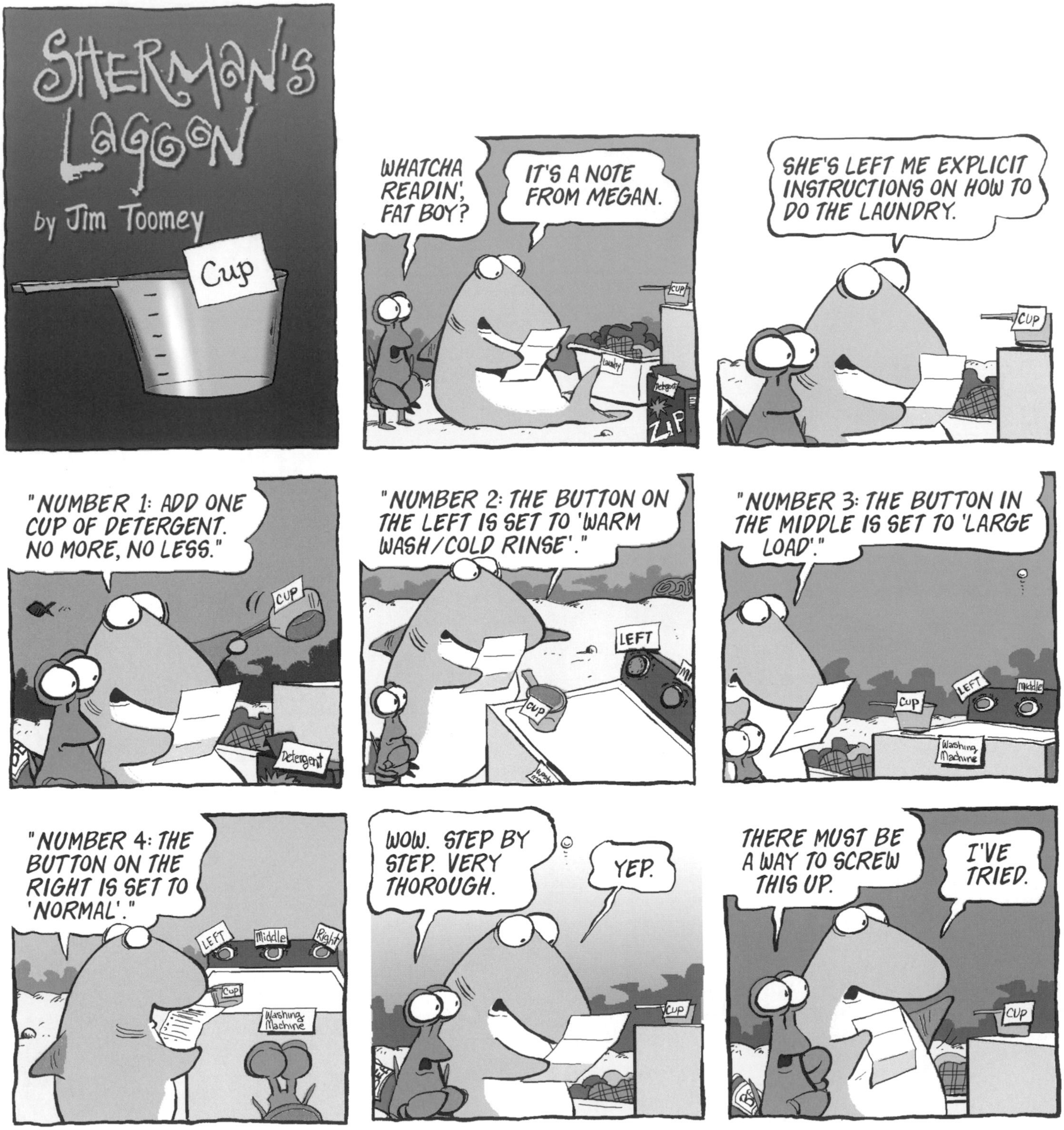
SHERMAN'S LAGOON
by Jim Toomey
Cup
WHATCHA READIN', FAT BOY?
IT'S A NOTE FROM MEGAN.
SHE'S LEFT ME EXPLICIT INSTRUCTIONS ON HOW TO DO THE LAUNDRY.
"NUMBER 1: ADD ONE CUP OF DETERGENT. NO MORE, NO LESS."
"NUMBER 2: THE BUTTON ON THE LEFT IS SET TO 'WARM WASH/COLD RINSE'."
"NUMBER 3: THE BUTTON IN THE MIDDLE IS SET TO 'LARGE LOAD'."
"NUMBER 4: THE BUTTON ON THE RIGHT IS SET TO 'NORMAL'."
WOW. STEP BY STEP. VERY THOROUGH.
YEP.
THERE MUST BE A WAY TO SCREW THIS UP.
I'VE TRIED.

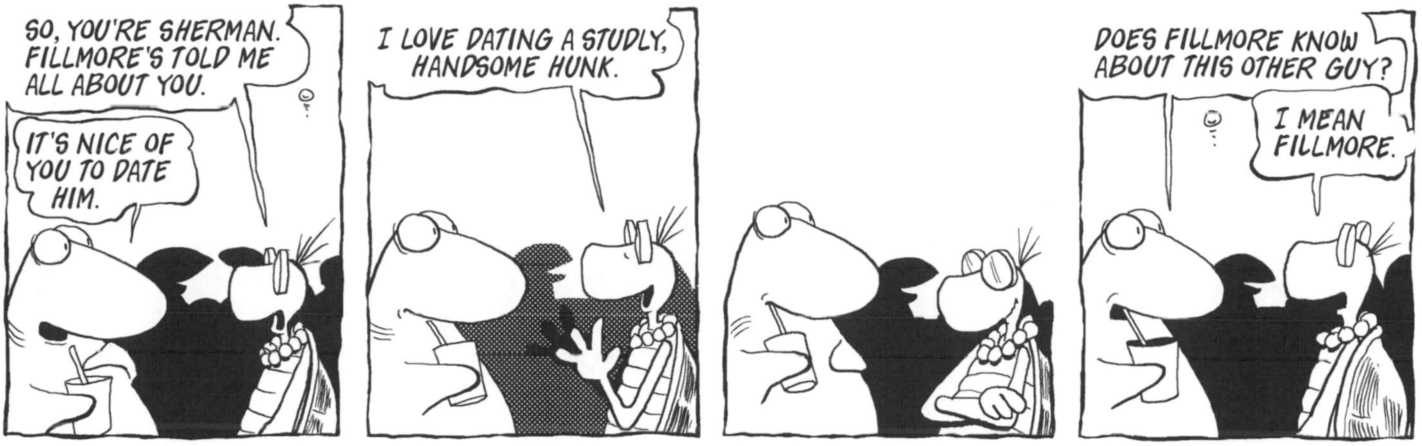
SO, YOU'RE SHERMAN. FILLMORE'S TOLD ME ALL ABOUT YOU.
IT'S NICE OF YOU TO DATE HIM.
I LOVE DATING A STUDLY, HANDSOME HUNK.
DOES FILLMORE KNOW ABOUT THIS OTHER GUY?
I MEAN FILLMORE.

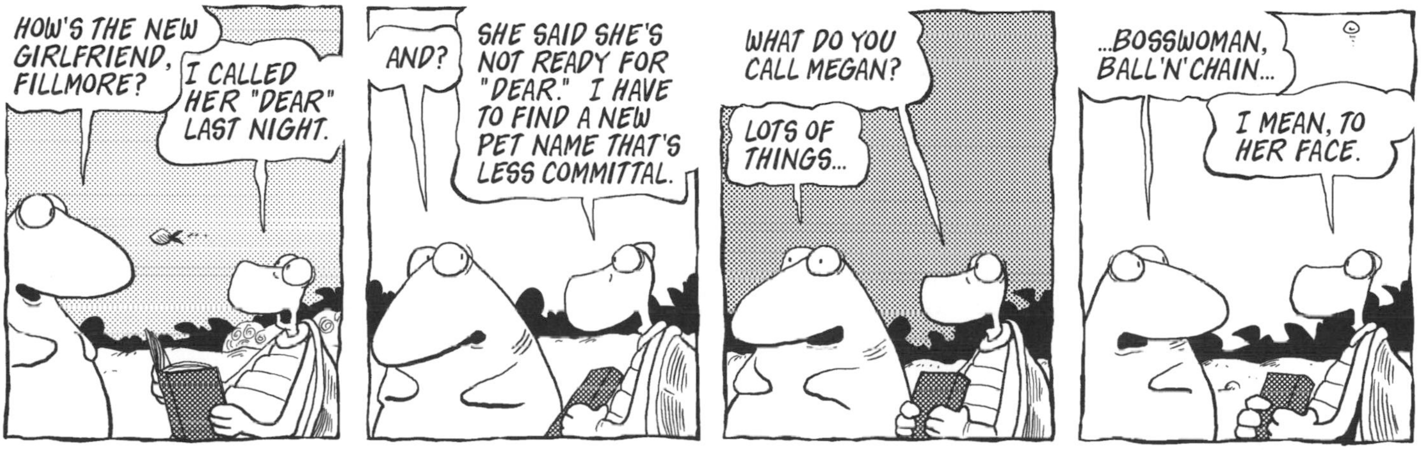
HOW'S THE NEW GIRLFRIEND, FILLMORE?
I CALLED HER "DEAR" LAST NIGHT.
AND?
SHE SAID SHE'S NOT READY FOR "DEAR." I HAVE TO FIND A NEW PET NAME THAT'S LESS COMMITTAL.
WHAT DO YOU CALL MEGAN?
LOTS OF THINGS...
...BOSSWOMAN, BALL'N'CHAIN...
I MEAN, TO HER FACE.

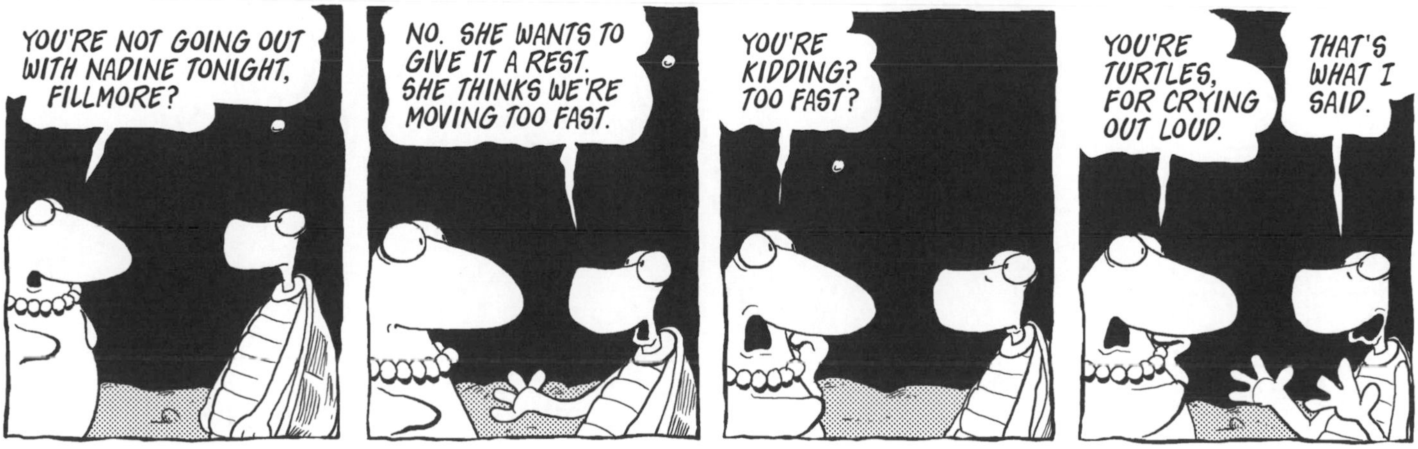
YOU'RE NOT GOING OUT WITH NADINE TONIGHT, FILLMORE?
NO. SHE WANTS TO GIVE IT A REST. SHE THINKS WE'RE MOVING TOO FAST.
YOU'RE KIDDING? TOO FAST?
YOU'RE TURTLES, FOR CRYING OUT LOUD.
THAT'S WHAT I SAID.

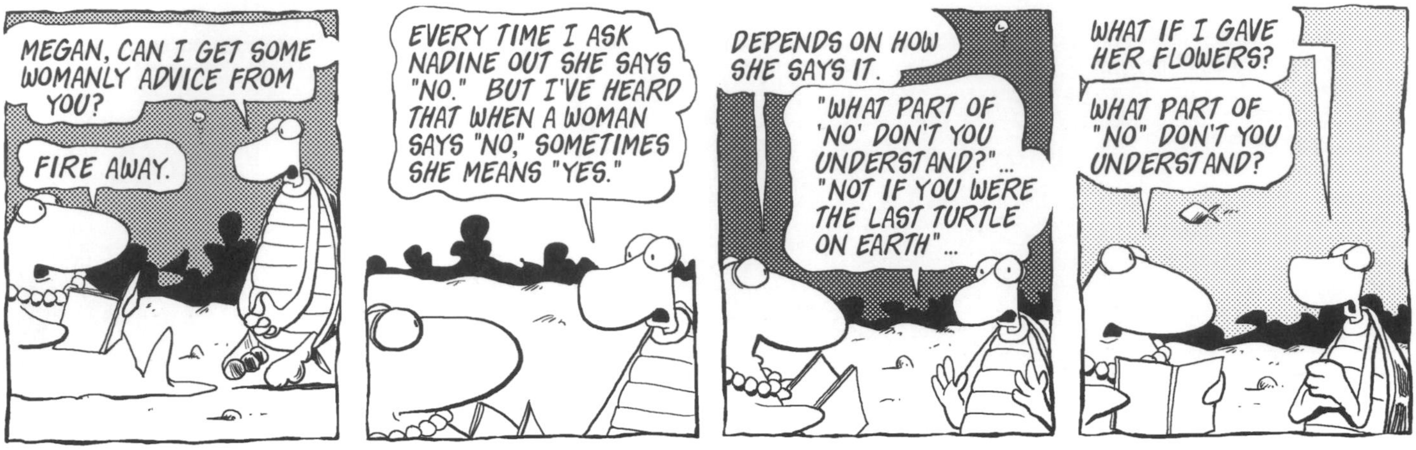
MEGAN, CAN I GET SOME WOMANLY ADVICE FROM YOU?
FIRE AWAY.
EVERY TIME I ASK NADINE OUT SHE SAYS "NO." BUT I'VE HEARD THAT WHEN A WOMAN SAYS "NO," SOMETIMES SHE MEANS "YES."
DEPENDS ON HOW SHE SAYS IT.
"WHAT PART OF 'NO' DON'T YOU UNDERSTAND?"... "NOT IF YOU WERE THE LAST TURTLE ON EARTH"...
WHAT IF I GAVE HER FLOWERS?
WHAT PART OF "NO" DON'T YOU UNDERSTAND?

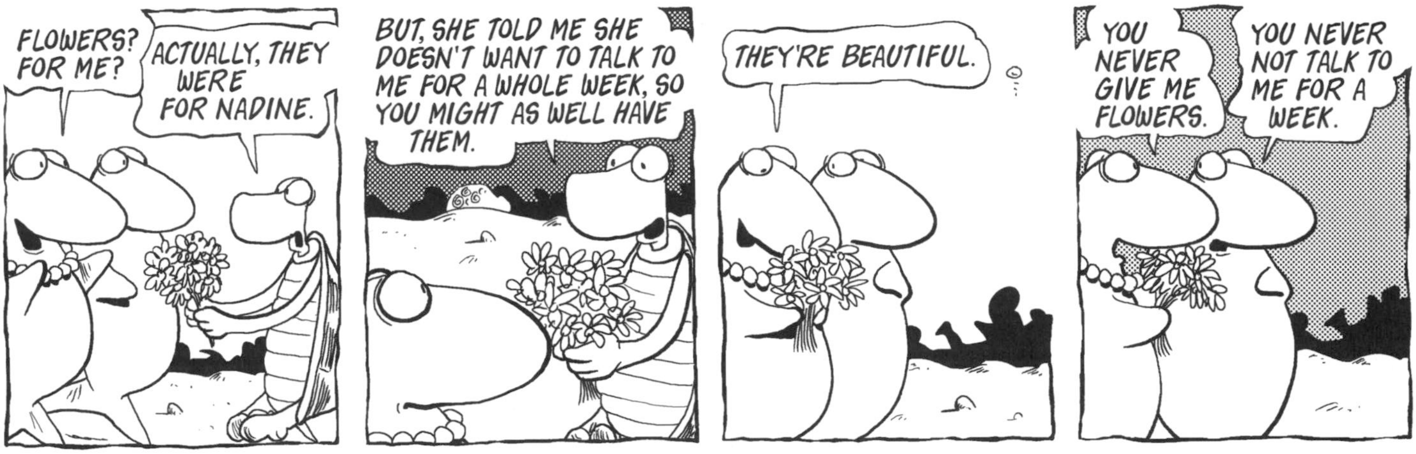
FLOWERS? FOR ME?
ACTUALLY, THEY WERE FOR NADINE.
BUT, SHE TOLD ME SHE DOESN'T WANT TO TALK TO ME FOR A WHOLE WEEK, SO YOU MIGHT AS WELL HAVE THEM.
THEY'RE BEAUTIFUL.
YOU NEVER GIVE ME FLOWERS.
YOU NEVER NOT TALK TO ME FOR A WEEK.

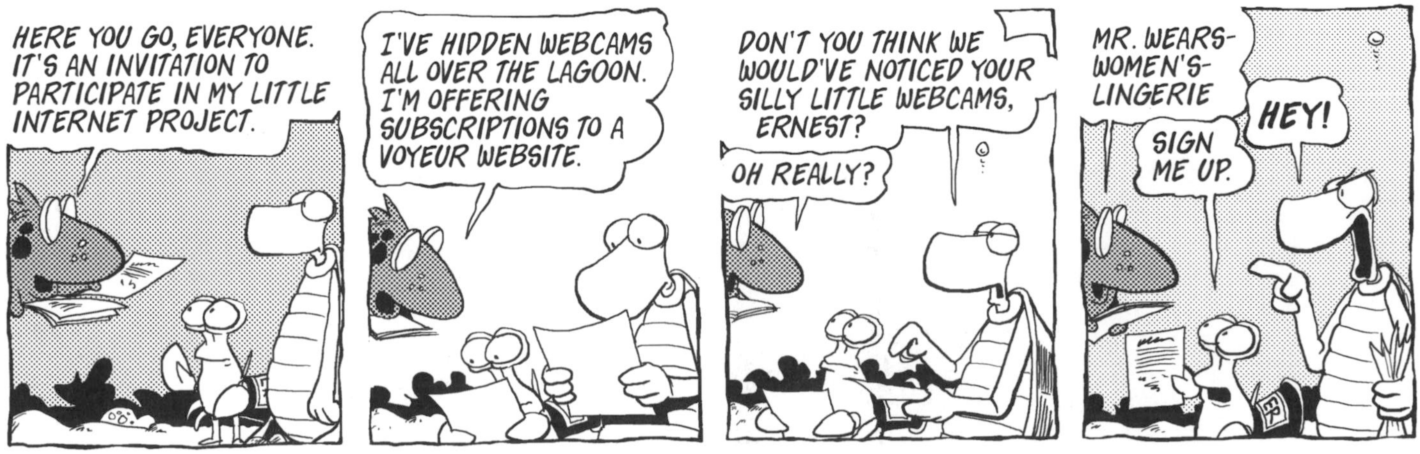
HERE YOU GO, EVERYONE. IT'S AN INVITATION TO PARTICIPATE IN MY LITTLE INTERNET PROJECT.
I'VE HIDDEN WEBCAMS ALL OVER THE LAGOON. I'M OFFERING SUBSCRIPTIONS TO A VOYEUR WEBSITE.
DON'T YOU THINK WE WOULD'VE NOTICED YOUR SILLY LITTLE WEBCAMS, ERNEST?
OH REALLY?
MR. WEARS-WOMEN'S-LINGERIE
SIGN ME UP.
HEY!

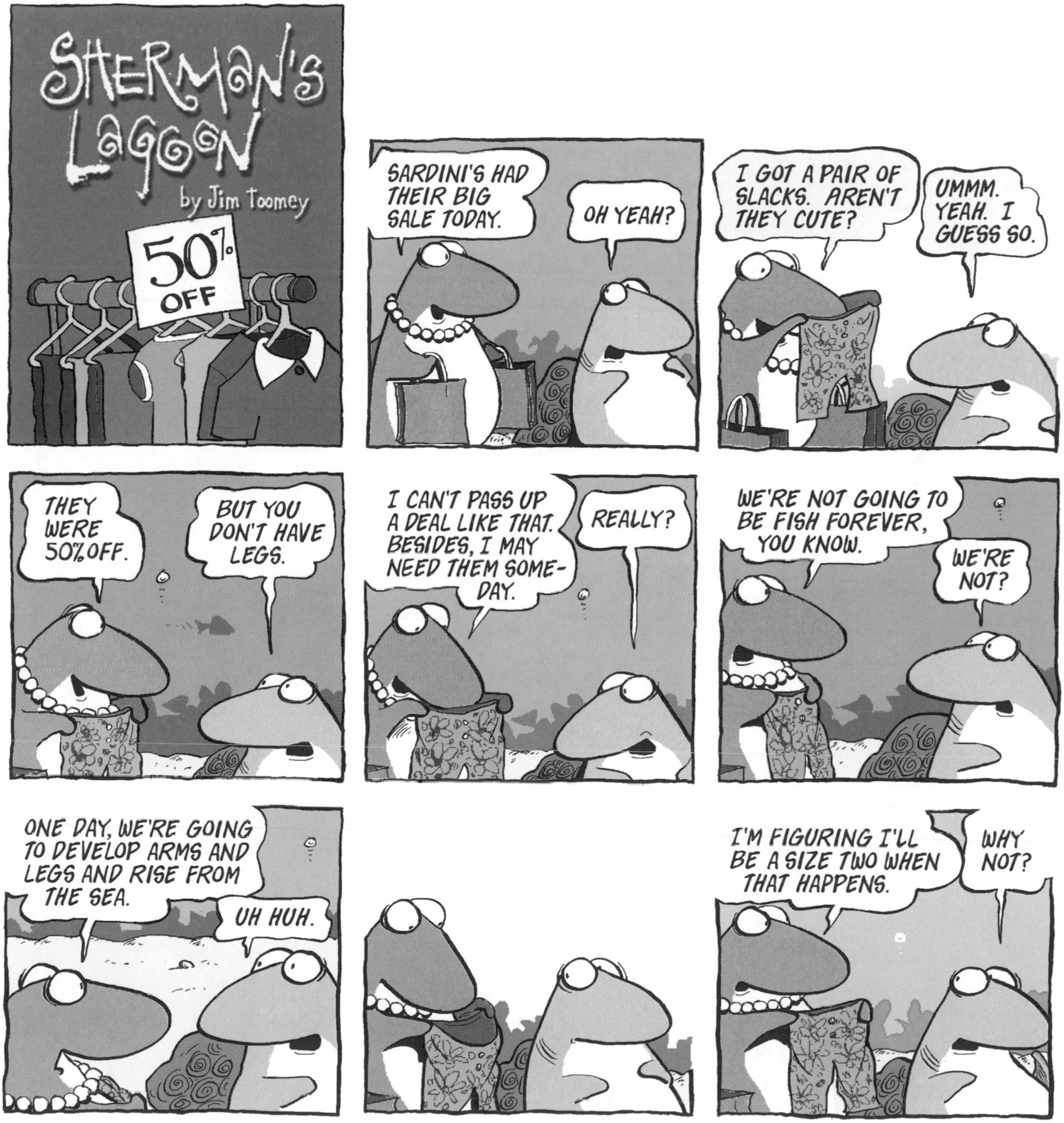
SHERMAN'S LAGOON
by Jim Toomey
50% OFF
SARDINI'S HAD THEIR BIG SALE TODAY.
OH YEAH?
I GOT A PAIR OF SLACKS. AREN'T THEY CUTE?
UMMM. YEAH. I GUESS SO.
THEY WERE 50% OFF.
BUT YOU DON'T HAVE LEGS.
I CAN'T PASS UP A DEAL LIKE THAT. BESIDES, I MAY NEED THEM SOME-DAY.
REALLY?
WE'RE NOT GOING TO BE FISH FOREVER, YOU KNOW.
WE'RE NOT?
ONE DAY, WE'RE GOING TO DEVELOP ARMS AND LEGS AND RISE FROM THE SEA.
UH HUH.
I'M FIGURING I'LL BE A SIZE TWO WHEN THAT HAPPENS.
WHY NOT?

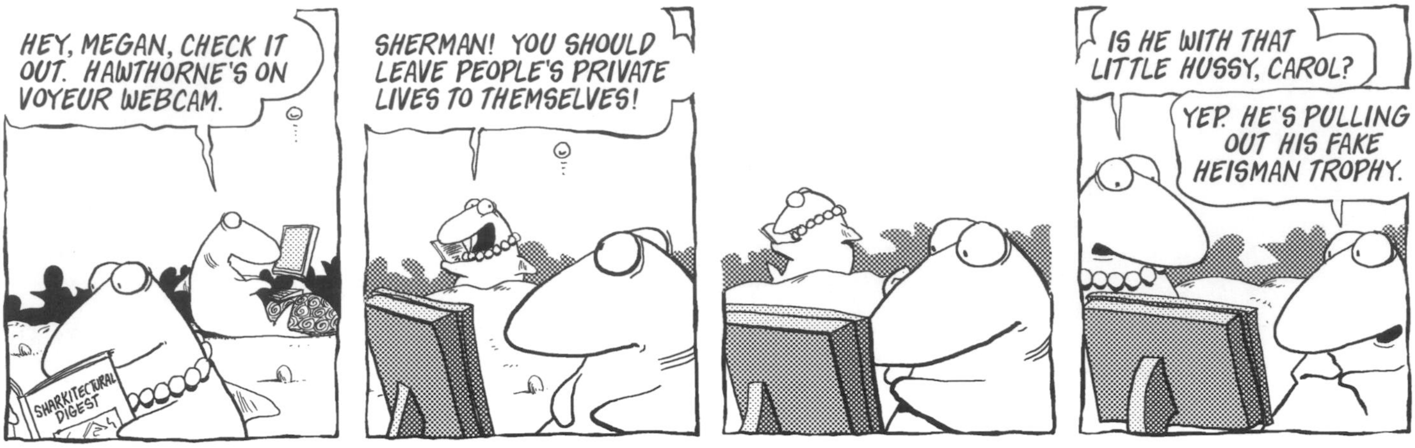
HEY, MEGAN, CHECK IT OUT. HAWTHORNE'S ON VOYEUR WEBCAM.
SHARKITECTURAL DIGEST
SHERMAN! YOU SHOULD LEAVE PEOPLE'S PRIVATE LIVES TO THEMSELVES!
IS HE WITH THAT LITTLE HUSSY, CAROL?
YEP. HE'S PULLING OUT HIS FAKE HEISMAN TROPHY.

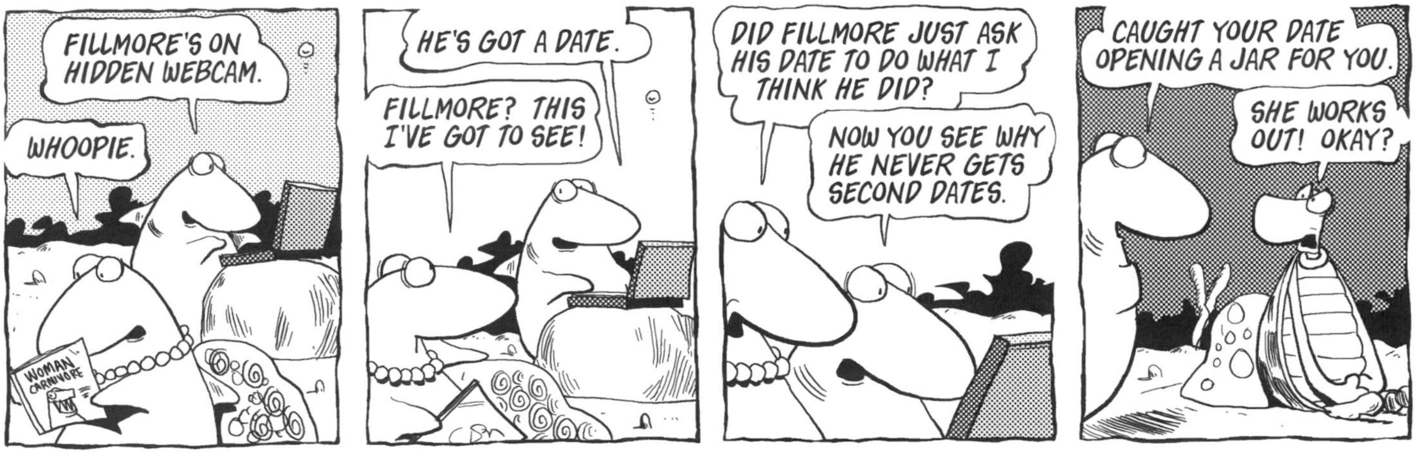
FILLMORE'S ON HIDDEN WEBCAM.
WHOOPIE.
WOMAN CARNIVORE
HE'S GOT A DATE.
FILLMORE? THIS I'VE GOT TO SEE!
DID FILLMORE JUST ASK HIS DATE TO DO WHAT I THINK HE DID?
NOW YOU SEE WHY HE NEVER GETS SECOND DATES.
CAUGHT YOUR DATE OPENING A JAR FOR YOU.
SHE WORKS OUT! OKAY?

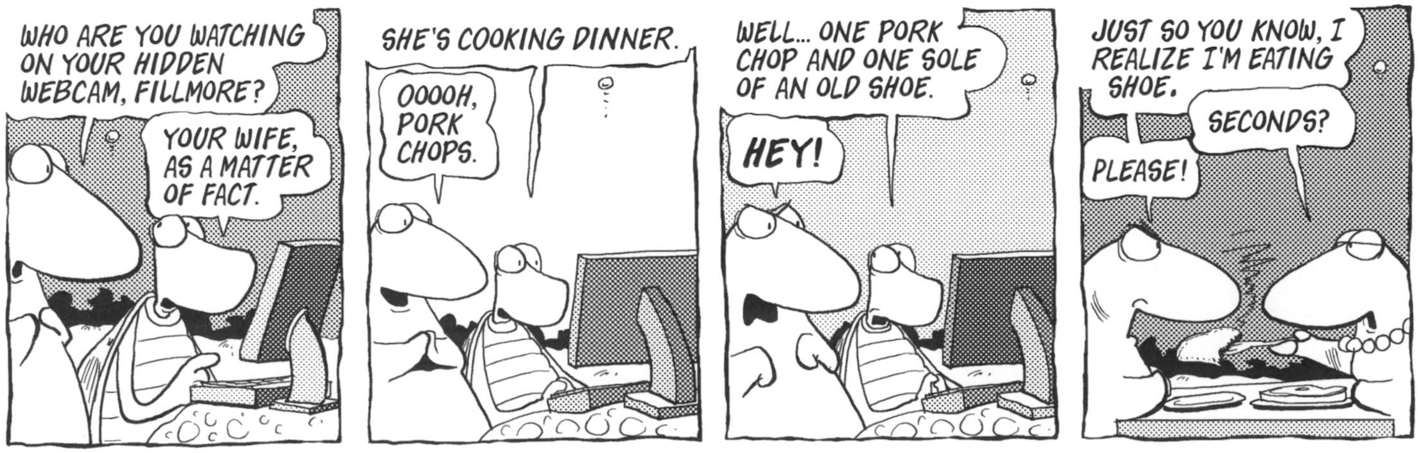
WHO ARE YOU WATCHING ON YOUR HIDDEN WEBCAM, FILLMORE?
YOUR WIFE, AS A MATTER OF FACT.
SHE'S COOKING DINNER.
OOOOH, PORK CHOPS.
WELL... ONE PORK CHOP AND ONE SOLE OF AN OLD SHOE.
HEY!
JUST SO YOU KNOW, I REALIZE I'M EATING SHOE.
SECONDS?
PLEASE!

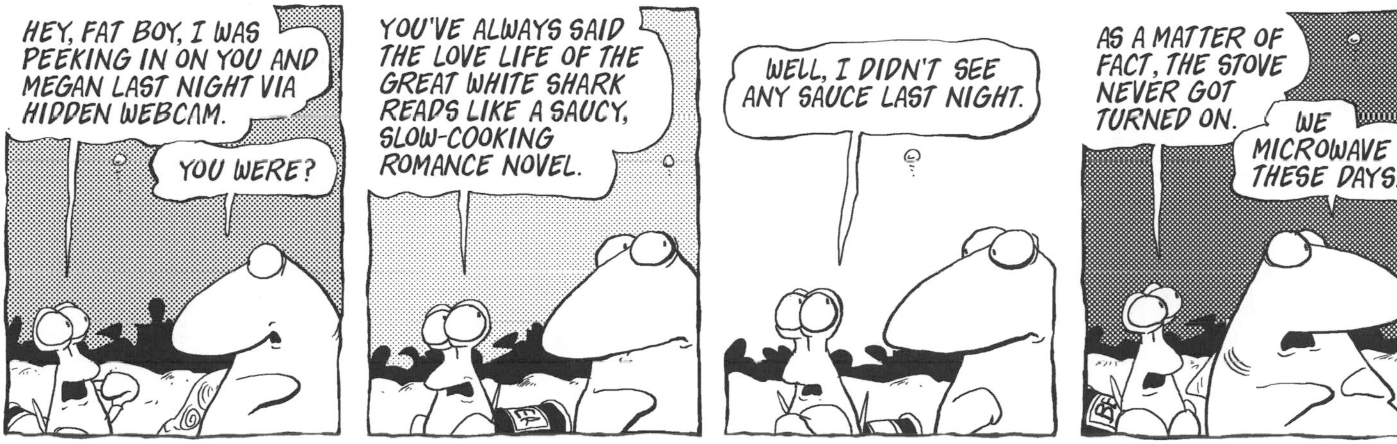
HEY, FAT BOY, I WAS PEEKING IN ON YOU AND MEGAN LAST NIGHT VIA HIDDEN WEBCAM.
YOU WERE?
YOU'VE ALWAYS SAID THE LOVE LIFE OF THE GREAT WHITE SHARK READS LIKE A SAUCY, SLOW-COOKING ROMANCE NOVEL.
WELL, I DIDN'T SEE ANY SAUCE LAST NIGHT.
AS A MATTER OF FACT, THE STOVE NEVER GOT TURNED ON.
WE MICROWAVE THESE DAYS.

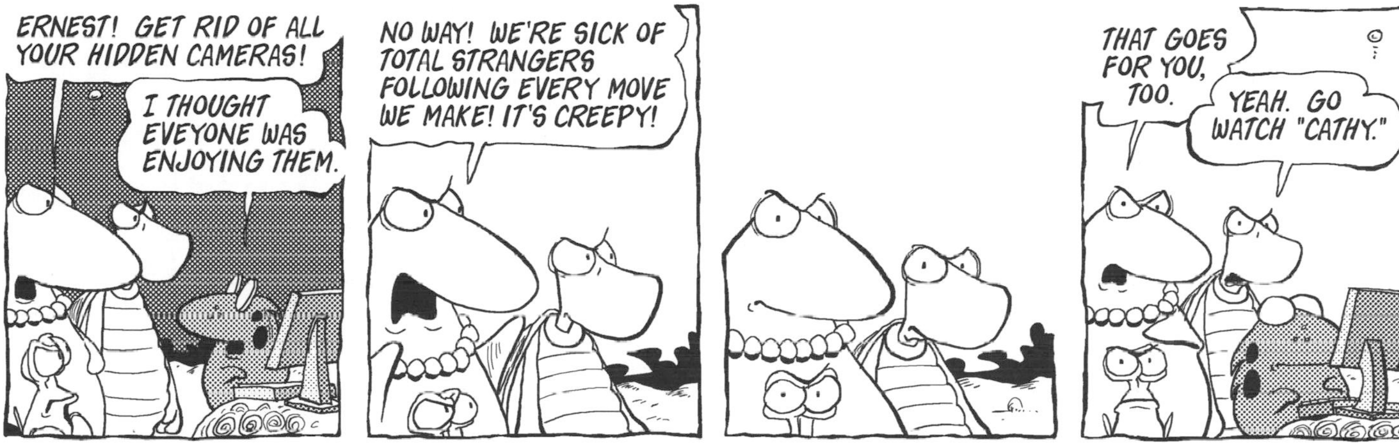
ERNEST! GET RID OF ALL YOUR HIDDEN CAMERAS!
I THOUGHT EVEYONE WAS ENJOYING THEM.
NO WAY! WE'RE SICK OF TOTAL STRANGERS FOLLOWING EVERY MOVE WE MAKE! IT'S CREEPY!
THAT GOES FOR YOU, TOO.
YEAH. GO WATCH "CATHY."

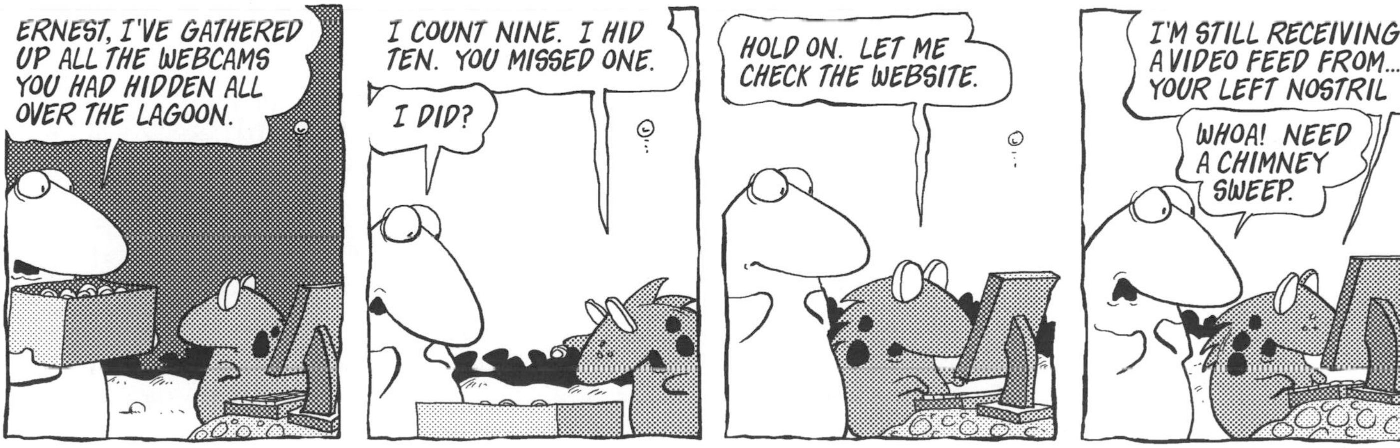
ERNEST, I'VE GATHERED UP ALL THE WEBCAMS YOU HAD HIDDEN ALL OVER THE LAGOON.
I COUNT NINE. I HID TEN. YOU MISSED ONE.
I DID?
HOLD ON. LET ME CHECK THE WEBSITE.
I'M STILL RECEIVING A VIDEO FEED FROM... YOUR LEFT NOSTRIL
WHOA! NEED A CHIMNEY SWEEP.

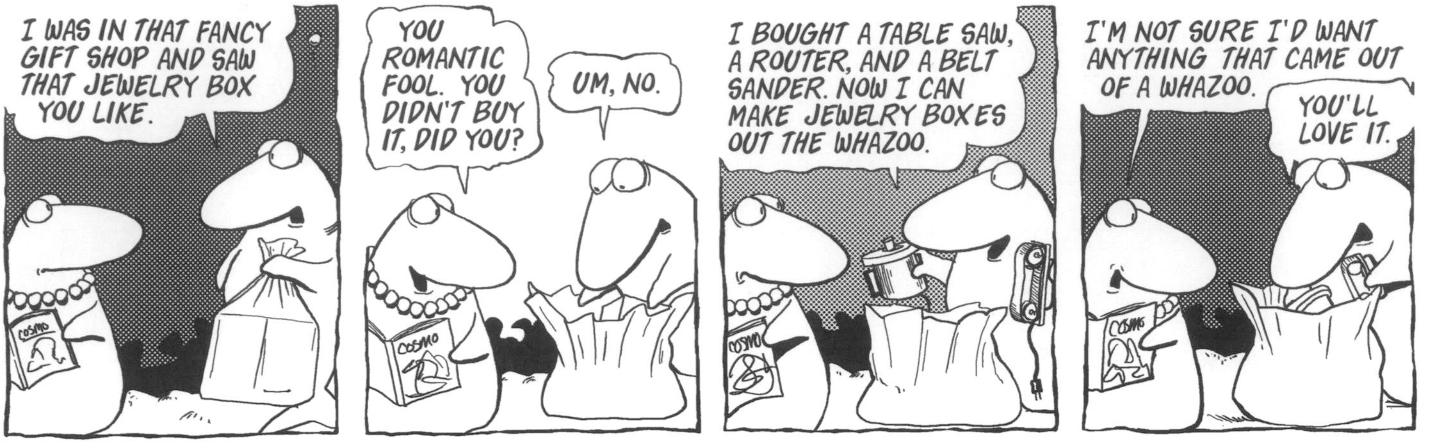
I WAS IN THAT FANCY GIFT SHOP AND SAW THAT JEWELRY BOX YOU LIKE.
COSMO
YOU ROMANTIC FOOL. YOU DIDN'T BUY IT, DID YOU?
UM, NO.
I BOUGHT A TABLE SAW, A ROUTER, AND A BELT SANDER. NOW I CAN MAKE JEWELRY BOXES OUT THE WHAZOO.
I'M NOT SURE I'D WANT ANYTHING THAT CAME OUT OF A WHAZOO.
YOU'LL LOVE IT.

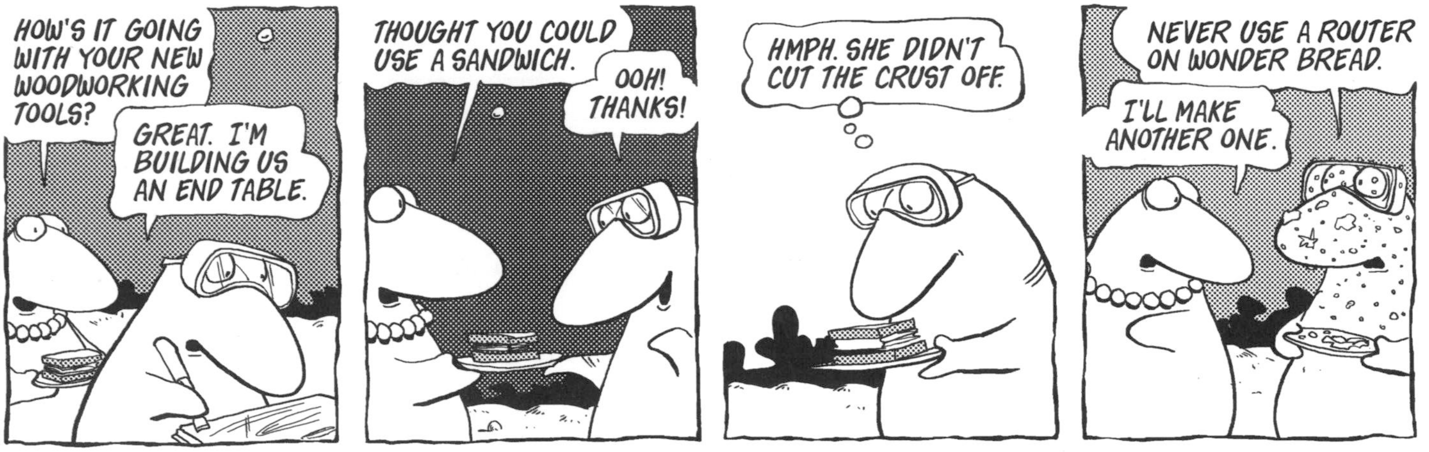
HOW'S IT GOING WITH YOUR NEW WOODWORKING TOOLS?
GREAT. I'M BUILDING US AN END TABLE.
THOUGHT YOU COULD USE A SANDWICH.
OOH! THANKS!
HMPH. SHE DIDN'T CUT THE CRUST OFF.
NEVER USE A ROUTER ON WONDER BREAD.
I'LL MAKE ANOTHER ONE.

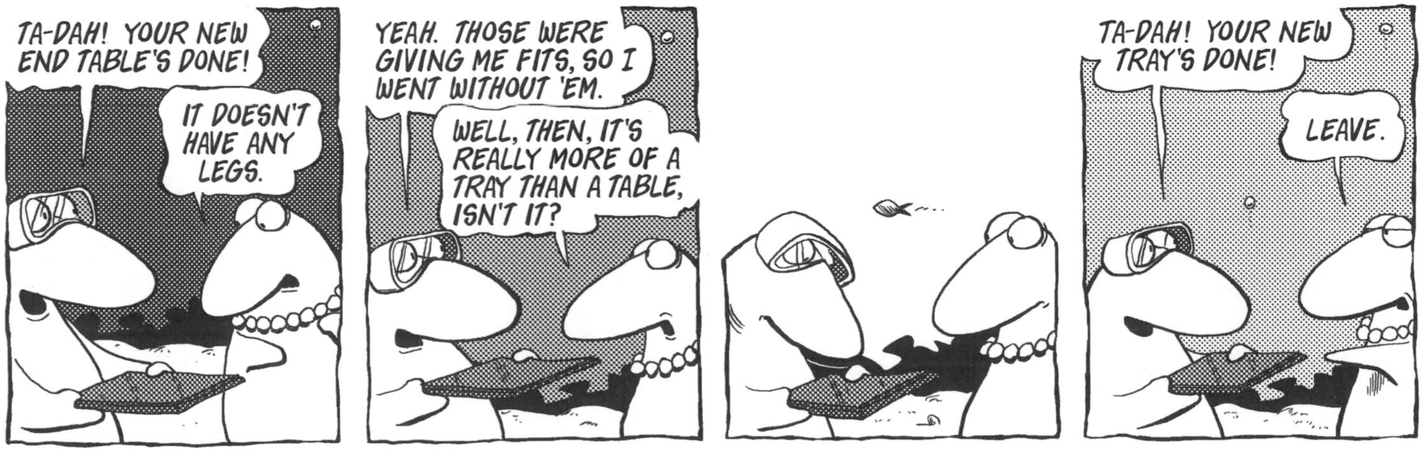
TA-DAH! YOUR NEW END TABLE'S DONE!
IT DOESN'T HAVE ANY LEGS.
YEAH. THOSE WERE GIVING ME FITS, SO I WENT WITHOUT 'EM.
WELL, THEN, IT'S REALLY MORE OF A TRAY THAN A TABLE, ISN'T IT?
TA-DAH! YOUR NEW TRAY'S DONE!
LEAVE.

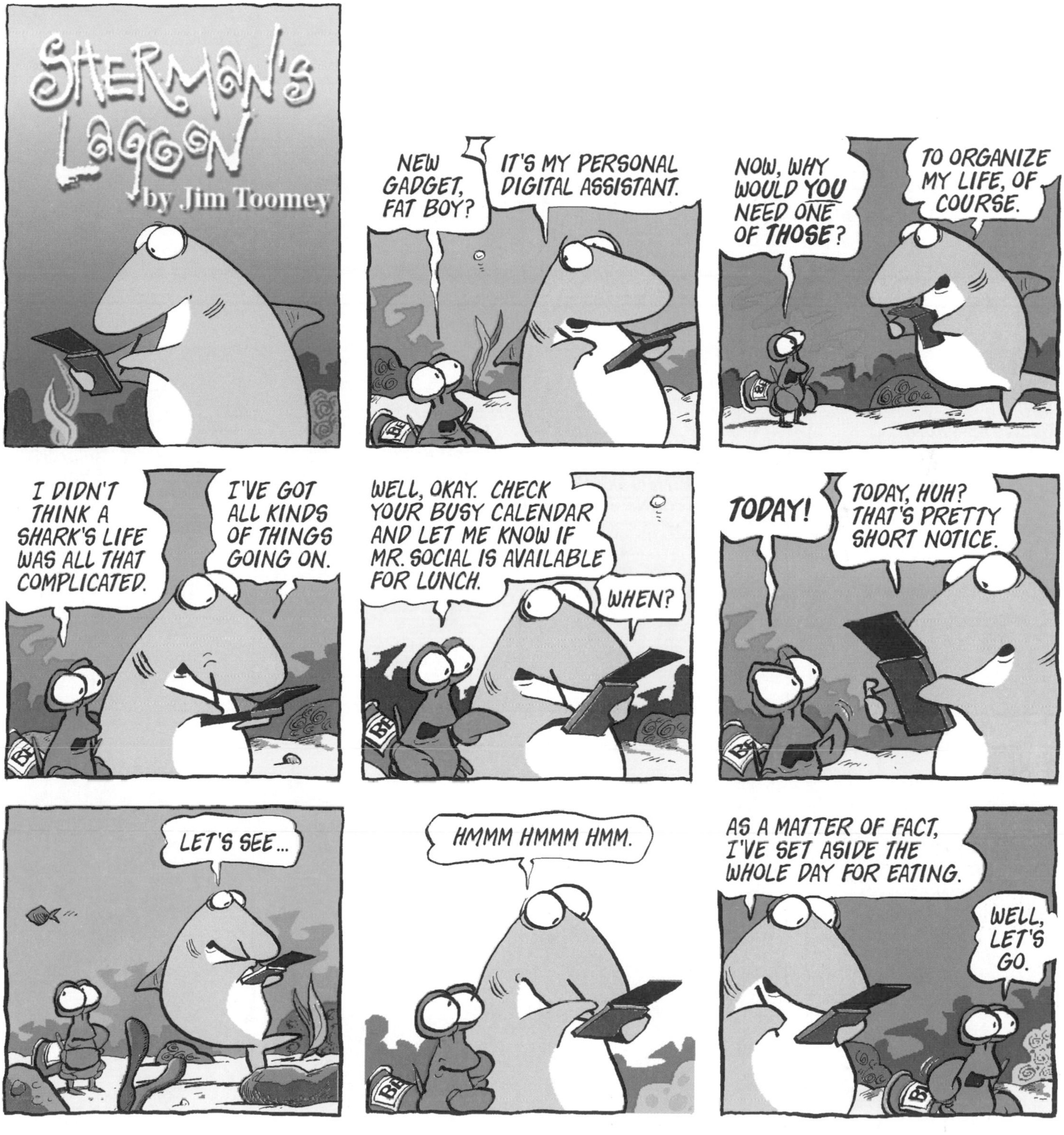
SHERMAN'S LAGOON
by Jim Toomey
NEW GADGET, FAT BOY?
IT'S MY PERSONAL DIGITAL ASSISTANT.
NOW, WHY WOULD YOU NEED ONE OF THOSE?
TO ORGANIZE MY LIFE, OF COURSE.
I DIDN'T THINK A SHARK'S LIFE WAS ALL THAT COMPLICATED.
I'VE GOT ALL KINDS OF THINGS GOING ON.
WELL, OKAY. CHECK YOUR BUSY CALENDAR AND LET ME KNOW IF MR. SOCIAL IS AVAILABLE FOR LUNCH.
WHEN?
TODAY!
TODAY, HUH? THAT'S PRETTY SHORT NOTICE.
LET'S SEE...
HMMM HMMM HMM.
AS A MATTER OF FACT, I'VE SET ASIDE THE WHOLE DAY FOR EATING.
WELL, LET'S GO.

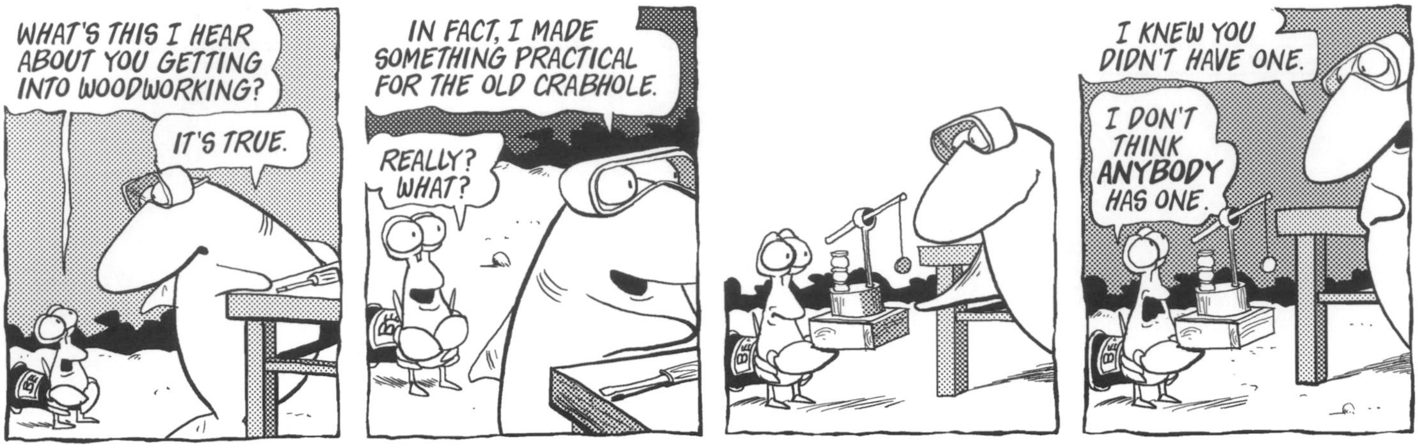
WHAT'S THIS I HEAR ABOUT YOU GETTING INTO WOODWORKING?
IT'S TRUE.
IN FACT, I MADE SOMETHING PRACTICAL FOR THE OLD CRABHOLE.
REALLY? WHAT?
I KNEW YOU DIDN'T HAVE ONE.
I DON'T THINK **ANYBODY** HAS ONE.

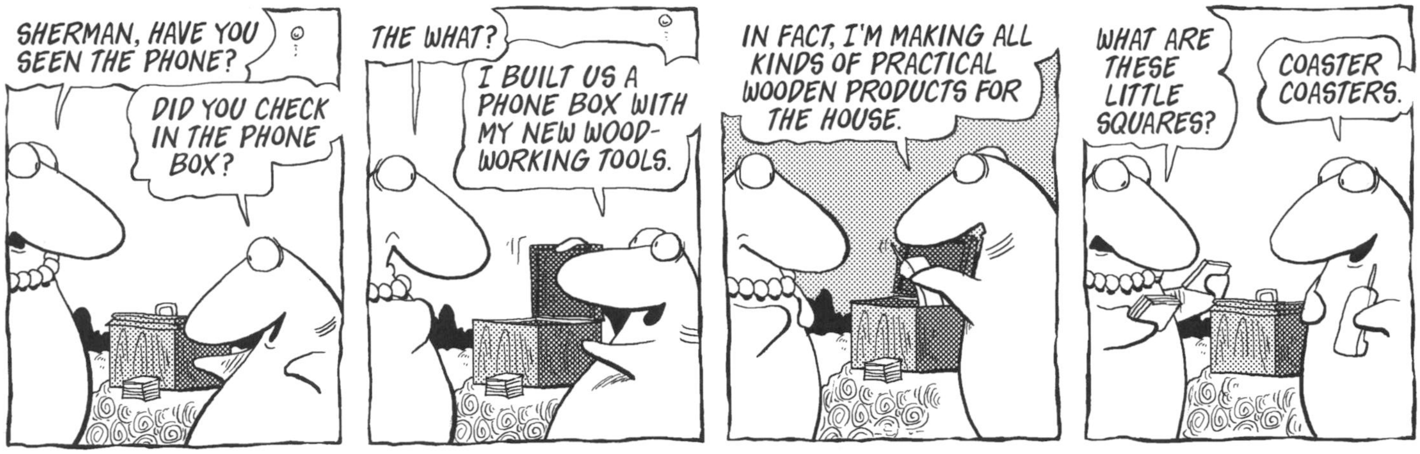
SHERMAN, HAVE YOU SEEN THE PHONE?
DID YOU CHECK IN THE PHONE BOX?
THE WHAT?
I BUILT US A PHONE BOX WITH MY NEW WOOD-WORKING TOOLS.
IN FACT, I'M MAKING ALL KINDS OF PRACTICAL WOODEN PRODUCTS FOR THE HOUSE.
WHAT ARE THESE LITTLE SQUARES?
COASTER COASTERS.

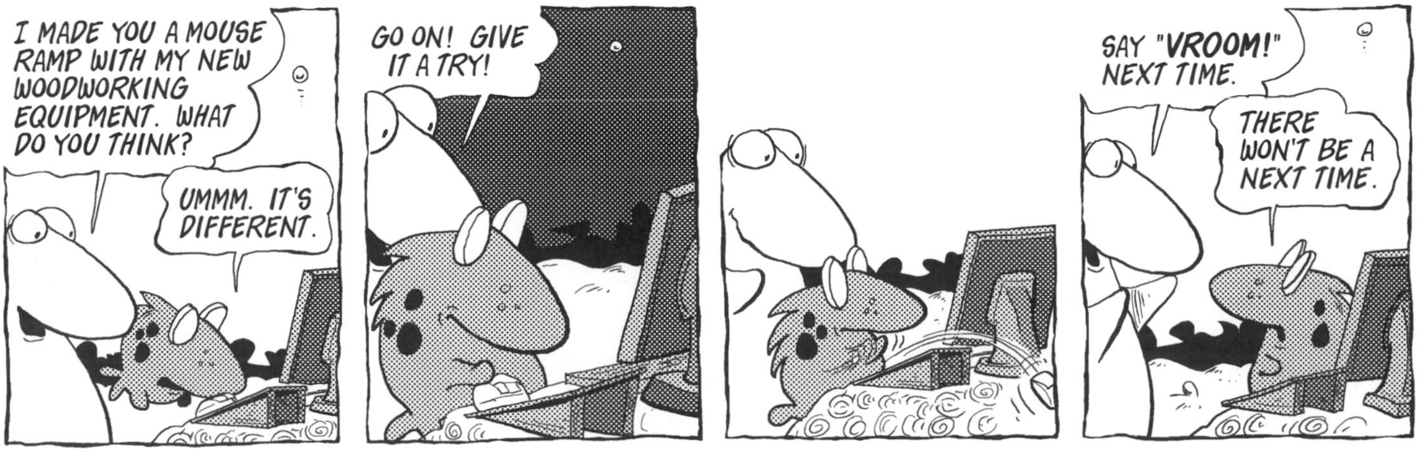
I MADE YOU A MOUSE RAMP WITH MY NEW WOODWORKING EQUIPMENT. WHAT DO YOU THINK?
UMMM. IT'S DIFFERENT.
GO ON! GIVE IT A TRY!
SAY "**VROOM!**" NEXT TIME.
THERE WON'T BE A NEXT TIME.

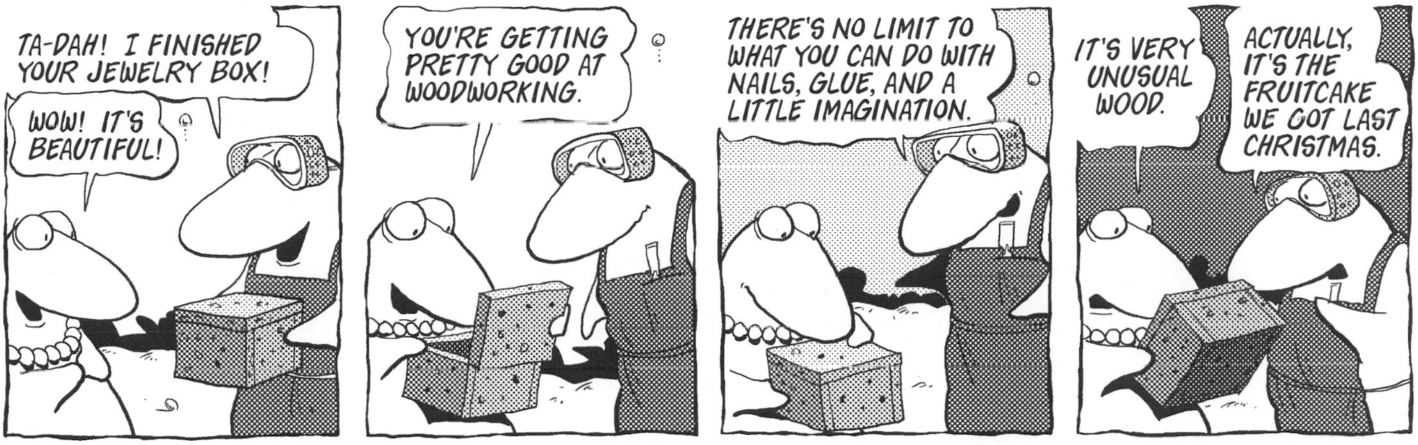
TA-DAH! I FINISHED YOUR JEWELRY BOX!
WOW! IT'S BEAUTIFUL!
YOU'RE GETTING PRETTY GOOD AT WOODWORKING.
THERE'S NO LIMIT TO WHAT YOU CAN DO WITH NAILS, GLUE, AND A LITTLE IMAGINATION.
IT'S VERY UNUSUAL WOOD.
ACTUALLY, IT'S THE FRUITCAKE WE GOT LAST CHRISTMAS.

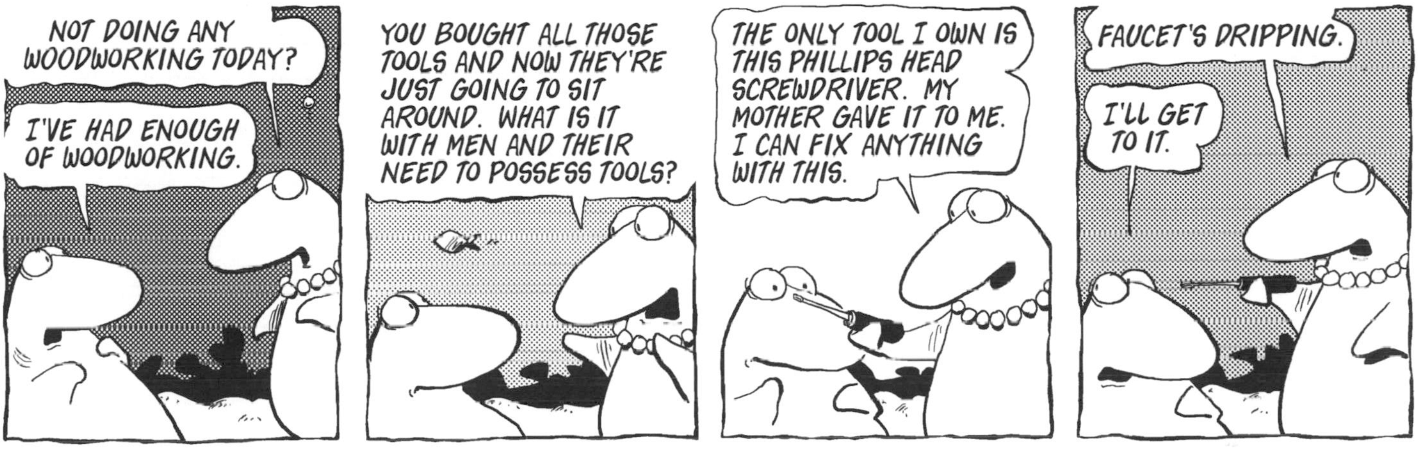
NOT DOING ANY WOODWORKING TODAY?
I'VE HAD ENOUGH OF WOODWORKING.
YOU BOUGHT ALL THOSE TOOLS AND NOW THEY'RE JUST GOING TO SIT AROUND. WHAT IS IT WITH MEN AND THEIR NEED TO POSSESS TOOLS?
THE ONLY TOOL I OWN IS THIS PHILLIPS HEAD SCREWDRIVER. MY MOTHER GAVE IT TO ME. I CAN FIX ANYTHING WITH THIS.
FAUCET'S DRIPPING.
I'LL GET TO IT.

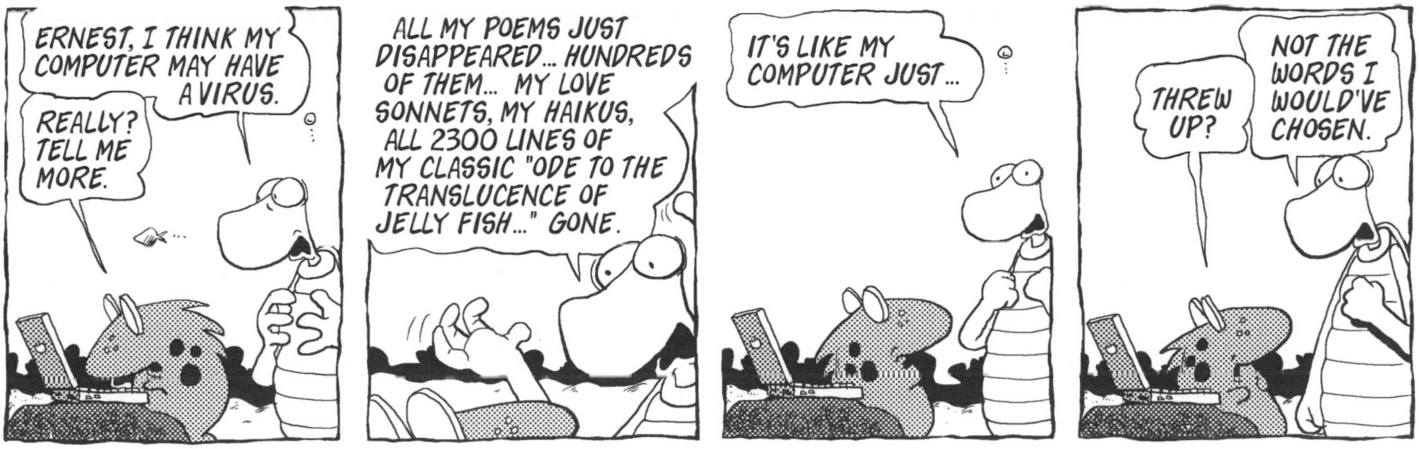
ERNEST, I THINK MY COMPUTER MAY HAVE A VIRUS.
REALLY? TELL ME MORE.
ALL MY POEMS JUST DISAPPEARED... HUNDREDS OF THEM... MY LOVE SONNETS, MY HAIKUS, ALL 2300 LINES OF MY CLASSIC "ODE TO THE TRANSLUCENCE OF JELLY FISH..." GONE.
IT'S LIKE MY COMPUTER JUST...
THREW UP?
NOT THE WORDS I WOULD'VE CHOSEN.

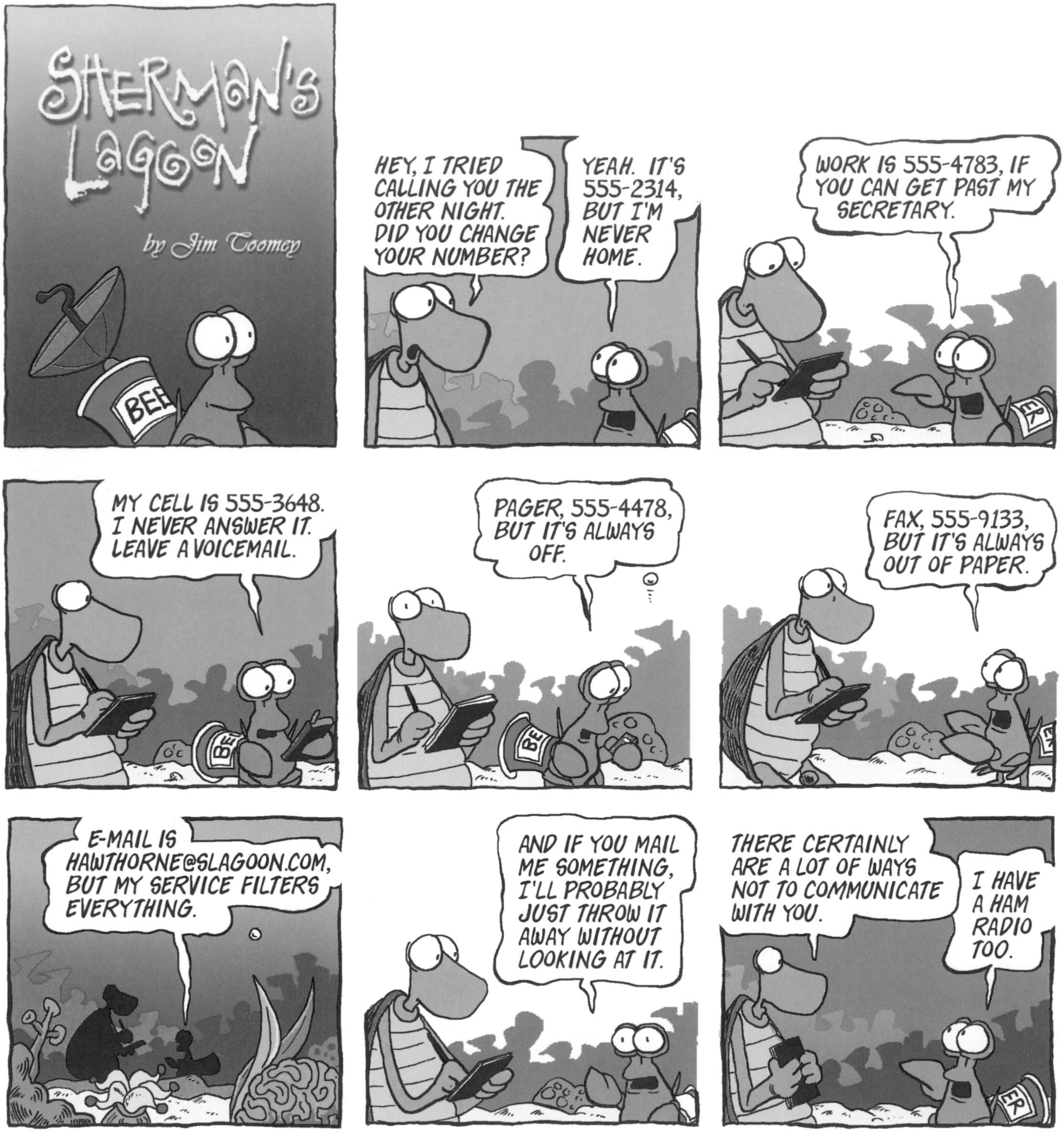
SHERMAN'S LAGOON
by Jim Toomey
BEER
HEY, I TRIED CALLING YOU THE OTHER NIGHT. DID YOU CHANGE YOUR NUMBER?
YEAH. IT'S 555-2314, BUT I'M NEVER HOME.
WORK IS 555-4783, IF YOU CAN GET PAST MY SECRETARY.
MY CELL IS 555-3648. I NEVER ANSWER IT. LEAVE A VOICEMAIL.
PAGER, 555-4478, BUT IT'S ALWAYS OFF.
FAX, 555-9133, BUT IT'S ALWAYS OUT OF PAPER.
E-MAIL IS HAWTHORNE@SLAGOON.COM, BUT MY SERVICE FILTERS EVERYTHING.
AND IF YOU MAIL ME SOMETHING, I'LL PROBABLY JUST THROW IT AWAY WITHOUT LOOKING AT IT.
THERE CERTAINLY ARE A LOT OF WAYS NOT TO COMMUNICATE WITH YOU.
I HAVE A HAM RADIO TOO.

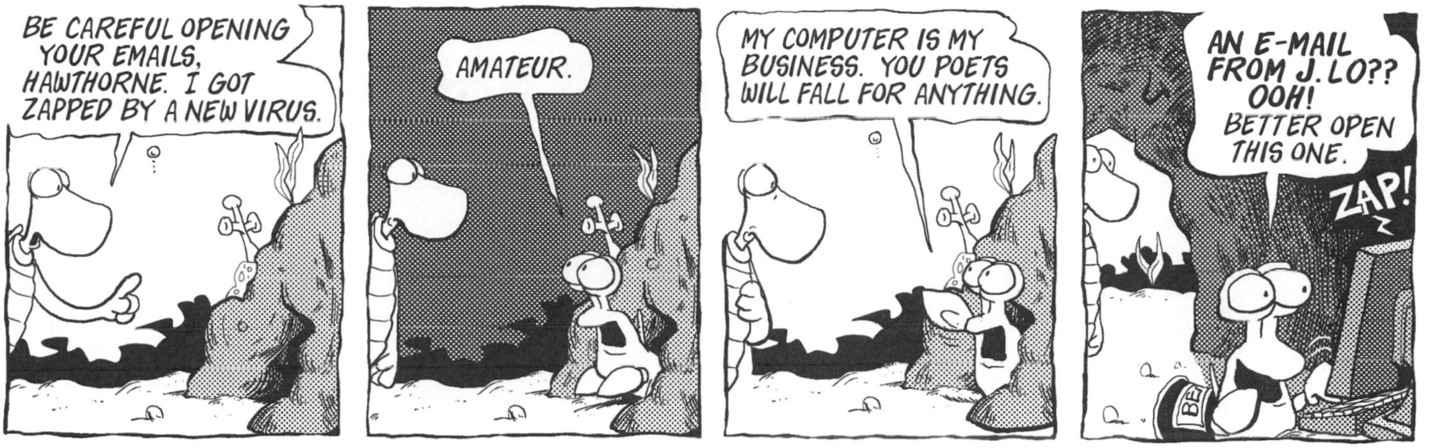
BE CAREFUL OPENING YOUR EMAILS, HAWTHORNE. I GOT ZAPPED BY A NEW VIRUS.
AMATEUR.
MY COMPUTER IS MY BUSINESS. YOU POETS WILL FALL FOR ANYTHING.
AN E-MAIL FROM J. LO?? OOH! BETTER OPEN THIS ONE.
ZAP!

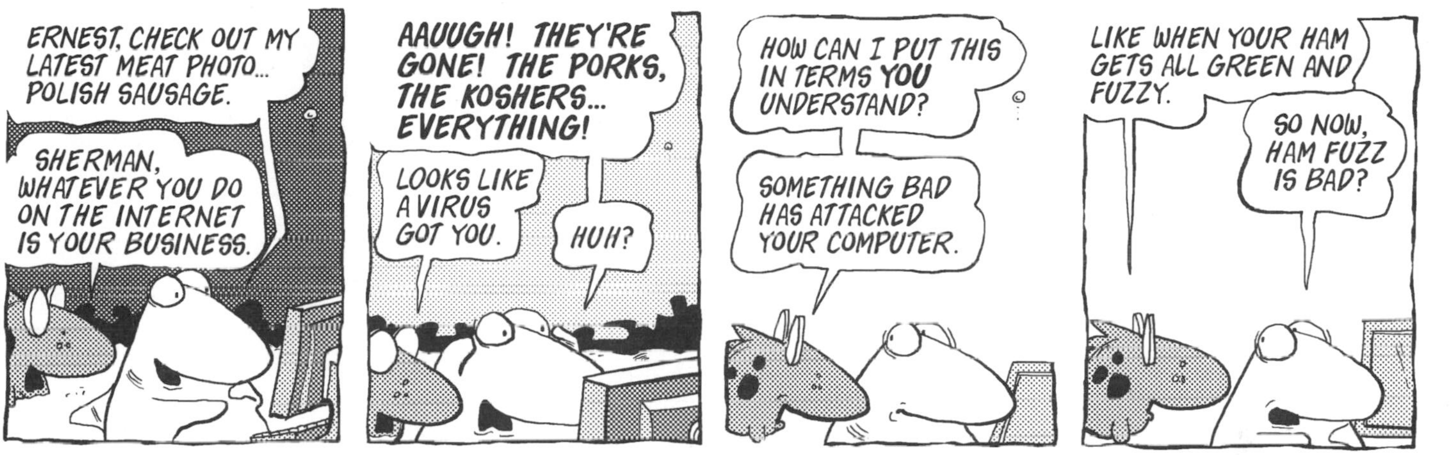
ERNEST, CHECK OUT MY LATEST MEAT PHOTO... POLISH SAUSAGE.
SHERMAN, WHATEVER YOU DO ON THE INTERNET IS YOUR BUSINESS.
AAUUGH! THEY'RE GONE! THE PORKS, THE KOSHERS... EVERYTHING!
LOOKS LIKE A VIRUS GOT YOU.
HUH?
HOW CAN I PUT THIS IN TERMS YOU UNDERSTAND?
SOMETHING BAD HAS ATTACKED YOUR COMPUTER.
LIKE WHEN YOUR HAM GETS ALL GREEN AND FUZZY.
SO NOW, HAM FUZZ IS BAD?

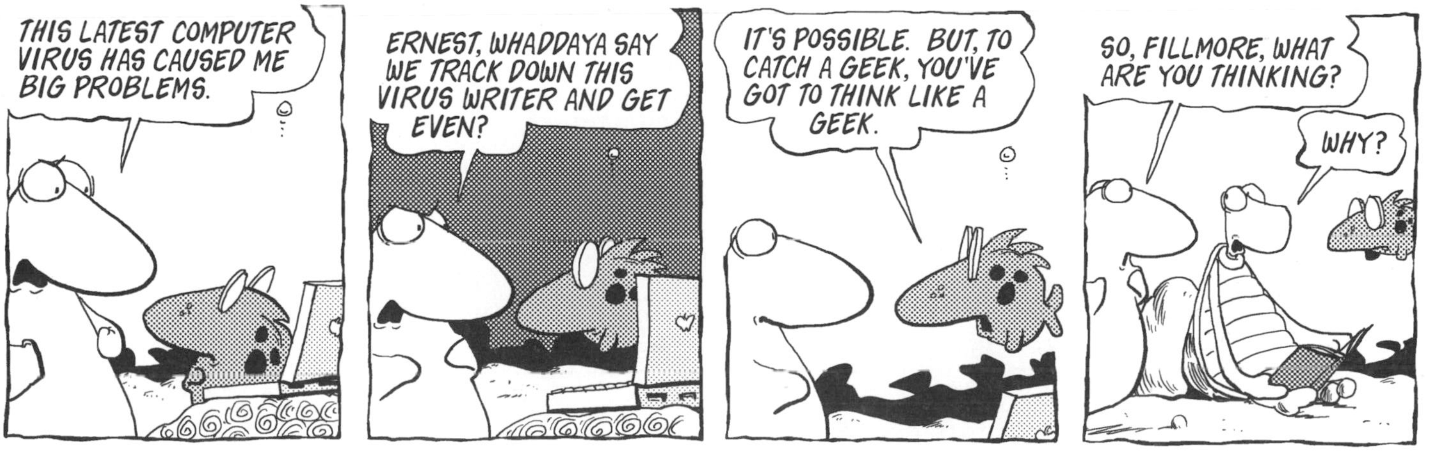
THIS LATEST COMPUTER VIRUS HAS CAUSED ME BIG PROBLEMS.
ERNEST, WHADDAYA SAY WE TRACK DOWN THIS VIRUS WRITER AND GET EVEN?
IT'S POSSIBLE. BUT, TO CATCH A GEEK, YOU'VE GOT TO THINK LIKE A GEEK.
SO, FILLMORE, WHAT ARE YOU THINKING?
WHY?

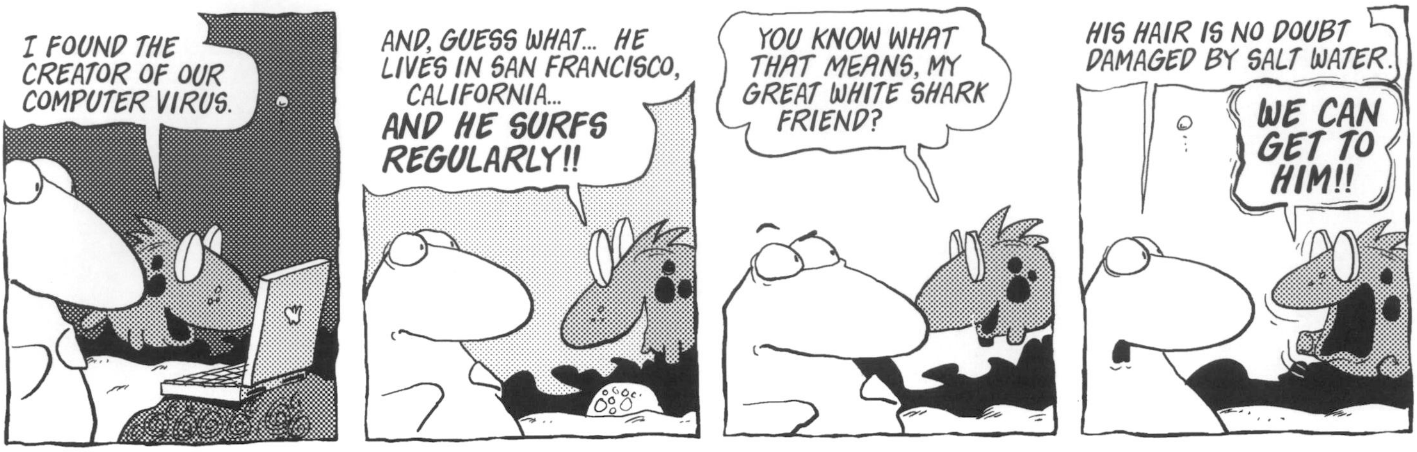
I FOUND THE CREATOR OF OUR COMPUTER VIRUS.
AND, GUESS WHAT... HE LIVES IN SAN FRANCISCO, CALIFORNIA... AND HE SURFS REGULARLY!!
YOU KNOW WHAT THAT MEANS, MY GREAT WHITE SHARK FRIEND?
HIS HAIR IS NO DOUBT DAMAGED BY SALT WATER.
WE CAN GET TO HIM!!

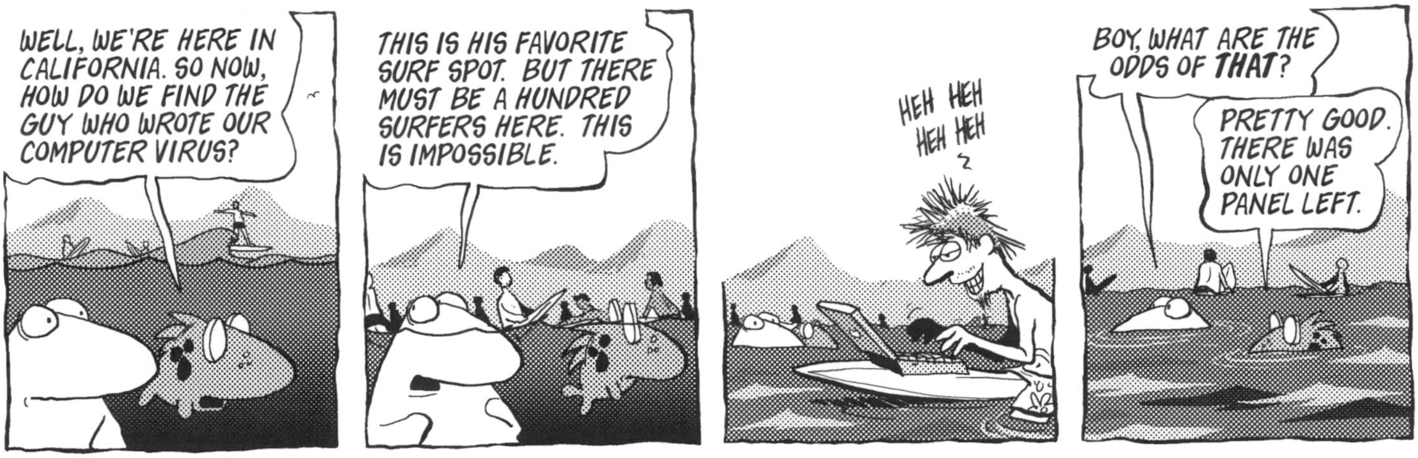
WELL, WE'RE HERE IN CALIFORNIA. SO NOW, HOW DO WE FIND THE GUY WHO WROTE OUR COMPUTER VIRUS?
THIS IS HIS FAVORITE SURF SPOT. BUT THERE MUST BE A HUNDRED SURFERS HERE. THIS IS IMPOSSIBLE.
HEH HEH HEH HEH
BOY, WHAT ARE THE ODDS OF THAT?
PRETTY GOOD. THERE WAS ONLY ONE PANEL LEFT.

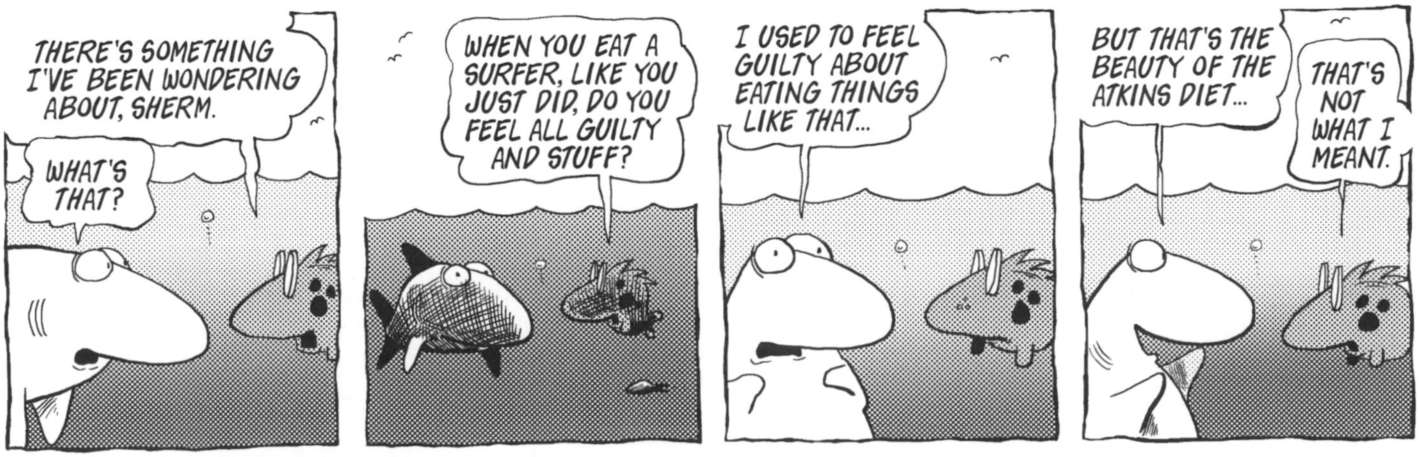
THERE'S SOMETHING I'VE BEEN WONDERING ABOUT, SHERM.
WHAT'S THAT?
WHEN YOU EAT A SURFER, LIKE YOU JUST DID, DO YOU FEEL ALL GUILTY AND STUFF?
I USED TO FEEL GUILTY ABOUT EATING THINGS LIKE THAT...
BUT THAT'S THE BEAUTY OF THE ATKINS DIET...
THAT'S NOT WHAT I MEANT.

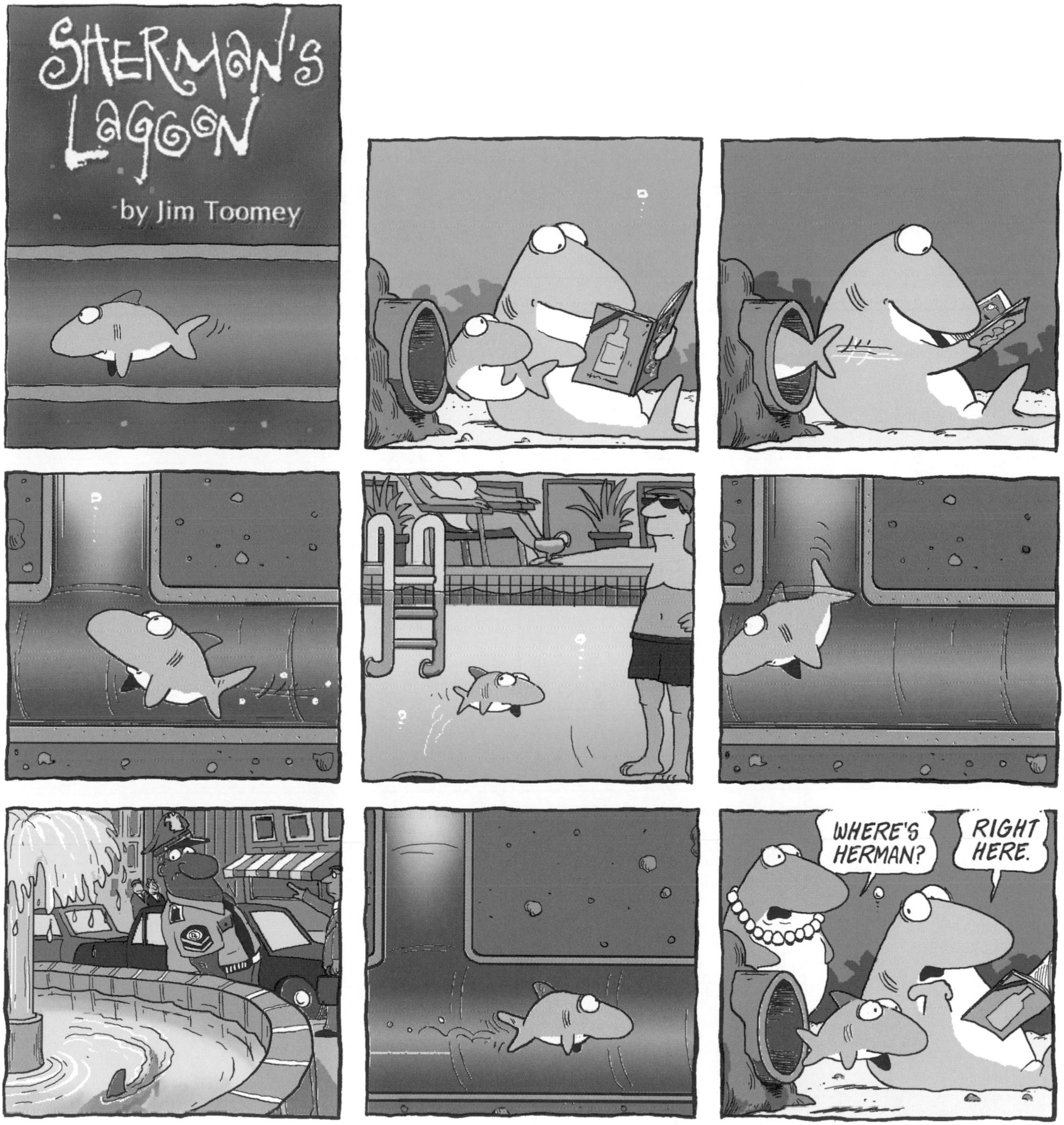
SHERMAN'S LAGOON
by Jim Toomey
WHERE'S HERMAN?
RIGHT HERE.

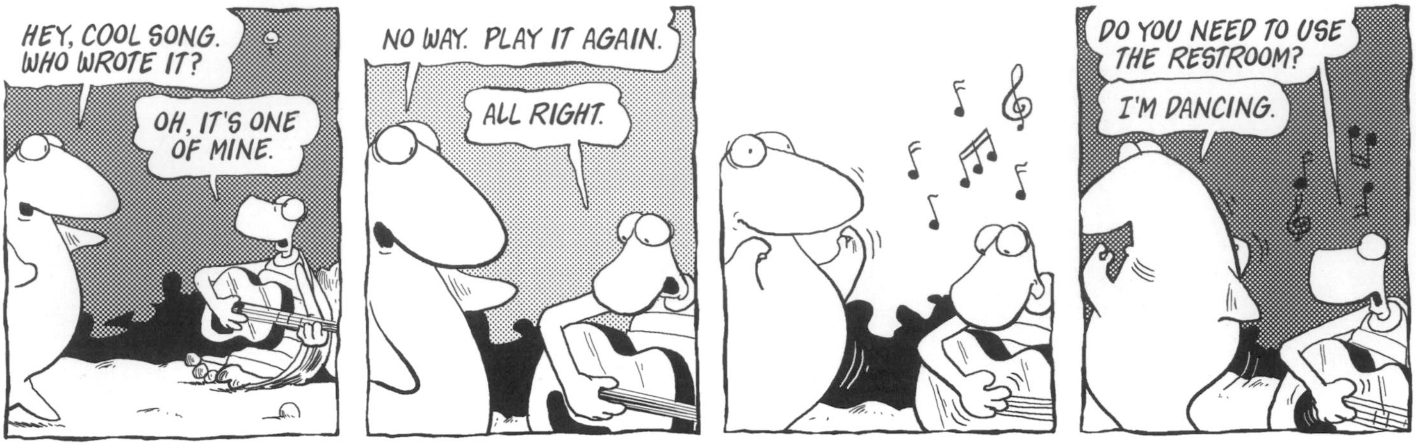
HEY, COOL SONG. WHO WROTE IT?
OH, IT'S ONE OF MINE.
NO WAY. PLAY IT AGAIN.
ALL RIGHT.
DO YOU NEED TO USE THE RESTROOM?
I'M DANCING.

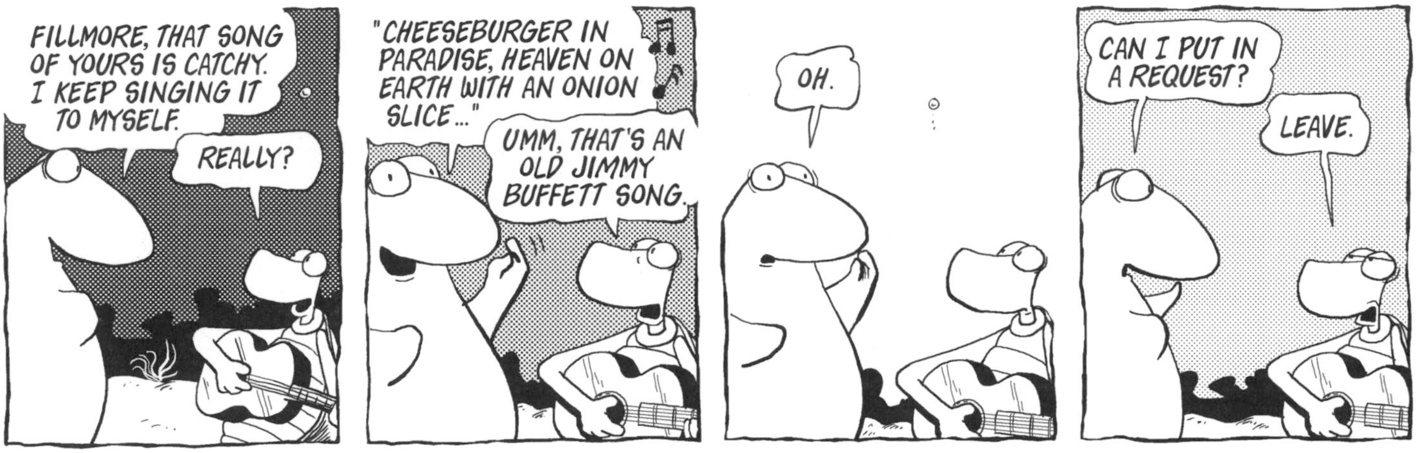
FILLMORE, THAT SONG OF YOURS IS CATCHY. I KEEP SINGING IT TO MYSELF.
REALLY?
"CHEESEBURGER IN PARADISE, HEAVEN ON EARTH WITH AN ONION SLICE..."
UMM, THAT'S AN OLD JIMMY BUFFETT SONG.
OH.
CAN I PUT IN A REQUEST?
LEAVE.

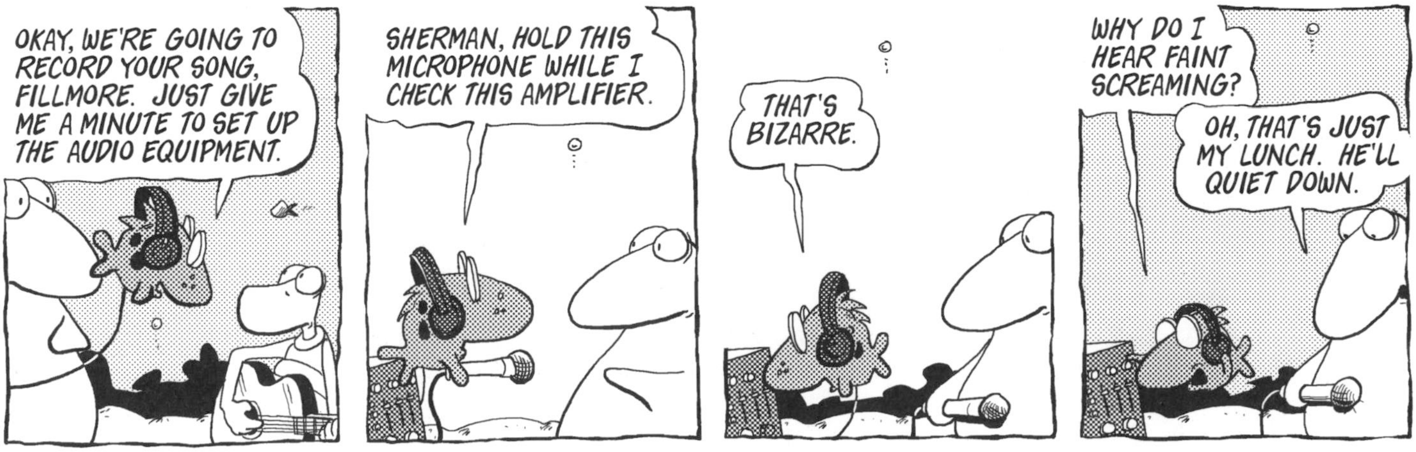
OKAY, WE'RE GOING TO RECORD YOUR SONG, FILLMORE. JUST GIVE ME A MINUTE TO SET UP THE AUDIO EQUIPMENT.
SHERMAN, HOLD THIS MICROPHONE WHILE I CHECK THIS AMPLIFIER.
THAT'S BIZARRE.
WHY DO I HEAR FAINT SCREAMING?
OH, THAT'S JUST MY LUNCH. HE'LL QUIET DOWN.

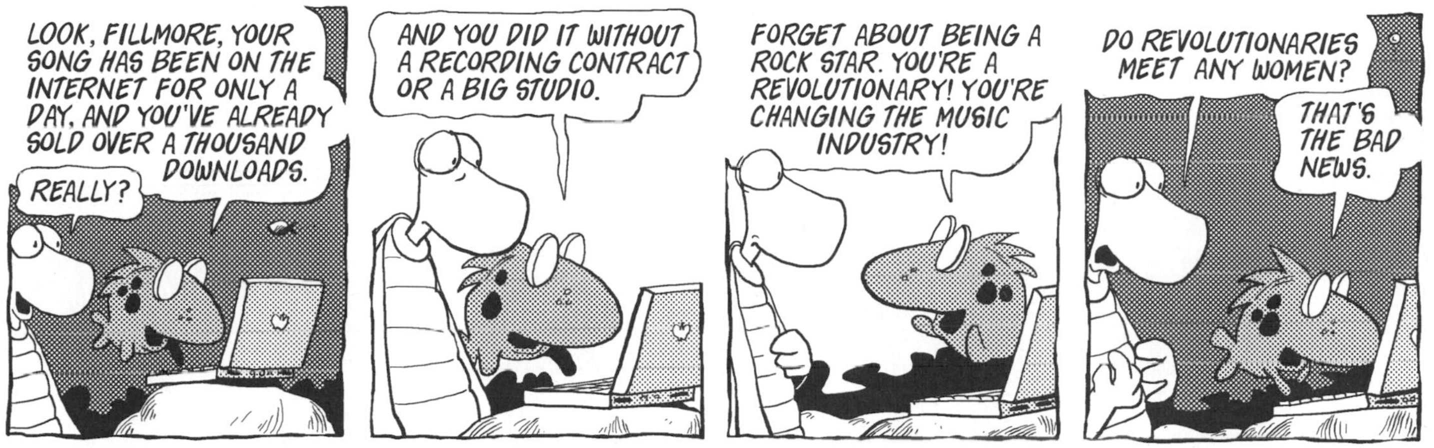
LOOK, FILLMORE, YOUR SONG HAS BEEN ON THE INTERNET FOR ONLY A DAY, AND YOU'VE ALREADY SOLD OVER A THOUSAND DOWNLOADS.
REALLY?
AND YOU DID IT WITHOUT A RECORDING CONTRACT OR A BIG STUDIO.
FORGET ABOUT BEING A ROCK STAR. YOU'RE A REVOLUTIONARY! YOU'RE CHANGING THE MUSIC INDUSTRY!
DO REVOLUTIONARIES MEET ANY WOMEN?
THAT'S THE BAD NEWS.

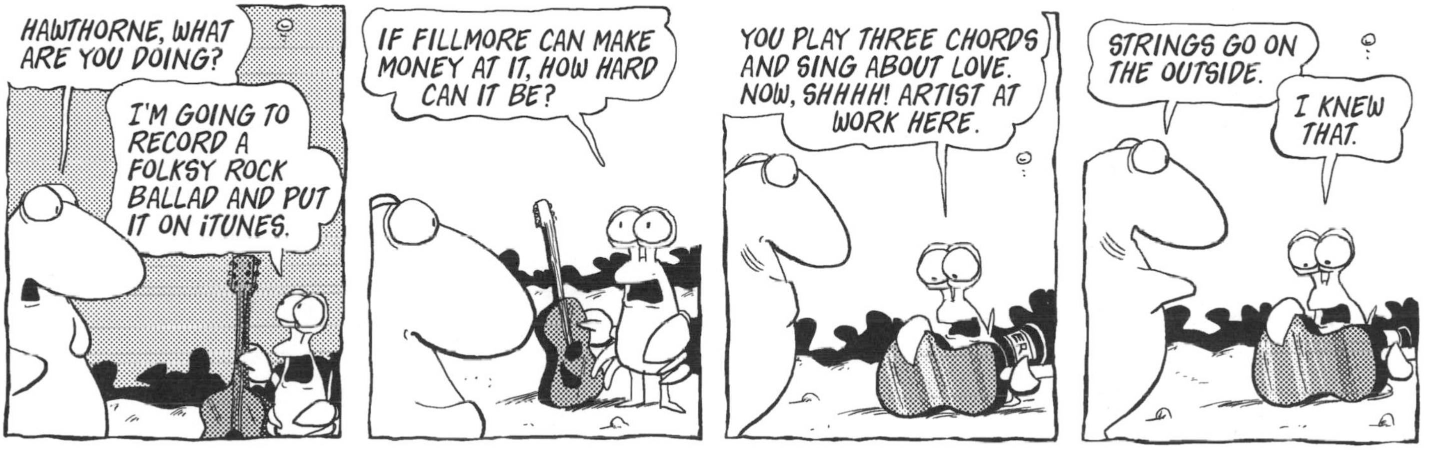
HAWTHORNE, WHAT ARE YOU DOING?
I'M GOING TO RECORD A FOLKSY ROCK BALLAD AND PUT IT ON iTUNES.
IF FILLMORE CAN MAKE MONEY AT IT, HOW HARD CAN IT BE?
YOU PLAY THREE CHORDS AND SING ABOUT LOVE. NOW, SHHHH! ARTIST AT WORK HERE.
STRINGS GO ON THE OUTSIDE.
I KNEW THAT.

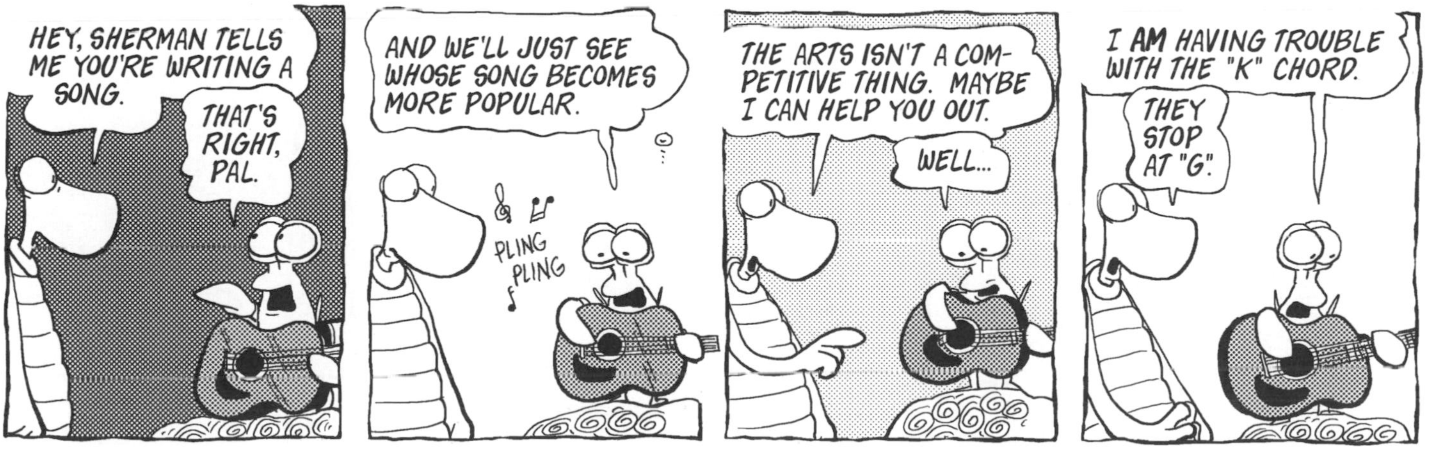
HEY, SHERMAN TELLS ME YOU'RE WRITING A SONG.
THAT'S RIGHT, PAL.
AND WE'LL JUST SEE WHOSE SONG BECOMES MORE POPULAR.
PLING PLING
THE ARTS ISN'T A COMPETITIVE THING. MAYBE I CAN HELP YOU OUT.
WELL...
I AM HAVING TROUBLE WITH THE "K" CHORD.
THEY STOP AT "G".

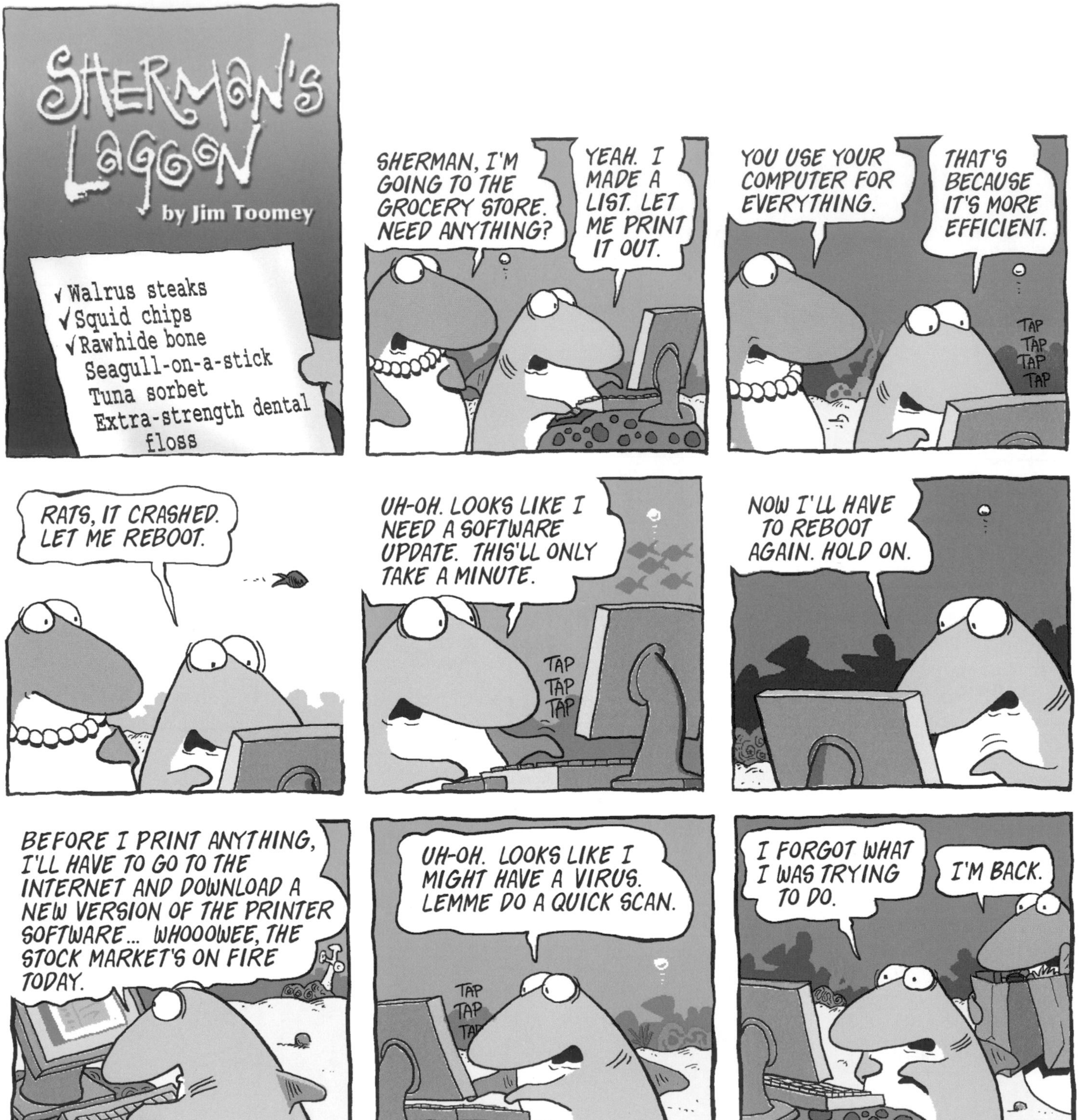

SHERMAN'S LAGOON
by Jim Toomey
✓Walrus steaks
✓Squid chips
✓Rawhide bone
Seagull-on-a-stick
Tuna sorbet
Extra-strength dental floss
SHERMAN, I'M GOING TO THE GROCERY STORE. NEED ANYTHING?
YEAH. I MADE A LIST. LET ME PRINT IT OUT.
YOU USE YOUR COMPUTER FOR EVERYTHING.
THAT'S BECAUSE IT'S MORE EFFICIENT.
TAP TAP TAP TAP
RATS, IT CRASHED. LET ME REBOOT.
UH-OH. LOOKS LIKE I NEED A SOFTWARE UPDATE. THIS'LL ONLY TAKE A MINUTE.
TAP TAP TAP
NOW I'LL HAVE TO REBOOT AGAIN. HOLD ON.
BEFORE I PRINT ANYTHING, I'LL HAVE TO GO TO THE INTERNET AND DOWNLOAD A NEW VERSION OF THE PRINTER SOFTWARE... WHOOOWEE, THE STOCK MARKET'S ON FIRE TODAY.
UH-OH. LOOKS LIKE I MIGHT HAVE A VIRUS. LEMME DO A QUICK SCAN.
I FORGOT WHAT I WAS TRYING TO DO.
I'M BACK.

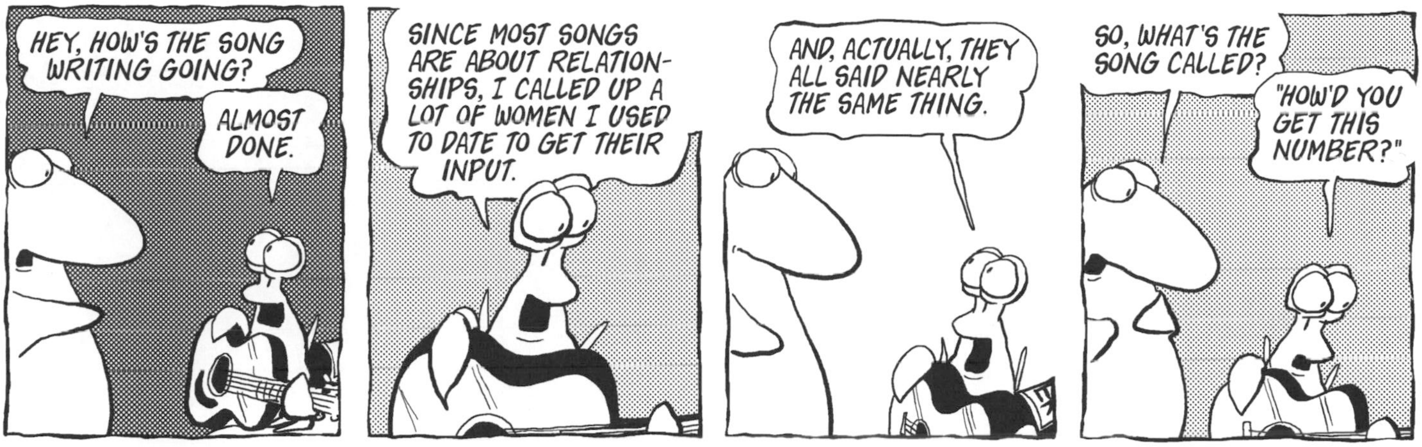
HEY, HOW'S THE SONG WRITING GOING?
ALMOST DONE.
SINCE MOST SONGS ARE ABOUT RELATIONSHIPS, I CALLED UP A LOT OF WOMEN I USED TO DATE TO GET THEIR INPUT.
AND, ACTUALLY, THEY ALL SAID NEARLY THE SAME THING.
SO, WHAT'S THE SONG CALLED?
"HOW'D YOU GET THIS NUMBER?"

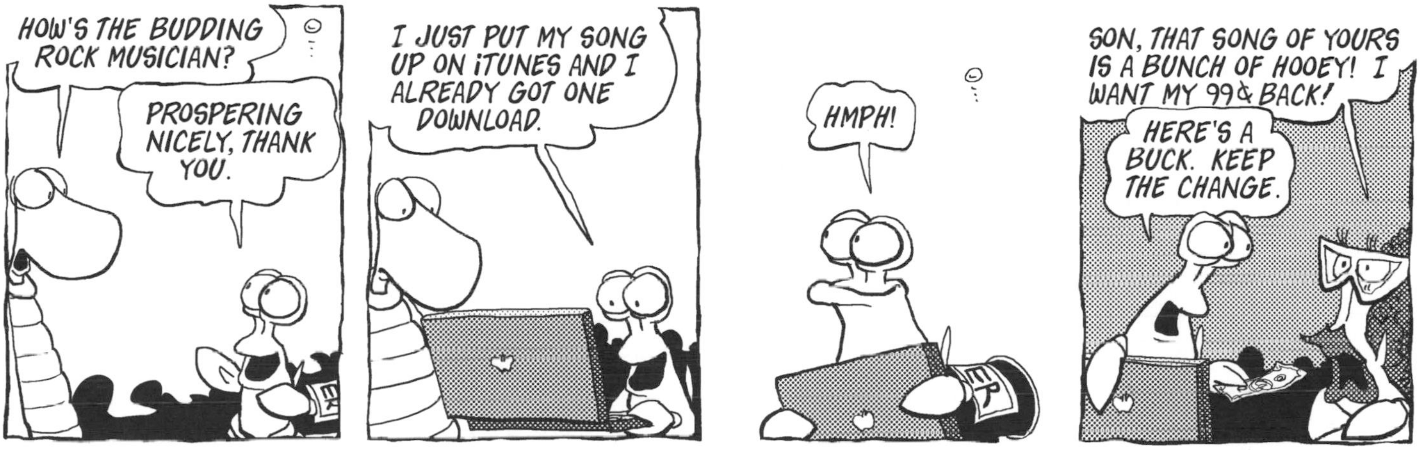
HOW'S THE BUDDING ROCK MUSICIAN?
PROSPERING NICELY, THANK YOU.
I JUST PUT MY SONG UP ON iTUNES AND I ALREADY GOT ONE DOWNLOAD.
HMPH!
SON, THAT SONG OF YOURS IS A BUNCH OF HOOEY! I WANT MY 99¢ BACK!
HERE'S A BUCK. KEEP THE CHANGE.

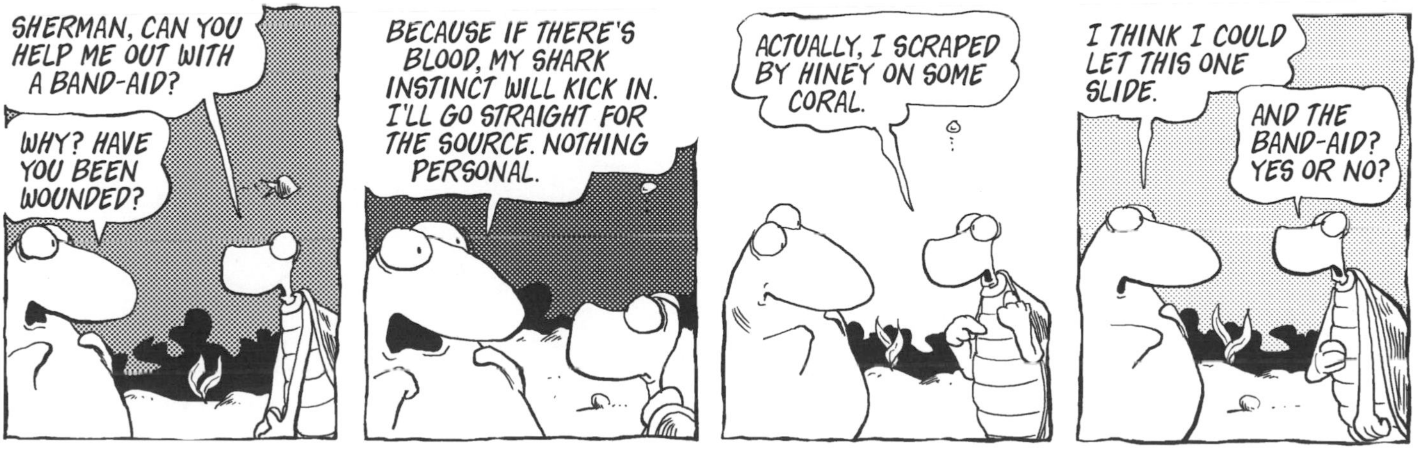
SHERMAN, CAN YOU HELP ME OUT WITH A BAND-AID?
WHY? HAVE YOU BEEN WOUNDED?
BECAUSE IF THERE'S BLOOD, MY SHARK INSTINCT WILL KICK IN. I'LL GO STRAIGHT FOR THE SOURCE. NOTHING PERSONAL.
ACTUALLY, I SCRAPED BY HINEY ON SOME CORAL.
I THINK I COULD LET THIS ONE SLIDE.
AND THE BAND-AID? YES OR NO?

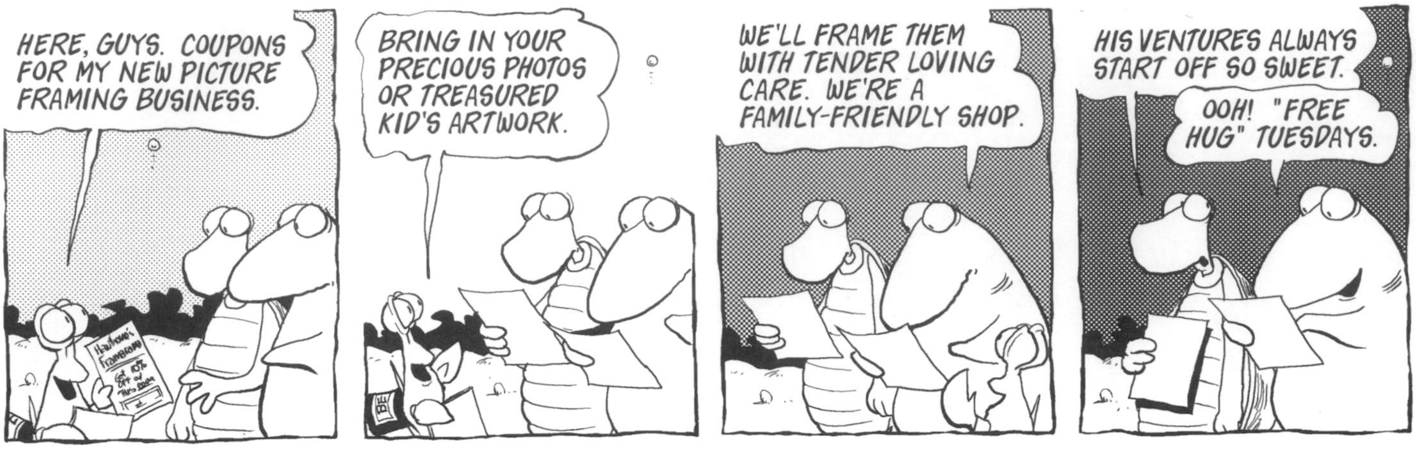
HERE, GUYS. COUPONS FOR MY NEW PICTURE FRAMING BUSINESS.
BRING IN YOUR PRECIOUS PHOTOS OR TREASURED KID'S ARTWORK.
WE'LL FRAME THEM WITH TENDER LOVING CARE. WE'RE A FAMILY-FRIENDLY SHOP.
HIS VENTURES ALWAYS START OFF SO SWEET.
OOH! "FREE HUG" TUESDAYS.

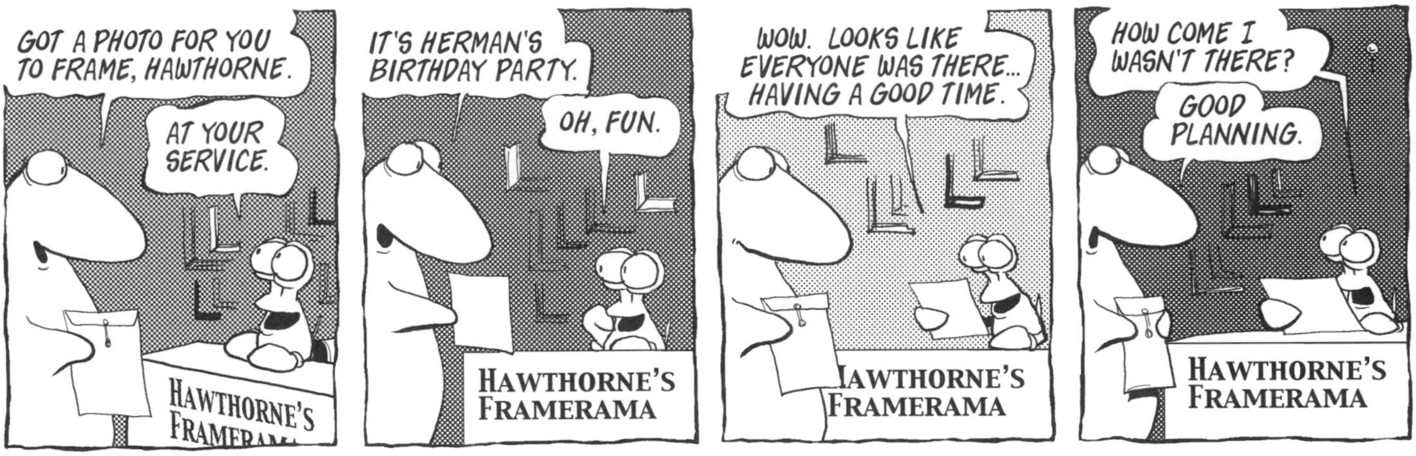
GOT A PHOTO FOR YOU TO FRAME, HAWTHORNE.
AT YOUR SERVICE.
IT'S HERMAN'S BIRTHDAY PARTY.
OH, FUN.
HAWTHORNE'S FRAMERAMA
WOW. LOOKS LIKE EVERYONE WAS THERE... HAVING A GOOD TIME.
HOW COME I WASN'T THERE?
GOOD PLANNING.
HAWTHORNE'S FRAMERAMA

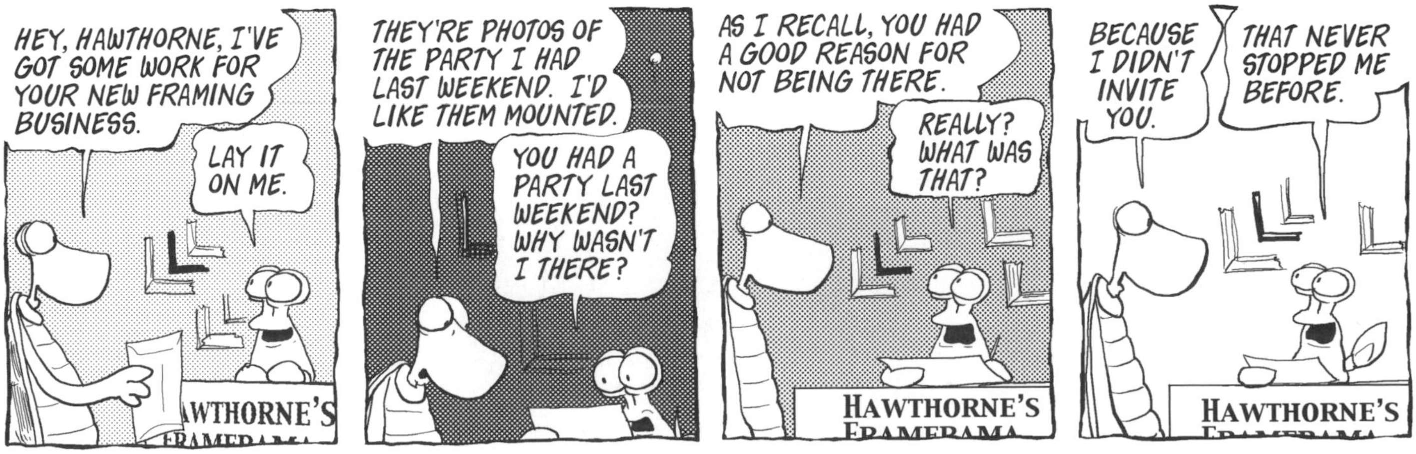
HEY, HAWTHORNE, I'VE GOT SOME WORK FOR YOUR NEW FRAMING BUSINESS.
LAY IT ON ME.
THEY'RE PHOTOS OF THE PARTY I HAD LAST WEEKEND. I'D LIKE THEM MOUNTED.
YOU HAD A PARTY LAST WEEKEND? WHY WASN'T I THERE?
AS I RECALL, YOU HAD A GOOD REASON FOR NOT BEING THERE.
REALLY? WHAT WAS THAT?
HAWTHORNE'S
BECAUSE I DIDN'T INVITE YOU.
THAT NEVER STOPPED ME BEFORE.
HAWTHORNE'S

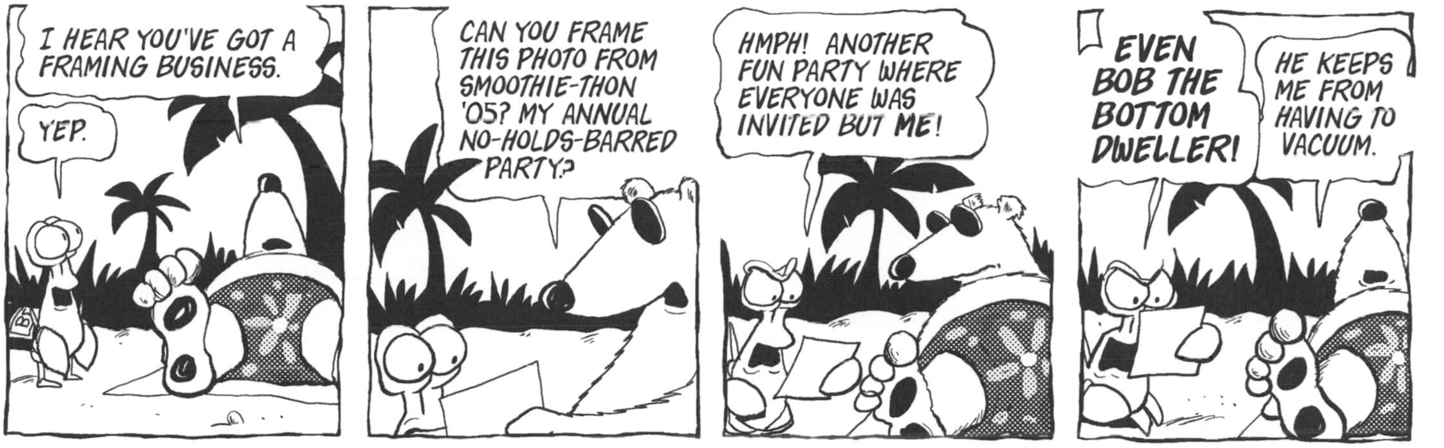
I HEAR YOU'VE GOT A FRAMING BUSINESS.
YEP.
CAN YOU FRAME THIS PHOTO FROM SMOOTHIE-THON '05? MY ANNUAL NO-HOLDS-BARRED PARTY?
HMPH! ANOTHER FUN PARTY WHERE EVERYONE WAS INVITED BUT ME!
EVEN BOB THE BOTTOM DWELLER!
HE KEEPS ME FROM HAVING TO VACUUM.

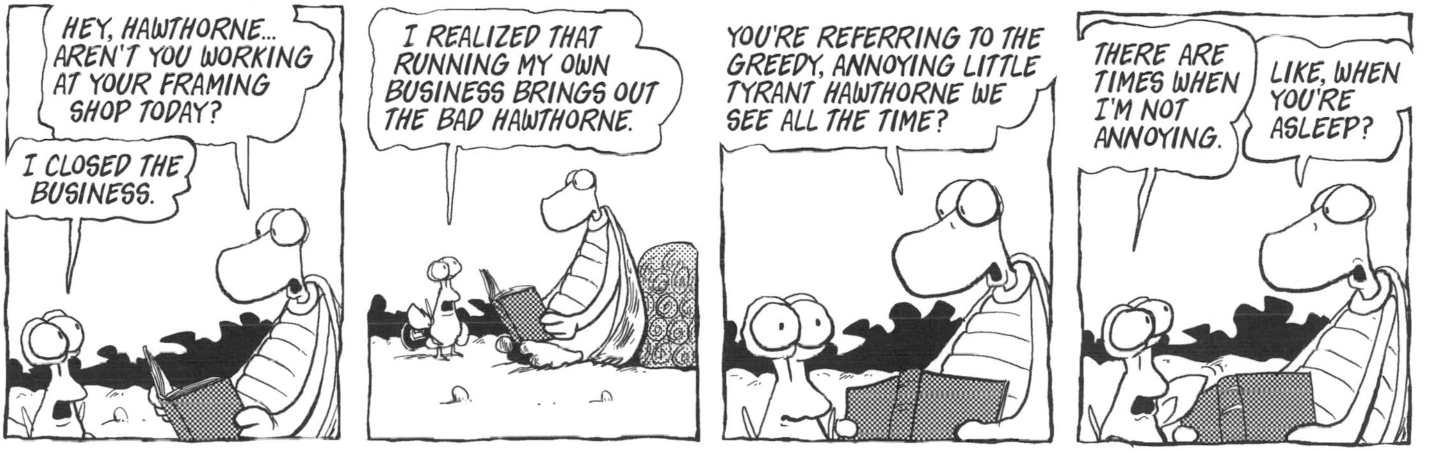
HEY, HAWTHORNE... AREN'T YOU WORKING AT YOUR FRAMING SHOP TODAY?
I CLOSED THE BUSINESS.
I REALIZED THAT RUNNING MY OWN BUSINESS BRINGS OUT THE BAD HAWTHORNE.
YOU'RE REFERRING TO THE GREEDY, ANNOYING LITTLE TYRANT HAWTHORNE WE SEE ALL THE TIME?
THERE ARE TIMES WHEN I'M NOT ANNOYING.
LIKE, WHEN YOU'RE ASLEEP?

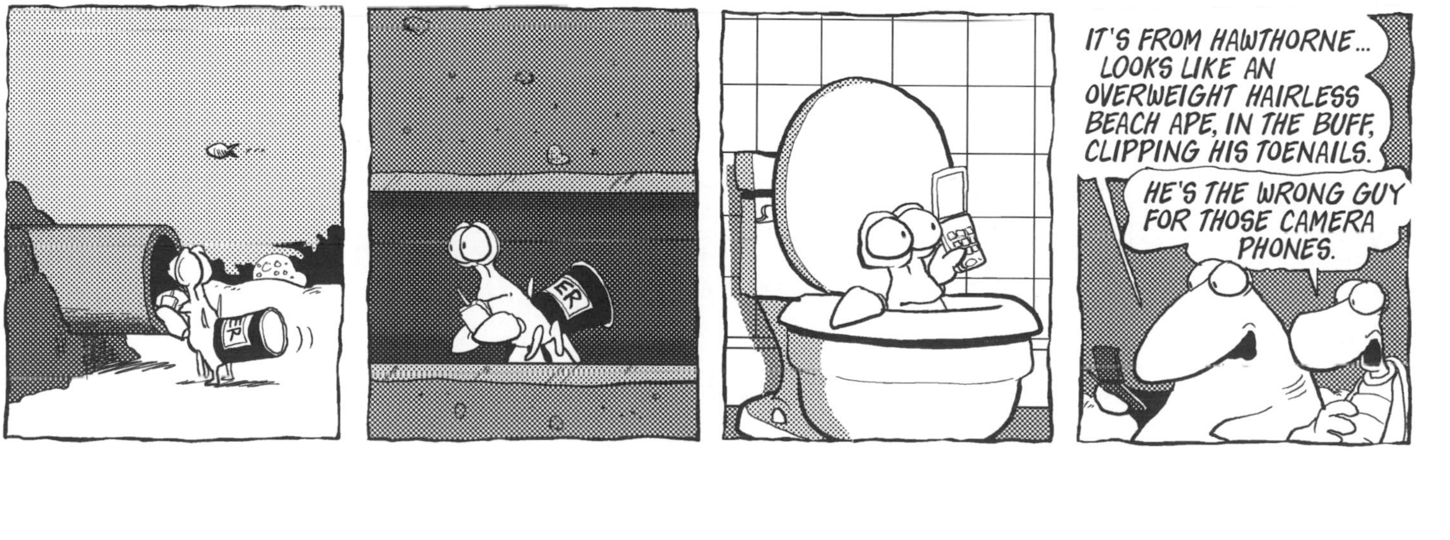
IT'S FROM HAWTHORNE... LOOKS LIKE AN OVERWEIGHT HAIRLESS BEACH APE, IN THE BUFF, CLIPPING HIS TOENAILS.
HE'S THE WRONG GUY FOR THOSE CAMERA PHONES.

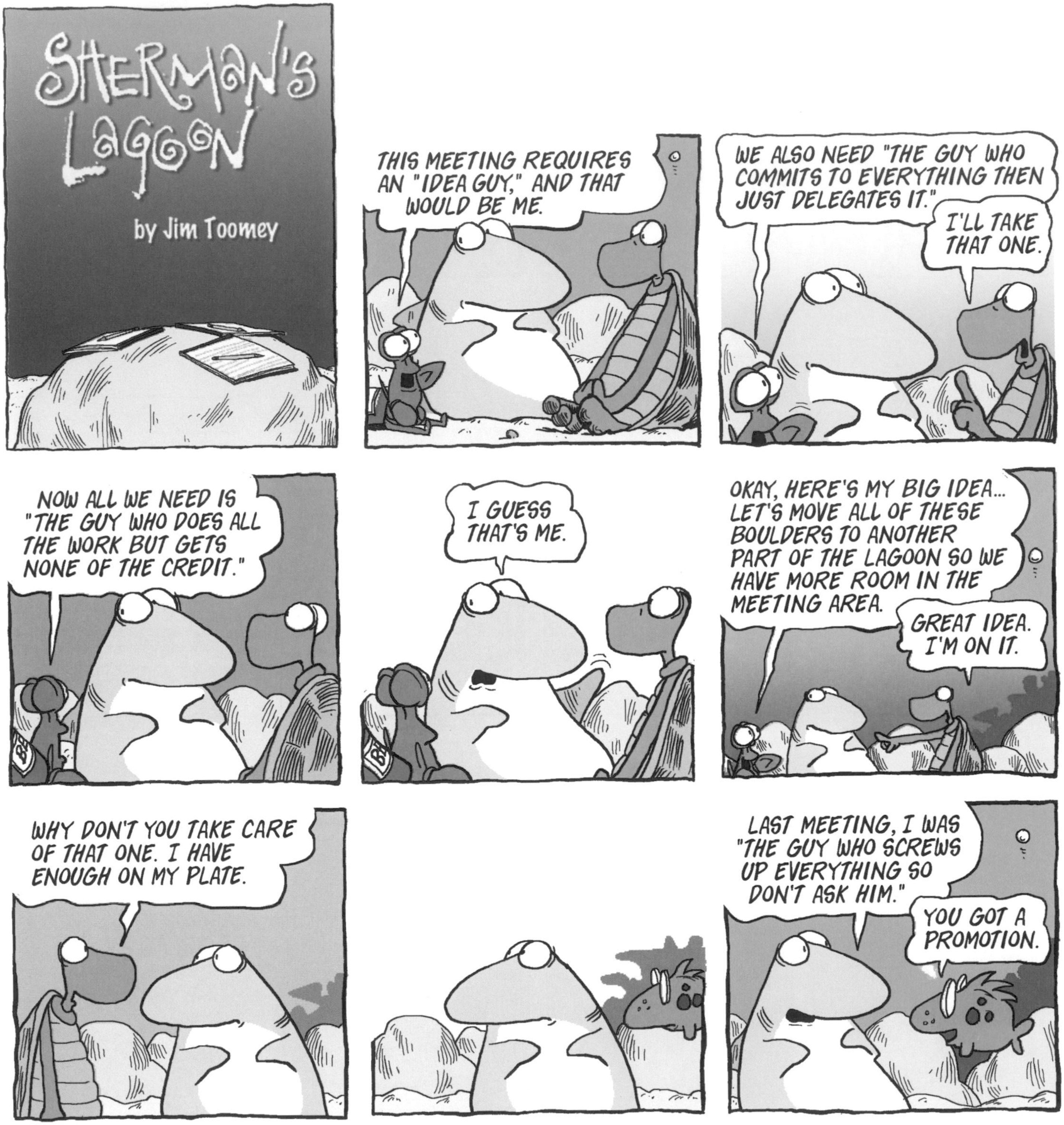
SHERMAN'S LAGOON
by Jim Toomey
THIS MEETING REQUIRES AN "IDEA GUY," AND THAT WOULD BE ME.
WE ALSO NEED "THE GUY WHO COMMITS TO EVERYTHING THEN JUST DELEGATES IT."
I'LL TAKE THAT ONE.
NOW ALL WE NEED IS "THE GUY WHO DOES ALL THE WORK BUT GETS NONE OF THE CREDIT."
I GUESS THAT'S ME.
OKAY, HERE'S MY BIG IDEA... LET'S MOVE ALL OF THESE BOULDERS TO ANOTHER PART OF THE LAGOON SO WE HAVE MORE ROOM IN THE MEETING AREA.
GREAT IDEA. I'M ON IT.
WHY DON'T YOU TAKE CARE OF THAT ONE. I HAVE ENOUGH ON MY PLATE.
LAST MEETING, I WAS "THE GUY WHO SCREWS UP EVERYTHING SO DON'T ASK HIM."
YOU GOT A PROMOTION.

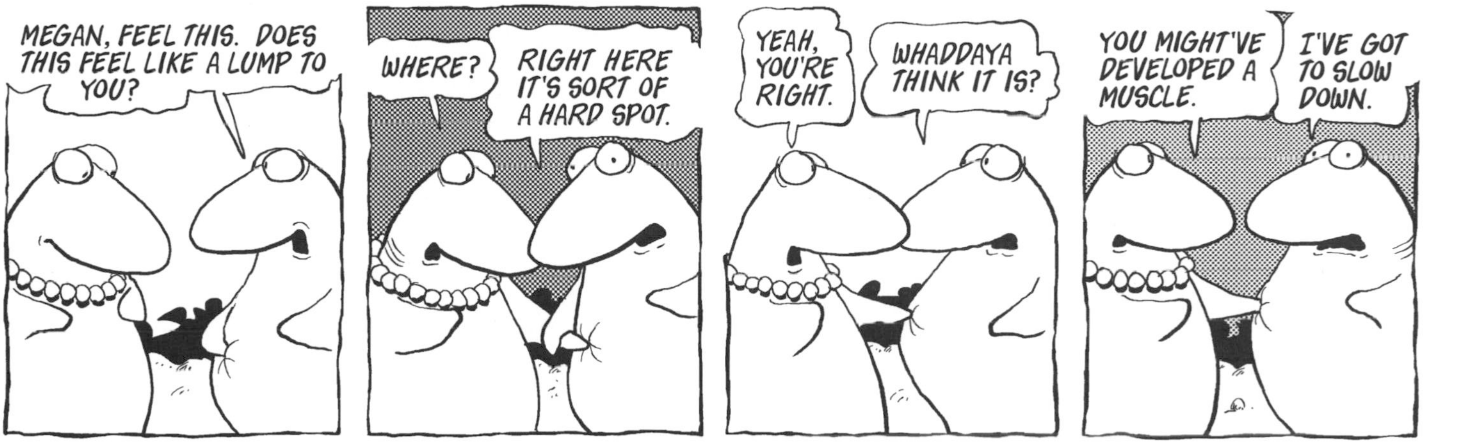
MEGAN, FEEL THIS. DOES THIS FEEL LIKE A LUMP TO YOU?
WHERE?
RIGHT HERE IT'S SORT OF A HARD SPOT.
YEAH, YOU'RE RIGHT.
WHADDAYA THINK IT IS?
YOU MIGHT'VE DEVELOPED A MUSCLE.
I'VE GOT TO SLOW DOWN.

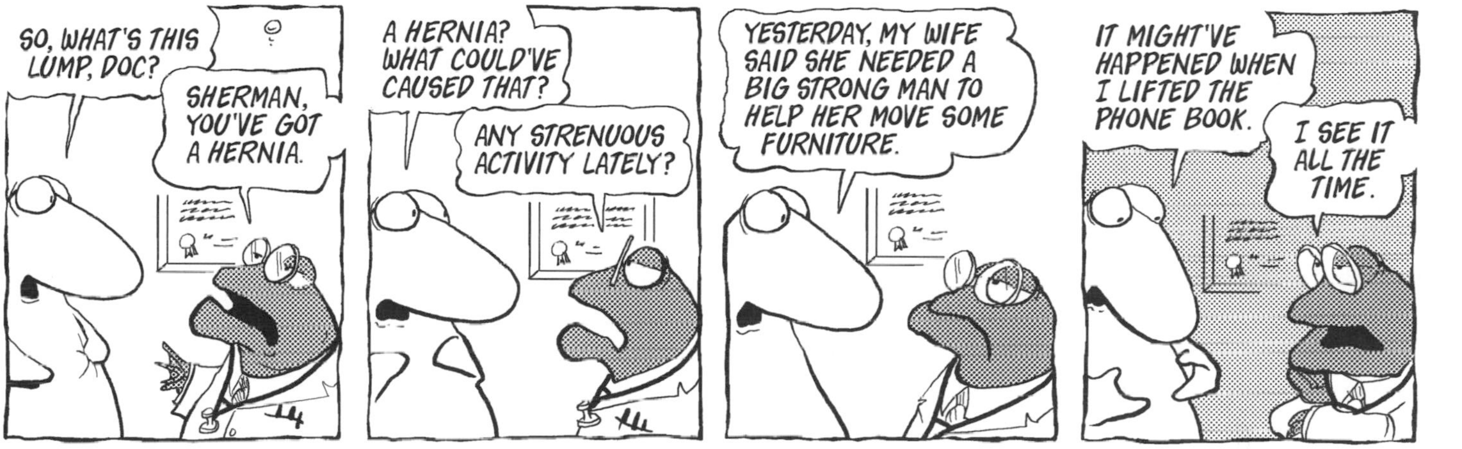
SO, WHAT'S THIS LUMP, DOC?
SHERMAN, YOU'VE GOT A HERNIA.
A HERNIA? WHAT COULD'VE CAUSED THAT?
ANY STRENUOUS ACTIVITY LATELY?
YESTERDAY, MY WIFE SAID SHE NEEDED A BIG STRONG MAN TO HELP HER MOVE SOME FURNITURE.
IT MIGHT'VE HAPPENED WHEN I LIFTED THE PHONE BOOK.
I SEE IT ALL THE TIME.

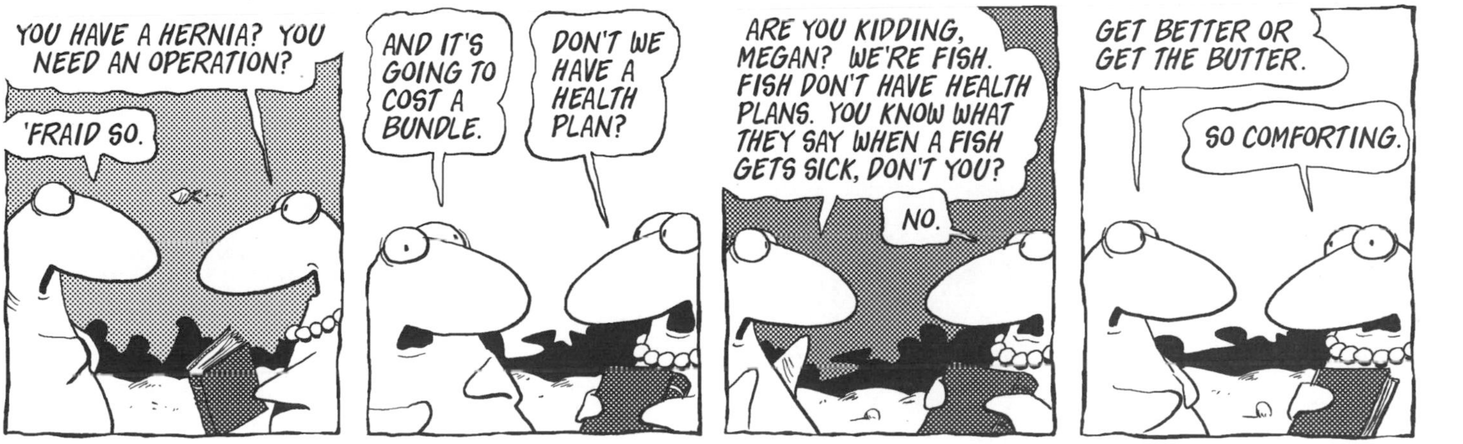
YOU HAVE A HERNIA? YOU NEED AN OPERATION?
'FRAID SO.
AND IT'S GOING TO COST A BUNDLE.
DON'T WE HAVE A HEALTH PLAN?
ARE YOU KIDDING, MEGAN? WE'RE FISH. FISH DON'T HAVE HEALTH PLANS. YOU KNOW WHAT THEY SAY WHEN A FISH GETS SICK, DON'T YOU?
NO.
GET BETTER OR GET THE BUTTER.
SO COMFORTING.

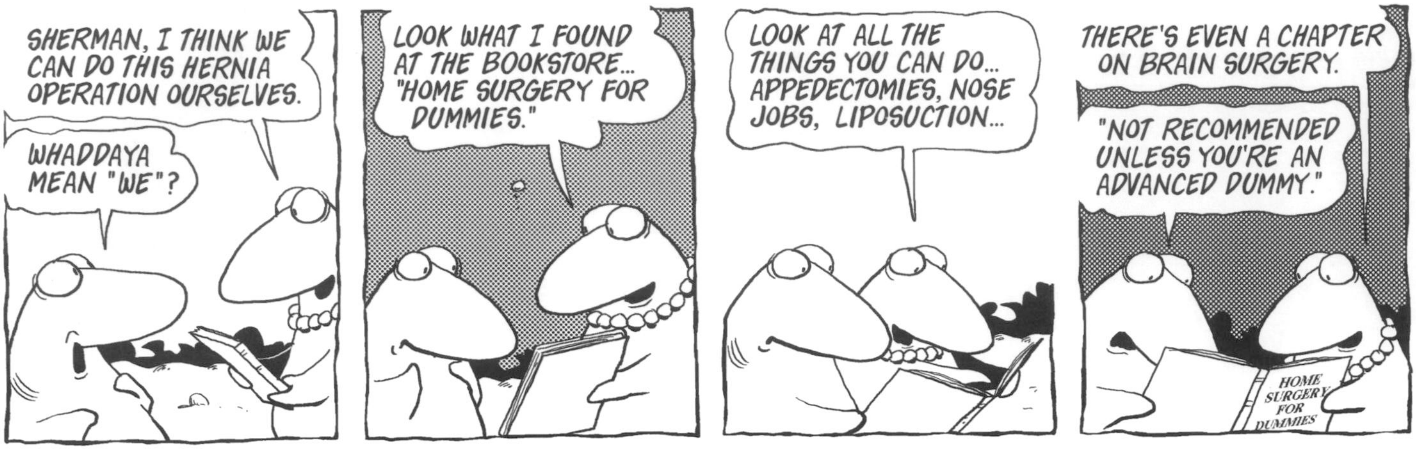
SHERMAN, I THINK WE CAN DO THIS HERNIA OPERATION OURSELVES.
WHADDAYA MEAN "WE"?
LOOK WHAT I FOUND AT THE BOOKSTORE... "HOME SURGERY FOR DUMMIES."
LOOK AT ALL THE THINGS YOU CAN DO... APPEDECTOMIES, NOSE JOBS, LIPOSUCTION...
THERE'S EVEN A CHAPTER ON BRAIN SURGERY.
"NOT RECOMMENDED UNLESS YOU'RE AN ADVANCED DUMMY."
HOME SURGERY FOR DUMMIES

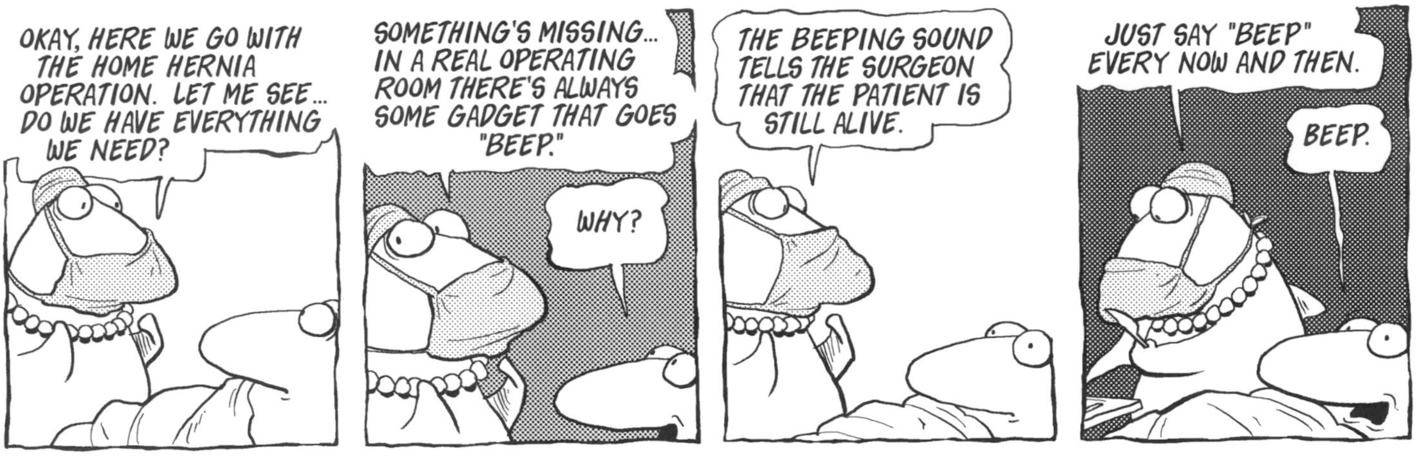
OKAY, HERE WE GO WITH THE HOME HERNIA OPERATION. LET ME SEE... DO WE HAVE EVERYTHING WE NEED?
SOMETHING'S MISSING... IN A REAL OPERATING ROOM THERE'S ALWAYS SOME GADGET THAT GOES "BEEP."
WHY?
THE BEEPING SOUND TELLS THE SURGEON THAT THE PATIENT IS STILL ALIVE.
JUST SAY "BEEP" EVERY NOW AND THEN.
BEEP.

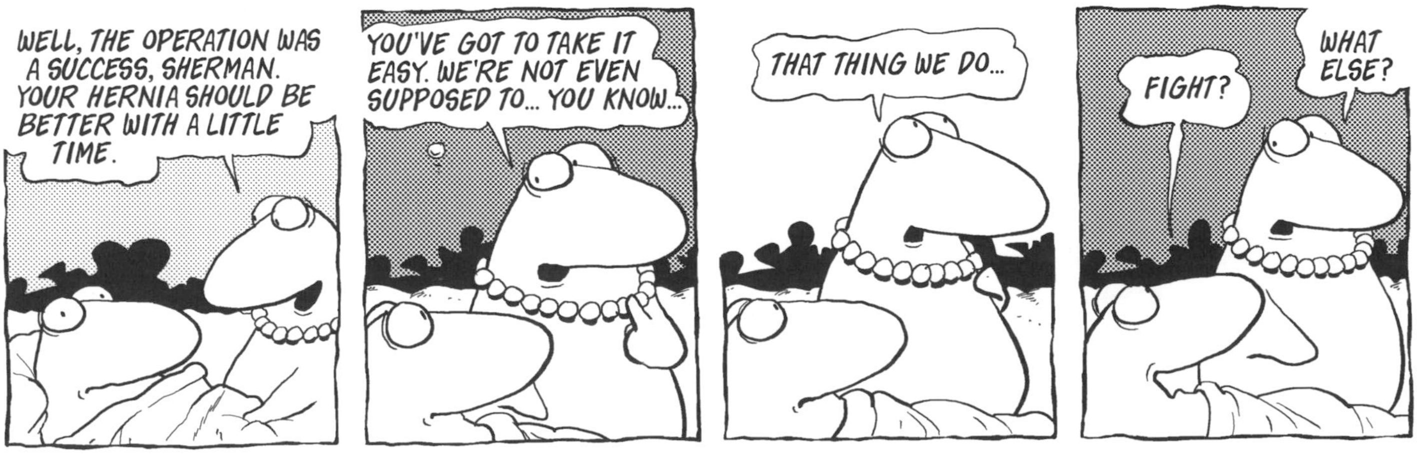
WELL, THE OPERATION WAS A SUCCESS, SHERMAN. YOUR HERNIA SHOULD BE BETTER WITH A LITTLE TIME.
YOU'VE GOT TO TAKE IT EASY. WE'RE NOT EVEN SUPPOSED TO... YOU KNOW...
THAT THING WE DO...
FIGHT?
WHAT ELSE?

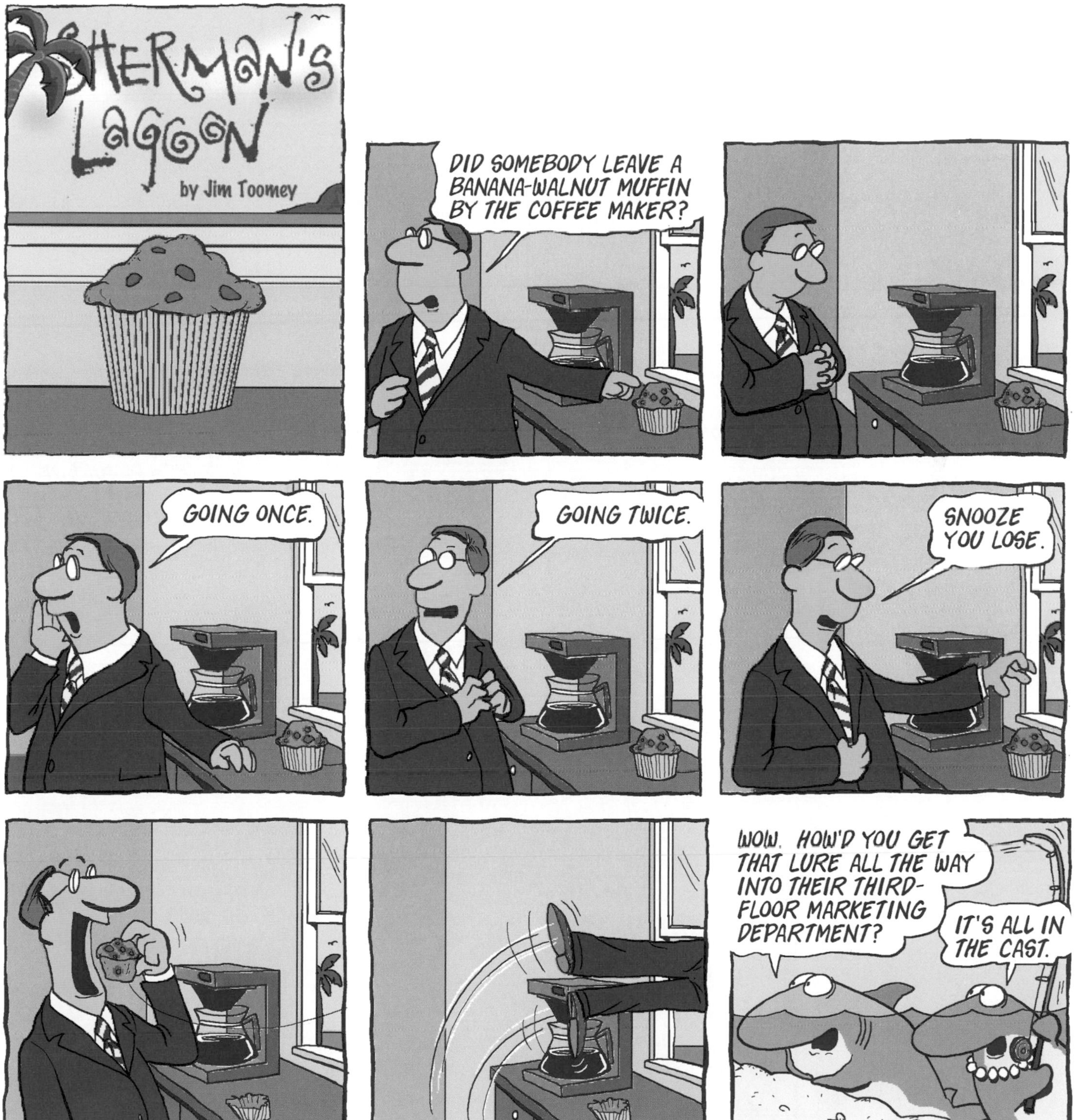
SHERMAN'S LAGOON
by Jim Toomey
DID SOMEBODY LEAVE A BANANA-WALNUT MUFFIN BY THE COFFEE MAKER?
GOING ONCE.
GOING TWICE.
SNOOZE YOU LOSE.
WOW. HOW'D YOU GET THAT LURE ALL THE WAY INTO THEIR THIRD-FLOOR MARKETING DEPARTMENT?
IT'S ALL IN THE CAST.

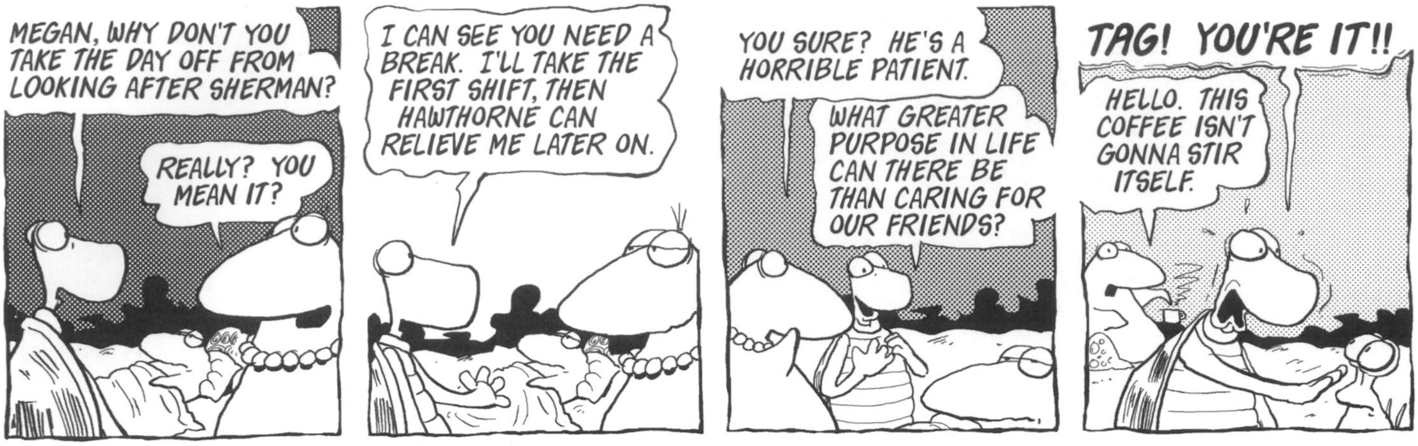
MEGAN, WHY DON'T YOU TAKE THE DAY OFF FROM LOOKING AFTER SHERMAN?
REALLY? YOU MEAN IT?
I CAN SEE YOU NEED A BREAK. I'LL TAKE THE FIRST SHIFT, THEN HAWTHORNE CAN RELIEVE ME LATER ON.
YOU SURE? HE'S A HORRIBLE PATIENT.
WHAT GREATER PURPOSE IN LIFE CAN THERE BE THAN CARING FOR OUR FRIENDS?
TAG! YOU'RE IT!!
HELLO. THIS COFFEE ISN'T GONNA STIR ITSELF.

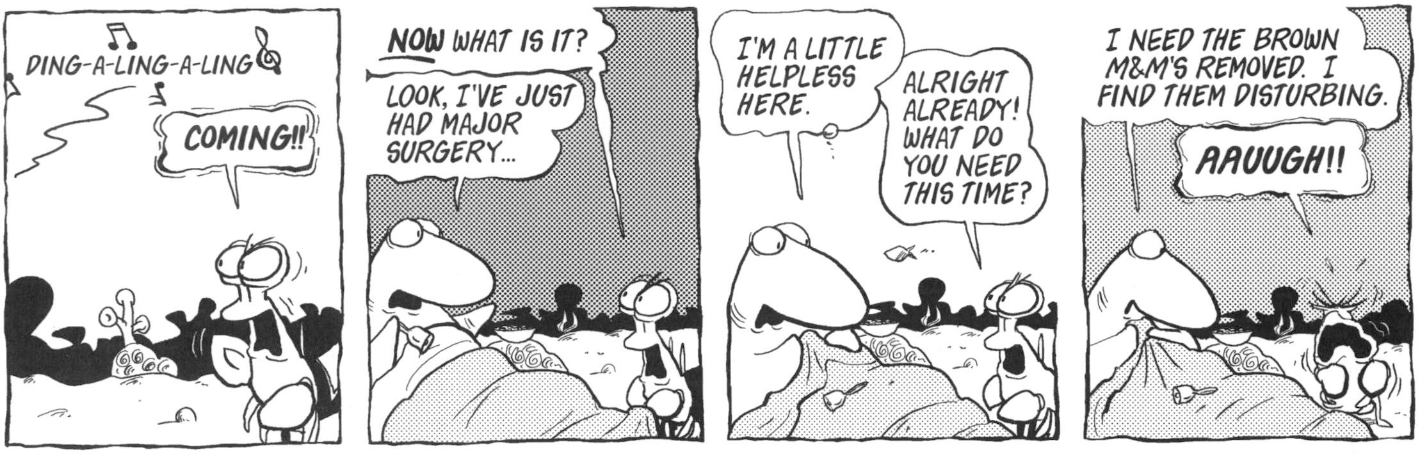
DING-A-LING-A-LING
COMING!!
NOW WHAT IS IT?
LOOK, I'VE JUST HAD MAJOR SURGERY...
I'M A LITTLE HELPLESS HERE.
ALRIGHT ALREADY! WHAT DO YOU NEED THIS TIME?
I NEED THE BROWN M&M'S REMOVED. I FIND THEM DISTURBING.
AAUUGH!!

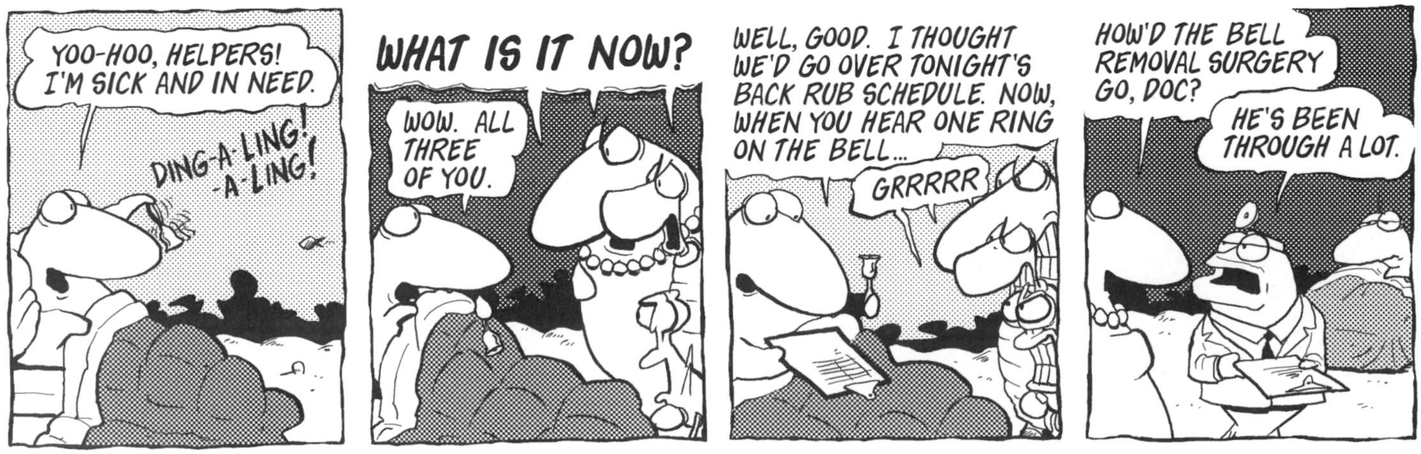
YOO-HOO, HELPERS! I'M SICK AND IN NEED.
DING-A-LING! -A-LING!
WHAT IS IT NOW?
WOW. ALL THREE OF YOU.
WELL, GOOD. I THOUGHT WE'D GO OVER TONIGHT'S BACK RUB SCHEDULE. NOW, WHEN YOU HEAR ONE RING ON THE BELL...
GRRRRR
HOW'D THE BELL REMOVAL SURGERY GO, DOC?
HE'S BEEN THROUGH A LOT.

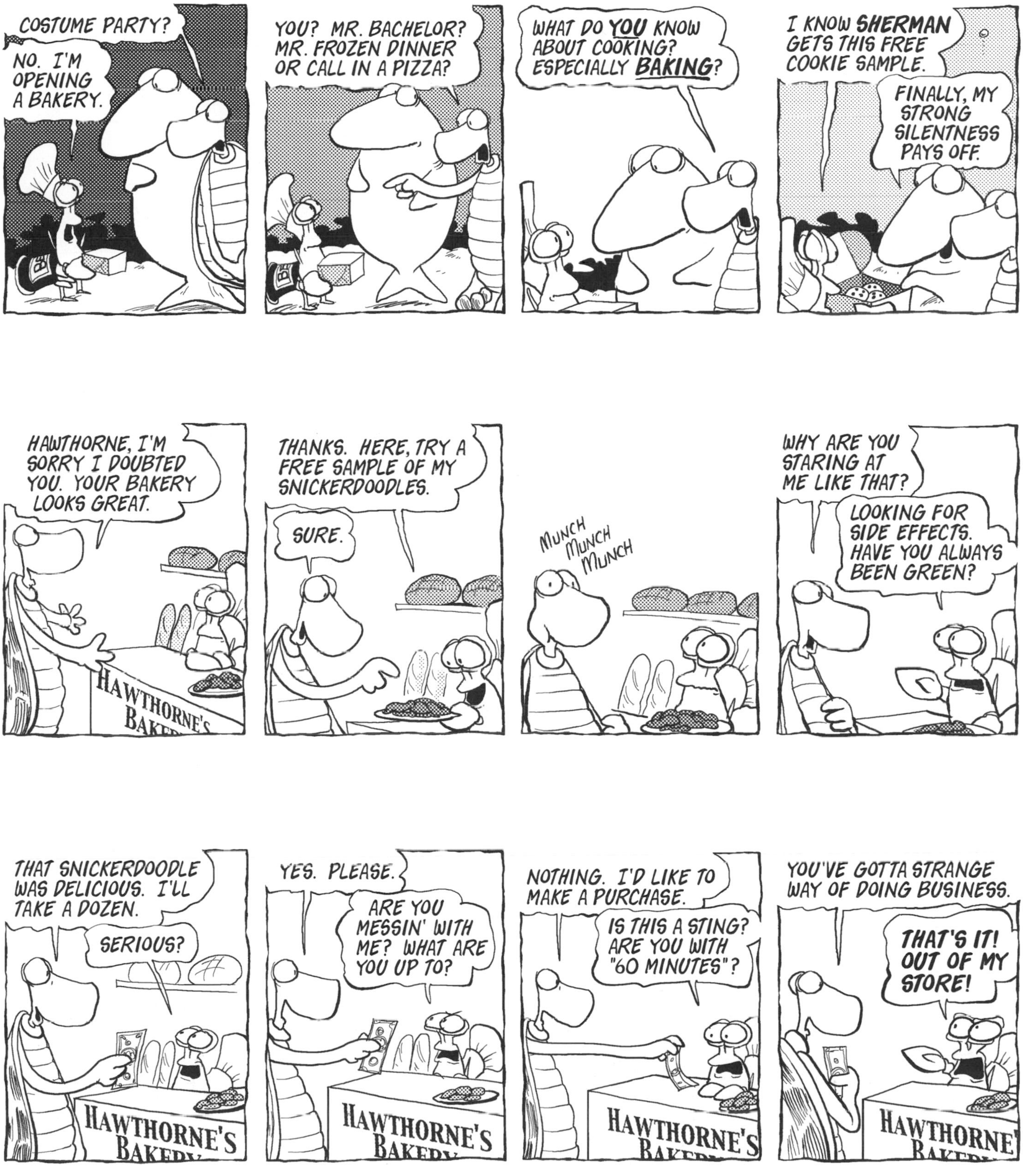
COSTUME PARTY?
NO. I'M OPENING A BAKERY.
YOU? MR. BACHELOR? MR. FROZEN DINNER OR CALL IN A PIZZA?
WHAT DO YOU KNOW ABOUT COOKING? ESPECIALLY BAKING?
I KNOW SHERMAN GETS THIS FREE COOKIE SAMPLE.
FINALLY, MY STRONG SILENTNESS PAYS OFF.
HAWTHORNE, I'M SORRY I DOUBTED YOU. YOUR BAKERY LOOKS GREAT.
HAWTHORNE'S BAKERY
THANKS. HERE, TRY A FREE SAMPLE OF MY SNICKERDOODLES.
SURE.
MUNCH MUNCH MUNCH
WHY ARE YOU STARING AT ME LIKE THAT?
LOOKING FOR SIDE EFFECTS. HAVE YOU ALWAYS BEEN GREEN?
THAT SNICKERDOODLE WAS DELICIOUS. I'LL TAKE A DOZEN.
SERIOUS?
HAWTHORNE'S BAKERY
YES. PLEASE.
ARE YOU MESSIN' WITH ME? WHAT ARE YOU UP TO?
HAWTHORNE'S BAKERY
NOTHING. I'D LIKE TO MAKE A PURCHASE.
IS THIS A STING? ARE YOU WITH "60 MINUTES"?
HAWTHORNE'S BAKERY
YOU'VE GOTTA STRANGE WAY OF DOING BUSINESS.
THAT'S IT! OUT OF MY STORE!
HAWTHORNE'S BAKERY

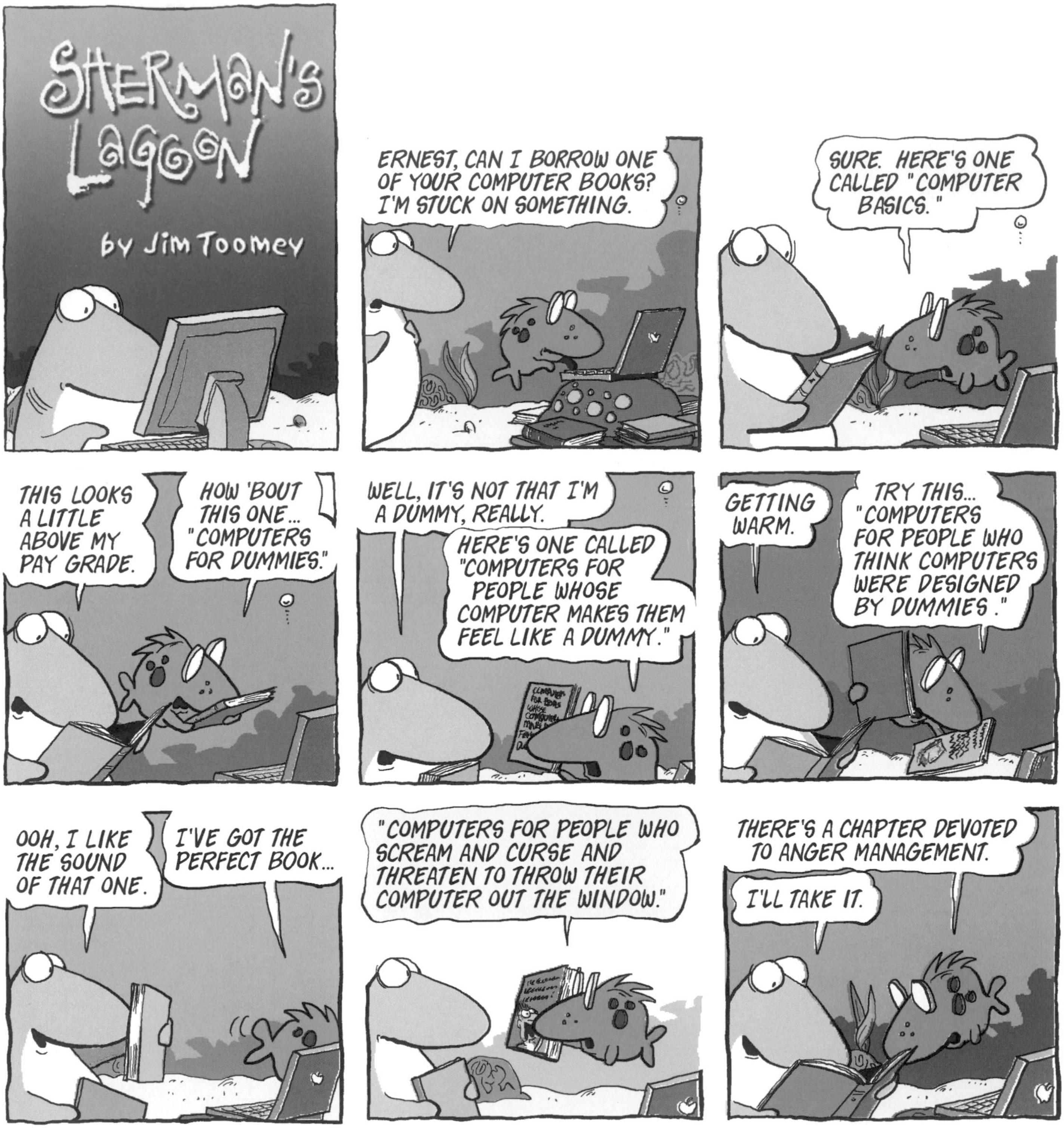
SHERMAN'S LAGOON
by JIM TOOMEY
ERNEST, CAN I BORROW ONE OF YOUR COMPUTER BOOKS? I'M STUCK ON SOMETHING.
SURE. HERE'S ONE CALLED "COMPUTER BASICS."
THIS LOOKS A LITTLE ABOVE MY PAY GRADE.
HOW 'BOUT THIS ONE... "COMPUTERS FOR DUMMIES."
WELL, IT'S NOT THAT I'M A DUMMY, REALLY.
HERE'S ONE CALLED "COMPUTERS FOR PEOPLE WHOSE COMPUTER MAKES THEM FEEL LIKE A DUMMY."
GETTING WARM.
TRY THIS... "COMPUTERS FOR PEOPLE WHO THINK COMPUTERS WERE DESIGNED BY DUMMIES."
OOH, I LIKE THE SOUND OF THAT ONE.
I'VE GOT THE PERFECT BOOK...
"COMPUTERS FOR PEOPLE WHO SCREAM AND CURSE AND THREATEN TO THROW THEIR COMPUTER OUT THE WINDOW."
THERE'S A CHAPTER DEVOTED TO ANGER MANAGEMENT.
I'LL TAKE IT.

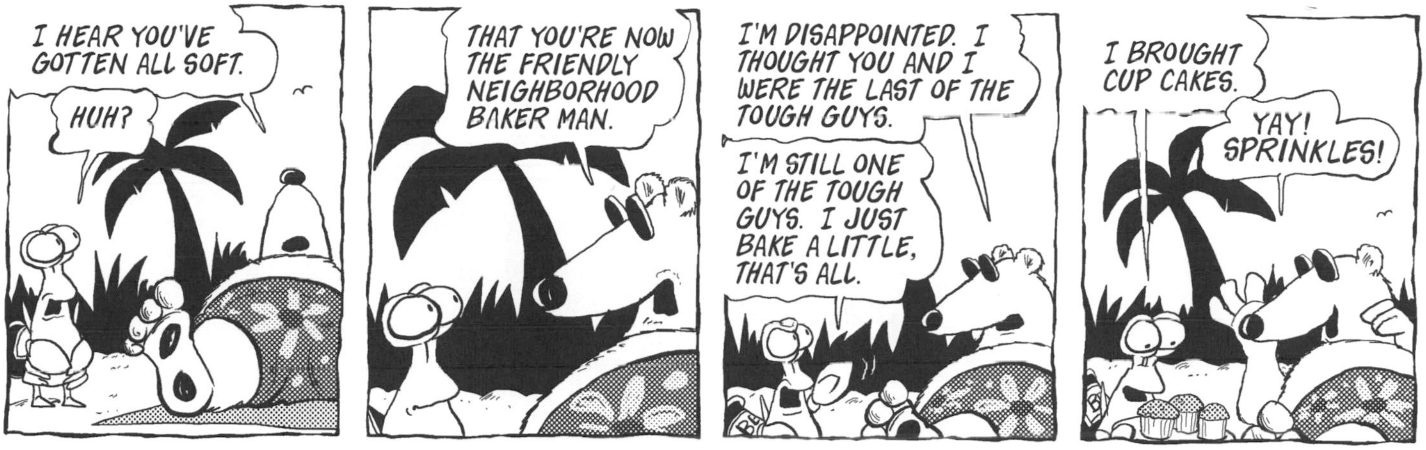
I HEAR YOU'VE GOTTEN ALL SOFT.
HUH?
THAT YOU'RE NOW THE FRIENDLY NEIGHBORHOOD BAKER MAN.
I'M DISAPPOINTED. I THOUGHT YOU AND I WERE THE LAST OF THE TOUGH GUYS.
I'M STILL ONE OF THE TOUGH GUYS. I JUST BAKE A LITTLE, THAT'S ALL.
I BROUGHT CUP CAKES.
YAY! SPRINKLES!

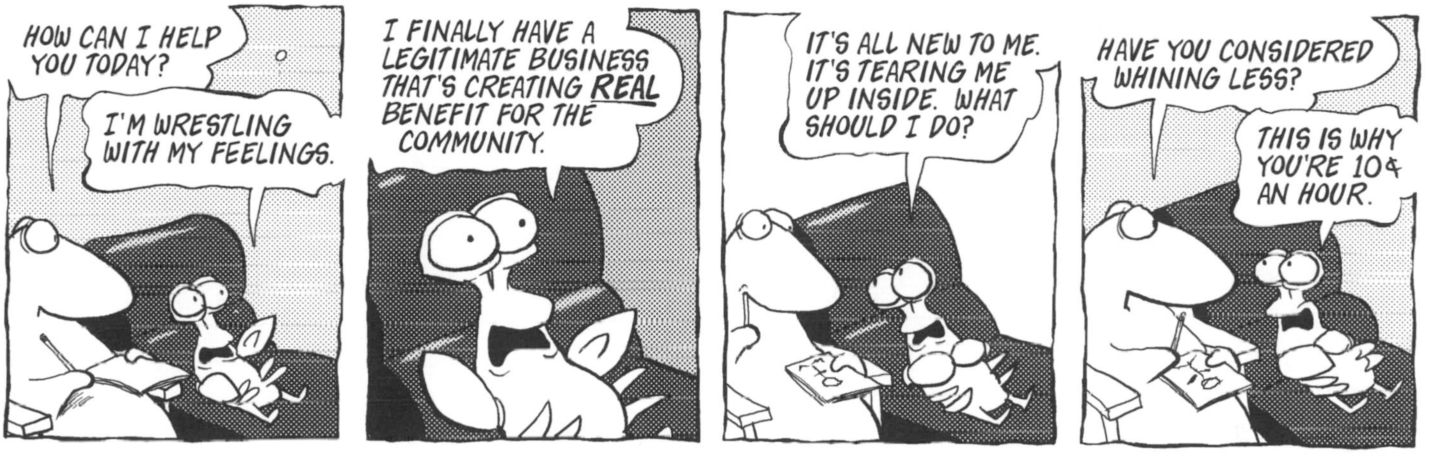
HOW CAN I HELP YOU TODAY?
I'M WRESTLING WITH MY FEELINGS.
I FINALLY HAVE A LEGITIMATE BUSINESS THAT'S CREATING REAL BENEFIT FOR THE COMMUNITY.
IT'S ALL NEW TO ME. IT'S TEARING ME UP INSIDE. WHAT SHOULD I DO?
HAVE YOU CONSIDERED WHINING LESS?
THIS IS WHY YOU'RE 10¢ AN HOUR.

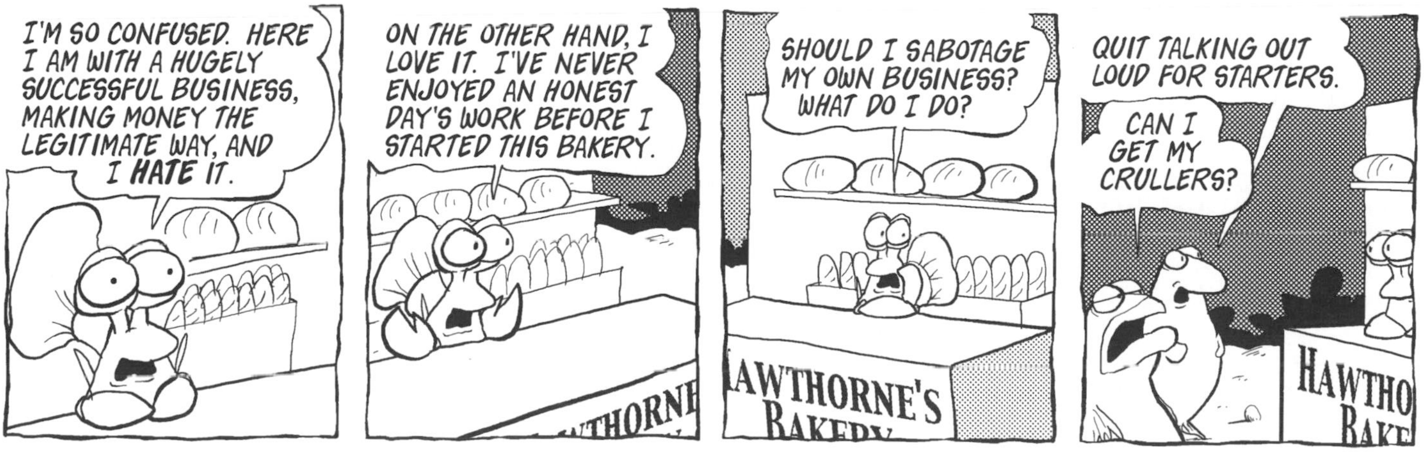
I'M SO CONFUSED. HERE I AM WITH A HUGELY SUCCESSFUL BUSINESS, MAKING MONEY THE LEGITIMATE WAY, AND I HATE IT.
ON THE OTHER HAND, I LOVE IT. I'VE NEVER ENJOYED AN HONEST DAY'S WORK BEFORE I STARTED THIS BAKERY.
SHOULD I SABOTAGE MY OWN BUSINESS? WHAT DO I DO?
HAWTHORNE'S BAKERY
QUIT TALKING OUT LOUD FOR STARTERS.
CAN I GET MY CRULLERS?

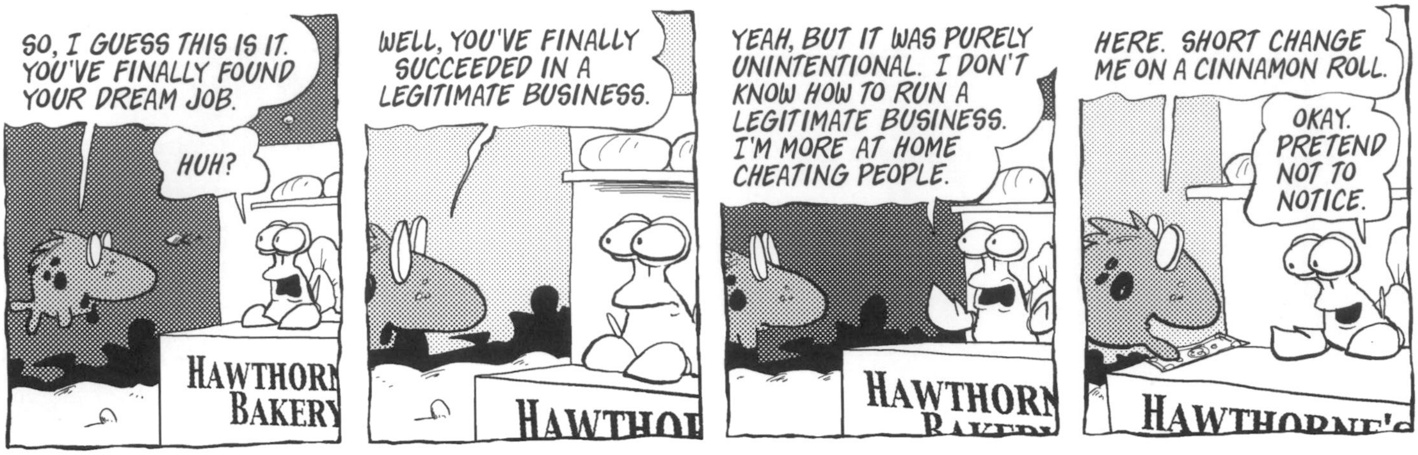
SO, I GUESS THIS IS IT. YOU'VE FINALLY FOUND YOUR DREAM JOB.
HUH?
WELL, YOU'VE FINALLY SUCCEEDED IN A LEGITIMATE BUSINESS.
YEAH, BUT IT WAS PURELY UNINTENTIONAL. I DON'T KNOW HOW TO RUN A LEGITIMATE BUSINESS. I'M MORE AT HOME CHEATING PEOPLE.
HERE. SHORT CHANGE ME ON A CINNAMON ROLL.
OKAY. PRETEND NOT TO NOTICE.
HAWTHORNE'S

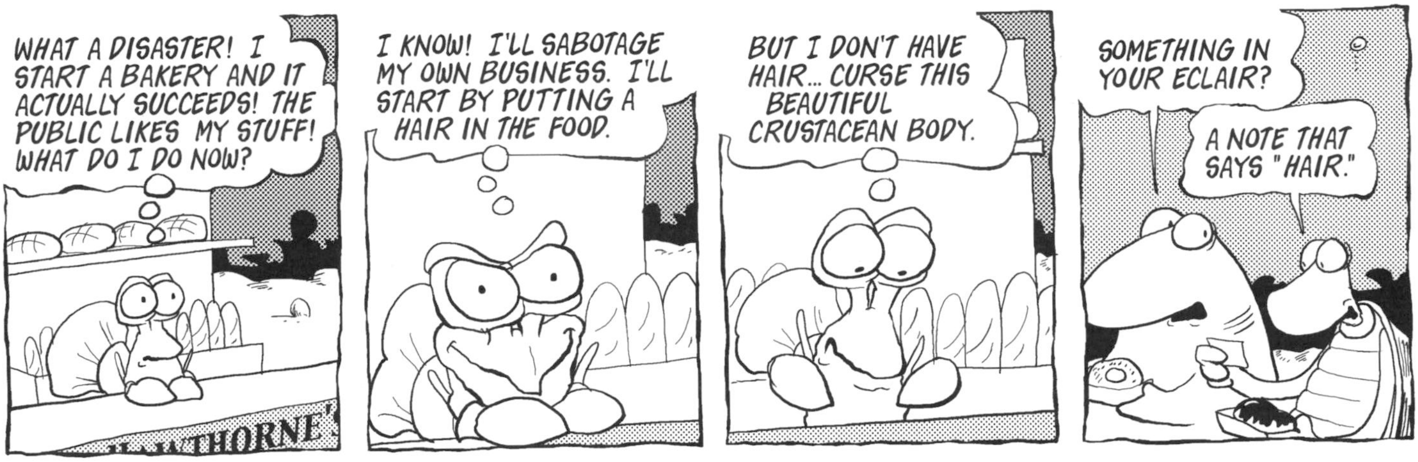
WHAT A DISASTER! I START A BAKERY AND IT ACTUALLY SUCCEEDS! THE PUBLIC LIKES MY STUFF! WHAT DO I DO NOW?
I KNOW! I'LL SABOTAGE MY OWN BUSINESS. I'LL START BY PUTTING A HAIR IN THE FOOD.
BUT I DON'T HAVE HAIR... CURSE THIS BEAUTIFUL CRUSTACEAN BODY.
SOMETHING IN YOUR ECLAIR?
A NOTE THAT SAYS "HAIR."

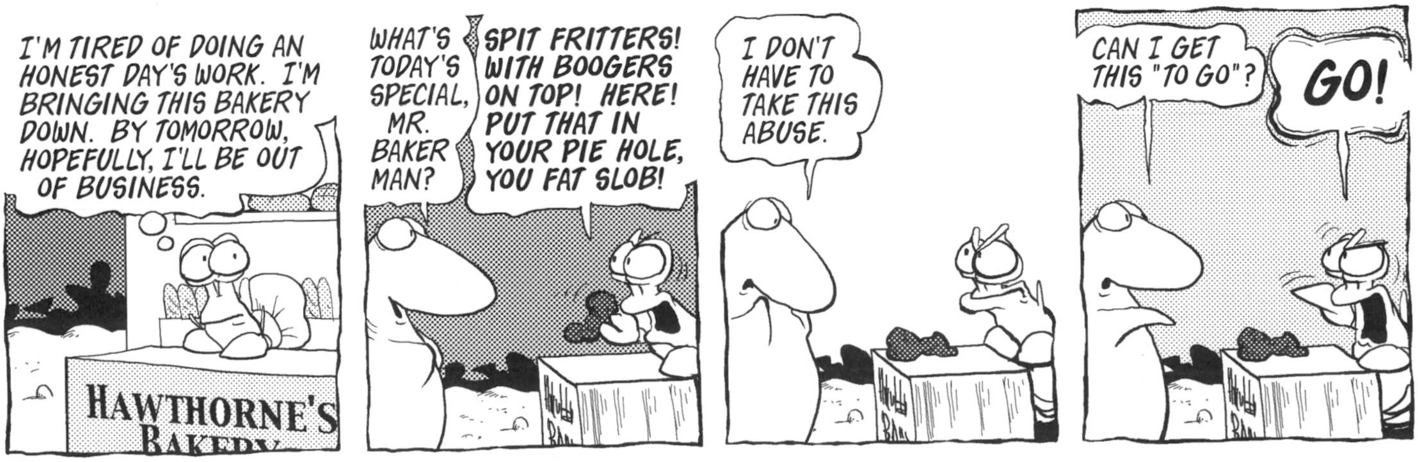
I'M TIRED OF DOING AN HONEST DAY'S WORK. I'M BRINGING THIS BAKERY DOWN. BY TOMORROW, HOPEFULLY, I'LL BE OUT OF BUSINESS.
HAWTHORNE'S
WHAT'S TODAY'S SPECIAL, MR. BAKER MAN?
SPIT FRITTERS! WITH BOOGERS ON TOP! HERE! PUT THAT IN YOUR PIE HOLE, YOU FAT SLOB!
I DON'T HAVE TO TAKE THIS ABUSE.
CAN I GET THIS "TO GO"?
GO!

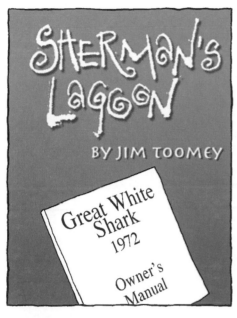

SHERMAN'S LAGOON

BY JIM TOOMEY

Great White Shark 1972 Owner's Manual

HEY, SHERM, YOU KNOW THAT LITTLE FIN YOU HAVE NEAR YOUR TAIL?

YEAH.

WHAT'S IT DO?

HUH?... UH... WHY DO YOU WANT TO KNOW?

JUST CURIOUS.

IT'S UH... IT'S A SPARE FIN... IN CASE THE OTHER ONE FALLS OFF.

YOU'RE JUST MAKING THAT UP.

LOOK. I'M A SHARK. I'VE GOT A TAIL ON ONE END AND A MOUTH ON THE OTHER. I SWIM, I EAT. WHY MAKE THIS MORE COMPLICATED THAN IT IS?

DON'T YOU HAVE AN OWNER'S MANUAL OR SOMETHING?

IT'S AROUND HERE SOME-WHERE.

HERE IT IS.

HERE WE GO. PAGE 64... "THE SECOND DORSAL FIN PROVIDES LATERAL STABILITY WHILE SWIMMING BACKWARDS."

Great White Shark 1972 Owner's Manual

I CAN SWIM BACKWARDS? LEMME SEE THAT THING.

YOU DIDN'T KNOW THAT?

WHO HAS TIME FOR OWNER'S MANUALS!

Great White Shark 1972 Owner's Manual

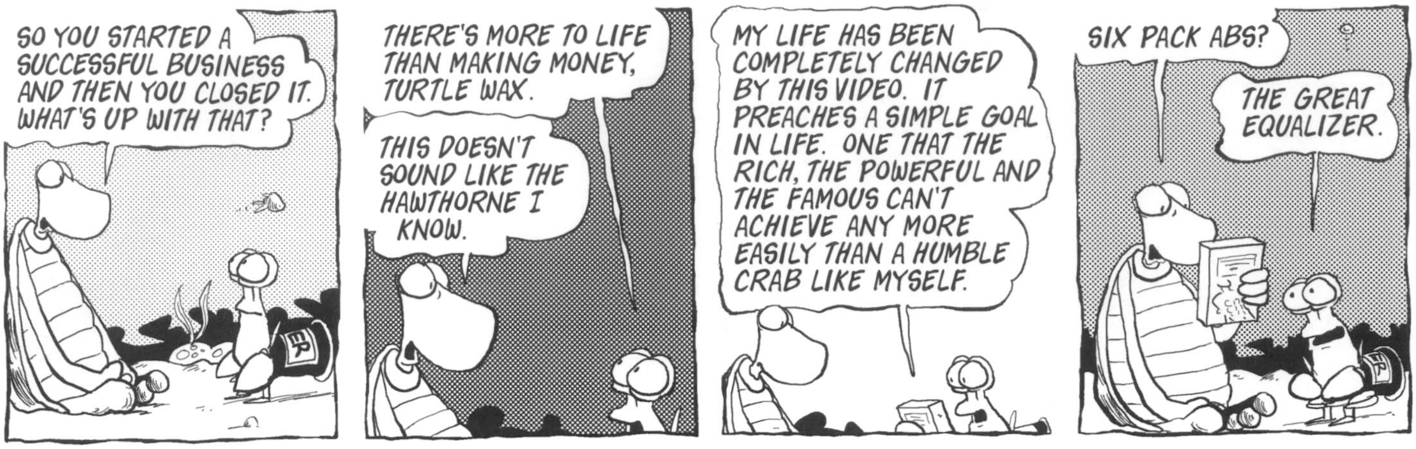
SO YOU STARTED A SUCCESSFUL BUSINESS AND THEN YOU CLOSED IT. WHAT'S UP WITH THAT?
THERE'S MORE TO LIFE THAN MAKING MONEY, TURTLE WAX.
THIS DOESN'T SOUND LIKE THE HAWTHORNE I KNOW.
MY LIFE HAS BEEN COMPLETELY CHANGED BY THIS VIDEO. IT PREACHES A SIMPLE GOAL IN LIFE. ONE THAT THE RICH, THE POWERFUL AND THE FAMOUS CAN'T ACHIEVE ANY MORE EASILY THAN A HUMBLE CRAB LIKE MYSELF.
SIX PACK ABS?
THE GREAT EQUALIZER.

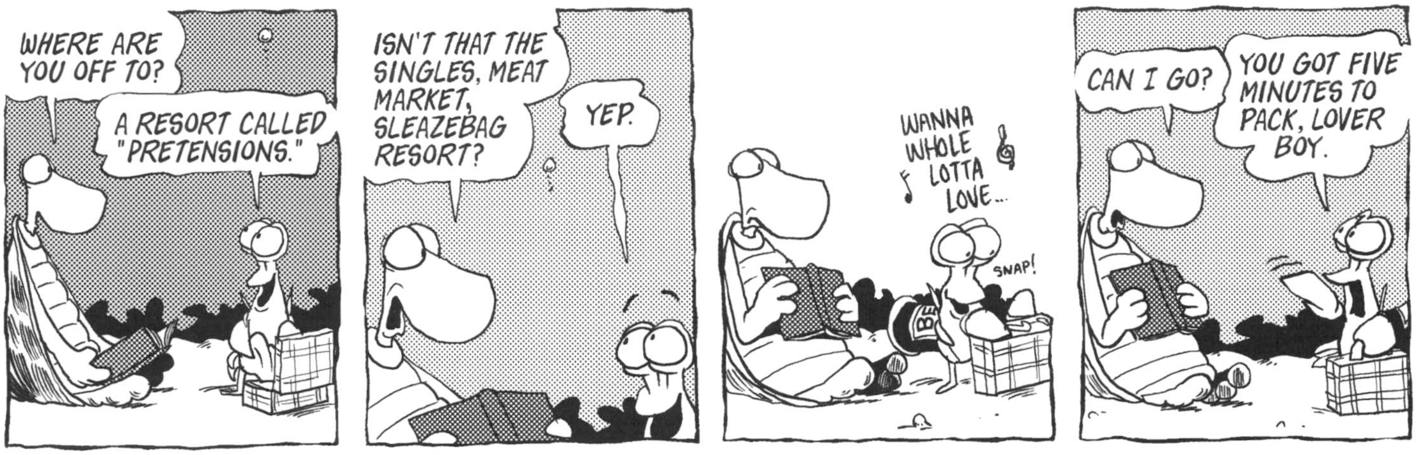
WHERE ARE YOU OFF TO?
A RESORT CALLED "PRETENSIONS."
ISN'T THAT THE SINGLES, MEAT MARKET, SLEAZEBAG RESORT?
YEP.
WANNA WHOLE LOTTA LOVE...
SNAP!
CAN I GO?
YOU GOT FIVE MINUTES TO PACK, LOVER BOY.

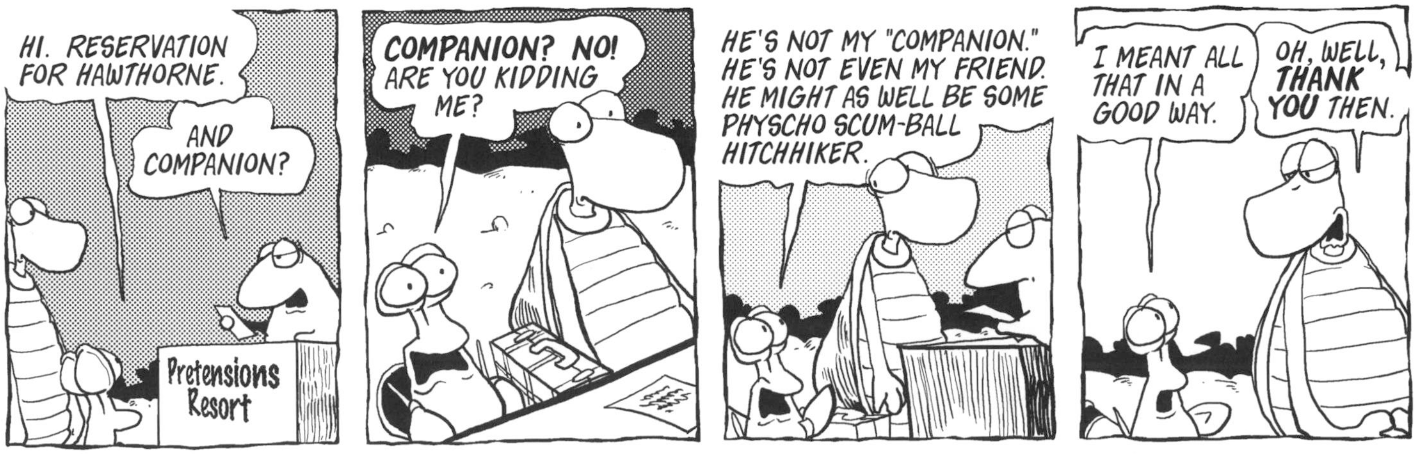
HI. RESERVATION FOR HAWTHORNE.
AND COMPANION?
Pretensions Resort
COMPANION? NO! ARE YOU KIDDING ME?
HE'S NOT MY "COMPANION." HE'S NOT EVEN MY FRIEND. HE MIGHT AS WELL BE SOME PHYSCHO SCUM-BALL HITCHHIKER.
I MEANT ALL THAT IN A GOOD WAY.
OH, WELL, THANK YOU THEN.

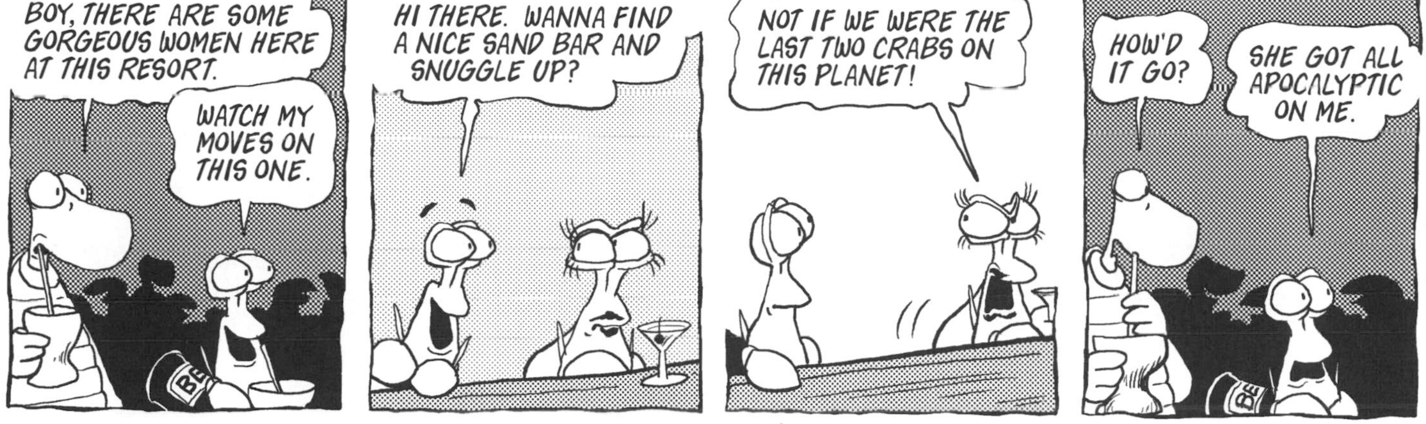
BOY, THERE ARE SOME GORGEOUS WOMEN HERE AT THIS RESORT.
WATCH MY MOVES ON THIS ONE.
HI THERE. WANNA FIND A NICE SAND BAR AND SNUGGLE UP?
NOT IF WE WERE THE LAST TWO CRABS ON THIS PLANET!
HOW'D IT GO?
SHE GOT ALL APOCALYPTIC ON ME.

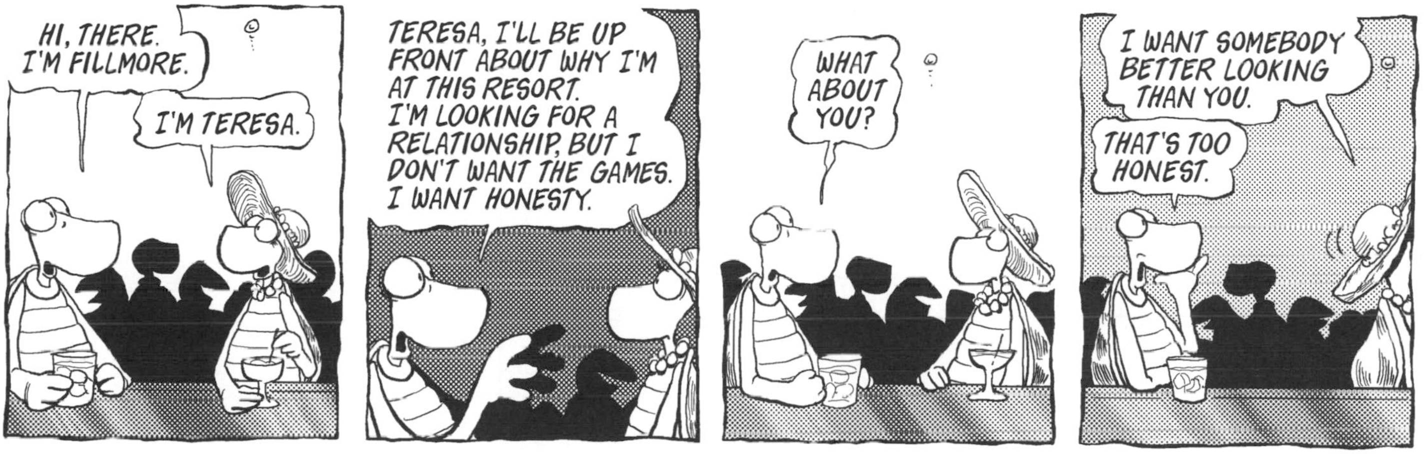
HI, THERE. I'M FILLMORE.
I'M TERESA.
TERESA, I'LL BE UP FRONT ABOUT WHY I'M AT THIS RESORT. I'M LOOKING FOR A RELATIONSHIP, BUT I DON'T WANT THE GAMES. I WANT HONESTY.
WHAT ABOUT YOU?
I WANT SOMEBODY BETTER LOOKING THAN YOU.
THAT'S TOO HONEST.

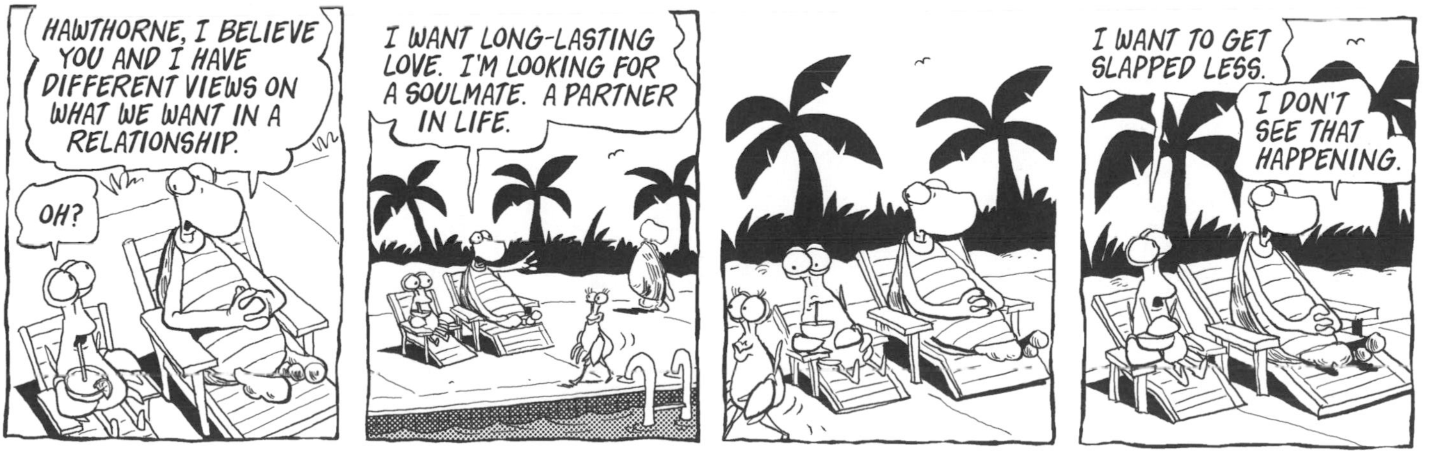
HAWTHORNE, I BELIEVE YOU AND I HAVE DIFFERENT VIEWS ON WHAT WE WANT IN A RELATIONSHIP.
OH?
I WANT LONG-LASTING LOVE. I'M LOOKING FOR A SOULMATE. A PARTNER IN LIFE.
I WANT TO GET SLAPPED LESS.
I DON'T SEE THAT HAPPENING.

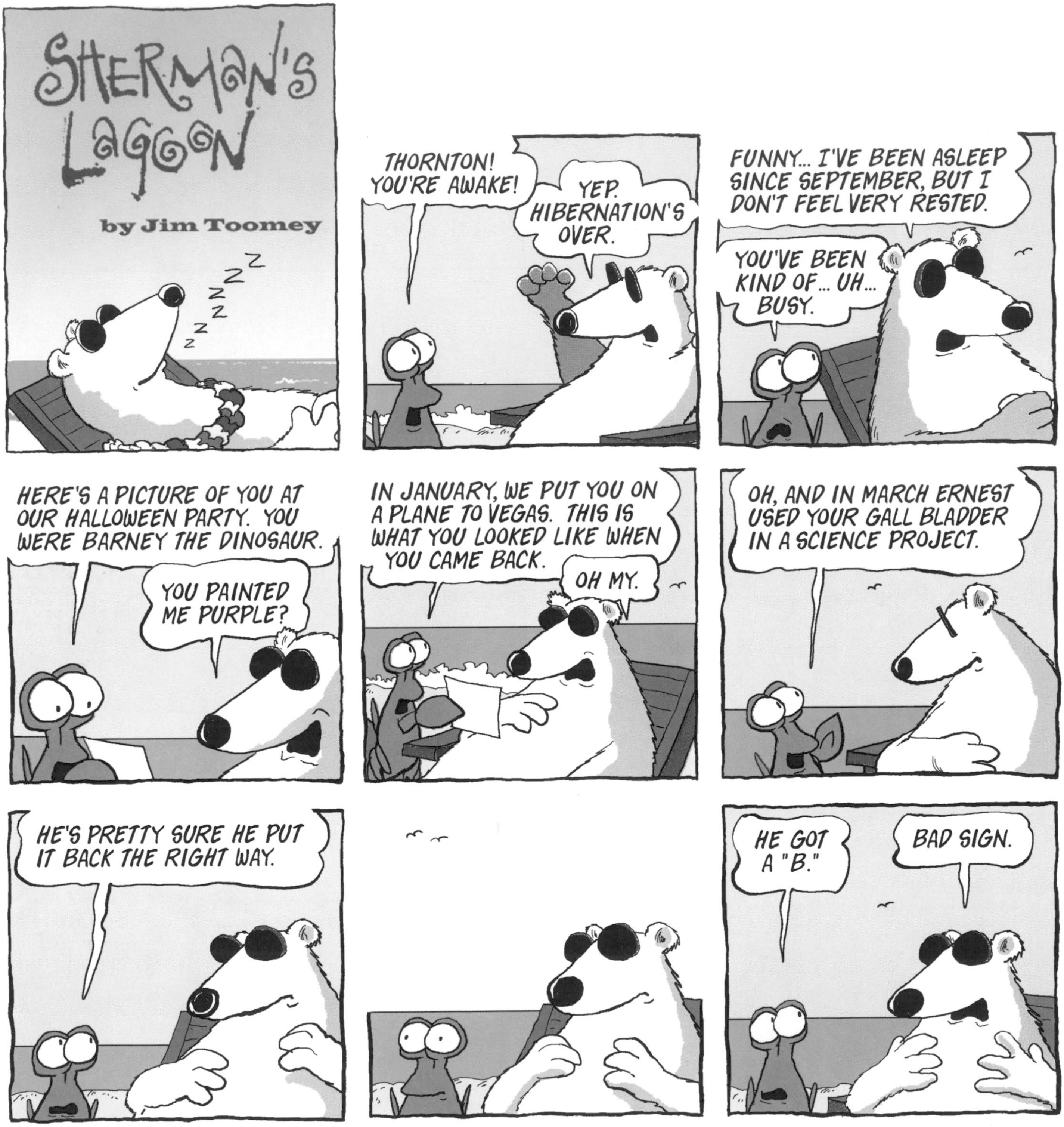
SHERMAN'S LAGOON
by Jim Toomey
Z Z Z Z Z Z Z
THORNTON! YOU'RE AWAKE!
YEP. HIBERNATION'S OVER.
FUNNY... I'VE BEEN ASLEEP SINCE SEPTEMBER, BUT I DON'T FEEL VERY RESTED.
YOU'VE BEEN KIND OF... UH... BUSY.
HERE'S A PICTURE OF YOU AT OUR HALLOWEEN PARTY. YOU WERE BARNEY THE DINOSAUR.
YOU PAINTED ME PURPLE?
IN JANUARY, WE PUT YOU ON A PLANE TO VEGAS. THIS IS WHAT YOU LOOKED LIKE WHEN YOU CAME BACK.
OH MY.
OH, AND IN MARCH ERNEST USED YOUR GALL BLADDER IN A SCIENCE PROJECT.
HE'S PRETTY SURE HE PUT IT BACK THE RIGHT WAY.
HE GOT A "B."
BAD SIGN.

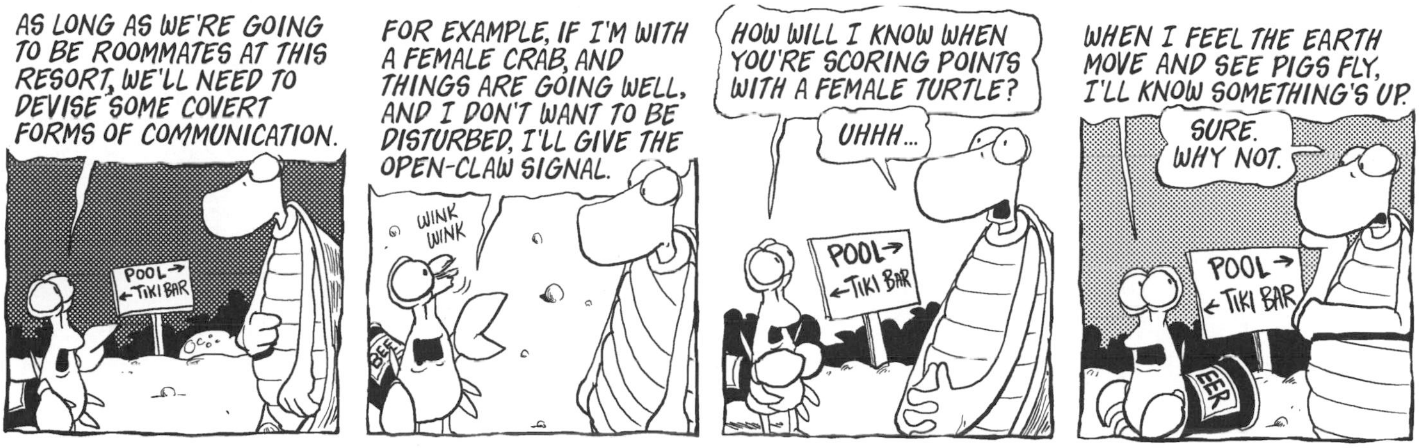
AS LONG AS WE'RE GOING TO BE ROOMMATES AT THIS RESORT, WE'LL NEED TO DEVISE SOME COVERT FORMS OF COMMUNICATION.
POOL →
← TIKI BAR
FOR EXAMPLE, IF I'M WITH A FEMALE CRAB, AND THINGS ARE GOING WELL, AND I DON'T WANT TO BE DISTURBED, I'LL GIVE THE OPEN-CLAW SIGNAL.
WINK WINK
HOW WILL I KNOW WHEN YOU'RE SCORING POINTS WITH A FEMALE TURTLE?
UHHH...
POOL →
← TIKI BAR
WHEN I FEEL THE EARTH MOVE AND SEE PIGS FLY, I'LL KNOW SOMETHING'S UP.
SURE. WHY NOT.
POOL →
← TIKI BAR

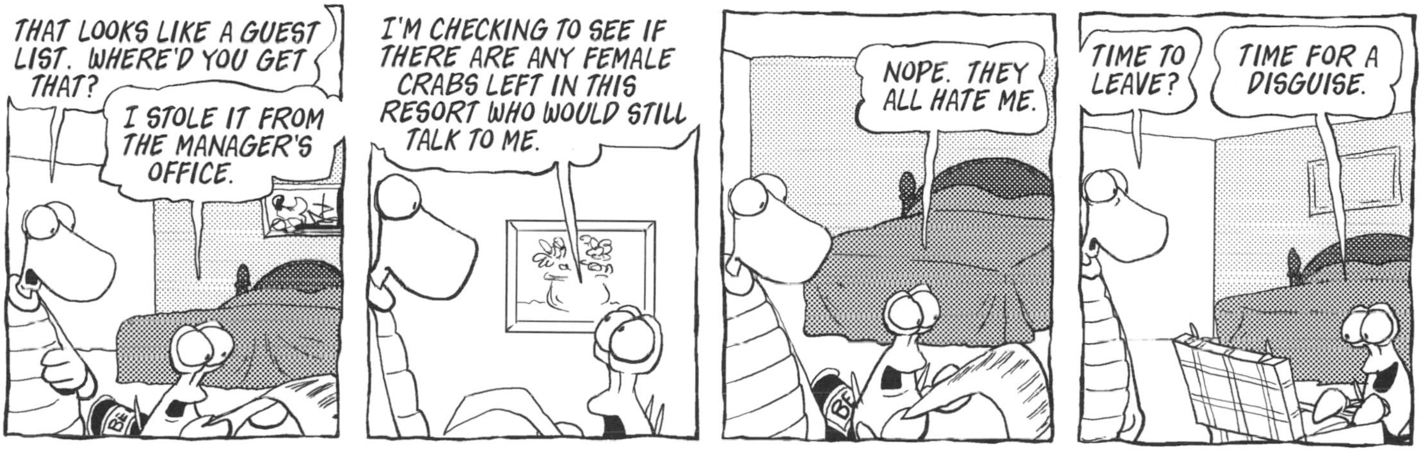
THAT LOOKS LIKE A GUEST LIST. WHERE'D YOU GET THAT?
I STOLE IT FROM THE MANAGER'S OFFICE.
I'M CHECKING TO SEE IF THERE ARE ANY FEMALE CRABS LEFT IN THIS RESORT WHO WOULD STILL TALK TO ME.
NOPE. THEY ALL HATE ME.
TIME TO LEAVE?
TIME FOR A DISGUISE.

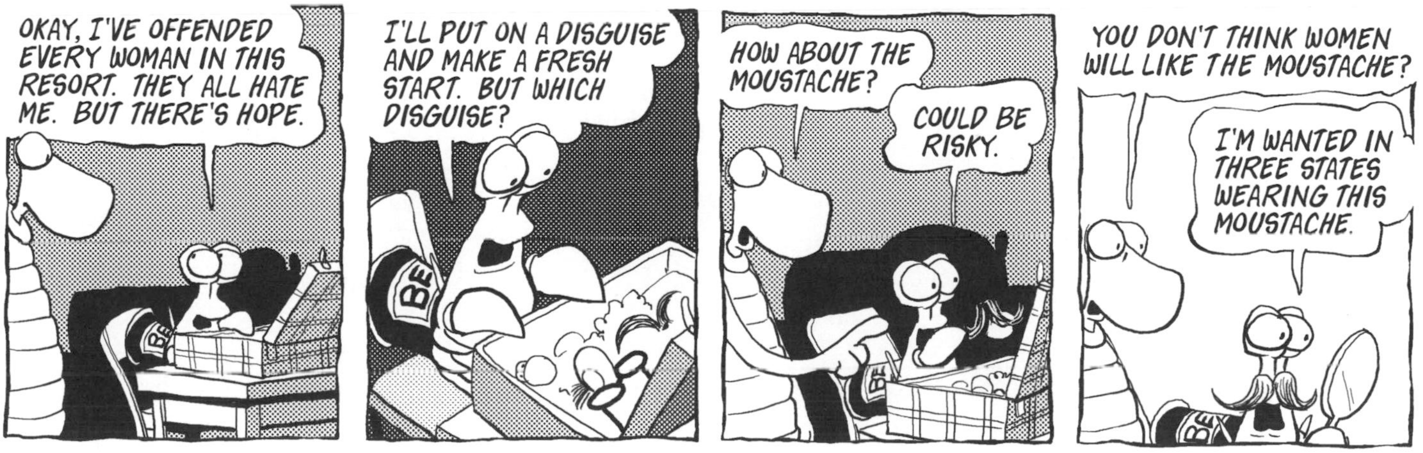
OKAY, I'VE OFFENDED EVERY WOMAN IN THIS RESORT. THEY ALL HATE ME. BUT THERE'S HOPE.
I'LL PUT ON A DISGUISE AND MAKE A FRESH START. BUT WHICH DISGUISE?
HOW ABOUT THE MOUSTACHE?
COULD BE RISKY.
YOU DON'T THINK WOMEN WILL LIKE THE MOUSTACHE?
I'M WANTED IN THREE STATES WEARING THIS MOUSTACHE.

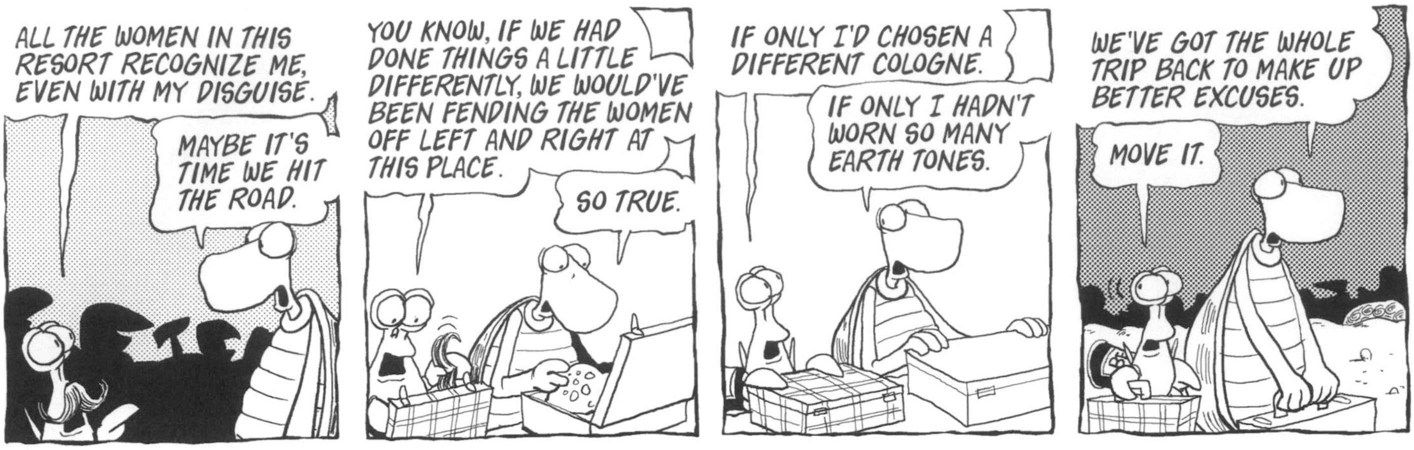
ALL THE WOMEN IN THIS RESORT RECOGNIZE ME, EVEN WITH MY DISGUISE.
MAYBE IT'S TIME WE HIT THE ROAD.
YOU KNOW, IF WE HAD DONE THINGS A LITTLE DIFFERENTLY, WE WOULD'VE BEEN FENDING THE WOMEN OFF LEFT AND RIGHT AT THIS PLACE.
SO TRUE.
IF ONLY I'D CHOSEN A DIFFERENT COLOGNE.
IF ONLY I HADN'T WORN SO MANY EARTH TONES.
WE'VE GOT THE WHOLE TRIP BACK TO MAKE UP BETTER EXCUSES.
MOVE IT.

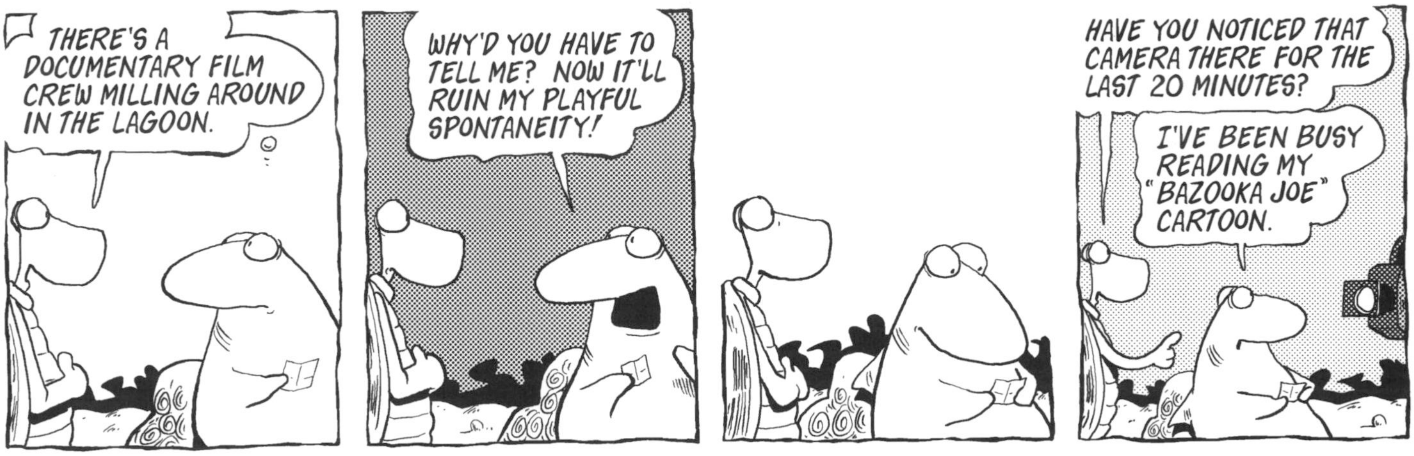
THERE'S A DOCUMENTARY FILM CREW MILLING AROUND IN THE LAGOON.
WHY'D YOU HAVE TO TELL ME? NOW IT'LL RUIN MY PLAYFUL SPONTANEITY!
HAVE YOU NOTICED THAT CAMERA THERE FOR THE LAST 20 MINUTES?
I'VE BEEN BUSY READING MY "BAZOOKA JOE" CARTOON.

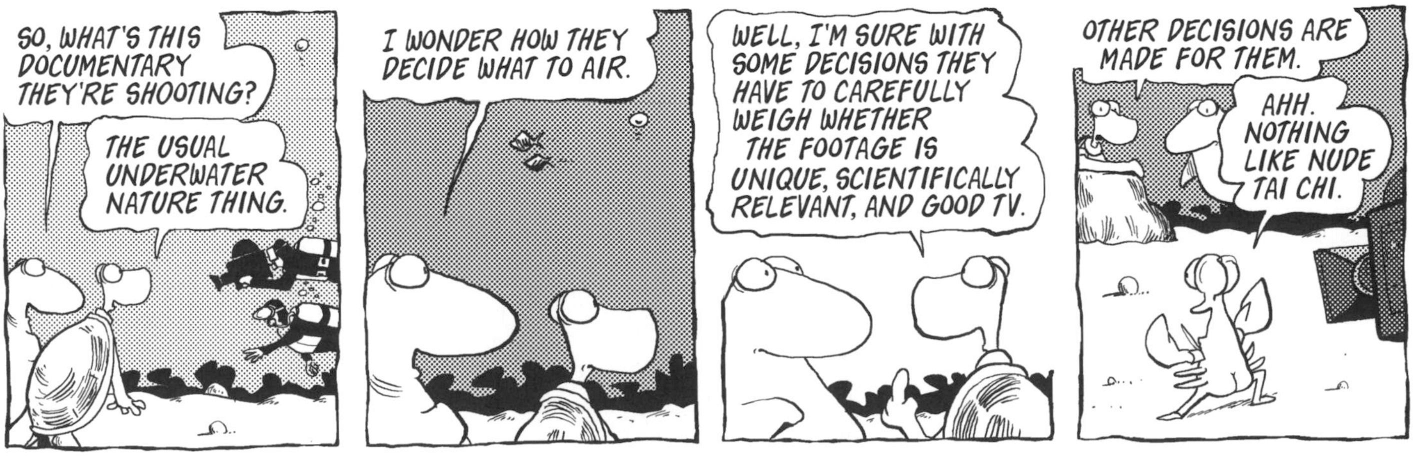
SO, WHAT'S THIS DOCUMENTARY THEY'RE SHOOTING?
THE USUAL UNDERWATER NATURE THING.
I WONDER HOW THEY DECIDE WHAT TO AIR.
WELL, I'M SURE WITH SOME DECISIONS THEY HAVE TO CAREFULLY WEIGH WHETHER THE FOOTAGE IS UNIQUE, SCIENTIFICALLY RELEVANT, AND GOOD TV.
OTHER DECISIONS ARE MADE FOR THEM.
AHH. NOTHING LIKE NUDE TAI CHI.

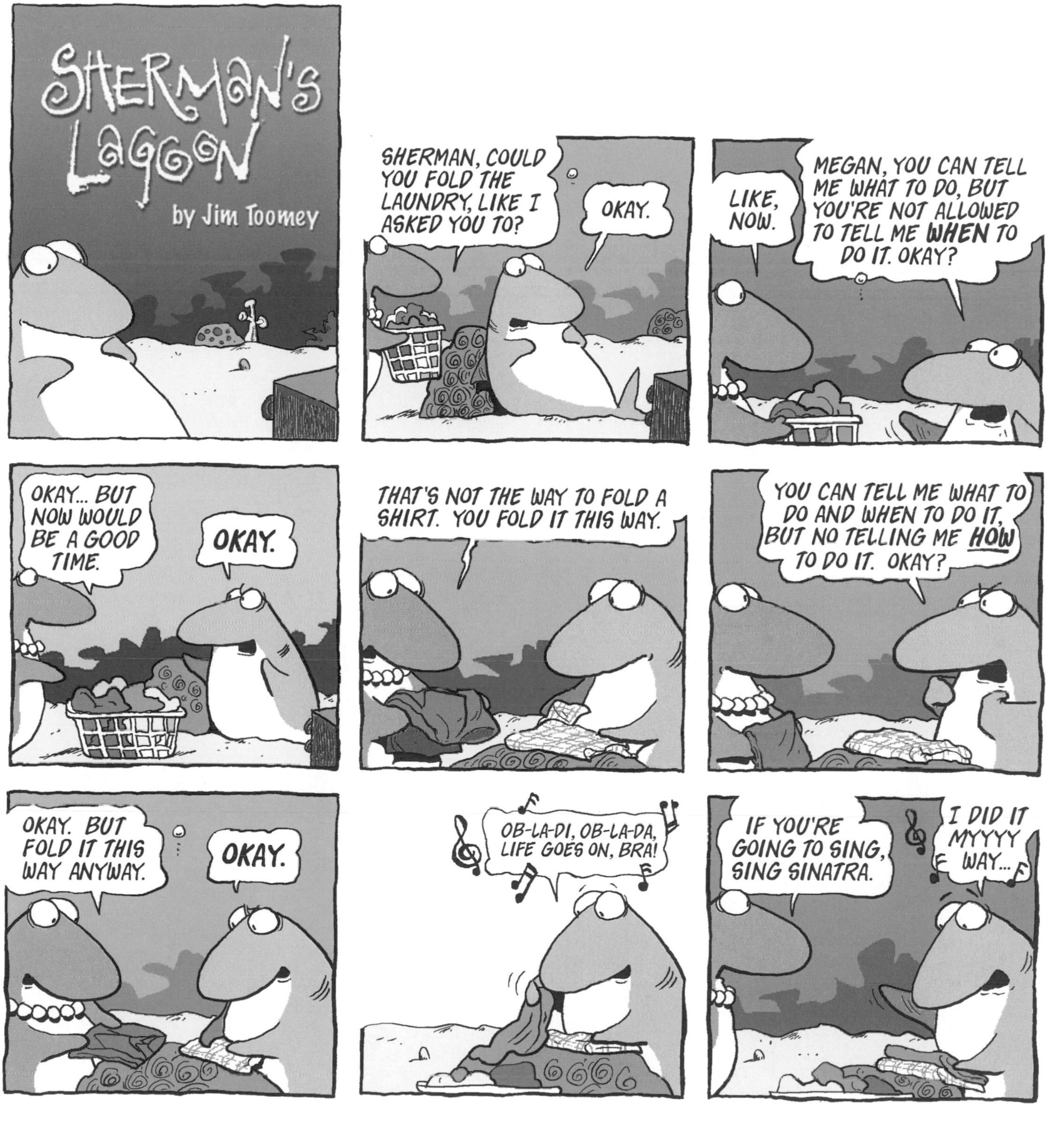
SHERMAN'S LAGOON
by Jim Toomey
SHERMAN, COULD YOU FOLD THE LAUNDRY, LIKE I ASKED YOU TO?
OKAY.
LIKE, NOW.
MEGAN, YOU CAN TELL ME WHAT TO DO, BUT YOU'RE NOT ALLOWED TO TELL ME WHEN TO DO IT. OKAY?
OKAY... BUT NOW WOULD BE A GOOD TIME.
OKAY.
THAT'S NOT THE WAY TO FOLD A SHIRT. YOU FOLD IT THIS WAY.
YOU CAN TELL ME WHAT TO DO AND WHEN TO DO IT, BUT NO TELLING ME HOW TO DO IT. OKAY?
OKAY. BUT FOLD IT THIS WAY ANYWAY.
OKAY.
OB-LA-DI, OB-LA-DA, LIFE GOES ON, BRA!
IF YOU'RE GOING TO SING, SING SINATRA.
I DID IT MYYYY WAY...

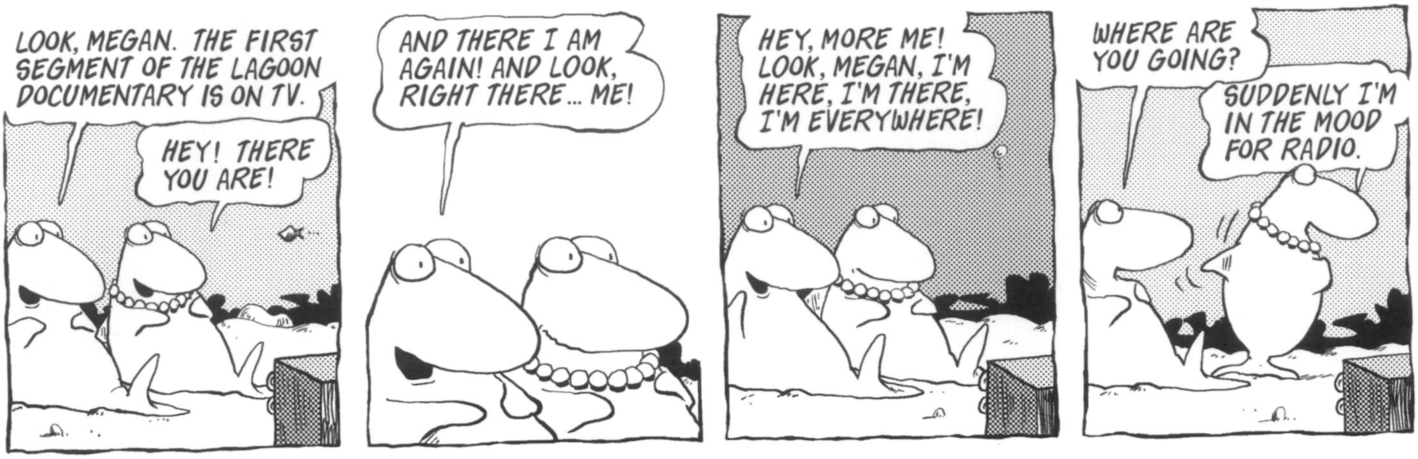
LOOK, MEGAN. THE FIRST SEGMENT OF THE LAGOON DOCUMENTARY IS ON TV.
HEY! THERE YOU ARE!
AND THERE I AM AGAIN! AND LOOK, RIGHT THERE... ME!
HEY, MORE ME! LOOK, MEGAN, I'M HERE, I'M THERE, I'M EVERYWHERE!
WHERE ARE YOU GOING?
SUDDENLY I'M IN THE MOOD FOR RADIO.

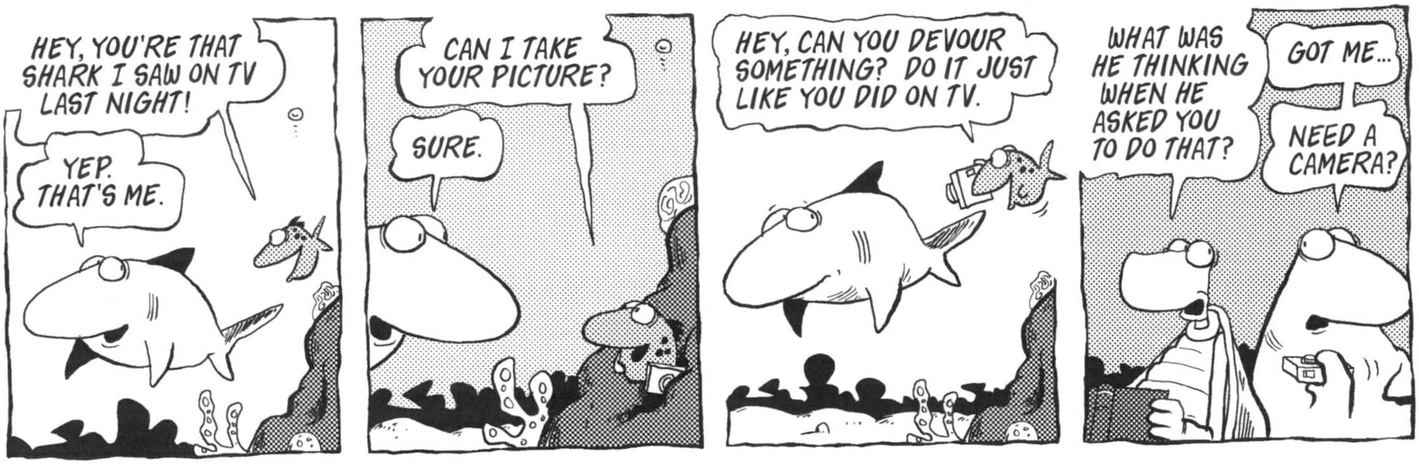
HEY, YOU'RE THAT SHARK I SAW ON TV LAST NIGHT!
YEP. THAT'S ME.
CAN I TAKE YOUR PICTURE?
SURE.
HEY, CAN YOU DEVOUR SOMETHING? DO IT JUST LIKE YOU DID ON TV.
WHAT WAS HE THINKING WHEN HE ASKED YOU TO DO THAT?
GOT ME...
NEED A CAMERA?

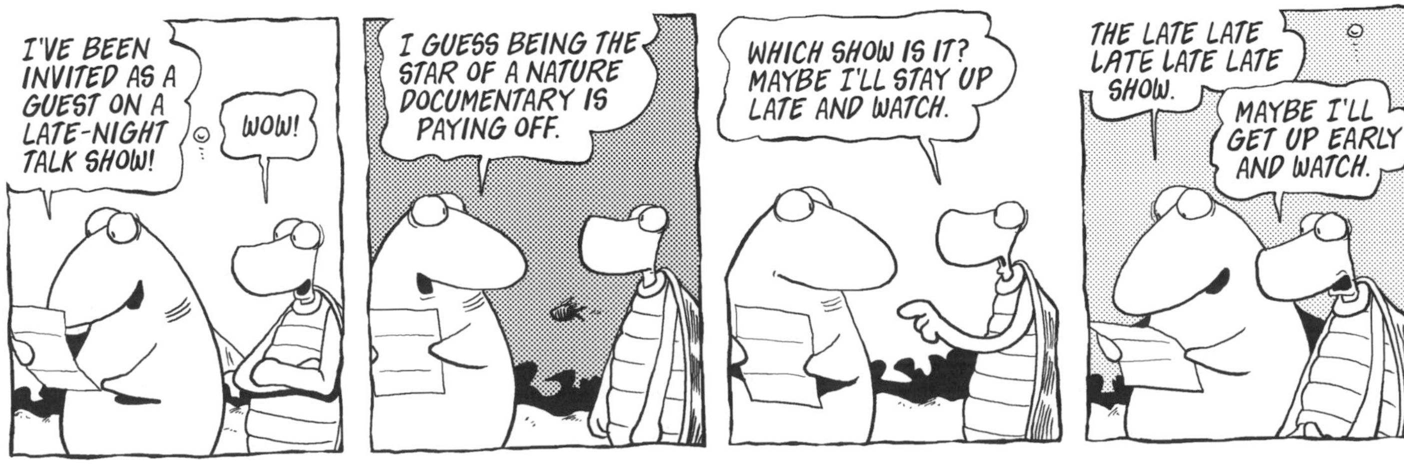
I'VE BEEN INVITED AS A GUEST ON A LATE-NIGHT TALK SHOW!
WOW!
I GUESS BEING THE STAR OF A NATURE DOCUMENTARY IS PAYING OFF.
WHICH SHOW IS IT? MAYBE I'LL STAY UP LATE AND WATCH.
THE LATE LATE LATE LATE LATE SHOW.
MAYBE I'LL GET UP EARLY AND WATCH.

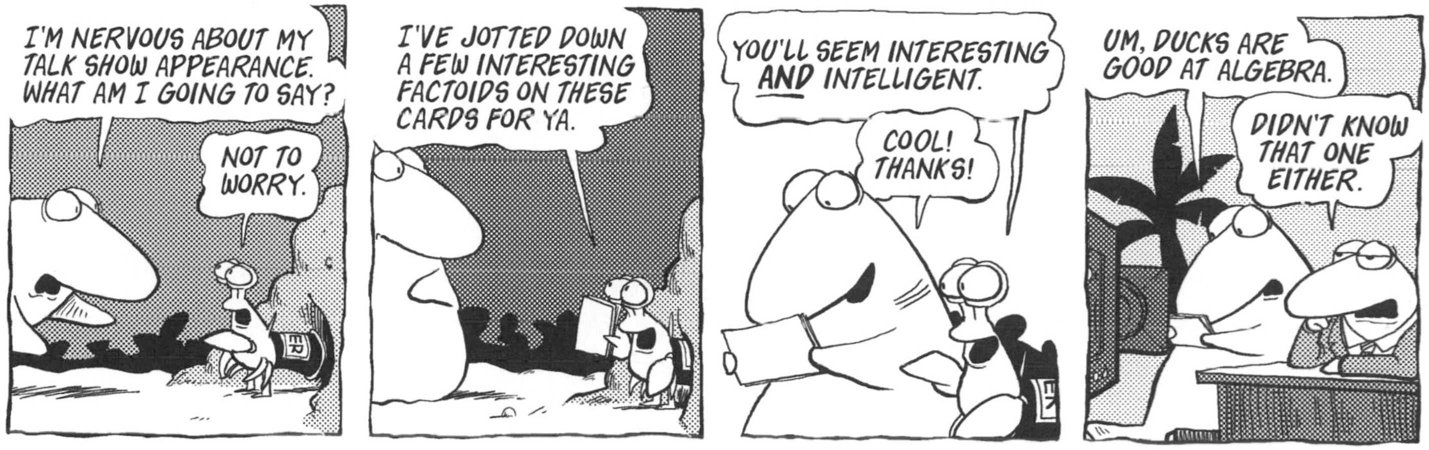
I'M NERVOUS ABOUT MY TALK SHOW APPEARANCE. WHAT AM I GOING TO SAY?
NOT TO WORRY.
I'VE JOTTED DOWN A FEW INTERESTING FACTOIDS ON THESE CARDS FOR YA.
YOU'LL SEEM INTERESTING AND INTELLIGENT.
COOL! THANKS!
UM, DUCKS ARE GOOD AT ALGEBRA.
DIDN'T KNOW THAT ONE EITHER.

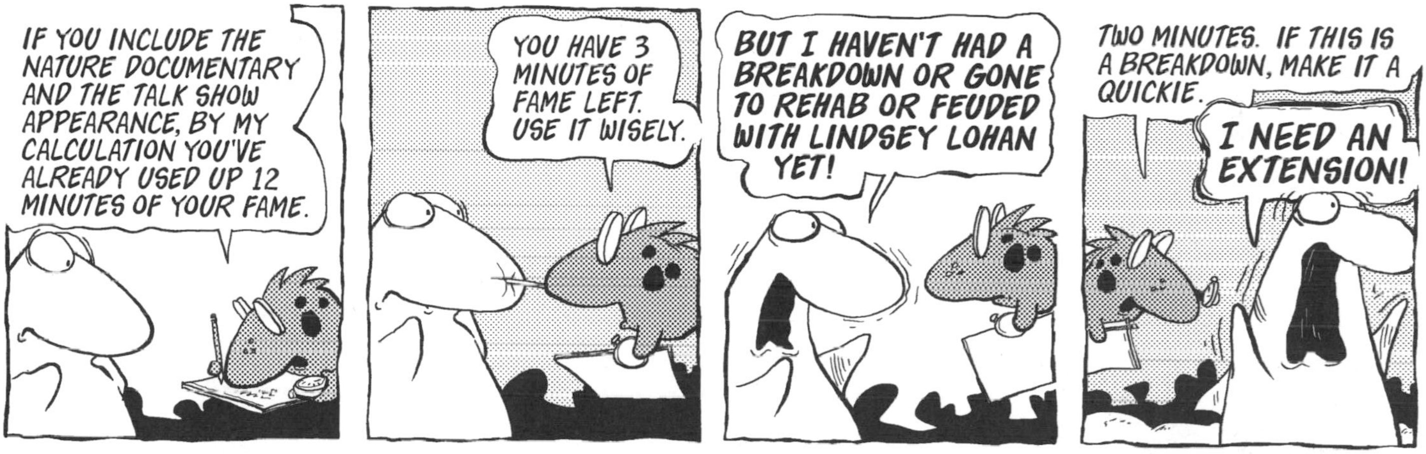
IF YOU INCLUDE THE NATURE DOCUMENTARY AND THE TALK SHOW APPEARANCE, BY MY CALCULATION YOU'VE ALREADY USED UP 12 MINUTES OF YOUR FAME.
YOU HAVE 3 MINUTES OF FAME LEFT. USE IT WISELY.
BUT I HAVEN'T HAD A BREAKDOWN OR GONE TO REHAB OR FEUDED WITH LINDSEY LOHAN YET!
TWO MINUTES. IF THIS IS A BREAKDOWN, MAKE IT A QUICKIE.
I NEED AN EXTENSION!

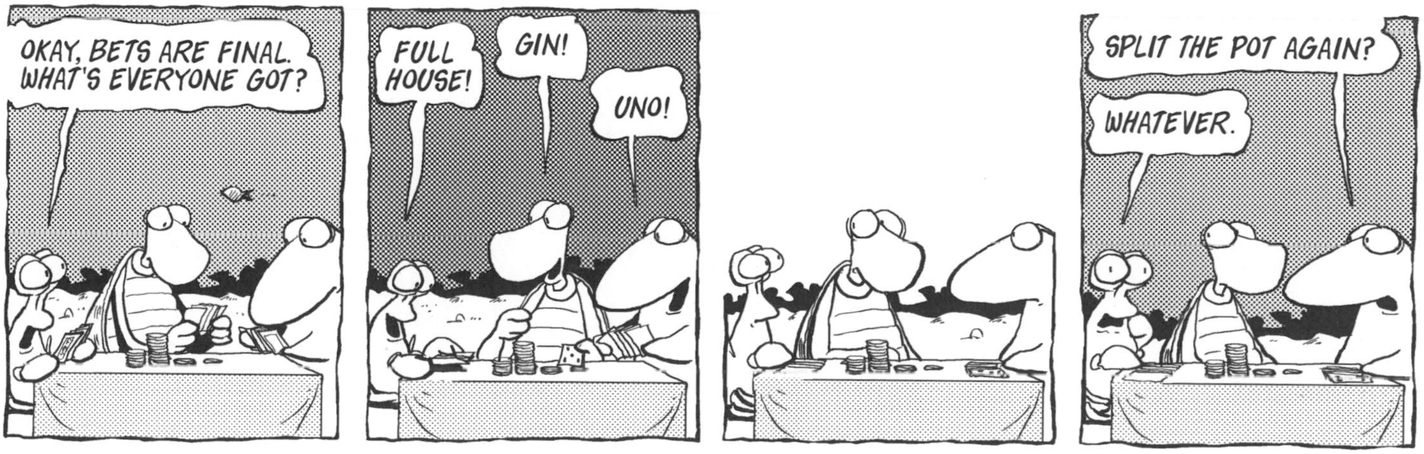
OKAY, BETS ARE FINAL. WHAT'S EVERYONE GOT?
FULL HOUSE!
GIN!
UNO!
SPLIT THE POT AGAIN?
WHATEVER.

SHERMAN'S LAGOON
by Jim Toomey

WOW, THAT'S SOME FANCY-SCHMANCY PIECE OF PLUMBING.

I DID IT MYSELF.

YOU'RE A DO-IT-YOURSELFER.

I GUESS YOU COULD SAY THAT.

I STARTED IT SIX MONTHS AGO. HAVEN'T GOTTEN AROUND TO FINISHING IT YET.

YOU'RE A START-IT-YOURSELFER.

NOT SURE IF I'M DOING IT RIGHT.

YOU'RE A TRY-IT-YOUR-SELFER.

IT'S SO MESSED UP NOW, I MAY HAVE TO GET A PLUMBER IN HERE.

YOU'RE A SCREW-IT-UP-YOUR-SELFER.

THAT'S GOING TO COST A FORTUNE.

OH, YOU'RE A TOO-CHEAP-TO-PAY-SOMEBODY-UNTIL-YOU-TRY-IT-AND-SCREW-IT-UP-YOURSELFER.

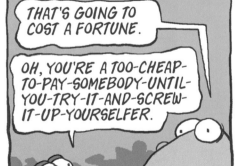

HAVE YOU SEEN THE PICTURE FRAME I'M WORKING ON?

YOU'RE A CHANGE-THE-SUBJECT-YOUR-SELFER.

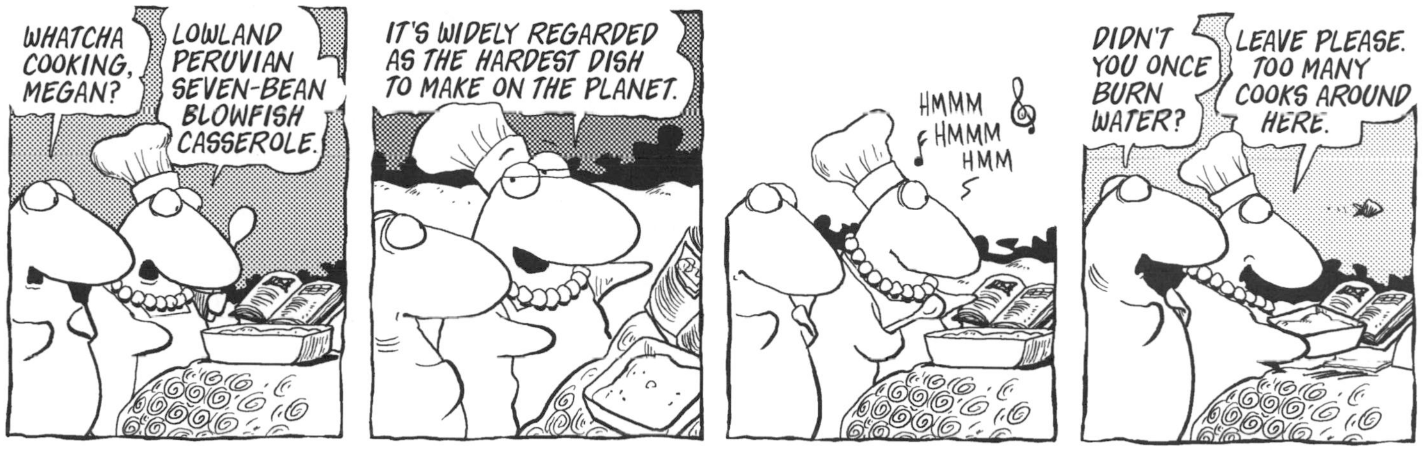
WHATCHA COOKING, MEGAN?
LOWLAND PERUVIAN SEVEN-BEAN BLOWFISH CASSEROLE.
IT'S WIDELY REGARDED AS THE HARDEST DISH TO MAKE ON THE PLANET.
HMMM HMMM HMM
DIDN'T YOU ONCE BURN WATER?
LEAVE PLEASE. TOO MANY COOKS AROUND HERE.

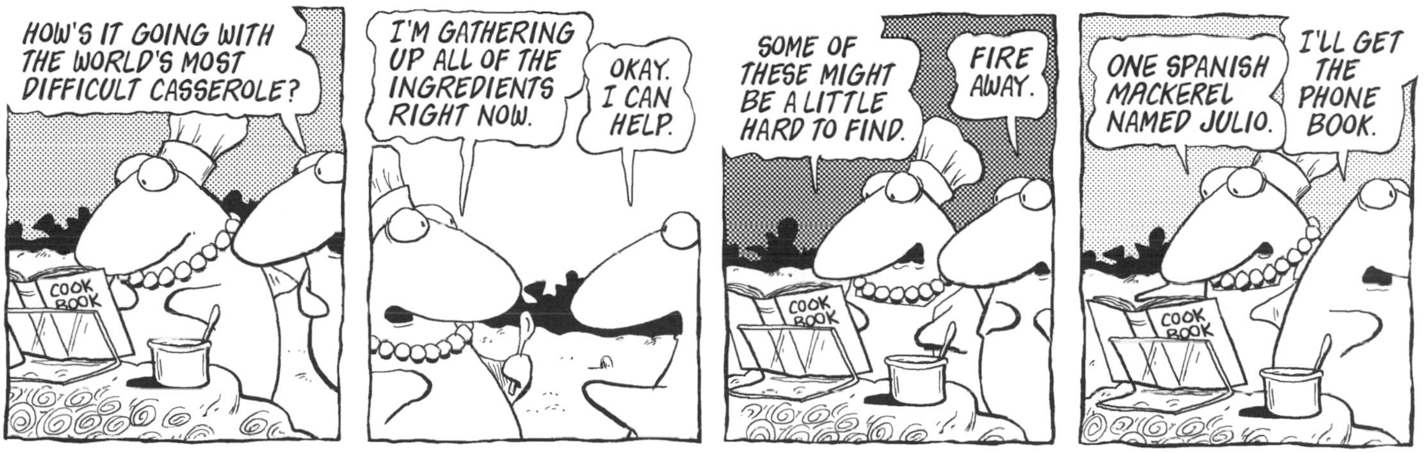
HOW'S IT GOING WITH THE WORLD'S MOST DIFFICULT CASSEROLE?
COOK BOOK
I'M GATHERING UP ALL OF THE INGREDIENTS RIGHT NOW.
OKAY. I CAN HELP.
SOME OF THESE MIGHT BE A LITTLE HARD TO FIND.
FIRE AWAY.
COOK BOOK
ONE SPANISH MACKEREL NAMED JULIO.
I'LL GET THE PHONE BOOK.
COOK BOOK

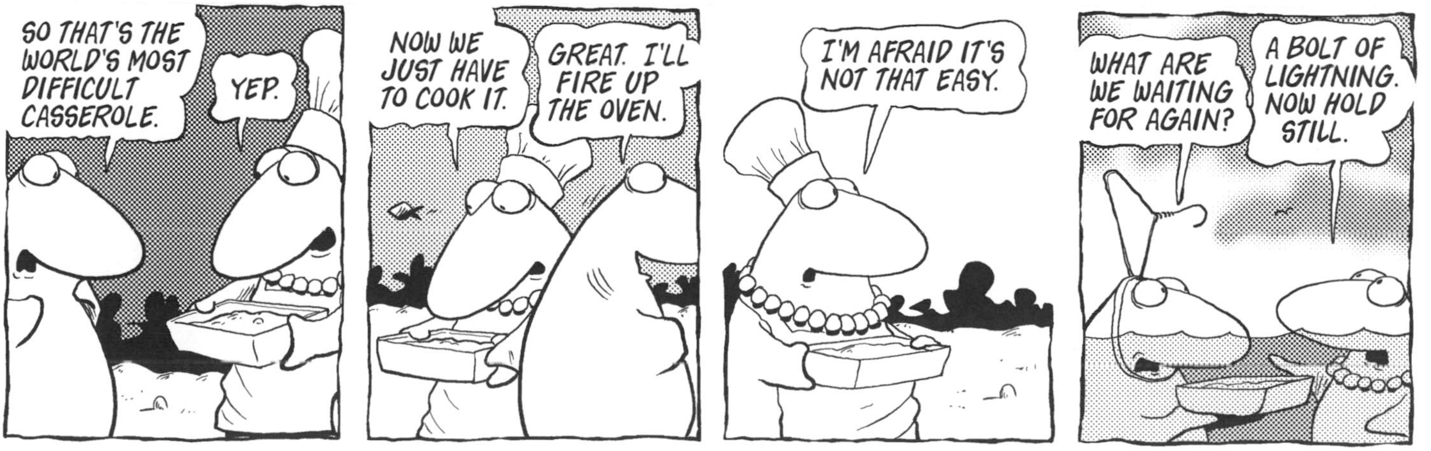
SO THAT'S THE WORLD'S MOST DIFFICULT CASSEROLE.
YEP.
NOW WE JUST HAVE TO COOK IT.
GREAT. I'LL FIRE UP THE OVEN.
I'M AFRAID IT'S NOT THAT EASY.
WHAT ARE WE WAITING FOR AGAIN?
A BOLT OF LIGHTNING. NOW HOLD STILL.

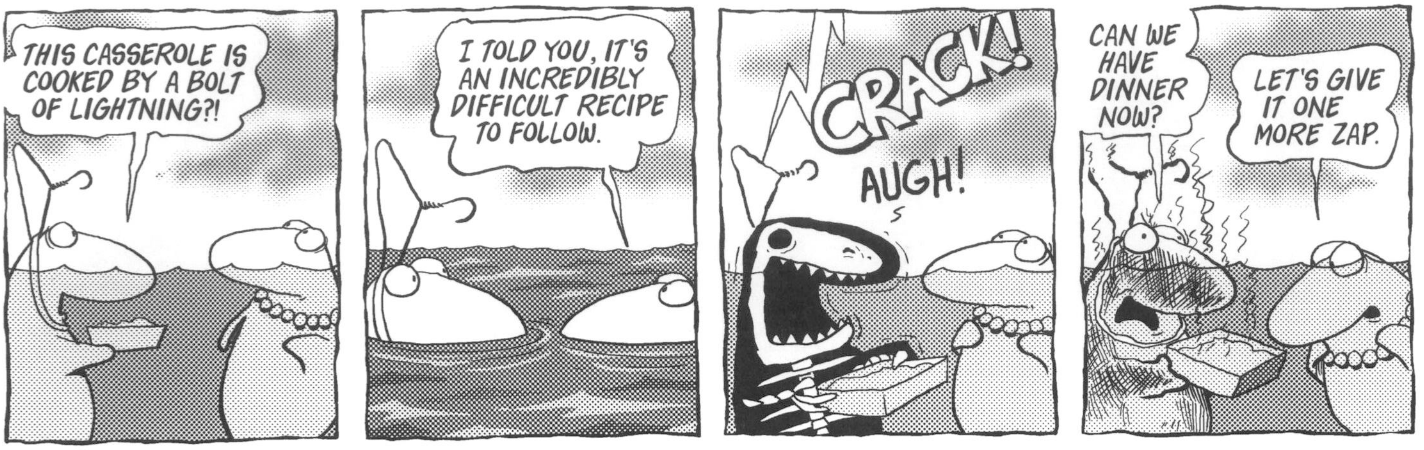
THIS CASSEROLE IS COOKED BY A BOLT OF LIGHTNING?!
I TOLD YOU, IT'S AN INCREDIBLY DIFFICULT RECIPE TO FOLLOW.
CRACK!
AUGH!
CAN WE HAVE DINNER NOW?
LET'S GIVE IT ONE MORE ZAP.

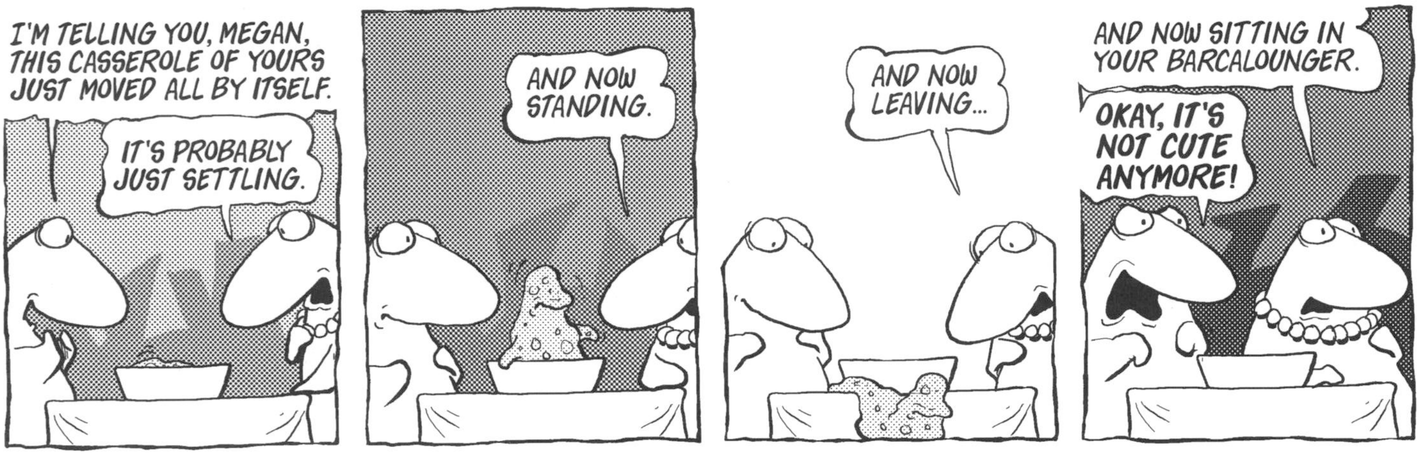
I'M TELLING YOU, MEGAN, THIS CASSEROLE OF YOURS JUST MOVED ALL BY ITSELF.
IT'S PROBABLY JUST SETTLING.
AND NOW STANDING.
AND NOW LEAVING...
AND NOW SITTING IN YOUR BARCALOUNGER.
OKAY, IT'S NOT CUTE ANYMORE!

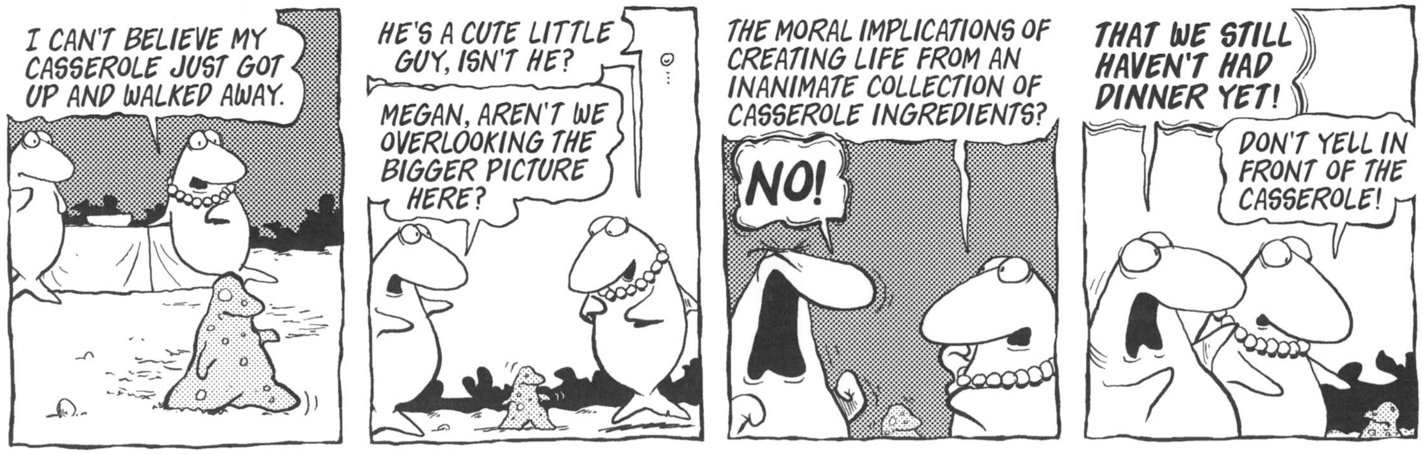
I CAN'T BELIEVE MY CASSEROLE JUST GOT UP AND WALKED AWAY.
HE'S A CUTE LITTLE GUY, ISN'T HE?
MEGAN, AREN'T WE OVERLOOKING THE BIGGER PICTURE HERE?
THE MORAL IMPLICATIONS OF CREATING LIFE FROM AN INANIMATE COLLECTION OF CASSEROLE INGREDIENTS?
NO!
THAT WE STILL HAVEN'T HAD DINNER YET!
DON'T YELL IN FRONT OF THE CASSEROLE!

SHERMAN'S LAGOON

by Jim Toomey

ISN'T LIFE A GRIND, FAT BOY?

WHADDAYA MEAN?

AS SOON AS YOU GET RID OF ONE PROBLEM, ANOTHER ONE POPS UP. IT'S LIKE A GAME OF "WHACK-A-MOLE."

THAT'S HOW WE MEASURE OUR SUCCESS, ISN'T IT? HOW MANY MOLES DID WE WHACK TODAY?

WE WHACK-A-MOLE OUR WAY THROUGH LIFE UNTIL ONE FINE DAY WHEN WE PUT THAT MALLET DOWN, FIND A ROCKING CHAIR, AND REFLECT ON ALL THE MOLES WE'VE WHACKED.

I HAVE A SUBPOENA FOR MR. SHERMAN T. SHARK.

WHACK!

THAT WHACK-A-MOLE THING, THAT WAS JUST A METAPHOR.

WHAT'S A METAPHOR?

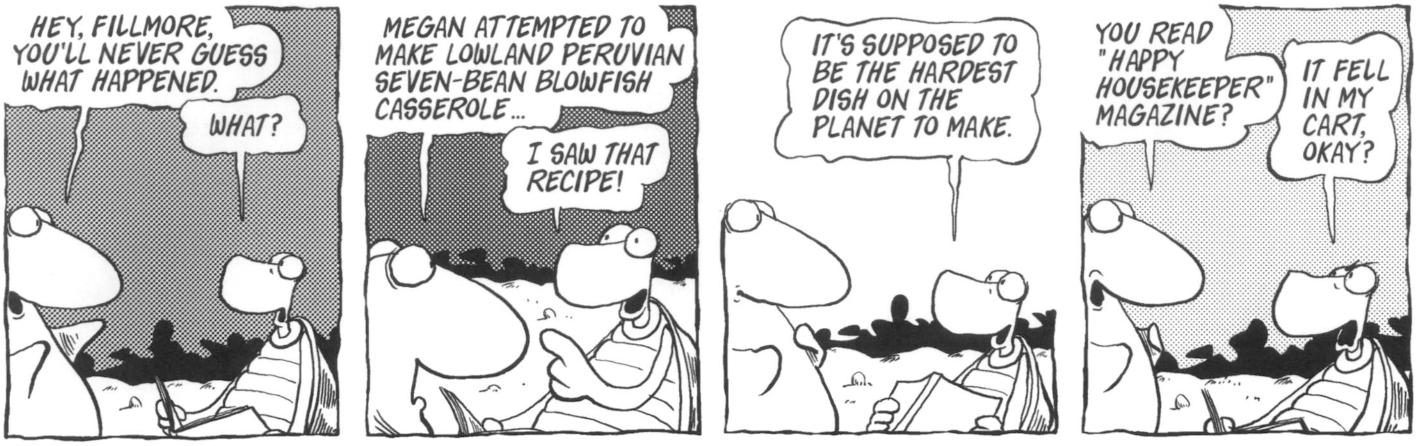
HEY, FILLMORE, YOU'LL NEVER GUESS WHAT HAPPENED.
WHAT?
MEGAN ATTEMPTED TO MAKE LOWLAND PERUVIAN SEVEN-BEAN BLOWFISH CASSEROLE...
I SAW THAT RECIPE!
IT'S SUPPOSED TO BE THE HARDEST DISH ON THE PLANET TO MAKE.
YOU READ "HAPPY HOUSEKEEPER" MAGAZINE?
IT FELL IN MY CART, OKAY?

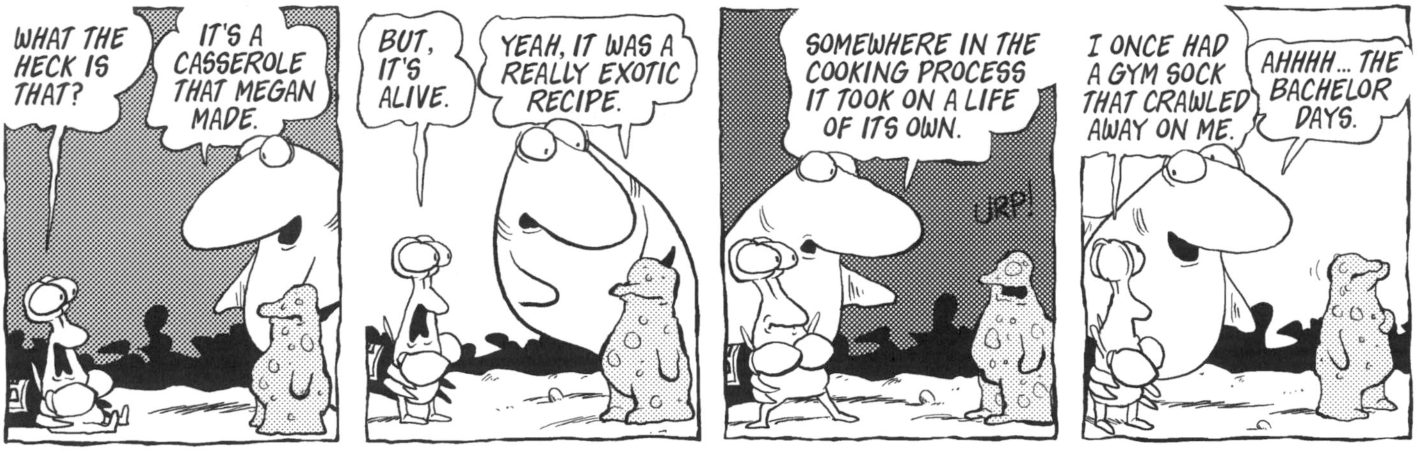
WHAT THE HECK IS THAT?
IT'S A CASSEROLE THAT MEGAN MADE.
BUT, IT'S ALIVE.
YEAH, IT WAS A REALLY EXOTIC RECIPE.
SOMEWHERE IN THE COOKING PROCESS IT TOOK ON A LIFE OF ITS OWN.
URP!
I ONCE HAD A GYM SOCK THAT CRAWLED AWAY ON ME.
AHHHH... THE BACHELOR DAYS.

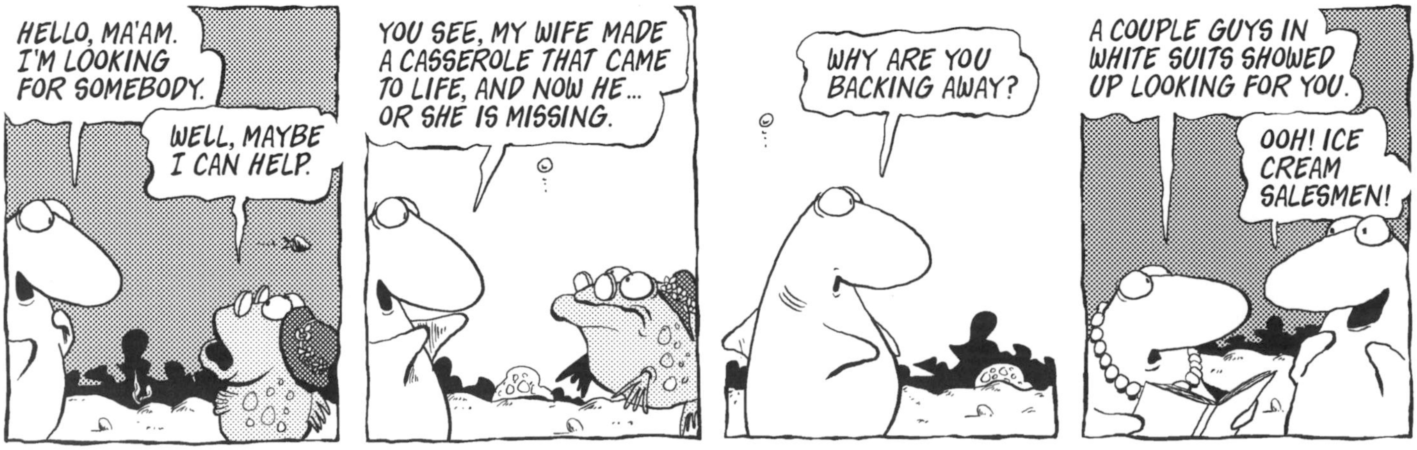
HELLO, MA'AM. I'M LOOKING FOR SOMEBODY.
WELL, MAYBE I CAN HELP.
YOU SEE, MY WIFE MADE A CASSEROLE THAT CAME TO LIFE, AND NOW HE... OR SHE IS MISSING.
WHY ARE YOU BACKING AWAY?
A COUPLE GUYS IN WHITE SUITS SHOWED UP LOOKING FOR YOU.
OOH! ICE CREAM SALESMEN!

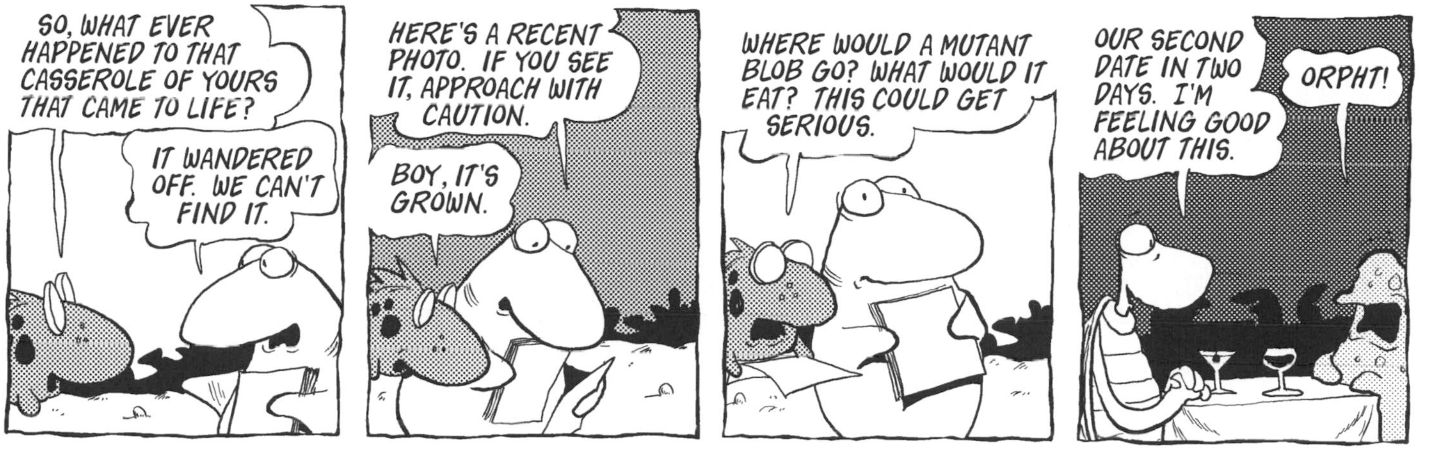
SO, WHAT EVER HAPPENED TO THAT CASSEROLE OF YOURS THAT CAME TO LIFE?
IT WANDERED OFF. WE CAN'T FIND IT.
HERE'S A RECENT PHOTO. IF YOU SEE IT, APPROACH WITH CAUTION.
BOY, IT'S GROWN.
WHERE WOULD A MUTANT BLOB GO? WHAT WOULD IT EAT? THIS COULD GET SERIOUS.
OUR SECOND DATE IN TWO DAYS. I'M FEELING GOOD ABOUT THIS.
ORPHT!

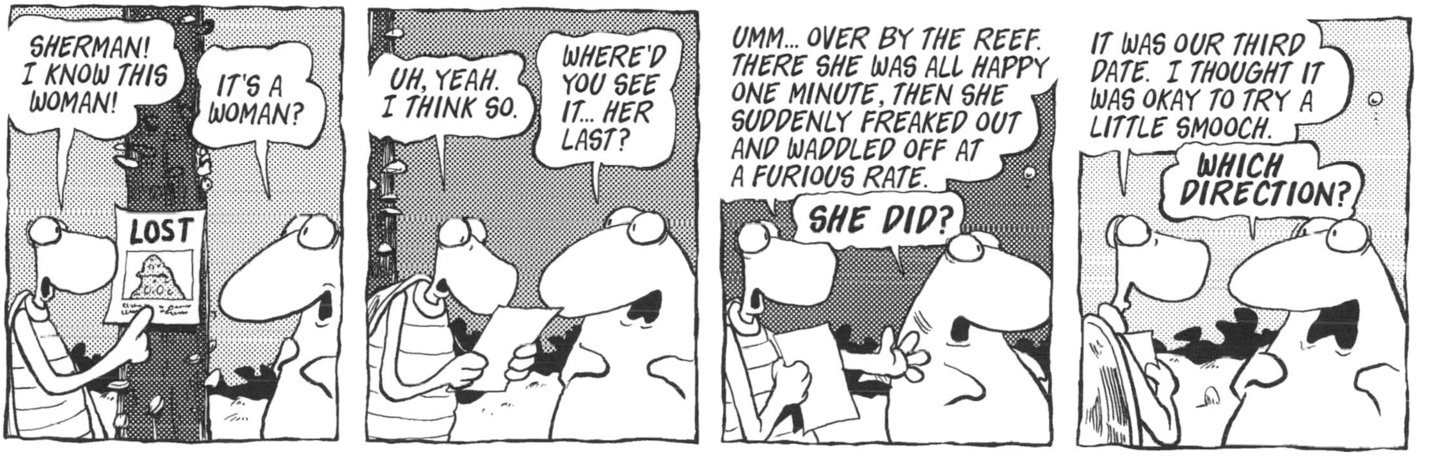
SHERMAN! I KNOW THIS WOMAN!
IT'S A WOMAN?
LOST
UH, YEAH. I THINK SO.
WHERE'D YOU SEE IT... HER LAST?
UMM... OVER BY THE REEF. THERE SHE WAS ALL HAPPY ONE MINUTE, THEN SHE SUDDENLY FREAKED OUT AND WADDLED OFF AT A FURIOUS RATE.
SHE DID?
IT WAS OUR THIRD DATE. I THOUGHT IT WAS OKAY TO TRY A LITTLE SMOOCH.
WHICH DIRECTION?

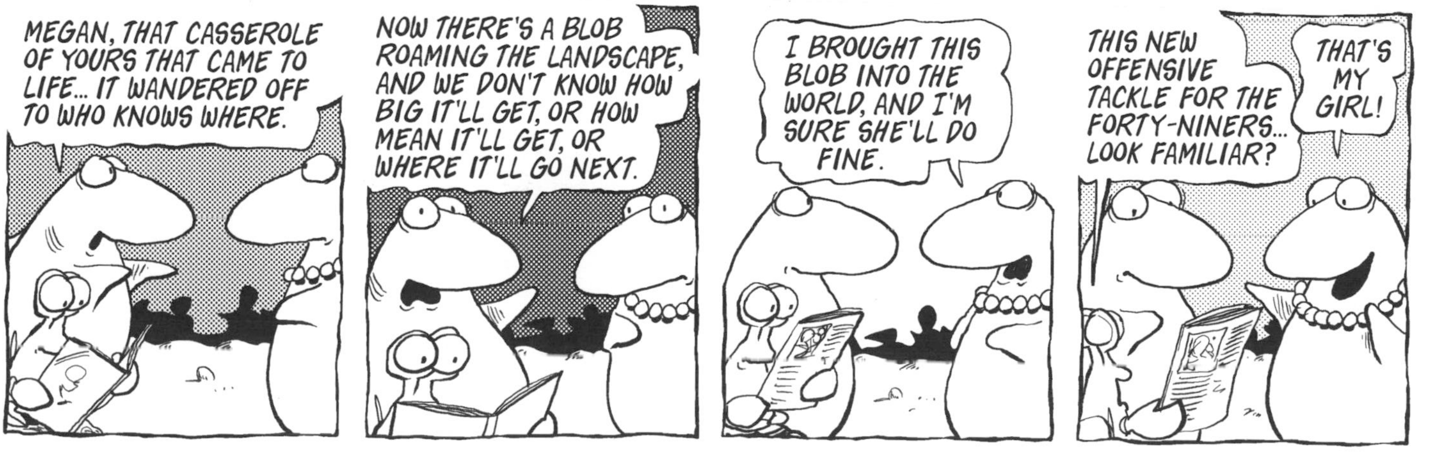
MEGAN, THAT CASSEROLE OF YOURS THAT CAME TO LIFE... IT WANDERED OFF TO WHO KNOWS WHERE.
NOW THERE'S A BLOB ROAMING THE LANDSCAPE, AND WE DON'T KNOW HOW BIG IT'LL GET, OR HOW MEAN IT'LL GET, OR WHERE IT'LL GO NEXT.
I BROUGHT THIS BLOB INTO THE WORLD, AND I'M SURE SHE'LL DO FINE.
THIS NEW OFFENSIVE TACKLE FOR THE FORTY-NINERS... LOOK FAMILIAR?
THAT'S MY GIRL!

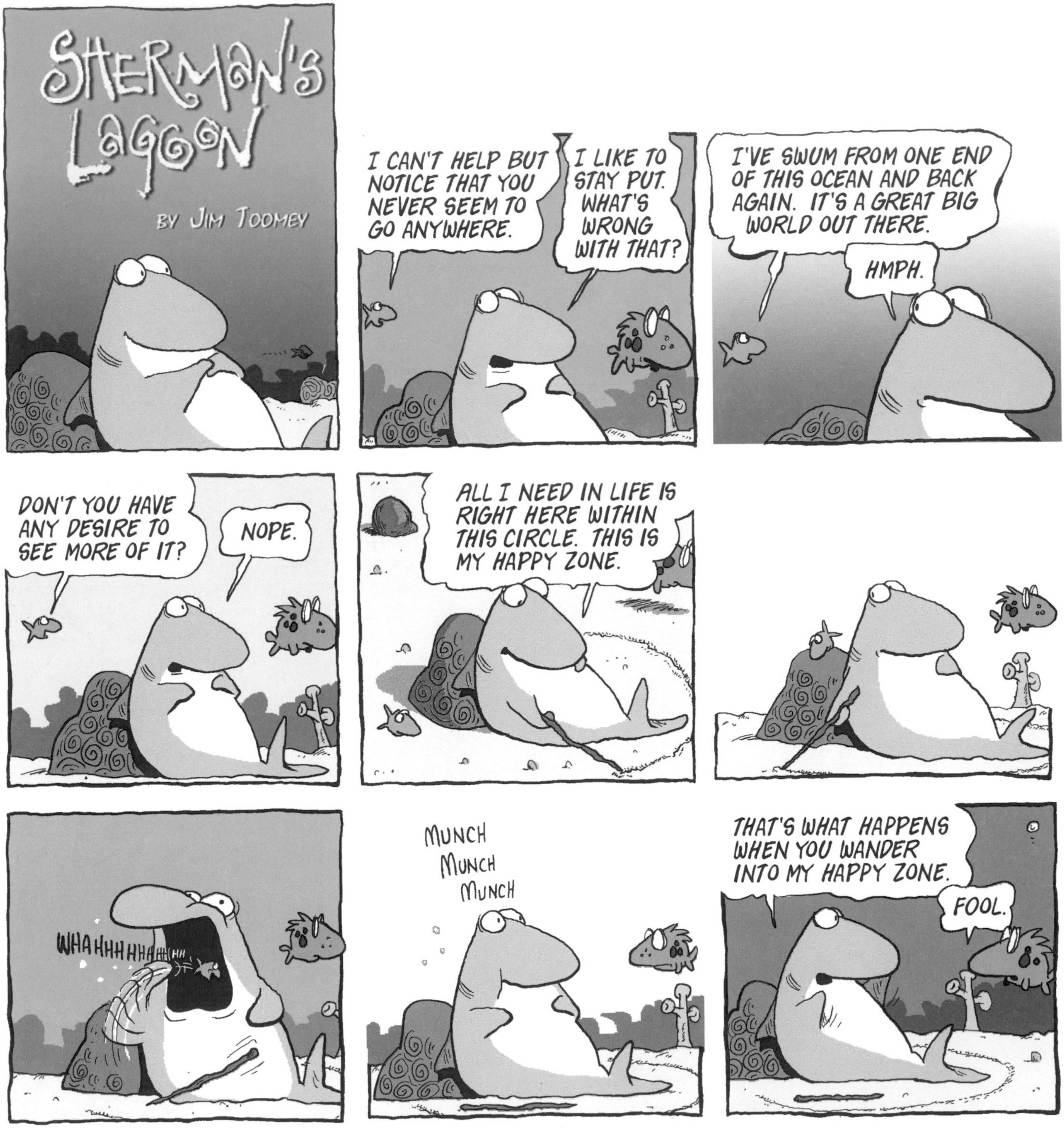
SHERMAN'S LAGOON
BY JIM TOOMEY
I CAN'T HELP BUT NOTICE THAT YOU NEVER SEEM TO GO ANYWHERE.
I LIKE TO STAY PUT. WHAT'S WRONG WITH THAT?
I'VE SWUM FROM ONE END OF THIS OCEAN AND BACK AGAIN. IT'S A GREAT BIG WORLD OUT THERE.
HMPH.
DON'T YOU HAVE ANY DESIRE TO SEE MORE OF IT?
NOPE.
ALL I NEED IN LIFE IS RIGHT HERE WITHIN THIS CIRCLE. THIS IS MY HAPPY ZONE.
MUNCH
MUNCH
MUNCH
THAT'S WHAT HAPPENS WHEN YOU WANDER INTO MY HAPPY ZONE.
FOOL.

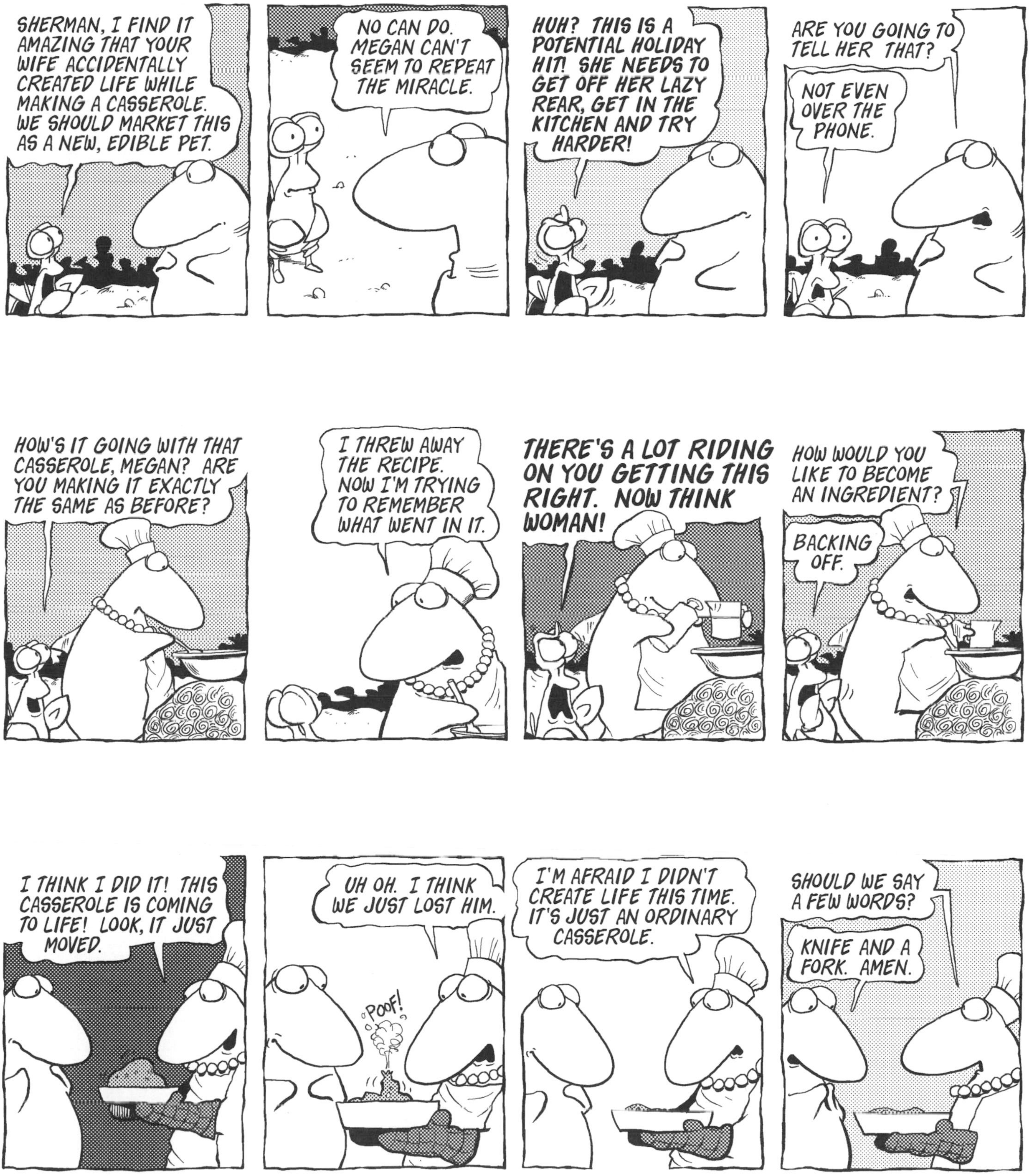
SHERMAN, I FIND IT AMAZING THAT YOUR WIFE ACCIDENTALLY CREATED LIFE WHILE MAKING A CASSEROLE. WE SHOULD MARKET THIS AS A NEW, EDIBLE PET.
NO CAN DO. MEGAN CAN'T SEEM TO REPEAT THE MIRACLE.
HUH? THIS IS A POTENTIAL HOLIDAY HIT! SHE NEEDS TO GET OFF HER LAZY REAR, GET IN THE KITCHEN AND TRY HARDER!
ARE YOU GOING TO TELL HER THAT?
NOT EVEN OVER THE PHONE.
HOW'S IT GOING WITH THAT CASSEROLE, MEGAN? ARE YOU MAKING IT EXACTLY THE SAME AS BEFORE?
I THREW AWAY THE RECIPE. NOW I'M TRYING TO REMEMBER WHAT WENT IN IT.
THERE'S A LOT RIDING ON YOU GETTING THIS RIGHT. NOW THINK WOMAN!
HOW WOULD YOU LIKE TO BECOME AN INGREDIENT?
BACKING OFF.
I THINK I DID IT! THIS CASSEROLE IS COMING TO LIFE! LOOK, IT JUST MOVED.
UH OH. I THINK WE JUST LOST HIM.
POOF!
I'M AFRAID I DIDN'T CREATE LIFE THIS TIME. IT'S JUST AN ORDINARY CASSEROLE.
SHOULD WE SAY A FEW WORDS?
KNIFE AND A FORK. AMEN.

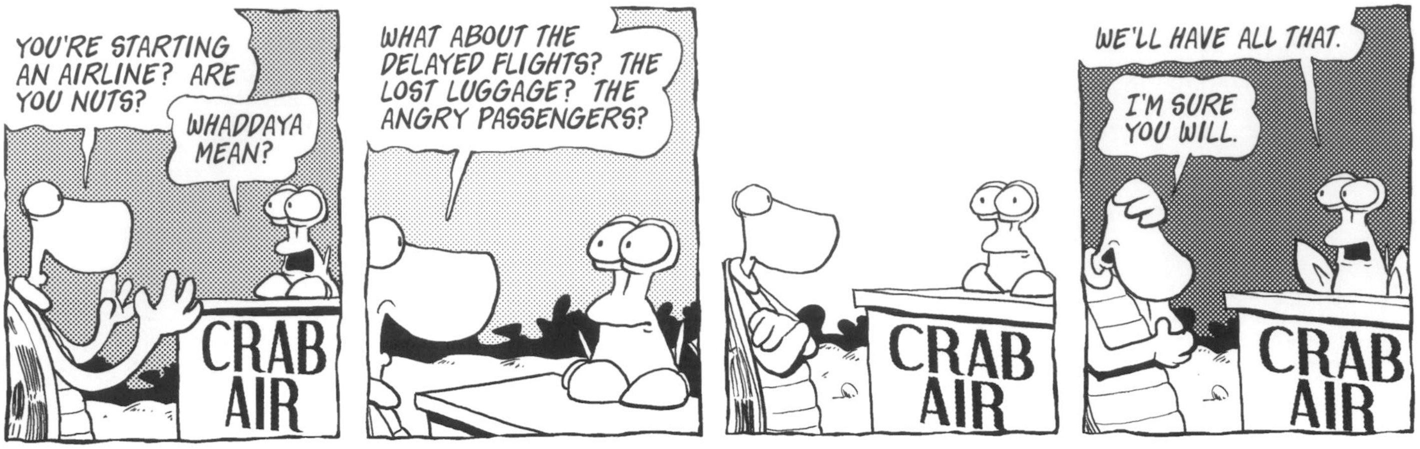
YOU'RE STARTING AN AIRLINE? ARE YOU NUTS?
WHADDAYA MEAN?
CRAB AIR
WHAT ABOUT THE DELAYED FLIGHTS? THE LOST LUGGAGE? THE ANGRY PASSENGERS?
CRAB AIR
WE'LL HAVE ALL THAT.
I'M SURE YOU WILL.
CRAB AIR

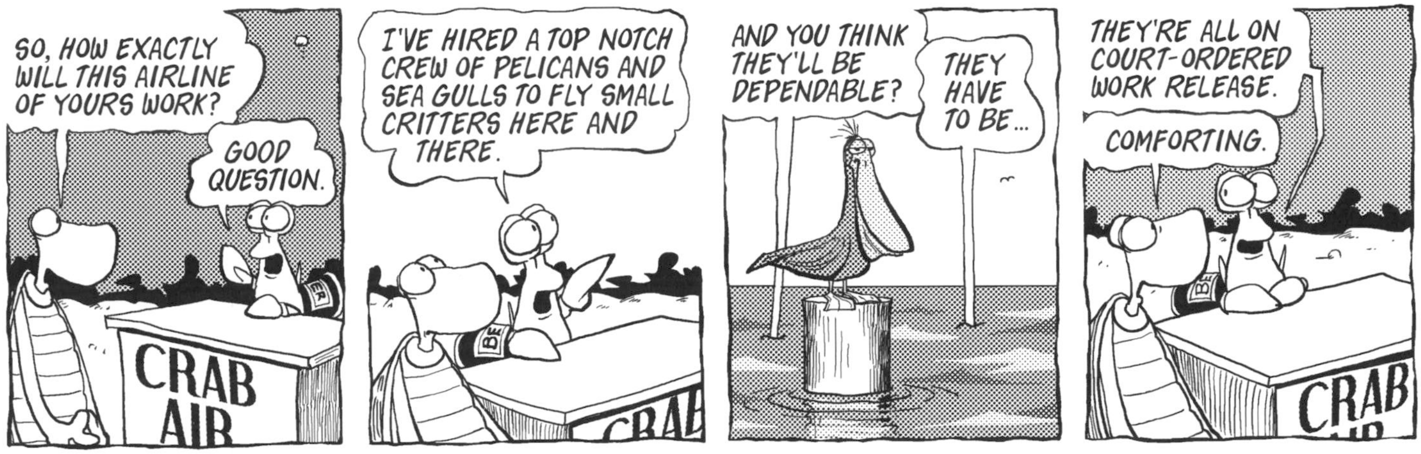
SO, HOW EXACTLY WILL THIS AIRLINE OF YOURS WORK?
GOOD QUESTION.
CRAB
I'VE HIRED A TOP NOTCH CREW OF PELICANS AND SEA GULLS TO FLY SMALL CRITTERS HERE AND THERE.
AND YOU THINK THEY'LL BE DEPENDABLE?
THEY HAVE TO BE...
THEY'RE ALL ON COURT-ORDERED WORK RELEASE.
COMFORTING.
CRAB

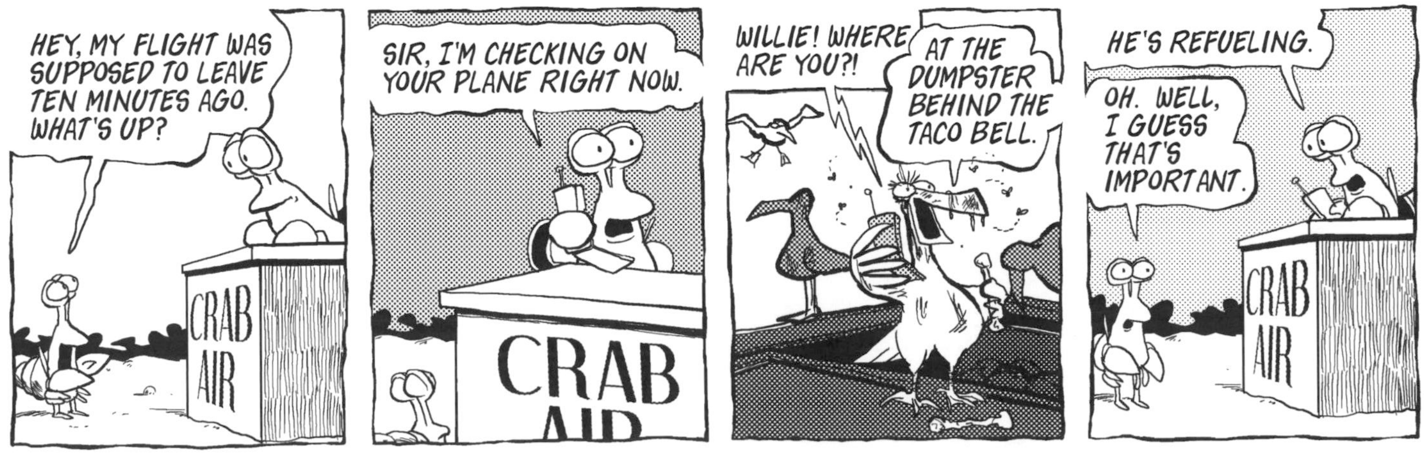
HEY, MY FLIGHT WAS SUPPOSED TO LEAVE TEN MINUTES AGO. WHAT'S UP?
CRAB AIR
SIR, I'M CHECKING ON YOUR PLANE RIGHT NOW.
CRAB
WILLIE! WHERE ARE YOU?!
AT THE DUMPSTER BEHIND THE TACO BELL.
HE'S REFUELING.
OH. WELL, I GUESS THAT'S IMPORTANT.
CRAB AIR

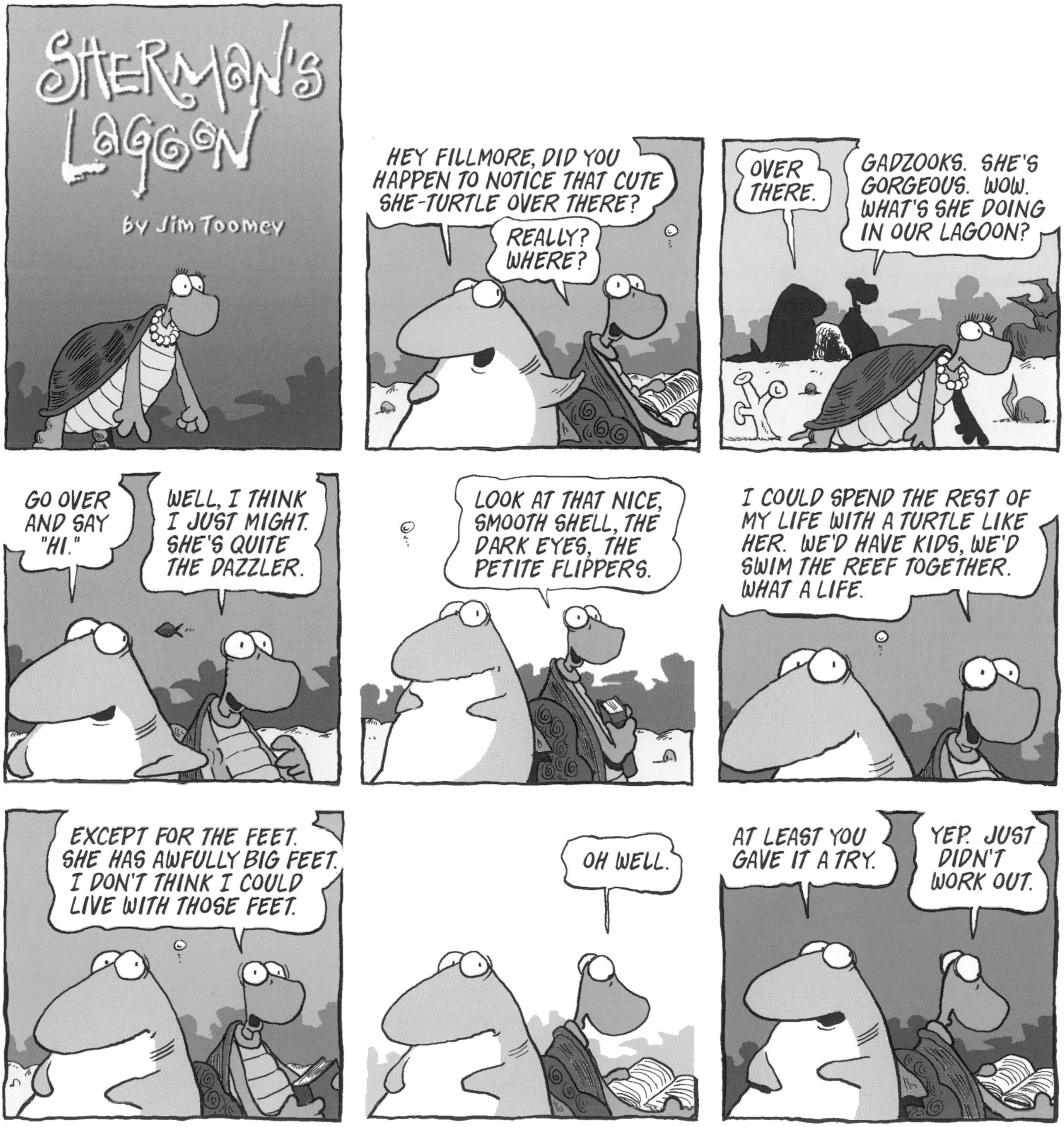
SHERMAN'S LAGOON
by Jim Toomey
HEY FILLMORE, DID YOU HAPPEN TO NOTICE THAT CUTE SHE-TURTLE OVER THERE?
REALLY? WHERE?
OVER THERE.
GADZOOKS. SHE'S GORGEOUS. WOW. WHAT'S SHE DOING IN OUR LAGOON?
GO OVER AND SAY "HI."
WELL, I THINK I JUST MIGHT. SHE'S QUITE THE DAZZLER.
LOOK AT THAT NICE, SMOOTH SHELL, THE DARK EYES, THE PETITE FLIPPERS.
I COULD SPEND THE REST OF MY LIFE WITH A TURTLE LIKE HER. WE'D HAVE KIDS, WE'D SWIM THE REEF TOGETHER. WHAT A LIFE.
EXCEPT FOR THE FEET. SHE HAS AWFULLY BIG FEET. I DON'T THINK I COULD LIVE WITH THOSE FEET.
OH WELL.
AT LEAST YOU GAVE IT A TRY.
YEP. JUST DIDN'T WORK OUT.

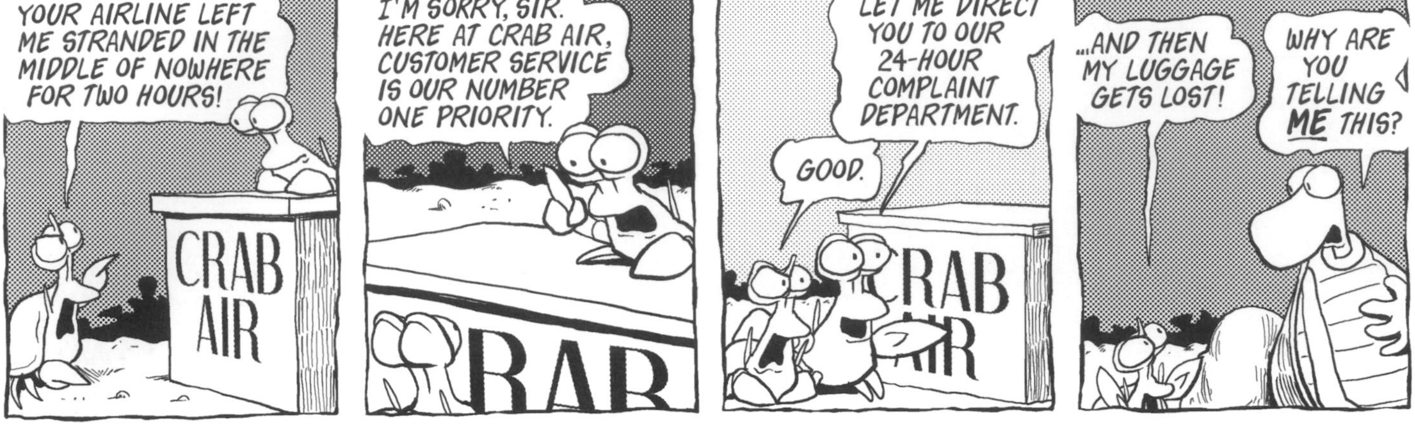
YOUR AIRLINE LEFT ME STRANDED IN THE MIDDLE OF NOWHERE FOR TWO HOURS!
I'M SORRY, SIR. HERE AT CRAB AIR, CUSTOMER SERVICE IS OUR NUMBER ONE PRIORITY.
CRAB AIR
LET ME DIRECT YOU TO OUR 24-HOUR COMPLAINT DEPARTMENT.
GOOD.
...AND THEN MY LUGGAGE GETS LOST!
WHY ARE YOU TELLING **ME** THIS?

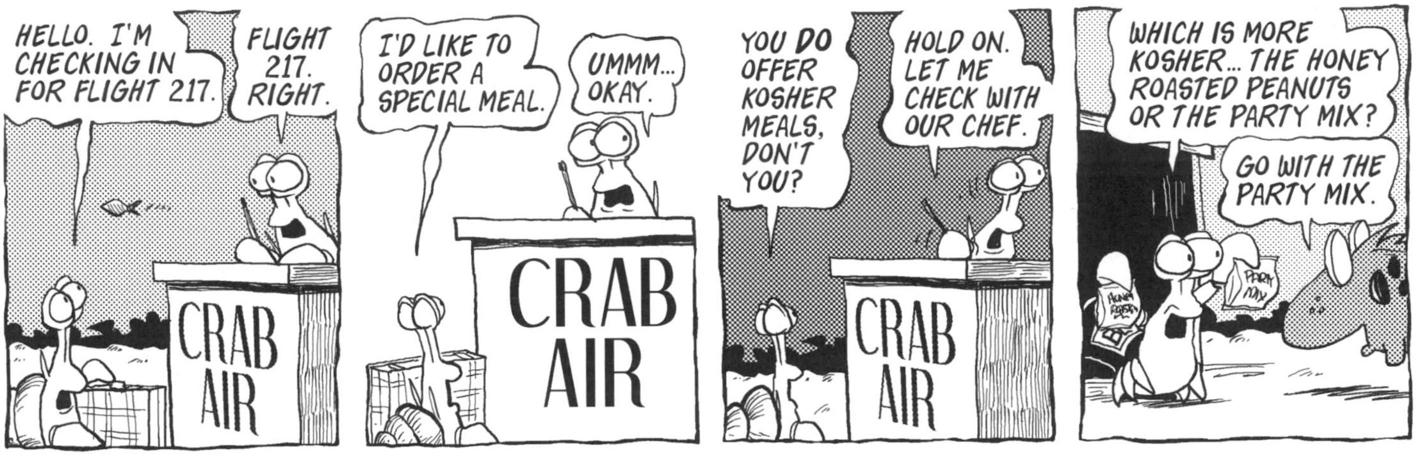
HELLO. I'M CHECKING IN FOR FLIGHT 217.
FLIGHT 217. RIGHT.
CRAB AIR
I'D LIKE TO ORDER A SPECIAL MEAL.
UMMM... OKAY.
YOU **DO** OFFER KOSHER MEALS, DON'T YOU?
HOLD ON. LET ME CHECK WITH OUR CHEF.
WHICH IS MORE KOSHER... THE HONEY ROASTED PEANUTS OR THE PARTY MIX?
GO WITH THE PARTY MIX.

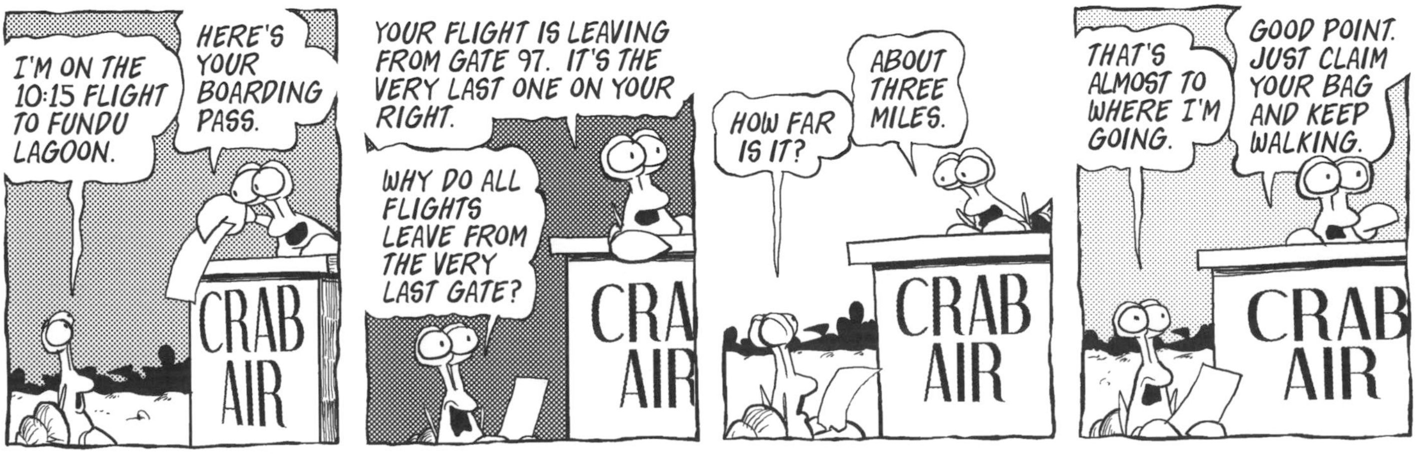
I'M ON THE 10:15 FLIGHT TO FUNDU LAGOON.
HERE'S YOUR BOARDING PASS.
CRAB AIR
YOUR FLIGHT IS LEAVING FROM GATE 97. IT'S THE VERY LAST ONE ON YOUR RIGHT.
WHY DO ALL FLIGHTS LEAVE FROM THE VERY LAST GATE?
HOW FAR IS IT?
ABOUT THREE MILES.
THAT'S ALMOST TO WHERE I'M GOING.
GOOD POINT. JUST CLAIM YOUR BAG AND KEEP WALKING.

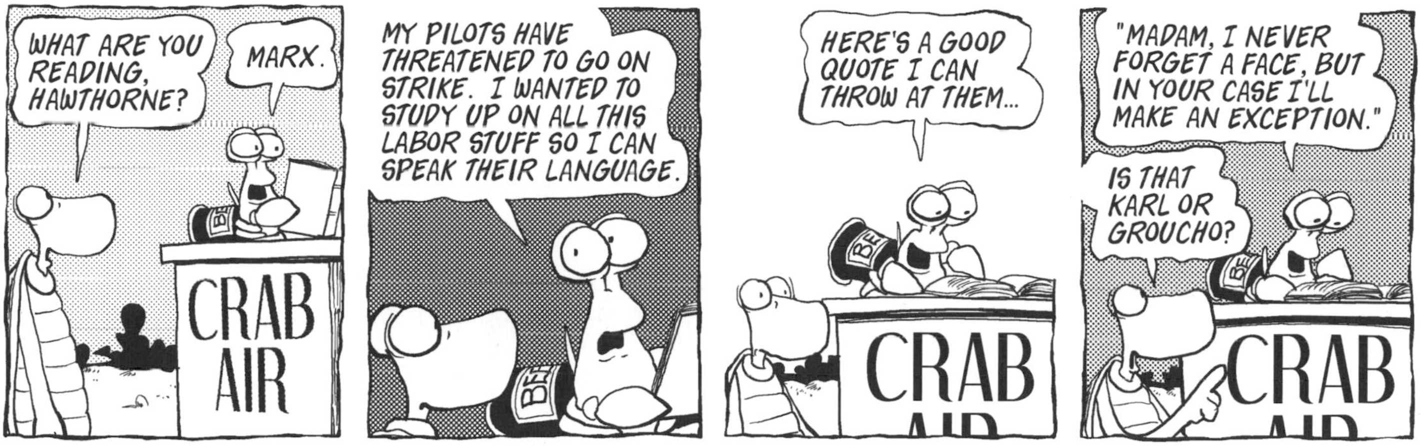
WHAT ARE YOU READING, HAWTHORNE?
MARX.
CRAB AIR
MY PILOTS HAVE THREATENED TO GO ON STRIKE. I WANTED TO STUDY UP ON ALL THIS LABOR STUFF SO I CAN SPEAK THEIR LANGUAGE.
HERE'S A GOOD QUOTE I CAN THROW AT THEM...
CRAB
"MADAM, I NEVER FORGET A FACE, BUT IN YOUR CASE I'LL MAKE AN EXCEPTION."
IS THAT KARL OR GROUCHO?
CRAB

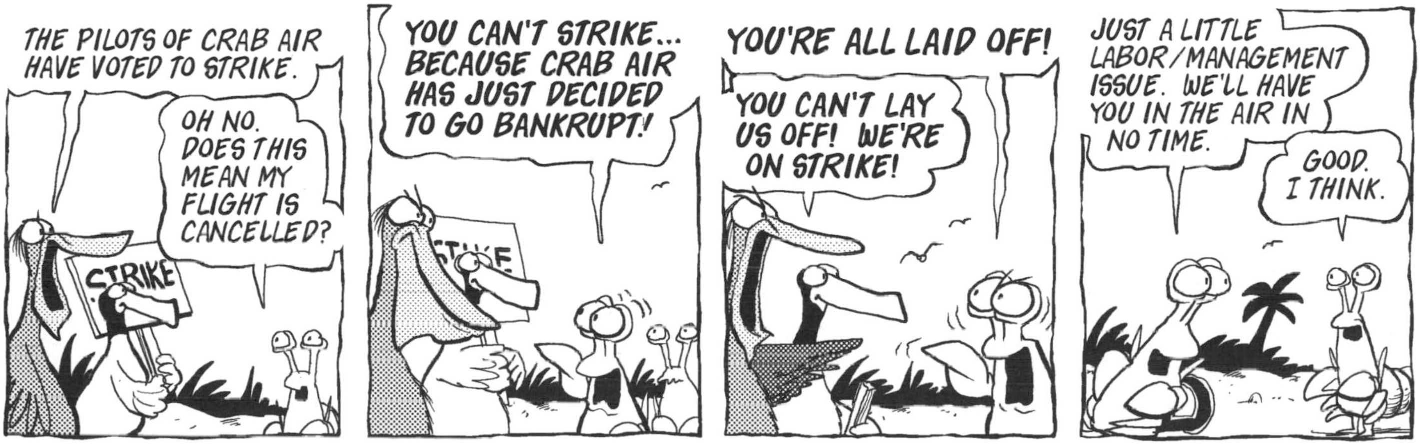
THE PILOTS OF CRAB AIR HAVE VOTED TO STRIKE.
OH NO. DOES THIS MEAN MY FLIGHT IS CANCELLED?
STRIKE
YOU CAN'T STRIKE... BECAUSE CRAB AIR HAS JUST DECIDED TO GO BANKRUPT!
YOU'RE ALL LAID OFF!
YOU CAN'T LAY US OFF! WE'RE ON STRIKE!
JUST A LITTLE LABOR/MANAGEMENT ISSUE. WE'LL HAVE YOU IN THE AIR IN NO TIME.
GOOD. I THINK.

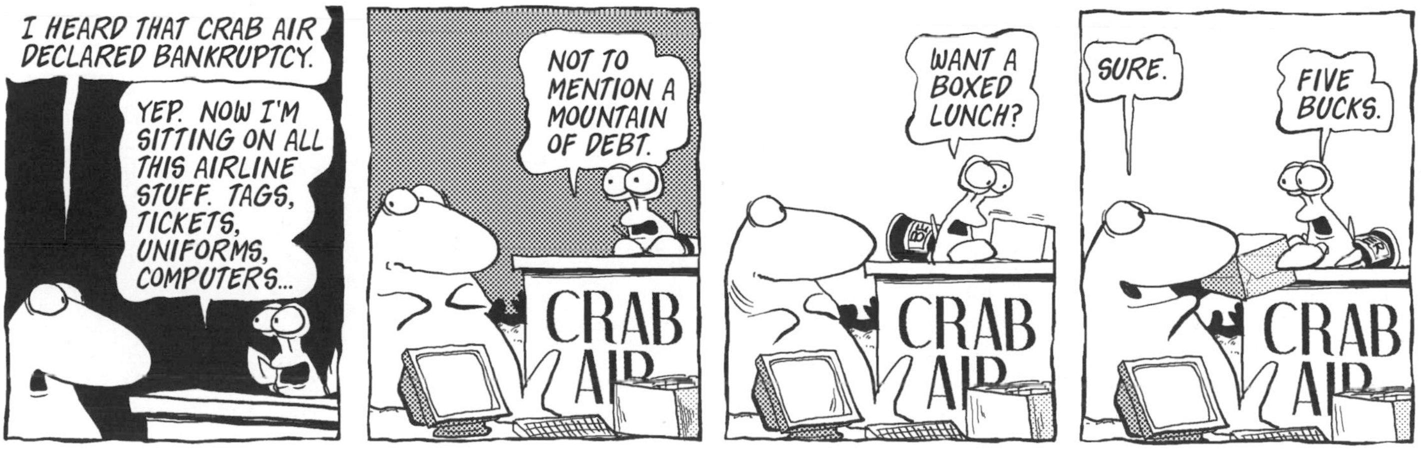
I HEARD THAT CRAB AIR DECLARED BANKRUPTCY.
YEP. NOW I'M SITTING ON ALL THIS AIRLINE STUFF. TAGS, TICKETS, UNIFORMS, COMPUTERS...
NOT TO MENTION A MOUNTAIN OF DEBT.
CRAB
WANT A BOXED LUNCH?
CRAB
SURE.
FIVE BUCKS.
CRAB

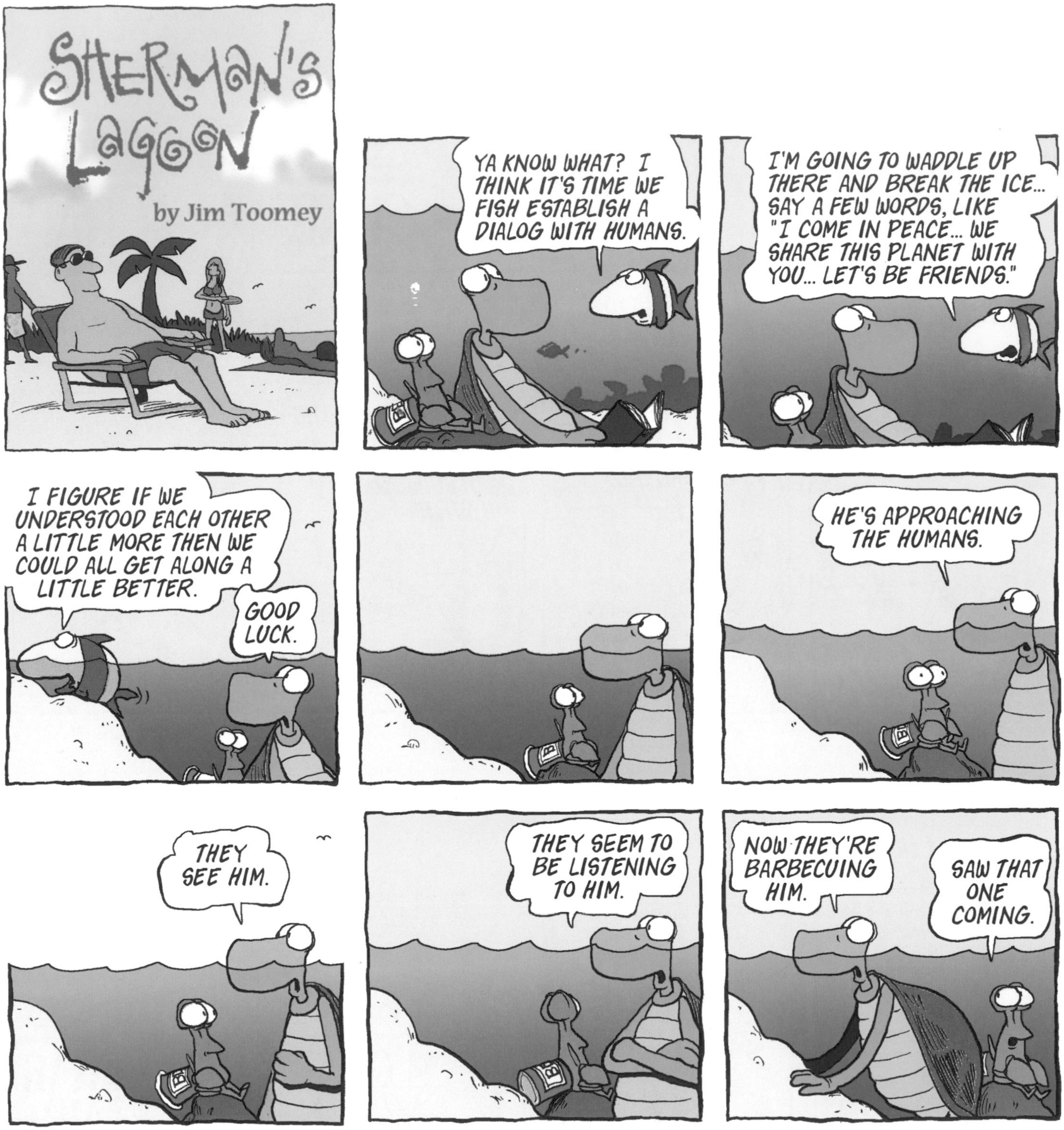
SHERMAN'S LAGOON
by Jim Toomey
YA KNOW WHAT? I THINK IT'S TIME WE FISH ESTABLISH A DIALOG WITH HUMANS.
I'M GOING TO WADDLE UP THERE AND BREAK THE ICE... SAY A FEW WORDS, LIKE "I COME IN PEACE... WE SHARE THIS PLANET WITH YOU... LET'S BE FRIENDS."
I FIGURE IF WE UNDERSTOOD EACH OTHER A LITTLE MORE THEN WE COULD ALL GET ALONG A LITTLE BETTER.
GOOD LUCK.
HE'S APPROACHING THE HUMANS.
THEY SEE HIM.
THEY SEEM TO BE LISTENING TO HIM.
NOW THEY'RE BARBECUING HIM.
SAW THAT ONE COMING.